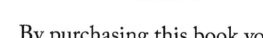

ISBN 978-0-260-01816-8
PIBN 10922548

This book is a reproduction of an important historical work. Forgotten Books uses
state-of-the-art technology to digitally reconstruct the work, preserving the original format
whilst repairing imperfections present in the aged copy. In rare cases, an imperfection in
the original, such as a blemish or missing page, may be replicated in our edition. We do,
however, repair the vast majority of imperfections successfully; any imperfections that
remain are intentionally left to preserve the state of such historical works.

9 7
July

MINNESOTA REPORTS

VOL. 127

CASES ARGUED AND DETERMINED

IN THE

UPREME COURT

OF MINNESOTA

JULY 24 DECEMBER 18, 1914

HENRY BURLEIGH WENZELL

REPORTER

LAWYERS' CO-OPERATIVE PUBLISHING CO.
ST. PAUL
1915

JUSTICES

OF

THE SUPREME COURT

OF MINNESOTA

DURING THE TIME OF THESE REPORTS

Hon. CALVIN L. BROWN, Chief Justice
Hon. GEORGE L. BUNN
Hon. PHILIP E. BROWN
Hon. ANDREW HOLT
Hon. OSCAR HALLAM

COMMISSIONERS
appointed under Laws 1913, p. 53, c. 62

Hon. MYRON D. TAYLOR
Hon. HOMER B. DIBELL

IRVING A. CASWELL, Esq., Clerk

ATTORNEY GENERAL
Hon. LYNDON A. SMITH

NOTE

. ————

By G. S. 1913, § 137, the reporter is required to report all cases decided by the court.

Pursuant to G. S. 1913, § 123, the headnote in each case is prepared by the justice or commissioner writing the opinion, except where otherwise noted.

With a few exceptions the cases are reported in the order of their decision. The date of the decision follows the title of each case. The numbers given below the date indicate the number of the case in the files of the clerk of court and the number of the case in the general term calendar, the calendar numbers being enclosed in ( ). The cases preceding the case on page 172 and those beginning on pages 223, 231, 234, 518, 519 and 537 are from the April, 1914, term calendar; the others are from the October, 1914, term calendar.

As required by G. S. 1913, § 137, when any Minnesota case has been printed in the periodical known as "The Northwestern Reporter," and is cited in any opinion in this volume, a reference to the book and page of that periodical where such case appears has been inserted in such opinion. A similar citation for each opinion in this volume has been given in a footnote.

In citations from the first twenty volumes of the Minnesota Reports the page of the original edition is given, preceded by the corresponding page of the edition by Chief Justice Gilfillan.

The footnotes in the present volume which are preceded by the word "Note" are inserted by the publisher pursuant to the terms of paragraph 4 of its contract dated May 8, 1909, with the Secretary of State.

CASES REPORTED

MINNESOTA CASES CITED BY THE COURT

BY ORDERS MADE IN OPEN COURT, THE OPINIONS WRITTEN BY THE COMMISSIONERS AND REPORTED IN THIS VOLUME WERE ADOPTED AS THE OPINIONS OF THE COURT BEFORE THEY WERE FILED, AND HAVE THE SAME FORCE AND EFFECT AS THOUGH WRITTEN BY A JUSTICE OF THE COURT.

FOR TABLE OF STATUTES CITED BY THE COURT, SEE INDEX, PAGES 611–614.

127 M.   (xx)

CASES

ARGUED AND DETERMINED

IN THE

SUPREME COURT OF MINNESOTA.

WILLIAM McMAHON v. ILLINOIS CENTRAL RAILROAD COMPANY.[1]

July 24, 1914.

Nos. 18,799—(272).

Negligence — verdict sustained by evidence.

1. Plaintiff was run over by a freight train of defendant. He testified that he was ordered by the conductor to go under the train to fix something that was dragging, and that while he was under the car for that purpose the conductor started the train without notice to him. This story is denied by the conductor. Some of the circumstances corroborate plaintiff. The evidence is sufficient to sustain the jury's finding that plaintiff's injury was caused by the negligence of the conductor.

Charge to jury.

2. An instruction that the violation of a penal statute, as to starting trains without signal, constituted a breach of duty owed by defendant to plaintiff, could not prejudice defendant where the employee on whom the statute imposes the duty of giving the signal is the engineer and the finding of the jury negatives negligence on the part of the engineer.

---

[1] Reported in 148 N. W. 446.

127 M.—1.

Same — refusal to charge.

    3. There was no error in charging the jury that, unless plaintiff was injured while under the car fixing a broken brake rod, there is no evidence as to how the accident happened, nor in refusing to charge that if he was not under the car for that purpose the verdict must be for the defendant. There was no theory advanced on the trial that the accident happened in any other manner, and the conduct of all parties has conceded that at the time plaintiff was injured he was under the car for the purpose claimed by him.

Offer to prove custom.

    4. An offer of evidence that on other roads it is customary for a train-man, before going under a train, to personally notify the engineer, was properly rejected since defendant's witnesses testified that personal notice to the engineer was not required on this division of defendant's road if the conductor was notified.

A train "on the road."

    5. A train made up ready for travel, in charge of a road crew, overdue to start, and which has attempted to leave the station, but is unable to make a heavy grade without application of additional power, which, however, is right at hand, is a train "on the road" as distinguished from a train "standing in a yard."

Damages not excessive.

    6. The damages awarded are not excessive.

    Action in the district court for Ramsey county to recover $81,000 for personal injury received while in the employ of defendant. The answer denied that plaintiff was ordered by defendant or any of its agents to go under the train for the purpose of making any repairs, and denied that defendant or its agents had any notice of the fact that plaintiff was under the train and alleged that the accident was caused wholly by plaintiff's negligence in going under the train without taking any precaution to see that it was not moved while he was thereunder. The case was tried before Orr, J., who denied defendant's motion for a directed verdict, and a jury which returned a verdict for $39,000 in favor of plaintiff. From an order denying its motion for a new trial, defendant appealed. Affirmed.

    Butler & Mitchell, for appellant.

    Henry Mahoney, Humphrey Barton and *Walter D. Corrigan,* for respondent.

HALLAM, J.

Plaintiff was a brakeman on one of defendant's trains. On the morning of October 16, 1912, he was run over and terribly injured. On the trial plaintiff had a verdict. Defendant appeals from an order denying its motion for a new trial.

1. Defendant contends that the evidence is not sufficient to sustain the verdict. The facts are as follows: Plaintiff's crew was about to take a train of 70 cars from Amboy to Clinton, in Illinois. The train was made up and started slowly. The grade was heavy and the train stalled and backed up again, apparently to get a fresh start. Plaintiff's story is that, about the time the train commenced to back up he saw marks on the ground indicating that something was dragging; that the following conversation between himself and the conductor, Edward Burns, then occurred: "I said: 'There is something dragging, Eddie.' * * * He said: 'Now we'll back up, and I'll stand here and watch and point out to you the car that is dragging, and you hurry up and fix it and we'll wait until you get it fixed.' And we both gave a back-up signal * * * . I stood and hung out the side of the caboose and watched Burns, and he was looking down at the cars, and he pointed and hollered and he said: 'There it is on that B. & O.' and I hollered 'All right, I'll fix it.'" Plaintiff testified that when the train stopped he took a wrench, got under the car, found a brake rod broken, and proceeded to detach it. While he was so engaged the train started, upon signal from the conductor, without warning to plaintiff, and he was injured. The conductor denies the above conversation *in toto*.

Plaintiff's case hangs on the truth of this story. The court in his charge so limited the issues. The charge reads as follows:

"If you are satisfied * * * that the conductor did give this order and that in the exercise of reasonable care the brakeman did undertake to make these repairs or to go under the car, and that the conductor gave a signal (to start) without any information from the flagman * * * or without knowing that he was in a place of safety, his act would be one of negligence," but that "if * * * he went there without being told by conductor Burns to do so and without notifying the conductor or the engineer of the fact that he intended to do so, he would then be the cause of his own injuries and could not recover."

The question presents only an issue of fact, which the jury resolved in favor of the plaintiff. The evidence is sufficient to sustain the verdict. One of these men testified falsely. The jury could tell better than we which told the truth. Some circumstances tend to corroborate plaintiff. It is strange that plaintiff, an experienced railroad man, should have gone under this car in the manner he did if no conversation had occurred. It is a fact that after backing the train the conductor allowed it to remain standing for several minutes during which time he left the train and went to the roundhouse 1,000 feet away. Subsequent inspection discovered the fact that there was a "B. & O." car in the train with a broken rod. Its dragging would make a mark that could be seen, and it required immediate attention. The conductor reported to his employer two days later that plaintiff was injured while removing this brake rod, and that plaintiff could have prevented the accident by "having understanding with engine crew," and further reported that plaintiff "apparently thought he had time to get under car and remove rod." Considering the positive testimony of plaintiff and all the attendant circumstances, we must hold the evidence sufficient to sustain a verdict for the plaintiff.

2. Much stress is laid upon the fact that the court charged the jury in substance that the violation of a certain penal statute of Illinois constituted a breach of legal duty owed by defendant to plaintiff, and that it might be considered as bearing on the question of defendant's negligence. This statute reads as follows:

"STARTING TRAIN WITHOUT SIGNAL: If any engineer on any railroad shall start his train at any station or within any city, incorporated town or village, without ringing the bell or sounding the whistle a reasonable time before starting he shall forfeit a sum not less than $10.00 nor more than $100.00 to be recovered in an action of debt in the name of the People of the State of Illinois and such corporation shall also forfeit a like sum to be recovered in the same manner." (Hurd's Rev. St. [Ill.] 1913, c. 114, § 70).

Defendant contends that this statute was intended for the pro-

tection of the public, such as persons at crossings, and not for employees, and that the charge was erroneous. It is not necessary to
determine whether the ruling of the court was correct because, if
it was erroneous, the error was without prejudice. The statute, so
far as it imposes a duty at all, imposes that duty on the engineer.
It could have bearing only on the negligence of the engineer. Had
the jury found the engineer negligent, then the question of the correctness of the court's construction of this statute would have been
material. But the jury did not find the engineer negligent. In
response to an instruction that if they found for the plaintiff, and
that the accident was due to and caused by the negligence of a fellow-
servant or co-employee or employees, "you must name in your verdict
the fellow-servant or servants of the plaintiff whose negligence caused
the accident." The jury returned this verdict: "Employee found
to be negligent, E. F. Burns, conductor." This is tantamount to a
finding that the engineer was not negligent and it renders immaterial any instruction which pertained only to the negligence of the
engineer.

3. Defendant assigns as error the charge of the court that the
contention of plaintiff that he was injured while under the car fixing
a broken brake rod "is the only contention as to how this accident
happened, and unless it happened under those conditions, there is
no evidence as to how it may have happened," and in refusing to
charge: "If you believe from the evidence that at the time of the
accident the plaintiff was not in fact under the cars for the purpose
of fixing the broken brake rod, your verdict must be for the defendant." Defendant's contention is: "There is abundant circumstantial evidence that he may not have gone under the cars at all
to fix the brake rod;" that it is more probable that plaintiff must
have started between the cars and accidentally fallen between them.

We agree with the trial court that if the accident did not happen
while plaintiff was under the car fixing the brake rod, the record
presents no evidence as to how it did happen. No witness suggests
any other theory. More than this, the conduct of all parties from
start to finish concedes the fact that plaintiff was injured while
under this car for the purpose mentioned. The conductor, who knew

more about the happening of the accident than any other man but
plaintiff himself, so reported two days after the accident, and he
testified on the stand that he had no doubt plaintiff was under the
train but that he did not know it at the time. Defendant's answer
in like manner concedes this fact and makes plaintiff's conduct in
going under the train the basis of a charge of contributory negligence. Notwithstanding all this, it would seem from the whole
charge, taken together, that the question whether this part of plaintiff's story was true, was submitted to the jury in connection with
the question whether the circumstances of his injury were as he
claimed. There was no error either in the instruction given or in
the refusal to charge as defendant requested on this point.

4. Defendant assigns as error the refusal of the court to receive
proof that on other railroads it was always customary before a
trainman went under a train, to personally notify the engineer,
and to receive from the engineer personal acknowledgment of notice
that the trainman was going under the train.

Proof of custom is some evidence as to whether an act is negligent.
What is usually done may be evidence as to what ought to be done.
General custom is not, as a matter of law, in itself due care, but it
is proper to show that the act claimed to be negligent was not done
in the usual mode of doing such things, for the amount or degree
of care required by men in general in similar circumstances is the
test of ordinary care. Steffenson v. Chicago, M. & St. P. Ry. Co.
51 Minn. 531, 53 N. W. 800; Kelly v. Southern Minn. Ry. Co.
28 Minn. 98, 9 N. W. 588; Armstrong v. Chicago, M. & St. P.
Ry. Co. 45 Minn. 85, 47 N. W. 459; Wiita v. Interstate Iron Co.
103 Minn. 303, 308, 309, 115 N. W. 169, 16 L.R.A.(N.S.) 128.
These principles are well settled, but, applying them to this case,
we cannot see that the rejected testimony would have been of any
assistance to the jury, *first,* because the conditions in the case were
peculiar by reason of the express order given by the conductor in
this case, and, *second,* because it affirmatively appears from the
testimony of several of defendant's witnesses that, whatever may
have been the custom elsewhere, the custom on this particular division
of the Illinois Central Railroad was not in accordance with the testi-

mony offered. The conductor and engineer on this train, and another witness who had been for 18 years a conductor on this same division, all witnesses for defendant, testified that it was the custom of employees to notify the *conductor or the engineer* before going under cars, notification to the conductor being deemed sufficient. In this case, if plaintiff's story is true, the conductor not only had notice, but directed the act to be done. There was no error in exclusion of this testimony.

5. The remaining assignments of error relate to the court's construction of a rule of defendant, known as rule 820. This rule provides that "Conductors must inspect the running gear and brake and draft rigging of trains as often and as closely as practicable while on the road, require their men to assist in such inspection, remedy as far as possible any defects discovered, and remove from the train cars which are unsafe to run." Defendant requested the court to charge the jury that this rule "does not require the conductor or members of his train crew to remedy defects while the train is standing in a yard where car repairers are employed and on duty for the purpose of making repairs." The yard at Amboy was such a yard. The court declined to give this request, but instead, after reading the rule, said: "This applies to being on the road and there has been testimony here relative to what 'on the road' means in the operation of trains. This means, as closely as practicable, and not absolutely. That is, what is reasonable under all the circumstances." Both the instruction and the refusal to charge are assigned as error. This whole subject could have no very important bearing on the case. If the conductor did order plaintiff under the car and then did give a signal to go ahead while plaintiff was obeying this order, defendant could not be heard to say that its duty toward plaintiff was diminished by the fact that the order he was obeying was unusual and one which he was not required by any rule to obey. If defendant's construction of this rule was correct, and it does not apply to such a train as this was, the fact is important only as throwing light on the probability of the story of plaintiff that the conductor ordered him under the car. We, however, find no error, technical or otherwise, either in the instruction given or

in the failure to give the instruction asked. We think this train was "on the road" as that term was used in the rule. It was fully made up, ready for travel, was in charge of a road crew, was due to start, past due in fact, had already made the attempt to leave the station, and was only prevented from doing so by insufficient motive power. The opinion testimony of brakeman Cummings fully confirms this view.

6. The damages are not excessive. Plaintiff suffered the loss of both arms and the virtual loss of a leg. The jury awarded $39,000. It is conceded that this amount, though very large, is not excessive, unless defendant is entitled to some deduction under the Federal law on account of the contributory negligence of the plaintiff. It is contended, however, that plaintiff was guilty of negligence as a matter of law, and that some deduction must accordingly be made. We cannot so hold. If plaintiff's story as to the orders given him by the conductor, which necessitated his going under the car, was true, the jury might find that plaintiff was not negligent at all. They found this story true when they returned their verdict for plaintiff.

Order affirmed.

JORGEN F. HEIBERG v. WILD RICE BOOM COMPANY.[1]

July 31, 1914.

Nos. 18,487—(65).

Navigable river — riparian rights subordinate to rights of state.
1. The rights of mill and other riparian owners upon navigable rivers are subordinate to the right of the state to improve the river for navigation,

---

[1] Reported in 148 N. W. 517.

Note.—As to the correlative rights of log owners and riparian owners, see notes in 41 L.R.A. 377, and 32 L.R.A.(N.S.) 376. And upon the question of liability for injuries to riparian owner by running of logs in stream, see notes in 41 L.R.A. 494; 64 L.R.A. 983, 986, and 35 L.R.A.(N.S.) 824.

and to the rights conferred upon logging corporations organized under section 6263, G. S. 1913, with the limitation that the rights so conferred must be exercised in a reasonable manner and so as not unnecessarily to injure or damage riparian rights.

Damages for building flooding dams.

2. The construction of flooding dams by such corporation is not unlawful, and no damages can be recovered therefor, unless the construction thereof and the conduct of the same be unreasonable.

Charge to jury — rights of logging company.

3. The charge of the court to the effect that defendant, a logging corporation, had no rights in or to the river in question, a navigable stream, superior or paramount to plaintiff, a mill owner, *held* error.

Injury to rights of riparian owner — evidence.

4. Evidence *held* insufficient to justify recovery for the alleged negligence of defendant in conducting a drive of logs, in consequence of which the logs were permitted to come in contact with the river bank, thus injuring plaintiff's riparian rights.

Action in the district court for Norman county to recover $7,000. The substance of the complaint is stated at the beginning of the opinion. The case was tried before Grindeland, J., who denied defendant's motions to dismiss the action and for a directed verdict upon each cause of action, and a jury which returned a verdict for $2,500 upon the first cause of action and $250 upon the second cause of action. From an order denying its motion for judgment in its favor notwithstanding the verdict or for a new trial, defendant appealed. Reversed and new trial granted.

Lind, Ueland & Jerome, for appellant.

Christian G. Dosland, for respondent.

BROWN, C. J.

The Wild Rice river has its origin or source in Eastern Mahnomen county, being supplied by various lakes and tributary streams of lesser importance, and flows in a westerly direction through Norman county and into the Red River of the North. Some 20 years or more ago plaintiff under authority of law constructed a dam across the stream at a point in Norman county, for the purpose of collecting and storing the water of the river in a mill pond to be used for power purposes in the operation of his flour mill, and an electric light plant, subsequently installed and operated in connection with the mill. Defendant is a corporation duly organized and existing under the provisions of section 6263, G. S. 1913, and was so organized as a public service corporation, and for the purpose of handling, transporting and driving logs down this river. As such it is clothed with all the power and authority vested in such corporations by the statute under which it was organized. It has so operated upon the river since its incorporation in March, 1908. Plaintiff claimed that it has so wrongfully, unlawfully and negligently conducted its operations upon the river as to cause injury and damage to him in the operation of his mill and light plant, and this action was brought to recover therefor. The complaint states two causes of action: (1) The wrongful, unlawful and unreasonable conduct of defendant in damming up certain tributaries of the river and thereby impounding and holding back the water and preventing it from flowing in its natural way past plaintiff's mill, thus depriving plaintiff of the power he would otherwise have; and (2) negligence in driving logs down the stream by means of which the logs were permitted, after passing through the sluiceway of the dam, to butt into the banks of the river adjacent to plaintiff's land, thereby digging away the sand and injuring his riparian rights. The defendant, by its answer, put in issue the allegation of the wrongful, unlawful and negligent conduct, and specially pleaded the authority granted to it by the statute under which it was organized and incorporated. Plaintiff had separate verdicts; upon the first cause of action for $2,500, and upon the second for $250. Defendant appealed from an order denying its alternative motion for judgment or a new trial.

The evidence tends to show, in respect to the first cause of action, and it is sufficient to justify the verdict, that during the years complained of, namely, 1910, 1911 and 1912, the defendant by constructing dams in some of the tributaries of the river impounded the waters therein and prevented them from flowing in the usual and natural way past plaintiff's mill, in consequence of which plaintiff was deprived of the use of the water for power purposes; and was compelled to install in the mill a steam power plant at considerable expense, and that before the installation of the same the mill remained idle for the lack of power to operate it, resulting in a loss of profits that he would have realized had defendant not so withheld the water by its dams.

It is contended by defendant that the river is a navigable stream, therefore a public highway, and that its rights therein and to the use thereof are paramount and superior to the rights of plaintiff or other riparian owners; that in constructing the dams complained of it exercised, as a public service corporation, a right expressly conferred by law, and that incidental or consequential injuries resulting therefrom to riparian owners are *damnum absque injuria,* for which no recovery can be had. The trial court declined to submit the case to the jury in harmony with these contentions, and did instruct that the parties possessed equal rights in the river, to be exercised by each with due regard to the other, and that defendant had no rights which were superior to those of plaintiff. Exceptions were duly noted. The contentions of defendant involve two distinct questions, namely: (1) The relative rights of the parties in and to the use of the river; and (2) the extent of defendant's liability for the alleged wrongful withholding of the water by its dams.

1. The charge of the court was in all respects correct, viewed from the standpoint of the common law, but the failure of the court to give effect to the statutory grant of power under which the defendant was conducting its operations we think was error. Defendant was incorporated under the provisions of chapter 89, p. 106, Laws 1905 (section 6263, G. S. 1913), and had taken possession of the river under the authority there conferred. That statute provides for the incorporation of logging companies, requires them to serve the public equally and reasonably, and for a reasonable compensation, and authorizes them to take possession of any navigable stream of water in the state suitable for the handling and floating of logs, to improve the same, and its tributaries, by straightening the banks thereof and deepening its channel, and to construct booms, sluiceways, flooding dams, and other works necessary to facilitate the driving of logs thereon.

The state has exclusive control of navigable lakes and rivers with-

in its borders, with full power and authority in the improvement
thereof for the purposes of navigation. It may delegate this authority to corporations organized for the purpose, and the corporation to which it is so delegated acts in a representative capacity
for the state, performing a public function. No person or corporation, whether riparian owner or otherwise, not so authorized, has
a right to make changes or alterations in such rivers, and any act
in that respect would amount to an unlawful interference with the
waterway and subject the wrongdoer to damages suffered as a result
thereof. By the statute referred to the legislature has expressly
granted to corporations organized thereunder authority in this respect, in broad terms, thus conferring upon them a power and right
not possessed by riparian owners or other persons. The power and
authority so granted, being for a public purpose and in aid of navigation, is superior and paramount to the rights of riparian owners.
The improvements made under the power, dams constructed, or
other works placed in the river, are not unlawful, and can be complained of by a riparian owner only when there appears an unreasonable encroachment upon his shore or mill dam rights. In other
words the riparian owner holds his land subordinate to the public
rights in the river, and subject to the power of the state to make
necessary improvements therein in the aid of navigation. Fish v.
Chicago G. W. R. Co. 125 Minn. 380, 147 N. W. 431; Minneapolis
Mill Co. v. Board of Water Commrs. 56 Minn. 485, 58 N. W. 33;
Doucette v. Little Falls Imp. & Nav. Co. 71 Minn. 206, 73 N. W.
847; Coyne v. Mississippi & R. R. Boom Co. 72 Minn. 533, 75 N.
W. 748, 41 L.R.A. 494, 71 Am. St. 508; Holyoke Water Power
Co. v. Connecticut River Co. 52 Conn. 570.

The charge of the court to the effect that defendant possessed no
rights in the river superior or paramount to plaintiff was, therefore,
error, and clearly prejudicial. The jury might well have concluded
from the instructions that, as defendant had no superior rights in
the matter, its conduct in constructing the flooding dams was unlawful and wrongful, rendering it liable for that reason alone. But
the act of defendant in damming the tributaries was not unlawful
nor wrongful, but the exercise of a right expressly conferred by

law, and for which no liability could attach except for unreasonably detaining the water, and unreasonably preventing it from flowing past plaintiff's mill. The question should have been submitted to the jury in this view of the legal rights of the parties.

2. The statute so extending this authority cannot be construed as a protection to the logging company for all injuries resulting to riparian owners. It serves as a protection to the extent the state would be free from liability for the same acts and no further. While it is well settled that injury and damage resulting from improvements in such rivers which are merely incidental or consequential are *damnum absque injuria* (Fish v. Chicago G. W. R. Co. 125 Minn. 380, 147 N. W. 431), the rule does not extend so far as to justify a taking of private property, or an unnecessary injury thereto. If it were construed so broadly it would clearly violate the constitutional guaranty that private property shall not be taken or damaged for public use without compensation first paid or secured. Weaver v. Mississippi & R. R. Boom Co. 28 Minn. 534, 11 N. W. 114; 2 Notes on Minn. Reports, 253. But limiting the exemption from liability to merely consequential injuries the statute is valid. Coyne v. Mississippi & R. R. Boom Co. 72 Minn. 533, 75 N. W. 748, 71 Am. St. 508; 4 Notes on Minn. Reports, 425; 41 L.R.A. 494, and note. In respect to all other injuries, resulting from such improvements, the liability of the logging company must be measured by the rule of reasonable use. It has the right to construct flooding dams in the river tributaries, but no right to unreasonably detain the water from the riparian or lower mill owners. What will amount to unreasonable conduct will necessarily be determined by the special facts of each particular case, and is for the jury to determine. The instructions of the court upon this feature of the case are not open to serious criticism. But for the error in the instructions as to the relative rights of the parties, from which the jury might conclude that as a matter of law the construction of the dams was in itself wrongful, there must be a new trial.

In view of this result we remark that the case has been considered and disposed of upon the theory that the river in question is a navigable stream. The case was tried below upon that theory and the contention of plaintiff in this court that it is not navigable is not sustained. If on the new trial it shall appear that the river is not navigable, within the meaning of the law, and can be made so only by artificial means, it is probable that an entirely different rule will control the rights of the parties. 1 Farnham, Waters, 365. It is unnecessary to enter into a discussion of the law upon that subject. The question is not presented. Nor is it important that defendant was not licensed to take possession of the river by the board of county commissioners as provided for by section 5433, G. S. 1913. Defendant's authority in the premises is granted by the statute under which it was incorporated, and by that, if the river be navigable, it must stand or fall.

3. The assignments of error relating to plaintiff's second cause of action do not require extended mention. It is claimed that, by reason of the negligence of defendant in handling a drive, the logs after passing through the sluiceway of plaintiff's dam were permitted to damage and injure the shore land by butting into the river banks. If this is not a consequential injury under the facts as presented (Coyne v. Mississippi & R. R. Boom Co. supra), for which no recovery can be had, we are of opinion, and so hold, that the evidence is wholly insufficient to justify the conclusion of negligence on the part of defendant. We are firmly impressed that the construction of plaintiff's dam diagonally across the river resulted in the creation of a whirlpool at the sluiceway, by reason of which the logs passing through the sluiceway were thrown into the whirlpool, and caused to jam the banks of the river, a condition for which defendant is not responsible. The evidence on the new trial may, however, entirely change the situation, and make the issue one for the jury.

This covers all assignments of error that require mention. And for the error pointed out there must be a new trial.

Order reversed and new trial granted.

C. N. SONNESYN v. HENRY HAWBAKER.[1]

July 31, 1914.

Nos. 18,630—(160).

Partnership — verdict sustained by jury.

1. Plaintiff procured the sale of a tract of land from a third party to defendant, the contract being taken in the name of defendant. The evidence sustains the finding of the jury that it was agreed between plaintiff and defendant that the land was bought for their joint benefit, and that, on plaintiff's procuring a sale, the parties should divide the net profits.

Same — statute of frauds.

2. Such a contract was in the nature of a partnership or joint adventure, and was not the sale to plaintiff of an interest in land, and was not within the statute of frauds.

Verdict negatives fraud of plaintiff — offer of evidence.

3. Evidence was received upon the question whether plaintiff committed a fraud upon the vendor by acting as agent and purchasing in his own interest, without the consent of the vendor, and the question was submitted to the jury, and they were instructed that if such conditions existed their verdict must be for defendant. The verdict for plaintiff is a finding that there was no such fraud, and defendant cannot obtain relief on that ground. The rejection of a certain offer of evidence of fraud and the denial of a motion to amend to allege such fraud, *held* not prejudicial error in view of the fact that it does not appear that further material evidence could have been produced.

Evidence of collateral facts.

4. The reception of certain evidence as to collateral facts was within the discretion of the trial court and was properly received as corroborative of plaintiff's testimony.

Demand for money — evidence admissible.

5. Evidence of a demand for money to which no reply is made may be received when the demand is made under such circumstances that a reply would ordinarily be made.

New trial — remarks of counsel.

6. Determination of the question whether improper remarks of counsel

---

[1] Reported in 148 N. W. 476.

were prejudicial rests largely in the discretion of the trial court. Counsel made improper remarks in his address to .the jury. The court directed him to desist and he did so and the court directed the jury not to con- sider such matters as were the subject of the remarks. The case pre- sented does not warrant this court in granting a new trial on this ground.

Record on appeal — original verdict conclusive.
7. The original verdict filed with the clerk is part of the record proper, and is no proper part of a settled case. If the verdict as incorporated in the settled case conflicts with the original verdict as so filed, the latter will be regarded in this court as the true verdict.

Action in the district court for Watonwan county to recover $2,- 640 for loss of one-half of the profits to be derived from the sale of certain premises. The case was tried before Pfau, J., who de- nied defendant's motion for a directed verdict, and a jury which returned a verdict for $3,331.71 in favor of plaintiff. From an order denying his motion for judgment notwithstanding the verdict or for a new trial, defendant apealed. Affirmed.

J. L. Lobben, S. B. Wilson, E. J. Hawbaker and *Henry W. Mead,* for appellant.

Hammond & Farmer, for respondent.

HALLAM, J.

Plaintiff was engaged in the land business at Butterfield, Waton- wan county, Minnesota. Defendant was a resident of Illinois, a man of means and an investor in southern Minnesota lands. Plain- tiff and defendant had had some land dealings prior to the transac- tion here in question. In 1909 one Peter Falk had for sale a farm near Butterfield. It had been on the market for some time at $36 an acre. In the summer he went to Dakota and, before going, raised the price to $45 an acre. Plaintiff had the land listed for sale but had no exclusive agency. It was listed with another agent also. Plaintiff had previously tried to interest defendant in this land. On defendant's arrival in Butterfield, in September, 1909, the subject of buying this land came up again. Defendant was not willing to negotiate at the new price of $45 an acre. After several conferences between plaintiff and defendant it was decided to prepare a contract of sale running from Falk to defendant at the old price of $36 an acre, to have defendant sign it and send it on to Falk with a check for $1,000, as a proposition which he might accept by signing and returning the contract. This was done, and Falk returned the contract signed. This contract called for further payments and delivery of a deed March 1, 1910.

It is conceded that there was some further negotiation between plaintiff and defendant as to the resale of the land. The parties are not agreed as to the nature of this negotiation. Plaintiff testified that it was agreed "he would go in with me on a half of the profits, and advance the money at 6 per cent interest, provided I would stand the loss, if there was any." Defendant's version is that he told plaintiff "if you sell this farm by the first day of January for $50 an acre I will give you half of the difference between $36 and $50 * * * . He said all right."

Plaintiff claims that in November, 1909, he made a resale of the land to one Fletcher Brown at $50 an acre, less $2 an acre commission to be paid another agent, took from Brown a written contract and received from him $500 earnest money; that he reported this sale to defendant and defendant then said he preferred to keep the land and to pay plaintiff the amount he would receive on consummation of such a sale, and that this was agreed to. Defendant denies this and denies that he was ever informed of a sale to Brown, or to anyone, or that any resale was ever made.

The jury found for plaintiff.

1. The questions whether the agreement was as plaintiff claims, whether the sale to Brown was in fact made, and whether defendant made the subsequent agreement to pay plaintiff the amount here demanded, are pure questions of fact with ample evidence to support a finding in favor of plaintiff. We accept the jury's determination of these facts in plaintiff's favor as final.

2. Defendant contends that the agreement as testified to by plaintiff was one for the conveyance to him of an interest in land, and was void because not in writing. It appears to us that the contract as testified to by plaintiff created a partnership or a joint adventure. Defendant contributed the capital. Plaintiff contributed his serv-

127 M.—2.

ices and assumed some financial obligation. The technical name
of the relationship created is not important. It was a joint enterprise for their mutual benefit. The agreement was a valid and binding one. It was not necessary that it be in writing. It is well settled
in this state that an agreement between two parties to purchase real
property for the purpose of selling again for a joint profit is a
contract in the nature of a partnership and is valid though not in
writing. Newell v. Cochran, 41 Minn. 374, 43 N. W. 84; Stitt v.
Rat Portage Lumber Co. 98 Minn. 52, 107 N. W. 824. An agreement to share profits or losses arising from the purchase and sale
of real estate is not a contract for the transfer or conveyance of an
interest in land. 20 Cyc. 237; Bates v. Babcock, 95 Cal. 479, 30
Pac. 605, 16 L.R.A. 745, 29 Am. St. 133; Babcock v. Read, 99
N. Y. 609, 1 N. E. 149; Bruce v. Hastings, 41 Vt. 380, 98 Am.
Dec. 592. It is not important that the contract related to only one
piece of land. The character of the contract and the relationship
it creates between the parties depends upon its terms, and not upon
the magnitude or extent of the transactions covered. Stitt v. Rat
Portage Lumber Co. 98 Minn. 52, 107 N. W. 824; Irvine v. Campbell, 121 Minn. 192, 141 N. W. 108. If the contracts as testified
to by plaintiff were in fact made, they then are valid and binding
contracts.

3. The next contention is that, if the purchase of this land from
Falk was part of a joint adventure, the contract was void, because
plaintiff was the agent of Falk, and a purchase in his own interest
was contrary to good morals and public policy. We need spend no
time discussing the proposition that an agent to sell cannot sell to
himself, and if he does so the principal may declare the contract
void. Whether one who is a partner in a purchase may avoid his
partnership agreement on the ground that the negotiation is a fraud
upon a third party may not be free from doubt, but we are not
troubled with that question here. A real estate agent with whom
land is listed for sale may buy from his principal if his principal
so wills it. The court submitted to the jury the question whether
plaintiff did in fact perpetrate a fraud on Falk. He instructed the
jury that, if plaintiff did do so, "he would not be entitled to recover

in this case," but that if "while he was acting for Peter Falk as agent to a certain extent and while he had this land listed with him for sale * * * it was understood that he would have the right to buy the land * * * if he had that understanding with Peter Falk, then he had the right to buy it for himself and can recover in this action." The jury, by finding a verdict in favor of plaintiff, necessarily found this issue in plaintiff's favor, that is, they necessarily found that plaintiff had an understanding with Falk that he had the right to buy for himself. The evidence sustains this finding. Plaintiff explicitly testified that Falk urged him to buy. Falk said: "He was to sell it, nothing else, whether he bought it or whether he sold it to some one else, I didn't care," and the evidence shows that Falk did not in fact pay plaintiff any agent's commission.

Defendant made offer of proof as follows: "We wish to make an offer at this time, to prove by this witness (Peter Falk) that the plaintiff through fraud induced Peter Falk to reduce the price on this land from $45 to $36 an acre, and that he represented to Mr. Falk that he had sold this land to one, other than himself; and that said Falk did not know at the time of the sale that the plaintiff claimed to be interested in such purchase and sale; and if the plaintiff's claim is true as made in this action he is advancing a fraud, which the law nor the courts will not permit or encourage, and if such facts are proved, it is urged by the defendant in this action, it prevents a recovery in this case." This offer was objected to and objection sustained. This ruling is assigned as error. In view of the theory on which the court submitted the case, the objection should have been overruled. We think it clear, however, that the error was without prejudice. Defendant's counsel did in fact examine Falk on this subject. He testified that he did not know plaintiff was buying for himself but, as above indicated, he said that whether plaintiff bought himself or sold to another was of no concern to him. The negotiation with Falk after consummation of the agreement with defendant was by telegram and letter, which were received in evidence. Defendant's offer does not make it clear that he could have proved by the witness any further facts than were put in evidence. In fact it seems quite apparent from Falk's testimony that he could not have done so.

Defendant assigns as error the refusal of the court to permit him to amend his answer so as to plead that plaintiff perpetrated a fraud on Falk. The motion to amend should probably have been granted. However, inasmuch as the evidence admissible under the amendment was received and the issue it would have raised was submitted to the jury, the refusal of the amendment could not prejudice the defendant.

4. It was proper to show that Falk did not pay plaintiff any commission on the sale. It had a tendency to corroborate the testimony of plaintiff as to the arrangement with defendant. Evidence as to the value of the land was likewise properly received. It may not have been of great probative value, but it was a collateral fact, having some tendency to corroborate the testimony of plaintiff as showing the reasonableness and probability of plaintiff's version of the negotiation between plaintiff and defendant. The reception of such testimony rests largely in the discretion of the trial court. Glassberg v. Olson, 89 Minn. 195, 94 N. W. 554; Dalby v. Lauritzen, 98 Minn. 75, 107 N. W. 826; Humphrey v. Monida & Yellowstone Stage Co. 115 Minn. 18, 131 N. W. 498. There was no abuse of discretion.

5. Defendant assigns as error the reception of "Exhibit D," a letter written by plaintiff to defendant making demand for the amount claimed, and stating the ground of his demand. This was properly received. Where a demand is made upon a party under such circumstances that he would naturally deny if he did not assent, the demand and failure to reply may be received as evidence in the nature of an admission tending to prove the justice of the demand. 1 Greenleaf, Ev. § 197, 2 Wigmore, Ev. § 1073; Murphey v. Gates, 81 Wis. 370, 51 N. W. 573.

6. It is claimed the court should grant a new trial on account of certain remarks of counsel as follows:

"You cannot make me believe that this man Hawbaker has acquired all these farms in Illinois, Iowa and Minnesota, and all his riches by the sweat of his brow. He is located in Watonwan county until he can get the increase on his land, then he will sell out and go back to Illinois. He is not a part of Watonwan county."

Upon exception taken to these remarks the court directed counsel to confine his remarks to the evidence, and he desisted. The court in his charge directed the jury to disregard such matters as were mentioned by counsel in these remarks. The remarks were improper, but we cannot think they prejudiced the jury. We have not before us the context. The trial court, "with much better opportunity than we have, has decided, in refusing a new trial, that they did not prejudice. The record would have to show a decided probability of prejudice to justify us in reversing that decision. The case, as presented, does not call on us to do so." Johnson v. Chicago, B. & N. R. Co. 37 Minn. 519, 35 N. W. 438.

7. It is urged that the damages awarded are excessive. The verdict, as shown by the settled case, is for $3,331.71, and is excessive by about $200. The original verdict filed with the clerk has been returned to this court, and it is plainly for $3,131.71, an amount not excessive. The original verdict controls and will be regarded by this court as the true verdict. The verdict is one of the "papers properly filed with the clerk," is part of the record proper, and should have been excluded from the settled case. G. S. 1913, § 7831; Peach v. Reed, 87 Minn. 375, 92 N. W. 229.

Order affirmed.

GRACE H. MERRIAM v. ROBERT H. MERRIAM.[1]

July 31, 1914.

Nos. 18,895—(292).

Injunction — divorce action in foreign state.
    Judgment was entered in a court in Minnesota in favor of the plaintiff,

[1] Reported in 148 N. W. 478.

Note.—The authorities on the general question as to injunction against action or proceeding in foreign jurisdiction are reviewed in notes in 21 L.R.A. 71 and 25 L.R.A.(N.S.) 267.

the wife of the defendant, in an equitable action for separate support.
The defendant, having become a resident and citizen of Illinois, brought
an action for divorce against the plaintiff in a court of that state.   It
is *held* that the trial court did not err in denying the plaintiff's application
for a temporary injunction restraining defendant from proceeding with his
action for divorce in Illinois.

Action in the district court for Ramsey county.   From an order,
Catlin, J., denying plaintiff's motion for an order requiring defendant to dismiss his action for divorce against plaintiff in the superior
court of Cook county, Illinois; denying plaintiff's motion for an
order restraining defendant from prosecuting that action in that
court; denying plaintiff's motion requiring defendant to pay plaintiff $250 on account of attorney's fees necessarily incurred by her
in defending the action in Illinois; denying plaintiff's motion to
pay her $250 attorney's fees in the present action, plaintiff appealed.
Affirmed.

B. H. Schriber, for appellant.

Stan J. Donnelly and *Stan Dillon Donnelly,* for respondent.

DIBELL, C.

This action is brought to restrain the defendant from prosecuting
an action against the plaintiff for divorce in the superior court of
Cook county, Illinois.   The plaintiff appeals from an order denying her application for a temporary injunction.

In an action brought by the plaintiff against the defendant in
the district court of Ramsey county, Minnesota, for separate support, judgment was entered on April 22, 1913, adjudging in substance that the defendant pay the plaintiff $125 per month, com-
mencing May 10, 1913, so long as plaintiff continued to live separate and apart from her husband.   This judgment was entered pursuant to a stipulation of the parties and an order of the court based
thereon.   It was an equitable action for separate support, not an
action for a limited divorce.   See Baier v. Baier, 91 Minn. 165, 97
N. W. 671.

The defendant claims that in October, 1912, he established his
residence in Chicago, and that he is now a resident and citizen of

Illinois. The evidence on the hearing of the motion was *prima facie* sufficient in proof of residence and citizenship in Illinois. In April, 1914, the defendant commenced an action for divorce in the superior court of Cook county and in that action the plaintiff in this action was served with process and has appeared and answered.

The defendant Robert H. Merriam was personally served in this state with process in the pending action. Without discussing what are the powers of a Minnesota court to restrain the defendant from proceeding with his divorce action in Illinois, it is quite clear that the court committed no error in refusing a temporary injunction. A temporary injunction in a case like this is issued with caution. Hawkins v. Ireland, 64 Minn. 339, 67 N. W. 73, 58 Am. St. 534; Freick v. Hinkly, 122 Minn. 24, 141 N. W. 1096, 46 L.R.A.(N.S.) 695, and cases cited.

The courts of Illinois will properly dispose of the litigation and will properly determine whether the plaintiff is in fact a resident and citizen of Illinois and entitled to a divorce there. If the judgment rendered in this court is in issue in the Illinois court, it will be construed properly, and full faith and credit will be given to it under the faith and credit clause of the Federal Constitution.

Order affirmed.

MINNESOTA CANAL & POWER COMPANY v. FALL LAKE BOOM COMPANY and Others.[1]

August 7, 1894.

Nos. 18,544—(94).

Eminent domain — exercise of the power.

1. The power of eminent domain rests exclusively in the legislature and can be exercised only as authorized by the legislature.

Same — taking by public service corporation.

2. Under the statutes relating to public service corporations, it is the

[1] Reported in 148 N. W. 561.

duty of the court to determine, in each particular case, whether the taking of the designated property is necessary for the purposes of the proposed enterprise, and whether such property may lawfully be taken for such purposes.

Same — diversion of water.

3. Such corporations cannot divert water from the navigable streams of one drainage basin into those of another drainage basin, if such diversion will impair the navigability of the streams from which the water is proposed to be taken.

Same — in aid of public use.

4. Private property can be condemned only when it can be made to subserve some public use. If the purpose for which it is sought to take private property cannot be accomplished, such taking will not subserve public purposes, is not necessary within the meaning of the statute, and is unauthorized.

Same — burden of proof.

5. The burden of showing that such purpose can be accomplished is upon the petitioner.

Same — finding sustained by evidence.

6. The evidence justifies the conclusion of the trial court that the purpose of the proposed enterprise cannot be accomplished without impairing the navigability of the navigable waters of the Birch lake drainage basin.

Petition to the district court for Lake county for the appointment of commissioners to assess and determine the damages to be paid to the owners of certain lands necessary for the construction and maintenance of certain reservoirs and canals and the diversion of the waters of Birch lake and its tributaries into the valley · of the St. Louis river and to the pipe lines and water wheels of petitioner's water power and electric plants at West Duluth. The petition was heard before Cant, J., who made findings and denied it. From the judgment entered pursuant to the order, petitioner appealed. Affirmed.

Tyler, Corneau & Eames and *Butler & Mitchell,* for appellant.

H. J. Grannis, J. N. Searles, J. A. P. Neal, Thomas J. Davis, Harris & Pearson, J. A. Wharton, Washburn, Bailey & Mitchell, Wilson G. Crosby, I. C. Buell, and *Willson & Morgan,* for respondents.

TAYLOR, C.

The petitioner and appellant, the Minnesota Canal & Power Co., was first incorporated some 20 years ago. Its business as defined in its amended articles of incorporation, or charter, is to generate and distribute electricity for public use, to supply the public with water, and to improve navigation. To accomplish these purposes it is authorized by its charter to construct, maintain and operate dams, reservoirs, canals, power plants, transmission lines, and all other works and appliances necessary or convenient therefor; and to acquire by purchase, condemnation or otherwise, any and all property and rights in property necessary or convenient for carrying on its operations. The charter also provides that all things authorized therein and done thereunder shall be "for public use on equal terms and for a reasonable compensation, subject to the supervision and control of the state of Minnesota."

The company, in a petition filed in the district court of Lake county, states that, in order to accomplish the object for which it was organized, it desires to construct and maintain a continuous navigable waterway from Birch lake to West Duluth capable of floating logs, timber, canal boats, barges and other water craft; that, by means of such waterway, it proposes to furnish water for public use, and also to create and operate, at West Duluth, a waterpower for generating electricity for public use; and asks the court to determine that the prosecution of such enterprise and the taking of the property, easements and rights necessary for the prosecution of the same are required by the public interests, and to appoint commissioners to ascertain the damages that will be sustained by the several property owners by reason of the construction of the proposed improvements and the taking of the property, easements and rights necessary therefor. The extent and nature of the enterprise is indicated in the following excerpt from the findings of the trial court:

"That the waters of Birch lake, Birch river, north and south branches of the Kawishiwi river, White Iron lake, Garden lake, Farm lake and the connecting streams and waterways between Fall lake and Basswood lake are navigable waters of the state of Minnesota and of the United States; that all of said waters are tributary to

Basswood lake and flow thence into and along and form a part of
the boundary waters between the United States and the Dominion
of Canada, along the line from Lake Superior to the Lake of the
Woods, and are discharged into the Lake of the Woods and thence
north, through connecting streams and lakes, into Hudson Bay.
* * *

"That the aforesaid waters, tributary to Basswood lake, are in
what is known as the Birch lake drainage basin, the area of which
basin is something more than 1,100 square miles; that between the
Birch lake drainage basin and the St. Louis river drainage basin, to
the south, is a height of land, forming a natural watershed. That
the waters to the north of said height of land drain into said Birch
lake drainage basin, and the waters to the south thereof drain into
the St. Louis river drainage basin. That the plans and purposes
of the petitioner contemplate the construction of a dam across Birch
river, at the outlet of Birch lake to the north, of sufficient dimensions
and so designed, as to raise the waters of Birch lake twenty feet
above the mean low water level thereof, and by the aid thereof and
of other dams and structures, to control and reservoir a considerable
portion of the waters of said Birch lake drainage basin and by means
of a canal cut through the said height of land, forming the watershed between said Birch lake drainage basin and said St. Louis
River drainage basin, the petitioner proposes to divert water, impounded in said Birch lake, by the aforesaid means, through said
canal and the Embarrass river, a tributary of the St. Louis river,
into the St. Louis river and to take said waters from the St. Louis
river, above the city of Cloquet and by means of a canal, some
twenty-four miles in length, to deliver said waters, by appropriate
appliances, at or in the vicinity of West Duluth, in said county of
St. Louis, for the purpose of generating electrical power for public
use, sale and distribution."

Two previous applications by this company to acquire substantially the same rights and privileges now in question have already
been considered and determined by this court; and a more complete
description of the purpose and scope of the enterprise will be found
in the opinions in those cases. In the first case (Minnesota Canal

& Power Co. v. Koochiching Co. 97 Minn. 429, 107 N. W. 405, 5 L.R.A.(N.S.) 638, 7 Ann. Cas. 1182), the application was denied, upon the ground that such an enterprise was not authorized by the statutes then in force, and upon the further ground that the petition then before the court sought to take the property, in part, for private purposes. The Revised Laws of 1905 amended the statutes, and thereafter the company amended its articles of incorporation and filed a new petition. A motion to dismiss this second application was granted by the trial court, on the ground that the petition did not state facts sufficient to authorize taking the property sought for the purpose of the enterprise. On appeal this court held (Minnesota Canal & Power Co. v. Pratt, 101 Minn. 197, 112 N. W. 395, 11 L.R.A.(N.S.) 105), that the company, under this petition and its amended charter, was entitled to exercise the power of eminent domain conferred upon public service corporations; that the statutes as amended authorized the diversion of water from one drainage basin to another, if such diversion would not interfere with navigation and was not forbidden by some state or Federal law; that the laws of Minnesota prohibited any such diversion of water which would interfere with the rights of navigation or with other public uses to which the waters were already devoted; that, as the case was before the court as upon demurrer to the petition, the allegations therein must be treated as true in determining the questions then under consideration; that the laws of Minnesota did not forbid the construction of the proposed works, if the company could prove at the hearing the following allegations of its petition: "That your petitioner's said works and the diversion of water as proposed by your petitioner will not interfere with the navigable capacity of any of said waters and will not interfere with any navigation of which they are capable, and your petitioner's works can and will be so conducted as not to interfere with such navigation or any public use thereof, but, on the contrary, so as to aid and facilitate the same and so as to increase and improve the navigable capacity of said waters;" that the Federal laws prohibited the construction of such works without first obtaining a permit therefor from the Secretary of War; and that the petitioner was not entitled to prosecute its enterprise, for the reason that it had failed to procure such permit. Thereafter the company procured such permit, inserted an allegation to that effect in its petition, and without any other substantial change therein, made the application now in question. After an extended hearing at which much evidence was taken, the trial court found against the petitioner on the facts and rendered judgment denying the application. The petitioner appealed.

The power of eminent domain rests exclusively in the legislature and can be exercised only as authorized by the legislature. The legislature has provided that a public service corporation may take property under this power, "if the proposed taking shall appear to be necessary and such as is authorized by law," and has imposed upon the courts the duty to determine these questions. G. S. 1913, §§ 6137, 6246, 5401. Although in all cases the propriety and expediency of condemning private property for public use is a purely legislative question, yet, under our statutes, it becomes the duty of the court to determine, in each particular case, whether the taking of the designated property is necessary for the purposes of the proposed enterprise, and whether such property may lawfully be taken for such purposes. In Re St. Paul & Northern Pacific Ry. Co. 34 Minn. 227, 25 N. W. 345; In re St. Paul & Northern Pacific Ry. Co. 37 Minn. 164, 33 N. W. 701; In re Minneapolis Railway Terminal Co. 38 Minn. 157, 36 N. W. 105; McGee v. Board of County Commrs. of Hennepin County, 84 Minn. 472, 88 N. W. 6; Minneapolis & St. L. R. Co. v. Village of Hartland, 85 Minn. 76, 88 N. W. 423; State v. Crosby, 92 Minn. 176, 99 N. W. 636. That analogous statutes devolve the determination of such questions upon the courts is held by the authorities generally. Portneuf Irrigating Co. v. Budge, 16 Idaho, 116, 100 Pac. 1046, 18 Ann. Cas. 674; Bigelow v. Draper, 6 N. D. 152, 69 N. W. 570; Town of Greenburg v. International Trust Co. 36 C. C. A. 471, 94 Fed. 755; Olmsted v. Proprietors of Morris Aqueduct, 46 N. J. Law, 495; Seattle & M. Ry. Co. v. State, 7 Wash. 150, 34 Pac. 551, 22 L.R.A. 217, 38 Am. St. 866; Rensselaer & S. R. Co. v. Davis, 43 N. Y. 137; Re New York Cent. Ry. Co. 66 N. Y. 407; City of Rome v. Whitestown Water Works Co. 113 App. Div. 547, 100 N. Y. Supp. 357; Wilmington

Canal & Reservoir Co. v. Dominguez, 50 Cal. 505; Spring Valley Waterworks v. Drinkhouse, 92 Cal. 528, 28 Pac. 621; City of Santa Ana v. Gildmacher, 133 Cal. 395, 65 Pac. 883; Sand Creek Lateral Irrigation Co. v. Davis, 17 Colo. 326, 29 Pac. 742; Montana Cent. Ry. Co. v. Helena & R. M. R. Co. 6 Mont. 416, 12 Pac. 916; Tracy v. Elizabethtown L. & B. S. R. Co. 80 Ky. 259; Riley v. Charleston Union Station Co. 71 S. C. 457, 51 S. E. 485, 110 Am. St. 579; Atlantic & B. R. Co. v. Penny, 119 Ga. 479, 46 S. E. 665; Stearns v. City of Barre, 73 Vt. 281, 50 Atl. 1086, 58 L.R.A. 240, 87 Am. St. 721; Jockheck v. Shawnee County, 53 Kan. 780, 37 Pac. 621.

That the petitioner possesses the power of eminent domain conferred upon public service corporations; that it seeks to take the property in question for public use; that its project involves diverting the water necessary therefor from navigable lakes and watercourses without ever returning it thereto; and that the laws of Minnesota forbid any diversion of such waters which will impair the present or future navigability of such lakes and watercourses, or which will interfere with any public use to which they are now devoted, has already been settled and determined, and such questions are not in controversy in this case. The principal controversy is whether the petitioner can carry out its enterprise without impairing the navigability of the streams from which the water for such enterprise would be diverted. The trial court found:

"That the waters of Birch lake, Birch river, north and south branches of the Kawishiwi river, White Iron lake, Garden lake, Farm lake and Fall lake, have, in the past, been used and are now being used for purposes of navigation and are capable of still greater use, in the future, for such purposes; that the aforesaid waters of Basswood lake and the boundary waters between the United States and the Dominion of Canada, to which the aforesaid waters in the state of Minnesota are tributary, have been in the past and are now used for navigation and are capable of still greater uses for navigation in the future. * * * That the plans and purposes of the petitioner contemplate, and, if carried out, would require the diversion of a large quantity of water from said Birch lake drainage basin. That the aforesaid diversion by the petitioner from said Birch lake drainage basin of the quantity of water contemplated in its petition or of a quantity of water sufficient to develop or carry on the project of petitioner, or to make such project feasible or practicable, would substantially interfere with and impair the navigable capacity of the aforesaid navigable waters, and would substantially interfere with the navigation thereof; and that the diversion of the water contemplated by petitioner or of any substantial amount of water from said Birch lake drainage basin such as would be necessary to supply a canal or develop a waterpower project by diverting water from the Birch lake drainage basin into a canal connecting with the Embarrass and St. Louis rivers would substantially interfere with and impair the navigable capacity of the aforesaid navigable waters and the navigation thereof. That said substantial interference with and impairment of the navigable capacity of the aforesaid navigable waters and with the navigation thereof applies to the waters within the state of Minnesota and also to the aforesaid boundary waters between the United States and the Dominion of Canada, to which the said waters in the Birch lake drainage basin are tributary, and that such diversion of said waters from the Birch lake drainage basin would substantially interfere with and impair the uses of said waters, both while the said waters are in the state of Minnesota and when they become a part of said boundary waters for present and also future purposes of navigation. That the diversion of said waters of the Birch lake drainage basin by means of dams and reservoirs as contemplated in the petition herein and the taking of such waters into the Embarrass and St. Louis rivers would substantially and *pro tanto* impair the navigable capacity of those waters and the use for navigation by the citizens of both the United States and Dominion of Canada of the boundary waters in their natural flow." The petitioner claims to have avoided the effect of these findings by providing in its petition for the diversion of "such portion of the waters of the said Birch lake drainage basin as may be required to carry out the purposes of this corporation and the diversion of which will not interfere with the navigation, navigable capacity or public use of the waters of the said Birch lake drainage basin and the various lakes and streams to which they are tributary."

It contends that, by reason of this provision in the petition, it can take only such quantity of water as may be taken without affecting the navigability of the streams from which the water is diverted; and that no question as to interference with navigation is involved in the case. It also contends that the question as to whether its enterprise will prove a business and financial success is not for the court to consider. While these contentions, in the main, are true, we cannot concede the conclusions drawn therefrom by the petitioner.

The petitioner desires to construct a navigable waterway perhaps 150 miles in length. The project contemplates the construction of a canal from the Birch lake drainage basin to the St. Louis river drainage basin, the improvement of the Embarrass and St. Louis rivers, and the construction of a canal from a point near Cloquet on the St. Louis river to Duluth. It also contemplates the construction of dams in the Birch lake drainage basin which will raise the waters of that lake 20 feet in height and will necessarily interfere with the works and property of the Fall Lake Boom Co. The present works of that company were constructed for the purpose of aiding navigation in the streams of this basin, and by means thereof it transports to mills and market large quantities of logs and timber each season. There are numerous waterpowers within this basin, and the Fall Lake Boom Co. and also other companies possess waterpowers therein, and are authorized by the statutes and by their charters to improve such powers and to generate electricity thereat for public use. It does not appear that any such use has yet been made of these waterpowers, but the construction of the petitioner's works will interfere with using them in the future for the purpose of creating power within this basin. We advert to these matters to show that extensive public interests are at least indirectly involved.

The basis of the petitioner's project and the first step toward accomplishing its purpose is the creation of a large reservoir in the Birch lake basin. Without such reservoir and the taking therefrom of sufficient water to operate its canal across the watershed, its purpose cannot be accomplished. According to its own figures, in

order to operate its proposed works to their full capacity, the petitioner will require three-fifths of all the water which naturally
flows from the Birch lake drainage basin. It urges, however, that,
if the taking of such quantity interferes with the navigable capacity
of the streams affected, it will take only such lesser quantity as will
not interfere therewith. To maintain and operate the proposed
canal between the Birch lake drainage basin and the St. Louis river
drainage basin so as to serve any public purpose will require a large
and substantial quantity of water. The water for this purpose must
all be drawn from the Birch lake basin. The trial court has found
that no substantial quantity of water can be diverted from that basin
without impairing the navigability of the waters therein. It necessarily follows that the proposed enterprise cannot be inaugurated and
carried on without interfering with such navigability. But the
petitioner insists that whether it will be able to obtain sufficient
water to carry on its enterprise is of no concern to the courts; and
that it has the right, at its option, to construct its works and to take
the chances of obtaining sufficient water to operate them. We cannot accede to this proposition. The vast property rights involved
can be condemned, under our statutes, only when they can be made
to subserve some public use. Unless it appears that by acquiring
the property in question the petitioner will be enabled to perform
some public service, it has no right to take such property. The burden is upon the petitioner to show that the property is needed for
and will serve a public purpose. Chicago, B. & N. R. Co. v. Porter,
43 Minn. 527, 46 N. W. 75; Minneapolis & St. L. R. Co. v. Village
of Hartland, 85 Minn. 76, 88 N. W. 423. The duty to determine
whether the property is to be taken for a public use, whether it is
necessary therefor, and whether it may lawfully be taken for the
purpose designated has been imposed upon the court. This necessarily includes the duty to determine whether the object of the
proposed enterprise can be lawfully and efficiently accomplished.
Whether the venture is likely to prove profitable or unprofitable is
not the question. That question must be determined by the petitioner for itself. But, before the court can find that the property
is being taken for and will be applied to a public use, it must find

that the purpose of the enterprise can be accomplished in the manner and through the means proposed. If the purpose of the enterprise cannot be accomplished, the taking of property therefor will not subserve public interests, and is not necessary for public purposes within the meaning of the statute. The statute does not authorize the exercise of the power of eminent domain unless it appears that the public purpose, for which alone property rights may be condemned, can be attained. McGee v. Board of Co. Commrs. of Hennepin County, 84 Minn. 472, 88 N. W. 6.

The right to lessen the navigable capacity of the streams of the Birch lake drainage basin has not been granted to the petitioner, and the statutes will not permit it to impair the navigability of such streams. The trial court has found, in effect, that the purpose of the proposed enterprise cannot be accomplished without impairing such navigability. The evidence justifies the conclusions drawn therefrom by the trial court, and it follows that the petitioner has no authority to take the property sought under the power of eminent domain.

The respondents raise several other objections to the prosecution of the proposed enterprise, but the conclusion reached upon the questions considered renders the determination of other questions unnecessary.

Judgment affirmed.

F. A. JOHNSON v. JOHN H. SLAPP.

EMIL NURMI v. COLE E. BENSON.[1]

August 14, 1914.

Nos. 18,927—(293).

Election contest — tie vote.

In a contest for the office of town clerk, and a contest for the office of

[1] Reported in 148 N. W. 593.

Note.—On the question of the decision of tie votes at elections, see note in 47 L.R.A. 551.

127 M.—3.

town supervisor, tried together, it is *held*, upon an examination of the evidence and a construction of certain ballots, that in each contest the contestant and contestee received an equal number of votes.

F. A. Johnson gave notice of contest against John H. Slapp from the canvass of votes at the election in the township of Trout Lake on March 10, 1914, which certified that F. A. Johnson received 29 votes for the office of town clerk and that John H. Slapp received 30 votes for that office. Emil Nurmi gave notice of contest from the canvass of votes at the same election which certified that Emil Nurmi received 29 votes for the office of supervisor and Cole E. Benson received 31 votes for that office. The district court for Itasca county appointed inspectors who recounted the ballots and made report that 27 votes had been counted for contestant Johnson for town clerk and 30 votes for contestee Slapp and 28 votes had been counted for contestant Nurmi and 30 votes for contestee Benson. The court made findings and ordered judgment that Johnson had been elected town clerk and there was a tie vote between Nurmi and Benson for the office of supervisor. From an order denying contestees' motions for amended findings and for a new trial, they appealed. Reversed on appeal of contestee Slapp and affirmed on appeal of contestee Benson.

C. C. McCarthy, for appellants.

Andrew Nelson and *George B. Sjoselius,* for respondents.

DIBELL, C.

At the election held in the town of Trout Lake in Itasca county on March 10, 1914, F. A. Johnson and J. H. Slapp were rival candidates for the office of town clerk. The court found that Johnson received 31 votes, and Slapp 30, and that Johnson was elected. Slapp appeals from the order denying his motion for a new trial.

The voting was by ballot. There was no official ballot. Johnson was a candidate on the "independent ticket," and Slapp on the "caucus ticket." Each voter was given two tickets, one of each kind. No provision was made for voting by a cross-mark. None was necessary. The names of competing candidates were not on the same ticket. A number of the voters, however, used cross-marks throughout their ballots, or occasionally, and sometimes a name was crossed out and another written in its place.

The ballots marked A, B, C, D and E are the ones important in the contest for clerk. As we understand it the court reached its result by counting ballots A, B, C and E for Johnson, and by holding that ballot D did not sufficiently indicate the intent of the voter, and was not a vote for either candidate.

Ballot A was a caucus ballot. The name of Slapp was crossed off and underneath it was written, though perhaps not quite accurately, the name "Alfret Johnson." It does not appear that there was any one else by the name of Johnson a candidate for the office. The evidence indicates that F. A. Johnson was commonly known as Alfred Johnson and that there was no other Alfred Johnson in the town. It was clearly enough a vote for F. A. Johnson.

Ballot B has the name of Slapp crossed out and a name which should be held as intended to be "Alfred Johnson" written underneath. It is a Johnson vote.

Ballot C is an independent ticket bearing the name of F. A. Johnson for town clerk. One large cross is placed over the ballot. It must be treated as evincing an intent to vote for all on the independent ticket or as evincing an intent to vote for no one. We think the former construction should be given it.

Exhibit D is an independent ticket containing the name of F. A. Johnson. Johnson's name is not stricken off, but opposite it is written a name, somewhat indistinctly, but clearly intended to be J. H. Slapp. The voter used a cross opposite the supervisor and opposite the constable without striking off the name.

This ballot, as we view it, evinces an intent to vote for Slapp. The Australian ballot system does not apply to a town election. A town election is governed by G. S. 1913, § 1122, et seq. (R. L. 1905, § 632, et seq.). One looking at the ballot, without technical rules of construction in mind, would conclude that the voter intended to vote for Slapp. This was the view of the trial court, for, as it aptly expresses it in its memorandum, "the intention of the voter is shown by the mere fact that he wrote the name 'J. H. Slapp.'" But the court thought itself bound by Newton v. Newell, 26 Minn.

529, 6 N. W. 346. In this we think it was in error. The statutory provision affecting the result in that case, G. S. 1878, p. 41, c. 1, § 19, relative to a greater number of names for one office than the number of persons required to fill it, is not involved here. All other ballots it counted correctly. Counsel cite Pennington v. Hare, 60 Minn. 146, 149, 62 N. W. 116, and Erickson v. Paulson, 111 Minn. 337, 126 N. W. 1097, in support of their contention that the ballot should not be counted for Slapp. These cases both arose under the Australian ballot system. They do not at all control the case at bar.

Ballot E is the same as ballot C and should be counted for Johnson.

The result is that Johnson and Slapp each received 30 votes.

At the same election Cole E. Benson and Emil Nurmi were rival candidates for town supervisor. Benson was on the caucus ticket and Nurmi on the independent ticket. The court found that each received 30 votes. Benson appeals from the order denying his motion for a new trial.

The court reached its result by counting ballots A, C, D and E for Nurmi, and ballot B for Benson.

Ballot A is a caucus ticket. Benson's name is stricken out and below it is written a name, which fairly may be interpreted to be that of Emil Nurmi. This should be counted for Nurmi vote.

Ballots C and E have been already considered and were properly counted for Nurmi.

No serious question is made but that the ballot D was correctly counted. Ballot B was a vote for Benson.

The court made a proper disposition of all the ballots before it on the contest for town supervisor.

Reversed on the appeal of Slapp and affirmed on the appeal of Benson.

CHARLES N. ORR and Others v. WILLIAM SUTTON and Others.[1]

July 17, 1914.

Nos. 18,433—(55).

Former appeal — decision conclusive.

1. A proposition decided upon a former appeal becomes the law of the case and should not be re-examined in a subsequent appeal in the same action.

Tender — finding — evidence.

2. The pleading and evidence required a finding on the issue of tender of payment by the judgment debtor of the judgment under which plaintiffs effected redemption. If the findings in this case are to be construed to the effect that, by direct authority of the judgment debtor, a tender in lawful money of the full amount of plaintiffs' judgment was not made to them personally prior to the time when they could use the same for redemption purposes, they are not justified by the evidence.

Right of judgment creditor to redeem.

3. No one in the line of redemptioners, nor an intermeddler, may by tender of payment of a judgment impair or destroy a judgment creditor's right to use the judgment to effect redemption.

Same — action to compel satisfaction of judgment.

4. To destroy a judgment creditor's right to use the judgment as a means for obtaining certain land through redemption, it is not indispensable that the judgment creditor, in addition to tender of payment, bring suit to compel satisfaction of the judgment and deposit the money tendered in court.

Same — tender of payment of judgment.

5. A tender by the judgment debtor of the full amount due on a judgment, under which the judgment creditor has filed an intention to redeem land, before the arrival of the time when the judgment could be used for such purpose, and under circumstances clearly disclosing that both parties appreciated the purpose of such tender, destroys the right of the judgment creditor to thereafter use the judgment as a basis for redeeming such land.

[1] Reported in 148 N. W. 1066.

Note.—Conclusiveness of prior decisions on subsequent appeals, see note in 34 L.R.A. 321.

Redemption by judgment creditor with notice of tender.

6. But if a redemption is made by a judgment creditor whose right to make it, though good on the face of the record, has, in fact, been destroyed by the tender of the payment of the judgment, the title of the purchaser at the sale nevertheless passes to him, if the holder thereof accepts the redemption money with full knowledge of the tender.

Estoppel — equities lacking — compliance with statute.

7. Assuming a valid tender proven, it is *held:*

(a) That the defendant Torinus, the holder of the title acquired through the mortgage foreclosure sale, by accepting the redemption money paid by plaintiffs, judgment creditors, with full knowledge of the facts showing that they had no right to redeem, thereby suffered plaintiffs to succeed to his title and cannot now question the validity of their redemption.

(b) That the evidence does not show any rights or equities which required the court to relieve the defendant William Sutton, junior to plaintiffs in the line of redemptioners, who attempted to redeem under a mortgage, recorded without the prepayment of the registry tax. Nor has Sutton alone, or in conjunction with any other defendant, any equities through which to attack plaintiffs' title.

(c) That the defendant Sauntry, the owner, after the expiration of the year of redemption, had no interest in the land so as to question plaintiffs' redemption, and his right to have the land applied to the payment of such of his debts as were liens thereon, depended entirely upon the lienholders making redemption in strict conformity with the statute.

Action in the district court for St. Louis county by Charles N. Orr, Herman F. Stark, Charles E. Collett, copartners as Orr, Stark & Collett, and Charles J. Spratt against William Sutton, Lyman Sutton, William Sauntry and his wife, Russell M. Bennett, Edmund J. Longyear, Louis E. Torinus and all other persons claiming any right, title, estate, interest or lien in the real estate described. The facts are set forth in the opinion.

The case was tried before Fesler, J., who made findings and ordered judgment in favor of plaintiffs, removing the cloud on their title and interest in the land by the record of the instruments mentioned in the opinion and restraining defendants from asserting any title or lien upon the title and interest of plaintiffs. From an order denying their motion for a new trial, defendants appealed. Affirmed.

J. N. Searles, Manwaring & Sullivan and *Butler & Mitchell,* for appellants.

William G. White and *Theodore Hollister,* for respondents.

HOLT, J.

Action to quiet title. William Sauntry owned an undivided half of valuable mining lands in St. Louis county, this state, which he mortgaged to secure the sum of $30,000. He defaulted and the mortgage was duly foreclosed by advertisement. The year for redemption expired on September 20, 1911. The rights acquired by the purchaser at the sale were on the last named date held by Louis E. Torinus, the sheriff's certificate having been duly assigned to him. The mortgagor was insolvent, and unsatisfied judgments existed against him. Transcripts of the following judgments were docketed in St. Louis county prior to September 21, 1911: (1) A transcript of a judgment in favor of Nathan E. Franklin for $8,243.34, docketed July 22, 1910. This judgment was assigned to Louis E. Torinus and proper record made on September 23, 1911; (2) a transcript of judgment in favor of Fred Rossiter for $1,589.35, docketed October 24, 1910; (3) a transcript of a judgment in favor of John J. Kilty for $329, docketed at 5:15 p. m. September 20, 1911, together with proper records showing an assignment of the judgment to William Sutton, September 18, 1911; and (4) a transcript of a judgment in favor of Robert W. Hunt & Co. for $741.38, docketed at 5:19 p. m. September 20, 1911, with proper records showing an assignment of this judgment to plaintiffs January 11, 1911. In the evening of September 20, 1911, William Sauntry executed a second mortgage on the land to William Sutton to secure a demand note for $50. It appears that this indebtedness represented a portion of attorney's fees owing to one Grannis from Sauntry which Grannis assigned to William Sutton. This mortgage was filed in the office of the register of deeds at 10 p. m. on the same day. But no mortgage registry tax was paid thereon until long afterwards. No registry number was placed on the mortgage, nor was it indexed until the next morning after it then had been taken to the county treasurer and he had certified thereon that it was exempt from taxation. Proper notices of intention to redeem were filed so that the respective judgment creditors were placed in line of redemptioners in the order above given and the mortgagee William Sutton last, provided each had a good right to redeem. Sauntry, the mortgagor and owner, did not redeem. Louis E. Torinus redeemed on September 25, 1911, as assignee of the Franklin judgment. Fred Rossiter the next in line did not offer to redeem. Nor did William Sutton make any attempt to redeem as assignee of the Kilty judgment. On October 5, 1911, plaintiffs, as assignees of the Robert W. Hunt & Co. judgment, redeemed; and on October 9, 1911, William Sutton in turn redeemed as mortgagee in the $50 mortgage mentioned. The sheriff upon each of these redemptions issued his certificate to the redemptioner. October 10, 1911, William Sutton, claiming to be the owner of the land under his redemption, mortgaged the same to Louis E. Torinus to secure the payment of $10,000. The complaint sets out the various matters very fully, alleges conspiracy between the defendants to circumvent plaintiffs and deprive them of their right to redeem, and asks that the claims of each defendant to the land be barred and the cloud cast upon plaintiffs' title by the Sutton redemption, the Torinus mortgage, and the records thereof be removed. In addition to Torinus, Sutton and Sauntry, the latter's wife and one Lyman Sutton are made defendants, also the lessees of the mine, but the latter are in no way affected. The court found plaintiffs to be the owners, that the defendants had no right, title or lien in or to the land, and directed judgment quieting title in plaintiffs and removing the cloud cast on their title by the record of the Sutton redemption and mortgage, and the mortgage to Torinus. Defendants appeal from the order denying their motion for a new trial.

The defendants contend for a new trial upon three grounds: (1) No mortgage registry tax was required upon the $50 mortgage under which Sutton redeemed, hence his redemption vested title in him; (2) plaintiffs lost their right to redeem by the tender of payment of their judgment prior to the time when such right could be exercised; (3) even if the tax be held applicable to this mortgage, equities will relieve defendants since its nonpayment was the result of an honest mistake induced by the conduct of the administrative officers of the state and county, and the tax was paid before the trial.

In a former opinion in this case (Orr v. Sutton, 119 Minn. 193, 137 N. W. 973, 42 L.R.A.[N.S.] 146) we held that this mortgage, upon which the registry tax imposed by chapter 328, p. 448, Laws 1907, was not paid before it was recorded, furnished no sufficient legal basis for redemption from the foreclosure sale here involved. This was following and applying the rule announced in State v. Fitzgerald, 117 Minn. 192, 134 N. W. 728, that all mortgages including those of $50 and less are subject to the registry tax. We are earnestly importuned to re-examine the question, on the ground that that decision is wrong and that the court was led astray, because counsel on both sides designedly took the position that the law violated the Constitution, unless it was held applicable to all mortgages however small. Even if the court, as now constituted, entertained doubts concerning the soundness of the Fitzgerald decision, a well-settled rule of law stands in the way of any re-examination of the question upon this appeal, for on this proposition our former decision herein is the law of the case and binding on us. There is nothing in the situation which calls for a deviation from this well-established doctrine. No application was made for reargument when the former appeal was determined. In Terryll v. City of Faribault, 84 Minn. 341, 87 N. W. 917, it is said: "The case was here on a former appeal and the notice of claim for damages was held sufficient. 81 Minn. 519, 84 N. W. 458. That decision, whether right or wrong, must be treated as the law of the case and the question cannot be re-examined at this time." The same rule was stated thus in Bradley v. Norris, 67 Minn. 48, 69 N. W. 624: "This court has the right to overrule the decision made on the former appeal in some other case, but in this case it must be followed." See also Schleuder v. Corey, 30 Minn. 501, 16 N. W. 401; Smith v. Glover, 50 Minn. 58, 52 N. W. 210, 912; Tilleny v. Wolverton, 54 Minn. 75, 55 N. W. 822; Maxwell v. Schwartz, 55 Minn. 414, 57 N. W. 141; St. Paul Trust Co. v. Kittson, 67 Minn. 59, 69 N. W. 625; Phelps v. Sargent, 73 Minn. 260, 76 N. W. 25; Piper v. Sawyer, 78 Minn. 221, 80 N. W. 970; Hibbs v. Marpe, 84 Minn. 178, 87 N. W. 363. To the same effect many authorities may be cited from other jurisdictions: Adams Co. v. B. & M. R. Co. 55 Iowa, 94, 2 N. W. 1054, 7 N. W. 471; Heffner v. Brownell, 75 Iowa, 341, 39 N. W. 640; Bem v. Shoemaker, 10 S. D. 453, 74 N. W. 239; Bolton v. Hey, 168 Pa. St. 418, 31 Atl. 1097; and Case v. Hoffman, 100 Wis. 334, 72 N. W. 330, 74 N. W. 220, 75 N. W. 945, 44 L.R.A. 728.

One of the main defenses pleaded is, plaintiffs were tendered payment of their judgment before the time arrived at which it might be used to effect redemption, therefore the one made by them was wrongful and of no validity to pass title. It is undisputed that on September 27, 1911, Lyman Sutton, accompanied by defendants' attorney, brought $785 in gold coin to plaintiffs' office and tendered the same to them personally in payment of the judgment held by them. The amount was sufficient and was verified by one of plaintiffs. Beyond quibble written authority from Sauntry to Lyman Sutton to make the payment was exhibited to plaintiffs. The money was not Sauntry's. It was furnished by Lyman Sutton. When plaintiffs refused to accept, Sutton placed the money in his safe, where it remained ready for plaintiffs until some time in the following December. Defendants insist a valid tender was proven and should have been definitely found by the court, and, in case the findings should be construed as negativing a tender, they contend the evidence does not justify the same. It is commendable to find only the ultimate facts. But in this case tender was set up as a specific defense or ground for contesting the validity of plaintiffs' redemption. Whether William Sauntry actually offered plaintiffs lawful money in sufficient amount to pay their judgment prior to their redemption, was a matter of pure fact. Whether such fact constituted a legal defense, is a question of law. The court below may have been satisfied of the existence of the fact, but may have concluded that the legal effect was of no consequence to defendants. This court may take a different view. It is thus apparent that an absence of a specific finding upon the issue of tender is not fair to defendants, nor, indeed, to plaintiffs were they appellants. It is true the request to make findings on this issue was not in the proper form (Hall v. Sauntry, 72 Minn. 420, 75 N. W. 420, 71 Am. St. 497), nevertheless tender was so important a matter to a right decision that the findings should not leave the fact of its being made in doubt. This is a case where a definite finding should have been made on this issue. Turner v. Fryberger, 99 Minn. 236, 107 N. W. 1133, 109 N. W. 229. Moreover, even if the findings, coupled with the court's refusal to amend the same to show tender, should be construed equivalent to a finding that tender was not proven, we are of opinion that the evidence as it now stands does not so warrant. The money was there. Plaintiffs were lawyers. They knew as well as defendants what it was intended for, and what was at stake. Their refusal to accept payment was no doubt a deliberate act with full knowledge of the situation. They took the chance of defendants not being able to establish that the tender was made by authority and direction of Sauntry, or else that the law did not give the debtor the right to stop plaintiffs at that time from resorting to the land for the satisfaction of their judgment. We shall therefore assume that plaintiffs were tendered payment of their judgment before the arrival of the time when they could use it for the purpose of redemption.

True, no one in the line of redemptioners, either ahead of or behind plaintiffs, nor any intermeddler, could extinguish or impair their right to redeem by offering to pay their judgment. The only one who possessed this right on September 27, 1911, was the judgment debtor. His right was absolute. It is immaterial who furnished him the money, or what his motives were, he was then entitled to pay the judgment or cause it to be paid, for the time had not arrived when plaintiffs could use it for redemption purposes.

It is asserted the tender was unavailing because when refused the only way to keep it good was to pay the money into court and begin an action to compel a satisfaction of the judgment. Section 7908, G. S. 1913, is cited. This provision does not in terms apply to this case. But we may admit that the procedure suggested by respondent is not improper. However, it is not absolutely necessary in order to give effect to the tender. The testimony shows that the gold was kept intact for plaintiffs for some time after this action was brought and the answer served. In the answer Sauntry still asserts a readiness to pay. At any time after Sutton's redemption plaintiffs could have received from the sheriff full payment of their judgment and all moneys paid by them in their attempt to redeem, including the wrongful payment of the Kilty judgment. We think the tender was kept good and the money is available now.   Dunn v. Dewey, 75 Minn. 153, 77 N. W. 793; Murray v. Nickerson, 90 Minn. 197, 95 N. W. 898.

The claim is also presented that the tender unaccepted was of no effect.   Harking back to the early case of Jackson v. Law, 5 Cow. (N. Y.) 248, Law v. Jackson, 9 Cow. (N. Y.) 641, text books and decisions state that a judgment lien cannot be discharged by tender. There must be actual payment.   The argument is that so long as the judgment remains a lien it furnishes a basis under the statute for the right to redeem.   But there is quite a unanimity among the authorities, in states where the mortgagee's estate is considered a lien or pledge merely, that a tender of the debt discharges the lien. Kortright v. Cady, 21 N. Y. 343, 78 Am. Dec. 145; Moore v. Norman, 43 Minn. 428, 45 N. W. 857, 9 L.R.A. 55, 19 Am. St. 247. That there are inherent differences in the quality of a judgment lien and a mortgage lien which justify the rule that a tender of payment of one does not discharge a tract of land from its lien, while it does as to the other, may be doubted.   The owner of the debt in either case may voluntarily release any real estate from the one as well as from the other without discharging any part of the debt.   Be that as it may, this court has recognized the distinction in Rother v. Monahan, 60 Minn. 186, 62 N. W. 263.   But that case also clearly establishes the principle applicable here, namely, that a tender of payment of a judgment by the judgment debtor destroys and extinguishes the right to make the judgment the basis for a redemption.   It may well be that, before any notice of intention to use the judgment as against any particular land is filed, a tender of payment does not impair or destroy the judgment creditor's right to make use of or enforce the judgment generally.   But when, after he has so done, the judgment debtor tenders payment, the creditor must accept the money and let that land alone.   Any further attempt to proceed against the land in question after such tender must be considered wrongful.   Mr. Justice Mitchell thus states the view of the court in the case cited: "The act of the defendant in attempting, under the circumstances, to use this judgment for redemption purposes was wholly in his own wrong. If, under similar circumstances, he had attempted to enforce the judgment by execution, a court would have unquestionably enjoined him from doing so, or, if a sale had been made on the execution, set it aside as wrongful, and an abuse of the process of the court, and compelled defendant to accept the tender and satisfy his judgment. Mason v. Sudam, 2 Johns Ch. (N. Y.) 172. The same principle applies where, as in this case, the defendant has wrongfully attempted, notwithstanding the tender, to use the statutory process of redemption for the purpose of collecting his judgment out of this land. It is wholly immaterial what the object of the debtor and mortgagor was in making the tender,—even if it was to prevent a redemption by defendant. He must be presumed to have some interest in preventing such a redemption. It may be that he had made some advantageous arrangement with the plaintiff, the holder of the certificate of sale. But what his intent or motive was it is not for the courts to inquire. He had a legal right to pay the judgment, and thereby prevent a redemption by defendant. Defendant's duty and only right, under the circumstances, was to accept the tender and satisfy the judgment. His refusal to do so and his attempt to use his judgment for redemption purposes were wrongful and a clear abuse of the statutory right of redemption. The court will, under such circumstances, set aside the attempted redemption, and compel defendant to do what he ought to have done in the first instance,—accept his money and satisfy his judgment." And we think it has been definitely determined in Roberts v. Meighen, 74 Minn. 273, 77 N. W. 139, that it is not necessary, in order to make the judgment creditor's attempt to redeem wrongful, that the judgment debtor prior to redemption bring the money into court and commence suit to compel satisfaction of the judgment. In that case payment was merely tendered, no money was brought into court and no action brought until after redemption. The point was distinctly made in appellant's brief that such tender was not sufficient to destroy the right to use the judgment as a basis for redemption. Chief Justice Start, who tried the case of Rother v. Monahan, supra, in the court below and therein adverted to the rule that tender of payment of a judgment does not release its lien on real estate, writes the opinion sustaining the court below in the ruling that the tender as made destroyed the right to use the judgment for redemption purposes.

Is any defendant in position to object to plaintiffs' redemption? When the owner fails to redeem from a mortgage foreclosure sale, the purchaser acquires the title the owner had when the mortgage was given. If lienholders redeem under the statutory provisions, the title acquired by the purchaser at the foreclosure sale is thereby vested in such redemptioners. Even when the redemptioner has no right to make it, or does not conform to the law in so doing, the title nevertheless passes to him, if the one from whom redemption is made accepts the redemption money, unless there exists some lienholder whose redemption is interfered with or prejudiced. Willard v. Finnegan, 42 Minn. 476, 44 N. W. 985, 8 L.R.A. 50; Todd v. Johnson, 50 Minn. 310, 52 N. W. 864; same case in 56 Minn. 60, 57 N. W. 320; Clark v. Butts, 73 Minn. 361, 76 N. W. 199. No doubt Torinus could have objected to plaintiffs' redemption, but he did not. By accepting the redemption money paid by plaintiffs he relinquished to them the title he had. He turned over his money to be used by Sutton in making the redemption from plaintiffs. There is nothing in the record to suggest that Torinus did not have full knowledge of the tender when he accepted and receipted for the money. And we think it follows from the authorities hereinbefore cited that the only person who may attack a redemption fair on the face of the record, but wrongful in fact, where the redemption money has been accepted by the one holding the title of the purchaser at the foreclosure sale, is one who has still some beneficial interest in the land, or one who, being a subsequent lienholder, has availed himself of the right to redeem strictly in accordance with the provisions of the statute.

Whether Torinus be regarded as acting for Sutton or for himself alone, the fact remains that plaintiffs' right to redeem was conceded by both in that their redemption money was accepted and in that both plant themselves on the redemption by which Sutton claims to have succeeded to the title plaintiffs secured by their redemption.

The defendant Sutton insists that in equity he should be relieved from the mistake he made in not paying the mortgage registry tax, notwithstanding the former decision that he had no legal statutory right to redeem. For the purpose of considering the equities urged, let us for the moment assume that the provisions of the redemption statute may be suspended or abrogated by the courts. The one who asks equitable relief, even against a wrongdoer, must show equities of some merit and clean hands. If we take plaintiffs on the one hand and Torinus and the Suttons on the other, we look in vain for any appealing equities. The Suttons sought the land. So did plaintiffs. Each party bought up judgments against Sauntry for the sole purpose, apparently, of thereby securing title to this land. William Sutton made no attempt to redeem under the Kilty judgment, but the money plaintiffs paid on that was also accepted and receipted for by Torinus, presumably under Sutton's direction, so that, on October 5, 1911, when Sutton attempted to redeem, the only equity or right he had was this $50 mortgage. It is perfectly obvious that the only reason for purchasing this small, stale claim against Sauntry was to circumvent plaintiffs who had outwitted him in the race to be the last in the line of redemptioners. Both Sauntry and the Suttons are very careful in the pleadings, as well as in the testimony, to deny any intent to obtain for Sauntry either the land or any beneficial interest whatever therein. Sauntry and his wife would be the only persons in all this company entitled to consideration in the search for equities, and they disclaim. Torinus got in to make $2,500, the Suttons to get the land, and when the means provided for that purpose slipped from under, this mortgage was obtained as a last resort. Neither the claim supporting the mortgage, nor the circumstances under which it was procured, furnish equities of merit.

It is also apparent that William Sutton was not misled by the interpretations placed on the mortgage registry law by either state or county officials, even if this should be held excusable. His attorneys counseled together on this proposition, evidently without placing reliance on the advice given, or the practice adopted, by any official. In fact, no attempt was made, on the night the mortgage was filed for record, to have the indorsement made on the mortgage by the proper official, that it was exempt from taxation in accordance with the custom adopted in St. Louis county.

Neither does it appear to us that William Sauntry may invoke equities to vest title in Sutton under his attempted redemption. Sauntry's failure to redeem terminated his estate in the land. His title had vested in Torinus as assignee of the purchaser at the foreclosure. It did not harm Sauntry if Torinus allowed plaintiffs to redeem without right. On the contrary Sauntry's debt to plaintiffs of over $700 was thereby effaced. If there had been any claim on the part of Sauntry that he had some beneficial interest in or to the land which the Suttons were assisting him to secure, the case might have been brought under the principle controlling in ˙Roberts v. Meighen, supra. But it is clear from the pleadings and from the evidence that both Sauntry and the Suttons take the position that Sauntry has no interest whatever in the land, that the redemption under the $50 mortgage was for the benefit of the Suttons alone, outside of the $2,500 bonus to Torinus, and that the sole ground upon which Sauntry contests plaintiffs' redemption is that he is entitled to have the land appropriated to pay his debts to the greatest possible extent. However, he could not compel Sutton to redeem. The right of Sauntry to have the land appropriated to the payment of the liens of his creditors was all the time subject to the condition that such creditors availed themselves of the redemption statute in strict conformity to its provisions. That was wholly within their choice. Hoover v. Johnson, 47 Minn. 434, 50 N. W. 475; State v. Kerr, 51 Minn. 417, 53 N. W. 719; Bartleson v. Munson, 105 Minn. 348, 117 N. W. 512. If Sutton because of noncompliance with the redemption laws failed to appropriate the land to the satisfaction of Sauntry's debts, and cannot be relieved, it would seem to follow that the only right which Sauntry now claims, namely, to have his $50 debt to Sutton wiped out, is also gone.

But we do not believe provisions of the redemption statute can be abrogated, or in particular cases relieved against by the courts in the absence of some agreement or act of waiver of the party whose rights are to be affected. No one will claim that, if through a mistake a mechanic's lien was filed too late, equity could relieve. Nor can an owner be heard to be relieved against his mistake in permitting the year of redemption to expire, or a creditor against the mistake or omission to file his lien as the statute requires, except in cases where the mistake or omission has been induced by the agreement or acts in the nature of waiver on the part of the person who is to be affected by the relief. No act of plaintiffs can be pointed to as inducing William Sutton or Torinus to accept the redemption money, or to refrain from paying the mortgage tax, or to take any other step to acquire the land. It is true, the mortgage without the tax paid was not a nullity, except as a basis for redemption. Cases like Forest Lake State Bank v. Ekstrand, 112 Minn. 412, 128 N. W. 455; Mason v. Fichner, 120 Minn. 185, 139 N. W. 485; State Bank of Boyd v. Hayden, 121 Minn. 45, 140 N. W. 132; Staples v. East St. Paul State Bank, 122 Minn. 419, 142 N. W. 721, are cited to the effect that equity will relieve against mistake in not paying the mortgage registry tax. But these cases relate to a reformation of instruments which defectively expressed the intention of the parties because of mutual mistake. In none did the court attempt to affect the rights of third parties who had neither taken part nor induced the transaction. In State v. Kerr, supra, it is said the court does not possess the power to enlarge the redemption statute: "The right of redemption is a strict legal right, to be exercised, if at all, in accordance with the terms of statute by which the right is conferred, unless waived or extended by the party whose interests are to be affected. * * * As a general rule, it may be said that when a valid legislative act has determined conditions on which rights shall vest or be forfeited, and no fraud has been practiced, no court can interpose conditions or qualifications in violation of the statute. The courts have no power to relieve against statutory forfeitures." When William Sutton attempted to use his $50 mortgage as a basis of redemption, the right had been forfeited because the mortgage was not legally on record. As tending in the same direction, see Bagley v. McCarthy Brothers Co. 95 Minn. 286, 104 N. W. 7; Brady v.

127 M.—4.

Gilman, 96 Minn. 234, 104 N. W. 897, 1 L.R.A.(N.S.) 835, 113 Am. St. 622.

So that, assuming the tender of payment of plaintiffs' judgment made their attempt to redeem wrongful, they nevertheless are now owners, because their redemption, fair on the face of the record, was acquiesced in by Torinus, from whom they redeemed by his accepting their money, thereby transferring the purchaser's title at the foreclosure sale to them; and as to William Sauntry he has foreclosed himself from attacking plaintiffs' title, because he disclaims all bene-eficial interest in or to the land through the Sutton redemption; and as to William Sutton, if Torinus acted for him, he is bound by the acceptance of plaintiffs' redemption money, and if he relies on his redemption, he had no legal or equitable right to make it.

Taking the view of the evidence most favorable to defendants on all controverted matters, we nevertheless reach the conclusion that the decision of the trial court must be affirmed.

PHILIP E. BROWN, J. (dissenting).

When the opinion in this case came to the writer the following dissent was prepared and submitted. Subsequently, pursuant to what seems to be the usual practice, the latter part of the main opinion was rewritten and enlarged. That the controversy may be brought to an end, the dissent is filed without alteration.

I dissent from the propositions that Sutton should not be relieved from the consequences of failing to pay the mortgage registry tax and that plaintiff is entitled to equitable relief.

An excusable mistake whereby one loses a valuable legal right gives rise to an equity, not only as against the person responsible for it or privy thereto, but also against anyone who will not be injured by its correction. Lane v. Holmes, 55 Minn. 379, 57 N. W. 132, 43 Am. St. 508. Orr would not, in legal contemplation be injured by judicial recognition of Sutton's redemption; for the sole purpose of the statute allowing a creditor to redeem is that his claim may be saved and paid, which would be accomplished in this case if plaintiffs' right to question Sutton's redemption were denied. The statute does not contemplate speculation in the mortgaged property with the view of obtaining title thereto, except as such is necessarily involved in efforts of creditors to save their claims and as incident to the end that the property shall go as far as possible towards payment of the mortgagor's debts. Sprague v. Martin, 29 Minn. 226, 13 N. W. 34. Hence neither Orr's nor Sutton's acts should be regarded as those of an owner seeking to protect his specific rights in property as such, and their respective redemptions should be considered solely with reference to their status as creditors attempting to save their claims, which, if valid, are entitled to due protection, regardless of amount. Aside from fraud, the desire of either to secure the land itself is immaterial, either for or against him, and the equities of each, if any, should rest in and be weighed by their standing as creditors. Thus tested, the circumstances disclosed on the trial presented no equity in Orr needing protection, for his rights as a creditor were conserved by Sutton's redemption; whereas Sutton had an equity arising from the fact that he would lose at least the security for his debt unless the mistake, whereby his attempt to redeem fell short of legal requirements, was corrected. That this mistake, though one of law, was excusable, seems unquestionable; for if Sutton was not equitably justified in accepting the prior practical construction placed upon the statute by the officers of the state, including the attorney general, it is difficult to conceive of such justification for any act attributable to an erroneous conception of the law. In a proper case, however, one may be relieved of the effect of a mistake of law. See Benson v. Markoe, 37 Minn. 30, 34, 33 N. W. 38, 5 Am. St. 816; Gerdine v. Menage, 41 Minn. 417, 421, 43 N. W. 91; Lane v. Holmes, supra; Truesdale v. Sidle, 65 Minn. 315, 67 N. W. 1004; Dodge v. Kennedy, 93 Mich. 547, 53 N. W. 795; Pomeroy, Eq. Jur. (3d Ed.) 839, 849. The rule established by these authorities is, as reiterated in Forest Lake State Bank v. Ekstrand, 112 Minn. 412, 416, 128 N. W. 455, that equity will relieve from a mistake of law where one party by availing himself thereof will secure without consideration an unjust advantage of the other party, who is blameless in the premises. Certainly it seems that Sutton's failure to pay the 50-cent registration tax comes within the rule, wherefore his redemption should be recognized and adjudicated effective, thereby preventing grave consequences as the result of trivial, and in no sense wilful, fault.

But assuming this position untenable, what is plaintiff's standing to seek equitable relief? What is he other than an intermeddler seeking speculative gain through his own wrong, thus attempting to pervert the redemption law? Legally he had a lien when he redeemed, for, under our decisions, the tender did not destroy that; but it was a naked, technical lien, existing merely because his wrong had not yet been remedied by wiping his judgment from the records. After the tender, or at least so long as it continued to be operative, no remedial right thereon remained against Sauntry except as to the money tendered. Rother v. Monahan, 60 Minn. 186, 188, 62 N. W. 263. Only as a creditor with a vested right to have the property applied to the satisfaction of his debt did he have any right to redeem. Sprague v. Martin, 29 Minn. 226, 232, 13 N. W. 34. After the tender, therefore, he had no better standing to redeem than one without a lien, who, as declared in Nelson v. Rogers, 65 Minn. 246, 248, 68 N. W. 18, has no such specific interest in the property as to constitute him a proper redemptioner under the statute. Such also is the rule declared applicable in the present case, so that "any further attempt to proceed against the land in question after such tender must be considered wrongful;" but nevertheless Orr's redemption is upheld because Torinus, the purchaser, accepted the money. In short, it is held, in effect, that one having no right to redeem may do so and thus acquire title to the land, if no one entitled to object does so. Upon the same reasoning it would seem that the necessity of a lien or some specific interest in the property as the basis of the right to redeem could be waived, which certainly is not the law as heretofore understood by this court. See Todd v. Johnson, 50 Minn. 310, 313, 52 N. W. 864. It is difficult to comprehend how this holding consists with the nature of the creditor's rights under the statute, after the year for redemption by the mortgagor has expired, such being the equitable substitute for his prior right to subject the property to execution (Powers v. Sherry, 115 Minn. 290, 294, 132 N. W. 210), or with the character of the relief sought, the same being essentially equitable (Mathews v. Lightner, 85 Minn. 333, 336, 88 N. W. 992, 89 Am. St. 558). To grant plaintiff any relief in the premises is not only to place a premium upon wrongful speculation by creditors, but also to forget that equity should not be oblivious to the stain on plaintiff's hands, nor need a complaining defendant to close its doors to one who comes limping upon a crutch of wrong. Had plaintiff alleged the facts regarding the tender his complaint would unquestionably have been demurrable, and he should not be held to be in any better position with the proofs in to the same effect.

But can it properly be said that none of the defendants are in position to object to plaintiff's redemption? Assuming that Sutton, as a subsequent lienholder, was not, and accepting as sufficient predicate for an estoppel or waiver, the statement of the court that "there is nothing in the record to suggest that Torinus did not have full knowledge of the tender when he accepted and receipted for the money" paid on plaintiff's redemption, the question of Sauntry's right still remains. Under the reasoning of Rother v. Monahan, supra, he could have maintained an action, after tender to restrain plaintiff from attempting to enforce the judgment for any purpose, and must have prevailed; from which it would seem to follow that he could resist its enforcement by objection to redemption. The only escape from this conclusion lies in the determination of the court, following Willard v. Finnegan, 42 Minn. 476, 44 N. W. 985, 8 L.R.A. 50, that after Sauntry's year of redemption expired he had no interest in the property to protect and was without right to question Orr's redemption or to take steps necessary to insure redemption by Sutton. Here it is the court seems to lose sight of Sauntry's rights, both legal and equitable. The mortgagor's rights were summarily disposed of in Willard v. Finnegan, supra, without discussion and seemingly with little consideration, whereas under the rule of Rother v. Monahan, supra, he "must be presumed to have had some interest in preventing such a redemption." This presumption should be conclusive for the reason, if no other, that the mortgagor is necessarily concerned in carrying out the policy of the law, declared in Martin v. Sprague, 29 Minn. 53, 56, 11 N. W. 143, 145, "to save the property of debtors from being sacrificed, and to enable debtors

to retain their property; or, if they shall fail to do so, then to secure
its application, so far as may be, to the payment of the demands of
creditors." To effect the latter purpose his interest extends beyond
the expiration of his redemption period; for to make the two co-
terminous would be to deny him the right to seek the accomplishment
of that end. As was said in the Rother case, it well may be that,
though he has lost the right to redeem, he may have some advantageous arrangement with a particular creditor looking to the saving of
the property or valuable rights therein, or else, it may be added, he
may require protection from the effect of prior covenants. See Allis
v. Foley, 126 Minn. 14, 147 N. W. 670. It may be that he can
neither redeem nor make any advantageous arrangement during the
year, but can thereafter secure valuable concessions from one creditor, though not from another. Should he then be deprived of the
right, by tender, to eliminate the latter from the succession of redemptioners, thus removing an obstacle to the effectuation of his
plans? Having an absolute right to make the tender, he should be
accorded the unconditional right to avail himself of the benefit thereof, without the expense, delay, annoyance and uncertainty incident to
litigation of an issue as to whether he will in fact be benefited, especially as against the creditor who has wrongfully refused such tender.
Though he cannot, after expiration of his redemption period, be regarded as having any title whatever to the property, as former owner
thereof he should be dealt with as leniently as possible and afforded
every opportunity consistent with the rights of others to save what
he can out of it, both for his own and his family's benefit. These
considerations should certainly outweigh the claims of one asserting
merely technical rights based upon a claim for money of which he
will not be deprived by their denial.

The injustice, departure from the settled policy of the redemption
law, and danger involved in the rule established by the majority
opinion would be clearer if Sutton's mortgage had secured $50,000
instead of $50. Yet the court's reasoning would require the same
holding in such case, including denial of the right of redemption to
one who, under very recent decisions, unquestionably had an equitable lien upon the property and was thus strictly within the statutory

designation of those entitled to redeem, and who, in matter of procedure, was generally, if not technically, within the law.

Finally, neither Sutton nor Sauntry should be deprived of any right here claimed because of Torinus' acceptance of the money paid on Orr's redemption.

I think the order should be reversed.

HALLAM, J. (dissenting).

I dissent.

It is conceded that the redemption by plaintiffs was void; that when, after tender to them of the amount of their judgment, they persisted in using this judgment for the purpose of redeeming the land of their debtor from a sale on a prior lien, such use of the judgment was wholly in their own wrong, and that, upon demand of a party having a proper interest to conserve, the court would set aside the attempted redemption and compel the plaintiffs to accept the tender and satisfy their judgment. Mitchell, J., in Rother v. Monahan, 60 Minn. 186, 62 N. W. 263.

The position of the majority of the court is that none of the defendants are in a position to take advantage of the admitted invalidity of plaintiffs' redemption and that accordingly plaintiffs must get the land; that these defendants who are manifesting such intense interest in this litigation either have no interest in the subject matter at all, or else they have by their conduct precluded themselves from asserting their rights.

To this I do not agree. I am of the opinion that William and Lyman Sutton, by virtue of their interest in the certificate from which plaintiffs' redemption was made, are in a position to object to the use of this judgment by plaintiffs for the purpose of redemption.

The relation of these defendants to the property is undisputed. Torinus held the sheriff's certificate from which plaintiffs attempted to redeem. It is conceded that Torinus was not the sole beneficial owner of this certificate. The fact is that William Sutton and Lyman Sutton had undertaken the task of redeeming the property of their uncle William Sauntry from the foreclosure sale and from other subsequent liens. They set about to raise the money to purchase the

sheriff's certificate of sale then held by the Weyerhaeusers, and also
what is known as the Franklin judgment. This required over $45,-
000, more money than they had. William Sutton furnished $15,800,
Lyman Sutton $12,980. Torinus loaned them $7,500. He was to
be repaid this amount in any event, and $10,000 if they got the prop-
erty. They borrowed the balance in small amounts from various
parties. These facts were undisputed, and the court was asked to so
find, but declined to do so. The Suttons were the real beneficial
owners of the sheriff's certificate from which plaintiffs undertook to
redeem. This is virtually conceded.

It follows that the Suttons may challenge this redemption by
plaintiffs, unless they have in some manner estopped or precluded
themselves from exercising that right. There is no claim of estoppel
in the proper sense of that term. They have done no act upon which
plaintiffs have in any sense relied. The claim is that, under the
doctrine of Willard v. Finnegan, 42 Minn. 476, 44 N. W. 476, 8
L.R.A. 50, Torinus, and all claiming under him, have waived their
right to object to the plaintiffs' redemption. Referring to plaintiffs'
brief on reargument, they say: "He (Torinus) cannot raise the question because he has accepted and retained the plaintiffs' money and
has thereby waived all irregularity and invalidity in the redemption
proceedings;" and again: "If Sutton was a joint owner with Torinus
then the act of his joint owner (in whose name the certificate for convenience had been placed) in accepting and retaining the money of
the plaintiffs certainly estopped him (Sutton) and the same result
must necessarily and logically follow if Lewis E. Torinus was holder
of the certificate as a sort of trustee." The alleged waiver or estoppel is predicated on these facts:

It is admitted that the money paid by plaintiffs to the sheriff was
received by Torinus and turned over by him to William Sutton, and
that William Sutton immediately used it for the purpose of an attempted subsequent redemption from plaintiffs under the $50 mort-
gage. The two Suttons were acting in unison, and the act of one
doubtless bound both. This act, plaintiffs claim, cut the ground
from under their feet and left them no standing to assail the invalidity of plaintiffs' redemption. Curiously enough, neither this al-

leged waiver nor the facts out of which it is claimed it arose were pleaded by plaintiffs, either in the complaint or reply. Had the case been tried on the pleadings, plaintiffs' case must surely have failed. Evidence of the facts mentioned was, however, received without objection and the failure to plead is accordingly not of vital importance.

The fact is, William Sutton also claimed a lien under his $50 mortgage subsequent to plaintiffs', if plaintiffs had any lien at all, and under this alleged subsequent lien he claimed a right to effect a subsequent redemption. It turned out that neither plaintiffs nor William Sutton under this latter alleged lien had any legal right to redeem. William Sutton and the others interested in the Torinus certificate could have resisted the claim of plaintiffs to redeem. But William Sutton did not want to stand on this ground alone. No one claims he was obliged to. He wanted also to assert his own right to redeem under his own alleged later lien. What he did do in effect was to take $45,000 or more left with the sheriff by plaintiffs and immediately handed it back to plaintiffs with the amount of their judgment added. It was therefore used to restore to plaintiffs what they had paid out in making redemption under their lien, and for no other purpose.

The intervention of the sheriff in these redemptions was not important. He was a mere conduit. The effect was the same as though Sutton had received the money from plaintiffs in person and in person handed it back to plaintiffs. The majority opinion holds this conclusive evidence of a waiver of the indisputable right that Sutton then had to assert that plaintiffs' redemption was void. The consequence of holding this conclusive of a waiver is of great importance in this case. It means that the Suttons were under the necessity of either standing solely upon their claim of the insufficiency of plaintiffs' redemption, or else raising another $45,000 to place in the sheriff's hands to await the outcome of a determination of that question of right. Such a requirement was onerous. We may infer from the methods the Suttons were obliged to use, and the number of persons upon whom they were obliged to draw to raise the first $45,000, that they could never have raised another similar amount at all. Persons who redeem without any right, as plaintiffs did, should not have it in their power to put a party, who of right owns property, to any such alternative. The Suttons might properly have said to plaintiffs: "Here is your money. If your redemption is wrongful you are entitled to your money back; if your redemption is valid, we still claim a right to redeem from you, and then you are entitled to the same amount plus the amount of your judgment lien. Here it is. It will serve no useful purpose to require us to g᾽ elsewhere and raise another $45,000 so as to leave with the sheriff for you two rolls of money, one for you to take if your redemption is valid, the other if it is void. It may be admitted there is some technical justification for such a proceeding. As a practical proposition, however, the placing of two such sums in the hands of the sheriff would simply impose on us a tremendous burden which would not benefit you. You could not have it all in any event. To require such a course would be to sacrifice substance to form."

Here is involved not the mere question of waiver of some technical formality in procedure, but the acquisition through an alleged waiver of the title to property of great value.

Waiver has been defined as "a technical doctrine introduced and applied by the courts for the purpose of defeating forfeitures." 40 Cyc. 254; Kierman v. Dutchess County Mut. Ins. Co. 150 N. Y. 190, 196, 44 N. E. 698. Waivers, where they operate to dispense with merely formal requirements in judicial procedure and to defeat forfeitures, are, and should be, favored, but where the sole effect of a waiver is, not to defeat forfeiture, or dispense with formality, but to deprive a party of some substantial property rights without any substantial consideration, i. e., in fact to work a forfeiture, a waiver should not be favored and should not be extended by the application of merely technical rules. In such cases it should be necessary, to make a waiver effective, that the party claiming it should have been led to act upon the facts going to make up the waiver to his detriment. Bigelow, Estoppel (6th ed.) §§ 730, 731. Had the Suttons not taken this redemption money, their title to this property would be secure. I am not willing to hold that the defendant William Sutton, by the act of merely receiving this redemption money and immediately tendering it back to plaintiffs, passed the title and interest of these parties to this valuable property to plaintiffs. No decided case has ever so held. In every case where the certificate holder has been held estopped, the record shows that he accepted and appropriated the money in such a way as to deprive the redemptioner of it.

Plaintiffs use the term "waiver" and I have done the same. This question is perhaps more properly a question of election than waiver. It is conceded that a man cannot ordinarily occupy inconsistent positions. By acceptance of benefits of a transaction he may bar himself from repudiating the transaction. Pederson v. Christofferson, 97 Minn. 491, 496, 106 N. W. 958. But the taking of one of two inconsistent positions will not always preclude the party taking it from later availing himself of the other, if no prejudice is done to anyone thereby. As to this, Mr. Bigelow, in his work on Estoppel, in treating the subject of "election and inconsistent positions generally" says: "However, the estoppel arising from accepting the benefits of a contract applies only when the party may accept or reject without serious inconvenience." This is an unquestioned rule as applied to contracts. Bigelow, Estoppel (7th ed.) p. 747; City of Cincinnati v. Cameron, 33 Oh. St. 336, 374; Zottman v. San Francisco, 20 Cal. 98, 81 Am. Dec. 96 (Field, C. J.); Potter v. Brown, 50 Mich. 436, 15 N. W. 540 (Cooley, J.); Black v. Dressell's Heirs, 20 Kan. 153 (Brewer, J.). As said by Field, C. J., in 20 Cal. 107, 81 Am. Dec. 96, "the party must also be in a situation where he is entirely free to elect * * *. The mere retention and use of the benefit resulting from the work where no such power or freedom of election exists, or where the election cannot influence the conduct of the other party with reference to the work performed, does not constitute evidence of acceptance." The same principle is applicable here. Defendants Sutton in this case had no real freedom of choice. The statutes did not permit them to wait until the regularity of plaintiffs' redemption could be tested before making redemption under their claimed subsequent lien. They were obliged to act within five days. They could not, without serious inconvenience, which as a practical proposition probably amounted to impossibility, leave this large fund in the hands of the sheriff, and at the same time avail themselves of their right to make or attempt to make their subsequent redemption. In my opinion they did not lose their right to question plaintiffs' void redemption by receiving from plaintiffs this money and forthwith offering to return it to them in the manner disclosed by the record in this case.

STATE v. ELIZA KORRER and Others.[1]

September 11, 1914.

Nos. 18,551—(4).

Navigable water.

1. A meandered lake, approximately 150 acres in extent, naturally suitable for boating, bathing, hunting, fishing and other beneficial public uses, on the shore of which is situated a village of 2,000 inhabitants, is a public or navigable body of water.

Navigable and non-navigable water.

2. Natural bodies of water are classed as navigable or non-navigable. The term navigable, as used in this connection, has been extended beyond its technical signification. It is unnecessary that the water should be capable of commerce of pecuniary value. The division of waters into navigable and non-navigable is but another way of dividing them into public and private waters. If a body of water is adapted for use for public purposes, it is a public or navigable water.

Rule of the English common law.

3. Under the English common law the crown owned the soil under the tide water and also the soil under the water of navigable rivers up to the point reached by the flow of the tide. The soil under fresh water rivers above tide water and the soil under fresh water lakes belonged to the owners of the shore land.

[1] Reported in 148 N. W. 617.

Note.—What waters are navigable, see note in 42 L.R.A. 305.

Title to land under water, see notes in 42 L.R.A. 161, and 1 L.R.A.(N.S.) 762.

Right of riparian owner to erect and maintain wharves, see note in 40 L.R.A. 635.

Rule in Minnesota.

4. In the United States each state determines for itself the question of the ownership of the soil underlying its public waters. The United States government never owned the soil under public waters, and its patent to the shore land does not pass title to the land under the water. This belonged to the states, and if the riparian owner has acquired it at all it is by the favor or concession of the state. In Minnesota the title of the proprietor of abutting lands extends to low-water mark. The title to the soil under the waters below low-water mark is held by the state, not in the sense of ordinary absolute proprietorship, but in its sovereign governmental capacity, for common public use, and in trust for the people of the state, for the public purposes for which they are adapted. This rule applies to all public waters, lakes as well as streams.

Riparian rights of owner of shore land.

5. The shore owner has well defined riparian rights in the adjacent water and the soil under it below low-water mark. These rights include the right of access, the right to accretions and relictions, the right to wharf out and the right, absolute as respects every one but the state, to improve, reclaim and occupy the surface of the submerged land out to the point of navigability for any private purpose.

Same — subject to the control of the state.

6. These rights are not unrestricted but are subject to the control of the state. The state has power to conserve the integrity of its public lakes and rivers. The riparian owner has no right against the protest of the state to destroy the bed of a public lake for the private purpose of taking ore therefrom.

Diversion of bed of lake from public use.

7. The question is not wholly one of interference with present public use. The fact that in the opinion of the court the portions of the lake in controversy are, during low-water mark, not capable of any substantial beneficial use does not prevent the state from objecting to its diversion to a private use foreign to the public uses of the water and the soil under it.

Right in soil between high and low-water mark.

8. The fee to the soil between high and low-water is in the abutting owner, subject to the right of the public to use or reclaim it for public purposes. The shore owner has the right, during periods of recession of water, to take ore from this space, provided the state does not require it for public purposes, and provided he shall not measurably interfere with the utilization of it for such prospective uses.

Action in the district court for St. Louis county against Eliza
Korrer, Edmund N. Korrer, Annie L. Korrer, John Brennan, White
Iron Lake Iron Co., Albert B. Coates, Martha R. Coates, and Euclid
Iron Mining Co. to enjoin defendants from interfering with the public waters of Longyear lake, from removing the iron ore under said
lake and the natural waters thereof, from removing the iron ore from
under that part of the bed of said lake which would be covered by the
waters thereof in the natural condition of said lake at the time of the
commencement of the action but for the erection by defendants of the
embankment or dump mentioned in the complaint, and for an accounting as to any ore unlawfully removed prior to or pending the
action. The case was heard before Cant, J., who made findings and
ordered judgment in favor of defendants. From the judgment entered pursuant to the order for judgment, plaintiff appealed. Reversed.

Lyndon A. Smith, Attorney General, and *C. Louis Weeks,* Assistant Attorney General, for appellant.

Crassweller, Crassweller & Blu, Washburn, Bailey & Mitchell,
John Brennan and *T. L. Doyle,* for respondents.

John R. Van Derlip, as *amicus curiæ,* filed a brief supporting the
position of respondents.

HALLAM, J.

The bed of Longyear lake contains deposits of iron ore both between high and low-water mark and below low-water mark. Defendants own land abutting on the lake. Upon their taking steps to remove the ore beneath the bed of the lake, and for that purpose to
fill in the lake bed from the shore to a point some distance below
low-water mark, the state brought this action to restrain them. Both
the state and the defendants claim a proprietary interest in the ore
underlying the bed of the lake. The real issue involved is whether
the state has such interest in this body of water and the bed thereof
that it may enjoin the defendants from filling in and reclaiming the
bed of the lake for the purely private purpose of removing the underlying ore. We shall address ourselves to this issue.

A consideration of this question requires some examination into the character of this lake and into the history of the rights of the government and of the riparian owner in waters of this character.

1. The first question is: What is the character of this body of water? The trial court found "that Longyear lake is a meandered public body of water * * * having an area of more than one hundred and fifty acres in extent * * * that within the entire natural limits of said lake the same during high water is naturally suitable for boating, bathing, hunting, fishing and other beneficial public uses; that on the shore of said lake and in the main on the westerly shore thereof * * * is situated the village of Chisholm, having a population of more than two thousand inhabitants." The finding in substance is that these facts constitute Longyear lake a "public body of water." This finding is sustained by the evidence.

2. Natural bodies of water are *classed* as navigable or non-navigable. The term "navigable," as used in this connection, has been extended beyond its technical signification and embraces many bodies of water not navigable in the ordinary sense of that term. The division of waters into navigable and non-navigable is but another way of dividing them into public and private waters, and navigable waters embrace all bodies of water public in their nature. It is not necessary that the water should be capable of commerce of pecuniary value. If a body of water is adapted to use for public purposes other than commercial navigation, it is held to be public water, or navigable water, if the old nomenclature is preferred. Boating for pleasure is considered navigation, as well as boating for mere pecuniary profit. "Navigability for pleasure is as sacred in the eye of the law as * * * navigability for other purposes." City of Grand Rapids v. Powers, 89 Mich. 94, 50 N. W. 661, 14 L.R.A. 498, 28 Am. St. 276. "Many, if not the most, of the meandered lakes of the state, are not adapted to, and probably will never be used to any great extent for, commercial navigation; but they are used—and as population increases, and towns and cities are built up in their vicinity, will be still more used —by the people for sailing, rowing, fishing, fowling, bathing, skating, taking water for domestic, agricultural, and even city purposes, cutting ice, and other public purposes which cannot now be enumerated or even anticipated. To hand over all these lakes to private owner-

ship, under any old or narrow test of navigability, would be a great wrong upon the public for all time, the extent of which cannot, perhaps, be now even anticipated." Mitchell, J. in Lamprey v. State, 52 Minn. 181, 199, 200, 53 N. W. 1139, 1143, 18 L.R.A. 670, 38 Am. St. 541. See also Chicago, M. & St. P. Ry. Co. v. City of Minneapolis, 115 Minn. 460, 133 N. W. 169, Ann. Cas. 1912D, 1029.

Applying these rules, it must be held that this lake is a public body of water and is governed by the law applicable to public or navigable fresh water lakes.

3. The next question is: What are the respective rights of the state and the riparian proprietors in such public waters? It has been said that under the early common law there was no assertion of public right in the waters or the soil under them, and that all land under water which could be profitably used passed by the grants of the crown into private ownership. Farnham, Waters & Water Rights, § 36, p. 166. This may be true, but this private right received no recognition in any early judicial decision and received very little attention from the early commentators. In the reign of Elizabeth a lawyer named Digges advanced the theory that the proprietorship of all tide water and tide land, together with accretions and relictions, was in the crown, and that all use of the shore below high-water mark by the adjacent proprietors was illegal. Farnham, Waters & Water Rights, § 36, p. 167. The assertion of this alleged right by the crown was much opposed, and the claim was modified by royal concession and later by legislation, so that the title of the crown was to be considered as held for public uses and subject to certain riparian rights. The theory that the crown owned the title to the soil of navigable rivers up to a point reached by the flow of the tide of the sea was probably an outgrowth of this same doctrine. As applied to rivers this theory received judicial recognition early in the reign of James I, when, in the case of The Royal Fishery of the Banne, Davis Rep. 55, 56 (Moore, H. & L. of Foreshore & Seashore, 248) it was held that "every navigable river, so high as the sea flows and ebbs in it, is a royal river." See also Bulstrode v. Hall, 1 Sid. 148. Whatever its origin, the rule that the soil of tidal navigable rivers belongs to the crown has been consistently followed for several centuries as the com-

mon law of England. Lord Adv. v. Hamilton (1852) 1 Macq. (H. of L.) 46.

This doctrine did not apply to navigable fresh-water streams above tide water or to fresh-water lakes. There were few such streams and practically no such lakes in England, and the law applicable to such bodies of water received scant attention. Apparently there were no judicial decisions clearly defining rights in fresh-water lakes or rivers prior to the separation of the colonies from England. It is worthy of note that Blackstone, in his Commentaries published on the eve of the Revolution, makes no mention of this subject at all. After the Revolution, and in 1787, there was published a manuscript, written more than 100 years before by the eminent jurist and commentator, Sir Matthew Hale. This contained the following: "Fresh rivers of what kind soever, do of common right belong to the owners of the soil adjacent; so that the owners of the one side have, of common right, the propriety of the soil, and consequently the right of fishing, *usque filum aquæ;* and the owners of the other side the right of soil or ownership and fishing unto the *filum aquæ* on their side. And if a man be owner of the land of both sides, in common presumption he is owner of the whole river, and hath the right of fishing according to the extent of his land in length. With this agrees the common experience." De Juris Maris, Part I, c. I. These views were not at once accepted as settling the law of England. In 1863 doubt was expressed as to whether the soil of lakes belongs to the owners of the land on either side *"ad medium filum aquæ."* Marshall v. Ullewater Steam Navigation Co. 3 Best & S. 742; and as late as 1883 Lord Denman said in Williams v. Wilcox, 8 Ad. & El. 336, that the question whether the soil of public navigable rivers above the flow of the tide was at common law in the crown or the owners of the adjacent land was "a point perhaps not free from doubt." The views of Sir Matthew Hale are now, however, recognized as the common law of England. Hindson v. Ashby (1896) L. R. 2 Ch. Div. 78; Orr Ewing v. Colquhoun, L. R. 2 App. Cas. 839; Scott v. Napier (H. of L.) 7 Ct. of Sess. Cas. 35 (1869) (a Loch of Scotland); Bristow v. Cormican (1878), L. R. 3 App. Cas. 641 (a Lough of Ireland).

4. In the United States the rule is not uniform. The common law of England, as it existed at the time of the separation of the colonies,' is followed here as far as applicable to our conditions. But, in the first place, the common law of England on this subject was not then well settled, and, secondly, the authorities are not agreed as to whether conditions are so similar here in this respect as to require the adoption of what is now established as the English rule. A classification of waters based upon the ebb and flow of the tide has been rejected in many cases as unsuited to our conditions, and it was long ago said by the United States Supreme Court: "If a distinction is made on that account, it is merely arbitrary, without any foundation in reason; and, indeed, would seem to be inconsistent with it." The Genesee Chief, 12 How. 443, 454, 13 L. ed. 1058. The most that has ever been said for this basis of classification is that it is a convenient test and easy of application. Cobb v. Davenport, 32 N. J. Law, 369; Woodcliffe Land Imp. Co. v. New Jersey S. L. R. Co. 72 N. J. Law, 137, 60 Atl. 44; Illinois Central R. R. Co. v. Illinois, 146 U. S. 387, 435, 13 Sup. Ct. 110, 36 L. ed. 1018. In another case that court declared that to permit private ownership of the beds of navigable waters was "at variance with sound principles of public policy." Barney v. Keokuk, 94 U. S. 324, 24 L. ed. 224. It is now well settled, however, that this is not a Federal question, but that each state must determine for itself the question of the ownership of the soil underlying its public waters. Barney v. Keokuk, 94 U. S. 324, 24 L. ed. 224. The result is much confusion. Courts of some states hold that title to the bed of navigable waters is in the riparian proprietor in a proprietary capacity. The Steamboat Magnolia v. Marshall, 39 Miss. 109; Kinkead v. Turgeon, 74 Neb. 580, 104 N. W. 1061, 109 N. W. 744, 1 L.R.A.(N.S.) 762, 7 L.R.A.(N.S.) 316, 121 Am. St. 740, 13 Ann. Cas. 43; Wilson v. Watson, 141 Ky. 324, 132 S. W. 563, 35 L.R.A.(N.S.) 227; Johnson v. Johnson, 14 Idaho, 561, 95 Pac. 499, 24 L.R.A.(N.S.) 1240; Admrs. of Gavit v. Chamber & Coats, 3 Ohio, 496. Others hold that the title to the bed of all navigable waters is in the state in a proprietary capacity. Chapman v. Kimball, 9 Conn. 38, 21 Am. Dec. 707. Others hold that the title to the beds of navigable rivers is in the state and the beds

of navigable lakes in the riparian owner. Cobb v. Davenport, 32 N. J. Law, 369. Others hold that the title to beds of navigable lakes is in the state and the beds of navigable rivers in the riparian owner. Seaman v. Smith, 24 Ill. 521; Illinois Cent. R. R. Co. v. City of Chicago, 173 Ill. 471, 50 N. E. 1104, 53 L.R.A. 408; Schulte v. Warren, 218 Ill. 108, 75 N. E. 783, 13 L.R.A.(N.S.) 745; Fletcher v. Phelps, 28 Vt. 257; Willow River Club v. Wade, 100 Wis. 86, 76 N. W. 273, 42 L.R.A. 305; State v. Gilmanton, 9 N. H. 461. Some courts hold, as we shall see more fully later on, that the title is in the state in its sovereign capacity in trust for the people.

In Minnesota the decisions bearing upon this subject are numerous. The earliest case is that of Schurmeier v. St. Paul & Pac. R. Co. 10 Minn. 59 (82), 88 Am. Dec. 59. This case is relied upon as adopting the rule of the English common law that the owner of land bordering on a navigable stream takes title to the middle of the bed of the stream. The case in fact involved the question of title to a so-called island which lay above low-water mark, and the decision of the court was that "a tract of land bounded on the Mississippi river extends at least to the low-water mark." The decision of this question determined the case. A majority of the court, however, took occasion to approve the English common-law rule as to the ownership of the beds of fresh-water streams. In this view Justice Berry did not concur, and the language of the majority of the court in this regard was not essential to a decision of the case.

On appeal to the Supreme Court of the United States, that court, referring to the provisions of the original act of May 17, 1796, providing for the sale of public lands, used the following pointed language: "The court does not hesitate to decide that Congress, in making a distinction between streams navigable and those not navigable, intended to provide that the common-law rules of riparian ownership should apply to lands bordering on the latter, but that the title to lands bordering on navigable streams should stop at the stream, and that all such streams should be deemed to be, and remain public highways." Railroad Co. v. Schurmeir, 74 U. S. (7 Wall.) 272, 288, 289 (19 L. ed. 74).

In St. Paul, S. & T. F. R. Co. v. First Division St. Paul & Pac.

R. Co. 26 Minn. 31, 49 N. W. 303, and Morrill v. St. Anthony Falls
Water Power Co. 26 Minn. 222, 2 N. W. 842, 37 Am. Rep. 399, this
court referred to its decision in the Schurmeier case as holding the
English common-law rule in force in this state, but, deferring to the
language of the United States Supreme Court in the same case on
appeal, held that in the case of lands acquired by patent from the
Federal government the title of the patentee "stops at the stream and
that the title to the beds of such streams is reserved to the government." The last portion of this statement, that the title is reserved
to the government, evidently meaning the Federal government, seems
unwarranted by the Federal decision relied upon, and is directly contrary to earlier Federal decisions which held that "the shores of navigable waters, and the soils under them, were not granted by the
Constitution to the United States, but were reserved to the states respectively; and the new states have the same rights, sovereignty and
jurisdiction over this subject as the original states." (Pollard's Lessee v. Hagan, 44 U. S. [3 How.] 212, 11 L. ed. 565; Mumford v.
Wardwell, 73 U. S. [6 Wall.] 423, 436, 18 L. ed. 756); and the
doctrine that the matter was controlled by act of Congress had already
been repudiated by the explicit declaration of the Federal court in
the later case of Barney v. Keokuk, 94 U. S. 324, 24 L. ed. 224, to
the effect that the determination of the rights of riparian proprietors
in public waters is a question which each state must decide for itself.
In view of this position of the Federal supreme court in the Pollard,
Mumford and Barney cases, the declarations that the title to the bed
of public waters was in the Federal government, or that the question
of such title was governed by Federal law, could not be allowed to
stand, and they were not followed in subsequent cases.

In Union Depot, St. Ry. & T. Co. of Stillwater v. Brunswick, 31
Minn. 297, 17 N. W. 626, 47 Am. Dec. 789, the subject was again
fully considered. This case involved the extent and nature of the
rights of the defendants, as riparian owners of land upon the shore
of the navigable waters of the river or lake of St. Croix. The subject
was fully considered and, so far as the title to the bed of the waters
was concerned, was plainly deemed an open question. The decisions
in St. Paul, S. & T. F. R. Co. v. First Division St. Paul & Pac. R.

Co. 26 Minn. 31, 49 N. W. 303, and Morrill v. St. Anthony Falls Water Power Co. 26 Minn. 222, 2 N. W. 842, 37 Am. Rep. 399, that the title to the bed was reserved in the Federal government, were not followed. Barney v. Keokuk was not cited, but the court accepted the doctrine of that case that the right of riparian owners in such cases "is wholly a matter for the state to determine the extent of its own rights." The Schurmeier case, 10 Minn. 59 (82), 88 Am. Dec. 59, was followed as settling the law "that the riparian owner has the fee to low-water mark," but was followed no further. The decision reached in the Brunswick case was that the title to the bed of the stream below low-water mark "vests in the state as a sovereign right." The failure of the court to follow the language of the majority in the Schurmeier case, 10 Minn. 59 (82), 88 Am. Dec. 59, as to ownership of the bed of the stream, was not apparently, as claimed by defendants, based upon the authority of Morrill v. St. Anthony Falls Water Power Co. 26 Minn. 222, 2 N. W. 842, 37 Am. Rep. 399, or St. Paul S. & T. F. R. Co. v. First Division St. Paul & Pac. R. Co. 26 Minn. 31, 49 N. W. 303, nor upon any misunderstanding of the effect of the Federal decisions, but rather upon what the court conceived to be the correct principle of law, for the court cites upon this point only the Pollard and Mumford cases, in which cases the doctrine of ownership in the state received decided approval. The decision in the Brunswick case that the state owns the bed of navigable waters settled the law on that subject, and it has been followed in a long line of cases. Miller v. Mendenhall, 43 Minn. 95, 44 N. W. 1141, 8 L.R.A. 89, 19 Am. St. 219; Hanford v. St. Paul & Duluth R. Co. 43 Minn. 104, 42 N. W. 596, 44 N. W. 1144, 7 L.R.A. 722; Bradshaw v. Duluth Imperial Mill Co. 52 Minn. 59, 65, 53 N. W. 1066; Lamprey v. State, 52 Minn. 181, 198, 53 N. W. 1139, 18 L.R.A. 670, 38 Am. St. 541.

At the risk of some repetition, the law on this branch of the case may be stated as follows:

When the American Revolution was concluded, the people of each state became themselves sovereign, and in that character held the absolute right to all their navigable waters and the soils under them for their own common use, and continued to do so subject only to the rights since surrendered by the Constitution to the general government. The soil under navigable waters was not granted by the Constitution to the United States, but was reserved to the states respectively, and the new states had the same rights. St. Anthony Falls Water Power Co. v. St. Paul Water Commrs. 168 U. S. 349, 359, 18 Sup. Ct. 157, 42 L. ed. 497. When the United States government issues its patent to public land bordering upon navigable water, the land under the water does not pass to the riparian proprietor by force of the patent, because the United States does not own it, but if the riparian owner acquires it at all it is by the concession or favor of the state which does own it. Barney v. Keokuk, 94 U. S. 324, 24 L. ed. 224; Hardin v. Shedd, 23 Sup. Ct. 685, 47 L. ed. 1156, 190 U. S. 508, 519; Franzini v. Layland, 120 Wis. 72, 81, 82, 97 N. W. 499. We conceive that the state of Minnesota has never conceded away its title as sovereign to its navigable waters or to the soil under them, and that the law of the state now is that the title of the proprietor of lands abutting upon navigable waters extends to low-water mark; that the title to the bed of the stream or body of water, below low-water mark, is held by the state, not, however, in the sense of ordinary absolute proprietorship with right of alienation but in its sovereign governmental capacity, for common public use, and in trust for the people of the state for the public purposes for which they are adapted.

This rule is not peculiar to this state, but is adopted in many other jurisdictions. Town of Brookhaven v. Smith, 188 N. Y. 74, 80 N. E. 665, 9 L.R.A.(N.S.) 326; Barnes v. Midland R. Terminal Co. 193 N. Y. 378, 85 N. E. 1093, 127 Am. St. 962; McLennan v. Prentice, 85 Wis. 427, 444, 55 N. W. 764; Rhode Island Motor Co. v. City of Providence (R. I.) 55 Atl. 696; Walbridge v. Robinson, 22 Idaho, 236, 125 Pac. 812, 43 L.R.A.(N.S.) 240; State v. Gerbing, 56 Fla. 603, 47 South. 353, 22 L.R.A.(N.S.) 337. And it is not far from the English rule now prevailing in respect to tidal waters. Gann v. Free Fishers, 11 H. L. Cas. 192; Attorney General v. Johnson, 2 Wils. Ch. 87; Attorney General v. Tomline, L. R. 14 Ch. Div. 58.

In Minnesota the rights of shore owners of land bordering on lakes are the same as those of owners of land bordering on rivers. Lamprey v. State, 52 Minn. 181, 53 N. W. 1139, 18 L.R.A. 670, 38 Am. St.

541. As to the Great Lakes and other larger lakes like Lake Champlain, it is agreed that the title to underlying soil is in the state. 1 Farnham, Waters & Water Rights, p. 264, § 58; State v. Franklin Falls Co. 49 N. H. 240, 250, 6 Am. Rep. 513. As to smaller lakes the rule, as above indicated, is not uniform. When a lake is so small in size as to constitute merely a pond and to be entirely upon the land of one individual, no question of public ownership is raised. Between this class of lakes or ponds and the Great Lakes there are a large number which are more or less useful to the public. There is a point in the diminishing size, below which no one can doubt that the title should be in the individual. Conversely, there is a point above which every one will agree that the title must be in the state. 1 Farnham, Waters & Water Rights, p. 265, § 58a. In the Minnesota cases no distinction is made between the rights of the owner of land abutting upon Lake Superior and the rights of owners of land upon public waters of smaller size. This court has made navigability the dividing line. All public or navigable waters are placed in the same class. The rules applied to Lake Superior are likewise applied to smaller lakes, provided only they are in the class of public waters. The shore owner of land on non-navigable or private lakes takes title to the middle of the lake. Lamprey v. State, 52 Minn. 181, 53 N. W. 1139, 18 L.R.A. 670, 38 Am. St. 541; Tucker v. Mortenson, 126 Minn. 214, 148 N. W. 60. But the shore owner of land on navigable or public lakes takes only to low-water mark.

5. But while the shore owner owns the fee only to low water mark, he has certain well defined rights in the water and the soil under it below low-water mark. These rights are designated riparian rights. Riparian rights are incident to the ownership, not of the bed of the water, but of the shore land. The riparian owner has the right to the use of the water and has the right of access to it for that purpose. To that end he may follow it as it recedes. He has the title to the reliction caused by the gradual recession of the water and to the accretion caused by the washing of sand, dirt and gravel ashore. The rights of riparian owners have received very full consideration by this court. They include the right of the riparian owner to build and maintain, for his own and the public use, suitable wharves, piers and landings,

on and in front of his land, and to extend the same therefrom into the river, to the point of navigability, even though beyond low-water mark, and to this end exclusively to occupy the surface of the bed of the water, subordinate and subject only to the rights of the public, and to such needful rules and regulations for their protection as may be prescribed by competent legislative authority. Brisbine v. St. Paul & Sioux City R. Co. 23 Minn. 114, 130. This private right of use and enjoyment is not limited to purposes connected with the actual use of the navigable water, but may extend to any purpose not inconsistent with the public right. Hanford v. St. Paul & Duluth R. Co. 43 Minn. 104, 111, 42 N. W. 596, 44 N. W. 1144, 7 L.R.A. 722. The riparian owner has, subject to this public right, the exclusive right of possession and the entire beneficial interest in the surface of the underlying soil. Union Depot, St. Ry. & T. Co. of Stillwater v. Brunswick, 31 Minn. 297, 302, 17 N. W. 626, 47 Am. Rep. 297. He has the exclusive right—absolute as respects *every one but the state,* and limited only by the public interests of the state for purposes connected with public uses—to improve, reclaim and occupy the surface of the submerged land, out to the point of navigability, for any private purpose, as he might do if it were his separate estate. Hanford v. St. Paul & Duluth R. Co. 43 Minn. 104, 118, 42 N. W. 596, 44 N. W. 1144, 7 L.R.A. 722. The exercise of such rights, though subject to state regulation, can be interfered with only for public purposes. The rights which thus belong to him as riparian owner of the abutting premises are valuable property rights of which he cannot be divested without consent, except by due process of law, and, if for public purposes, upon just compensation. Brisbine v. St. Paul & Sioux City R. Co. 23 Minn. 114, 129.

6. Throughout all of these cases runs the thread of reserved state control. All of them were controversies between private parties. In all of them is distinctly recognized the power of the state to regulate and control the use of the water, particularly below low-water mark. While the Minnesota cases recognize the right to use the bed of the stream or lake for purposes not connected with the actual use of the water, we know of no case in Minnesota or elsewhere where the right of the riparian proprietor has been recognized as possessing the right

of utilizing the bed of a public body of water below low-water mark for purely private purposes disconnected with the use of the water, to the extent of destroying its existence, and against the protest of the state.

It may be noted that no decided case has ever sustained the title of the riparian owner to the minerals under public waters or the right to remove them under any circumstances. In most of the cases in which such questions have arisen the state is held to be the owner of the underlying soil in its proprietary capacity. Steele v. Sanchez, 72 Iowa, 65, 33 N. W. 366, 2 Am. St. 233; Brandt v. McKeever, 18 Pa. St. 70; Taylor v. Commonwealth, 102 Va. 759, 47 S. E. 875, 102 Am. St. 865; Lord Adv. v. Wemyss (1900) L. R. App. Cas. 50; See, also, Gould, Waters, § 10. In such cases it is held that "the state and it alone has the right to develop those hidden sources of wealth." Taylor v. Commonwealth, 102 Va. 776, 47 S. E. 875, 102 Am. St. 865. In Florida the rule as to title to the soil under navigable waters is substantially the same as in this state, and the rights of riparian owners are made by statute at least as large as they are in this state. In the case of State v. Black River Phosphate Co. 32 Fla. 82, it was held that the riparian owner had no right to take phosphate from the bed of a navigable river under any circumstances, except by consent of the state duly given by the law-making power and upon such terms and conditions as it may prescribe (p. 114). We need not in this case go even this far. Under the law of this state the state owns the soil under public waters in a sovereign not a proprietary capacity, but still the state owns it and the shore owner does not. Whether the riparian owner has any beneficial interest in the minerals underlying the bed of the lake where they can be removed without destroying the lake bed, we are not called upon to determine. We do hold that the state has the power to conserve the integrity of its public lakes and rivers and that riparian rights of the shore owner do not include the right to fill and destroy the bed of a navigable lake for the purpose of taking ore therefrom, against the protest of the state. Manifestly if the lake can be filled in for this private purpose it may be filled in for any private purpose, as for agriculture or grazing, upon a showing of greater utility being subserved by such private use. The propriety of filling in the public lakes and streams of the state for such private purposes, is not primarily a judicial question. Other authorities bearing upon this particular question are not numerous, nor altogether direct, but we think they point to the conclusion just stated. In Gould, Waters (3d ed.) § 179, it is said:

"Riparian owners upon navigable *fresh* rivers and lakes may construct, in the shoal water in front of their land, wharves, piers, landings, and booms in aid of and not obstructing navigation. This is a riparian right, being dependent upon title to the bank and not upon title to the river bed. Its exercise may be regulated or prohibited by the state."

In Farnham, Waters & Water Rights, page 528, § 113, it is said as to the right of a riparian owner to wharf out:

"This right is subject to public regulation, and, if the public good requires that no wharves or piers shall be constructed at any particular place, they may be forbidden."

In Lincoln v. Davis, 53 Mich. 375, 19 N. W. 103, 51 Am. Rep. 116, where it is held that "the title to the soil under the navigable waters of the Great Lakes became vested in the state as sovereign," it was held that "the state can forbid any erections in navigable waters, and on navigable streams and along the Great Lakes can fix the distance beyond which private erections cannot be maintained."

In Attorney General v. Smith, 109 Wis. 532, 85 N. W. 512, it was held that a structure built by a riparian owner upon the bed of a navigable lake, not in aid of navigation, is an invasion both of the state's title and the rights of the public, and that it may be suppressed at the suit of the state.

City of St. Paul v. Chicago, M. & St. P. Ry. Co. 63 Minn. 331, 63 N. W. 267, 65 N. W. 649, 68 N. W. 458, 34 L.R.A. 184, bears upon this question. Defendant built a freight house on a public levee under license given by the city council, on condition that the city engineer be of the opinion that the same shall in no manner interfere with the navigation of the river. It was held that the state holds the levee in its sovereign capacity in trust for the public, for the purposes for which it was dedicated, that, if the freight house was used without reference to traffic with craft navigating the river, its construction would constitute a diversion of the property to a use foreign to that to which it was dedicated, and that the license for its construction was void and might be revoked. These cases are not directly in point, but we think they sustain the principle we have laid down.

We have not overlooked the finding of the trial court that in recent years the depth of the water in the lake has been substantially lessened so that during low water the portion here in controversy is not capable of any substantial beneficial use, and that the water is occasionally so low that it is incapable of any public use whatever. The question is not wholly one of interference with present public use. In City of St. Paul v. Chicago, M. & St. P. Ry. Co. 63 Minn. 330, 63 N. W. 267, 65 N. W. 649, 68 N. W. 458, the court said: "Neither does it appear whether there exists any present public necessity for the use of this land for levee purposes. This last consideration would, of course, not be controlling, for the fact that the land is not presently needed for levee purposes would not prevent the city or state, as the trustee of the public, from objecting to a diversion of the property to a use wholly foreign to or inconsistent with that to which it was dedicated."

It was said by Cooley, C. J., by way of illustration, in Attorney General v. Evart Booming Co. 34 Mich. 462, 473: "A highway usually includes within its limits more than is ever made use of for public purposes; but, as it is set apart for public use, provided there shall be occasion, the appropriation by an individual is unlawful, though it occasion no present inconvenience to any one, and it may be abated because the result of its being persisted in might be to obscure and, possibly, in the end, to defeat the public right altogether, and thus preclude enjoyment by the public in case the use of that which was inclosed should ever be needed for highway purposes."

The conclusion is that the defendants have no right to take ore from the bed of Longyear lake below low-water mark and for that purpose to fill in the bed of the lake.

8. The remaining question is as to the rights of the parties in the space between high and low water. We are of the opinion that within this space the riparian owner has a qualified right to mine. Many courts and text writers lay down the rule that the title of the riparian owner stops at high-water mark. Others hold that his title

extends to low-water mark. This is a matter for each state to determine for itself. In this state it has been settled for nearly 50 years that the title of the riparian owner extends to low-water mark. Schurmeier v. St. Paul & Pac. R. Co. 10 Minn. 59 (82), 88 Am. Dec. 59; Union Depot, St. Ry. & T. Co. v. Brunswick, 31 Minn. 297, 17 N. W. 626, 47 Am. Rep. 789; Hanford v. St. Paul & Duluth R. Co. 43 Minn. 104, 111, 42 N. W. 596, 44 N. W. 1144, 7 L.R.A. 722; Village of Wayzata v. Great Northern Ry. Co. 50 Minn. 438, 52 N. W. 913; In re Minnetonka Lake Improvement, 56 Minn. 513, 58 N. W. 295, 45 Am. St. 494; Gniadck v. N. W. Imp. & Boom Co. 73 Minn. 87, 75 N. W. 894; Reeves v. Backus-Brooks Co. 83 Minn. 339, 86 N. W. 337. While the title of a riparian owner in navigable or public waters extends to ordinary low-water mark, his title is not absolute except to ordinary high-water mark. As to the intervening space his title is limited or qualified by the right of the public to use the same for purpose of navigation or other public purpose. The state may use it for any such public purpose, and to that end may reclaim it during periods of low water, and protect it from any use, even by the riparian owner, that would interfere with its present or prospective public use, without compensation. Restricted only by that paramount public right the riparian owner enjoys proprietary privileges, among which is the right to use the land for private purposes. Hanford v. St. Paul & Duluth R. Co. 43 Minn. 104, 112, 42 N. W. 596, 44 N. W. 1144, 7 L.R.A. 722; In re Minnetonka Lake Improvement, 56 Minn. 513, 520, 58 N. W. 295, 45 Am. St. 494; Gniadck v. N. W. Imp. & Boom Co. 73 Minn. 87, 75 N. W. 894; State v. District Court of Kandiyohi County, 119 Minn. 132, 137 N. W. 298; People v. Jones, 112 N. Y. 597, 20 N. E. 577. The rights of the riparian owners are accordingly distinctly different in and to the space between high and low-water mark from what they are below low-water mark.

Applying the foregoing principles to this case, it appears to us:

That the defendants have the right during periods of recession of water to take ore from the space between high and low-water mark, provided the state does not require the use of this space for authorized public purposes, and provided they shall not measurably interfere with the utilization of such space for such prospective public uses.

That the state is entitled to an injunction restraining the defendants from taking ore below low-water mark and from filling in or in any manner interfering with the bed of the lake below that point.

Judgment reversed and case remanded with directions to proceed in accordance with this opinion.

On November 20, 1914, the following opinion was filed:

PER CURIAM.

Defendants White Iron Lake Iron Company, John Brennan, Eliza Korrer, and Annie L. Korrer move for a reargument of the case. The state and the defendant Euclid Iron Mining Company both petition that further direction be given the trial court to the end that proper judgment may be given relative to the rights of the parties in certain ore which has already been taken from the bed of Longyear lake.

It will be borne in mind that the defendants Eliza Korrer and Annie L. Korrer were and are the owners of the shore land, that they gave a mining lease to the defendant White Iron Lake Iron Company, that this company in turn gave a mining lease to defendant Albert B. Coates, and this lease was assigned to the Euclid Iron Mining Company.

After the commencement of the action, and before the trial thereof, a stipulation was made between the state and defendant Euclid Iron Mining Company, which recited that, upon a certain area of Longyear lake below the low-water mark, the waters had been by said defendant forced back by an embankment, and that a body of ore within this area had already been stripped and prepared for mining, and it was stipulated that said defendant might remove the ore so stripped, and that said defendant should pay the state 60 cents per ton for ore it should so remove and which it should be finally adjudged did not at the beginning of the action belong to the fee owners of the shore land.

On this stipulation the trial court ordered that the Euclid Iron

Company be permitted to remove the ore so stripped and uncovered, and that it should pay to the state 60 cents per ton for ore which it might remove from said area, "for which, under the final determination of the court in this action, it is under no obligation to pay royalty to the fee owners and those claiming under them."

The trial court made no finding that any ore was in fact removed by the Euclid Company from this area. In fact the taking of evidence bearing on the right to ore taken from such area and to an accounting therefor was reserved until the rights of the parties should be further determined. We are assured, however, that ore was taken out of this area pursuant to this stipulation and order.

A majority of the court construe this stipulation as giving the state the right to an accounting only in the event the state is found to be the owner in a proprietary capacity of the mineral underlying Longyear lake. The decision of this court explicitly holds that the state owns the bed of this lake below low-water mark, "not, however, in the sense of ordinary absolute proprietorship with the right of alienation but in its sovereign governmental capacity, for common public use, and in trust for the people of the state for the public purposes for which they are adapted." From this it necessarily follows that the state has no right to recover the value of the ore, and no right to an accounting under the stipulation.

Whether the law-making power of the state and the shore owner may by joint action provide for the mining of the ore under the waters of this lake, is a question here not presented and it is not decided.

The several applications for a rehearing are denied.

JOHN P. POGUE v. GREAT NORTHERN RAILWAY COMPANY.[1]

September 25, 1914.

Nos. 18,713—(224).

Negligence — evidence.

1. There is evidence in this case that defendant was negligent in operating a train without a headlight on the engine, and without giving proper signals of its approach.

Same — unlighted train approaching highway crossing.

2. A person approaching a railroad track in a lighted automobile in the dark of evening will not be held negligent as a matter of law in not seeing a train approaching without a headlight, where his view is obscured until he is within less than 30 feet of the track, and there is testimony that he looked as soon as he could but did not see the train until it was upon him.

Conflicting testimony of witness at former trial.

3. Testimony on a former trial is not conclusive against the party giving it, where his testimony on the later trial is corroborated, even though his explanation of the discrepancy may not impress this court with favor.

Highway crossing — looking and listening for trains.

4. A railroad track is in itself a danger signal. The duty of a traveler approaching a railroad track to look and listen for trains is the rule. It is only under exceptional circumstances that he is relieved of this duty. Failure of the railroad company to give expected signals may excuse him in relaxing somewhat in his vigilance, but it does not dispense with vigilance altogether. An instruction which gives the jury to understand that the traveler may wholly omit the duty of looking and listening, simply because he hears none of the customary or required signals of the approach of the train, is erroneous.

Same — imperfect hearing.

5. Any circumstance which impedes the exercise of the sense of hearing renders more imperative the duty of the traveler to use his sense of sight.

[1] Reported in 148 N. W. 889.

Note.—Failure to give customary signals at railroad crossing as excusing performance of duty to look and listen, see note in 3 L.R.A.(N.S.) 391.

Action in the district court for Beltrami county to recover $10,000 for personal injury received in driving plaintiff's automobile across defendant's track, and $1,000 for injury to the machine. The answer specifically denied that defendant was guilty of negligence of any kind and alleged that, if plaintiff suffered any personal injury or his automobile was damaged by reason of any collision with defendant's train, it was due to lack of ordinary care on the part of plaintiff and not to any carelessness of defendant. The case was tried before Wright, J., who denied defendant's motion to dismiss the action, and a jury which returned a verdict for $3,500 in favor of plaintiff. From an order denying its motion for judgment notwithstanding the verdict or for a new trial, defendant appealed. Reversed and new trial granted.

M. L. Countryman and *A. L. Janes,* for appellant.
Marshall A. Spooner and *John F. Gibbons,* for respondent.

HALLAM, J.

Plaintiff, driving an automobile in the little village of Wilton, came into collision at a street crossing with a freight train of defendant. This action was brought to recover damages. Plaintiff had a verdict. Defendant asks for judgment notwithstanding the verdict or for a new trial.

Defendant is not entitled to judgment notwithstanding the verdict.

1. There was evidence, proper to be submitted to the jury, tending to prove the negligence of defendant. The collision occurred close to 6 p. m., on the twenty-eighth of October. The headlight of the engine was not lighted. There is also evidence that no bell was rung until almost the moment of the accident, and that no crossing whistle was blown. The question whether the defendant was negligent in these particulars was one of fact for the jury.

2. It is contended that the evidence is conclusive that plaintiff was guilty of contributory negligence. We cannot so hold. Plaintiff's view of the train was obscured by a long string of box cars on an intervening track. The distance between these standing cars and the passing train was less than 30 feet. Not until he passed these

cars could he have a clear view of the approaching train. Plaintiff's testimony as given on this trial was to the effect that, after passing these standing cars, he stopped his automobile and looked up and down the track, did not see anything, and went ahead; that he did not discover the train until "just like a flash of your eye it was right there, and then a blow." It is conceded that if this testimony is believable, plaintiff was not guilty of contributory negligence. The evidence is conflicting as to just how dark it was. Plaintiff's witnesses testified that it was very dark. There is some evidence that the evening was cloudy and gloomy. The lights of the village were lighted. The lights on plaintiff's automobile were lighted. There is evidence that the trainmen were giving signals with lighted lanterns. The trainmen themselves deny this, but it is admitted that they lighted their lanterns for this purpose at Solway, the station above. If it was as dark as plaintiff now claims, it is not unbelievable that he might look and still fail to see the approaching engine beyond the range of his own lights.

3. The doubt as to this branch of the case arises from the fact that upon a former trial plaintiff testified that he did see the train approaching when he was 12 or 14 feet from the track, and that he could have stopped his car in three or four feet, but that he was "flustered" and did not stop. Plaintiff's counsel does not question that such conduct would have been contributory negligence. We are not impressed with plaintiff's explanation as to how he came to give this testimony on the former trial, which is to the effect that he was intoxicated from drinking liquor to relieve his pain, and was guessing, but it appears to us that inasmuch as his testimony on this trial is somewhat corroborated, his former testimony is not conclusive against him.

We are not confronted with the question whether this contradiction in plaintiff's testimony on the two trials is ground for granting a retrial of the case, for we are of the opinion that a new trial should be granted upon another ground.

4. The court instructed the jury as follows:

"Now, if you should find in considering this testimony that no bell was rung, that no whistle was blown, and if you should take into

127 M.—6.

consideration the weather and find, as some of the witnesses have testified, that the wind was blowing strongly from the southeast, and you should find that the plaintiff approached the crossing and failed to stop, look and listen, you would have a right to take into consideration all those things; the absence of a headlight, if you found that such headlight was needed, that it was dark enough for it and that there wasn't any, to determine the ultimate question as to whether or not he was negligent in not stopping, looking and listening."

This instruction does not correctly state the law. The law is well settled that a person about to cross a railroad track at a public high-way must look and listen for approaching trains, unless he is in some way prevented from doing so without fault of his own. Wardner v. Great Northern Ry. Co. 96 Minn. 382, 104 N. W. 1084. A railroad track is in itself a danger signal, warning one about to go upon it to use his sense of sight and hearing, to the extent of his opportunity, to discover approaching trains. Woehrle v. Minn. Transfer Ry. Co. 82 Minn. 165, 169, 84 N. W. 791, 52 L.R.A. 348. It is also well settled, however, that the duty to look and listen is not an absolute one, that a higher vigilance is required under some circumstances than under others, and that circumstances may be such as to relieve the traveler from the duty altogether. But the duty to look and listen is the rule. It is only under exceptional circumstances that the traveler is relieved of this duty. There were no exceptional circumstances in this case which would wholly excuse plaintiff from looking and listening, unless it can be said that the failure of defendant to give proper signals and its failure to have the headlight burning are such circumstances.

There are cases which hold that a person cannot rely upon signals to remind him of danger, that the failure of the traveler to look and listen is negligence or not, according to the circumstances, but that the negligence of the employees of a railroad company in failing to whistle or ring a bell is no excuse for negligence on the part of the person about to cross in failing to use his senses to discover danger. Sandberg v. St. Paul & Duluth R. Co. 80 Minn. 442, 83 N. W. 411;

Carlson v. Chicago & N. W. Ry. Co. 96 Minn. 504, 105 N. W. 555, 4 L.R.A.(N.S.) 349, 112 Am. St. 655.

On the other hand, numerous cases hold that when a traveler is approaching a railroad track he may, in regulating his own conduct, have a right to presume that the railroad company will act with proper care in giving signals of the approach of its trains. Loucks v. Chicago, M. & St. P. Ry. Co. 31 Minn. 526, 18 N. W. 651; Hutchinson v. St. Paul, M. & M. Ry. Co. 32 Minn. 398, 21 N. W. 212; Hendrickson v. Great Northern Ry. Co. 49 Minn. 245, 51 N. W. 1044, 16 L.R.A. 261, 32 Am. St. 540.

We think these cases may be harmonized, and that the rule deducible from them is that the traveler may, in regulating his conduct, have some regard to the presumption that the railroad company will give proper signals, and, if he hears none, the same preparedness and caution will not be expected of him as would be required in case proper signals were given; but he cannot in any case wholly omit the duty of looking and listening simply because he hears none of the customary or required signals of the approach of a train. Newstrom v. St. Paul & Duluth R. Co. 61 Minn. 78, 63 N. W. 253; Klotz v. Winona & St. Peter R. Co. 68 Minn. 341, 71 N. W. 257; Woehrle v. Minn. Transfer Ry. Co. 82 Minn. 165, 84 N. W. 791, 52 L.R.A. 348. In other words, the failure of the defendant to give expected signals may excuse a traveler in relaxing somewhat in his vigilance, but it has never been held to dispense with vigilance altogether. If such were the law, then there would be little left of the rule which requires the traveler to look and listen, for the rule is only applied as bearing upon the question of his contributory negligence, and that question is never reached, unless there is some negligent act or omission in the operation of the train. The vice of the instruction is in this: It gave the jury to understand that, even if plaintiff wholly failed to look and listen, they might still find that he was not negligent, because of the failure of defendant to give signals, or because of the blowing of a strong wind. This, as we have above indicated, is not the law. The failure of defendant to give signals would not excuse plaintiff from looking and listening for approaching trains.   We are of the opinion that this error was not cured by other portions of the charge.

5. It should also be said that the jury might fairly infer from the charge that the existence of a wind "blowing strongly from the southeast" would tend to relieve plaintiff from his duty of vigilance. On the contrary, this circumstance impeding the exercise of the sense of hearing rendered more imperative the duty of plaintiff to use his sense of sight.   Marty v. Chicago, St. P. M. & O. Ry. Co. 38 Minn. 108, 35 N. W. 670; Schneider v. Northern Pacific Ry. Co. 81 Minn. 383, 84 N. W. 124.

Order reversed and new trial granted.

LOUIS THORESON and Others v. GEORGE SUSENS.[1]

September 25, 1914.

Nos. 18,720—(232).

Consolidation of school districts — posting notice.

1. The last day for posting notices of election in proceedings for the consolidation of school districts, under G. S. 1913, §§ 2686–2694, was Monday, February 10. The notices were tacked up on Sunday, February 9, but remained up on Monday, the tenth. The notices were valid.

Same.

2. Where such a notice is left posted on Sunday, the court may presume that it remained posted on Monday, there being no evidence to the contrary.

Objection to question — opinion of witness.

3. An objection that a question is incompetent, irrelevant and immaterial, does not raise the point that it is improper as calling for an opinion of the witness on the whole issue in the case.

Louis Thoreson, Oscar Gahlon and Edward O'Brien appealed to the district court for Douglas county from an order consolidating school districts Nos. 22 and 15 in that county into a district to be

---

1 Reported in 148 N. W. 891.

known as Consolidated School District No. 15. George Susens, as county superintendent of schools, filed an answer to the complaint of the appellants. The appeal was heard before Parsons, J., who made findings and dismissed the appeal. From an order denying the motion of appellants for amended findings and for judgment in their favor or for a new trial, they appealed. Affirmed.

George L. Treat and *Henry T. Ronning,* for appellants.

Hugh E. Leach, County Attorney, *C. J. Gunderson* and *Constant Larson,* for respondent.

HALLAM, J.

This appeal involves the validity of an election in proceedings for the consolidation of two school districts, pursuant to chapter 207 p. 268, Laws 1911 (G. S. 1913, §§ 2686–2694). The principal contention is that no lawful notice of the election was given.

The statute provides that the county superintendent shall "cause ten days' posted notice to be given in each district affected." The term "posted notice" means "the posting, at the beginning of the prescribed period of notice, of a copy of the notice * * * in a manner likely to attract attention, in each of three of the most public places in the * * * district." G. S. 1913, § 9412, subd. 14. The election was held February 20, 1913. The notices of election were posted in one district on Sunday, February 9, and the contention is that this rendered the notices void. Counsel for appellant argues at length that the tacking up of an election notice on Sunday is "labor," and is forbidden by our Sunday laws. G. S. 1913' §§ 8752–8753. We shall not enter into a discussion of this question, since it seems to us that it is quite immaterial. It is not as though personal service of notice were required, and such personal service were made on Sunday. Nor is this case at all like the cases where a legal notice is published in a Sunday newspaper. No importance attaches here to the act of tacking up the poster. This act is no part of the giving of the notice. The requirement that the county superintendent shall "cause ten days' posted notice to be given" means that the notice must be up ten days before the election. No posting was necessary until Monday, February 10. The important consideration is that these notices remained and were posted on that day. This satisfies the requirement of the statute. Pelton v. Muntzing, 24 Colo. App. 1, 131 Pac. 281.

The evidence is direct that two of these notices remained posted on Monday. As to the third, there is no direct evidence, but the court invoked the rule that, where a fact of a continuing nature is shown to exist, there is a presumption that it continues to exist for a reasonable time, unless the contrary is shown, and found as a fact that the third notice also remained posted. Appellant, again urging that the act of tacking up the notice on Sunday was unlawful, contends that there can be no presumption of a continuance of a condition based upon an unlawful act. Were we to concede the unlawfulness of the act, the result contended for would not follow, for there may be a presumption of continuance of an unlawful act or condition. State v. Worthingham, 23 Minn. 528; In re Terry's Estate, 58 Minn. 268, 59 N. W. 1013. But there can be nothing unlawful in the fact of this notice remaining posted. The court properly determined that the rule of presumption of continuance applied.

Exception is taken to the ruling of the court in receiving in evidence the opinion of certain witnesses as to whether the consolidation of these two districts would be for the best interest of the territory affected. The objection here urged is that in admitting this testimony the court submitted to these witnesses the whole issue in the case. No such ground of objection was urged on the trial. It cannot accordingly be considered on this appeal. A party will not be permitted to review rulings of the trial court in admitting evidence, unless on the trial he advises the court of his ground of objection. Some of the questions to which exception is taken were not objected to on the trial at all. Others were objected to as incompetent, irrelevant and immaterial. Clearly this did not advise the trial court that counsel meant to rely on the ground of objection here urged. Larson v. Anderson, 122 Minn. 39, 141 N. W. 847; Lyon v. City of Grand Rapids, 121 Wis. 609, 99 N. W. 311.

Some of these questions were objected to, on the ground that the witnesses had not shown themselves qualified to testify on the subject. These witnesses showed thorough familiarity with all the facts, and ample foundation was laid for their testimony.

Order affirmed.

JOHN O'BRIEN v. GREAT NORTHERN RAILWAY COMPANY.[1]

October 2, 1914.

Nos. 18,715—(229).

Damages not excessive.

In an action by a railway switchman 29 years old, with an earning capacity of $105 a month, a verdict for $2,050 for injuries consisting of the loss of two teeth, a serious ankle sprain, aggravation of appendical trouble, and alleged injury to the back, sustained as against the contention that it was excessive.

Action in the district court for Anoka county to recover $21,000 for injury received while employed by defendant as a switchman. The case was tried before Giddings, J., and a jury which returned a verdict for $2,050 in favor of plaintiff. From an order denying its motion for a new trial, defendant appealed. Affirmed.

Cobb, Wheelwright & Dille and *C. M. Bracelen,* for appellant.

Thomas D. Schall, T. D. Sheehan and *B. C. Thayer,* for respondent.

PHILIP E. BROWN, J.

On April 16, 1913, plaintiff, aged 29 years, a switchman in defendant's employment, fell from a defective car, on his back, across a steel rail. Defendant conceded liability, and the jury fixed the damages at $2,050. The sole claim is that this was excessive.

Plaintiff suffered the loss of two teeth and an ankle sprain from

[1] Reported in 148 N. W. 893.

which he had nearly recovered at the time of the trial, six months later. In addition it appeared that shortly after the accident he was seriously sick in his stomach and, symptoms of appendicitis thereafter developing, an operation disclosed that the organ was diseased prior to the accident, but the evidence was concededly sufficient to warrant a recovery for aggravation of such condition from the fall. The value of the physician's services for the operation was $200. At the time of the accident plaintiff was earning $105 a month, and he claimed an injury to his back which, according to the physicians testifying in his behalf, would prevent him from performing hard labor for from 8 to 12 months after the trial. The evidence warranted the jury in finding that plaintiff's back was weak and painful at the time of the trial, rendering it necessary for him to continue to wear an elastic bandage which had been procured for him at the suggestion of and by one of defendant's surgeons. Defendant grounds its claim of excessiveness almost entirely upon the testimony of its medical witnesses that plaintiff's sufferings, if any, in his back, were attributable to his having a natural condition known as double flat foot, that is flatness of both feet, easily remediable simply by use of a support for the arches of the feet, which would relieve the trouble and enable plaintiff to go to work at once. The testimony of these witnesses as to the condition of plaintiff's feet is not disputed and must be taken as true; but the jury were not required to accept as correct their conclusions as to the cause of his suffering, for one of them admitted that rigidity of the muscles of plaintiff's back, which the testimony tended to show still existed, could not be referred to the condition of the feet, and accounted therefor on the theory that it was feigned, which, of course, made a question for the jury. Moreover, it did not appear that plaintiff had suffered any pain, illness or inconvenience prior to the accident.

In actions for personal injuries there is necessarily much uncertainty respecting the nature and character of the injury complained of, which, together with the damages, must, as a rule, be left to the jury and trial court.

We find no occasion for interference with the verdict.

Order affirmed.

INTERNATIONAL REALTY & SECURITIES CORPORATION v. E. F. VANDERPOEL and Others.[1]

October 2, 1914.

Nos. 18,722—(225).

Election of remedies.

1. Bringing an action to rescind an executory contract for fraudulent misrepresentations as to the quality of the land, and thereafter voluntarily dismissing such action because the right to rescind had been lost by laches, is not such an election of remedies as will debar plaintiff from subsequently bringing an action to enforce specific performance of such contract.

Damages for fraud.

2. As damages for the fraud cannot be applied upon the purchase price unless the vendee so elects, they do not operate as payment thereon until he has made such election.

Land contract — statutory notice to rescind — reinstatement.

3. Where the vendor has given the statutory notice to terminate the contract for nonpayment of overdue instalments and the time limited by statute for making such payment has expired, the vendee cannot reinstate the contract by thereafter electing to apply his claim for damages in discharge of such instalments.

Measure of damages.

4. The amount of damages recoverable for fraudulent misrepresentation as to the quality of the property sold is the difference between the purchase price and the value of the property in its true condition.

Action in the district court for Dodge county against E. F. Vanderpoel, Eugene N. Best and Eva M. Best, his wife, to ascertain the amount of damages sustained by plaintiff on account of the fraudulent representations by defendant Vanderpoel in the sale of land, for an accounting between plaintiff and defendant Vanderpoel under the contracts mentioned, and for specific performance by defendants upon the performance by plaintiff of its part of the contract. The facts are stated in the opinion. Defendants' motion for judgment on the

[1] Reported in 148 N. W. 895.

pleadings in their favor (1) on the issue of the right of plaintiff to
relief by way of a decree for specific performance; (2) on the issue
of the right of plaintiff to relief by way of damages; (3) on the issue
of title and right of possession to the lands in question; (4) on all
the issues made by the pleadings, was granted, Hale, J. From the
judgment entered pursuant to the order for judgment, plaintiff appealed. Affirmed.

Roberts & Strong, for appellant.

M. H. Boutelle, E. N. Best and *A. M. Higgins,* for respondents.

TAYLOR, C.

On November 23, 1910, defendant Vanderpoel contracted to sell
280 acres of land to plaintiff for the sum of $60,800. The purchase
price was payable in instalments as follows: $6,000 at the execution
of the contract; $4,000 on or before March 1, 1911; $5,000 on or
before November 1, 1911; $5,800 on or before May 1, 1912; and
$40,000 on or before May 1, 1918. Deferred payments bore interest
at the rate of six per cent per annum payable November 1, 1911, and
annually thereafter. The contract also provided that time was of
the essence thereof; that the vendor could declare the contract null
and void in case of any default on the part of the vendee; that until
such default the vendee should have possession of the property; and
that in case of such default the vendee should surrender possession of
the property to the vendor on demand. After the execution of the
contract, defendant Vanderpoel conveyed his interest therein, together with the title to the land, to defendant Eugene N. Best as security for advances made to him by Best. Plaintiff paid the instalment of the purchase price due at the execution of the contract and
the instalment due March 1, 1911, and procured an extension of the
time for paying the two next instalments until December 1, 1912, but
never paid them.

On December 24, 1912, plaintiff brought an action to rescind the
contract and to recover back the payments already made, on the
ground that it was induced to enter into the contract by false and
fraudulent representations on the part of Vanderpoel as to the character and condition of the land. The defendants answered and

among other things denied specifically all the charges as to misrepresentation.   Thereafter, and in February, 1913, plaintiff sought to amend the complaint so as to change the action from one for rescission to one for specific performance.   The trial court would not permit the amendment and thereupon plaintiff voluntarily dismissed the action.

On January 27, 1913, the defendants served notice on plaintiff as provided by statute (now section 8081, G. S. 1913) that the contract would be cancelled and terminated 30 days from the service thereof, unless all overdue principal and interest were paid prior to the expiration of such 30 days.   The instalments of the principal and interest then past due and unpaid aggregated the sum of $14,455.28. Plaintiff neither made nor tendered payment, but, about three weeks after the expiration of the time limited by statute for the making of such payment, and shortly after the dismissal of the former action, began the present action to enforce specific performance of the contract.   Rescission and specific performance are inconsistent remedies and the election of one is an abandonment of the other.   Defendants, at the outset, contend that plaintiff by bringing the former action for rescission made an election of that remedy which is binding upon it and a bar to the present action.   Plaintiff contends that the bringing of such an action does not constitute a valid and binding election until a recovery is had therein.   As plaintiff voluntarily dismissed the former action before trial, for the reason that through laches it had lost its right to rescind, we think that the bringing of that action was not such an election as would bar plaintiff from bringing the present action.   Spurr v. Home Ins. Co. 40 Minn. 424, 42 N. W. 206, 207; In re Van Norman, 41 Minn. 494, 43 N. W. 334; Marshall v. Gilman, 52 Minn. 88, 53 N. W. 811.

Plaintiff rightly and necessarily concedes that it is not entitled to specific performance, unless the overdue instalments were paid or discharged within the time limited therefor by the statute.   But plaintiff makes the same charge of fraud alleged in the former action and contends, in effect, that the damages sustained by reason of the alleged misrepresentations paid and discharged the overdue instalments. We are unable to concur in this conclusion.

When plaintiff discovered the fraud it had the right, at its option, either to repudiate and annul the contract and recover back the payments already made, or to affirm the contract and seek redress for the fraud in damages. If plaintiff elected to affirm the contract, it had the right, if seasonably exercised, either to recover damages in an independent action for deceit, or to recoup such damages against the claim of the vendor for the unpaid portion of the purchase price. The choice of remedies rested with plaintiff. Damages for the fraud could not be applied upon the purchase price, unless plaintiff affirmed the contract instead of rescinding it, and also elected to apply them thereon instead of recovering them as an independent claim. It necessarily follows that such damages could not operate as a payment upon the purchase price until plaintiff, by some appropriate proceeding, caused them to be applied thereon. 34 Cyc. 758; 19 Enc. Pl. & Pr. 738.

Plaintiff does not contend, and it cannot be held, that the unsuccessful attempt to amend the complaint in the former action, the denial of which was acquiesced in by the plaintiff, operated as a valid and binding election to apply the damages for the fraud upon the delinquent payments, and they have never been so applied, unless the bringing and prosecution of the present action accomplished that result.

By force of the statute the contract terminated 30 days after service of the notice given by the vendor, unless the delinquent payments were made prior thereto. The statute is absolute and at the end of the prescribed time all rights of the parties under the contract ceased. Olson v. Northern Pacific Ry. Co. 126 Minn. 229, 148 N. W. 67. The proceeding is in effect a statutory foreclosure of the contract, and a tender of payment made after the expiration of the 30 days is of no avail. Sylvester v. Holasek, 83 Minn. 362, 86 N. W. 336. An attempt to apply a claim for damages as payment can be given no greater effect than can be given to a tender of actual payment. Plaintiff made no election to apply its claim for damages in discharge of the delinquent payments, until after the time for making payment had expired. It was then too late. The statutory foreclosure terminated the right to enforce specific performance and no act of plaintiff thereafter could reinstate it.

As the above conclusion is decisive of the case, a discussion of the other questions raised is unnecessary. But, as plaintiff alleged that the land, if it had been as represented, would have been worth $7.50 per acre more than the contract price, and sought to recover this anticipated profit as a part of its damages, it is proper to call attention to the rule, firmly established in this state, that the amount of damages recoverable for fraudulent misrepresentation as to the quality of the property sold is the difference between the purchase price and the value of the property in its true condition.

At the trial defendants moved for judgment on the pleadings. The admitted facts entitled them to such judgment and the court correctly granted the motion and rendered judgment in accordance therewith.

Judgment affirmed.

C. D. MASTIN v. A. W. MAY and Another.[1]

October 2, 1914.

Nos. 18,732—(227).

Forcible entry and unlawful detainer.
  1. Proceedings under the forcible entry and detainer statute, to recover the possession of land alleged to be unlawfully and forcibly detained, cannot be maintained against a person who peaceably and under claim of right entered into possession of the property, and does not forcibly detain the same. Davis v. Woodward, 19 Minn. 137 (174), followed and applied.

Same — ejectment.
  2. The unlawful detention, unaccompanied with force, where the original possession was taken peaceably and under claim of right, is not sufficient to authorize proceedings under section 7657, G. S. 1913. Ejectment is the remedy in such cases.

[1] Reported in 148 N. W. 983.

From a judgment in justice court in favor of plaintiff, defendants appealed to the district court for Dakota county. The appeal was heard before Hodgson, J., who made findings and ordered judgment that the action be dismissed. From the judgment entered pursuant to the order for judgment, plaintiff appealed. Affirmed.

S. R. Child and *Albert Schaller,* for appellant.

Charles R. Pye and *C. S. Lowell,* for respondents.

BROWN, C. J.

The short facts in this case are as follows: Plaintiff as the owner of certain real property entered into negotiations to sell the same to defendants. Pending the negotiations defendants went into possession of the premises, whether with the knowledge and consent of plaintiff does not appear but, as found by the trial court, peaceably and under claim of right under the oral arrangements of the parties as to the sale. They so entered into possession on October 16, 1912, and have since retained the same. The negotiations for the sale were not completed and were abandoned, and on November 1, 1912, some two weeks after defendants entered into possession of the property, plaintiff demanded that they vacate the same, which defendants refused to do, claiming to have certain rights under the attempted sale, by way of compensation for improvements made upon the premises during the time of their possession. Thereafter, in December, 1912, plaintiff brought this proceeding under the forcible entry and detainer statute to regain possession. There was a judgment for plaintiff before the justice and defendants appealed to the district court. The cause was tried in that court without a jury and the court made findings of fact, substantially as above stated, and, further, "that the entry upon said lands by the defendants was made in a peaceable manner; that the detention of said premises after the first day of November, 1912, by the defendants was unlawful but not forcible or held with strong hands." As conclusion of law the court found that plaintiff was not entitled to maintain the proceeding and that it should be dismissed. Judgment of dismissal was subsequently entered, and plaintiff appealed.

The only question presented is whether the facts stated present a case for proceedings under the forcible entry and detainer statute, or whether plaintiff's remedy was in ejectment.

Our statutes, like those of many of the other states, limit the right to resort to forcible entry proceedings to recover the possession of land, other than the instances specially provided for by section 7658, G. S. 1913, (1) to cases where there has been an unlawful or forcible entry thereon, and (2) where there has been a peaceable entry, and a subsequent unlawful and forcible detention of the premises. If the possession be taken unlawfully or forcibly, the proceeding will lie without regard to the question whether the subsequent possession is maintained by force or violence. If the entry into possession be under claim of right or peaceably, then the proceeding cannot be maintained, unless the possession thus taken be "unlawfully and forcibly" detained. The *unlawful* detention is not, standing alone, sufficient, where the proceeding is founded upon section 7657, G. S. 1913. Davis v. Woodward, 19 Minn. 137 (174). The statute, with some modifications, is but declaratory of the common law upon the subject, and was designed to provide a speedy remedy to recover the possession of land unlawfully taken or forcibly and unlawfully detained from the person entitled thereto. It was not intended as a substitute for ejectment (O'Neill v. Jones, 72 Minn. 446, 75 N. W. 701), and is only applicable to the cases specially provided for by the statute. In the case at bar the record does not present facts showing either an unlawful or forcible entry of the land in question, the findings negative either theory, and plaintiff cannot recover upon that ground. The case presented is one showing a peaceable entry, pending negotiations for the purchase of the land, and a wrongful or unlawful withholding possession after abandonment of the negotiations, unaccompanied by force or violence. There is no showing of a forcible detention of the land, and therefore plaintiff cannot prevail on that theory of the statute. This was expressly so held in the case of Davis v. Woodward, 19 Minn. 137 (174), supra. The ruling there made is in harmony with the authorities generally. Fults v. Munro, 202 N. Y. 34, 95 N. E. 23, 37 L.R.A.(N.S.) 600, Ann. Cas. 1912D, 871, and note 875; 19 Cyc. 1135. The proceeding cannot be resorted to for the purpose of removing a mere trespasser, who entered into possession peaceably under claim of right and asserts no right of possession by force or violence. Castro v. Tewkbury, 69 Cal. 562, 11 Pac. 339; Wood v. Phillips, 43 N. Y. 152; Smith v. Reeder, 21 Ore. 541, 28 Pac. 890, 15 L.R.A. 172; Foster v. Kelsey, 36 Vt. 199, 84 Am. Dec. 676. The findings of the court to the effect that the entry of defendants was peaceable and under claim of right and not retained by force or a strong hand, dispose of the case and render the forcible entry statute inapplicable. The remedy of plaintiffs was in ejectment.

Judgment affirmed.

JOHN F. FITZPATRICK v. CORA B. FITZPATRICK.[1]

October 2, 1914.

Nos. 18,755—(241).

Divorce — findings sustained by evidence.

1. In an action for divorce on the ground of cruel and inhuman treatment, it is *held* that the evidence supports the findings of the trial court and, further, that the divorce was not granted on the consent of the parties.

Alimony — judgment modified.

2. An award of alimony *held* not out of proportion to what is reasonable and fair, in view of the facts presented, but that the judgment should be modified to secure the relief intended to be granted, namely, life support of the wife.

Action for divorce in the district court for Ramsey county. The case was tried before Stanton, J., who made findings and ordered judgment in favor of plaintiff for an absolute divorce and granted alimony to defendant as stated at the end of the opinion. From the judgment entered pursuant to the order for judgment and from the order denying her motion for a new trial, defendant appealed. Order denying new trial affirmed. Judgment affirmed as modified.

[1] Reported in 148 N. W. 1074.

George B. Edgerton, for appellant.
Butler & Mitchell and *R. G. O'Malley,* for respondent.

BROWN, C. J.

Action for divorce in which plaintiff had judgment and defendant appealed. The action was predicated, by the allegations of the complaint, upon the alleged cruel and inhuman treatment of plaintiff by defendant. Defendant by answer denied the allegations of the complaint, and interposed a cross-complaint, and alleged therein cruel treatment of her by plaintiff, and she prayed for a limited divorce with alimony. At the trial below the court dismissed defendant's cross-complaint for lack of evidence to support the same, found the allegations of plaintiff's complaint substantially true, including the allegations of cruel and inhuman treatment, and ordered judgment of absolute divorce, making no order, however, respecting the care and custody of the children. The court also gave judgment in favor of defendant in the sum of $50,000, as personal alimony and suit money, which was declared a specific lien upon certain described real property owned by plaintiff. Defendant subsequently moved for a new trial, on the ground, among others, that the finding of cruel and inhuman treatment by defendant toward plaintiff was not sustained by the evidence, and that the award of alimony was inadequate. The motion was denied, and there was an appeal from that order as well as from the judgment.

The 28 assignments of error, so far as argued in the briefs, present but two questions, namely: (1) Whether the findings of cruel and inhuman treatment on the part of defendant toward plaintiff are sustained by the evidence, and (2) whether, in view of the value of the property owned by plaintiff and the situation and circumstances of the parties as disclosed by the record, the award of alimony to defendant is inadequate?

1. The first question does not require extended discussion. After a full and careful examination of the record we have reached the conclusion, though not without some hesitation, that the findings of the trial court should be sustained. It would serve no useful purpose to spread upon the record a detailed statement of the evidence, tend-

127 M.—7.

ing as it does to disclose grievous misconduct on the part of both husband and wife, and we refrain. The evidence brings the case within the rule of Williams v. Williams, 101 Minn. 400, 112 N. W. 528, and Bechtel v. Bechtel, 101 Minn. 511, 112 N. W. 883, 12 L.R.A.(N.S.) 1100. The contention of defendant that the findings were prompted and the divorce granted upon the consent of the defendant, given by her counsel in open court, is not sustained. While her counsel did state to the court at the conclusion of the trial, and after the court had announced that the cross-complaint would be dismissed upon the merits, that defendant would consent to an absolute divorce in favor of plaintiff, the trial court promptly declined to act thereon, and announced that a divorce could not be granted upon that ground. From this we conclude that the learned trial judge was guided in reaching a conclusion in the action by the evidence and the evidence alone. The evidence in corroboration of plaintiff was sufficient. Clark v. Clark, 86 Minn. 249, 90 N. W. 390.

2. The parties were married in March, 1892, and thereafter continued to live together as husband and wife until a short time prior to the commencement of the action. Four children were born to them, three sons and one daughter, the latter, the last to come to the home, being of the age of about 14 years; the ages of the boys range from 15 to 21 years. At the time of the trial of the action plaintiff was 56 and defendant 50 years of age. Plaintiff is an attorney and counsellor at law, and as such he has for many years occupied a prominent and conspicuous place in the ranks of the profession of the state, enjoying a lucrative law practice. By method of economy and prudent investments he has accumulated, since the marriage with defendant, a considerable property, the value of which, according to the testimony of some of the witnesses exceeds the sum of $350,000; the court below, however, acting conservatively, found the value thereof to be the sum of $280,000. His gross annual income from his law practice and investments exceeds $11,000. The court awarded to defendant, under authority of the statutes in such case made and provided, first, a life estate in the family homestead, valued at $4,500, together with the household furniture and effects;

and, second, the sum of $50,000 as alimony, payable, two payments of $1,000 each within the time stated in the findings, and the balance, or $48,000, in quarterly payments of $750 each, with interest on the deferred payments after they became due and payable. It was provided and ordered that the amount so awarded should be treated as including all costs and expenses of the action, and the judgment was declared a lien upon certain specified real property, subject to discharge upon substituting in its place under approval of the court suitable security for the payment of the instalments as they became due.

We are unable to concur in the contention that the trial court should have awarded to defendant a full one-third of plaintiff's property. The statutes provide (section 7128, G. S. 1913) that such award shall be made in cases of this kind as the situation of the parties, the circumstances of the case, and the ability and financial worth of the husband, the court shall deem fair and just, "not exceeding in value the one-third thereof." While the court might in a particular case grant to the wife the full one-third of the husband's property, there are reasons why that conclusion should not be reached in the case at bar. Defendant is given a life estate in the family homestead, fully furnished, and an annual allowance of $3,000. The four children of the marriage must be supported by plaintiff, and the allowance made is for the sole benefit of defendant, no part of which is she under any legal obligation to expend for their care. If the custody and education of any of the children had been by the court committed to her care, she probably might insist that the allowance was inadequate. And though the younger children, and probably all of them, will remain with the mother, at the family home, plaintiff will without doubt perform all his obligations ·in respect to their comfort and support. So that with the homestead and an annual income of $3,000, if continued during her life, we think defendant has no serious cause for complaint. The amount will provide fully for all her comforts. Such a result was intended by the trial court, as disclosed by its memorandum attached to the findings and order for judgment; wherein it was said: "It would * * * be unjust and unreasonable, in view of the character and situation of the parties, and all of the circumstances of the case   *   *   *   to fix her permanent alimony in any sum less than an amount certain to be adequate to provide for her liberally during her lifetime."

But it may seriously be doubted whether the form of the order and judgment will accomplish that end, and secure to defendant a life time support. The award of $50,000 was granted as "personal alimony," is subject to revision by the court, and is not a fixed sum to be paid as a distributive share of plaintiff's property. Haskell v. Haskell, 116 Minn. 10, 132 N. W. 1129; Blake v. Blake, 68 Wis. 303, 32 N. W. 48. The general rule, supported by the weight of authority, in respect to an award of alimony in a definite sum of money, payable in instalments at future dates, in the absence of some statute or provision in the decree to the contrary, is that the allowance terminates at the death of either party. 1 Ruling Case Law, 933; Wilson v. Hinman, 182 N. Y. 408, 75 N. E. 236, and notes to the report of that case in 108 Am. St. 820, and 2 L.R.A. (N.S.) 232. We have no statute in this state covering this subject, and if the rule stated applies here, a question we do not stop to determine, then the period during which the alimony must be paid under this decree depends for its continuance upon the life of plaintiff and not upon the life of defendant; the reverse of what was intended by the court below. We fully concur with the trial judge, and for reasons stated by him, that defendant is entitled, under the facts of this case, to liberal support from plaintiff during the remainder of her life, and to effect this end, conclude that the judgment appealed from should be so modified that the matter will be put beyond future controversy. To this end the judgment will be so modified as to direct the payment by plaintiff to defendant during the remainder of her life the sum of $3,000 annually, payable in quarterly instalments of $750 each, commencing on the first day of January, 1915, with interest on each instalment after maturity at the rate of six per cent per annum; that the judgment be declared a lien upon the real property described therein, as now provided subject to discharge as therein stated, and that the judgment and the right of defendant to have and receive the payments shall continue after the death of plaintiff, should defendant survive him, and be a charge upon and against his estate. The clause of the judgment limiting the amount to $50,000, should be omitted. The payments are limited to the life of defendant and may amount to more or less than that sum, depending on the length of time that she may live. We conclude further, and this will cover all prior allowances of suit money, including the costs of the action and attorney's fees, that the judgment be further modified by eliminating therefrom the two payments of $1,000 each, and substituting in the place thereof a direction and order that plaintiff pay to defendant, in addition to the quarterly payments commencing January 1, 1915, within 30 days from the date of the modified decree, the sum of $3,000, without deduction on account of payments heretofore made under the order of the court below, the same to be in full of all costs and disbursements of the action and the items heretofore ordered paid by this court. With these modifications the judgment appealed from will be affirmed, and the cause remanded with direction to the court below to proceed accordingly.

The order denying a new trial is affirmed.

BUNN, J., took no part.

On October 8, 1914, the following opinion was filed:

PER CURIAM.

It appearing that subsequent to the filing of the opinion herein defendant has been paid the sum of $200, on account of alimony awarded by the court below, and it further appearing that in fairness this amount should be deducted from the $3,000 ordered paid by the decision of this court, it is ordered that the opinion be modified by reducing the payment ordered made within thirty days to the sum of $2,800.

STATE ex rel. FRANK MURPHY v. HENRY WOLFER.[1]

October 2, 1914.

Nos. 19,047—(297).

Commutation of life sentence — allowance for good conduct.

  1. A prisoner sentenced to the state prison for life, whose sentence is commuted to one for a term of years, is entitled to diminution of that sentence by reason of good conduct, commencing on the day of his arrival in prison, and not from the time of commutation of his sentence.

Habeas corpus.

  2. It is the practice of this court to refuse to issue writs of *habeas corpus* in ordinary cases and unless the circumstances are exceptional. In view of the importance of the case and the importance of an early final determination of it, this original proceeding is entertained.

Upon the relation of Frank Murphy this court granted a writ of *habeas corpus* directed to Henry Wolfer, as warden of the state prison at Stillwater, requiring him to show cause why relator was detained in custody. Relator discharged.

Harold J. Richardson, for relator.

Lyndon A. Smith, Attorney General, for respondent.

HALLAM, J.

On October 23, 1893, the relator, Frank Murphy, was sentenced to the state prison for life. On October 30, 1893, he commenced serving his term, and he has ever since been imprisoned. On July 24, 1914, the state board of pardons commuted the sentence to imprisonment for the term of 30 years. During the time of relator's imprisonment his conduct has been such that, if his sentence had been originally for the term of 30 years, he would now be entitled to his liberty, under the law relating to the diminution of sentences by rea-

[1] Reported in 148 N. W. 896.

Note.—Construction and effect of statutes providing for reduction of term of sentence for good behavior, see note in 34 L.R.A. 510.

son of good conduct in prison. The only question in the case is whether the relator is entitled to credit by reason of good conduct prior to the commutation of his sentence.

The statute provides:

"Every convict sentenced for a definite term other than life * * * may diminish such term as follows:

"First—For each month, commencing on the day of his arrival, during which he has not violated any prison rule or discipline, and has labored with diligence and fidelity, five days.

"Second—After one year of such conduct, seven days for each month.

"Third—After two years of such conduct, nine days for each month.

"Fourth—After three years, ten days for each month for the entire time thereafter." G. S. 1913, § 9309.

There is very little in the decided cases that throws much light upon the construction of this statute. A few principles applicable to the case are, however, well settled. It is well settled that a commutation of a sentence is a substitution of a less for a greater punishment. After commutation the commuted sentence is the only one in existence, and the only one to be considered. After commutation, the sentence has the same legal effect, and the status of the prisoner is the same, as though the sentence had originally been for the commuted term. Johnson v. State (Ala.) 63 So. 163; In re Hall, 34 Neb. 206, 209, 51 N. W. 750; 5 Opinions of Atty. Gen. (U. S.) 370; Lee v. Murphy, 22 Gratt. (Va.) 789, 799; In the Matter of Victor, 31 Oh. St. 206, 208. It should logically follow that when a prisoner's sentence is reduced from a life sentence to "a definite term other than life" he is brought within the language of the statute allowing a diminution of such a definite term for good time. This view is sustained by the decision in In re Hall, 34 Neb. 206, 51 N. W. 750, and it seems to us correct in principle.

The contention of the state is, not that the prisoner is not entitled to credit for "good time" at all, but that the "good time" credited to him is to be computed from the time of the commutation of his sentence. We find no warrant in the language of the statute for this construction. The statute is explicit as to the time when the computation of credit for good conduct commences. When credit for "good time" is allowed to a prisoner at all, it commences, by the express terms of the statute, "on the day of his arrival" in prison. In Re McMahon, 125 N. C. 38, 34 S. E. 193, a case which seems to sustain the contention of the state, the statute construed differs from ours in this particular.

The view of the state further appears to be that the theory of the allowance of good time is that it is something which, if ever credited at all, must be credited from month to month as it is earned, and that, inasmuch as it could not be credited in this manner as long as the prisoner was serving a life sentence, it is not available in diminution of the commuted sentence. This is not the theory of the statute. Good time is not really credited to the prisoner at all until enough has been earned to give him his liberty. Up to that time all benefit to the prisoner on account of good time is liable to forfeiture by reason of a provision that the board of control "in view of the aggravated nature and frequency of offenses, may take away any or all of the good time previously gained." G. S. 1913, § 9309. Nor is it true that good time cannot under any circumstances be credited from time to time to a person serving a life sentence. Another statute provides that "no convict serving a life sentence shall be paroled until he has served thirty-five years, less the diminution which would have been allowed for good conduct had his sentence been for thirty-five years." G. S. 1913, § 9319.

We do not, however, regard these considerations of primary importance. We base our decision on the proposition that the fair construction of section 9309 is that every prisoner serving a sentence for a fixed term of years, whether it be an original or a commuted sentence, is entitled to a diminution of that sentence by reason of good conduct, "commencing on the day of his arrival" in prison. It follows that the relator has completed his sentence and is entitled to be discharged from prison.

In this case the original writ of *habeas corpus* was issued out of this court, running to the respondent in Washington county. This court, as well as the district court, may, subject to certain restrictions, issue an original writ of *habeas corpus*. G. S. 1913, § 8284. We are not unmindful of the decision In re Doll, 47 Minn. 518, 50 N. W. 607, to the effect that the statute contemplates that the application for the writ should be addressed to a court or judge in the county where the prisoner is restrained, if there be one present and willing to act, and it has been the practice of this court to refuse to issue writs of *habeas corpus* in ordinary cases and unless the circumstances are exceptional. But in this case relator and respondent joined in consent to the commencement and determination of this proceeding in this court, and, in view of the importance of this case and the importance of an early final determination of the question presented, since several other similar cases await the result of this one, this original proceeding is entertained.

Relator discharged.

BROWN, C. J., took no part.

A. H. BJORGO and Another v. FIRST NATIONAL BANK OF EMMONS and Another.[1]

October 9, 1914.

Nos. 18,625—(162).

Adverse rulings not reviewable on appeal, when.

1. A party whose motion for new trial has been granted is not aggrieved by the order so that the rulings adverse to him on the trial may be reviewed on his cross-appeal.

Notice of appeal.

2. The notice of plaintiffs' appeal from the order granting their motion for a new trial does not in terms embrace an appeal from the court's orders on the demurrers interposed, even if such orders were appealable.

Bank draft — payee put on inquiry.

3. The fact that a bank draft issued by a small village bank was made

[1] Reported in 149 N. W. 3.

payable to the order of the defendant bank, is *held* sufficient to put the
defendant bank on inquiry as to the ownership of the proceeds before paying the same to the person presenting the draft.

Action in the district court for Freeborn county to recover $600.
The case was tried before Kingsley, J., who sustained the demurrer
of defendant Rasmussen to the complaint and overruled the demurrer
of plaintiffs to the separate answer of defendant bank, and dismissed
the case on the merits when the plaintiffs rested.   From the order
granting plaintiffs' motion for a new trial on the sole ground that
it was a question for the jury whether the draft mentioned in the
opinion was so drawn that on presentation to the payee it was sufficient to put the payee upon notice as to the character of the transaction between plaintiffs and Mr. Haugan, which notice, upon inquiry,
would have led to knowledge that Mr. Haugan was not entitled to the
proceeds of the draft, defendants appealed.   From the same order
refusing to grant a new trial upon any other grounds set out in plaintiffs' motion, plaintiffs appealed.   Affirmed on both appeals.

T. A. Kingland and *Mayland & Peterson,* for plaintiffs.
Henry A. Morgan and *John F. D. Meighen,* for defendants.

HOLT, J.
The plaintiffs allege, in substance, that on or about February 21,
1911, one B. B. Haugan was soliciting subscriptions for stock in a
corporation then organized by him and two other persons; that
Haugan represented to plaintiffs that the corporation had an option
on certain lands in Texas; that until the corporation should procure
title to these lands the money paid for subscriptions to stock should
be deposited in the defendant bank; that the bank and its cashier,
the defendant Rasmussen, on February 25, 1911, knew of these
representations and that subscriptions were thus obtained and money
paid thereon conditionally; that on last named date plaintiffs
subscribed for 20 shares of stock in the corporation, and about said
date deposited in the defendant bank $600 by draft drawn to the
order of and delivered to the bank, as a deposit to pay for said shares
of stock when the corporation should obtain title to the Texas lands

which was to be acquired on June 1, 1911; that said Haugan and one of the other two incorporators and officers of the corporation absconded about March 1, 1911; that the title to said land has never been acquired by the corporation and the option has expired, and that plaintiffs' demand for payment of the $600 has been refused. The defendant Rasmussen demurred, and the demurrer was, by a verbal order, sustained at the time the case was reached for trial, but before the introduction of any testimony. In its answer the bank admits the demand for the money, and alleges that B. B. Haugan presented at its banking house in the usual course of business a six hundred dollar draft, being the draft referred to in the complaint, drawn upon the Commercial National Bank of Chicago by the Kensett Bank of Iowa, dated February 25, 1911, and payable to the order of the defendant bank, and that, at the request of Haugan, in good faith without knowledge or notice that plaintiffs, or either of them, claimed any interest in the draft or the proceeds, the defendant bank paid the full sum of $600 to Haugan. Other allegations of the complaint were denied. Plaintiffs interposed a demurrer to the answer, which was overruled by a verbal order at the same time that the demurrer of the defendant Rasmussen was submitted. The evidence of the alleged agreement between plaintiffs and Haugan as to how the proceeds of the draft should be disposed of having been excluded, in the absence of any proof that the bank had any knowledge thereof, and the form of the draft not being deemed sufficient notice to charge the bank with negligence in following Haugan's directions in paying the money, the court dismissed the case on the merits. Thereafter plaintiffs moved for a new trial alleging various errors, among others the rulings of the demurrers. The court granted a new trial upon the sole ground that it was for the jury to say whether the fact that the draft was made payable to the defendant bank was sufficient to put the bank "upon notice as to the character of the transaction between the plaintiffs and Mr. Haugan * * * which notice upon inquiry would have led to knowledge that Mr. Haugan was not entitled to the proceeds of said draft." Both parties appeal.

There is nothing to plaintiffs' appeal. It is clear that having obtained what they asked, a new trial, they are not aggrieved. If the record shows errors which necessitate a new trial, the order will stand, although the error assigned as the sole ground by the court for its action should be no error at all. The order overruling plaintiffs' demurrer to the bank's answer is not appealable, even if it could be said to be embraced within the scope of the notice of appeal. But we do not think their notice is so framed that the rulings on either demurrer are properly before us. When the defendant Rasmussen's demurrer was sustained, he dropped out as a party, so that the subsequent trial, dismissal and order granting a new trial, did not affect him. Therefore the only question for review relates to the correctness of the order granting a new trial, challenged by the appeal of the bank.

The contention of plaintiffs that the order is, as to the bank, not appealable, is not sound, for the order expressly states that it was granted exclusively upon an error occurring at the trial and is thus within the terms of the statute. Section 8001, subd. 4, G. S. 1913.

We come then to the question whether the dismissal on the merits was error. The basis of plaintiffs' cause of action is perhaps somewhat obscure. It is alleged that the money paid for stock subscriptions should be deposited in the defendant bank, but there is no allegation that it was the money of the several subscribers. The reasonable inference is rather that it belonged to the corporation, but was to remain in the bank until the title of certain land was acquired by it. Nor is it alleged that plaintiffs' subscription was conditional. The gist of the allegations is that plaintiffs made a special deposit with the bank of $600, which was to pay for the shares of stock purchased by them when the corporation acquired the land mentioned. This, however, is not deemed material, under the view taken by the majority of the court, for the defendant bank admits collecting the draft and cashing it, or paying the proceeds to Haugan who presented the same. The question is, was there sufficient evidence in the fact that the draft was payable to the order of the defendant bank to put the bank on inquiry as to the ownership or disposition of the proceeds, so that it justified a submission of the bank's liability to the jury when plaintiffs rested? Nothing appeared on the face of the draft disclosing plaintiffs' interest. And, in that, the case at bar differs from Bristol Knife Co. v. First Nat. Bank, 41 Conn. 421, 19 Am. Rep. 517, and Sims v. U. S. Trust Co. 103 N. Y. 472, 9 N. E. 605, relied on by plaintiffs, where checks made payable to the bank (held liable) indicated who was the owner of the funds. We, however, think the fact that the draft being payable to the bank, instead of to Haugan, who presented it and claimed ownership, was so out of the ordinary mode of doing business, if Haugan was entitled to the proceeds, that it placed a duty upon the bank to take some precautions before paying out the money. It is therefore considered that the court erred when dismissing the case on the merits and properly granted a new trial.

The writer would concur in this disposition of the appeal were it not for these facts appearing: Plaintiffs pleaded a special deposit, they intrusted Haugan to make it for them without disclosing, on the face of the draft or otherwise, their identity or ownership of the funds; the cashier of this bank knew Haugan, knew that he was taking subscriptions for shares of stock and receiving payment, having himself bought and paid Haugan for stock a few days before; there was not the slightest proof, or offer of proof, that, had the defendant bank communicated with the drawer bank, any information could have been obtained as to plaintiffs' ownership, or alleged agreement with Haugan; and furthermore, the plaintiff Bjorgo testified that Haugan bought the draft from the bank, paying therefor to the extent of $300 with the personal check of Bjorgo executed and delivered to Haugan in payment of his part of the stock subscription. It seems to me, taking the whole evidence as it stood when the court dismissed the case, it did not justify a recovery. Plaintiffs had chosen Haugan to do their business with the bank without disclosing themselves; the bank was in a measure justified in acting on his directions; it undoubtedly paid out the money in good faith, believing Haugan owned it or had authority to obtain the same, and, I think, the rule "that, where one of two innocent persons must suffer from the act of a third person, he shall sustain the loss who had enabled the third party to do the injury" should protect the bank here, the same as in the very similar case of Timpson v. Allen, 149 N. Y. 513, 44 N. E. 171, where the rule was stated as above and applied.

On both appeals the order of the court is affirmed.

ADAM SIKORSKI v. GREAT NORTHERN RAILWAY COMPANY and Another.[1]

October 9, 1914.

Nos. 18,716—(228).

Contributory negligence.

In this action to recover for injuries received by plaintiff while attempting to cross between cars of a train standing on a crossing, it is *held* that it conclusively appears from the evidence that plaintiff was guilty of contributory negligence.

Action in the district court for St. Louis county to recover $8,300 for personal injury. The answer, among other matters, alleged that whatever injuries were sustained by plaintiff were by reason of his negligent and foolhardy conduct in attempting to pass between the cars of the train, with the engine attached, which was then being operated by defendant railway company. The case was tried before Dancer, J., who denied defendant's motion to direct a verdict in its favor, and a jury which returned a verdict for $3,368. From an order granting defendant's motion for judgment in its favor notwithstanding the verdict, plaintiff appealed. Affirmed.

Andrew Nelson and *George B. Sjoselius,* for appellant.

Baldwin, Baldwin & Holmes, for respondent.

BUNN, J.

This action was to recover for personal injuries.

There was a verdict for plaintiff, but, upon defendant's motion in the alternative for judgment or a new trial, the trial court ordered

[1] Reported in 149 N. W. 5.

Note.—Contributory negligence in attempting to cross a train standing on a crossing, see notes in 13 L.R.A.(N.S.) 1066; 34 L.R.A.(N.S.) 466.

judgment for defendant notwithstanding the verdict. Plaintiff appealed from this order.

The accident in which plaintiff received his injuries occurred in the city of Superior, Wisconsin, at the intersection of West Sixth street and defendant's tracks, which cross the street at substantially right angles. The street is a much used public thoroughfare, and hundreds use the crossing daily. Plaintiff lived south of the tracks and a block from the crossing. On the evening of November 12, 1912, he left his home, intending to cross the tracks at Sixth street and purchase some tobacco at a store on the other side. When he reached Sixth street plaintiff saw that a string of cars blocked the crossing. When he reached a point 10 feet from the tracks he "looked to the right and to the left" and saw "nothing else but cars." The cars were on the southerly or east bound main track. As a matter of fact it was a live train; there was an engine attached, but it was around a curve and the view of it was obstructed by the cars. There were tail lights on the caboose. It was dark and plaintiff could see but half a block in either direction. He testified that he did not see the engine, or the tail lights on the caboose. He waited, according to his testimony, for 10 minutes, and then started to go between the cars by seizing the grab iron and stepping on the coupling. The cars started suddenly and plaintiff was thrown to the ground and dragged some distance, receiving the injuries complained of.

The ground upon which the trial court held that plaintiff could not recover was his contributory negligence. As we have concluded that the order appealed from must be sustained upon this ground, it is unnecessary to discuss or decide whether there was any evidence of negligence on the part of defendant that was the proximate cause of the accident. The charges in this respect were (1) blocking the crossing for an unreasonable length of time, (2) starting the train without warning by bell or whistle.

That plaintiff was guilty of negligence that contributed to cause his injuries conclusively appears from the evidence. His effort to show his justification for believing that the string of cars blocking the crossing was not a live train with an engine attached was a failure.

The cars were on the main east bound track, where strings of cars were not left standing without engines. Traffic was heavy and trains frequent. He must have known that he could not see the engine from where he looked. The case is therefore controlled by Wherry v. Duluth, M. & N. Ry. Co. 64 Minn. 415, 67 N. W. 223. We are unable to accede to the proposition that plaintiff was justified in concluding, or in fact concluded, that no engine was attached. The undisputed facts show plaintiff's act simply as the conduct of one weary of waiting and in a hurry for his tobacco. He probably thought he could safely enough take the risk, but he took his chances.

It is sought to differentiate this case from the Wherry case, in the evidence here tending to show a custom to ring a bell or sound a whistle before starting a train that blocks a crossing. But the evidence negatives the theory that plaintiff relied at all on the absence of signals. His claim was that he saw no engine, no lights on the caboose, no trainmen about, and thought it was an abandoned string of cars. He in fact waited for 10 minutes before venturing to attempt to cross between the cars. Conceding, without deciding, that the evidence of a custom to signal was sufficient to make a *prima facie* case of negligence on defendant's part, there is no evidence that plaintiff was relying on any such custom. On the whole, we are safe in saying that no fact or circumstance was shown that tends to relieve plaintiff from the charge of negligence. The case of Amann v. Minneapolis & St. L. R. Co. 126 Minn. 279, 148 N. W. 101, is so clearly distinguishable from the present case that we need not point out the difference. We have not overlooked the decisions from other courts cited in support of both sides. The Wherry case is the law of this state, and we see no occasion to overrule it. See also Helback v. Northern Pacific Ry. Co. 125 Minn. 155, 145 N. W. 799.

We do not decide whether the order in this case is appealable.

Order affirmed.

T. P. ROACH v. OLE HALVORSON.[1]

October 9, 1914.

Nos. 18,729—(235).

Collateral security — title of holder.

1. The transfer of negotiable paper for value and in the usual course of business, as collateral security, vests in the holder a valid title, similar in all respects to that held by an unconditional indorsee.

Evidence — admissions by former owner of note.

2. The general rule that admissions of a former owner of property in disparagement of his title, made after he has parted with the title and possession, cannot be received in evidence against his successor in interest, applies to commercial paper.

Hearsay.

3. Under the rule admissions made by the payee of a negotiable promissory note after he has transferred the same to a third person, tending to show that the note was by him obtained in fraud, are hearsay and inadmissible against the indorsee in an action against the maker.

Action in the district court for Rock county to recover $3,599.36. The case was tried before Nelson, J., who denied plaintiff's motion for a directed verdict in his favor, and a jury which returned a verdict in favor of defendant. From an order denying his motion for a new trial, plaintiff appealed. Reversed and new trial granted.

A. J. Daley, for appellant.

C. H. Christopherson, for respondent.

BROWN, C. J.

This action was brought to recover upon a promissory note given by defendant to the American & Canadian Land Co. a copartnership doing business in the state of Iowa, and by the payee transferred to

[1] Reported in 148 N. W. 1080.

Note.—Holder of bill or note as collateral security as a bona fide holder, see note in 31 L.R.A.(N.S.) 288.

127 M.—8.

plaintiff as collateral security.   Defendant interposed in defense that the note was procured from him by the Land Co. by fraud and fraudulent representations and was wholly without consideration. Plaintiff in reply put in issue the allegations of fraud and fraudulent representations, and affirmatively alleged that the note was duly indorsed and delivered to plaintiff in the usual course of business, before maturity, and as collateral security for a loan of money then made to the Land Co., and that plaintiff had no notice or knowledge of the acts of fraud alleged in the answer.   Defendant had a verdict and plaintiff appealed from an order denying a new trial.

The assignments of error in this court challenge certain rulings of the trial court in the admission and exclusion of evidence, the instructions of the court to the jury, and the sufficiency of the evidence to support the verdict.

1. The law controlling the rights of the parties is well settled in this state.   The holder of a negotiable promissory note, delivered to him by the payee as collateral security, in the usual course of business for value and before maturity, stands in the same position as an unconditional indorsee, and is presumed to be a *bona fide* holder.   First Nat. Bank of Rochester v. Bentley, 27 Minn. 87, 6 N. W. 422; 2 Notes on Minn. Reports, 94; First Nat. Bank of Morrison v. Busch, 102 Minn. 365, 113 N. W. 898.   The defense of fraud in the procurement of the note is available to the maker, and, when he pleads and proves the same on the trial, the presumption of *bona fides* in the holder in effect disappears, and the burden is cast upon him to establish his good faith in fact.   If he succeeds in this, he is entitled to recover notwithstanding the fraud, precisely as an unconditional indorsee may recover under a like state of facts, at least to the extent of the secured indebtedness.   In other words, when the good faith is in fact shown the defense of fraud fails.   This is settled law in this state (Cummings v. Thompson, 18 Minn. 228 (246); 1 Notes on Minn. Reports, 746), and the trial below proceeded in harmony therewith.   Two issues were accordingly litigated, namely: (1) Whether the note in suit was procured by fraud and fraudulent representations, and without consideration, and (2) whether plaintiff was in fact a *bona fide* holder of the same, without notice of the fraud.

The verdict for defendant necessarily answered both questions in favor of defendant.

2. The assignments of error having reference to the admission of evidence may all be considered together, for with one exception they present substantially the same question. The note in suit was given to the Land Co. in part payment for certain land the company then agreed to sell and convey to defendant, which defendant claims the company represented that it owned, whereas, in fact, that the company had no title and could not convey the same, and never did so convey to him. Substantially all the evidence of the admission of which plaintiff complains, was clearly admissible. It was not necessary to connect plaintiff with the fraud, and the statements and representations made by the agents of the Land Co. at the time of and leading up to the final consummation of the transaction were properly received, insofar as they tended to show the alleged fraud. And, without referring to the evidence and the various assignments in detail, we affirm that no error was committed in this feature of the case, save as now to be mentioned.

3. The note was signed and delivered on February 13, 1911, for the sum of $3,200, and was due and payable on or before two years from that date. It was indorsed and transferred to plaintiff by the payee on March 14, 1912, and plaintiff at all times since has retained the same. At the time of the transfer and delivery of the note to plaintiff he loaned to the payee the sum of $3,000, and the transfer was so made as collateral security for its repayment. At the trial plaintiff expressly disclaimed the right to recover anything in excess of the amount of that loan. Defendant called a witness in his behalf, who was permitted to testify to a conversation had by him with one of the payees of the note, a member of the copartnership, in April, 1912, long after the note had been transferred to plaintiff, in which the payee admitted facts tending to show that the note was obtained by fraud, that the Land Co. did not own the land for which the same was given and were unable to convey it to defendant. This evidence was objected to as incompetent and hearsay, and the order overruling the objection is assigned as error. In admitting this evidence the court erred.

It was incumbent upon defendant to establish the allegations of fraud in the procurement of the note by legal and competent evidence, and plaintiff had the right to insist that he do so, for if there was no fraud he was entitled to recover whether a *bona fide* holder within the law merchant or not. The evidence of the witness was at most nothing more than bringing into the case the unsworn admissions of one of the payees of the note, made long after he had parted with the title, and for the purpose of establishing an important element in the alleged fraud. Plaintiff had the right, under the facts here disclosed, to have the witness produced, or his deposition taken. It is well settled law in practically all of the states of this country, and of England, that declarations and admissions of a former owner of property, tending to defeat his title, made after a transfer thereof to a third person, are inadmissible against his transferee or successor in interest. 1 Dunnell, Minn. Dig. § 3417; Burt v. McKinstry, 4 Minn. 146 (204), 77 Am. Dec. 507; 1 Notes on Minn. Reports, 108. The rule applies to commercial paper, and forbids the payee thus to defeat the title of his transferee, by declarations and admissions made after the transaction. 2 Jones, Ev. p. 408; 8 Cyc. 255; 1 Am. & Eng. Enc. (2d ed.) and cases cited in note on page 685; Patton v. Gee, 36 Ark. 506; Head v. Shaver, 9 Ala. 791; Buckman v. Barnum, 15 Conn. 67; National Bank of Athens v. Exchange Bank of Athens, 110 Ga. 692, 36 S. E. 265; Gillighan v. Tebbets, 33 Me. 360; Zimmerman v. Kearney County Bank, 57 Neb. 800, 78 N. W. 366, and numerous other authorities cited in Jones, Evidence, supra. There are exceptions to the rule, none of which, however, are applicable to this case, and for the error in admitting the evidence there must be a new trial. That the evidence was prejudicial is clear.

This sufficiently covers the case, and we need not refer to the assignments challenging the instructions to the jury, except to say that the reference in the charge to a *failure* of consideration was evidently an inadvertence. A mere failure of consideration would not constitute a defense to the action if plaintiff was a *bona fide* holder. To constitute such defense a total want of consideration must be shown. If the charge contains other technical errors they will be corrected on the new trial.

Order reversed and new trial granted.

MARTIN MOE v. PHILIP G. KEKOS and Another.[1]

October 9, 1914.

Nos. 18,731—(236).

Judgment notwithstanding verdict — questions for jury.

On the evidence in this case the questions were for the jury, and it was error to grant judgment notwithstanding the verdict.

Action in the municipal court of Minneapolis to recover $222.25, balance due under a contract of hiring. The case was tried before Bardwell, J., who denied defendants' motion that the court instruct the jury plaintiff should not recover to exceed $4.75, and that he recover no damage whatever for the alleged breach of contract, and a jury which returned a verdict for $152.24 in favor of plaintiff. Defendants' motion for judgment notwithstanding the verdict and in favor of plaintiff for the sum of $4.75 was granted. From the judgment entered pursuant to the order for judgment, plaintiff appealed. Reversed.

Harry Rauch and *Richard & Coe,* for appellant.
Lane & Malmberg, for respondents.

BUNN, J.

Action to recover damages for breach of a contract by defendants to employ plaintiff as a shoemaker for a stated period. The trial before a jury resulted in a verdict of $152.24 in favor of plaintiff. Defendants moved for judgment notwithstanding the verdict, or for a new trial. The trial court granted judgment as asked. Such judgment was entered and plaintiff appealed therefrom to this court.

The question is whether it appeared as a matter of law from the evidence that plaintiff was entitled to recover nothing more than the sum of $4.75, admittedly due, or whether the case was for the jury.

Plaintiff and a disinterested witness testified that the oral contract

[1] Reported in 149 N. W. 8.

of employment was that plaintiff was to work as a shoemaker for defendants from November 12, 1912, until April, 1913, at $15 per week; that the hiring was for a definite time. Defendant Philip Kekos denied in his testimony that any time was agreed upon, and claimed that he agreed to employ plaintiff as long as his work was satisfactory. Plaintiff was discharged December 10, 1912. The trouble that led to this was a shoe that defendant gave plaintiff with instructions to sew on a half sole. Defendant accused plaintiff of nailing on the sole, instead of sewing it, and immediately discharged him.

We are satisfied that both issues—the terms of the contract of employment, and the sufficiency of defendant's reason for discharging plaintiff, including the truthfulness of the charge made, were on the evidence questions for the jury. We think the trial court erred in granting the motion for judgment.

Judgment reversed.

JOHN WATRE v. GREAT NORTHERN RAILWAY COMPANY.[1]

October 9, 1914.

Nos. 18,733—(237).

Finding sustained by evidence.

1. Jury's finding that the flooding of plaintiff's land was due to defendant's negligence, sustained.

Evidence excluded.

2. Trial court *held* not to have abused its discretion in excluding evidence of the amount of rainfall at distant points.

[1] Reported in 149 N. W. 18.

Note.—Liability of railroad company for conducting surface water through its embankments and onto the property of an adjoining owner, see note in 12 L.R.A.(N.S.) 680.

Right to flow of surface water generally, see note in 21 L.R.A. 593.

Damages — evidence.

3. Evidence *held* to afford a sufficient basis for a reasonable approximation of the portion of the damage attributable to defendant's acts.

Refusal to instruct jury.

4. Refusal of instruction upon the necessity of differentiating the loss occasioned by defendant's negligence from that due to other causes, *held* not reversible error.

Construction of court rule 9.

5. Under rule 9 of this court, where the sufficiency of the evidence to sustain the verdict is challenged, the portions of the record printed must be in substantial conformity with the settled case and not be in the nature of a bill of exceptions.

Action in the district court for Grant county to recover $1,000 for damage caused by the diversion of surface water from its natural watershed. The answer alleged that in building its railway and in making excavations therefor defendant exercised all the care that was reasonable under the circumstances and that any embankments, grades, ditches or excavations that were made were only such as were necessary and, if any surface water escaped from its right of way upon the land of plaintiff, the same was caused not through any negligence on its part, but by reason of defendant's lawful acts in the employment of its own property for the purposes for which it was intended. The facts are stated in the opinion. The case was tried before Flaherty, J., and a jury which returned a verdict for $550 in favor of plaintiff. From an order denying its motion for judgment notwithstanding the verdict or for a new trial, defendant appealed. Affirmed.

M. L. Countryman and *A. L. Janes,* for appellant.

E. J. Scofield, for respondent.

PHILIP E. BROWN, J.

Action to recover damages for the destruction of growing crops in the years 1907 and 1908, claimed to have been caused by defendant's unlawful diversion of and flooding by surface waters. Plaintiff had a verdict and defendant appealed from an order denying its alternative motion.

Plaintiff, in the years stated, owned the southwest quarter of the southwest quarter of section 3, in North Ottawa township, Grant county. His crops growing thereon were destroyed by surface water in June, 1907 and 1908. His land was quite level, sloping to the west, and that west of it was also level. Defendant's railway line ran about east a few rods north of plaintiff's north line, and about two miles east of his premises intersected a gravel ridge forming a watershed which, previously to the construction of defendant's line and the excavations shortly to be mentioned, caused waters falling upon a large area to the east thereof to flow to the south, clear of plaintiff's lands. Defendant had two sand pits in the west side of the ridge, one immediately north and the other just south of its track. The north one was 50 or 60 acres in extent, and the south one about 80 acres. They were from three to five feet deep. The south pit had not been used for a number of years, but the other was being worked in May and June, 1907 and 1908. Defendant had excavated the gravel in the pits below the bottom of a ravine or coulee immediately east of the ridge, through which surface waters had theretofore been accustomed to run south. After the excavation these waters, in times of very heavy rainfall, ran over the eastern rim of the south pit and collected therein, escaping through a cut made by defendant in the west rim some two miles east of the south line of plaintiff's land. In the north pit defendant had constructed an opening through the sand ridge into the coulee, for the purpose of taking water therefrom into the pits for use in its engines, and had also placed obstructions in the coulee. This pit was drained by a 12x24 inch culvert laid under a sidetrack which branched from the main track near the west edge of the pit and extended to the east side thereof, which was several feet higher than the west. This culvert was the only outlet from the pit and emptied into defendant's borrow pit on the north side of its track. The two pits were not connected by any opening. The land north and south of plaintiff's and easterly to the ridge is flat, with natural drainage to the south and west. From the sand pits westerly it falls rapidly 18.3 feet in the first mile, 14.7 feet in the second, and in the third to plaintiff's west line, 4.3 feet. There were borrow pit ditches on both sides of defendant's track, with culverts at the highway crossings, claimed by plaintiff to be inadequate, and three bridges between the sand pits and plaintiff's west line, one being directly north of plaintiff's land, which was bounded on the south by a graded section line highway, a like highway being on the north line of the same section. Both of these highways extended from west of plaintiff's premises easterly to the sand pits, their ditches being so constructed as to carry the water west to an artificial ditch. North and south of defendant's track were graded section line roads between sections 1 and 2, 2 and 3, and 3 and 4, and with ditches on each side draining from north to south.

The months of May and June in both years mentioned were very wet, with heavy rains in June, and, just previous to the flooding of plaintiff's land in 1908, there was a very heavy but not unprecedented rainfall, the lands in the localities mentioned being thereafter covered with water. On plaintiff's land, however, the water stood for two or three weeks. After these rains water from the north sand pit ran through the culvert mentioned and over the side track and from the cut in the south pit, reaching plaintiff's lands through the railway and highway ditches.

The evidence was amply sufficient to establish the facts as recited, so far as they may be regarded as disputed, and summarizing its effect, in connection with the opinion evidence, we hold that it warranted the jury in finding: (a) That defendant, for purposes of its own, diverted and collected water from the natural course of drainage and, by cutting through the divide, cast it upon plaintiff's premises where otherwise it would not have gone; (b) that, while the rains in 1907 and 1908 were heavy, they were not so unusual and extraordinary in that locality as to exempt defendant from liability as for *vis major* or such as defendant was not bound to anticipate and guard against; (c) that the continued standing of water on plaintiff's land was attributable to defendant's acts.

1. Defendant contends that it had the right to drain its south pit through the artificial cut in its west rim, and also the right to take water from the coulee into its north pit for use in its engines, and to drain this pit into its borrow pits, and that it fully performed all duties, by constructing ditches along its right of way sufficient to

carry off all ordinary volumes of surface water coming from the
coulee into the sand pits or otherwise collecting therein.

If it be admitted that defendant had the legal right to collect
waters in its pits and to drain them to the west, yet, under numerous
decisions of this court, a duty was imposed to use all reasonable means
to avoid injury therefrom to the property of others, which duty is
governed by the same principles as that of individuals. Howard v.
Illinois Central R. Co. 114 Minn. 189, 130 N. W. 946. Whether it
took such precautions in obstructing the flow of water in the coulee
and in maintaining its ditches, were questions for the jury, whose
findings thereon, necessarily included in the verdict, are sustained
by the evidence.

2. Error is assigned as to the court's refusal to permit defendant
to show the amount of rainfall at Morris, 38 miles from plaintiff's
land, during May and June, 1908. It was admitted, however, that
rains sometimes occurred at Morris when none would fall upon
plaintiff's land, and even without this the remoteness of the evidence
is apparent. Evidence must afford a basis for relief over and above
mere conjecture and be more than remotely relevant. No general
test has been established for determining whether it is too slight,
conjectural or remote. These questions must be left largely to the
judgment of the trial court. Thayer, Evidence, 516. It is doubtful if the exclusion of the evidence was prejudicial, but that aside we
find no reversible error in the court's action.

3. It appeared that plaintiff must have suffered some loss directly
from rains and from waters for which defendant was not responsible,
but the principal damage was evidently occasioned by water standing
on his land for several weeks. The court carefully limited the recovery to damages caused by defendant's negligent acts, thus establishing the law of the case as to plaintiff. Defendant, however, insists that the evidence warrants no rational deduction differentiating
these losses, and requested an instruction to the effect that, if the
jury were unable to determine the damages severally, they should
award nominal damages only, error being assigned because it was
not given. In the nature of things damages under such circumstances as here disclosed cannot be ascertained with mathematical

certainty, nor is it necessary that they should be in order to entitle
plaintiff to a recovery. A liberal discretion is vested in the jury to
determine, from all the facts shown, what part was caused by defendant's acts. Of course a jury cannot act without evidence, and
there must be some basis upon which to found an award; but mere
difficulty in getting at the amount of damages is no reason for denying them altogether. The principle is well illustrated in cases where
owners of dogs are held liable for the losses respectively occasioned
by their own animals, and for none other, though the dogs acted together, slight circumstances being deemed sufficient to afford a basis
for apportionment of the aggregate damage. Another illustration is
in case of trespass by cattle of different owners. The rule is well
stated in Sellick v. Hall, 47 Conn. 260, where the total damage was
caused by an overflow attributable partly to defendant's wrongful
acts and partly to city drainage.

"It may be very difficult," said the court at page 274, "for a jury
to determine just how much damage the defendant is liable for and
how much should be left for the city to answer for; but this is no
more difficult of ascertainment than many questions which juries are
called upon to decide. They must use their best judgment, and make
their result, if not an absolutely accurate one, an approximation to ac-
curacy. And this is the best that human tribunals can do in many
cases."

See also Sedgwick, Damages (9th ed.) § 36a, p. 40.

In the case before us no insuperable difficulty confronted the jury
in arriving at a reasonably accurate approximation of plaintiff's loss
caused by defendant's acts alone. Nor was it error to refuse defendant's requested instruction. Its substance was fairly covered by the
charge given. Moreover, it was inaccurate in ignoring the rule of
approximation, and, standing alone, gave the jury no workable rule.

4. The record in this case does not comply with rule 9 of this
court (139 N. W. viii.). It is practically a bill of exceptions; and
where, as here, the sufficiency of the evidence to sustain the verdict is
challenged, it is a material and unwarrantable deviation from the
rule, adding greatly to the labor of the court. The portion of the
evidence printed must be in substantial conformity with the settled

case. The insufficiency of the record in the present case, being the
first instance of the kind since the adoption of the rule, has been
overlooked; but our action in this regard must not be taken as a
precedent.

Order affirmed.

ADOLPH SUCKER v. S. H. CRANMER and Another.[1]

October 9, 1914.

Nos. 18,737—(238).

Redemption from mortgage sale — taxes paid — subrogation.

A mortgage, containing stipulations that the mortgagees might pay taxes
and charge the amount to the mortgagors, or at his option buy and hold
in his own right tax title on the mortgaged premises, was foreclosed and
at the sale plaintiff, the assignee of the mortgagee, bid in the premises for
the amount of the debt and expenses of sale; while the year of redemption
was running plaintiff redeemed from tax sales and paid taxes to prevent
the penalty from being added, but through inadvertence failed to file and
furnish the affidavit required by section 8172, G. S. 1913, so that defendants,
the mortgagors, within the year, redeeming as owners, did so without
reimbursing plaintiff. In this action to recover of defendants the sums
thus paid by plaintiff subsequent to the sale and to enforce a lien therefor
against the land, it is *held:*

That, even though the court cannot restore the statutory remedy lost
through plaintiff's failure to comply with the requirements of the statute,
and though it be conceded, without so deciding, that under the terms of
the mortgage and the facts of the case no personal claim exists against
defendants, still plaintiff's payment of the tax liens was, under the mortgage and statute, authorized and lawful, so that in equity he should be
subrogated to the rights of the holders of such liens.

Action in the district court for Hennepin county to recover $425.-
16 paid by plaintiff, and that the amount so paid with interest and
costs of the action be decreed to be a specific lien against the real es-

1 Reported in 149 N. W. 16.

tate described. From an order, Jelley, J., sustaining defendant's demurrer to the complaint, plaintiff appealed. Reversed.

H. R. Hewitt and *C. J. Cahaley,* for appellant.

S. H. Cranmer, for respondents.

HOLT, J.

Plaintiff is the assignee of a real estate mortgage executed by defendants. The latter covenanted to pay the taxes and keep the buildings insured for further security, until all obligations under the mortgage were discharged, and, in case of failure to perform these covenants, it was provided that the mortgagee might effect the insurance and pay the taxes, and the sums so disbursed should be charged against the mortgagors, or the then owner of the premises, and should become an additional lien, secured by the mortgage and enforced at the same time and in the same manner as the original indebtedness, or, the mortgagee might at his option purchase and hold solely in his own right any and all such taxes or tax titles on the premises. Default was made and the mortgage was foreclosed. Plaintiff became the purchaser, having bid in the property for enough to wipe out the debt and expenses of sale. After the sale, and while the year of redemption was running, plaintiff paid $267.61 in redemption of tax certificates, acquired by Hicks & Co. on the mortgaged premises subsequent to the execution of the mortgage, and he also paid $112.80 taxes, about to be subjected to the statutory penalty, all on account of the failure of defendants to perform their covenant in regard to taxes. There was also a payment for fire insurance, but, since the allegations in respect thereto are admittedly insufficient or erroneous, no consideration will be given that item. The defendants, as owners, made redemption within the year, but, inasmuch as the plaintiff had failed to file or furnish the affidavit specified in section 8172, G. S. 1913, defendants paid nothing towards reimbursing plaintiff for the said amounts disbursed by him subsequent to the foreclosure sale. The above facts, except as to the payment for insurance, were appropriately alleged in plaintiff's complaint, and also that the failure to comply with the provisions of said section 8172 was due to plaintiff's mistake and inadvertence. He asks for personal judgment against defendants, that the amount be decreed a lien against the land, and for such other relief as to the court may seem just and equitable. The case is here on appeal from the order sustaining the defendants' demurrer to the complaint. The question presented is, has a mortgagee, who, at the foreclosure sale bid in the property for the full amount of the debt then due, but, while the year of redemption ran, disbursed money in payment of taxes and in redemption from tax sales, no remedy if he has failed to file and furnish an affidavit in accordance with section 8172, G. S. 1913, when redemption is made by the mortgagor, as owner, without reimbursement for such tax payments, the mortgage containing a provision that the mortgagee may pay delinquent taxes and charge the amount to the mortgagor or the then owner or at his option secure tax title to the property?

It is to be noted that in this case the foreclosure never became complete because the mortgagors redeemed. The sale thereby became of no effect. It was annulled. However, the power of sale became exhausted, at least as a means to enforce the collection of any part of the debt due or collectable at the time of the foreclosure. Loomis v. Clambey, 69 Minn. 469, 72 N. W. 707. And we may concede, without so deciding, that the payment of the taxes did not create an instalment of the mortgage coming due subsequent to the foreclosure, so that there may be a reforeclosure therefor. It may also be conceded that, where a statutory remedy has been lost through omission to observe a prescribed requirement, courts have no power to restore the same, unless the one seeking to reap an advantage therefrom in some manner induced the omission. The defendants are not charged with any conduct which caused or induced plaintiff to neglect to file the required affidavit.

The defendants confidently contend that plaintiff has no personal claim against them for the taxes paid, and has no redress whatever since he failed to obtain it under the provisions of said section 8172. The decisions cited by them do not foreclose the question. In Spencer v. Levering, 8 Minn. 410 (461), where the statement is made that there is no personal liability against the mortgagor for failure to pay taxes, it does not appear that any agreement existed in regard thereto. Nor did Martin v. Lennon, 19 Minn. 45 (67),

65 Am. St. 576, or Nopson v. Horton, 20 Minn. 239 (268), involve any agreement between the litigants in regard to the taxes. Cases from other jurisdictions do not reach the point because of dissimilarity of mortgage stipulations, of statutes and of facts. Those tending to sustain defendants' position that no express or implied agreement can be spelled out which authorizes a recovery against them are: Johnson v. Payne, 11 Neb. 269, 9 N. W. 81; Kersenbrock v. Muff, 29 Neb. 530, 45 N. W. 778; Walton v. Bagley, 47 Mich. 385, 11 N. W. 209; Vincent v. Moore, 51 Mich. 618, 17 N. W. 81; Swan v. Emerson, 129 Mass. 289; Semans v. Harvey, 52 Ind. 331; Horrigan v. Welmuth, 77 Mo. 542; Stone v. Tilley, 100 Tex. 487, 101 S. W. 201, 10 L.R.A.(N.S.) 678, 123 Am. St. 819, 15 Ann. Cas. 524. However in Hogg v. Longstreth, 97 Pa. St. 255, the supreme court of Pennsylvania held that a mortgagee may pay the taxes and sue the mortgagor, whose duty it was to pay them, in assumpsit. In the case at bar it must be observed that defendants stipulated that, in case of default in payment of taxes, plaintiff, the assignee of the mortgagee, might pay them and charge the amount to the defendants; that the payment was not made until after the foreclosure; that the statute (section 8172) permitted plaintiff to make the payment when it was made and gave a lien on the land therefor, and that the foreclosure never became complete so that the purchaser could be said to have taken the title as it stood at the time of the sale, charged with these taxes. The defendants at all times remained the owners of the mortgaged premises. It has been held that a mortgagee, who has paid taxes to protect his interests prior to the foreclosure sale, may reimburse himself from the proceeds of the sale, although no mention was made in the foreclosure notice, or the proceedings were so irregular that no claim could be made that the lien given by the statute, or by the usual terms of the mortgage, was enforced in the foreclosure proceeding. Gorham v. Nat. Life Ins. Co. 62 Minn. 327, 64 N. W. 906; Hamel v. Corbin, 69 Minn. 223, 72 N. W. 106. Taxes paid by plaintiff during the year of redemption should, as to these defendants, stand in as good position since the

enactment of section 8172, as did the taxes paid by the holder of the mortgage in the two cases last referred to.

It would therefore seem to follow that at least plaintiff was not a volunteer or intermeddler when he redeemed from the tax certificates held by Hicks & Co. and when he, during the year of redemption, paid the subsequent taxes in order to avoid the imposition of the penalty. The statute gave him the right to make the payment and have a lien therefor. His mortgage executed by defendants permitted him to make the payment and charge the amount to them as owners of the land, and it further authorized him to purchase and hold tax titles upon the land in his own right. Under this situation it would be a gross injustice to permit defendants to profit several hundred dollars from plaintiff's mistake or inadvertence. Regardless of the right to a personal judgment, we think plaintiff is entitled to be subrogated to the position of Hicks & Co. and the state as to these taxes. Taxes are a perpetual lien until paid. Hicks & Co., as holders of the tax certificates, held this lien, by virtue of which they had also the right to pay subsequent taxes and acquire a lien therefor. Section 2125, G. S. 1913. We perceive no good reason why defendants should be heard to object to such subrogation. There is ample authority for the proposition that one who has paid taxes to protect his own rights, and not as a volunteer or intermeddler, may be subrogated to the rights of the state or of the one who had acquired the state's rights. Pratt v. Pratt, 96 Ill. 184; Sharp v. Thompson, 100 Ill. 447, 39 Am. Rep. 61; Cockrum v. West, 122 Ind. 372, 23 N. E. 140; John v. Connell, 61 Neb. 267, 85 N. W. 82; Fiacre v. Chapman, 32 N. J. Eq. 463; Title Guarantee & Trust Co. v. Haven, 196 N. Y. 487, 89 N. E. 1082, 1085, 25 L.R.A.(N.S.) 1308, 17 Ann. Cas. 1131. In this state in two cases where subrogation was permitted there were included, in the lien allowed, amounts paid for taxes. Emmert v. Thompson, 49 Minn. 386, 52 N. W. 31, 32 Am. St. 566; and Elliott v. Tainter, 88 Minn. 377, 93 N. W. 124.

In our opinion the facts pleaded show that plaintiff, in reference to the payment of taxes and redeeming from the tax certificates of Hicks & Co., did so lawfully, under both contract and statute, to protect his interest in the land; and justice requires that he be substituted to the liens held by Hicks & Co. and the state, notwithstanding these have been cancelled. "This doctrine (of subrogation) is applied when such lien has been discharged under a mistake of the real situation, to save the party who has made the payment from loss if such payment and discharge would otherwise give the owner of the land an unconscionable and inequitable advantage over the person who had paid the same." Elliott v. Tainter, supra. If the defendants or third parties have equities which may prevent plaintiff from obtaining relief, they do not appear from the complaint. The payment being made subsequent to the foreclosure, it cannot very well be contended that there is a splitting up of a cause of action, for the right to subrogation did not exist prior to the foreclosure proceeding.

Order reversed.

PETER N. FOLTMER v. FIRST METHODIST EPISCOPAL CHURCH OF ST. CLOUD and Others.[1]

October 9, 1914.

Nos. 18,745—(242).

Building contract — construction of "mill work."

The contract for the construction of a church building provided that certain of the windows of the building should be set with art or cathedral glass. A subcontractor agreed to furnish all "mill work" for the structure. It is *held* that, on the evidence presented to the court below, the question whether the contract to furnish the "mill work" included the cathedral glass should have been disposed of by the trial court as a question of fact, or mixed law and fact, and a finding made thereon.

Action in the district court for Stearns county to foreclose plaintiff's lien for $833.50 for materials upon the real estate of defendant corporation. The case was tried before Roeser, J., who made findings that plaintiff was not obliged under his contract to furnish the

---

[1] Reported in 148 N. W. 1077.

127 M.—9.

art or cathedral glass provided for in the specifications, but was bound to set the art glass in the window frames and to supply certain rolling curtains provided in the plans and specifications, and ordered judgment in favor of plaintiff for the sum of $578.50 and a lien upon the premises, and directed a sale of the real estate to satisfy the amount due and an allowance of $25 as attorney's fees. From an order denying their motion for a new trial, defendants appealed. Remanded with directions.

J. D. *Sullivan,* for appellants.

R. B. *Brower,* for respondent.

BROWN, C. J.

Defendant Steckling was awarded the contract for the construction of the Methodist Church at St. Cloud, and he in turn entered into a contract with plaintiff, under and by which plaintiff contracted and agreed to furnish all "mill work" for the building. Subsequent to the completion of the edifice this action was brought by plaintiff, the subcontractor, to foreclose a mechanic's lien which he had perfected against the building for material furnished by him. Judgment was ordered for plaintiff and defendants appealed from an order denying a new trial.

The real controversy in the action is between plaintiff and defendant Steckling. By his contract plaintiff agreed to furnish all mill work for the building for the sum of $1,600. Certain of the windows were, according to the plans for the building, to be set with art or cathedral glass, the value of which was fixed by the specifications at $300. Defendant Steckling, as contractor for the entire building, was under obligation to the church society to furnish this glass, as well as all other material. He contended on the trial that plaintiff's contract to furnish the "mill work" included this glass, and that, since he did not furnish it, the amount of his claim should be reduced to the extent of its value, namely, $300. If not so reduced, then the amount must be paid by Steckling. Plaintiff claims that his contract to furnish the mill work did not include this glass, and that he was under no obligation to furnish the same. So the case, as here presented, narrows down to this single issue: Did plaintiff's contract impose upon him the obligation to furnish the cathedral glass ?

The term "mill work" as used in building contracts has a well defined and well understood meaning. As applied to window sash, it includes ordinary glass properly set into the sash and ready to be placed in position in the building. This seems to be conceded by plaintiff. Whether the term includes glass of the kind here in question, art or cathedral glass, was a disputed question on the trial. Both parties called witnesses upon the subject, who gave their opinion, either as builders and contractors, or as mill workers, that cathedral glass was included in the term and that it was not. The witnesses were not agreed. Their opinions were expressed with reference to this particular contract which simply called for "mill work," in connection with the specifications forming a part of the building contract, and not from any usual or common custom in respect to the subject. The evidence as thus presented was conflicting, presenting a question of fact. The trial court did not consider it, and held as a matter of law that cathedral glass was not included within plaintiff's contract, and judgment was ordered for the full amount of his claim.

We are of opinion, and so hold, that the question whether cathedral glass was included within plaintiff's contract, to furnish the "mill work" of the building, should not on this record have been disposed of as a matter of law from a construction of the contract alone. If the case had been submitted upon the written contract, together with the building plans and specifications, no doubt the question would have resolved itself into one of construction for the court. And though if it be conceded that the contract, as found in written specifications, is not ambiguous, and therefore not open to parol explanation, a concession not entirely free from doubt, we are quite clear that the evidence above referred to, showing a diversity of opinion among the builders and mill workers upon the question, all of which was offered and received without objection, made the rights and obligations of the parties thereunder sufficiently uncertain as to require a consideration of the evidence and a finding upon the issue, one way or the other, as one of fact or mixed law and fact. Such a finding was requested by defendant and refused by the court. In this we hold that the learned trial court erred.

There would seem, however, no reason for granting a new trial of the action, thus prolonging the litigation and adding further expense to the litigants, and the cause will be remanded with directions to the court below to find, upon the present record, as a question of fact whether plaintiff's contract included the cathedral glass, and to direct the entry of judgment in accordance therewith. We are not to be understood, however, as directing any particular finding upon the question. The court below will make the finding according to its own views of the evidence, construed in connection with the written contracts, and all the facts disclosed by the record.

The allowance of attorney's fees was within the discretion of the court.

The cause is remanded accordingly.

NIKOLE DIMETRE v. RED WING SEWER PIPE COMPANY.[1]

October 9, 1914.

Nos. 18,751—(233).

Rule of "gravel pit" cases not applicable.

1. The rule of the "gravel pit" cases does not apply where the embankment consists of material of such adhesiveness, or so placed or supported, that it may reasonably be expected to withstand the effect and operation of the law of gravitation.

[1] Reported in 148 N. W. 1078.

Note.—Servant's assumption of risk of changing conditions of the working place during progress of the work, see notes in 19 L.R.A.(N.S.) 340; 28 L.R.A. (N.S.) 1267.

Assurance to servant of safety by master or coservant, see notes in 48 L.R.A. 542; 23 L.R.A.(N.S.) 1014; 30 L.R.A.(N.S.) 453.

Servant relying on master's assurance of safety — contributory negligence.

2. Where the master directs the servant to perform specific work and assures him that he can do so in safety, if the servant, in reliance upon such assurance, proceeds to perform the work, he is usually not chargeable either with contributory negligence or with a voluntary assumption of the risk, unless the danger be so obvious and imminent and so apparent to the ordinary mind that it would be unreasonable for him to rely upon the assurances given him.

Same — question for jury.

3. Whether it would be unreasonable for the servant to rely upon the assurances given him is a question for the jury, unless the court can say that reasonable minds could reach only one conclusion. The present case is within the rule requiring the question to be submitted to the jury.

Action in the district court for Goodhue county by the administrator of the estate of Andrew Naum, deceased, to recover $7,500 for the death of his intestate while in the employ of defendant. The answer alleged that the death of the intestate was caused by reason of his negligence or solely by reason of the risks and dangers incident to the business in which the deceased was then engaged. The case was tried before Johnson, J., who denied defendant's motion to dismiss the action and its motion for a directed verdict in its favor, and a jury which returned a verdict for $1,600 in favor of plaintiff. From an order denying its motion for judgment notwithstanding the verdict or for a new trial, defendant appealed. Affirmed.

A. A. Tenner and *F. M. Wilson,* for appellant.

C. P. Diepenbrock and *Mohn & Mohn,* for respondent.

TAYLOR, C.

Andrew Naum, an Albanian 18 years of age, while at work for defendant in its clay pit, was buried beneath a mass of clay and earth which fell from the bank or wall of the pit, and sustained injuries which resulted in his death. Plaintiff as administrator of his estate brought this action for damages and recovered a verdict. Defendant made the usual alternative motion for judgment notwithstanding the verdict or for a new trial and appealed from the order denying the motion.

Defendant contends that the facts bring the case within the rule established in the so-called "gravel pit" cases, and that plaintiff cannot recover, for the reason that Naum was chargeable with contributory negligence and had assumed the risks. Plaintiff contends that the instant case does not come within the rule applied in the "gravel pit" cases, for the reason that the bank in question was composed mainly of hard, adhesive and tenacious clay, not likely to give way or fall, and for the further reason that defendant's foreman with full knowledge of the attending conditions had assured Naum that it was safe to work at the foot of the bank and ordered him to do so.

The witnesses do not agree as to the height of the bank or wall of the pit at the place of the accident. Plaintiff's witnesses estimate it as about 15 feet; defendant's witnesses as at least 20 feet. From the bottom to a height of about seven feet, it consisted of "pipe clay" and was nearly perpendicular. Above this clay was a four or five inch layer of what is designated as "iron rock." Above the "iron rock" was a layer of sand, or sandy material, which sloped back considerably and was estimated by plaintiff's witnesses as between two and four feet in thickness. Above the sandy layer were about six feet of "brick clay" and common soil, the face of which was nearly perpendicular and projected two or three feet beyond the upper surface of the sandy layer. While the testimony discloses some common soil in this topmost layer, the quantity was evidently small, as the witnesses on both sides continually refer to this layer as "brick clay." During the noon hour on the day of the accident, the crew, of which Naum was a member, passed over the top and near the edge of the bank on their way to and from dinner, and observed a crack along the top four or five feet back from the edge and several feet in length. They made no examination of this crack and whether Naum saw it does not appear, except by inference from the fact that he passed by with the other members of the crew. They discussed the danger among themselves and then informed the foreman of the crack and that it was dangerous to work under that bank. The foreman went to the top of the bank and after making an examination told the crew that there was no danger and to proceed with their work. They did so. Late in the afternoon the overhanging bank fell and Naum was caught beneath it and killed. The falling mass came wholly from the upper portion of the bank. The layers of "iron rock" and of "pipe clay" remained in place, showing that the slide was not caused by the work in which the crew were engaged during the afternoon. Some sand had dropped or trickled down during the afternoon but apparently not in sufficient quantities to attract attention. The hard and adhesive character of the so-called "brick clay" is indicated by the fact that after it had fallen to the bottom of the pit it still remained in large, hard chunks,—some of them so large that it required two or three men to lift them from the unfortunate Naum.

The embankments considered in the gravel-pit cases were composed of material likely to slide or fall in the absence of lateral support, and it was held that the workman is presumed to have "the knowledge which common observation forces on the most ordinary intellect," and to have known the effect and operation of the law of gravitation, and that by working upon or at the foot of such an embankment he took the chance of being injured in case it should fall. Olson v. McMullen, 34 Minn. 94, 24 N. W. 318; Pederson v. City of Rushford, 41 Minn. 289, 42 N. W. 1063; Swanson v. Great Northern Ry. Co. 68 Minn. 184, 70 N. W. 978; Reiter v. Winona & St. Peter R. Co. 72 Minn. 225, 75 N. W. 219; Kletschka v. Minneapolis & St. Louis R. Co. 80 Minn. 238, 83 N. W. 133; O'Neil v. Great Northern Ry. Co. 101 Minn. 467, 112 N. W. 625. But where the embankment consists of material of such adhesiveness, or so placed or supported, that it may reasonably be expected to withstand the effect and operation of the law of gravitation, the rule does not apply. Hill v. Winston, 73 Minn. 80, 75 N. W. 1030; Lund v. E. S. Woodworth & Co. 75 Minn. 501, 78 N. W. 81; Kohout v. Newman, 96 Minn. 61, 104 N. W. 764; Wolf v. Great Northern Ry. Co. 72 Minn. 435, 75 N. W. 702.

Where the master directs the servant to perform specific work at a specific place and assures him that he can do so in safety, and the servant, pursuant to such order and in reliance upon such assurance, proceeds to do the work and is injured, his conduct does not, ordinarily, amount either to contributory negligence or to a voluntary assumption of the risks incident to the performance of the work. The servant is usually justified in assuming that the knowledge, experience and judgment of the master are superior to his own; and, even if the undertaking appear to him to be hazardous, he may rely upon the assurances of the master, presumably based upon such superior knowledge, without being chargeable either with contributory negligence or with a voluntary assumption of the risks, unless the danger be so obvious and imminent and so apparent to the ordinary mind that it would be unreasonable to rely upon the master's assurances of safety. Chicago Anderson Pressed Brick Co. v. Sobkowiak, 148 Ill. 573, 36 N. E. 572; Illinois Steel Co. v. Schymanowski, 162 Ill. 447, 44 N. E. 876; Consolidated Coal Co. v. Shepherd, 220 Ill. 123, 77 N. E. 133; Keegan v. Kavanaugh, 62 Mo. 230; Stephens v. Hannibal & St. J. R. Co. 96 Mo. 207, 9 S. W. 589, 9 Am. St. 336; Monahan v. Kansas City Clay & Coal Co. 58 Mo. App. 68; Swearingen v. Consolidated Troup Mining Co. 212 Mo. 524, 111 S. W. 545; Brown v. Lennane, 155 Mich. 686, 118 S. W. 581, 30 L.R.A.(N.S.) 453; McKee v. Tourtellotte, 167 Mass. 69, 44 N. E. 1071, 48 L.R.A. 542; Central Coal & Iron Co. v. Thompson, 31 Ky. Law R. 276, 102 S. W. 272; Bush v. West Yellow Pine Co. 2 Ga. App. 295, 58 S. E. 529; Starr v. Kreuzberger, 129 Cal. 123, 61 Pac. 787, 79 Am. St. 92; Daley v. Schaaf, 28 Hun (N. Y.) 314; Chadwick v. Brewsher, 15 N. Y. Supp. 598; Baccelli v. New England Brick Co. 138 App. Div. 656, 122 N. Y. Supp. 856; Van Dusen Gas & Gasoline Engine Co. v. Schelies, 61 Oh. St. 298, 55 N. E. 998; Wurtenberger v. Metropolitan St. Ry. Co. 68 Kan. 642, 75 Pac. 1049; Lane Brothers & Co. v. Bott, 104 Va. 615, 52 S. E. 25; Allen v. Gilman, McNeil & Co. 127 Fed. 609; Haas v. Balch, 56 Fed. 984, 6 C. C. A. 201; Cook v. St. Paul, M. & M. Ry. Co. 34 Minn. 45, 24 N. W. 311; Nelson v. St. Paul Plow Works, 57 Minn. 43, 58 N. W. 868; Anderson v. Pitt Iron Mining Co. 103 Minn. 252, 114 N. W. 953; Nustrom v. Shenango Furnace Co. 105 Minn. 140, 117 N. W. 480; Manks v. Moore, 108 Minn. 284, 122 N. W. 5; Arnold v. Dauchy, 115 Minn. 28, 131 N. W. 625.

In the instant case the presence of the sandy layer in the embankment, the projection of the upper layer of brick clay beyond the sandy layer, and the existence of the crack along the top and four or five feet from the edge of the upper layer, pointed to danger and excited apprehension on the part of the crew. On the other hand the material of which the bank was composed, except the sandy layer, was hard and adhesive, and had remained in its then position for some time. The work in which the crew were engaged did not undermine the bank or change its condition. According to the testimony of the superintendent it was the duty of the foreman to look out for dangerous places, tell the men when there was danger, and see that they did not get hurt. Defendant, in effect, undertook to ascertain when danger was impending and to give the men timely warning. When the men expressed their apprehensions to the foreman, he examined both the bank and the crack, and then told them that the bank was safe and to "go to work there." They relied upon this assurance, and proceeded with the work of loading the pipe clay upon the "skip" for removal from the pit, and were so engaged at the time of the accident. Naum, a youth of little experience and unable to talk English, was naturally influenced to some extent by the conduct of the other members of the crew.

Whether, in view of all the circumstances, the danger was so obvious and imminent and so apparent to the ordinary mind that Naum could not reasonably rely upon the assurances of safety given by the foreman, was a question for determination by the jury and not by the court. Such questions can be determined by the court only when the court can say that all reasonable minds would concur in the conclusion reached. We cannot say that this is such a case and the order appealed from is affirmed.

ALBERT A. JOHNSON v. LEWIS H. STARRETT and Others.[1]

October 9, 1914.

Nos. 18,771—(246).

Mechanic's lien.

1. Coal and gasolene for generation of power, dynamite for blasting, lubricant, lighting materials and supplies, and materials for erection of a tool-house, furnished excavating contractors, *held* lienable under G. S. 1913, § 7020, as being contributions to the improvement of defendant's realty. Supplies for and repairs and parts of the excavating machinery, *held* not lienable, being merely contributions to the personal property of the contractors.

Same.

2. Materials furnished in good faith for the improvement of realty may be lienable though not actually used in the work.

Action in the district court for Hennepin county against Lewis H. Starrett and Abraham L. Cornman, doing business as Starrett & Cornman, and Hennepin Avenue Methodist Episcopal Church, to foreclose a lien for $451.12 for materials furnished defendant corporation and by a sale of the premises therefor. The Schurmeier Wagon Co. and others intervened. The case was tried before Hale, J., who denied the motion of defendant church for the dismissal of the intervener's claims, and made findings and ordered judgment in favor of plaintiff and the several interveners, granting each of them a lien and directing a sale of the property to pay the same. From an order denying the motion of defendant Hennepin Avenue Methodist Episcopal Church for the vacation of the findings and the substitution of others in their stead, or for a new trial, defendant Hen-

[1] Reported in 149 N. W. 6.

Note.—Right to mechanics' lien for explosives furnished contractor, see note in 2 L.R.A.(N.S.) 288.

Lien for materials furnished for structure, but not actually used, see note in 31 L.R.A.(N.S.) 749.

nepin Avenue Methodist Episcopal Church appealed. Affirmed as to
one intervener. Reversed with directions as to the other interveners.

L. K. Eaton and *Willard R. Cray,* for appellant.

*George W. Hanson, Norton M. Cross, W. W. Todd, James C.
Melville* and *H. C. Mackall,* for respondents.

PHILIP E. BROWN, J.

The trial court held that plaintiff and the interveners were all
entitled to liens on defendant's realty for materials furnished, for
the full amounts claimed. Defendant appealed from an order denying a new trial. The undisputed facts are:

Defendant, being the owner of a lot in Minneapolis, contracted on
December 4, 1912, with Starrett & Cornman, for its excavation by
them for the purpose of erecting a church. The terms of the contract do not appear. Between that date and March 5, 1913, the contractors were engaged in doing the excavating. The work was done
with a portable steam-power excavating machine known as a whirly,
which was owned by the contractors and operated day and night.
The earth, as excavated and lifted by the machine, was loaded upon
motor trucks and carried away. Plaintiff furnished the contractors
the coal used in generating the steam-power for the whirly, and
intervener Manhattan Oil & Linseed Co. sold the gasolene used in
the motor trucks; both of these fuels being sold to the contractors for
the purposes stated and delivered on the premises. Intervener Gard-
ner Hardware Co. sold them materials of the value and for the purposes next stated, namely, $9.81, for lumber used in building an
office or toolhouse on defendant's premises; materials and supplies
used in connection with the light plant of the machine, $19.25;
dynamite, $173.50; supplies and repairs for and parts of the power
engine, $119.51; materials for the dump platform of the whirly,
$6.99; and supplies, materials, and parts of the machine, $89.46.
Intervener Schurmeier Wagon Co. furnished the contractors forg-
ings, iron work, and labor in repairing the machine, of the value of
$94.57. Intervener W. K. Morrison & Co. furnished them materials
for the like purpose, to the amount of $42.56, and also $3 worth of
rope grease to be used in lubricating the pulleys. After the excava-

tion was completed the machine, with its appurtenances, was removed from the premises. One-half the ground excavated consisted of clay, which the contractors were unable advantageously to blast or remove with shovel and pick, and which was more economically removable by use of the machine.

The sole question involved is: Were the several items mentioned lienable? Defendant, relying largely on decisions from other jurisdictions, insists upon a negative answer as to all. Upon the questions involved, however, foreign decisions, while instructive, are not of their usual weight; for, aside from the fact that this court has already determined some of the questions decided, the statutes considered are not alike and the rules of statutory construction and policy affecting the foundation of the determinations in some of the cases are at variance with our holdings. The opinions in Indiana, Massachusetts, Pennsylvania, and California, are notable in these regards. The Indiana statute is not given a liberal construction as being remedial. Cincinnati, R. & M. v. Shera, 36 Ind. App. 315, 73 N. E. 293. The Pennsylvania court regards mechanic's lien laws as class legislation, the scope of which should not be unnecessarily enlarged by too liberal construction. Oppenheimer v. Morrell, 118 Pa. St. 189, 12 Atl. 307. Massachusetts and California, and also Pennsylvania, seem to be committed to the doctrine that liens cannot be allowed for materials incidentally promoting the construction of buildings, but only for such as enter into the construction and become a part of the structure. For example, their courts exclude forms for holding concrete in place during process of building and temporary scaffolding. But Massachusetts nevertheless awards a lien for gunpowder used in building an aqueduct. Geo. H. Sampson Co. v. Com. 202 Mass. 326, 86 N. E. 911. And California reaches the same conclusion regarding oil furnished for and applied on the threads of joints of pipe used in the structure, and also for soapstone used as a lubricant in order to facilitate the pulling of electric wires through the pipes in the building, both of which obviously do not remain as a part of the permanent structure. Pacific Sash & Door Co. v. Dumiller, 162 Cal. 664, 124 Pac. 230. California, likewise, in accord with the great weight of authority (note, 2 L.R.A.[N.S.]

288), holds explosives lienable. California Powder Works v. Blue Tent, Consol. Hydraulic Gold Mines, 22 Pac. 391, 3 Cal. Un. Cas. 145; Giant Powder Co. v. San Diego Flume Co. 78 Cal. 193, 20 Pac. 419. Wisconsin, adhering to the doctrine of liberal construction, holds that materials used directly upon the work or structure and instrumental in producing the final result, are lienable if actually consumed in the use, though not physically incorporated therein, but apparently excludes coal used in portable engines, and oil used in lubricating building machinery. Barker & Stewart Lumber Co. v. Marathon Paper Mills Co. 146 Wis. 12, 130 N. W. 866. On the other hand, in New York, Tennessee, Kentucky, Missouri and Kansas, a much more liberal view is taken. See Schaghticoke Powder Co. v. Greenwich & J. Ry. Co. 183 N. Y. 306, 7 N. E. 153, 2 L.R.A.(N.S.) 288, 111 Am. St. 751, 5 Ann. Cas. 443, 73 App. Div. 20; Zipp v. Fidelity & Deposit Co. 76 N. Y. Supp. 386; Hercules Powder Co. v. Knoxville, L. F. & J. R. Co. 113 Tenn. 382, 83 S. W. 354, 67 L.R.A. 487, 106 Am. St. 836; Avery v. Woodruff, 144 Ky. 227, 137 S. W. 1088, 36 L.R.A.(N.S.) 866; Darlington Lumber Co. v. Wesley Construction Co. 161 Mo. App. 723, 141 S. W. 931; Chicago Lumber Co. v. Douglas, 89 Kan. 308, 131 Pac. 563, 44 L.R.A.(N.S.) 843. See also City Trust Safe Deposit & Surety Co. v. U. S. 147 Fed. 155, 77 C. C. A. 397. Many other cases to like effect might be added.

Our policy as to and construction of lien laws is well expressed in Emery v. Hertig, 60 Minn. 54, 57, 61 N. W. 830, 831, wherein it is said:

"It is sufficient for us to say that, whatever may be the conflicting decisions of other tribunals, we are of the opinion that no narrow or limited construction of our mechanic's lien law should be indulged in by the courts, and that the labor and industry of the country should not be hampered by technicalities or harsh interpretations of what was evidently intended to be a just law for the benefit of our industrial pursuits, which tends so materially to the building of cities and towns, and is the embodiment of so much natural justice. He whose property is enhanced in value by the labor and toil of others should be made to respond in some way by payment and full satisfaction for what he has secured.   To accomplish this result is the intent of the lien law."

These statutes must also have a reasonable and practical construction.   Howes v. Reliance Wire-Works Co. 46 Minn. 44, 48 N. W. 448; Lindquist v. Young, 119 Minn. 219, 138 N. W. 28.   Both the language quoted and the cases last cited accord with the report of the commission of statutory revision in New York, wherein it is said:

"The underlying principle of all legislation of this character is that a person who, at the request or with the consent of the owner of real property, enhances its value by furnishing materials or performing labor for the improvement thereof, should be deemed to have acquired an interest in such property to the extent of the value of such materials or labor.   This principle should be applicable generally to improvements of real property."   Schaghticoke Powder Co. case, supra, 183 N. Y. 310, 312, 76 N. E. 154, 155, 2 L.R.A.(N.S.) 288, 111 Am. St. 751, 5 Ann. Cas. 443.

In the same decision it is said:

"It is a familiar rule that in the construction of statutes their language must be adapted to changing conditions brought about by improved methods and the progress of the inventive arts."

Our statute reads:

"Whoever contributes to the improvement of real estate by performing labor, or furnishing skill, material, or machinery, for any of the purposes hereinafter stated * * * shall have a lien * * * for the price or value of such contribution * * * upon the land * * * ; that is to say for the erection * * * of any building, * * * thereon or for * * * excavating the same."   G. S. 1913, § 7020.

From a practical standpoint we think it cannot be justly said, under the plain terms of the statute, that those furnishing the coal, gasolene and dynamite did not "contribute to the improvement" of defendant's property by "furnishing material for excavating the same."   Clearly the work of the whirly and motor trucks contributed to the improvement of defendant's property, and, as the coal and gasolene furnished the motive power for its accomplishment, the contractors would have been entitled to a lien therefor.   But it is said that these materials were not furnished to excavate defendant's premises or for them, but, on the contrary, for use in and as a part of the plant and equipment of the contractors for the purpose of creating power and therefore were not lienable. This contention, we think, is too restricted both as to the facts and law. It ignores both the policy and settled construction of the statute and also modern methods employed in performing building contracts. Both the coal and gasolene were materials and both were components of the resultant achievement. Had the excavation and removal of the earth been done by manual labor, the right to a lien therefor would be undoubted, and we cannot differentiate such a case from one where the same result is reached by other and modern methods. The value of defendant's property was thereby enhanced, and it can make no difference that this was accomplished by use of power obtained from materials furnished by the lien claimants instead of by common labor. See Fay v. Bankers' Surety Co. 125 Minn. 211, 146 N. W. 359. Had the improvement necessitated the pumping of water, the strained construction and refined reasoning necessary to exclude a lien for fuel used in generation of power for the pump would, perhaps, be more apparent. The rule as to explosives should be applied to the items for coal and gasolene, and the trial court's determination as to them is sustained, as is also, by a parity of reasoning, its disposition of the claims for dynamite, rope grease, and materials and supplies for the light plant. The fact that it does not appear that the dynamite was actually used is unimportant, for materials furnished in good faith for a particular improvement are lienable, though not used. See authorities cited in note 10 of the statute quoted. The claim for the tool-house materials was likewise properly allowed. Lindquist v. Young, supra, 222, 138 N. W. 28. The other items, we hold, were not lienable. All were for supplies for, or repairs and parts of, the excavating machinery and engine, which were mere tools used in the work. These did not contribute to the improvement of defendant's realty, but to the personal property of the contractors. Furthermore, from aught that appears, they survived the performance of the work and remained the property of the contractors. They were not essentially different from repairs for tools requisite for an ordinary workman's labor on the job. Rosman v. Bankers Surety Co. 126 Minn. 435, 148 N. W. 454, is not in point.

Order affirmed as to plaintiff and intervener Manhattan Oil & Linseed Co., reversed as to the other interveners, with directions to the trial court to amend its conclusions of law so as to disallow the Schurmeier Wagon Co.'s claim of lien, and to reduce intervener W. K. Morrison & Co.'s lien to $3, and that of intervener Gardner Hardware Co. to $202.56.

CAPITAL TRUST COMPANY v. GREAT NORTHERN RAILWAY COMPANY.[1]

October 9, 1914.

Nos. 18,776—(250).

Witness — conflicting testimony — setting aside verdict.

1. The testimony of a witness which concededly made defendant's negligence a question for the jury, in this a personal injury action, was not so discredited by prior written statements and reports, or by his cross-examination, that a verdict based thereon, and approved by the trial court, should not stand. The jury have a right to consider the circumstances under which such statements are made.

Survival of cause of action.

2. When a person lives an appreciable length of time after receiving an injury through a defendant's negligence, even though in a state of unconsciousness, his cause of action survives under section 9 of the Federal Employer's Liability Act. Testimony that plaintiff's intestate, after the injury, moaned and breathed for ten minutes justified the court in submitting the question of the survival of his cause of action to the jury.

Damages not excessive.

3. The damages recovered *held* not excessive since the jury might have found that his death was not instantaneous.

[1] Reported in 149 N. W. 14.

Note.—Survival of right of action under Federal Employer's Liability Act, see note in 47 L.R.A.(N.S.) 66.

Action in the district court for Ramsey county by the administrator of the estate of William M. Ward, deceased, to recover $35,000 for the death of its intestate. The case was tried before Olin B. Lewis, J., and a jury which returned a verdict for $4,462.50 in favor of plaintiff. From an order denying its motion for judgment in its favor notwithstanding the verdict or for a new trial, defendant appealed. Affirmed.

M. L. Countryman and *A. L. Janes,* for appellant.

Samuel A. Anderson and *A. F. Storey,* for respondent.

HOLT, J.

While working for defendant, a carrier of interstate commerce, William M. Ward, a switchman, was killed. The administrator of his estate brought this action under the Federal Employer's Liability Act to recover damages, the claim being that Ward's injuries and death resulted from defendant's negligence. Plaintiff received a verdict, and defendant appeals from the order denying its alternative motion for judgment or a new trial.

Appellant claims that the testimony establishing its negligence is so discredited that a verdict based thereon should not be permitted to stand; that the proof of instantaneous death was conclusive, and hence the court erred in submitting the question of the survival of Ward's cause of action to the jury which, if found true, permitted the damages to be measured by the loss of Ward's earning capacity and not by the pecuniary loss to his beneficiaries; and that the damages are excessive.

The circumstances attending the fatality are in brief these: Ward, an experienced switchman, was engaged, under a foreman, one Rogers, and crew, in distributing a string of 14 cars, in an extensive switchyard in Minneapolis. The cars were to be "kicked" from the lead track and switched onto the proper yard tracks. In the operation the locomotive was in the rear pushing the cars west, and it was necessary to speed up sufficiently so that, when a car from the forward end was uncoupled, the momentum would be sufficient to carry it beyond the intended switch to its destination, the remaining cars would be stopped before reaching the switch, or else the

127 M.—10.

switch would be set against them. If the car, or cars, to be "kicked" were loaded, it was the duty of one of the switchmen to get to the brakes so as to stop at the right place. Rogers was on the ground directing, through signals, the movements of the train and, to some extent, the work of the crew. One man, called the pin puller, uncoupled the car or cars to be "kicked" at the proper time and place, and another attended the switch. As stated the cars were being pushed west in obedience to Rogers' signal to "kick" the forward car, an empty box car. At the time, Ward was observed standing on the running board at the middle of the next box car (one witness states it might have been on the third from the first), looking toward Rogers. A few seconds thereafter he was seen falling over the forward end of the second car, the first car, just prior to that moment having been uncoupled, had moved away several feet from the balance of the cars which were being slowed down, or abruptly checked, as claimed by plaintiff. He was run over and died, if not immediately, within ten minutes.

The negligence claimed was high speed, and the giving of the slow-down signal by Rogers so quickly after the uncoupling that Ward, who understood his duty to be to get onto the uncoupled car and ride it to its destination, did not have time to reach it from where he was standing before the cars parted; also that when Rogers had given the cut-off signal, he signalled the engineer for a quick check of speed, so that the car on which Ward was walking, or standing, was stopped so abruptly and violently as to throw Ward over the end. Counsel for defendant frankly concedes that a case for the jury upon defendant's negligence is made by the testimony of Holden, the switchman who was standing on the ground near Rogers, and who, upon observing the signals and the probability that Ward would not be able to get on the "kicked" car, rushed forward and boarded it in such hurry as almost to trip the pin puller. But it is said, Holden's story is so discredited by his written statements of the occurrence made soon thereafter to defendant and its claim agent, and by his cross-examination, that the verdict should not be permitted to stand. No witness observed Ward the few moments elapsing between the time the car was uncoupled and when he was seen pitching over the end of the car on which he had been riding. Defendant contends that since the switchman, McDonough, testified that he told Ward that the car then "kicked" was an empty and that the foreman had instructed the crew that empties "kicked" need not be ridden to destination, it is conclusively established that Ward knew or ought to have known that he had no business to try to get on that car. But the acts of the men then present testify to the contrary. Ward evidently considered it his duty to make that car, otherwise he would have remained at the middle and could not possibly have been pitched over the end however sudden the check. When Holden observed the signals of Rogers, he evidently thought it some one's duty to board the car, for he did, and there is no evidence that either Rogers or McDonough then attempted to call him back. Ward is dead and cannot speak. Rogers, the person who gave the signals and saw Ward's position, was not produced as a witness. Defendant sought to account for his absence, but the jury were not bound to find that such diligence in securing his attendance was shown that no inferences favorable to plaintiff's theory of the case should be drawn as to the facts within Rogers' knowledge. As to the claim that the written statements of Holden above referred to, and his cross-examination, wholly discredit his testimony, we observe that the only part in the written statements tending in that direction is to be found in this language "the accident was not due to any rough handling as these cars were switched the same as all others." We think a jury is justified in taking into consideration the circumstances usually surrounding reports and statements of accidents made by an employee to an employer or his claim agent. There may be reasons, that appear good to the servant at the time, why the giving of full details should be unnecessary. Some, because of an aversion to appear as a witness if a suit results, may make as noncommittal report as possible. Others may omit an important detail, thinking its legal bearing trivial. Again, a servant's desire to retain his place may be sufficiently persuasive to him to induce only a partial disclosure of his knowledge, if he thinks himself or a foreman or fellow-servant at all to blame. And, unless compelled by the authority of the law, many persons would hesitate to make written statements which charge any fellow-being with having been, even remotely, the cause of the death of another. May not also the statement when made in response to a claim agent's questions be somewhat directed, shaded or circumscribed by the questions and the secret purpose of the questioner? We think Holden's veracity was for the jury. There was no inherent improbability in his testimony, nor was it controverted by conceded physical facts.

Ward's injuries were received subsequent to the amendment of 1910 of the Federal Employer's Liability Act, and we do not understand that defendant challenges the correctness of the instructions of the court as to the proper damages in case Ward's cause of action survived. There being no conscious suffering, nor any expenses for medical attendance, the court limited the recovery, in case he was not instantly killed, to the lost earning capacity. There was testimony that Ward, though unconscious, lived some moments after being removed from the train. The court instructed the jury that, if they found that he lived an appreciable length of time after the injury, his cause of action survived. The defendant contends that, since Ward "never regained consciousness and had no conscious period of suffering, there is no reason why the action should * * * survive;" and that "the theory of a survival of an action is that there was a period of time during which the deceased could have brought an action in his own behalf." By that, we assume, it is meant that there should have been a physical possibility to begin an action in his behalf before his death. The authorities cited do not support the contention. In Kearney v. Boston & W. Ry. Co. 9 Cush. (Mass.) 108, a cause of action was held not to survive where "it is in evidence that there was only a momentary, spasmodic struggle, and the death instantaneous." In the later case of Hollenbeck v. Berkshire Ry. Co. 9 Cush. (Mass.) 478, Chief Justice Shaw says: "The accruing of the right of action does not depend upon intelligence, consciousness, or mental capacity of any kind, on the part of the sufferer." Chief Justice Bigelow in Bancroft v. Boston & W. Ry. Co. 11 Allen, 34, says: "The continuance of life after the accident, and not insensibility and want of consciousness, is the test by which to determine whether a cause of action survives." "If the intestate lived after he was struck, though the time might be brief, the cause of action survived." Tully v. Fitchburg R. Co. 134 Mass. 499. To the same effect is St. Louis, I. M. & S. Ry. Co. v. Dawson, 68 Ark. 1, 56 S. W. 46; Beeler v. Butte & London Copper Development Co. 41 Mont. 465, 110 Pac. 528; Kellow v. Central Iowa Ry. Co. 68 Iowa, 470, 23 N. W. 740, 27 N. W. 466, 56 Am. St. 858; Oliver v. Houghton County St. Ry. Co. 134 Mich. 367, 96 N. W. 434, 101 Am. St. 607, 3 Ann. Cas. 53; Ely v. Detroit United Ry. Co. 162 Mich. 287, 127 N. W. 259. The case of Dillon v. Great Northern Ry. Co. 38 Mont. 485, 100 Pac. 960, is not in point, for there was a stipulation that death was instantaneous. In the case of Kellow v. Central Iowa Ry. Co. supra, the jury answered in the affirmative the question: "Was the death of the deceased of that nature commonly known as instant death?" Nevertheless the court held that such finding did not determine that a cause of action did not accrue to him before his death. The deceased was on a railroad train that was wrecked; when found in the wreck he breathed, but died before he could be removed. The court said: "If he survived the injury but for a single moment, the cause of action accrued to him as certainly as it would have done if he had lived for a month or a year thereafter." One of defendant's witnesses testified that Ward breathed when taken from under the car; Holden's testimony was that, when he reached Ward after returning from riding the "kicked" car into the yard, which consumed about five minutes, he moaned and continued to breathe and live from three to five minutes longer. We think the testimony made the survival of Ward's cause of action a jury question.

If the jury found that Ward lived an appreciable length of time after the injury, and we conclude the evidence so warrants, it cannot be said that the damages are excessive.

Order affirmed.

I. T. WRIGHT and Another v. H. K. MAY.[1]

October 9, 1914.

Nos. 18,781—(261).

Auctioneer's license — act valid.

    The statutes of this state (G. S. 1913, §§ 6083 to 6088), providing that the county board or auditor may license any voter in its county as an auctioneer, and providing a penalty for selling property at auction without such license, violate neither section 2, art. 4, of the Constitution of the United States, section 1 of Fourteenth amendment to the Constitution of the United States, or section 2, art. 1, of the state Constitution, nor are they invalid as delegating legislative power to the county board or county auditor.

Action in the district court for Yellow Medicine county to recover $64.02 for services as auctioneers. From an order sustaining defendant's demurrer to the complaint, Qvale, J., plaintiffs appealed. Affirmed.

Johnson & Lende, for appellants.

T. J. Law, for respondent.

BUNN, J.

Plaintiffs, who were residents of South Dakota, performed services for defendant at his request as auctioneers. Defendant resides in Yellow Medicine county, Minnesota, and the services were performed in the sale in that county of personal property of defendant. This action was brought to recover $64.02, the agreed price of such services. A demurrer to the complaint was sustained and plaintiffs appealed.

The sole question involved is the constitutionality of G. S. 1913, §§ 6083 to 6088. Section 6083 provides that the county board or

[1] Reported in 149 N. W. 9.

Note.—Discrimination against nonresidents by statute or ordinance imposing license tax on auctioneers, see note in 40 L.R.A.(N.S.) 290.

auditor may license *any voter in its county* as an auctioneer. Section 6088 provides:

"If any person shall sell or attempt to sell any property at auction without being licensed as an auctioneer as herein provided, he shall be guilty of a misdemeanor."

It is plain that plaintiffs, being residents of South Dakota, were not and could not be licensed as auctioneers as provided by the act. If the statutory provisions referred to are constitutional, plaintiffs concede they are not entitled to recover for their services. If the provisions are unconstitutional, it is clear that the complaint states a cause of action.

The constitutional provisions which it is claimed the law violates are: Section 2, art. 4, of the Constitution of the United States, providing that the citizens of each state shall be entitled to all the privileges and immunities of citizens in the several states; section 1 of the Fourteenth amendment, providing that no state shall make or enforce any law which shall abridge the privileges or immunities of citizens of the United States, nor deny to any person within its jurisdiction the equal protection of the laws; section 2, art. 1, of the Constitution of Minnesota providing that "no member of this state * * * shall be * * * deprived of any of the rights or privileges secured to any citizen thereof."

The law in question denies the right of privilege of engaging in the occupation of auctioneer to all but voters. It excludes nonresidents of the state and residents who are aliens.

It is conceded that the business or calling of an auctioneer is one that is subject to legislative regulation. It is equally true, on the other hand, that the business is a lawful and useful one. City of Mankato v. Fowler, 32 Minn. 364, 20 N. W. 361; City of Duluth v. Krupp, 46 Minn. 435, 49 N. W. 235; Village of Minneota v. Martin, 124 Minn. 498, 145 N. W. 383. The right to regulate and license the business of auctioneering does not include the right to prohibit, but, as stated by Mr. Justice Holt in the case last cited, "it is nevertheless true that frequently individuals must subordinate their rights to a certain extent to the demands of the public welfare." As pointed out in the opinion in the Martin case, the occupation of the auctioneer, like that of the peddler, is liable to abuse, and in our large cities has become more or less of a nuisance, requiring regulation to the point of restraint.

Granting to the legislature, as we must, the right to regulate and control the vocation of auctioneering, to require a license and the payment of a substantial fee therefor, to limit the number of persons employed in such business, to require a bond, and an accounting, we see that regulation may go far without transgressing any constitutional safeguard of the rights of the individual. However the right of the individual to engage in the business may not be taken from him under the guise of regulation. Nor may the legislature authorize a license to one man and deny it to another, unless there is some reasonable ground for the distinction, unless, in short, licensing the second might reasonably result in harm to the public.

There are important distinctions between the business of an auctioneer and that of a peddler. The auctioneer does not sell his own goods; he acts, in making a sale at auction, primarily as the agent of the seller; when the property is struck off, he becomes also the agent of the purchaser, at least to the extent of binding him by his memorandum of sale. 4 Cyc. 1041. He is liable to the seller for a loss due to his negligence, or to his deviating from instructions, as well as for money paid him by purchasers. He is liable to a purchaser under certain circumstances. We can see good ground for refusing a license to a resident of another state in the difficulty that might be encountered in compelling him or his bondsmen to respond in case he rendered himself liable to either seller or purchaser. The case of State v. Nolan, 108 Minn. 170, 122 N. W. 255, in which an ordinance of the city of Hastings requiring a license of "itinerant merchants and transient vendors," exempting from its operation residents of the city, was held unconstitutional, is therefore not controlling.

Nor are other cases where laws have been held invalid that discriminated against nonresidents when there were plainly no evils to correct and no reason to apprehend injury to the public by freely permitting nonresidents to engage in the business within the state. Such are the authorities cited in the brief of plaintiff, and in the opinion in the Nolan case. We are unable to say that the legislature had no grounds for the discrimination made against nonresidents or that the classification was arbitrary and hold that the law does not, in this respect, violate the Federal Constitution or the Fourteenth amendment.

A more difficult question is whether the exclusion of resident aliens renders the act violative of the Fourteenth amendment or of section 2, art. 1, of the state Constitution. The Fourteenth amendment applies to aliens as well as citizens. A statute arbitrarily forbidding aliens to engage in ordinary kinds of business to earn their living would be unconstitutional. Yick Wo v. Hopkins, 118 U. S. 356, 6 Sup. Ct. 1064, 30 L. ed. 220. But where the calling or occupation is one which, though lawful, is subject to abuse, and likely to become injurious to the community, there is good authority for holding that the state may limit it to its own citizens and deny the right to all others. Commonwealth v. Hana, 195 Mass. 262, 81 N. E. 149, 122 Am. St. 251, 11 Ann. Cas. 514, 11 L.R.A.(N.S.) 799, and note. In the case cited, the supreme court of Massachusetts upheld a law of that state restricting the granting of peddlers' licenses to citizens and those who have declared their intention to become such. In Tragreser v. Gray, 73 Md. 250, 20 Atl. 905, 9 L.R.A. 780, 25 Am. St. 587, it was held that a state could deny to persons not citizens of the United States the right to sell spirituous liquors within its borders. These cases are cited with approval in Patmore v. Pennsylvania, 232 U. S. 138, 34 Sup. Ct. 281, 58 L. ed. 539, in which it was held that a statute of Pennsylvania, making it unlawful for unnaturalized foreign born . residents to kill wild game, except in defense of person or property, and to that end making the possession of shot guns and rifles unlawful, was not unconstitutional under the due process and equal protection provisions of the Fourteenth amendment. Mr. Justice Holmes, after stating the right of the state to classify with reference to the evil to be prevented, said:

"The question therefore narrows itself to whether this court can say that the legislature of Pennsylvania was not warranted in assuming as its premise for the law that resident unnaturalized aliens were the peculiar source of the evil that it desired to prevent. * * * Obviously the question so stated is one of local experience on which this court ought to be very slow to declare that the state legislature was wrong in its facts. * * * If we might trust popular speech in some states it was right—but it is enough that this court has no such knowledge of local conditions as to be able to say that it was manifestly wrong."

It is at this point that the court refers to Tragreser v. Gray and Commonwealth v. Hana.

There are authorities apparently to the contrary. Templar v. State Board of Examiners, 131 Mich. 254, 90 N. W. 1058, 100 Am. St. 610; State v. Montgomery, 94 Me. 192, 47 Atl. 165, 80 Am. St. 386. The former case held unconstitutional a law which prohibited issuing a barber's license to an alien, the latter a law like the one held valid in Commonwealth v. Hana.

While we are not able to see plainly that resident unnaturalized aliens were "the peculiar source of the evil" that the legislature desired to prevent when it enacted the law in question, nevertheless it may have been so. To again quote Mr. Justice Holmes:

"This court ought to be very slow to declare that the state legislature was wrong in its facts." "It is enough that this court has no such knowledge of local conditions as to be able to say that it was manifestly wrong." It may be that the evil or some part of it lay in the fact that foreigners, without the interest in the welfare of the state and county that the citizen has, perhaps irresponsible, were acting as auctioneers, to the harm of the public.

For a decision pointing out the evils which laws licensing and regulating the business have been enacted to correct, we refer to People v. Grant, 126 N. Y. 473, 27 N. E. 964. With some hesitation we reach the conclusion that denying to aliens the right to act as auctioneers does not contravene the due process or equal protection provisions of the Fourteenth amendment, or the provisions of article 1, section 2, of the state Constitution. This conclusion is at least not weakened by the fact that the law in question has stood without question for 50 years. It is strengthened by the idea that under the act an auctioneer may to a certain extent be considered as an administrative officer of the state. People v. Grant, supra. In this respect the cases upholding laws prescribing citizenship as a requirement for admission to the bar are analogous. See authorities cited in note to Commonwealth v. Hana, 11 L.R.A.(N.S.) 799. Our statute (G. S. 1913, § 4946) makes citizenship and residence in the state a prerequisite to the admission to the bar of graduates of law schools. We may also call attention to G. S. 1913, § 4964, providing that no certificate for a certified public accountant shall be granted to any person other than a citizen of the United States, or person who has in good faith declared his intention of becoming such citizen.

The claim is made that the law is unconstitutional because it delegates legislative power to the county board or auditor. The argument is based upon the use of the word "may." It is contended that the statute grants to the county board and the auditor the absolute and arbitrary power to license or refuse to license as an auctioneer any voter who applies and pays the fee. It is probably true that there is some discretion in the licensing officer, but this does not amount to a delegation of legislative power. It is rather an administrative or executive function, and a delegation of such functions does not violate the constitutional provision. 1 Dunnell, Minn. Digest, § 1600, and cases cited.

We hold that the law in question is valid, and that the demurrer was rightly sustained.

Order affirmed.

STATE ex rel. JAMES M. FURLONG v. HENRY McCOLL and Another.[1]

October 9, 1914.

Nos. 19,066—(298).

Municipal corporation — removal of subordinate.
  1. The St. Paul City Charter, by amendment effective June 1, 1914, gives

[1] Reported in 149 N. W. 11.

to heads of departments the right to remove subordinates by the methods prescribed in the chapter on civil service. This provision restricts the right of removal inherent in the power to appoint, and there is no right of removal except upon compliance with the requirements of the civil service chapter.

Classified civil service — removal of employee.

2. The amended charter contains a chapter regulating what is known as the classified civil service, provides that appointments to positions in the classified service shall be based on merit, and provides that the comptroller shall frame rules subject to the approval of the council, which rules shall provide "for discharge * * * only when the person * * * discharged * * * has been presented with the reasons for such discharge * * * specifically stated in writing, and has been allowed a reasonable time to reply thereto in writing." This provision is self-executing, and it became operative when the amended charter went into effect.

Same — construction of charter.

3. This provision does not contemplate that the officer sought to be removed shall be accorded a formal trial, but it does contemplate that removals shall only be for some cause touching the fitness and qualifications of the officer to discharge the duties of the office. The cause is to be determined by the removing officer, and his determination is quasi-judicial, and may be reviewed on *certiorari*. The fact that the removing officer does not assume to proceed under the provisions which the charter required him to follow, does not alter the case. The writ lies even if the action was arbitrary and without jurisdiction and void.

Relator can contest irregular removal.

4. The amended charter provides that "all persons holding positions in the classified service of the city as established by this charter, at the time it takes effect, shall retain their positions until discharged, reduced, promoted or transferred in accordance therewith." Under this provision the right of the relator to hold his office is confirmed, and it cannot be urged against his right to contest an irregular removal that he was over age when appointed.

Upon the relation of James M. Furlong, the district court for Ramsey county granted its writ of *certiorari* directed to Henry McColl, as commissioner of public safety of the city of St. Paul, and to the city of St. Paul, to review their action in dismissing relator. The respondent commissioner made return and the matter was heard before Brill, J., who quashed the writ. From the judgment entered pursuant to the order quashing the writ, relator appealed. Reversed.

Keller & Loomis, for appellant.

O. H. O'Neill, for respondents.

HALLAM, J.

Certiorari to review the action of the commissioner of public safety of the city of St. Paul in dismissing relator from the police force. The St. Paul charter in its present amended form went into effect June 1, 1914. The commissioner of public safety is the head of the police department. Relator was a lieutenant of police when the amended charter went into effect. On August 4, 1914, the commissioner undertook to remove the relator by sending him a written notice in the following terms: "You are hereby notified that on this day you were removed, to take effect the 5th day of August, 1914, from the police department of this city for incompetency and inefficiency."

This attempted removal was ineffective.

The charter contains a chapter regulating the "civil service" and dividing the civil service of the city into classified and unclassified. The classified service includes relator. The charter provides that "all persons holding positions in the classified service of the city as established by this charter, at the time it takes effect, shall retain their positions until discharged, reduced, promoted or transferred in accordance therewith." Section 104.

It then provides that "all heads of departments having the power of appointing assistants, subordinates or employees shall have power to remove said officers under the resolutions and by the methods provided in the chapter on civil service." Section 477.

Section 101 makes the city comptroller civil service commissioner, and he is authorized to frame rules and regulations for the classified service, to be approved by the common council. It provides numerous things which the rules must contain; among others they must provide:

"For discharge or reduction, either in rank or compensation, after appointment or promotion, only when the person to be discharged

or reduced has been presented with the reasons for such discharge
or reduction, specifically stated in writing, and has been allowed
a reasonable time to reply thereto in writing. The reasons and the
reply must be filed as a public record with the commissioner."
(Subd. L.)

No rules had been framed when this alleged removal was made.
Respondent commissioner contends that, until such rules were framed
and approved, the provisions of the civil service chapter were wholly
inoperative, and that the commissioner possessed in the meantime
an unrestricted power of removal as incident to his power to appoint.
It may be conceded that the power of removal is an incident of the
power to appoint unless it be otherwise provided. Parish v. City of
St. Paul, 84 Minn. 426, 87 N. W. 1124, 87 Am. St. 374. But this
charter does otherwise provide, for here the power of removal has
been in terms denied the commissioner, except in accordance with
the civil service chapter. If that chapter has not become operative,
the power of removal does not exist at all.

We think, however, that subdivision L of the civil service chapter
became operative regardless of the adoption of rules; in other words,
that the provisions of subdivision L are self-executing and were
operative as soon as the amended charter went into effect.

Much has been written in effort to furnish a test by which to
determine whether constitutions and charters imposing limitations
and conditions upon legislation are self-executing. No test easy of
application has yet been furnished. Whether a provision is self-
executing must be determined from a consideration both of the language used and of the intrinsic nature of the provision itself. In
general, it is said that prohibitory provisions in a Constitution or
charter are usually self-executing to the extent that anything done
in violation of them is void; so is any provision that indicates that
it was intended as a present enactment, complete in itself as defini-
tive legislation not contemplating subsequent legislation to carry it
into effect. It is not important that other legislation may be contemplated to supplement it. If the provision is to be operative
at all events, and the nature and extent of the rights conferred and
the liabilities imposed are fixed by it, so that they can be determined

by examination and construction of its terms, and the provision
itself furnishes a complete working rule of conduct, it will be held
self-executing, and the legislative authority will not be required to
go through the perfunctory process of passing it in order to give
it vitality. See Willis v. Mabon, 48 Minn. 140, 50 N. W. 1110,
16 L.R.A. 281, 31 Am. St. 626; Cleary v. Kincaid, 23 Idaho, 789,
131 Pac. 1117. In People v. Roberts, 148 N. Y. 360, 42 N. E.
1080, 31 L.R.A. 399, it was held that a constitutional provision requiring appointments to be made according to merit and fitness, to
be ascertained, so far as practical, by competitive examinations, and
providing that "laws shall be made to provide for the enforcement of
this section," was held self-executing, and it was said: "If the
legislature should repeal all the statutes and regulations on the subject of appointments in the civil service, the mandate of the Constitution would still remain and would so far execute itself as to
require the courts in a proper case to pronounce appointments made
without compliance with its requirements illegal." The matter may
not be free from doubt, but we are of the opinion that Subdivision L
is of the same class. It is absolutely mandatory in its terms. The
charter contemplates that it be supplemented by other rules, but, if
rules were adopted which wholly failed to embody this mandatory
requirement, there could be no doubt this provision would still be
in force. We think it was intended to be effective as soon as the
amended charter became operative. If this were not true, the power
of removal vested in heads of departments was wholly suspended
until such time as the comptroller should act in the framing of rules.
Any such construction would give the comptroller the power to sus-
pend indefinitely this power of removal by failure to frame any
rules at all. We cannot hold that such was the intent of the framers
of the charter. We hold that at the time the commissioner of public safety acted in this matter he had the power to remove the relator,
but that before he could effect such removal he was obliged to comply
with Subdivision L of section 101, and to present relator with the
reasons for such removal, specifically stated in writing, and to allow
him a reasonable time to reply thereto in writing. Not having done
so, his attempted removal of relator was void.

It is contended that relator has mistaken his remedy, and that a review of the action of the commissioner cannot be had by *certiorari*. It is well settled that *certiorari* lies to review the proceedings of municipal officers and commissions when their proceedings are judicial or quasi-judicial in their nature and there is no right of appeal. It is not always easy to determine whether the action of such municipal officer or commission is or is not judicial. In general, it may be said that to render their proceedings judicial or quasi-judicial, they must affect the rights or property of the citizen in a manner analogous to that in which they are affected by the proceedings of courts acting judicially. State v. Clough, 64 Minn. 378, 380, 67 N. W. 202. If the charter gave a right to a formal trial of charges before removal, there is no doubt that an order of removal would be a quasi-judicial act and that *certiorari* would lie. State v. Common Council of City of Duluth, 53 Minn. 238, 55 N. W. 118. If the commissioner has a right of removal, absolute, notwithstanding the facts or the explanations given, then the proceeding has no semblance of a judicial proceeding and cannot in this manner be reviewed. We must accordingly determine the character of the duty of the commissioner under these provisions of the charter.

Respondent contends that the power of the commissioner is absolute, and that the purpose of the provision which requires him to state the grounds for removal and to give the subordinate a chance to answer, is simply to put the commissioner on record. We think the provision is of more use than this. New York has for many years had a statute containing similar provisions for removal of subordinate municipal officers and employees. It was early held that, while these provisions gave no right to a formal trial, they were intended as a substantial limitation of the general power of removal, and that under these provisions removals can be made only for cause and the process for removal prescribed by statute must be pursued. The cause must be some delinquency or incapacity touching the fitness and the qualification of the officer to discharge the duties of the office; the removing officer may act upon his own knowledge of the facts or upon information furnished him by others, and, upon such knowledge and information and the showing made by the subordinate, he is to judge whether cause for removal exists. In so doing, he must exercise a discretion which the courts cannot control. Such discretion is not, however, unlimited, and it can only be exercised in the manner prescribed by law. People v. Board of Fire Commissioners, 72 N. Y. 445; People v. Thompson, 94 N. Y. 451, 462. The right of the removing officer is in substance "a right to judge" the subordinate, and upon the decision, if favorable, to remove him. People v. Campbell, 82 N. Y. 247, 252. See also Truitt v. Philadelphia, 221 Pa. St. 331, 70 Atl. 757.

We adopt and follow the foregoing as the correct construction of the provisions of the charter of the city of St. Paul, and hold that the charter provisions referred to contemplate removals only for cause, the determination of which is for the commissioner. It should follow on principle that the proceeding is quasi-judicial and that *certiorari* will lie to review this action, and we so hold.

People v. Brady, 166 N. Y. 44, 59 N. E. 701, is cited as authority for the proposition that *certiorari* will not lie. This case was decided in 1901. For 23 years the courts of New York had been reviewing the action of the removing authorities upon writs of *certiorari*. People v. Board of Fire Commissioners, 72 N. Y. 446; People v. Board of Fire Commrs. of New York, 73 N. Y. 437; People v. Campbell, 82 N. Y. 247; People v. Thompson, 94 N. Y. 451. In some of these cases the order of removal had been reversed. True, the right of review by *certiorari* had never been in terms determined, because the right had never been questioned. In the Brady case, the statute had been complied with. Notice had been given and explanations made. The court said: "The sole question to be determined upon this appeal is whether the learned court below had any power to interfere with the action of the defendant *when it appeared that he complied with the statute by filing a statement of his reasons in writing, which, upon their face, justified the removal after the relator had an opportunity for explanation.*" The conclusion reached was that the court "had no power under the circumstances of this case, to review the defendant's action in removing the relator," and while it is stated that the action of the defendant in removing the relator was not a judi-

127 M.—11.

cial proceeding in any legal sense, the court adds that "the writ of *certiorari* does not lie to review his action except, possibly, in cases where he has not complied with the law in filing written reasons and affording the subordinate an opportunity for explanation." It will be observed that the court, in terms, declined to hold that *certiorari* was not a proper remedy in a case like this, where the removing officer fails to accord to the person removed the right to be advised in writing of the charges against him and the right to answer the same.

We cannot hold that the fact that the commissioner did not assume to proceed under the provisions of Subdivision L of section 101 of the charter, affects the right to review his action by *certiorari*. It is not the procedure he did follow, but the procedure the law required him to follow, that determines the applicability of the proceeding. In all cases where the writ is invoked there is some alleged deviation from the requirements of the law. The extent of the deviation is not material. The writ lies even if the action was arbitrary and without jurisdiction and void. Hagerty v. Shedd, 75 N. H. 393, 74 Atl. 1055; Combs v. Dunlap, 19 Wis. 591.

Respondent contends that the relator was never legally entitled to hold the office of lieutenant of police, and therefore should not be allowed to question the legality of the proceedings to remove him. This contention is based on a charter provision, in force at the time of his appointment, that "no person shall be eligible to appointment as a police officer, policeman or patrolman who is not * * * under the age of 35 years," and relator was beyond that age when appointed. (Section 368, charter of 1900). We are of the opinion that the provisions of section 104 confirmed relator in his office, and that he was a lawful incumbent of the office at the time of his attempted removal.

Judgment reversed.

JOHN C. JEWISON v. EMIL DIEUDONNE and Others.[1]

October 16, 1914.

Nos. 18,703—(222).[2]

Customer not a bare licensee on premises.

1. Where plaintiff, a farmer, was injured by an automobile, while he was passing through the rear portion of a village automobile repair and farm implement shop in order to transact business in the front, the fact that he reached the place where he was injured by passing through a rubbish-strewn alley and the rear entrance of the building, did not, upon the facts of the case, constitute him a bare licensee so as to preclude him from invoking the rights of one upon premises by invitation.

Question for jury.

2. Whether an employee of the repair shop who was handling the automobile at the time of the accident was guilty of negligence, *held* for the jury.

Same — contributory negligence.

3. The question of negligence on plaintiff's part was also for the jury.

Partnership between defendants.

4. The fact that two of defendants were sued as copartners did not make a recovery necessarily depend upon the establishment of such relation.

Same.

5. Where there is a holding out of a partnership relation concerning the control of a place where business is transacted, and an invitation extended under such circumstances of publicity as to warrant the inference that a person, subsequently injured therein through the negligence of an employee of those in charge, must have had the right to believe that those extending the invitation were in control of the premises, a recovery may be had without regard to the actual existence of the partnership relation; liability in such case, however, depending not wholly upon the doctrine of estoppel nor that of *respondeat superior*, but upon the assumption of a definite status with reference to the property and a specific relation to the person injured, to which the law attaches direct and positive duties.

---

[1] Reported in 149 N. W. 20.　　　　[2] April, 1914, term calendar.

Note.—Liability of partnership for torts, see note in 51 L.R.A. 463.

Action in the district court for Waseca county to recover $25,750 for personal injury from an automobile owned and in the control of defendants. The case was tried before Childress, J., who when plaintiff rested denied the motion of defendants Dieudonne to dismiss the action as to them and at the close of the testimony their motion for a directed verdict. That part of the charge to the jury which referred to the subject of invitation to the plaintiff [see page 167] was as follows:

"If the plaintiff was a bare licensee upon the premises, the proprietor was not bound to exercise any care towards him except to refrain from wanton and wilful negligence. Was the plaintiff on the premises with the consent and invitation, express or implied, of the proprietor? If so, the proprietor was bound to exercise a reasonable degree of care to avoid injuring him. If you find from the evidence that it was plaintiff's habit and the habit and practice of others to go on to these premises as the plaintiff did, and this practice was known to the proprietor and he made no objection to it, and the plaintiff was there by reason of such custom, then you may find that the plaintiff was there by the invitation and consent of the proprietor. If you find such to be the case, then it was the proprietor's duty to exercise ordinary care under the circumstances as they existed for the safety of the plaintiff, and the test of such care should be what an ordinarily careful and prudent man engaged in work of that kind under the same or similar circumstances would have done."

The jury returned a verdict for $6,250 in favor of plaintiff. From an order denying their separate motions for judgment notwithstanding the verdict or for a new trial, defendants appealed. Affirmed.

J. P. Kyle and *P. McGovern,* for appellants.

L. D. Rogers and *Moonan & Moonan,* for respondents.

PHILIP E. BROWN, J.

Action against defendants Dieudonne as partners and defendant Nyquist as their alleged employee, to recover damages for personal injuries claimed to have been caused by the latter's negligence while plaintiff was in a shop conducted under the firm name of E. Dieudonne & Son. A verdict was returned against all defendants, and each of them appealed from an order denying their applications for judgment notwithstanding or for a new trial.

The accident occurred in the village of Janesville, in the afternoon of September 5, 1912. It is undisputed that in 1885 defendant Emil Dieudonne, to whom we will hereafter refer by his Christian name, opened a farm implement business on his own account and under his name, in the village mentioned, and so continued to operate it until 1900, in which year his son Eugene became of age and was associated with him therein, the firm thereafter being so conducted for the period of five years, under the name of E. Dieudonne & Son. Defendants claim that in 1905 this partnership was dissolved by Emil's withdrawal, the son continuing the business alone, and that since then the father has had no interest in the same, except as a creditor, and has taken no part in its management. It was conducted at all times in a building, owned by Emil but rented to Eugene after the dissolution, which fronted on the graded and paved main street of the village, the main entrance opening upon the sidewalk. The building was 42 feet wide and 90 feet deep, and situated in the center of the block, on a lot 140 feet deep, extending back to a 20-foot unpaved, ungraded, littered alley bisecting the block. Up to 1910 it had been used entirely for the sale and exhibition of farm machinery, having an office in front and a board floor, on a level with the sidewalk, running back its entire length. After the alleged dissolution and prior to 1910 the business of repairing automobiles was conducted in the rear part, and in the latter year all the board floor except about 37 feet in front was taken out, the level lowered two and one-half feet, and a cement floor substituted. The rise between the two floors was not boarded up and there were no permanent steps connecting them; a movable step, consisting of boxes being used for this purpose and being shoved under the board floor when space was needed. The area of the cement floor was divided into two compartments, one used as a garage and the other as a repair shop, with an entrance through a door opening to the rear. Nothing was kept for sale in these compartments, nor was either fitted up for the reception of customers, and the workmen there employed were engaged solely in repairing automobiles. Adjoining the office articles were kept for exhibition, including repairs for machinery.

On the day of the accident plaintiff, a farmer residing near Janesville, entered the building through the rear door, for the purpose of exchanging some mower repairs he had obtained on the previous day. Defendant Nyquist, an employee in the repair shop, was then engaged in the garage in repairing a defective automobile belonging to defendant Eugene, and, as plaintiff was about to enter, he backed the machine out through the door, noticing plaintiff and another man enter just after he came out. Stopping the automobile outside the entrance, but leaving the motor running very fast and without applying the brakes, on the supposition that the machine was not in gear, but not in fact knowing where the defect was, he proceeded with his work. He then stepped into the car and as he did so it started to move forward and, not being under control, ran into the garage. Plaintiff, who at this time was passing through the rear of the building in order to reach the office, was struck by the machine when near the temporary step and injured. He was familiar with the premises and their uses, and he and others had frequently entered the building through the rear for the purpose of transacting business in the front.

1. Defendants insist that plaintiff was a mere licensee, to whom no duty was owing except to refrain from wilfully injuring him while on the premises, and hence in no event is entitled to recover against any of them. We have set out the location and details with reference to the construction and use of the building, because these matters were elaborately covered by the testimony given on the trial and are also relied upon to establish the point mentioned. But it clearly appears that the building was such as is ordinarily used in the villages of the state for exhibition of farm implements and automobile repairs, and, taking into consideration the business transacted in it, its location, and the use made by patrons of the rear door, we cannot say that a customer like plaintiff, when entering from the rear, would have no better standing than a bare licensee. The fact that the alley was unimproved and strewn with rubbish such as is usually found in such places is not of importance; for farmers, who of necessity are often confronted with such conditions, would naturally be frequent

customers of the business conducted in the front of the building, and the persons in charge must have known that the condition of the alley would not, and did not, prevent them from using the rear entrance when more convenient than the front. Plaintiff was entitled to the rights of one who comes upon the premises of another by invitation. We find no reversible error in the instructions in this regard.

2. The further claims that, as a matter of law, defendant Nyquist's negligence was not established and that plaintiff should be held to have been negligent, are not sustained. We deem the recital of the facts stated concerning the manner in which the automobile was handled a sufficient refutation of the first, and the question of plaintiff's negligence was so plainly for the jury that the second does not merit discussion.

3. Defendants also contend that, because the Dieudonnes are sued as partners, unless such relationship was established no recovery can be sustained against any of defendants. Tort feasors, however, are jointly and severally liable, and G. S. 1913, § 7897, provides that "when two or more are sued as joint defendants, and the plaintiff fails to prove a joint cause of action against all, judgment may be given against those as to whom the cause of action is proved." See Miles v. Wann, 27 Minn. 56, 6 N. W. 56; Huot v. Wise, 27 Minn. 68, 6 N. W. 425; Fryklund v. Great Northern Ry. Co. 101 Minn. 37, 111 N. W. 727.

4. The complaint, in addition to alleging that defendants Dieudonne were copartners, charged that they conducted their business in the building wherein the accident occurred, and had done so for a long time previous thereto, inviting plaintiff to come there and trade, and that plaintiff had for a long time been a customer, entering their place of business under such invitation for the purpose of trading; and defendants admitted that, subsequently to the alleged dissolution of the partnership, the business was continued under the same firm name, this being permitted by Emil in order to give his son credit, and that with his knowledge and without protest advertisements over the name "E. Dieudonne & Son" were thereafter published in a newspaper of the village, soliciting patronage. Furthermore, it appeared that plaintiff had, for a number of years both before and after the dis-

solution, been a customer of the business, and no proof was made that
he had notice or knowledge of the dissolution. But the court, nevertheless, held and charged that plaintiff could recover only in case an
actual partnership relation existed, and defendants insisted that the
evidence does not warrant a finding of such, and further that, this being an action in tort, the instruction given by the court was correct.
We sustain defendants' first claim and hold the evidence insufficient
to establish a partnership. This conclusion necessitates consideration
of the second contention as to the correctness of the instruction. It
has long been settled that a merchant, who keeps his place of business
open to customers and invites and permits them to enter therein to
trade, owes them the duty of exercising reasonable care to keep the
premises safe for their ingress, progress and egress. Corrigan v. Elsinger, 81 Minn. 42, 83 N. W. 492. Under this rule, if the alleged
partnership had been established, Emil's liability would be clear. The
rule, however, has been further developed, and in the case cited it was
held that this duty was nondelegable and could not be shifted upon a
contractor engaged in making repairs, whose negligence caused the
accident. In Mastad v. Swedish Brethren, 83 Minn. 40, 85 N. W.
913, 53 L.R.A. 803, 85 Am. St. 446, it was held that a person having
the management and control of a public place of amusement, which he
invited the public to attend for pay, was bound to exercise reasonable
care to protect his patrons from assaults and insults from one becoming intoxicated with liquor which he there sold him. In Thompson
v. Lowell, L. & H. St. Ry. Co. 170 Mass. 577, 49 N. E. 913, 40 L.R.A.
345, 64 Am. St. 323, a street railway company was held liable for an
injury to a spectator, by reason of the negligent management of a
stage exhibition at a pleasure resort owned by it and on its line, though
the exhibition was conducted exclusively by an independent contract-
or hired by the company for that purpose, and though the latter was
not interested in the performance or its management, except insofar
as patrons were induced, through its advertisements, to use its line in
reaching the place of amusement. See also Richmond & M. Ry. Co.
v. Moore, 94 Va. 493, 27 S. E. 70, 37 L.R.A. 258. Considering the
rule as applied in the cases cited, to which many others of like effect
might be added, what is its underlying motive? Does liability result

because of ownership or actual occupation or management, or does it flow from *the invitation* extended to the public by one who has clothed himself with all *indicia* of the right to extend the same, coupled with apparent ownership or control? Defendants rely largely upon Smith v. Bailey, L. R. 2 Q. B. (1891) 403, and certain text books approving it, which criticise and refuse to follow Stables v. Ely, 1 Carr & P. 614, wherein it appears to have been held that one who allowed his cart to go out with his name on it held himself out to the world as liable for injuries occasioned by the negligence of anyone driving it. We agree that both the Smith case and the text authorities cited are sound in principle, but think they are not decisive of the present inquiry, if at all in point. In both the Smith and the Stables cases the accident happened on the highway, without the element of invitation and the duties incident thereto. In cases like the present one the gist of liability lies in the invitation, when extended under the circumstances indicated in the question. It does not rest wholly in estoppel but upon the assumption of a definite status—of control or ownership—with reference to the property, and a specific relation —involved in the invitation—towards the person injured; neither of which the defendants here attempt to deny. Nor, as we have seen, does it depend upon the doctrine of *respondeat superior*. See also Pollock, Torts (8th ed.) 74, 75. Where, as in this case, there is a holding out of a partnership relation concerning the control of a place where business is transacted, and an invitation to patronize extended under such circumstances of publicity as to warrant the inference that a person, subsequently injured therein through failure to exercise due care for his safety, must have had the right to believe that those extending the invitation were in control of the premises, liability results without regard to the existence of the partnership relation. Any other rule would enable those who have allowed invitations to be extended to the public in their names to escape liability for nonperformance of the duties they have thereby assumed by setting up ownership or control of the place in some irresponsible person.

The finding of the jury as to negligence and damages, when considered in connection with the undisputed facts, establishes liability on the part of defendant Emil, irrespective of the actual existence of the alleged copartnership, and there is nothing in the assignments of error showing sufficient prejudice to the rights of defendants to render this conclusion unjust. Hence the order is affirmed.

BUNN, J.

I dissent from the proposition that Emil Dieudonne is liable in this case. It was necessary, in my opinion, to establish a partnership in fact, and this the evidence failed to do. There was a "holding out," but my view is that this does not create a liability, under the facts here, either on the doctrine of estoppel or that of invitation. The fact that the firm name remained "E. Dieudonne & Son" had nothing to do with the happening of the accident to plaintiff. It does not appear that in going upon the premises, which were not inherently dangerous, plaintiff was relying upon the exercise of care on the part of the elder Dieudonne. The doctrine of invitation, upon which the majority opinion predicates liability, has no application, in my opinion, where the party sought to be held is not in fact in possession or control of the premises.

HALLAM, J.

I do not concur in the rule of liability adopted in paragraph four of the foregoing opinion. It must be remembered that Emil Dieudonne is sought to be held liable, not for any act of his own, but for the act of one employed by his son, Eugene Dieudonne. It appears to me there are only two possible theories on which Emil Dieudonne can be held liable for the act of his employee. One is that there was an actual partnership between himself and his son, the other that there was a partnership by "holding out." The opinion holds that the evidence is not sufficient to establish actual partnership. This leaves only the question of partnership by "holding out." Some courts have expressed doubts as to liability by holding out as a partner in any case of personal tort. It seems to me that such liability may exist, but that, like liability to contract creditors, it must rest on estoppel; that is, where a person is not a partner in fact, but merely permits himself to be held out as such, those, and only those, who have dealt with the firm in reliance upon his conduct can take advantage of it.

It should not be said that, because one not a partner is willing to assume liability to those who give credit in reliance on his name, he must thereby assume responsibility to the whole world to keep the partnership premises in safe condition. The doctrine of liability to the whole world by holding out was in a few early cases applied to liability on contract, but it has long since been repudiated. Bates, Partnership, §§ 92, 93, and cases cited. It is equally inapplicable to liability in tort. Lindley, Partnership (7th ed.) p. 79; Sherrod v. Langdon, 21 Iowa, 518; Maxwell v. Gibbs, 32 Iowa, 32.

If plaintiff had known Emil Dieudonne was not a partner, surely it could not be said Emil Dieudonne would be liable to him; nor could he be held liable to one who had no knowledge at all of his relations with the firm. Neither should he be held liable to one who knew of his conduct, unless such person has dealt with the firm on the faith of his conduct.

Such cases as bear on this subject have generally held that liability of one as a partner by holding out is more restricted in case of tort than contract. Shapard v. Hynes, 104 Fed. 449, 45 C. C. A. 271, 52 L.R.A. 675. The decision in this case establishes much the broader rule of liability in tort cases.

This case differs from the line of cases cited to which belong Corrigan v. Elsinger, 81 Minn. 42, 83 N. W. 492; Mastad v. Swedish Brethren, 83 Minn. 40, 85 N. W. 913, 53 L.R.A. 803, 85 Am. St. 446; Thompson v. Lowell, L. & H. St. Ry. Co. 170 Mass. 577, 49 N. E. 913, 40 L.R.A. 345, 64 Am. St. 323; Richmond & M. Ry. Co. v. Moore, 94 Va. 493, 27 S. E. 70, 37 L.R.A. 258. In all those cases was involved an invitation by the party in possession and control of premises, which involved the correlative obligation to keep the premises in safe condition, and to use due care to protect the invitee from injury at the hands of others. If defendant Emil Dieudonne had been in fact in possession and control of these premises, these cases would apply. But he was not. The case rests upon the claim that he held himself out as being in such possession and control in common with his son, and this claim in turn rests on evidence that he

held himself out as a partner.   The whole case accordingly falls back
on an alleged partnership by holding out, which it seems to me is
based only on estoppel.

The majority opinion uses the language that the liability of defendant Emil Dieudonne "does not rest wholly in estoppel," but I do not
understand this to mean that proof of an estoppel is considered essential to defendant Emil Dieudonne's liability.   The question whether
an estoppel was made out, the opinion does not at all discuss or decide.
I dissent from the principle established by the opinion, that one may
predicate liability in tort on an "invitation" upon which he has not
acted or relied.

FRANK J. RADEMACHER v. PIONEER TRACTOR MANUFACTURING COMPANY.[1]

October 16, 1914.

Nos. 18,778—(41).[2]

Fire — negligence of defendant — evidence.

   1. Plaintiff's intestate was killed by fire in defendant's factory. The
portion burned consisted of a frame building with a shingled roof. It was
the custom of defendant's employees to burn rags and greasy waste in the
heating furnace. Just before the fire the furnace was full and ready to be
fired. A few hours after the fire it was found to be empty. In the meantime smoke was seen indicating a fire in the furnace. The burning of the
rubbish usually emitted sparks. The fire started on the shingled roof. The
inside of the building was lined with tar paper, and in it were various
forms of combustible material. The evidence is sufficient to sustain a finding that the rubbish in the furnace was burned by defendant and emitted
sparks which caused the fire, and that the origin and spread of the fire was
due to negligence on the part of defendant.

[1] Reported in 149 N. W. 24.   [2] October, 1914, term calendar.

Note.—Presumption as to exercise of due care by person found to have been
killed through alleged negligence of another, see note in 16 L.R.A. 261.

Contradictory evidence — jury not bound to believe all.

2. After the fire deceased was found lying near his bench on the second floor of the burned building. He had been seen in various parts of the factory not long before. He was also seen at his bench a matter of a few minutes before the fire. He had left no unfinished work elsewhere. Escape was not easy for persons at or near his bench. It is presumed that he was exercising care for his own safety. The evidence sustains a finding that he was at the bench when the fire started. Two witnesses testified to seeing him elsewhere when the fire started, and one of them that he ran into the building when it was burning. The testimony of these witnesses is contradicted in many particulars and it contains some inherent improbabilities, and the jury were not bound to believe it.

Charge to jury.

3. The charge, taken as a whole, fairly submitted the case to the jury and contains no reversible error.

Action in the district court for Winona county by the administrator of the estate of Frank Rademacher, deceased, to recover $7,500 for the death of his intestate while in the employ of defendant. The answer alleged that there were no risks or dangers incident to decedent's employment which he did not know or appreciate, or were not readily observable, and that he assumed the risks and dangers as the result of which he came to his death. The case was tried before Snow, J., and a jury which returned a verdict for $5,000 in favor of plaintiff. From an order denying its motion for judgment in its favor notwithstanding the verdict or for a new trial, defendant appealed. Affirmed.

Bracelen & Cronin, for appellant.

Webber & Lees and *W. J. Smith,* for respondent.

HALLAM, J.

Plaintiff was employed as a millwright in one of the buildings in defendant's factory in Winona. On July 2, 1913, he lost his life in a fire in the factory. On trial of this action for damages, plaintiff, the administrator of his estate, had a verdict. Defendant moved in the alternative for judgment notwithstanding the verdict or for a new trial. Both being denied, defendant appealed.

The claim of plaintiff is, that this fire was caused by defendant's negligence, that deceased was entrapped while at work in a second-story room, and without fault on his part was overcome by fire and smoke. Defendant denies negligence and claims deceased was employed in another building when the fire broke out, and lost his life in a reckless attempt to get his tools from the burning building.

We see nothing in this case but questions of fact. They were fairly submitted to the jury, and the jury has settled them in favor of plaintiff.

1. First, as to the cause of fire. The factory consisted of two buildings 18 feet apart, a brick building and a two-story frame building. The frame building was burned. On the second story of this building was the workbench of deceased. The fire started on the shingled roof of this building. The weather was hot and dry. It was the custom of the defendant in the summer time to dump refuse and waste, some of it combustible, into the fire box of the heating furnace, and there burn it. A few hours before the fire the fire box was full of "old rags and * * * greasy stuff." Soon after the fire the smoke stack of the furnace was observed smoking and the fire box was empty. Some of the rubbish was of a character likely to emit sparks. The inside walls and ceiling or rafters of the second story were lined with tar paper; there is evidence of oily waste and other combustible material being upon this floor, and that oil, paint and gasolene were kept and used there. All these things facilitated the spread of the fire.

We think the jury might fairly infer that the rubbish in the furnace was burned and that the building took fire from sparks from the smoke stack. No other reasonably probable theory is suggested by the evidence.

There is no direct evidence as to who started the fire in the furnace, but, under the practice prevailing, it was due to be fired by some employee of defendant. The jury might infer that the usual course of business was followed and that the rubbish was fired by some person in defendant's employ.

The jury might well find that the accumulation of this combustible material for burning in this manner was, under the circumstances, negligence. They might also find that the interior construction of this shop, and the permission of combustible material about the factory at the time when the rubbish was liable to be fired, constituted negligence.

In other words, the evidence is sufficient to sustain a finding that the origin and rapid spread of the fire were due to negligence on the part of defendant. There is also evidence of negligence in failure to provide sufficient means of escape in case of fire.

2. The next question is whether this negligence of defendant was the cause of the death of deceased, or whether his death was due, as defendant claims, to his own rash act in running into this building for his tools after the fire was well under way. This resolves itself into a question whether deceased was at or in the vicinity of his workbench at the time of the breaking out of the fire. We think that the jury might find that he was.

There is no direct testimony on the part of plaintiff as to where deceased was at the time the fire broke out. He was subject to call from five or six foremen, and his presence anywhere in either building would not be strange. He had been seen about both buildings at times not long before the fire. Of course no one could trace his course. Early in the morning he had been directed to crate for shipment two separate pieces of machinery in the brick building. He had wholly finished one job and had not started on the other. His bench was his regular station and he had been seen there only a matter of minutes before the fire. After the fire, his body was found on the floor near his bench. There was evidently little time for escape for one near his bench after the fire was discovered. There was no stairway in this building. His bench was in the end of the building, remote from the regular exit, which consisted of a bridge across to the brick building, and which was the only easy means of escape. Other younger and more active men thereabout escaped only by jumping out of second-story windows or hanging out until help came. Deceased was a man 55 years old, very heavy, slow moving and not active, and if he was at his bench when the fire first broke out it is not strange that he failed to escape. Then, too, we have the presumption ever present that the deceased exercised due care to save himself from death, a presumption founded on a law of nature, the

universal and insistent instinct of self preservation.   Lewis v. Chicago, St. P. M. & O. Ry. Co. 111 Minn. 509, 511, 127 N. W. 180.

There is evidence of two witnesses that after the fire was under
way they saw deceased on the ground floor of the brick building.
One of these men testified that deceased ran out of the first floor door
of the brick building, then made some exclamation about his tools
which were at his bench and declared his purpose of going in to get
them.   The testimony of these two witnesses contained some inherent improbabilities and it is contradicted in many respects.
There was no practical way for deceased to go from the place where
these men said they saw him to the place where his body was found,
except by going up a flight of stairs, then across the bridge or gangway connecting the second stories of the two buildings, and down
through the frame building a distance of about 60 feet to the bench.
On this bridge or gangway a number of employees were fighting fire.
None of them saw deceased cross.   In fact it seems impossible, in
view of the rapidity with which the fire spread, that he could, after
the fire started, have gone from the place where these men testified
they saw him and reached the place where his body was found.   These
witnesses might have been mistaken as to the identity of the man they
saw.   One of them described this man as having a full beard.   Deceased had not a full beard.   Another employee, said by these witnesses to have been with deceased at the time, was in court but was
not called to corroborate them.   These are but a few of the circumstances that throw doubt on the testimony of these two witnesses.

We think the jury might reject the testimony of these witnesses
(Hawkins v. Sauby, 48 Minn. 69, 50 N. W. 1015), and might find
that deceased was at his bench when the fire started, and that he was
guilty of no negligence.

3. We find no reversible error in the charge.   It is contended the
court erred in submitting all of the claims of negligence above referred to to the jury.   We think there is some evidence to sustain
them all.   Some of these alleged acts of negligence, such as the
presence of paints, oils and gasolene about the shop, would not in
themselves be ground of action, and would not be negligence at all
except for other circumstances involving danger of fire.   But we

think the court made clear to the jury that they must find some acts of negligence which would be sufficient to cause the fire and the death of deceased. One or two isolated portions of the charge are now pointed out, which in themselves might seem to authorize recovery on less proof, but these were not excepted to on the trial or at all and are therefore not before this court for review.

Order affirmed.

MARY KLEIN v. JOHN FRERICHS.[1]

October 16, 1914.

Nos. 18,904—(26).

Trover and conversion — defense not proven.

1. In an action for conversion of a team, if plaintiff proves title, the defendant has not made out a defense by showing merely that the team, taken under a writ of replevin from plaintiff's husband, was afterwards returned because rebonded by him.

Unauthorized chattel mortgage — title to team.

2. The defendant claimed title through a chattel mortgage executed by plaintiff's husband, but failed to show any authority from plaintiff, either direct or by way of estoppel, to mortgage the team. Such being the case, no prejudicial error can be asserted by defendant on the immaterial issue whether the mortgage purported by its terms to include this team. If plaintiff proved ownership she was entitled to a verdict regardless of what was included in her husband's unauthorized mortgage.

Action in the district court for Jackson county. The facts are stated in the opinion. The case was tried before Quinn, J., and a jury which returned a verdict for $318 in favor of plaintiff. From an order denying his motion for a new trial, defendant appealed. Affirmed.

O. J. Finstad, for appellant.

Wilson Borst, for respondent.

1 Reported in 149 N. W. 2.
127 M.—12.

HOLT, J.

Plaintiff sued for the conversion of a team of mares, one five and the other six years old. The defense was that the mares belonged to her husband who mortgaged them when two years of age to defendant; that, after default in the chattel mortgage, defendant caused the mares to be taken from the possession of plaintiff's husband on a writ of replevin; that thereupon her husband rebonded the team and it was returned to the husband's possession and received and accepted by him and plaintiff; that thereafter in the trial of the replevin action plaintiff took part and assisted her husband in trying to establish the ownership of the mares in herself, but that the verdict was in favor of this defendant that he was entitled to the possession under his mortgage; and that said action is still pending. Defendant also pleaded facts which would tend to estop plaintiff from disputing his title under the mortgage. The appeal is from the order denying defendant a new trial after verdict against him.

Plaintiff's asserted title to the mares originated when they were very young colts. The evidence was that a few days after the one was foaled its mother died; the mother of the other refused to nourish it. Thereupon plaintiff's husband, the owner of the dams or these colts, told plaintiff that if she would bring up the colts on cows' milk she could have them. She accepted the offer, and thus raised the colts, being the mares in controversy. They remained on the farm occupied and cultivated all the time by her husband and family. They were fed from the products of the farm and were worked thereon the same as other similar stock.

There is no contention, and none could well be made, that plaintiff's ownership of the team, when seized under the writ of replevin in the action against her husband, was not for the jury. But defendant insists that the charge of the court was, in general, too favorable to plaintiff, so that the jury failed to reach a just result. It is probably true that the charge would have been better balanced and less open to a suspicion of partiality if less of the testimony and claims of plaintiff and her witnesses had been repeated therein. But on the issue of ownership we find no such over statement of the testimony favorable to plaintiff that we may say that prejudice resulted to defendant.

No defense was attempted under the allegations that plaintiff had concluded herself by her participation in, and the result of, the replevin suit. Nor does the evidence show her cause of action destroyed by a return and acceptance of the mares after the conversion. All that the record discloses is that, a few days after the mares were taken on the writ of replevin, they were rebonded by the defendant in that action, plaintiff's husband, and returned to him on the farm he and his family occupied. A return of the team under these circumstances did not, of itself and alone, absolve defendant from liability to plaintiff, were she the owner. But the court left to the jury to say whether she accepted and took it into her possession so as to defeat a recovery. In that connection the court stated that the return by defendant to plaintiff should be "free and clear from any obligation or claim of the husband's or any other person's." This statement is not accurate, for it is plain that if her husband, or some one else, had a claim against the mares previous to defendant's taking under the writ, he was not to redeliver them free from such claim. But we deem the misstatement of no consequence. The return was not a voluntary act of defendant undoing the wrong done to plaintiff's property rights. The law substituted the bond for the property and in consequence thereof the mares were returned. The evidence in reality made no issue of a return to and acceptance by plaintiff of the property taken under the writ, so that the inaccuracy in the charge of the court cannot be reversible error, even if it should not be passed by as one of those unintentional slips of the tongue which sometimes find place in an unwritten charge and upon which error cannot be predicated unless the court's attention was directed thereto at the time.

The defense of estoppel was not submitted to the jury. No fault is found because thereof. Nor could there be. There was no evidence that plaintiff knew of the chattel mortgage until long after it was given, and no testimony whatever that she ever consented that her property be included therein, or ever knew that it purported to cover the team in question. If she owned the same, the husband's unauthorized mortgage thereon did not affect her ownership in the least.   Unless she proved ownership she would fail even if the mortgage did not include this team.   Under this situation it became wholly immaterial whether the mortgage covered either mare.   McCarvel v. Phenix Ins. Co. 64 Minn. 193, 66 N. W. 367.   Therefore no reversible error can be predicated upon the reception of certain testimony that Henry Frerichs, one of the mortgagees in the chattel mortgage under which defendant claims title, was informed, when making a list of the property to be mortgaged, that plaintiff owned the animals in controversy.   The submission of the question whether the mortgage given by plaintiff's husband in terms embraced this team was giving the defendant an unwarranted chance to win.   But that aside, had the question been in the case properly, we think, there was no error in the admission of the testimony referred to.

We find no prejudicial error which warrants a reversal.

Order affirmed.

FRANK F. SEAMAN v. MINNEAPOLIS & RAINY RIVER RAILWAY COMPANY.

J. C. SULLIVAN and Another v. MINNEAPOLIS & RAINY RIVER RAILWAY COMPANY.[1]

October 23, 1914.[2]

Nos. 18,666, 18,667—(196, 197).

Case followed.

1. Decision in Sullivan v. Minneapolis & R. R. Ry. Co. 121 Minn. 488, adhered to.

Discrimination in freight rates.

2. Contracts made prior to statutory rate regulation *held* no justification for downward departure from freight tariffs thereafter established, whereby

plaintiffs, shippers who were charged with the legal rates for the same services, were discriminated against.

Subsequent payment by shipper not a defense to action.

3. The favored shipper's alleged payment to defendant of the difference between the discriminatory rate and the regular tariff, after the discriminations complained of had occurred, *held* no defense against the disfavored shipper's right to recover.

Competitive business essential to recovery.

4. Business competition is essential to a recovery of rate differentials by a shipper who is discriminated against, where no proof is made of damage other than the difference in the rates charged.

Same — evidence.

5. Evidence *held* to show business competition, between plaintiff Seaman and a favored shipper, within the rule requiring such competition where rate differentials are sought to be recovered, but the contrary was established in the Sullivan case.

Computation of rate differentials.

6. Rate differentials allowed as damages for discriminations in freight charges must be computed upon the basis of equal tonnage, but such discriminations should be considered with reference to a reasonable time before and after the disfavored shipment, and hence may arise from shipments on different dates.

Interstate commerce.

7. Under the facts disclosed, plaintiff Seaman's shipments were, to a considerable extent not precisely ascertainable, interstate commerce, to which the Federal rule of damages applied.

Two actions in the district court for Itasca county against defendant railway company to recover $4,500 and $5,366, respectively, for unlawful discrimination in freight rates. The facts are stated in the opinion. The cases were tried before Stanton, J., who at the close of the testimony in the Seaman case denied defendant's motion to dismiss the action and in each case denied defendant's motion to direct a verdict in its favor. The jury returned a verdict for $3,445.24 in favor of plaintiff Seaman and for $5,650.43 in behalf of plaintiffs Sullivan, Kolliner and Irvine, copartners under the name of J. J. J. Log & Cedar Co. From orders denying its motions for judgment in its favor notwithstanding the verdicts or for new trials, defendant appealed. Reversed on both appeals, with directions to reduce the amount of the verdict in the Sullivan case to nominal damages.

Powell & Simpson and *Ernest C. Carman,* for appellants.

George H. Spear, for respondents.

PHILIP E. BROWN, J.

Separate actions to recover for unlawful discriminations in freight rates. After verdict for plaintiff in each, defendant appealed from orders denying its alternative motions for judgment or new trial.

The substance of the complaint in the Sullivan case is stated in the opinion (121 Minn. 488, 142 N. W. 3, 45 L.R.A.[N.S.] 612) sustaining it on demurrer, and like averments appear in the Seaman case, except that no claim is made therein for a recovery because of defendant's free hauling of lumbering supplies for others. The facts proved in the two cases are sufficiently similar to render joint consideration desirable.

1. Plaintiffs offered no evidence in either case of damages, other than the difference between the schedule rate paid by them and the less rate allowed the favored shipper. Since the decision in the Sullivan case, supra, the Supreme Court of the United States, in Pennsylvania R. Co. v. International Coal Mining Co. 230 U. S. 184, 33 Sup. Ct. 893, 57 L. ed. 1446, has held that payment by a carrier to one shipper of an unlawful rebate gives another shipper, not so favored, no right of action under the Interstate Commerce Act to recover like rebates on his shipments, nor any right to recover at all in the absence of other evidence of damages. We concede that this decision cannot be reconciled with ours. In the Sullivan case we are urged, on the one hand, to adhere to our determination there reached, both under the doctrine of the law of the case and on the ground that our decision is correct, while, on the other hand, we are asked to recede therefrom because its fallacy is demonstrated by the Federal case cited.

If defendant's contention be correct, the rule adopted should be abrogated. Defendant claims in this connection that, notwithstanding the statement to the contrary in the Sullivan decision, our rate-regulating statutes do provide a civil remedy for discrimination in rates, which was overlooked both by court and counsel on the former appeal, and to substantiate this contention quotes the latter part of R. L. 1905, § 1986, as follows:

"Any common carrier or warehouseman who shall do or cause to be done any act in this chapter forbidden, or fail to do any act therein enjoined, or who shall aid or abet in any such act or neglect, shall be liable in damages to any person injured thereby; and in any action for such damages the plaintiff, if he recover, shall be allowed by the court a reasonable attorney's fee, to be taxed and allowed in addition to statutory costs."

But the first part of this section reading:

"Nothing in this chapter shall be construed to abridge or limit the duties and liabilities of common carriers or warehousemen, or the remedies now existing at common law or by statute, and the provisions of this chapter are in addition thereto," nullifies the force of the contention and clearly indicates not only that the legislature had in mind the existence of common-law liability and remedy, but intended to preserve them in addition to those created by the statute.

We have given the opinion in the Federal case such careful attention as is due all declarations emanating from that high court. The decision, however, was reached only after reargument, reverses the determinations of both the circuit court and the circuit court of appeals, and the opinion failed to convince Mr. Justice Pitney, as is evidenced by his vigorous dissent. It is also in conflict with the decisions of many other able courts. The law is not an exact science, differences of opinion are inevitable, and counsel have not heretofore claimed or conceded infallibility for the decisions of any court. Our previous convictions are strengthened by the fact that, in Texas & P. R. Co. v. Interstate Commerce Com. 162 U. S. 199, 233, 16 Sup. Ct. 80, 40 L. ed. 940, the court with which we differ declared, with reference to passenger rates:

"Nor is there any legal injustice in one person procuring a particular service cheaper than another," and again, in Parsons v. Chicago & N. W. R. Co. 167 U. S. 447, 17 Sup. Ct. 887, 42 L. ed. 231, one of the mainstays of the decision in 230 U. S. 184, 201, 33 Sup. Ct. 893, 57 L. ed. 1446, that where a reasonable freight rate is charged a person he has no right to complain because another is given a smaller rate; though, in the case under discussion, conceding the holding of Interstate Commerce Com. v. Baltimore & O. R. Co. 145 U. S. 263, 275, 12 Sup. Ct. 844, 36 L. ed. 699, that prior to congressional action "the weight of authority in this country was in favor of an equality of charge to all persons for similar services."

Cogent reasons, we think, exist for not subscribing to the doctrines of the cases reported in 162 U. S. 199, 16 Sup. Ct. 666, 40 L. ed. 940, and 167 U. S. 447, 17 Sup. Ct. 887, 42 L. ed. 231, above referred to. Unless current history is to be belied, the theory of their pronouncements laid the foundation for monopolistic fortunes, the greatest ever known, built up through systems of rebates where, as in the present cases, the same persons were often stockholders in the railroad company and its favored shippers. We are not prepared either to admit the soundness of these declarations, as applied to public service corporations, or, with the knowledge since acquired of their effect, to incorporate the doctrine thereby promulgated into the law of this state. Nor are we impressed with the view that the penalties imposed on carriers for violations of rebating statutes constitute a panacea for rebating evils or are, as stated in 230 U. S. 206, 33 Sup. Ct. 893, 57 L. ed. 1446, "a terror to evil doers." Experience, we think, has proved the contrary, and, curiously, in the same case where this statement is made it appeared that defendant had "made a practice of paying rebates" both to plaintiff and other shippers.

The former opinion is adhered to.

2. Defendant's line is about 70 miles long and located wholly in Itasca county. It was originally constructed by the Itasca Lumber Co., an Illinois corporation owning tributary timber lands, as a private logging railway. In 1904 this corporation sold the road to defendant, a Minnesota railway corporation, which has since then operated it as a common carrier. When the sale was made it was agreed, as a part of the purchase price of the line, that defendant would thereafter transport the lumber company's logs at a specified rate, less than the tariff subsequently established, and at the same time, also as a part of the purchase price, defendant assumed a like contract theretofore existing between the Itasca Co. and the Deer River Co. Defendant seeks, under these contracts, to justify the discriminations

complained of; it being claimed that as such agreements were, when made, not contrary to statute or illegal, they have since continued lawful. The contention is not sustained.

"If one agrees to do a thing," says Mr. Parsons, "which it is lawful for him to do, and it becomes unlawful by an act of the legislature, the act avoids the promise." Parsons, Cont. (9th ed.) 827.

In Louisville & N. R. Co. v. Mottley, 219 U. S. 467, 31 Sup. Ct. 265, 55 L. ed. 297, 34 L.R.A.(N.S.) 671, it was held that an agreement by an interstate carrier to issue annual passes for life, in consideration of release of a claim for damages, though entered into prior to Federal regulation, was thereby rendered unenforcible.

The proposition that our rate legislation rendered these contracts inoperative, we consider too clear to require further discussion or citation of authority.

3. It appeared that the stockholders of the Itasca Co. and the Deer River Co. were the same persons. In December, 1911, after the alleged discriminations complained of, the state brought action against this defendant to recover taxes claimed to have been evaded under the contracts mentioned. Thereafter, and after the pending actions were commenced, defendant paid the state a large sum in settlement of its demand, and in connection therewith the Itasca Co. claims it paid defendant the difference between the freight charges actually paid by it, and also by the Deer River Co., and the tariff rates, including those for transporting the lumbering supplies carried free for the Itasca Co. This transaction is said to be a complete defense to each of these actions. If defendant had, in good faith, extended credit for the amount of the established tariff freight charges, and payment had been made pursuant thereto, a different question would be presented. But here plaintiffs' rights of action, if any, for defendant's unlawful acts, accrued prior to such payment, and could not be defeated by the expedient resorted to. The question of the making of this alleged payment should not have been submitted to the jury.

4. In the Sullivan case, while the complaint alleged the relation of competitors as between plaintiffs and the Itasca Co., the proof negatived the averment, and it affirmatively appeared from the uncontradicted testimony of one of plaintiffs that the logs shipped, for which

reparation in freight charges paid by plaintiffs was sought, were not plaintiffs' but the property of the Northland Pine Co., and were logged and shipped by the former under a contract with the latter, wherein it was provided that payment for the services to be rendered was to be based upon a stipulated compensation plus the established tariff rate. A majority of the court hold that the favored and disfavored shippers must have been competitors, in order to sustain a recovery for substantial damages, competition being deemed an essential ingredient of each of plaintiffs' causes of action. Wherefore, the absence of such having been established, damages of the kind here sought were disproved; which adversely disposes of plaintiffs' claim of the applicability of the doctrine of the law of the case. Defendant, however, owed the duty of charging all shippers the schedule rate, and its violation entitled plaintiffs to nominal damages.

5. Defendant's claim that business competition between plaintiff and the favored shipper was not established in the Seaman case cannot be sustained in point of fact; for both shippers were dealing in forest products in the same general market, shipping from practically the same place, and must be said to have been competitors within any reasonable meaning of the term.

However, on this record, defendant's claim that Seaman's shipments were, to a considerable extent, not precisely ascertainable interstate commerce, is sustained. While it appeared that no joint rates had been established by defendant, whose line was wholly within the state, and the Great Northern Railway Co., the connecting interstate carrier, and that cars going beyond defendant's terminal at Deer River were rebilled by the shipper over the latter road, the charges being paid to Deer River, yet the tracks of the two companies were connected, and a considerable portion of the shipments involved was loaded on defendant's line at the point of origin of the freight, in cars belonging to the Great Northern Co., obtained upon the shipper's requisition, for the purpose of transporting the products to predetermined destinations in other states, to which they went through without reloading. These facts bring the shipments in question within the holding of Texas & N. O. R. Co.

v. Sabine Tram Co. 227 U. S. 111, 33 Sup. Ct. 229, 57 L. ed. 442, and render applicable, to the exclusion of our own, the Federal rule of damages.

6. Rate differentials allowed as damages for discrimination in freight rates must be computed upon the basis of equal tonnage; but discriminations should be considered not merely with reference to the precise time of shipments, but to a reasonable time before and after the disfavored shipment; otherwise, if a discriminatory rate were allowed a shipper on shipments completed in July, another shipping in June or August would be remediless.

Orders reversed on both appeals, with directions to reduce the amount of the verdict in the Sullivan case to nominal damages.

On November 21, 1914, the following opinion was filed:

PER CURIAM:

In applications for reargument plaintiffs call attention, among other things, to the following statement in the opinion: "Rate differentials allowed as damages for discrimination in freight rates must be computed upon the basis of equal tonnage;" which it is claimed does not furnish a workable rule in either case, because as to some of the products they were charged full tariff rates on certain items and an arbitrary rate as to each unit of others, while the favored shipper received the same service at so much per car, which was less than the rates charged plaintiffs.

The applications are denied. We deem it advisable to say, however, that by "equal tonnage" it was not intended to always require proof of equal poundage or arbitrarily to establish weight as the standard of comparison, but merely to limit the recovery to the differentials on the same amount of service.

LOUIS NELSON v. SAMUEL HALLAND.[1]

October 23, 1914.

Nos. 18,774—(21).

Automobile — duty of driver when meeting horses.
    1. It is the duty of the person operating an automobile upon a public highway, when meeting a team of horses being driven thereon, to exercise reasonable care to avoid frightening the team, and, if necessary, to slow down or stop his car, as the situation presented may require.

Same — failure to give signal.
    2. The operator of the automobile is not relieved from this duty by the failure of the driver of the team to signal him to stop his car. Whether the failure to so signal will constitute contributory negligence will depend upon the facts presented in the particular case.

Verdict sustained by evidence.
    3. Evidence *held* to support the verdict.

Action in the district court for Clay county to recover $200. The case was tried before Nye, J., who denied defendant's motion to direct a verdict in his favor, and a jury which returned a verdict for $88 in favor of plaintiff. Defendant's motion for judgment notwithstanding the verdict or for a new trial was denied. From the judgment entered pursuant to the verdict, defendant appealed. Affirmed.

F. H. Peterson, for appellant.
Christian C. Dosland, for respondent.

BROWN, C. J.
    1. Plaintiff's team of horses was being driven along the highway by his son; defendant was operating his automobile upon the same

[1] Reported in 149 N. W. 194.

Note.—Duty and liability of operator of automobile with respect to horses encountered on the highway, see notes in 1 L.R.A.(N.S.) 233; 14 L.R.A.(N.S.) 251; 48 L.R.A.(N.S.) 946.

highway in an opposite direction. When the team and the automobile met, the horses became frightened, unmanageable, and ran out of the road into a shallow ditch extending parallel therewith, and one of the horses received such injuries from violent exertions to escape the automobile that he subsequently died. In this action to recover the value of the horse, defendant was charged with negligence in operating his car at an excessive rate of speed, and in making no effort, by stopping his car or otherwise, to avoid an accident, when he knew that the horses were frightened and likely to get beyond the control of the driver. Plaintiff had a verdict and defendant appealed.

The assignments of error challenge the sufficiency of the evidence to support the verdict.

The evidence tends to show that the highway in question is a straight level prairie road with shallow ditches on each side; that plaintiff's horses were ordinarily gentle, but on this occasion showed signs of fright at the automobile at a considerable distance before meeting it; that on approaching the car the driver reined the team partly out of the road; that defendant saw, or with reasonable care could have seen, that the horses were so frightened, notwithstanding which he proceeded at a high rate of speed past the team, without checking the car, or making any effort to avoid further fright to the horses; the horses were thus caused to plunge into the adjoining ditch in an effort to escape what to them seemed impending danger. It further appears that, at the time of the approach of the automobile and when the horses showed signs of fright, the driver made no sign to defendant to stop or slow up the automobile, but directed his efforts toward controlling his horses, which he was unable to do.

While there is some conflict in the evidence on some of the facts stated, we think, and so hold, that it was sufficient to sustain the jury in finding them substantially as outlined. And that the case thus made established the negligence charged seems quite clear. Defendant had the right to operate his automobile on the highway and was not an insurer against the fright of horses·passing over the road at the same time. He was charged with the exercise of reasonable care to avoid frightening them, and if necessary to prevent an accident and injury from such fright to slow down or stop his automobile. This duty or obligation is imposed by law upon any person operating an automobile upon the public streets or country roads (Ploetz v. Holt, 124 Minn. 169, 171, 144 N. W. 745; Pfeiffer v. Radke, 142 Wis. 512, 125 N. W. 934; Cumberland Tel. & Tel. Co. v. Yeiser, 141 Ky. 15, 131 S. W. 1049, 31 L.R.A.[N.S.] 1137), and must be performed whether the driver of the team signals the automobile operator to slow down or not. Chisty v. El-liott, 216 Ill. 31, 74 N. E. 1035, 1 L.R.A.(N.S.) 215, 108 Am. St. 196, 3 Ann. Cas. 487; Strand v. Grinnell Auto. Garage Co. 136 Iowa, 68, 113 N. W. 488. There is no rule of fixed liability in such case, for the question of negligence on the part of the operator of the automobile, and the failure of the driver of the team to signal, usually resolve themselves into issues of fact for the jury. Such is the situation in the case at bar. Whether defendant, on the evidence presented, exercised reasonable care to avoid injury to plaintiff's team, and whether the driver of the team contributed to the accident by failing to signal defendant to stop the car, were questions of fact and properly submitted to the jury.

It is further contended that the death of the horse was not shown to have been caused by the misconduct of defendant; in other words, that defendant's alleged failure to slow down or stop his car was the proximate cause of the death of the horse. We think that this question was also one for the jury. That the horse was badly fright-ened and violently exerted himself when the car approached is made clear by the evidence. It further appears that immediately after the occurrence the horse was found bleeding at the nose and mouth. The animal was taken to plaintiff's home, turned into the pasture, and thereafter within 24 hours died. The animal was ex-amined after death by a veterinary who found the lungs filled with blood, and he expressed an opinion that this condition was caused by a ruptured blood vessel, and that the rupture was brought about by the violent exertions of the horse at the time of the accident. The evidence made the question of proximate cause one for the jury. There was no suggestion that the horse was injured in any other manner.

Judgment affirmed.

STATE ex rel. CITY OF ST. PAUL v. ST. PAUL CITY RAILWAY COMPANY.[1]

October 23, 1914.

Nos. 18,826—(88).

Street railway — ordinance to build line valid.
1. An ordinance requiring defendant, a street railway corporation, to construct a new and additional car line, enacted under the authority reserved by the terms of the franchise granted to defendant, *held* not to violate any of the constitutional rights of defendant.

Public convenience — findings sustained by evidence.
2. The findings of the trial court that the proposed new line was justified by public necessity and convenience *held* sustained by the evidence.

Power of city to require double track.
3. Under the reserved authority of the city to order the construction of new lines of street railway, the city may direct whether the new line shall be a single or double track line; and defendant possesses under its franchise no vested right or option to determine the character of the line in this respect.

Upon the relation of the city of St. Paul the district court for Ramsey county granted its writ of *mandamus* requiring defendant to proceed and construct forthwith a double track line of street railway upon St. Clair street from West Seventh street to Oxford street, in the city of St. Paul, and when so constructed to operate cars thereon, or show cause why it had not done so. Defendant made return and answer to the writ and prayed that a peremptory writ be denied. The case was heard before Kelly, J., who made findings and ordered judgment granting relator a peremptory writ. From the judgment entered pursuant to the order for judgment, respondent appealed.

Affirmed.

N. M. Thygeson and *W. D. Dwyer,* for appellant.

O. H. O'Neill, for respondent.

1 Reported in 149 N. W. 195.

BROWN, C. J.

By ordinance No. 1227, defendant, a street railway corporation, was duly granted a franchise to construct and operate lines of street railway upon the streets of the city of St. Paul. The ordinance constitutes defendant's franchise. It was accepted by the company, and thereafter lines of railway were constructed upon streets designated in the ordinance, and defendant now operates its cars thereon. Section 18 of the ordinance expressly reserved to the city the right to order the construction and operation of new and additional lines upon streets other than those mentioned in the ordinance wherein sewers had been laid, and imposed upon the company the obligation to construct the same within one year from the date of the order. In May, 1910, the city council duly enacted ordinance No. 2905, by which the company was ordered and required to construct a new line upon St. Clair street from West Seventh to Oxford street. The defendant refused to comply with the order, and this proceeding in *mandamus* was commenced by the city to compel compliance therewith. Defendant interposed in justificatioh of its refusal (1) that there was no public necessity for the proposed new line, and that the ordinance requiring its construction was a violation of the state and Federal constitutional rights of defendant and therefore void; and (2) that, since the ordinance orders the construction of a double track line on the street in question, it deprives defendant of the option granted by its franchise to construct either a single or double track, and for this additional reason that it violates defendant's constitutional rights, both state and Federal, particular reference being made to the Fourteenth amendment and section 10 of article 1 of the Federal Constitution.

The cause was before us on a former appeal. 122 Minn. 163, 142 N. W. 136. That appeal was taken from an order sustaining a demurrer to that portion of defendant's answer setting forth the claim that the proposed new line was not justified by public interests. The facts are fully stated in the former opinion. We there held that, while the franchise ordinance and its acceptance by the company constituted a contract between the city and the company, section 18 thereof, reserving in the city the right to order the construction of new lines, should not be construed as vesting in the city arbitrary authority in the matter, and that the right of the city to so order new lines should be limited to such as were reasonably necessary for the public convenience. In other words, in construing the contract we applied the general rule applicable to all municipal regulations of public service corporations, namely, that of reasonableness to the exclusion of arbitrary action. The question whether the order for the new line was void as depriving defendant of its claimed option to construct a single or double track was not presented or considered on the former appeal. The cause was remanded, and the trial below proceeded in harmony with the views of the former opinion. The trial court found as a fact that there was reasonable public necessity for the proposed new line, and held further that defendant had no vested option to construct, in response to an order under section 18, a single or double track, and that the kind and character of track to be constructed was a matter within the discretion of the city council. Judgment was entered accordingly and defendant again appealed.

This appeal presents the questions: (1) Whether the finding of public necessity is sustained by the evidence; and (2) whether the court erred in holding that the city was within its rights in ordering the construction of a double track on the street in question.

1. The first question does not require extended discussion. The question whether public interests require an improvement of this kind is one largely of fact, and addressed primarily to the judgment and discretion of the city council, whose determination thereof will be interfered with by the courts only when arbitrary and clearly unreasonable. State v. St. Paul City Ry. Co. 117 Minn. 316, 135 N. W. 976, Ann. Cas. 1913D, 139. The question in this case was fully presented to the city council in the first instance, in the consideration of the propriety of enacting the ordinance requiring the new line, again to the district court in this proceeding, each tribunal concluding that the public interests justified the new line. Our examination of the evidence discloses nothing upon which to base a conclusion that the city council acted arbitrarily in the matter, or that the findings of the court affirming the action of the council are not supported by sufficient competent evidence. We have no alterna-

tive therefore but to sustain the ordinance, and we do so without discussion of the evidence. It is sufficient to say that we have examined
it with the result stated.

2. Section 1 of the ordinance granting to defendant its street car
franchise enacted as follows:

"Section 1. There is hereby granted to the St. Paul City Railway
Company, its successors and assigns, the authority, right and privilege to build, equip, maintain and operate street railway lines, *with
single or double tracks,* with all necessary sidetracks and switches,
poles, wires, conduits and appliances over and along the streets and
avenues in the city of St. Paul hereinafter mentioned, to wit:"

Following this general grant numerous streets and avenues of the
city are named as those upon which the company might lay its tracks
and operate its cars, designating also the time within which the lines
should be completed and the system in operation. Sections 2 to 17
inclusive define, with some particularity, the rights and obligations
of the respective parties, in respect to the operation of the street
cars, the care of the streets occupied by the company, and the authority of the city to regulate from time to time the conduct in the
respects stated therein. Section 18, as heretofore noted, reserves
to the city the right and authority to require new or extended car
lines to be constructed and operated by the company, and this proceeding is founded thereon.

The only question upon this branch of the case is whether the option given to the company by section 1 to construct a single or double
track, extends by necessary implication to new lines or extensions
ordered by the city under section 18. We think, and so hold, that
the intention of this contract was to vest in the company the right to
elect whether to install a single or double track system of street railway under the franchise, and to vest also in the city, by section 18,
the right to order such extensions as would conform generally to the
system adopted by the company. The system so adopted by the company was a double track, and it thus extends, for the most part, at
least as to all principal lines, throughout the city. And it seems fairly clear that in ordering a new line which conforms to that general
system the council did not exceed the authority possessed by it un-

der section 18. It follows that none of the constitutional rights of defendant, either state or Federal, have been invaded and the judgment appealed from must be affirmed.

Judgment affirmed.

BUNN, J., took no part.

LAMPERT LUMBER COMPANY v. MINNEAPOLIS & ST. LOUIS RAILROAD COMPANY.[1]

October 23, 1914.

Nos. 18,831—(74).

Carrier — evidence to explain bill of lading.

Upon an issue as to the amount of coal delivered to a carrier for transportation, testimony of competent witnesses is admissible to prove that figures in the weight column of the bill of lading are trade abbreviations.

Action in the municipal court of Minneapolis to recover $13.90. The answer was a general denial. The case was tried before Montgomery, J., who directed a verdict in favor of defendant. From an order denying its motion for a new trial, plaintiff appealed. Reversed.

Kerr, Fowler, Ware & Furber, for appellant.
W. H. Bremner and *F. M. Miner,* for respondent.

PHILIP E. BROWN, J.

Action to recover from defendant, the last of several connecting carriers, the value of part of a carload of coal claimed to have been lost in transit, and the freight charges paid thereon.

On the trial plaintiff proved defendant's delivery of the car to it, and payment of tariff charges on 60,000 pounds, although it contained only 51,700. In order to show the net pounds received by

[1] Reported in 149 N. W. 133.

the initial carrier, plaintiff offered and the court received in evidence a standard form of bill of lading issued by it, wherein the load was described as "Lump Coal," and its weight as

"Gross 818
"Tare 318
"Net   600"

This instrument constituted an important item in making out plaintiff's case, as it evidenced the receipt of the coal by the first carrier and the agreement of affreightment, and constituted the contract between plaintiff and all carriers participating in the transportation. If it be read understandingly and the figures quoted be interpreted in accordance with plaintiff's claims, then the burden of proof devolved upon defendant to establish that the loss did not result from a cause for which it was responsible. 1 Dunnell, Minn. Dig. § 1356, 101 Am. St. 396b. Plaintiff offered to show by competent witnesses that these figures were abbreviations for hundred weight. The court, however, excluded the testimony, and directed a verdict for defendant on the ground that plaintiff had failed to prove the amount of coal delivered to the initial carrier. This was error. The rejected evidence was competent to show that the figures were mere trade abbreviations, having a recognized meaning. Maurin v. Lyon, 69 Minn. 257, 72 N. W. 72, 65 Am. St. 568. With this evidence in, plaintiff's *prima facie* case would have been made out.

Order reversed.

BETTY MARCUS and Another v. NATIONAL COUNCIL OF KNIGHTS AND LADIES OF SECURITY.[1]

October 23, 1914.

Nos. 18,876—(22).

Mutual benefit insurance — issues involved.
  1. The pleadings in this case raise the question of waiver of nonpayment

1 Reported in 149 N. W. 197.

of assessments, of waiver of a law of the order requiring members of a dissolved council to take certain steps to preserve their membership, and waiver of proofs of death.

Expulsion of member — burden of proof.

2. Defendant notified deceased that she was expelled from membership and her certificate cancelled, and that no further assessments would be received from her. The burden is on the defendant to prove that its repudiation of its contract was rightful. Its assertion of due expulsion in its notice of repudiation of membership furnishes no evidence of expulsion, even though the plaintiff offers the notice of repudiation in evidence.

Same — tender of assessments.

3. After such notice, no further tender of assessments by deceased was necessary to keep her certificate in force. Her obligation to the defendant was not thereby discharged. The conduct of defendant simply waived payment of assessments at the time stipulated in the contract. Under such circumstances, if the member stands on the contract and seeks to enforce it, he must discharge his obligation of payment as a condition to such enforcement, and, should the society change its attitude and again recognize the contract, the member must continue to discharge the obligations of the contract if he would continue it in force.

Waiver by conduct.

4. The conduct of defendant in repudiating the contract of deceased relieved her from making application to join another council on dissolution of the council to which she belonged, and waived the requirement that plaintiffs make proofs of death and of their claim on blanks to be furnished by defendant.

Action by deceased not a bar to this action.

5. The bringing of an action by deceased for damages for breach of contract, in the absence of proof that judgment was entered or some benefit received by deceased or some detriment suffered by defendant, does not bar an action by the beneficiaries of deceased to recover under the term of the contract.

Action in the district court for Ramsey county to recover $2,000 upon defendant's policy or certificate of insurance upon the life of Getal Segal. The case was tried before Olin B. Lewis, J., and a jury which returned a verdict in favor of plaintiffs for the amount demanded. From an order denying its motion for judgment in its favor notwithstanding the verdict or for a new trial, defendant appealed. Affirmed.

William G. White, for appellant.
A. J. Hertz and *James E. Markham,* for respondents.

HALLAM, J.

1. This action is brought to recover the face of a beneficiary certificate issued by defendant to one Getal Segal. Defendant interposed an answer, an amended answer, and an amendment to the amended answer. The first amended answer alleged that in April, 1910, deceased was tried upon charges before the national executive committee of the order and was expelled from the order and her beneficiary certificate cancelled, and that she acquiesced in the judgment of expulsion. The amendment to the amended answer alleged that in April, 1910, the local council to which she belonged was dissolved and its charter forfeited; that the laws of the order provide that when a local council is dissolved, any member thereof desiring to retain his membership must within 60 days make application for a national council card, and present said card to some local council and be admitted as a member thereof; that deceased failed to do this; that after April, 1910, she paid no assessments; that the laws of the order provide for notice of proofs of death and of the claimant's rights upon blanks furnished by the national secretary of defendant, and that plaintiffs made no such proofs of death.

Plaintiffs replied, alleging that the charges preferred were false and were made for the purpose of avoiding defendant's obligation to deceased and to plaintiffs; that deceased was never permitted to answer said charges nor to be heard thereon, and that the alleged trial was arbitrary, unauthorized, oppressive and void; that defendant waived the provisions of the laws of the order requiring proofs of death or presentation of claim, and took and maintained the position that the contract of deceased was terminated by reason of the pretended expulsion.

The laws of the order do require the prompt monthly payment of assessments. It is admitted deceased paid none between April and the time of her death in November, 1911. They require a member of a dissolved council to take the steps alleged to preserve his membership. It is admitted that she did not do so. And they require proofs of death and of claimant's claim upon blanks furnished by defendant. It is admitted no proofs were made. Plaintiffs claim the facts alleged in the answer constitute a waiver of all of these provisions. Defendant contends that they are not pleaded as a waiver of any default, except that arising from failure to make proofs of death. We do not agree with this contention. The allegation of the unauthorized repudiation of the contract is general and may be regarded as responsive to all the defenses alleged in the answer.

2. The failure of deceased to pay any assessments from April, 1910, to the time of her death, would naturally forfeit her membership unless excused. It appears, however, that after the alleged trial, and on April 22, 1910, the national secretary of the order notified deceased that she had been expelled and advised her that no further payments would be received from her. Although this alleged expulsion lay at the bottom of all the controversies between these parties, and was the only defense alleged in the original answer, strangely enough, no attempt was made to prove it on the trial.

Defendant contends the burden is on plaintiffs to show that its refusal to recognize the membership of deceased was wrongful. The law is otherwise. Forfeitures are never presumed and must be proved by the person asserting them. Cornfield v. Order Brith Abraham, 64 Minn. 261, 66 N. W. 970; Kulberg v. National Council of Knights and Ladies of Security, 124 Minn. 437, 145 N. W. 120.

Defendant further contends that inasmuch as the letters notifying deceased of the repudiation of her membership were offered in evidence by plaintiffs, plaintiffs are bound by the statements made in them that deceased was duly expelled from the order and her certificate cancelled. Clearly this is not the law. The expulsion of deceased cannot be proved by defendant's assertion of it. Where an insurance society repudiates the contract of one of its members and makes a declaration in writing of its repudiation, its own assertion in such writing that its conduct was rightful, furnishes no evidence in its favor to that effect.

The result is, the court is obliged to regard the refusal of defendant to accept further payments from deceased as wrongful, and as an inexcusable breach of the contract between them.

3. The defendant having clearly indicated its intention to refuse to receive from deceased any further assessments or to recognize her membership in any manner, the subsequent tender of assessments was not necessary to keep her certificate in force. Ibs v. Hartford Life Ins. Co. 121 Minn. 310, 319, 141 N. W. 289; Kulberg v. National Council of Knights and Ladies of Security, 124 Minn. 437, 145 N. W. 120; Guetzkow v. Michigan Mut. Life Ins. Co. 105 Wis. 448, 81 N. W. 652; Byram v. Sovereign Camp, Woodmen of World, 108 Iowa, 430, 79 N. W. 144, 75 Am. St. 265.

Defendant's counsel argues at length that the governing body of the defendant society had no power to waive the payment of assessments by deceased. He predicates his argument on the assumption that the effect of such waiver was to permanently excuse deceased from future payment of assessments, and nevertheless keep her certificate in force. If the effect were as counsel assumes, then his argument would doubtless be well founded. But it is not. The action of the society did not relieve the deceased of her obligation to pay assessments. Even repeated tenders of all assessments as they became due would not affect this result. Tender never discharges an obligation. It simply excuses the person owing it from the consequences of failure to make payment at the time the contract requires. The declaration of a beneficiary society that it will not receive further payments from a member, simply excuses the member from payment at the time and in the manner required by his contract, but if he stands on his contract and seeks to enforce it, he must discharge his obligation of payment as a condition to such enforcement. If the member acquiesces in the repudiation of the contract by the society, then he loses all rights under it, for a repudiation of a contract by one party, acquiesced in by the other, is tantamount to a rescission. See Marcus v. National Council of Knights and Ladies of Security, 123 Minn. 145, 143 N. W. 265. On the other hand, should the society change its attitude and again recognize the contract as a valid and subsisting one, then the member must continue to discharge the obligations it imposes on him if he would have it continue

in force. Langnecker v. Trustees of Grand Lodge A. O. U. W. of
Wis. 111 Wis. 279, 283, 87 N. W. 293, 55 L.R.A. 185, 87 Am. St.
860. If the beneficiaries of the member sue on the contract after
the member's death, they must make good the member's obligations
by payment of all dues and assessments, or suffer a deduction of the
amount thereof from their recovery. Kulberg v. National Council
of Knights and Ladies of Security, 124 Minn. 437, 145 N. W. 120.
In this view of the nature and effect of the conduct of defendant's
officers as a waiver, there can be no more doubt of their power to waive
prompt payment in such a case as this than in a case where payment
is made one day after it becomes due.

4. This conduct in attempting to terminate her membership likewise excused deceased from attempting to comply with the law of the
order which requires a member, when his council is dissolved, to
make application within 60 days for a transfer card to some other
council and obtain admittance as a member thereof.

The conduct of defendant in repudiating the membership of deceased likewise excused the default of plaintiffs in failing to submit
proofs of death. It is well settled that a disavowal of liability by
the insurer, on other grounds, after death of the alleged member,
dispenses with the necessity of making proofs of death. 2 Bacon,
Ben. Soc. & Life Ins. § 413; Alexander v. Grand Lodge, A. O. U.
W. 119 Iowa, 519, 93 N. W. 508. It is likewise the law that, if the
insurer during the lifetime of the insured declares a forfeiture of
the insurance contract and continues its disavowal of the contract
up to the time of death of the deceased, such action on its part
amounts to a waiver of the provisions of the contract requiring
proofs of death. Equitable Life Assur. Soc. v. Winning, 58 Fed.
541, 7 C. C. A. 359.

5. Copy of a summons and complaint was left with the insurance
commissioner purporting to be in a suit brought by Getal Segal
against this defendant to recover damages for breach of the insurance contract. Defendant contends that this conduct was an election by her to choose that particular remedy and to bar the right of
recovery on the part of the plaintiffs in the present action. The jury,
under instructions from the trial court, found that no action was

ever in fact commenced. Whether the evidence sustains this finding we need not stop to inquire, for if such an action was commenced it was no bar to this one. We are not favored with the facts as to the disposition made of this action claimed to have been commenced over four years ago, but it is clear that we cannot assume either that it resulted in a judgment in favor of the plaintiff or that the plaintiff derived any benefit therefrom or defendant suffered any detriment. The rules governing cases of this sort are well settled. A person may have two courses open to him to redress a single wrong, but he can never have double redress. The two courses may be so inconsistent that the choice of one is an irrevocable waiver of the other as soon as the choice is made, as, where property is taken in proceedings instituted without jurisdiction, the owner may repudiate the proceeding or appear in it and assert his rights. The latter course waives beyond recall the right to question jurisdiction. Rheiner v. Union Depot, Street Ry. & T. Co. 31 Minn. 289, 17 N. W. 623. See Pederson v. Christofferson, 97 Minn. 491, 496, 106 N. W. 958. In order that the commencement of an action which is not prosecuted to judgment and which results in no benefit to plaintiff or detriment to defendant, shall have the effect to bar any other remedy the plaintiff may have, the remedies must proceed from opposite and irreconcilable claims of right, and must be so opposite or inconsistent that a party cannot logically assume to follow one without renouncing the other. Bowen v. Mandeville, 95 N. Y. 237; Mills v. Parkhurst, 126 N. Y. 89, 26 N. E. 1041, 13 L.R.A. 472; Stier v. Harms, 154 Ill. 476, 40 N. E. 296; Patterson v. Swan, 9 Serg. & R. (Pa.) 16; Morris v. Rexford, 18 N. Y. 552, 557. But a party may have alternative remedies which are not so inconsistent. An example of this is the alternative right to bring action for damages for breach of contract or demand full or specific performance. These remedies are both predicated on the existence of the contract, and the mere commencement of one will not be a bar to the other. Connihan v. Thompson, 111 Mass. 270; Slaughter v. La Campagnie Francaises Des Cables Tel. 119 Fed. 588, 57 C. C. A. 19; see Bitzer v. Bobo, 39 Minn. 18, 38 N. W. 609; Spurr v. Home Ins. Co. 40 Minn. 424, 42 N. W. 206; Johnson v. Town of Clontarf, 98 Minn. 281, 108 N.

W. 521. This is the principle applicable to the facts of this case. The remedy on the contract to recover the amount of the insurance and that for damages for the breach of the contract are both in affirmance of the contract. They are alternative remedies but not inconsistent. Both cannot be carried to judgment and satisfaction, but the mere commencement or pendency of one is not a plea in bar in the other.

Order affirmed.

VICTOR CARLSON v. PETER SMITH, Jr.[1]

October 23, 1914.

Nos. 18,892—(50).

Assignment of judgment.

1. The statute providing for filing of assignments of judgments with the clerk of court, and for a docket entry thereof, affects the validity of assignments only as to subsequent purchasers and attaching creditors. As between the parties, an assignment of a judgment is valid without compliance with those formalities.

Finding sustained by evidence.

2. The evidence is sufficient to sustain a finding that a judgment against plaintiff and his co-surety was assigned to defendant.

Alias execution — presumption.

3. An original writ of execution must be returned before an *alias* writ can issue. Where the evidence shows the original writ returned and the *alias* writ issued on the same day, it will be presumed, in the absence of evidence to the contrary, that these acts were done in such order as to render both valid.

Execution sale — order of court — clerk's signature on copy.

4. No order of court is necessary for the issuance of an *alias* writ of execution.

The fact that the copy of the execution served on the judgment debtor does not bear the signature or seal of the clerk of the court, does not invalidate a sale of real estate made under the execution.

[1] Reported in 149 N. W. 199.

Same — failure to make return after sale.

   5. No formal levy is necessary to be made on real estate in order to sell the same on execution. Failure of the sheriff to make return after the execution sale, does not invalidate the sale.

Action in the district court of Hubbard county to determine adverse claims to certain real estate. The answer set up the judgment and execution sale mentioned at the beginning of the opinion and prayed that defendant be adjudged to be the owner of the property. The reply set up the payment of $1,000 by Schmidt to Mackey in full satisfaction of the judgment and thereafter the issue of an *alias* execution while the original execution was still unreturned and outstanding, and alleged that the execution sale in question was made upon such wrongful *alias* execution and was void. The case was tried before Stanton, J., who made findings and ordered judgment that defendant was the owner in fee of the real estate described free of any lien except the right of plaintiff to redeem the premises from the sheriff's sale in question within one year from April 20, 1912. From the judgment entered pursuant to the order for judgment, plaintiff appealed. Affirmed.

John L. Brown, for appellant.
Daniel De Laury, for respondent.

HALLAM, J.
Plaintiff Carlson and J. P. Schmidt were co-sureties on a bond to one Mackey. On August 5, 1911, Mackey procured a joint judgment against them for $1,184.17, and procured an execution and caused levy to be made upon the property of Schmidt. After some negotiations, Mackey agreed to accept $1,000 in settlement of his judgment. On February 29, 1912, J. P. Schmidt procured this amount and paid it over, and an assignment of the judgment was taken in the name of his son, the defendant Peter Smith, Jr. There is evidence that J. P. Schmidt directed that this assignment be made to defendant in payment for services rendered since defendant became of age. On March 1, 1912, the first execution was returned by the sheriff half satisfied, and on the same day a new execution was

issued and land of this plaintiff was sold thereunder to satisfy the remaining half of the judgment. Plaintiff brings this action to quiet title to the land sold, on the ground that the sale was void. The execution was in due form, due notice of sale was given, the sale was regularly conducted, and it is not questioned that as between himself and his co-surety plaintiff Carlson ought in justice to pay his share of this judgment, but some objections are raised to the procedure followed which, it is claimed, invalidate the sale. We consider these objections without merit.

1. It is contended that the answer did not allege facts sufficient to show that defendant had a valid lien upon this land. The point of the contention is, that the answer simply alleged that the assignment of the judgment was "filed in said proceeding," whereas, it is contended, it should be filed with the clerk and an entry thereof made in the docket. The statute provides that no assignment of a judgment shall be valid "as against a subsequent purchaser * * * in good faith for value, or against a creditor levying upon or attaching the same, unless it is filed with the clerk and an entry thereof made in the docket." G. S. 1913, § 7909. This statute in clear terms affects the validity of the assignment only as to such parties as are therein designated, that is, subsequent purchasers and attaching creditors. As between the parties to the judgment, an assignment is valid though not so filed and entered. Swanson v. Realization & Deb. Corp. 70 Minn. 380, 73 N. W. 165.

2. It is contended the facts show a payment of the judgment by J. P. Schmidt, and that it follows that the assignment of it to defendant was void. The court found that the judgment was "sold, assigned and transferred" to defendant. This signifies a purchase of the judgment for a consideration, and the evidence is sufficient to sustain this finding. We do not wish to be understood as inferring that the assignment would have been invalid if J. P. Schmidt had in fact paid the judgment against himself and his co-surety. Felton v. Bissel, 25 Minn. 15; Ankeny v. Moffett, 37 Minn. 109, 33 N. W. 320.

3. The next contention is that the *alias* writ was prematurely issued. The original writ was returned March first and the *alias* writ issued the same day. Doubtless the original writ must be returned

before the *alias* writ can issue, and the contention is that the law will not consider fractions of a day, that upon the facts stated the first writ is conclusively presumed to be an outstanding writ during the whole of the day of its return unless there is affirmative evidence to the contrary. We do not so understand the law. Acts required to be done in sequence may usually be done on the same day, and where they are so done it will be presumed, in the absence of evidence to the contrary, that they were done in such order as to render them both valid. Haven v. Foster, 14 Pick. (Mass.) 534, 548; Ivy v. Yancey, 129 Mo. 501, 509, 31 S. W. 937. The evidence in this case simply showing that the original writ was returned and the *alias* writ issued the same day, it will be presumed that these acts were done in the proper order, that is, that the original writ was first returned.

4. It is contended that proper formalities were not observed in the procurement of this *alias* writ. No particular formalities were required. No order of court was necessary. Johnson v. Huntington, 13 Conn. 47; Ex parte McManaman, 16 R. I. 358, 16 Atl. 148, 1 L.R.A. 561. The *alias* writ was under the seal of the court and subscribed by the clerk, as required by statute. G. S. 1913, § 7924. The copy served on the judgment debtor was not signed or sealed. This court has held that this omission does not invalidate the sale, and we are not disposed to depart from this rule. Duford v. Lewis, 43 Minn. 26, 44 N. W. 522.

5. It is urged that "no return of any levy was signed by said sheriff." No formal levy is necessary to be made on real estate. Hutchins v. Co. Commrs. of Carver County, 16 Minn. 1 (13); Duford v. Lewis, 43 Minn. 26, 44 N. W. 522. The sheriff must of course make a return after sale. G. S. 1913, § 7925. The record before us is not altogether clear, but it would appear that such a return was made in proper form and signed. However, we do not regard this as material in this case. Omission of an act of this sort required to be done by the sheriff after sale cannot reach back and avoid the sale. Millis v. Lombard, 32 Minn. 259, 20 N. W. 187.

Judgment affirmed.

BERTHA McKNIGHT v. MINNEAPOLIS STREET RAILWAY COMPANY.[1]

October 23, 1914.

Nos. 19,058—(23).

Judgment a bar to subsequent action.

1. A single and entire cause of action cannot be split up into several suits, and the judgment in a suit brought upon such cause of action is a bar to a second suit thereon, although the complaint in the second suit may set forth grounds for relief which were not set forth in the complaint in the first suit.

Negligence — basis of cause of action.

2. In suits based upon negligence, the cause of action is the violation of the ultimate duty to exercise due care that another may not suffer injury.

Judgment a bar to subsequent action.

3. A judgment, rendered in a suit brought by a passenger to recover for injuries sustained while alighting from a street car, is a bar to a subsequent suit brought by the same passenger against the same defendant to recover for the same injuries, although the particular acts of negligence charged may be different in the two suits, as the cause of action in both suits is the violation of the ultimate duty to afford safe egress from the car.

Action in the district court for Hennepin county to recover $25,-500 for personal injury received while a passenger upon one of defendant's street cars. The answer set up a former action between the parties upon the same cause of action wherein judgment was duly docketed, upon the merits thereof, against the plaintiff in this action in the sum of $71 and in favor of defendant. The case was tried before Hale, J., who made findings and ordered judgment dismissing the action. From an order denying her motion for a new trial, plaintiff appealed. Affirmed.

Francis B. Hart, for appellant.
John F. Dahl, for respondent.

[1] Reported in 149 N. W. 131.

TAYLOR, C.

Plaintiff was a passenger upon one of defendant's street cars and while alighting therefrom fell and was injured. She brought an action against defendant for damages, in which she charged that defendant caused the accident by suddenly and negligently closing the gates and starting the car while she was in the act of alighting. After a trial lasting several days the jury returned a verdict for defendant, and thereafter judgment was duly entered thereon in favor of defendant. Subsequently she brought the present action against the defendant for damages for the same injury, and in this action charged that the car was provided with a defective step and that she caught her foot on the defect in the step and fell in consequence thereof. The trial court held that the judgment in the first action barred a recovery in the present action, and the only question for decision is whether the trial court was correct in so holding.

In Thompson v. Myrick, 24 Minn. 4, decided in 1877, the court held that a judgment decides "every matter which pertains to the cause of action or defense set up in the action, or which is involved in the measure of relief to which the cause of action or defense entitles the party, even though such matter may not be set forth in the pleadings, so as to admit proof and call for an actual decision upon it;" that "where the cause of action is entire and indivisible the judgment determines all the right of the parties upon it, although it may be but partially presented to the court;" that "all claim for relief, special or general, upon the same cause of action or defense, is disposed of and determined by the judgment, when the particular circumstances justifying such relief are not pleaded, as effectually as when they are fully set out;" and that such judgment is a bar to a second suit, if such second suit "presents no new cause of action, but only new grounds for relief upon the same cause of action."

The rule announced in that decision, and which, in later cases, has been summarized in the statement that "a single and entire cause of action cannot be split up into several suits," has been consistently followed ever since. Geiser Threshing Machine Co. v. Farmer, 27

Minn. 428, 8 N. W. 141; Pierro v. St. Paul & N. P. Ry. Co. 39 Minn. 451, 40 N. W. 520, 12 Am. St. 673; Bazille v. Murray, 40 Minn. 48, 41 N. W. 238; Northern Trust Co. v. Crystal Lake Cemetery Assn. 67 Minn. 131, 69 N. W. 708; O'Brien v. Manwaring, 79 Minn. 86, 81 N. W. 746, 79 Am. St. 426; King v. Chicago, M. & St. P. Ry. Co. 80 Minn. 83, 82 N. W. 1113, 50 L.R.A. 161, 81 Am. St. 238; Gilbert v. Boak Fish Co. 86 Minn. 365, 90 N. W. 767, 58 L.R.A. 735; H. W. Wilson Co. v. A. B. Farnham & Co. 97 Minn. 153, 106 N. W. 342; Liimatainen v. St. Louis River D. & Imp. Co. 119 Minn. 238, 137 N. W. 1099; Kinzel v. Boston & Duluth F. L. Co. 124 Minn. 416, 145 N. W. 124.

The decisions cited and relied upon by plaintiff do not establish a different rule. In West v. Hennessey, 58 Minn. 133, 59 N. W. 984, the court held that the cause of action in the first suit was not the same as in the second suit, although both arose out of the same transaction. In the second suit plaintiff sought to recover damages sustained through false representations made by defendant and relied upon by plaintiff. No question of fraud or false representations was involved in the first suit. In Village of Wayzata v. Great Northern Ry. Co. 67 Minn. 385, 69 N. W. 1073, it was held that a judgment defining the rights of defendant in respect to the use of the streets of the village in connection with a passenger station and boat landing maintained by it in the village, was not conclusive as to its rights in such streets in an action brought after it had removed its station and boat landing to a point outside the village. In Swanson v. Great Northern Ry. Co. 73 Minn. 103, 75 N. W. 1033, a demurrer had been sustained on the ground that the complaint failed to state a cause of action, and it was held that the judgment rendered pursuant thereto did not bar a subsequent suit in which the cause of action alleged was valid and sufficient. In Rossman v. Tilleny, 80 Minn. 160, 83 N. W. 42, 81 Am. St. 247, plaintiff failed in a suit to recover the contract price for performing certain work, for the reason that he had not completed the work; and the judgment therein was held not to bar a subsequent suit for the reasonable value of the services rendered, it appearing that plaintiff had been prevented from completing the contract by the act of de-

127 M.—14.

fendant. In Kaaterud v. Gilbertson, 96 Minn. 66, 104 N. W. 763, it was held that a judgment in favor of defendant in a suit to have a deed declared a mortgage and to redeem therefrom, did not bar a subsequent suit to enforce specific performance of an oral contract to convey to plaintiff the same land involved in the former suit. In Stitt v. Rat Portage Lumber Co. 101 Minn. 93, 111 N. W. 948, where plaintiff failed to recover upon a certain express contract, the judgment therein was held not a bar to a subsequent action upon a different contract, although both contracts related to the same transaction. In Marshall v. Gilman, 52 Minn. 88, 53 N. W. 811, it was held that an action for rescission which failed because plaintiff had waived his right to rescind, did not bar an action for deceit growing out of the same transaction.

In the above cases the court held that the two suits were based upon different causes of action, and therefore that the prosecution of the second was not barred by the judgment in the first. In the discussion as to whether the two causes of action were the same, it is stated in some of the cases, perhaps without making it entirely clear, that the designated test should be applied to the ultimate cause of action and not to the particular facts alleged in the pleadings, that the "test as to whether a former judgment is a bar is to inquire whether the same evidence will sustain both the former and the present action." Plaintiff invokes this rule and insists that this test shows that the present suit is not barred by the judgment in the former suit. She argues that, as she did not allege and hence could not prove the defect in the step in the former suit, and has not alleged and hence cannot prove the negligent starting of the car in the present suit, the present suit is not based upon the same cause of action as the former. This does not necessarily follow. In arriving at this conclusion plaintiff overlooks the rule stated in Thompson v. Myrick, supra, and repeatedly reiterated in later cases, that the judgment decides "every matter which pertains to the cause of action * * * even though such matter may not be set forth in the pleadings, so as to admit proof" thereof; and that "all claim for relief, special or general, upon the same cause of action or defense, is disposed of and determined by the judgment, when the particular circumstances justifying such relief are not pleaded, as effectually as when they are fully set out;" and that such judgment bars a second suit which "presents no new cause of action, but only new grounds for relief upon the same cause of action." The test is not whether the two complaints are so drawn that the same evidence would be admissible under both, but whether the same evidence which will sustain the cause of action upon which a recovery is sought in the second suit, would also have sustained the cause of action upon which a recovery was sought in the first suit. Whether the instant case falls within or without the rule depends upon whether the wrong for which redress is sought is the same wrong for which redress was sought in the former suit, and not upon whether the complaint sets forth grounds for relief which were not set forth in the former complaint. The case of Liimatainen v. St. Louis River D. & Imp. Co. 119 Minn. 238, 137 N. W. 1099, is decisive of the present case. It is there said that "one action only lies to redress a single wrong, or, as frequently expressed, a single tort gives rise to a single cause of action, and a plaintiff cannot be permitted to indulge in unnecessary litigation by splitting up a cause of action and prosecuting more than one suit thereon;" and the decision in Columb v. Webster Mnfg. Co. 84 Fed. 592, 28 C. C. A. 225, 43 L.R.A. 195, holding that a judgment for defendant, in a suit to recover for personal injuries, barred a subsequent suit between the same parties to recover for the same injuries, although additional acts of negligence were alleged in the second suit, was approved. It is further stated in the Liimatainen case that "a cause of action for wrong is predicated upon the violation of an ultimate duty, and, though the performance of such duty may require the doing or omission of many separate and distinct acts, the omission or doing of which would constitute a violation of the ultimate duty, it is nevertheless the violation of the latter, and not the specific acts or omissions, which constitutes the actionable wrong."

In suits based upon negligence, the cause of action is the violation of the ultimate duty to exercise due care that another may not suffer injury. In the instant case plaintiff was a passenger upon defendant's street car, and it was the duty of defendant to afford her safe egress therefrom.   Her claim for damages is grounded upon the charge that defendant violated such duty.   The violation of this duty constitutes her cause of action.   In the first suit she charged that defendant violated this duty by suddenly starting the car while she was in the act of alighting.   In the present suit she charges that defendant violated such duty by providing a defective step for her to use in descending from the car.   Both suits are based upon the violation of the ultimate duty to afford safe egress from the car.   The second suit "presents no new cause of action, but only new grounds for relief upon the same cause of action," and under the authorities cited is barred by the judgment in the former suit.   It follows that the decision of the trial court was correct and must be affirmed. So ordered.

GEORGE A. McKINLEY v. NATIONAL CITIZENS BANK OF MANKATO.[1]

October 30, 1914.

Nos. 18,242—(49).

Costs against intervener.

1. Where an intervener claiming a lien on property for negligent loss of which the action is brought, reiterates the allegations of the complaint in the action and becomes practically a coplaintiff, he is liable, under G. S. 1913, § 7766, jointly with plaintiff for costs, upon the setting aside of separate verdicts in their favor, including the expense of a transcript and two copies of the testimony.

Taxation of costs.

2. The trial court's determination, made on conflicting affidavits, as to the number of folios charged for, cannot be disturbed.

From an order of the clerk of the district court for Crow Wing county taxing costs and disbursements in favor of the defendant and

1 Reported in 149 N. W. 295.

against the National Citizens Bank of Mankato, as intervener, the intervener appealed to the district court. The taxation was sustained, Stanton, J. From the judgment for $574.06, entered pursuant to the order for judgment, the National Citizens Bank of Mankato appealed. Affirmed.

C. E. Phillips and *Lorin Cray,* for appellant.

A. D. Polk, for respondent.

PHILIP E. BROWN, J.

Plaintiff brought an action to recover damages for defendant's negligent loss of logs, etc., and for conversion of certain equipment. Appellant intervened, claiming a lien on the logs, etc., and, reiterating the charge of defendant's negligence, but making no claim as to the equipment, demanded judgment against defendant, to the exclusion of plaintiff, for $8,000. Separate verdicts were returned in favor of plaintiff and intervener for over two and six thousand dollars respectively. Thereafter the court set the verdicts aside and granted defendant a new trial. Subsequently the action was dismissed on plaintiff's motion, and thereupon, over intervener's objection, costs were taxed and allowed against it and plaintiff jointly, which was later affirmed on intervener's appeal and judgment entered against it and plaintiff jointly therefor; whereupon intervener appealed to this court.

The errors assigned relate only to the right of defendant to costs against intervener; the latter asserting that no costs resulted from the intervention, and hence, under G. S. 1913, § 7766, it was liable for none. This contention is predicated, so far as the facts are concerned, upon those already stated and also the following, disclosed by the record: Intervener was permitted to file its complaint on the preliminary call of the calendar of the term at which the cause was tried, and defendant's answer was allowed to stand as the answer thereto, no other pleadings being made. A large number of witnesses were examined by plaintiff and defendant, but none were sworn, examined or cross-examined by or on behalf of intervener, except that, by cross-examination of plaintiff, it established its lien and right to recover to the extent thereof if plaintiff prevailed, whereupon it was stipulated between them that this should be effected by separate verdicts. Intervener took no further part in the trial except to counsel with plaintiff's attorney. The court charged that a verdict could be rendered for intervener only in case the jury found that plaintiff was entitled to recover against defendant. The claim is also made that all witnesses were called simply to support or controvert the allegations of the complaint.

The statute cited reads that in case of intervention "all the issues shall be determined together, and if the intervener's claim be not sustained he shall pay the costs resulting therefrom." Recoveries for costs and disbursements being purely statutory, the questions involved turn upon the interpretation to be given this provision, which, however, must be read in the light of the purpose intended to be subserved by the allowance of costs generally, namely, compensation or indemnity for expenses incurred in enforcing a legal or resisting an illegal claim. Johnson v. Chicago, M. & St. P. Ry. Co. 29 Minn. 425, 430, 13 N. W. 673. While, therefore, the statute plainly declares that a defeated intervener shall pay only such costs as result by reason of the intervention, it does not follow that intervener's claim of nonliability in the present case can be sustained. It voluntarily became a party to the action, asserted the same cause of action, and had equal right with plaintiff to be heard in respect thereto. Bennett v. Whitcomb, 25 Minn. 148, 150. It was entitled to any appropriate relief under the issues presented determinable in its favor, and, speaking generally, had all the rights of a party to an action. Note, 123 Am. St. 312, etc; 30 Cyc. 139. Granting that the witnesses called by defendant merely testified upon the issues raised by the complaint in the action, yet the evidence thus adduced was equally material to the issue made by intervener's reiteration of the allegations thereof, and defendant necessarily had to contend on the trial against the claims of both plaintiff and intervener. The extent of the latter's participation in the trial is of slight consequence, and cannot be considered a determinative factor. We hold that intervener, having become practically a co-plaintiff, so that defendant was required to defend against both it and plaintiff in order to escape liability to either, there is joint liability for costs.

The statute should not be construed so as to allow intervener to attempt to benefit by the litigation without incurring the ordinary liabilities incident thereto. See Reay v. Butler, 99 Cal. 477, 33 Pac. 1134; Spruill v. Arrington, 109 N. C. 192, 13 S. E. 779; note, 16 Am. Dec. 184.

After verdicts, defendant obtained a transcript and two copies of the testimony in order to move for a new trial, the expense whereof was included in the cost bill over special objection. These were legitimate expenditures in accord with common practice. The necessity of attacking two verdicts instead of one resulted from the nature of the intervention. Nor can we disturb the court's determination, made on conflicting affidavits, as to the number of folios charged for. Other items in the bill were not specially objected to.

Judgment affirmed.

CHARLES A. IKENBERRY v. NEW YORK LIFE INSURANCE COMPANY.[1]

October 30, 1914.

Nos. 18,702—(29).

Life insurance — payment of first premium.

1. The evidence examined and *held* to make the payment of the first premium on a life insurance policy and its delivery to and receipt by the insured questions of fact for the jury.

Evidence of litigant's conduct.

2. While the conduct of a person, subsequent to an alleged transaction, may be used against him to disprove the position he takes in a litigation involving the same transaction, it may not be offered to corroborate or prove the correctness of such position.

Admission against interest — evidence inadmissible.

3. When it appeared that a purported sender of a telegram was in a state of coma from a paralytic stroke so that it was impossible for her to

[1] Reported in 149 N. W. 292.

have caused or directed a message to be sent, the telegram is properly excluded when offered as an admission against interest.

Same — evidence of collateral matters.

4. In the reception in evidence of acts or conduct in collateral matters tending to prove admissions against interest upon an issue in litigation, the trial court must exercise discretion and consider whether, in view of surrounding circumstances, the matter offered is likely to aid the jury. No abuse of such discretion is found in the ruling excluding the will of plaintiff's testate in which no mention is made of this insurance payable to her estate.

Conversations with decedent — agent not interested party.

5. The agent of defendant, who negotiated the insurance, to whom the insured made and delivered a note for the amount of the first premium, and to whom the defendant sent the policy after its issue, is *held* not interested in the event of the action so as to prevent his testifying to conversations with the insured, now deceased.

Action in the district court for Hennepin county by the administrator with the will annexed of the estate of Mary Elizabeth Cooke, deceased, to recover $5,000 upon defendant's policy upon the life of his testate. The case was tried before Booth, J., who at the close of the testimony denied defendant's motion to dismiss the action and its motion for a directed verdict, and a jury which returned a verdict in favor of plaintiff for $5,645.83. From an order denying its motion for judgment notwithstanding the verdict or for a new trial, defendant appealed. Affirmed as to motion for judgment. Reversed as to motion for new trial.

James H. McIntosh and *Brown & Guesmer,* for appellant.
M. H. Boutelle and *N. H. Chase,* for respondent.

HOLT, J.

The defendant appeals from an order denying it judgment notwithstanding, and also denying a new trial, a verdict having been awarded plaintiff upon a policy of insurance alleged to have been issued by defendant upon the life of plaintiff's testate payable to her estate.

The contention is that no contract of insurance was ever consummated. At the solicitation of E. T. Harris, the agent of defendant, plaintiff's testate, Mary E. Cooke, on March 11, 1911, applied for an insurance policy on her life in the defendant company. She gave a note for the amount of the first premium, due in six months and payable to the order of the agent. The defendant accepted the application, at least subject to the correction of an answer in the written application, made out and sent the policy to the agent. It never came into the manual possession of Mrs. Cooke. As supporting the defense that no insurance was ever effected, the defendant claims that there was ambiguity in the application as to the kind of policy she desired, and that her signature to a correction thereof was necessary before the policy could be delivered; also that, because she was unable to pay her note before due, as was contemplated in her arrangement with the agent, the policy was to be returned and another of later date substituted. Mrs. Cooke suffered a paralytic stroke on August 19, 1911, and was taken to a hospital, where she died on the twentieth of the following month. The application signed by Mary E. Cooke contained this provision: "I agree as follows: 1. That the insurance hereby applied for shall not take effect unless the first premium is paid and the policy delivered to and received by me during my lifetime." It would serve no useful purpose to set out or analyze the testimony touching the issue of the acceptance of Mrs. Cooke's note as payment of the first premium, nor the one whether the mailing of the policy by defendant to its agent was a delivery to and receipt thereof by Mrs. Cooke under the terms of the application. Under section 3607, G. S. 1913, Harris must be "held to be the company's agent for the purpose of collecting or securing the premiums" on the policy, whatever the stipulations might be in the contract of insurance or, for that matter, in the agent's contract of employment with defendant. By written admissions of Harris, while attempting to obtain advance payments on the note, the policy was considered to have taken effect; this, of course, implies both payment of the first premium, so far as defendant is concerned, and the delivery of the policy by it. Suffice to say that an attentive examination of the evidence convinces us that both the payment of the first premium and the delivery of the policy, the two decisive propositions which determined whether the policy was in effect, were not for the court, but were rightly and under clear and accurate instructions submitted to the jury. Defendant is not entitled to judgment notwithstanding the verdict.

We have examined the numerous assignments of error urged as grounds for a new trial, but find none meriting notice except the ones now to be considered relating to rulings on the offer of evidence. An inquiry as to the efforts of Harris to ascertain whether Mrs. Cooke's note for the first premium was bankable was properly excluded, if for no other reason than this, that at the time no evidence had been received as to any conditions under which the note was accepted as payment of the first premium. Nor was error made in excluding the proof of the absence of attempts on the part of Harris to negotiate or collect the alleged collateral note of $1,000 given him subsequent to March 11, 1911, by Mrs. Cooke, for that note was not due until some time in 1912. But, apart from these reasons, there was no error, for while the conduct of a person subsequent to an alleged transaction may be used as an admission against him, he should seldom, if ever, be permitted to offer testimony of that kind to support the position he maintains in the litigation. Such evidence comes too close to self-serving declarations. It cannot be used even in rebuttal of admissions against interest by word or act. "An admission by a party against his interest, at one time, cannot be rebutted by proof of a statement made in his own favor at another time." Marvin v. Dutcher, 26 Minn. 391, 4 N. W. 685.

A telegram received by Harris purporting to have been sent by Mary E. Cooke, we think, was rightly excluded, for it appeared clearly that Mrs. Cooke could not have sent it, or caused it to be sent. For more than three days previous to that time Mrs. Cooke had been in a state of coma from the stroke and continued in that condition during several days thereafter. For the same reason a letter written, during this time, to defendant by attorneys employed by Mrs. Cooke's daughter or son-in-law without her knowledge, or ability to know, could not bind her or her estate, and was properly rejected.

Some few days before death Mrs. Cooke recovered sufficiently to make a will by which she disposed of, apparently, all her possessions. Therein the property and legatees were described with some particularity, but without any reference to this insurance. The will was offered as tending to prove that Mrs. Cooke did not deem the insurance in existence. It was excluded. While the subsequent acts indicative of her understanding that the policy was not in force are admissible as admissions against interest, we would be loath to hold the exclusion of this will prejudicial error. The trial court exercises some discretion as to the extent to which the conduct of a party litigant subsequent to the making of an alleged contract may be inquired into, for the purpose of proving or disproving its existence. In so doing the court must also give consideration to the probability of the particular act, sought to be shown, furnishing a legitimate aid to the jury. In view of the illness of Mrs. Cooke and the surrounding circumstances, we are not prepared to say that the court exceeded a wise discretion in the matter of the exclusion of the will. And this applies also to rulings in respect to what Mrs. Cooke, Harris, and certain officers of defendant did subsequent to March 11, 1911, with reference to other collateral matters as throwing light upon the main issue—was the policy in force?

We have, however, concluded that the learned trial court was in error when ruling that section 8378, G. S. 1913, prohibited E. T. Harris from testifying as to conversations or admissions of Mrs. Cooke. The statute is: "It shall not be competent for any party to an action, or any person interested in the event thereof, to give evidence therein of or concerning any conversation with, or admission of, a deceased or insane party or person relative to any matter at issue between the parties, unless" etc. The disability of a person to testify in a case because of interest which existed at common law has been removed by statute, save in certain instances, one of which is found in the provision quoted. The uniform holding ever since Chadwick v. Cornish, 26 Minn. 28, 1 N. W. 55, has been that the provision is in the nature of an exception to the general rule of receiving all available testimony and should be construed strictly. Keigher v. City of St. Paul, 73 Minn. 21, 75 N. W. 732. Finn v. Modern Brotherhood of America, 118 Minn. 307, 136 N. W. 850. Harris was not a party. Was he interested in the event of the litigation so as to be disqualified? It has been held that the interest here referred to must be such "that [the

witness] has something to gain or lose by the direct legal operation
and effect of the judgment to be rendered therein, or that the record
thereof can be used for or against him, as evidence" upon the fact in
issue in some other action. Marvin v. Dutcher, 26 Minn. 391, 4 N.
W. 685. The party must make the incompetency appear clearly.
Perine v. Grand Lodge A. O. U. W. 48 Minn. 82, 50 N. W. 1022.
Harris had no pecuniary, legal, certain or immediate interest in the
event of the cause of action itself such as must exist under the decisions last cited. He would not gain or lose by direct legal effect of the
judgment herein. There is no way of ascertaining whether or not the
jury found that defendant, by its course of conduct, impliedly authorized Harris to accept notes in payment of premiums. His interest in
the event is not certain but contingent. A contingent or remote interest in the result or event of the action does not bring a witness within
the provision of the statutory prohibition. It has been held that a
wife's interest in her husband's real estate (exclusive of the homestead) is not such an interest as will debar her from testifying to a
conversation with a deceased person, where such conversation involves
an issue of the title of such real estate. Madson v. Madson, 69 Minn.
37, 71 N. W. 824. An agent who transacted the business for the sur-
vivor of two contracting parties is not precluded from testifying to
the conversations in regard thereto with the deceased party, where
such business becomes an issue in litigation. Darwin v. Keigher, 45
Minn. 64, 47 N. W. 314. And yet it is apparent that an agent is
nearly always interested in the event of a lawsuit, where the issue between two contracting parties may depend on the agent's acts or authority, for, if it be established therein that he exceeded his authority,
the result may be that no contract was effectuated or, if one was made,
that the agent is liable over for the damages suffered by the principal
because thereof. But nevertheless such interest in the event is contingent or remote. It is not rendered certain by the judgment in an
action to which the agent is not a party. It is also worthy of consideration that, if the liability over of an agent to his principal, or a
servant to his master, should be held a disqualifying interest under the
statute, the number of instances will be unduly increased, in which it

will be possible to prevent the actual facts from being developed in a lawsuit.   In O'Toole v. Faulkner, 34 Wash. 371, 75 Pac. 975, brought against a street railway to recover for the death of plaintiff's intestate caused by the motorneer's negligence in the operation of the defendant's street car, it was held that the motorneer's liability over was not such an interest in the event as would render his testimony of conversations with the deceased after the injury inadmissible under a statute similar to ours.

Plaintiff relies upon Williams v. Empire Mut. Annuity & Life Ins. Co. 8 Ga. App. 303, a parallel case to the one at bar as to the facts, to sustain the exclusion of Harris' testimony as to the conversations with Mrs. Cooke.   But the statute of Georgia is not the same as ours. It reads (Subds. 4, 5 of section 5269, Code 1895) : "Where a person not a party, but a person interested in the result of the suit, is offered as a witness, he shall not be competent to testify, if as a party to the cause he would for any cause be incompetent.   No agent or attorney-at-law of the surviving or sane party at the time of the transaction testified about, shall be allowed to testify in favor of a surviving or sane party, under circumstances where the principal, a party to the cause could not testify."   The case of Whitlow's Adm'r v. Whitlow's Adm'r, 109 Ky. 573, 60 S. W. 182, also cited by plaintiff, comes under a statute essentially different from ours; it provides that "no person shall testify for himself concerning any verbal statement of, or any transaction with, or any act done, or omitted to be done by, one who is * * * dead when the testimony is offered to be given." The case in our court which is nearest to holding that Harris had such an interest in the event of the litigation that he was incompetent to testify to the conversation with Mrs. Cooke is Beard v. First Nat. Bank of Minneapolis, 39 Minn. 546, 40 N. W. 842, a suit upon a certificate of deposit issued by defendant to plaintiff's intestate, where the defendant called a son of the deceased to prove a *donatio mortis causa* of the certificate to him, but he was held interested in the result, having indorsed the certificate and received the money upon it, and therefore liable to the bank if his title was not good.   However we observe that he was directly and pecuniarily interested in the validity of the title claimed by him in the instrument involved in the action. A similar direct pecuniary interest seems to have rendered the witness incompetent in Kells v. Webster, 71 Minn. 276, 73 N. W. 962.

But it is contended that Harris may be prejudiced by the use of the record for or against him. It is true that if hereafter, in an action by or against Harris, it becomes necessary to prove the existence of the judgment in this action it may be done by the mere introduction of the record. But such use thereof may be made against all the world. We think the true test is stated in Feitl v. Chicago City Ry. Co. 211 Ill. 279, 71 N. E. 991, where the proposition is fully and clearly discussed, namely: Can the record be used against him to prove the truth of the facts upon which the judgment was founded? 40 Cyc. 2280, 2281. A moment's reflection will disclose that the judgment in this case cannot be used to prove or disprove any fact which may render Harris liable over to defendant or any one else. Its introduction will not tend to prove that the note of Mrs. Cooke was taken in payment of the premium or that Harris exceeded his authority or that he, for any reason, should be held liable to the insurance company. It could only be introduced to prove the fact that a judgment was upon a certain date entered for a certain amount in favor of one and against the other of the parties litigant. We hold that Harris was not disqualified by reason of interest in the event of this action, nor because the record of the judgment herein can be used for or against him as evidence of any of the facts in issue, in this litigation, in some other proceeding based on the same issues.

For the error pointed out a retrial must be had. The order appealed from is affirmed insofar as it denied judgment notwithstanding and is reversed insofar as it denied a new trial.

LUEY HORBACH v. CATHERINE HORBACH.[1]

October 30, 1914.

Nos. 18,724—(226).[2]

Widow's allowance of personalty.

Under subdivision 1, R. L. 1905, § 3653 (G. S. 1913, § 7243), the widow is entitled to the allowance of personal property to the amount of $500 provided thereby, though she assents to her husband's will at the time of its execution and accepts its provisions in lieu of the provisions made for her by law, the subdivision cited providing that she shall receive such allowance as well when she takes the provisions made by her husband's will as when he dies intestate.

From an order of the probate court granting the petition of Catherine Horbach, widow of Daniel Horbach, deceased, that she be allowed personal property of decedent of the appraised value of $500, Luey Horbach, as executor of the last will and testament of said decedent, and in his own behalf as one of the heirs, legatees and devisees of said decedent, appealed to the district court for Dakota county. The appeal was heard before Hodgson, J., who made findings and ordered judgment affirming the order of the probate court. From the judgment entered against him Luey Horbach, as executor of the last will and testament of decedent, appealed. Affirmed.

P. H. Keefe, for appellant.
Albert Schaller, for respondent.

DIBELL, C.

Daniel Horbach bequeathed to his wife Catherine Horbach $400. He devised the rest of his estate, including his homestead, to his three children. The will provided that the bequest to his wife was "in lieu of any provisions made for her by the laws or statutes of the

---

[1] Reported in 149 N. W. 303.   [2] April, 1914, term calendar.

state of Minnesota." At the time of the execution of the will Mrs. Horbach assented thereto and accepted the provisions of it in lieu of any provisions made for her by the laws or statutes of the state, and particularly declared that she waived any right given her by statute in the homestead of her husband.

After her husband's death she selected personal property to the value of $500 and petitioned that it be set aside for her. The probate court made an order setting it aside. Upon appeal to the district court the order was affirmed. This appeal is from the order of the district court affirming the order of the probate court.

By subdivision 1, R. L. 1905, § 3653 (G. S. 1913, § 7243), it is provided, among other things, that the wife shall be entitled to personal property amounting to $500, to be selected by her. It was under this section that Mrs. Horbach claimed the right to select the personal property. The subdivision of the section of the statute cited contains this provision:

"She shall receive such allowances when she takes the provisions made for her by her husband's will, as well as when he dies intestate."

The precise question is whether, when the wife at the time of execution of the will assents to it and accepts its provisions in lieu of the provisions made for her by statute, she may still claim her statutory allowance of $500. We hold that she may. There is nothing in the case to make the result different from the ordinary case of an election to take under the will. When she takes under her husband's will she still has the absolute right to the allowance specified in subdivision 1. So far as we are advised the question presented has not been decided in this state. The conclusion we have reached was forecasted by the decision in Blakeman v. Blakeman, 64 Minn. 315, 67 N. W. 69.

Order affirmed.

WILLIAM L. CHRISTENSON and Others v. MARY MADSON.[1]

October 30, 1914.

Nos. 18,736—(54).[2]

Life insurance — recovery by beneficiary — matters of defense.

1. Where a person procures insurance upon the life of another, it is the general rule that he must prove an insurable interest in such life in order to recover upon such policy; but, where a person insures his own life and appoints another to receive the proceeds of such insurance, the appointee establishes a *prima facie* right to recover by proving the contract of insurance and the happening of the event upon which it is to become payable. If facts exist which preclude such recovery they are matters of defense.

Mutual benefit insurance — who may be beneficiaries.

2. The classes of persons eligible as beneficiaries under policies issued by a fraternal association are to be determined by the rules adopted for the express purpose of governing such matters, and not by general statements made for the purpose of indicating the general object of such association, and restrictions limiting the classes who may be so designated must be expressed in positive terms and cannot be inferred from general statements.

Construction of by-laws.

3. The by-laws of the association having provided that policies may be made payable to the affianced wife of the insured, a policy so payable is valid, although the object of the association, as stated in its constitution, is to provide insurance for the surviving relatives of its members.

Evidence.

4. Under the evidence in this case, the court did not err in refusing to find that immoral relations existed between the insured and his beneficiary.

Action in the district court for Hennepin county by the children and sole heirs of James P. Christenson, deceased, against Mary Madson, substituted by order of court for Danish Brotherhood in

---

[1] Reported in 149 N. W. 288.   [2] October, 1914, term calendar.

Note.—Validity of life insurance for benefit of betrothed wife, see note in 19 L.R.A. 187.

Insurable interest of woman in life of intended husband, see note in 53 L.R.A. 825.

127 M.—15.

America, to recover $1,000 upon its certificate upon the life of James
P. Christenson. The case was tried before Jelley, J., who made findings and ordered judgment in favor of defendant. From an order
denying their motion for a new trial, plaintiffs appealed. Affirmed.

Jay W. Crane, for appellants.

Grotte & Bowen, for respondent.

TAYLOR, C.

On June 7, 1909, James P. Christenson procured the Danish
Brotherhood in America, of which he was a member, to issue to him
a benefit certificate for $1,000 payable, upon his death, to defend-
ant, Mary Madson, as his betrothed. He paid all the assessments
upon the certificate until his death which occurred in December,
1912. In October, 1911, he delivered the certificate to Mary Madson, the beneficiary therein named, who has ever since retained it,
but he was never married to her. He had been previously married
and had grown-up children, but his wife had procured a divorce from
him on April 5, 1909. After his death, his children brought this
suit against the brotherhood to recover the amount of the certificate.
The brotherhood admitted liability under the certificate, paid the
money into court, and caused Mary Madson to be substituted as defendant.

The suit proceeded to trial between the children as plaintiffs and
Mary Madson as defendant, and she will be referred to as defendant
hereafter. The case was tried by the court without a jury. The
court, among other things, found that defendant was the affianced
wife of James P. Christenson; that both the law and the rules of the
order authorized the issuance of benefit certificates payable to the
affianced wife of the insured; and that the certificate in controversy
was, by its terms, payable to defendant as such affianced wife. The
court thereupon directed that judgment be entered to the effect that
defendant was entitled to the proceeds of the certificate, and that
the money paid into court be delivered to her. Plaintiffs appealed
from an order denying their motion for a new trial.

1. Plaintiffs insist that the evidence is not sufficient to sustain
the finding that defendant was betrothed to Christenson. His death

debarred her, a party in interest, from testifying as to conversations between them, and the only evidence to support the finding is the fact that the certificate, by his direction, was made payable to her as his betrothed. Plaintiffs invoke the rule, frequently stated in the books, that the beneficiary under a policy of life insurance, in order to recover thereon, must allege and prove an insurable interest in the life of the insured. This rule is based upon the theory that a policy, issued to one who has no interest in the continuation of the life of the person insured, is both a gambling contract, and a contract which creates a motive for desiring the termination of such life, and is therefore against public policy and void. The rule is applied very generally where the insurance is procured by the beneficiary and the suit is consequently founded upon a contract between the beneficiary and the insurer; but where the insured himself procures the insurance, the contract is between him and the insurer, not between the beneficiary and the insurer, and his interest in his own life sustains the policy and need not be proven. In such case he has the right to appoint the person to whom the proceeds of the policy shall go, and, if he make such appointment, the one so appointed takes by virtue of the contract between the insured and the insurer, not by virtue of a contract between the insurer and the appointee, and in order to recover thereon it is sufficient for the appointee to prove the contract and the happening of the event which entitles him to the benefit thereof. If there be facts which preclude the appointee from recovering, they should be alleged and proven as a defense. In other words, if the insured himself procured the issuance of the policy and caused the beneficiary to be named therein, the policy is *prima facie* evidence that the beneficiary so named is entitled to the proceeds thereof at the death of the insured; but, if the insured did not procure the issuance of the policy, the beneficiary thereunder must allege and prove the facts entitling him to receive such proceeds. In Campbell v. New England Mut. Life Ins. Co. 98 Mass. 381, the court say:

"The policy in this case is upon the life of Andrew Campbell. It was made upon his application; it issued to him as 'the assured;' the premium was paid by him; and he thereby became a member of the defendant corporation. It is the interest of Andrew Campbell in his own life that supports the policy. The plaintiff did not, by virtue of the clause declaring the policy to be for her benefit, become the assured. She is merely the person designated by the agreement of the parties to receive the proceeds of the policy upon the death of the assured. The contract (so long as it remains executory), the interest by which it is supported, and the relation of membership, all continue the same as if no such clause were inserted. Fogg v. Middlesex Ins. Co. 10 Cush. 337, 346; Sandford v. Mechanics' Ins. Co. 12 Cush. 541; Hale v. Mechanics' Ins. Co. 6 Gray, 169 [66 Am. Dec. 410]; Campbell v. Charter Oak Ins. Co. 10 Allen, 213; Forbes v. American Ins. Co. 15 Gray, 249 [77 Am. Dec. 360]. It was not necessary, therefore, that the plaintiff should show that she had an interest in the life of Andrew Campbell, by which the policy could be supported as a policy to herself as the assured." The same rule is recognized by other courts. Ætna Life Ins. Co. v. France, 94 U. S. 561, 24 L. ed. 287; Provident Life Ins. & Inv. Co. v. Baum, 29 Ind. 236; Milner v. Bowman, 119 Ind. 448, 21 N. E. 1094, 5 L.R.A. 95; Prudential Ins. Co. v. Hunn, 21 Ind. App. 525, 52 N. E. 772, 69 Am. St. 380; Union Fraternal League v. Walton, 109 Ga. 1, 34 S. E. 317, 46 L.R.A. 424, 77 Am. St. 350; Foresters of America v. Hollis, 70 Kan. 71, 78 Pac. 160, 3 Ann. Cas. 535; Guardian Mut. Life Ins. Co. v. Hogan, 80 Ill. 35, 22 Am. Rep. 180; Massachusetts Mut. Life Ins. Co. v. Kellogg, 82 Ill. 614; Scott v. Dickson, 108 Pa. St. 6, 56 Am. Rep. 192; Hill v. United Life Ins. Assn. 154 Pa. St. 29, 25 Atl. 771, 35 Am. St. 807; Brennan v. Prudential Ins. Co. 148 Pa. St. 199, 23 Atl. 901; Heinlein v. Imperial Life Ins. Co. 101 Mich. 250, 59 N. W. 615, 25 L.R.A. 627, 45 Am. St. 409; Fairchild v. Northeastern Mut. Life Assn. 51 Vt. 613; Bursinger v. Bank of Watertown, 67 Wis. 75, 30 N. W. 290, 58 Am. Rep. 848; Dolan v. Supreme Council, 152 Mich. 266, 16 L.R.A.(N.S.) 555, 15 Ann. Cas. 232, and note appended thereto.

2. Plaintiffs contend that defendant entered into meretricious relations with Christenson and by so doing terminated the betrothal. There is no finding that any improper relations existed between them. Plaintiffs made a motion to amend the findings by inserting

therein a statement that defendant became the mistress of Christenson. The court denied this application, and, under the evidence, it cannot be held that the court erred in so doing. As the existence of the alleged improper relations has not been established, it is not necessary to determine whether the marriage engagement would be broken by subsequent cohabitation without being married.

3. Plaintiffs further claim that the constitution of the Danish Brotherhood in America excludes the betrothed of the insured from the class of persons to whom benefit certificates may be made payable. The brotherhood is incorporated under the laws of the state of Nebraska. The certificate in question was issued in the state of Minnesota to a citizen of Minnesota. The laws of both Nebraska and Minnesota provide that such certificates may be made payable to the affianced wife of the insured; and the by-laws of the Danish Brotherhood contain a like provision. But plaintiffs contend that this provision of the by-laws violates the constitution of the brotherhood and is void. The provisions of the constitution upon which plaintiffs rely are the following:

"Sec. 2. The object of the Danish Brotherhood is to work toward a union among the Danes in America; to perpetuate the memories from Denmark and to strengthen each other in true brotherhood; to help one another by financial aid to sick and needy members; to help unemployed brothers to employment, and to provide for an insurance and guarantee fund, whereby every brother will have a guaranty that his surviving relatives, in case of his death, will receive a sum as stipulated by law, and to aid the local lodges, in cases where long continued sickness or some accident makes extra assistance necessary.

"Sec. 5. In case of the death of a brother, the brotherhood, according to the constitution and by-laws, shall provide for the payment to his surviving relatives of such sum as is described in his certificate of membership, and which, according to the constitution and by-laws, is his rightful due, either $250, $500 or $1,000, according to the scale after which he has paid, while the assessment, which every member must pay to this object, must not exceed the provisions described in the by-laws."

These sections of the constitution merely give a general outline of the purpose of the brotherhood. They contain no prohibitory or restrictive language, and were not intended to mark out and limit, except in a general way, the nature and extent of the power to make contracts.

To determine whether a certain person may lawfully be appointed as beneficiary, we must look to the rules and regulations adopted for the purpose of pointing out and defining who may, and who may not, become such beneficiaries. Such questions are to be determined by the provisions established for the express purpose of governing such matters, and not by the general phrases used in setting forth the general purpose of the association. This is true although the specific regulations are found in the by-laws and the general language in the constitution. Of course mandatory provisions in the constitution, and prohibitions and limitations therein must be observed; but the statement of the purpose of the organization, couched in general terms, is not ordinarily intended to restrict and define with exactness the powers of the association. The restrictions and limitations upon the powers of the association are usually contained in provisions, either in the constitution or the by-laws, adopted for the express purpose of outlining, limiting and defining such powers; and whether the association has power to make a particular contract is ordinarily to be determined by reference to such specific regulations, and not by reference to the general language used to express the general object for which the association was formed. Vanasek v. Western Bohemian Fraternal Assn. 122 Minn. 273, 142 N. W. 334, 49 L.R.A.(N.S.) 141; Walter v. Hensel, 42 Minn. 204, 44 N. W. 57.

It is also the general rule that restrictions limiting the classes who may be designated as beneficiaries must be expressed in specific and positive terms, and cannot be inferred from general statements contained in either the constitution or by-laws. Pleasants v. Locomotive Engineers Mut. Life & Accident Ins. Assn. 70 W. Va. 389, 73 N. E. 976, Ann. Cas. 1913E, 490, and cases cited in note appended thereto.

The constitution of the Danish Brotherhood contemplates the

existence of appropriate by-laws. The by-law in question expressly provides that the insured may make his benefit certificate payable to his fiancée. There is no other specific provision in respect to this matter; and, as the constitution contains no prohibitory or restrictive language, the phrase, "surviving relatives," used in stating the general object of the brotherhood, cannot be construed as invalidating such by-laws or forbidding the insured to make his certificate payable to his affianced wife.

Order affirmed.

BESSIE DALEY v. HORACE A. TOWNE and Others.[1]

October 30, 1914.

Nos. 18,740—(234).[2]

Covenant to repair — obvious defects — liability of landlord.

1. When a landlord does not covenant to keep the demised premises in repair, and such defects as exist therein are obvious, and there is no concealment, and the defects do not constitute a nuisance, the lessee takes the risk of their safe occupancy, and the landlord is not liable to him for an injury sustained in their use or to one occupying under him.

Directed verdict.

2. Applying this doctrine it is *held* that the court properly directed a verdict for two of the defendants occupying the position of landlords.

Action in the district court for Ramsey county to recover $10,500 for personal injury. The case was tried before Catlin, J., who granted the motions of defendants Towne and Joesting to direct verdicts in their favor and denied a similar motion by defendant

[1] Reported in 149 N. W. 368.   [2] April, 1914, term calendar.

Note.—Liability of landlord for personal injury to tenant or member of his family from defect in premises, see notes in 34 L.R.A. 824; 34 L.R.A.(N.S.) 798; 48 L.R.A.(N.S.) 917.

Whitford.   The jury returned a verdict for $5,000 against defend-
ant Whitford.   From the order denying her motion for a new trial
as to defendants Towne and Joesting, plaintiff appealed.   Affirmed.

Drill & Drill and *H. A. Loughran,* for appellant.

Flannery & Cooke and *Butler & Mitchell,* for respondents.

DIBELL, C.

The defendant Towne owned a four story building in St. Paul.
In 1906 he leased it for five years, commencing May 1, 1908, to the
defendant Joesting.   Afterwards, in October, 1910, the lease was
extended to April 30, 1918.   In August, 1911, Joesting sublet the
second and third floors to one Pinckney for a term expiring September 1, 1916.   Pinckney, in October, 1912, assigned the lease to
the defendant Whitford with the consent of Joesting.   In all of the
leases there was a covenant on the part of the lessees to repair, and
in the assignment to Whitford the latter assumed the covenants of
the prior leases.

Whitford used the premises as a rooming-house.   Plaintiff was
a guest, renting a room on the third floor from week to week.   About
two o'clock in the morning of January 10, 1913, she was injured.
Her claim, sufficiently substantiated by evidence, is that she started
from somewhere on the third floor to go to the toilet room and opened
or went through a door which led into a skylight just above the
bath-room of the second floor.   She fell through into the bath-room
and was seriously injured.   Her claim is that the door over the skylight was open, or off its hinges, so that she was misled.

The court directed a verdict for the defendants Towne and Joesting.   The plaintiff had a verdict against the defendant Whitford.
The plaintiff appeals from the order denying her motion for a new
trial as to the defendants Towne and Joesting.

1. The general principles of law applicable are fairly well settled.

When the landlord does not agree to repair, and such defects in the
premises as exist are obvious, and there is no concealment of their
condition, and the situation is not such as to create a nuisance,
the lessee takes the risk of their safe occupancy, and the landlord is
not liable to him or to one claiming under him.   This is the rule

stated in Harpel v. Fall, 63 Minn. 520, 65 N. W. 913, to which the later cases refer as authority. There Chief Justice Start said:

"Where the owner of land demises it with a nuisance upon it, he is presumed to authorize its continuance, and is liable to third persons subsequently injured thereby. For example, where a house is in such a ruinous condition at the time of the demise that it subsequently falls upon and injures an adjacent building or persons or property lawfully therein, he is liable for the injuries. But this rule has no application to injuries to tenants or subtenants of the owner where the defects were obvious at the time of the demise, and the lessor is guilty of no deceit in the premises, and has not covenanted to make repairs. * * * It is well settled that in the absence of any covenant or agreement in the lease to repair, and where there is no fraud, misrepresentation, or concealment by the lessor, there is no implied warranty on his part that the leased premises are fit for the purposes for which they are rented, or covenant to put them in repair or to keep them so. * * *

"A corollary of this proposition is that where there is no agreement to repair leased premises by the landlord, and he is not guilty of any fraud or concealment as to their safe condition, and the defects in the premises are not secret, but obvious, the tenant takes the risk of their safe occupancy; and the landlord is not liable to him or to any person entering under his title, or who is upon the premises by his invitation, for injuries sustained by reason of the unsafe condition of the premises."

This and later cases are reviewed and the same doctrine announced in Ames v. Brandvold, 119 Minn. 521, 138 N. W. 786.

2. Applying the doctrine of these cases, and of others cited later, the direction of a verdict in favor of Towne and Joesting must be sustained.

There is some evidence that the door leading from the hall into the light-well was off its hinges, and lying on the skylight, prior to the time of the lease from Towne to Joesting. If so, it was easily observable. Prior to the leasing to Pinckney, in August, 1911, and long prior to the accident, Joesting observed the condition of the door. He was not misled. He was under covenant to keep in repair. He at once caused the door to be nailed up. This appears by credible evidence which should not be disregarded. It was prior to the Pinckney lease. Upon taking possession Pinckney made an inspection and found the condition of the light-well and the door entering it. No difficulty was found in ascertaining the presence and condition of the light-well. This was 16 months prior to the plaintiff's injury. The defect which resulted in her injury was of later origin.

The case at bar is not a case where the landlord covenants to repair and negligently fails to do so (Good v. Von Hemert, 114 Minn. 393, 131 N. W. 466; Barron v. Liedloff, 95 Minn. 474, 104 N. W. 289); nor a case where the premises are let with a nuisance upon them (Isham v. Broderick, 89 Minn. 397, 95 N. W. 224); nor a case where the landlord retains general control over passageways, halls, and the like, and there is thus imposed upon him the duty of keeping in repair (Williams v. Dickson, 122 Minn. 49, 141 N. W. 849; Farley v. Byers, 106 Minn. 260, 118 N. W. 1023, 130 Am. St. 613). It is substantially controlled by Harpel v. Fall, *supra*.

Order affirmed.

E. F. GILLESPIE v. GREAT NORTHERN RAILWAY COMPANY.[1]

October 30, 1914.

Nos. 18,747—(240).[2]

Accident at highway crossing — contributory negligence — trainmen's rules.

In an action by the plaintiff to recover damages for the death of his

1 Reported in 149 N. W. 302.   2 April, 1914, term calendar.

Note.—Presumption as to exercise of due care by person found to have been killed through alleged negligence of another, see note in 16 L.R.A. 261.

Burden of proof as to contributory negligence generally, see note in 33 L.R.A. (N.S.) 1085.

Duty and liability of railroad company toward person going onto its property to pass around train blocking crossing, see note in 5 L.R.A.(N.S.) 775.

intestate, who was run over and killed by a car of the defendant which was blocking a crossing, and was put in motion by cars switched against it as he was crossing behind it, it is *held:*

(1) That the question whether the plaintiff's intestate was guilty of contributory negligence was one of fact and was properly submitted to the jury.

(2) That the court was in error in submitting to the jury the question whether the defendant, by the act of its conductor, was guilty of wilful or wanton negligence.

(3) That the private rules of a railroad company, adopted for the guidance of its trainmen not known to the deceased, are inadmissible in an action to recover damages caused while he was crossing the tracks behind a string of cars blocking the crossing.

Action in the district court for Isanti county by the administrator of the estate of Emmett Niles, deceased, to recover $7,560 for the death of his intestate. The case was tried before Giddings, J., and a jury which returned a verdict for $7,500. From an order denying its motion for judgment in its favor notwithstanding the verdict or for a new trial, defendant appealed. Reversed and new trial granted.

Cobb, Wheelwright & Dille, for appellant.
Godfrey G. Goodwin and *Albert F. Pratt,* for respondent.

DIBELL, C.

This action was brought by the plaintiff to recover damages sustained by the death of his intestate, Emmett Niles. There was a verdict for the plaintiff. The defendant appeals from the order denying its alternative motion for judgment or for a new trial.

The defendant's railroad runs in a general northerly and southerly direction through Cambridge. The greater part of the village is located on the west of the main line track as is also the depot. At the east of the main line track is the passing track. Still further to the east is the industry track. At the west of the main line track, and at the west of the depot, is the house track.

On the day of the death of the plaintiff's intestate a local train on its way north was switching at Cambridge. It was about six o'clock in the evening. Three cars had been left on the main track blocking the crossing which passed from the east to the west north of the depot. The trainmen were making a flying switch at the north, working two cars over from the industry track and getting them down to the three on the crossing, pulling them down attached to the front of the engine, and using the house track on which to run the engine as the cars continued south on the main track. Just prior to this Niles was at one of the potato warehouses at the east and the north of the depot. He had business at the depot. He went across the passing track and along to the end of the most southerly one of the three cars blocking the crossing, and then started to pass across the main track toward the depot. As he was attempting to cross, the two cars which had been shoved down in making the flying switch struck the three cars standing on the crossing, causing them to move a few feet, and the most southerly one knocked him down and ran over him, the accident resulting in his death a few minutes later.

It is conceded that the jury might, under the evidence, properly find the defendant guilty of negligence. The evidence in support of such finding is ample.

1. The first contention of the defendant is that Niles was, as a matter of law, guilty of contributory negligence.

We do not agree with this contention. When Niles started to the depot the crossing was blocked by the three cars and the engine was switching somewhere to the north. A presumption must be indulged that he exercised reasonable care for his safety. The evidence does not show that he did not make a reasonable observation before he passed behind the car, nor does it show that he did not make a reasonable observation at a practical time before reaching and crossing the passing track. Under the liberal rule now prevailing the question of his negligence was clearly one for the jury. Nelson v. Minneapolis & St. L. R. Co. 123 Minn. 350, 143 N. W. 914; Green v. Great Northern Ry. Co. 123 Minn. 279, 143 N. W. 722; Knudson v. Great Northern Ry. Co. 114 Minn. 244, 130 N. W. 994. We have no quarrel with the finding of the jury that he was not negligent and the court was not in error in submitting the question.

2. The court submitted to the jury the question whether the defendant was guilty of wilful or wanton negligence.

The claim in this connection is that the conductor, who stood somewhere at the north of the crossing, failed to do something which he should have done for Niles' protection after seeing him in a place of danger. He saw Niles and endeavored to attract his attention. Apparently he did not hear. The conductor supposed, or at least he says he supposed, that Niles went around southerly of the three cars and crossed safely over. At the time the two cars were coming from the north. He gave his attention to them, to see if there was sufficient clearance at the house switch, and did not know of Niles' injury until he saw the men pulling him out. We are unable to see that the conductor, after noticing Niles in what was a place of danger unless he was aware of the situation, failed to do anything which he should have done so as to justify a finding that his conduct was wilfully negligent. In submitting the question of wilful negligence to the jury the court was in error.

3. The plaintiff offered in evidence certain private rules adopted by the defendant company for the guidance of its trainmen in the operation of its trains. The test of the liability of a railway company to persons on public highways, or crossing its tracks, is fixed by the law and not by the rules which the company chooses to prescribe for the conduct of its employees. At least twice it has been held error to receive in evidence the rules of the company for the guidance of its employees upon the issue of the liability of the company for an injury to a pedestrian ignorant of them. Fonda v. St. Paul City Ry. Co. 71 Minn. 438, 74 N. W. 166, 70 Am. St. 341; Isackson v. Duluth Street Ry. Co. 75 Minn. 27, 77 N. W. 433. Counsel for the plaintiff urge that these rules were properly brought out on cross-examination, that in general they required nothing of the railroad additional to that imposed by the law, and that they were in no event prejudicial. It is quite clear that these rules did not come into the case as legitimate cross-examination. Whether they required more of the defendant than the law requires, or whether they were in fact prejudicial, we do not stop to discuss; but it is apparent to one familiar with trial work that an inquiry whether the em-

ployees of the defendant were obeying its rules might easily confuse
the jury in its investigation of the issues upon which liability depended.   These errors will not arise again.

Order reversed and new trial granted.

CARL BERNDT v. WILLIAM BERNDT.[1]

October 30, 1914.

Nos. 18,764—(61).[2]

Ejectment — proof of contract of sale — finding.

 1. Action in ejectment.   Defense, that defendant is in possession under
an oral contract of sale, with such part performance as to take the case out
of the statute of frauds.   The court found no oral contract was made.   To
entitle the defendant to the relief asked for, such contract must be clearly
proved and its terms so specific and distinct as to leave no reasonable doubt
of their meaning.   The finding should not be set aside unless it is manifestly
and palpably against the weight of the evidence.   The evidence is conflicting
and it well sustains the finding of the trial court, and the finding must be
sustained.

Plaintiff entitled to maintain action.

 2. Before the commencement of this action plaintiff sold the land to other
parties under contract which provided for payment of the price, delivery of
a deed, and delivery of possession at a time fixed.   That time arrived soon
after commencement of this action.   Payment has not yet been made and
no deed given.   The purchasers are accordingly not yet entitled to possession.
Ejectment is a possessory action.   Plaintiff is entitled to the possession of
the land and is entitled to maintain ejectment.

Action in the district court for Watonwan county.   The case was
tried before Pfau, J., who made findings and ordered judgment in
favor of plaintiff.   From an order denying his motion for amended
findings of fact and conclusions of law or for a new trial, defendant
appealed.   Affirmed.

---

1 Reported in 149 N. W. 287.   2 October, 1914, term calendar.

J. W. Seager and *J. L. Lobben,* for appellant.
Hammond & Farmer and *S. B. Wilson,* for respondent.

HALLAM, J.

Plaintiff and defendant are father and son. Plaintiff, the father, owned a 200-acre farm in Watonwan county. One year he rented it to the defendant, his son. They did not agree, and the next year a mutual friend, Charles Duryea, interceded, rented the land of the father and sublet it to the son. This arrangement was followed for two seasons. Toward the end of the second season, and in September, 1911, the father announced to Duryea that he was going to sell the farm. Duryea urged him to give his son the first chance to buy. The father remonstrated at first, stating that the son could never pay for it, but, at the instance of Duryea, consented to meet with the son and talk it over. They met. Plaintiff testified that as a result of the interview he said to his son: "I will give you a chance up to the fall, and if we can get along togedder, I sell you the farm at $55 an acre, and if we can's get along, then I says you have to pay rent. * * * If he got it * * * I say you have to pay me * * * every year $600 * * * interest * * * he have to pay me 5 per cent * * * I tell him dis way, if we go and make papers out, a deed, that we make it that way that he never could sell the land or put a mortgage on it * * * and when he is dead it goes to the children."

The son testified that the agreement, though verbal, was an absolute and present agreement to sell the farm for $55 an acre, payable $750 a year, without interest, the first payment to be made in the fall of 1912. He admits, however, that a contract was to be drawn when the first payment was made and that the land was to go to the children after his death. The son continued in possession during the season of 1912 under this agreement. Father and son disagreed and the father notified the son early in the season that he could not have the farm, and in September sold the farm to other parties, Hanson and Wenstrum, and later commenced this action in ejectment. The defense is that an oral contract of sale was made and that there was such part performance as to take the case out of the statute of frauds. The court found that no contract was made. Defendant asks us to set aside this finding as not sustained by the evidence.

If we bear in mind the principles which govern such cases, the determination of this question becomes easy. It is an old established rule that "to entitle a party to the specific performance of an alleged contract to convey real property, the contract must be clearly proved, and its terms should be so specific and distinct as to leave no reasonable doubt of their meaning." Lanz v. McLaughlin, 14 Minn. 55 (72); Kileen v. Kennedy, 90 Minn. 414, 97 N. W. 126; 2 Story, Eq. Jur. § 764. This rule is applied even when the alleged contract is in writing. It goes without saying that a rule no less strict is applied when the alleged contract is oral. Burke v. Ray, 40 Minn. 34, 41 N. W. 240; Koch v. Fischer, 122 Minn. 123, 142 N. W. 18; Brown v. Brown, 47 Mich. 378, 11 N. W. 205; 2 Story, Eq. Jur. § 764.

While the defendant does not ask in the present action for a decree for specific performance of his alleged contract, yet the effect of granting the relief he does ask for is in substance much the same, for he asks the court to find that the alleged contract was made and to adjudge his possession rightful by reason thereof, and the principles above stated are substantially the principles which the trial court was obliged to apply in arriving at the decision it did that no contract at all was made.

In reviewing that decision this court is to be guided by the principle that the finding should not be set aside, unless it is manifestly and palpably against the weight of the evidence. Wann v. Northwestern Trust Co. 120 Minn. 493, 497, 139 N. W. 1061. Applying this principle, the trial court must clearly be sustained. If plaintiff's testimony is true, there was no contract. There are circumstances tending to corroborate plaintiff. Defendant testifies to a contract. He is corroborated by some testimony in the nature of admissions said to have been made by plaintiff. The questions involved were purely questions of fact. The findings of the court are well sustained by evidence and should not be disturbed.

2. It is urged that plaintiff cannot maintain this action because

of the contract of sale which he gave to Hanson and Wenstrum. This contract of sale was dated August, 1912. This action was commenced in February, 1913. An examination of the contract makes it very apparent that it does not bar the right of plaintiff to commence and maintain this action. Ejectment is a possessory action, and may be maintained by any person entitled to possession. Atwater v. Spalding, 86 Minn. 101, 90 N. W. 370, 91 Am. St. 331. Plaintiff, as legal owner, has the right of possession, unless this contract with Hanson and Wenstrum has deprived him of it. The contract has not done so. The contract provided that the vendor should deliver a warranty deed upon full performance by the purchaser; that the purchase price of the land over and above earnest money of $500 and a mortgage encumbrance then on the property should be paid March 12, 1913; that the purchasers should have possession March 12, 1913. Right of possession had not passed from plaintiff when this action was commenced, in February, 1913. Nor did it pass on March 12, 1913. The obligation of payment on one side and delivery of deed and of possession on the other, were concurrent. The evidence is that the purchase price has not yet been paid and no deed has been given. Plainly Hanson and Wenstrum have no right either to a deed to the land or the possession of the land until payment has been made. See Buell v. Irwin, 24 Mich. 145. Plaintiff is the person entitled to the possession of this land, and he is entitled to maintain ejectment against the defendant, who wrongfully withholds possession.

Order affirmed.

J. R. BLOCHER v. MAYER BROTHERS COMPANY.[1]

October 30, 1914.

Nos. 18,779—(42).

Parol evidence to explain written contract.

1. The contract set out in the opinion *held* ambiguous and uncertain in

---

1 Reported in 149 N. W. 285.
127 M.—16.

its terms, as respects the subject matter of the litigation, and that parol evidence was admissible in explanation of the same.

2. The construction of the contract, the same being ambiguous and the parol evidence in explanation thereof not being conclusive of the intention of the parties, was properly submitted to the jury.

Action in the district court for Blue Earth county to recover $1,250 under a contract for payment of royalties. The case was tried before Pfau, J., who denied defendant's motion to dismiss the action and its motion for an instructed verdict in its favor, and a jury which returned a verdict in favor of defendant. From an order denying his motion for judgment notwithstanding the verdict or for a new trial, plaintiff appealed. Affirmed.

Miles Porter, George E. Perley and *Tim A. Francis,* for appellant.
C. O. Dailey, for respondent.

BROWN, C. J.

Action to recover certain royalties claimed to be due plaintiff from defendant under the contract hereafter referred to, in which defendant had a verdict, and plaintiff appealed from an order denying a new trial.

The facts in brief are as follows: One Larson was the holder of a patent device known as the Cyclone Disc Sharpener. In January, 1912, he entered into a contract with defendant, a corporation, under which defendant undertook and agreed to manufacture and sell a certain number of the machines annually and to pay Larson a fixed royalty for each machine sold. The contract was subsequently assigned to plaintiff who thereby succeeded to the rights of Larson. The issue presented on the trial, aside from that of fraud set up in the answer which does not seem to have been seriously litigated, was whether defendant was required to manufacture each year the number of machines mentioned in the contract, and to pay royalties thereon, or whether the royalty payments were intended to be limited to the number of machines actually sold by defendant. The contract was in writing and on the theory that it was ambiguous and uncertain in its terms the trial court admitted parol evidence in explanation thereof, and submitted the question of construction to the jury.

By their verdict for defendant the jury found that the parties intended by the contract to impose upon defendant the obligation to pay for machines sold only, and not for those manufactured and not sold.

Two principal questions are presented on this appeal, namely: (1) Whether the trial court erred in admitting parol evidence in explanation of the contract; and (2) whether there was error in submitting the construction of the contract to the jury. We think both questions should be answered in the negative.

1. The contract, insofar as here material, provides as follows: ·

"That the party of the first part (Larson) having a patent number 865627 on what is known as the Cyclone Disc Sharpener, and is desirous that party of the second part manufacture and sell the same and to pay him a royalty of ten ($10) dollars for each machine manufactured and sold. The party of the second part agrees to manufacture at least fifty of said machines on or before February 15th, 1913, and to manufacture at least one hundred of said machines every year thereafter during the continuance of this agreement, and to pay ten ($10) dollars royalty on each machine so manufactured and sold as hereafter stated. The party of the second part agrees to make a report to party of the first part immediately after the sale of each machine giving the name and postoffice address of the purchaser. * * * The party of the second part agrees to make settlement for all royalty not later than sixty days after date of shipment. * * * It is further understood and agreed between the parties that settlement, as per contract in amount, shall be had and made for all machines sold on the 15th day of February, 1913, and annually thereafter, and party of the second part agrees to pay royalty on all machines manufactured as per contract in amount, prior to said date of settlement within sixty days, that is on February 15th, 1913, royalty on at least fifty machines will have to be paid within sixty days, and annually thereafter royalty will have to be paid on at least one hundred machines within sixty days after the date of settlement."

The contract contains other and further stipulations and agreements between the parties, but the foregoing embraces all thereof bearing upon the payment of royalties. It will be noticed that by the language of the forepart of the contract, as above set out, defendant was obligated to pay a royalty on all machines sold, and its liability would seem there to be clearly limited, and to exclude the payment of royalties on machines not sold. While the latter part of the quotation, though somewhat involved, states that the royalty "will have to be paid" on all machines manufactured. The two clauses are inconsistent and render the contract as a whole doubtful and uncertain. In other words, in respect to the agreement for the payment of royalties it is ambiguous and open to parol explanation. There was no error therefore in the admission of the evidence offered by defendant for that purpose. 1 Dunnell, Minn. Dig. §§ 3397, et seq. From this it necessarily follows, the evidence not being conclusive upon the question of the intent of the contract, that the construction thereof was properly submitted to the jury. 1 Dunnell, Minn. Dig. § 1841.

This disposes of the principal questions in the case and results in an affirmance. The other assignments of error present no ground for a new trial, and there was no error in the charge or refusals to charge the jury.

Order affirmed.

PETER MARSHALL v. CHICAGO, ROCK ISLAND & PACIFIC RAILWAY COMPANY.[1]

October 30, 1914.

Nos. 18,805—(69).

Evidence of custom — instruction to jury — verdict.
> Where the court in an action to recover for personal injuries, instructed the jury that plaintiff could not recover, unless a custom existed to give warning of the danger, and there is no evidence tending to prove the existence of such custom, a verdict for plaintiff cannot be sustained.

[1] Reported in 149 N. W. 296.

Action in the district court for Waseca county to recover $3,000 for personal injury sustained while in the employ of defendant. The case was tried before Childress, J., who when plaintiff rested denied defendant's motion to dismiss the action and at the close of the testimony defendant's motion to direct a verdict in its favor, and a jury which returned a verdict for $1,500. From an order denying its motion for judgment notwithstanding the verdict or for a new trial, defendant appealed. Reversed and new trial granted.

Edward C. Stringer, McNeil V. Seymour and *Edward S. Stringer,* for appellant.

Moonan & Moonan, for respondent.

TAYLOR, C.

Plaintiff recovered a verdict for personal injuries, and defendant appealed from an order denying its alternative motion for judgment notwithstanding the verdict or for a new trial.

At the time of the accident, a bridge crew, of which plaintiff was a member, were engaged in removing from a trestle bridge a bent or row of piling which had become decayed to such an extent that it was to be replaced by new material. In constructing the bridge a heavy timber had been placed across the top of the bent or row of piling as a cap, and had been fastened to the piling by drift bolts driven through the cap and into the top of each pile near its center. In removing the piles, the crew cut them off eight or ten feet below the cap timber, pushed or pulled the lower end of the upper piece free from the lower piece which was embedded in the ground, and then worked the upper piece loose from the drift bolt which held it to the cap timber. At all times prior to the accident, the upper piece, after it had been pulled free from the lower piece, had been held suspended by the drift bolt, which fastened it to the cap timber, until the men by twisting it and moving it back and forth worked it loose from such bolt. At the time of the accident plaintiff, unassisted, pulled the upper piece of one of the piles free from the lower piece, and it dropped down upon him dislocating his ankle. Subsequent examination disclosed that the wood around the drift bolt was rotten and the top of the pile cracked or split.

The complaint, among other things, alleged that it was the custom for the foreman to examine the cap timber and the top of the piles to ascertain whether they were rotten, and if they were, to give warning of that fact; and that he failed to give such warning concerning this pile. The trial court submitted the case to the jury solely upon the question as to whether such custom existed and had not been observed in this instance. Consequently the verdict of the jury is necessarily based upon a finding that such custom existed.

A careful examination of the record forces us to the conclusion that there is no evidence to sustain this finding. The only evidence bearing upon the question is the testimony of plaintiff himself. His testimony fairly construed amounts only to this: That whenever the foreman observed a dangerous situation he called attention to the danger; but that he had never, at any time, either when at work upon this bridge or upon other bridges, given warning that the top of any pile was rotten or defective, or the drift bolt loose. Such testimony is wholly insufficient to sustain a finding that a custom existed to give warning whenever the top of a pile was rotten or defective.

The court instructed the jury that: "You must find that there was a custom of the foreman to examine the tops of this piling and warn the men when the same was rotten and, if there was no such custom, the plaintiff cannot recover and your verdict must be for the defendant." As there is no evidence tending to prove such custom, it was error to submit the case to the jury upon such issue, and the verdict, which, under such instruction, is necessarily based upon a finding that such custom existed, cannot be sustained. It does not conclusively appear, however, that plaintiff has no cause of action, and the circumstances do not require that judgment be directed notwithstanding the verdict; but the order denying a new trial must be reversed and a new trial granted.

So ordered.

JOSEPH GERONIME and Others v. GERMAN ROMAN CATHOLIC AID ASSOCIATION OF MINNESOTA.[1]

October 30, 1914.

Nos. 18,850—(104).

Mutual benefit association — forfeiture of membership.

A death benefit certificate issued by a mutual aid association, wherein it was provided that all obligations thereunder should cease if the member "at the time of his death belonged to a secret non-Catholic aid association or for any reason could not be considered as a rightful and reputable member of his respective society or this association," *held*, when construed, as required, most favorably to assured, not forfeited by his membership in a secret aid association open to Roman Catholics, sanctioned by their actual membership, and not shown to have been disapproved by that church, though in no way affiliated therewith.

Action in the district court for Ramsey county to recover $1,000 upon defendant's benefit certificate upon the life of Barth Geronime, deceased. The facts are stated in the opinion. The case was tried before Dickson, J., who granted plaintiffs' motion for a directed verdict in their favor for the amount demanded. From an order denying its motion for judgment notwithstanding the verdict or for a new trial, defendant appealed. Affirmed.

O. E. Holman, for appellant.
Douglas, Kennedy & Kennedy, for respondent.

PHILIP E. BROWN, J.

Action by the beneficiaries to recover on a mutual benefit insurance certificate issued by defendant upon the life of Barth Geronime. Plaintiffs prevailed, and defendant appealed from an order denying its alternative motion.

The facts are undisputed. Assured made written application for admission to defendant order, declaring therein that he was a prac-

[1] Reported in 149 N. W. 291.

tical Catholic and not a member of any secret non-Catholic benevolent association, and agreeing that these statements should be the basis of the contract between himself and defendant. Pursuant thereto he become a member of one of defendant's subordinate societies, and in 1908 received a certificate of insurance in the sum of $1,000. It was written in the German language and, according to the translation, provided, among other things not material, that if the member "at the time of his death belonged to a secret non-Catholic aid association or for any reason could not be considered as a rightful or reputable member of his respective society or this association," according to their constitution and by-laws, all obligations under the certificate should cease. In 1911 assured became a member of and received a $600 insurance certificate from the Mystic Workers of the World, a secret, nonsectarian aid association, whose membership was in no way restricted by considerations of religious belief or affiliation, but which in fact included Roman Catholics, both laymen and clergymen. Nor was it in anywise controlled by or connected with any church. Assured paid all dues and assessments required by both orders up to the time of his death, which occurred in 1912, and was never suspended or expelled from either. There is nothing in the record to indicate that assured was not at all times after he joined defendant's society and association "a rightful" and "reputable member" thereof. The sole defense was that his membership in the other association constituted a violation of the first quoted clause of the contract, thus working a forfeiture of the certificate. It is but fair to say at the outset that defendant's case has been candidly presented, for the purpose of obtaining an authoritative construction of these words, rather than to avoid liability. That this may be accomplished assured's application for membership in the defendant society, already referred to, will be considered as being in evidence, though, upon plaintiffs' objection, it was excluded on the trial.

Plaintiffs' contention that the clause in question is invalid as being against public policy is not sustained (Barry v. Catholic Knights, 119 Wis. 362, 96 N. W. 797); which brings us to the defense based thereon.

No controlling case has been found, and therefore the determination of this question depends upon the application of rules of construction and such aid as may be derived from decisions considering analogous contracts. Such provisions are rarely read literally, one of the most striking examples of the liberal interpretations indulged in favor of the assured being the restricted operation, under judicial construction, of suicide clauses. 2 Dunnell, Minn. Dig. § 4811. In Cook v. Modern Brotherhood of America, 114 Minn. 299, 131 N. W. 334, this court sustained a recovery, and held that the assured, a mining brakeman, whose duty it was to spot "stripping cars," was not a "railway freight brakeman" or "switchman" within a prohibition of the policy, nor engaged in an occupation the duties of which required him "to perform any of the duties belonging * * * to such prohibited occupation," though his employer used a freight engine and system of railway tracks of standard gauge in its mining operations. Similarly, in Hendrickson v. Grand Lodge, A. O. U. W. 120 Minn. 36, 138 N. W. 946, while not expressly so deciding, the court strongly intimated that a common laborer, by accepting temporary employment as a bartender for several weeks, did not thereby "enter into the business or occupation of selling at retail intoxicating liquors as a beverage," within a benefit association by-law imposing a forfeiture therefor.

"The certificate," said Chief Justice Start, in the first case cited, page 302, "if there be any fair doubt as to its meaning, must be construed most strongly against the defendant; for the language used was selected by it for its own benefit."

This declaration accords with the general rule. 29 Cyc. 67. But the doctrine of these cases and the rule stated cannot be invoked unless the words of the policy, when given their fair and ordinary meaning presumptively in the minds of the parties, fail to make the intent clear as to at least some of the language used, and leave that degree of uncertainty which would justify honest differences of opinion and argument between intelligent men as to their meaning. Graves v. Knights of Maccabees, 199 N. Y. 397, 401, 92 N. E. 792, 139 Am. St. 912. Finally:

"If it be left in doubt, in view of the general tenor of the instrument and the relations of the contracting parties, whether given words were used in an enlarged or restricted sense, other things being equal, that construction should be accepted which is most beneficial to the promisee." Bacon, Ben. Soc. (3d ed.) § 179.

The prefix "non" denotes mere negation or absence of the thing or quality to which it is applied, and no doubt the word "catholic," wherever used in the policy, means Roman Catholic, in which sense we also will hereinafter employ it. This, however, does not solve the question; for, as we have seen, literality is not decisive. The inquiry must be: Is there such uncertainty as to what a non-Catholic aid association is, within the purview of the policy, that ordinarily intelligent persons might honestly differ in regard thereto? In our opinion there is such. In other words, we think it fairly debatable whether these words were used in a restricted or an enlarged sense, that is, whether they were intended to exclude assured from membership in any secret aid association not composed exclusively of Catholics, as is contended by defendant, or merely to proscribe connection with organizations objectionable to the Catholic Church or discriminating against its members and adherents. Reading the forfeiture clauses together in accordance with the familiar rule, and remembering that it does not appear that defendant was connected with the Catholic Church or that either the laws of the latter or of defendant interdicted membership in associations of the character of the Mystic Workers, it may well be doubted that forfeiture of a policy on account of such membership was contemplated, when assured might, notwithstanding his connection with the last named association, properly be considered a rightful and reputable member of defendant society and allowed to remain therein until his death. No motive is disclosed for prohibiting membership in societies open to Catholics, sanctioned by their actual membership, not disapproved by the church, and of which assured's priest might have been a member; and, construing the provision in question, as we must, most favorably to assured, we decline to declare the forfeiture relied on to defeat recovery herein.

Order affirmed.

HJALMAR RUSTAD v. GREAT NORTHERN RAILWAY COMPANY.[1]

October 30, 1914.

Nos. 18,918—(151).

Liability as warehouseman — question for jury.

Upon an issue as to the liability of the defendant railway company for the destruction of the property of the plaintiff by fire when in its possession as warehouseman, after reaching its shipping destination, it is *held* that it did not, as a matter of law, establish its freedom from negligence, and that the court properly submitted the case to the jury.

Action in the district court for Pennington county to recover $1,-150. The facts are stated in the opinion. The case was tried before Grindeland, J., who denied defendant's motions for dismissal of the action and for a directed verdict in its favor, and a jury which returned a verdict for $660. From the judgment entered pursuant to the order for judgment, defendant appealed. Affirmed.

M. L. Countryman and *A. L. Janes,* for appellant.

G. Halvorson, for respondent.

DIBELL, C.

This is an appeal by the defendant from a judgment in favor of the plaintiff in an action to recover damages for the loss by fire of property shipped by the plaintiff over the railroad of the defendant and in its possession at the time. The case was here before and is reported in 122 Minn. 453, 142 N. W. 727. Upon that appeal, which was by the plaintiff from an order refusing a new trial, we held that the facts made a question for the jury upon the liability of the defendant for the destruction by fire of the property of the plaintiff while in its possession as warehouseman. The trial court had held that there was no liability. A new trial was therefore granted. Upon the new trial the plaintiff had a verdict.

[1] Reported in 149 N. W. 304.

The facts appearing at the former trial will be found by reference to the opinion. They are substantially the same on this trial. There may be added these: In the afternoon of the day of the fire the inspector of the defendant broke the seals of the car, made a casual examination, and closed the door. He directed the warehouseman to seal it. He did so some time before six o'clock. At that time he opened the door sufficiently to identify the car by its contents, closed it, and attached the seals. The door was not locked from the time the inspector opened it until sealed. There was no other merchandise in the car.

The merchandise was packed with sisel and burlap. The fire occurred along in the evening. It concededly originated from the inside. It smouldered there for a considerable time before breaking out.

The duty of the defendant in respect of showing its freedom from negligence was stated on the former appeal. The facts are not more favorable to the defendant than on the former trial. It cannot be said as a matter of law that the defendant sustained the burden of proof; and the trial court properly submitted the case to the jury.

Judgment affirmed.

STATE v. PEOPLE'S ICE COMPANY.[1]

October 30, 1914.

Nos. 18,931—(7).

Appeal after voluntary payment of fine.

    The defendant, a foreign corporation, indicted for a violation of the statute prohibiting an unlawful combination in restraint of trade, sought an opportunity to change its plea of not guilty to guilty and receive sentence. The sentence immediately imposed was a fine which was at once paid. Six months thereafter, lacking a few days, this appeal was taken. Upon the state's motion to dismiss the appeal it is made to appear that appellant

[1] Reported in 149 N. W. 286.

paid the fine voluntarily with the intention to abide by and comply with the sentence of the court, and hence the appeal should be dismissed.

The People's Ice Company was indicted by the grand jury of Ramsey county of unlawfully entering into a combination in restraint of trade which tended to control and regulate the price of ice, was tried in the district court for Dakota county before Johnson, J., and a jury, convicted and sentenced to pay a fine of $2,000. From the judgment and sentence the People's Ice Company appealed. The state made a motion to dismiss the appeal on the ground that prior to the taking of the appeal the appellant voluntarily paid the judgment, and that under such circumstances an appeal does not lie from a judgment imposing a fine.

John F. Fitzpatrick, for appellant.

Lyndon A. Smith, Attorney General, and *C. Louis Weeks,* Assistant Attorney General, for respondent.

HOLT, J.

The state moves to dismiss the appeal for the reason that appellant, subsequent to the judgment and prior to the appeal, voluntarily paid the fine, the only penalty imposed by the judgment.

The appellant contends that it has the statutory right to appeal within six months after the judgment is pronounced; that the satisfaction of the judgment does not affect this right to appeal; that the payment of a fine cannot be held voluntary, since appellant had property subject to execution; and that, since the stay of execution on appeal in a criminal case is a matter of grace and not of right, the payment of the fine should not be held to be in any sense voluntary or an acquiescence in the sentence. There is much force in these contentions fortified by decisions holding that, even in the absence of statutory provisions, a litigant in a civil action, who pays a judgment rendered against him, may still prosecute his appeal and in case of reversal recover back the amount paid in satisfaction of the judgment. The analogy is strong between the right to appeal in a civil action, as affected by the payment of the judgment, and the one to appeal in a criminal case where the sentence has been carried out.

Johnston v. State, 172 Ala. 424, 55 South. 226, Ann. Cas. 1913E, 296; People v. Marks, 64 Misc. (N. Y.) 679, 120 N. Y. Supp. 1106; Barthelemy v. People, 2 Hill (N. Y.) 248, and the note to State v. Conkling, in 45 Am. St. 271. In Commonwealth v. Fleckner, 167 Mass. 13, 44 N. E. 1053, it is said: "We should be slow to suppose that the legislature meant to take away the right to undo the disgrace and legal discredit of a conviction merely because a wrongly convicted person has paid his fine or served his term. * * * Of course the payment of the fine in accordance with the sentence was not a consent to the sentence but a payment under duress." The authorities which hold to the contrary proceed on the theory that, when the sentence is executed either by imprisonment or payment of the fine, there no longer exists a judgment from which to appeal. The suit is ended. To this effect may be cited: State v. Westfall, 37 Iowa, 575; Commonwealth v. Gipner, 118 Pa. St. 379, 12 Atl. 306; People v. Leavitt, 41 Mich. 470, 2 N. W. 812; Madsen v. Kenner, 4 Utah, 3, 4 Pac. 992; Washington v. Cleland, 49 Ore. 12, 88 Pac. 305, 124 Am. St. 1013, and cases cited in note to Johnson v. State, 30 Ann. Cas. 300.

It is not necessary to determine which line of authorities should be followed, for we are persuaded that here appellant voluntarily paid the fine and fully acquiesced in the sentence. There can be no purpose to remove the stigma of conviction by this appeal, for appellant pleaded guilty to the offense charged. The appeal can involve nothing but the propriety of a fine or the amount thereof. The state shows that Mr. Wells, the president of the appellant, a foreign corporation, had been found guilty upon a trial under an indictment charging him, this appellant, and others with an unlawful combination in restraint of trade, an offense under section 8973, G. S. 1913. He had obtained a stay. While the stay was pending he and the attorneys for appellant sought the prosecuting attorney and expressed the desire to have the whole matter settled. To that end they prevailed upon the prosecuting attorney to arrange with the judge who tried the case to come to the county seat of Dakota county, the place of trial, and hold a special term for that purpose. This was done. Wells, or his attorneys, requested that the stay as to him be vacated and sentence imposed. He was fined and paid the fine. He also, as president of appellant, withdrew appellant's plea of not guilty and entered a plea of guilty. The sentence was a fine of $2,-000. At once Wells produced the money and paid the fine. This occurred on December 13, 1913. No dissent to the form of the sentence, or to the amount of the fine was then suggested. Thereafter nothing occurred to indicate that appellant was in any manner aggrieved by the sentence until June 11, 1914, when this appeal was taken. Appellant, in the meantime, acquiesced in the entry of judgment ousting it from doing business in the state, in an action brought by the attorney general, because of its acknowledged violation of the statute. We hold that the whole course of appellant in procuring a special session of court to be held so as to allow it to change its plea to guilty, its payment of the fine without the slightest suggestion that either a fine, or the amount thereof, was not proper, and the long delay in taking the appeal, tends to show that the payment was voluntary, to the end that the whole prosecution should be terminated and settled. The state and prosecuting authorities were led to believe and act on that understanding. And we fully believe that the president of appellant, when he entered the plea of guilty for it and immediately produced the $2,000 in cash and paid the fine imposed, did so with the full intention, acting for appellant, to abide by and satisfy the sentence of the court. This is more of a voluntary payment than the facts disclosed in De Graff v. County of Ramsey, 46 Minn. 319, 48 N. W. 1135. This money was at once paid to the proper officers, presumably distributed to the proper funds, and has undoubtedly been used. This is and of itself may not be material, for we may well say that the sense of fairness is so well developed in the public conscience that the legislature would make provision to reimburse one who under legal compulsion has paid into the state treasury or to public funds money which in justice and right should not have been paid; but it is a circumstance to be considered in determining whether the payment of the fine imposed was voluntary, for appellant was represented by a capable officer, and able attorneys and knew that public authorities would receive, distribute and use the money for designated purposes.

The appeal should be and it is dismissed.

IMPERIAL ELEVATOR COMPANY v. W. M. BENNETT.[1]

November 6, 1914.

Nos. 18,524, 18,525—(24, 25).

Fraudulent transfer by debtor — finding sustained by evidence.

    1. A debtor assigned to a creditor as security for his debt the proceeds of an insurance policy on property that had been destroyed by fire. It is *held* that a finding of the trial court that there was no intent to defraud creditors is sustained by the evidence.

Same — intent to defraud.

    2. In the absence of an actual intent to defraud creditors, a transfer by a debtor to a creditor of property to pay or secure a valid debt, though it may be a preference, is not deemed fraudulent in law, unless some insolvent or bankrupt law makes it so, and then only in aid of an insolvent or bankruptcy proceeding. The assignment in this case was not fraudulent in law.

Subrogation — mechanic's lien — proceeds of fire insurance.

    3. Where the owner of real estate insures his interest therein against loss by fire, in the absence of contract obligation the holder of a mechanic's lien on the property has, after a loss by fire, no claim upon the proceeds of the insurance money.

Action in the district court for Hennepin county for $1,423.04, to obtain judgment that the assignment from defendant to Jennie M. Thompson was fraudulent and void, to impress the proceeds of the policy of fire insurance issued by the garnishee company with an equitable lien, and to require it to be turned over to plaintiff to the full extent of its claim. Jennie M. Thompson intervened. The Fidelity-Phenix Fire Insurance Co. of New York was garnisheed. The facts are stated in the opinion. The action was tried before Booth, J., who made findings and ordered judgment in favor of the intervener for the sum of $2,000, and interest, and in favor of plaintiff for the amount demanded. From an order denying its motion for a new trial and a motion to make findings as proposed by plain-

[1] Reported in 149 N. W. 372.

tiff, except in so far as the proposed amendments were adopted by the court, plaintiff appealed. Affirmed.

Mercer, Swan & Stinchfield, for appellant.

Arthur M. Higgins, for respondents.

BUNN, J.

Defendant Bennett owned lots 4 and 5 in Way's plat of the Townsite of Le Beau, South Dakota, together with a hotel then situated on lot 4. June 15, 1908, he borrowed $1,000 of the intervener, Jennie M. Thompson, and gave her his note for said sum payable in two years with six per cent interest. He and his wife executed and delivered to the intervener a mortgage to secure the note covering lot 4, which mortgage was recorded June 16, 1908. A year later and on July 19, 1909, Bennett, for value received, executed and delivered a second $1,000 note to the intervener, payable in two years, with seven per cent interest. July 30, 1909, Bennett and his wife executed and delivered to the intervener a mortgage to secure this note; this mortgage covered lots 4 and 5, and was recorded October 15, 1909. The mortgage of June, 1908, contained no agreement by the mortgagor to keep the buildings on the premises insured, but there was a clause in the mortgage of July, 1909, by which the mortgagor agreed to keep the premises insured to the extent of $1,000 for the benefit of the mortgagee.

Between June 1 and November 10, 1909, plaintiff sold and delivered to defendant Bennett building material for use by him in the construction of improvements and additions to the hotel. Bennett gave two notes to plaintiff for the material furnished, one for $937 on June 1, 1909, and the other for $589.05 on November 10, 1909. Plaintiff, on November 10, 1909, filed with the proper officer what would correspond to a lien statement under the laws of Minnesota, and admittedly then had under the South Dakota laws a lien on lots 4 and 5 for the amount due and unpaid for the materials furnished.

September 6, 1910, the garnishee insurance company issued to Bennett a policy insuring him against loss or damage by fire to the building then situate on lots 4 and 5 to the extent of $2,000, and against loss or damage to the personal property then contained in

127 M.—17.

the building to the extent of $500. The policy when delivered did not have attached a clause making the loss payable to the intervener. September 8, 1910, the insured property was entirely destroyed by fire. September 13, 1910, the agent for the insurance company, at the request of Bennett, indorsed upon the policy a clause making the loss, if any, payable to the intervener as her interest might appear. The loss of defendant by the fire was, on September 13, adjusted by the company at the full amount of the policy. On the same day Bennett executed and delivered to the intervener a written assignment of his claim against the insurance company.

Plaintiff then commenced this action against the defendant Bennett, asking judgment against him in the sum of $1,423.04, judgment that the assignment to intervener was fraudulent and void, and that the court impress the insurance money with an equitable lien and require it to be turned over to plaintiff to the full extent of his claim. The insurance company was garnished, and disclosed an indebtedness to defendant of $2,500, but subject to the claim thereto of Jennie M. Thompson. This money was paid into court. Mrs. Thompson filed a complaint in intervention, claiming the whole of the insurance money. Plaintiff filed its answer and cross-bill alleging the assignment from Bennett to Mrs. Thompson to be fraudulent and void, and claiming an equitable lien upon the insurance money paramount to any claim of the intervener.

A trial of the issues thus made resulted in a decision that the intervener was entitled to the insurance money to the extent of her claim, $2,000 and interest, and that plaintiff was entitled to the balance. Findings were filed both in the main action and in the garnishment action. Plaintiff moved for amended findings and conclusions, and for a new trial. These motions were denied, and plaintiff appealed from the orders.

The first contention of plaintiff is that the intervener established no right or claim to the fund, and therefore that plaintiff was entitled to be paid in full out of it, because of the garnishment. If the premises are correct, the conclusion would follow. The question therefore is: Had Mrs. Thompson, prior to the garnishment, a valid claim against this insurance money?

Her claim is under the "loss payable" clause indorsed upon the policy, and under the assignment by Bennett to her after the fire. This "loss payable" clause, as before stated, was indorsed upon the policy after the loss occurred. The trial court found as a fact that this was done pursuant to directions given the insurance company by Bennett, given prior to the execution of the policy, to make the loss payable to the intervener. Plaintiff argues that the agent of the company had no authority to change the company's obligations by attaching this clause after the fire. But the finding, which is sustained by the evidence, removes any such question. In any event the intervener had an equitable lien to the insurance money under the clause in the mortgage by which Bennett agreed to keep the property insured for her benefit. Ames v. Richardson, 29 Minn. 330, 13 N. W. 137.

The main contention of plaintiff on this branch of the case is that the indorsement of this clause, together with the assignment by Bennett to the intervener of all the former's claim to the insurance money, was fraudulent in law and in fact, as against Bennett's creditors. It is argued that Bennett was insolvent when he made the assignment; that the assignment was of $2,500, whereas he was under no obligation to secure Mrs. Thompson for more than $1,000, and that it was understood that Bennett should get back the balance of the $2,500 after the debt to Mrs. Thompson was paid. The trial court found as a fact that there was no fraud. There was a preference, it is true, but we are clear that the circumstances are not such that we can say the finding is not sustained by the evidence, or that there was fraud in law. The debt to the intervener was an honest one and was overdue. Bennett, at the time of the transfer, had insurance aggregating $6,000, though he in fact collected but $4,000. The assignment was undoubtedly given as security. The intervener had no knowledge of any fraudulent intent, and in fact Bennett had no such intent. It is well settled in this state that the payment of or securing an honest debt by a debtor is not deemed fraudulent in law, though it operates as a preference, and though it does in fact hinder and delay other creditors, unless some insolvency or bankruptcy law makes such transfer invalid, and then only in aid of an insolvency or bankruptcy proceeding. Crookston State Bank v. Lee, 124 Minn. 112, 144 N. W. 433; Dyson v. St. Paul Nat. Bank, 74 Minn. 439, 77 N. W. 236, 73 Am. St. 358.

As there was no actual intent to defraud, we hold that the assignment by Bennett to the intervener was valid as against plaintiff, and entitled intervener to payment of her claim out of the fund garnished, unless plaintiff had an equitable lien on such fund that was paramount to the claim of the intervener.

Under the laws of South Dakota, plaintiff had a lien on the building. This lien was clearly superior to the lien of the intervener's second mortgage, and apparently, under the statutes of South Dakota, superior to the lien of the prior mortgage. This may be conceded for the purposes of this case. This conclusion makes it unnecessary to consider the point that the second mortgage was not entitled to record, as, whether this is true or not, we start with the premise that plaintiff's lien on the building was paramount to the intervener's lien under either mortgage. The question is whether, when the building was destroyed by fire, plaintiff's lien attached in equity to the proceeds of the insurance. If it did, it would follow that the assignment by Bennett to the intervener could not operate to destroy this lien. If the lien did not in equity attach to the insurance money, the intervener's claim is clearly superior.

Plaintiff relies upon the principle that a court of equity, whenever it is necessary in order to prevent justice being defeated, will treat the money derived from property as it would the property itself. This principle has been frequently applied to cases where property upon which there was a lien has been sold under a paramount lien, under legal or judicial process or under a testamentary power paramount to the lien. Ness v. Davidson, 49 Minn. 469, 52 N. W. 46, is a good illustration of this doctrine. There real estate upon which there was a mechanic's lien was sold under a testamentary power that was paramount to the lien, the execution of which power discharged the lien from the land. It was held that the sale was in effect a conversion of the land into money, and that the proceeds should be charged with the payment of the debt. But plainly the principle has no application to a case where the property is insured by the owner for his own or another lienor's benefit, and where this act of the owner results in there being insurance money when the property is destroyed by fire. There has been no sale under a paramount lien under legal or judicial process, or under a testamentary or other power paramount to the lien. The owner was under no obligation to insure the property for the benefit of the lienor, and did not do so. The lienor had an insurable interest and might have protected his rights by insurance. The case of Elgin Lumber Co. v. Longman, 23 Ill. App. 250, relied upon by plaintiff, contains an obiter statement favorable to the contention that a mechanic's lien on land may attach to the proceeds of insurance thereon taken out by the owner, but this statement is opposed both to reason and authority. In Ames v. Richardson, 29 Minn. 330, 13 N. W. 137, this court said that it was well settled that, in the absence of an agreement by the mortgagor to insure for the benefit of his mortgagee, the latter has no right to any advantage whatever from an insurance upon the mortgaged property effected by the former for his own benefit. This is the universal rule as far as we know. A fire insurance policy is a mere personal contract of indemnity against a loss by the person insured. It does not attach to the property or go with the same as an incident. 19 Cyc. 583, 883, and cases cited. The City of Norwich, 118 U. S. 468, 6 Sup. Ct. 1150, 30 L. ed. 134; Farmers Loan & Trust Co. v. Penn Plate Glass Co. 186 U. S. 434, 22 Sup. Ct. 842, 46 L. ed. 1234. We perceive of no reason why the rule should be different in the case of a mechanic's lien than it is in the case of a mortgage. In either case it is the interest of the owner and not the interest of the lienor or mortgagee that is insured. In the absence of contract, or of facts constituting an estoppel, the insured is entitled to the insurance money, and it cannot be taken from him and given to a lien owner or mortgagee, on any doctrine of equity such as plaintiff relies on. 19 Cyc. 887, and cases cited.

Orders affirmed.

JOSEPH MATZ v. MARTIN MARTINSON.[1]

November 6, 1914.

Nos. 18,746—(56).

Intoxication — failure to disaffirm contract.

1. A contract entered into by a person in such a state of intoxication that he is unable to comprehend its terms is voidable but not void. If, after having knowledge of and comprehending its terms, he affirms it, it becomes valid and binding. His failure to disaffirm it within a reasonable time after having such knowledge is deemed an election to affirm it.

Same — estoppel by conduct.

2. Where defendant executed a promissory note for a valid pre-existing debt, and, for at least five years after full knowledge of the transaction, recognized the note as valid and repeatedly promised to pay it, he cannot thereafter interpose as a defense thereto that he was intoxicated when he signed it, and testimony to prove such intoxication may properly be stricken from the record.

Striking out evidence — statute.

3. Section 7998, G. S. 1913, does not deprive the court of the power to strike out immaterial evidence, nor require it to submit to the jury questions having no bearing upon the outcome of the suit. Where the court states the case as it is, explains the rules of law which apply and permits the jury to return such verdict as they may deem proper under the circumstances, the court has fully performed the duty imposed upon it by this statute.

Action in the district court for Wilkin county to recover a balance of $488.70 upon a promissory note. The answer alleged that on the day mentioned defendant was intoxicated and deprived of his reason and understanding, and while so intoxicated plaintiff, taking an undue advantage of his condition, induced him to sign his name to the note. The case was tried before Flaherty, J., who granted de-

[1] Reported in 149 N. W. 370.

Note.—Validity of contract made with intoxicated person, see notes in 54 L.R.A. 440; 2 L.R.A.(N.S.) 666; 25 L.R.A.(N.S.) 596.

fendant's motion to strike out all the evidence on behalf of the defendant bearing on the question of his intoxication, and a jury which returned a verdict for the amount demanded. From an order denying his motion for a new trial, defendant appealed. Affirmed.

Leonard Eriksson, for appellant.

Lewis E. & D. J. Jones, for respondent.

TAYLOR, C.

This is a suit upon a promissory note. The defense interposed is that defendant was so drunk when he signed it that he was incapable of entering into a contract. At the close of the evidence all testimony tending to prove such drunkenness was stricken out on motion of plaintiff. The testimony so stricken out would have supported a finding by the jury that defendant was intoxicated to the extent claimed, and consequently the action of the court in striking it out presents the question as to whether the fact of such intoxication was a defense to the suit.

1. The note together with a chattel mortgage upon some horses was executed on January 10, 1906. Defendant had previously mortgaged the horses to a third party. He subsequently sold them, and apparently applied the proceeds upon the first mortgage. He paid none of such proceeds to plaintiff. Plaintiff made no attempt to enforce his mortgage, and never received anything thereunder. He made several threats to prosecute defendant criminally for selling mortgaged property, but no prosecution was ever instituted. Defendant, at the trial, admitted and testified that he was informed of the note and mortgage and knew that he had executed them on January 11, 1906, the next day after their execution; that the note was given for a prior debt and that he owed such debt; that after knowing that he had executed the note, he repeatedly promised to pay it; that he made two payments upon it, one of $50 in September, 1908, and another of $50 in October, 1908; and that he made no claim to plaintiff that the note was invalid, because executed while he was intoxicated, until some time in the spring of 1913. His wife testified that one of plaintiff's attorneys came to the house at a time when her husband was absent; and that, in response to an inquiry

as to whether they could make a payment upon the note, she informed him that they would not pay it as her husband was intoxicated when he signed it. She was unable to fix the date of this conversation with any definiteness, but stated that it occurred some two years before the trial. As the trial took place in December, 1913, this conversation probably occurred some time in 1911. It is not claimed that there was any act repudiating the note prior to this conversation; but defendant contends that this conversation, and the statement, which he himself made in the spring of 1913, constituted a disaffirmance of the note and absolved him from any obligation to pay it.

Although a party may repudiate a contract entered into when he was in such a state of intoxication that he could not comprehend its terms, it is well settled that such contract is not void but voidable only. If, after becoming sober and comprehending its terms, he affirms it, it becomes valid and binding. If he elects to repudiate it, he must give notice thereof with reasonable promptness. He is allowed a reasonable time after he understands the nature and effect of the transaction in which to disaffirm it; but, if he takes no steps to disaffirm it within a reasonable time after he has such knowledge, he is deemed to have ratified it. Carpenter v. Rodgers, 61 Mich. 384, 28 N. W. 156, 1 Am. St. 595; J. I. Case Threshing Machine Co. v. Meyers, 78 Neb. 685, 111 N. W. 602, 9 L.R.A.(N.S.) 970; Kelly v. Louisville & N. R. Co. 154 Ala. 573, 45 South. 906; Strickland v. Parlin & Orendorf Co. 118 Ga. 213, 44 S. E. 997; Spoonheim v. Spoonheim, 14 N. D. 380, 104 N. W. 845; Fowler v. Meadow Brook Water Co. 208 Pa. St. 473, 57 Atl. 959; 17 Am. & Eng. Enc. (2d ed.) 401.

The note in controversy was given for a valid debt previously contracted. Defendant does not claim any defense to the debt, nor that he was overreached in any manner. He recognized the note as a valid and binding obligation for fully five years, and during that time made numerous promises, both verbally and by letter, that he would pay it. The record shows conclusively that he ratified the execution of the note after having full knowledge of the transaction. Therefore whether he was intoxicated when he signed it became wholly immaterial, and evidence tending to show such fact was properly stricken from the record.

2. Defendant complains of the manner in which the case was submitted to the jury. He offered no defense except the claim that the note was invalid because signed while he was intoxicated. As already pointed out his subsequent ratification of the note precluded him from asserting this defense. When the case went to the jury plaintiff's note stood admitted, and there was no evidence tending to show any defense to it whatever. Plaintiff moved the court to direct a verdict in his favor. Defendant objected under chapter 245, page 336, Laws of 1913. The trial judge endeavored to follow this statute. He denied plaintiff's motion. He called the attention of the jury to the note, and to the defense of intoxication, and gave them two forms of verdict. He told them that the testimony as to intoxication had been stricken out and was not to be considered by them. He further told them to take the note and, if plaintiff was entitled to recover, to return a verdict for the amount thereof, but that he did not direct a verdict for plaintiff.

Defendant contends that withdrawing the evidence as to intoxication from the jury infringed the rights secured to him by the statute. This somewhat unusual statute reads as follows:

"When at the close of the testimony any party to the action moves the court to direct a verdict in his favor, and the adverse party objects thereto, such motion shall be denied and the court shall submit to the jury such issue or issues, within the pleadings on which any evidence has been taken, as either or any party to the action shall request, but upon a subsequent motion, by such moving party after verdict rendered in such action, that judgment be entered notwithstanding the verdict, the court shall grant the same if, upon the evidence as it stood at the time such motion to direct a verdict was made the moving party was entitled to such directed verdict." Section 7998, G. S. 1913.

It may be noted in passing that defendant made no request for the submission of any issue to the jury, but merely objected to the granting of plaintiff's motion. This statute has no reference to the reception or rejection of evidence, and in no way changes or restricts the power of the court to determine questions arising in respect thereto. The court has precisely the same power to receive, exclude and strike out evidence that it had before the passage of the statute. Evidence offered for the purpose of proving facts which, if established, would not affect the result of the action, may properly be excluded or stricken out as immaterial.

The statute contemplates the existence of questions which are for the jury to determine, and which have a bearing upon the result of the action. Such questions may arise either because the facts are in controversy, or because different conclusions may be drawn from the undisputed facts. But if there be no such questions, there are no issues for submission to the jury. The court is not debarred from stating to the jury the rules of law which govern the case, and should do so. He performs his full duty under the statute when he states the case to the jury as it actually is, explains the rules of law which apply, and directs them to return such verdict as they may deem proper under the circumstances. Whether the court no longer possesses the power to direct a verdict in any case, if objection be made thereto, is neither involved nor decided herein.

The record in the present case discloses no error affecting any substantial right of defendant and the order denying a new trial is affirmed.

HENRY L. SIMONS v. EMIL MUNCH and Others.[1]

November 6, 1914.

Nos. 18,780—(43).

Construction of judgment.

1. In arriving at the meaning of a judgment or decree, it is improper to rely wholly on the literal reading of clauses severed from the sentence in which they are placed. The judgment as a whole should be considered in

[1] Reported in 149 N. W. 304.

interpreting any particular clause or sentence therein, and if so considered there be any doubt, or it be open to two constructions, the pleadings and findings or verdict may be resorted to, and that construction given which harmonizes with the record. *Held*, that the trial court properly construed the judgment and decree herein.

Contempt — findings sustained by evidence.

2. The findings of fact are amply sustained by the proof, and show that respondent has not been guilty of violation of the injunctional part of the judgment. Upon such findings the contempt proceeding was properly dismissed, and appellants are not prejudiced by the order refusing to set aside the findings and dismissal.

Certain of the interveners in the above entitled action obtained from the district court for Pine county an order directing the Pine City Electric Power Co. to show cause why it should not be punished for contempt in failing to obey the judgment as to the provision with regard to interfering with the natural flow of water in Snake river and why it should not indemnify the same parties for the resulting damage. The matter was heard before Dancer, J., acting for the judge of the Nineteenth judicial district, who denied defendant's motion to dismiss the proceedings on the ground that the court had no jurisdiction to enjoin defendant and made findings dismissing the order to show cause. From an order denying the motion of interveners for new findings of fact and conclusions of law, Ignatius Chelmik and T. J. Mider, plaintiffs and interveners, appealed. Affirmed.

Thomas C. Daggett and *James A. Manahan,* for appellants.
J. N. Searles and *George H. Sullivan,* for respondent.

HOLT, J.

Many years ago Henry L. Simons brought an action in ejectment for the possession of lands abutting Snake river, above the outlet of Cross lake, alleging that the defendants by means of a dam, known as the Chengwatonna dam, maintained a few hundred feet below the outlet of said lake, set the water back in the river, and the lake above for which it was an outlet, so as to overflow the plaintiff's lands and deprive him of their use. During the protracted litigation Pine City Electric Power Co. became the owner of the dam and was made party to the suit, together with a number of owners of lands abutting the river and lakes above the dam who intervened, setting forth a cause of action in ejectment for their lands substantially like plaintiff's. All asked also for damages for the unlawful usurpation of their lands. Among the interveners were appellants I. Chelmik and J. T. Mider. Final and separate judgments and decrees in favor of plaintiff and each intervener were entered. The history of this dam litigation in this court may be found in 100 Minn. 114, 110 N. W. 368, 107 Minn. 370, 120 N. W. 373, 121 N. W. 878; 115 Minn. 360, 132 N. W. 321, and 118 Minn. 528, 136 N. W. 1028. The judgments so entered provided and decreed: "That none of the defendants and none of the interveners above named allied with defendants has any right, title, interest or easement in or to or lien upon any part of said lands, that each and all of said defendants and allied interveners be and hereby are permanently enjoined from maintaining the so-called Chengwatonna dam across Snake river, in said county and state, from interfering with the natural flow of water in said river, and from in any way obstructing its current, but no execution or judgment shall issue for the recovery of said lands prior to April 1st, 1912."

In May, 1913, the appellants procured an order from the court directing the respondent to show cause why it should not be punished for contempt in failing to obey the judgment as to the provision above set forth and why it should not indemnify appellants for the resulting damage. At the hearing voluminous testimony from experts and nonexperts was submitted. The court made these controlling findings of fact: That respondent on March 31, 1912, began removing the dam and prosecuted the work diligently and so that it no longer interferes with the natural flow of the water in the river to any appreciable extent; and that before removing said dam respondent "erected what is now called the new Chengwatonna dam across said Snake river, approximately two thousand feet below the site of the original or the old Chengwatonna dam heretofore mentioned, which new Chengwatonna dam as so erected and as so maintained by said defendant (respondent) until the 30th day of June, 1912, interfered with the flow of the water in Snake river, but not to such an extent as to flood the lands of said Chelmik or Mider and other interveners or plaintiff in this action, or as to raise the water abutting said lands of any of them." It was also found that on June 30, 1912, respondent sold the dam to another company, and since such date has not interfered in any way with the natural flow of water in the river. Upon these findings an order was made dismissing the order to show cause. Thereafter appellants moved the court to set aside the findings and order of dismissal and to substitute proposed findings and an order adjudging respondent guilty. They appeal from the order denying their motion.

Respondent makes the point that the order is not appealable. Inasmuch as the controversy has been fully argued on the merits and it is highly desirable that needless litigation over the new dam be averted, if possible, we have concluded to pass by respondent's objection especially since it will not be prejudiced by so doing.

Appellants take their stand upon a literal interpretation of these detached clauses in the judgment, enjoining respondent "from interfering with the natural flow of water in said river, and from in any way obstructing its current." They claim that this prohibits respondent from interfering with the current at any place in Snake river. Such construction appears to us strained and unreasonable. It would be more proper to say that these clauses forbid every interference with the natural flow or current of the river that will affect the use or possession of the lands mentioned in the first part of the sentence. We see readily that the purpose of the judgment was to exclude respondent from claiming the right or easement of flowage in these lands of appellants, particularly the right of flowage by the old dam involved in the litigation. True it is, that where the language of a judgment or decree is clear and unambiguous, neither the pleadings nor the findings or verdict, nor matters de hors the record may be resorted to to change the meaning. It must stand and be enforced as it speaks. But when the meaning is obscure, doubtful or ambiguous, the judgment roll or record may always be examined for the purpose of rendering certain that which may be open for construction or interpretation. We look for harmony between the pleadings, findings and decree. If the latter be not absolutely clear or certain, we may expect more clearness when read in the light of the issues raised and the facts found. It is well settled that resort may be had to the pleadings and issues joined thereunder to explain and limit the language of the judgment. Pomona Land & Water Co. v. San Antonio Water Co. 152 Cal. 618, 93 Pac. 81. See also Watson v. Lawson, 166 Cal. 235, 135 Pac. 961; Drach v. Isola, 48 Colo. 134, 109 Pac. 748; Sharp v. McColm, 79 Kan. 772, 101 Pac. 659; Attorney General v. New York, N. H. & H. Ry. Co. 201 Mass. 370, 87 N. E. 621; Haskall v. Kansas Natural Gas Co. 224 U. S. 217, 32 Sup. Ct. 442, 56 L. ed. 738. "In case of doubt regarding the signification of a judgment, or any part thereof, the whole record may be examined for the purpose of removing the doubt." 1 Freeman, Judgments. § 45. "To ascertain the meaning of a judgment entry it is always permissible to read it in the light of the entire record." Burke v. Unique Printing Co. 63 Neb. 264, 88 N. W. 488. If, instead of isolating the injunctional clauses referred to, the whole sentence wherein they are found is read and a reasonable interpretation be given thereto, we think there is no difficulty in arriving at the same meaning arrived at by the trial court. This was in substance that the injunctional part of the judgment was intended to restore permanently to the appellants possession of their lands, insofar as there had been an encroachment or taking by means of the waters held back or impeded by the old Chengwatonna dam, and that neither by that dam, nor by any other dam or means, should respondent thereafter interfere with the natural flow of the water past the abutting lands of appellants, or be permitted to flood the same to any extent. And if we desire confirmation we have but to examine the pleadings and findings. The only object of the action on the part of the plaintiff and allied interveners was to remove the waters cast upon their lands by the maintenance of the old Chengwatonna dam, and for damages suffered therefor. Appellants had and can have no right in this action to ask more than protection from interference with the natural flow of the water past their premises. It is not to be assumed that appellants sought or obtained abatement of the old dam because of interference with the public right of navigation, for such an action would not lie unless appellants showed special injury in that direction. Viebahn v. Board of Co. Commrs. of Crow Wing County, 96 Minn. 276, 104 N.

W. 1089, 3 L.R.A.(N.S.) 1126. Neither pleadings nor judgment
involve such issue. The course of Snake river from the old dam to
the outlet into St. Croix river is many miles. It would savor entirely
too much of the dog in the manger proposition to enjoin respondent,
or any one else, from using the waters of the river for any purpose
to which it may be adapted as it passes lands not owned by appellants,
when such use in no manner affects the lands of the appellants situated miles above. Suppose Snake river extended in a precipitous
course several hundred miles below Cross lake, could it be a reasonable contention that the decree prohibited interference with the current in the river by any dam however small and however remote from
appellants' lands? Surely not. Since, as before stated, the pleadings
do not allege special injury to appellants from any interference with
the navigability of the river, a judgment prohibiting respondent from
impeding the flow at every place therein would not be warranted.
When a judgment admits of two constructions, "that one will be
adopted that is consonant with the judgment that should have been
rendered on the facts and the law of the case." 1 Black, Judgments,
§ 3.

The construction placed on the judgment by the trial court does
not contradict the language of any particular clause but harmonizes
the whole judgment, especially when read in connection with the
pleadings and findings. The material findings as hereinbefore set
forth are amply supported by the evidence; and upon these findings
respondent was entitled to a dismissal of the contempt proceedings.
Therefore no prejudicial error could result to appellants from the
order refusing to vacate the dismissal. This view renders unnecessary a consideration of other questions presented.

Order affirmed.

SAID MALOOF v. CHICAGO GREAT WESTERN RAILROAD COMPANY and Others.[1]

November 6, 1914.

Nos. 18,786—(45).

Death by wrongful act — finding — evidence.

In an action for personal injuries resulting in the death of plaintiff's intestate, it is *held* that the evidence justifies a finding that the defendant construction company and its foreman negligently put the plaintiff's intestate at work pushing a car which was being pinched out from one end of a string of cars, without taking proper precaution for his safety, and that they were properly found liable for his death, caused by being caught between the bumper of the car he was pushing and the one next behind it, the movement being caused by a switching crew running some cars into the rear of the string of cars.

Action in the district court for Ramsey county by the administrator of the estate of Joseph Namie Hodge, deceased, to recover $7,500 for the death of his intestate while in the employ of defendant Hoy & Elzy Co. The case was tried before Olin B. Lewis, J., who granted the motion of defendant Dumbrowsky and that of the railroad company to dismiss the action as to them and denied motions of the other defendants to dismiss the action as to them, and a jury which returned a verdict for $3,800 in favor of plaintiff. From an order denying their motions for judgment notwithstanding the verdict or for a new trial, defendants Hoy & Elzy Co. and J. W. Souter appealed. Affirmed.

Barrows, Stewart & Ordway, for appellants.
O'Brien, Young & Stone, for respondent.

DIBELL, C.
Action to recover damages for the death of plaintiff's intestate. The case was dismissed as to the defendant railroad company.

[1] Reported in 149 N. W. 284.

There was a verdict against the defendants Hoy & Elzy Co. and J. W. Souter. The defendants appeal from the order denying their alternative motion for judgment or a new trial.

The only question is whether the evidence sustains the verdict.

The deceased Hodge was in the employ of the defendant Hoy & Elzy Co. The defendant Souter was the company's foreman. The company was constructing a roundhouse for the defendant railroad company. About a quarter before seven on the morning of the accident Souter and a gang of men, which included Hodge, started to work. The railroad company had switched out a string of some 18 or 20 cars on the industry track near which was the roundhouse. The third car from the west end of the string of cars was for the defendant's use. The two at the west end were not. The defendant wanted to get the third car and spot it near the roundhouse. Under the direction of Souter the most westerly car was pinched some 40 or more feet west. Then under his direction the men started pinching the second car from the west, and had proceeded a few feet, Hodge pushing with his hands on the bumpers, when a switching crew which was working over at the east let some cars down against the string of cars causing them to move westerly a few feet. Hodge was caught between the bumpers of the second and third cars and was killed.

The jury might have found that Souter, when he directed the men to pinch out the cars, knew or should have known that the switching crew had not finished with this string of cars; that he knew or should have known that a switching crew might run cars against them, and that he negligently failed to make proper provision for the safety of the men engaged under his direction in spotting the car.

This brings the case within the general rule that the master must exercise reasonable care in furnishing a safe place of work for his servant and the particular application of it, which finds expression in the statement that where the master orders a servant into a place of danger to do specific work he owes him the affirmative duty of exercising reasonable care for his protection while there. Hess v. Adamant Mnfg. Co. 66 Minn. 79, 68 N. W. 774; Dizonno v. Great Northern Ry. Co. 103 Minn. 120, 114 N. W. 736; Lohman v.

Swift & Co. 105 Minn. 148, 117 N. W. 418; Aho v. Adriatic Mining
Co. 117 Minn. 504, 136 N. W. 310, and cases cited; Nilsson v.
Barnett & Record Co. 123 Minn. 308, 143 N. W. 789, and cases
cited.

From the same accident arose the case of Koury v. Chicago Great
Western R. Co. 125 Minn. 78, 145 N. W. 786. There the verdict
was for the plaintiff. On appeal a new trial was granted. The
case is now cited. It gives no help. In that case there was an
entire absence of proof of the cause of the moving of the string of
cars, or of knowledge in the defendants that a movement might occur.
As stated in the opinion:

"What caused these cars to move is left wholly in the field of
conjecture. * * * Neither does it appear that they (defendants)
had any knowledge or notice that it was about to take place, or any
reason to anticipate that it might occur."

The evidence sustains the verdict.

Order affirmed.

MINNESOTA FARMERS MUTUAL INSURANCE COMPANY v. JOHN DJONNE.[1]

November 6, 1914.

Nos. 18,808—(72).

Insurance — fraud of agent.

In this action to recover an assessment against a member of a Farmers
Mutual Insurance Co. it is *held* that the evidence sustains the verdict of
the jury, to the effect that defendant was induced to make application for
the insurance by fraudulent representations on the part of the agent of
plaintiff who solicited the application. *Held*, further, that plaintiff was
bound by such representations, and that defendant was not guilty of negligence.

[1] Reported in 149 N. W. 371.

Action transferred to the district court for Lac qui Parle county
to recover an assessment of $17.68 levied upon defendant as mem-
ber of plaintiff company.   The case was tried before Qvale, J., who
denied defendant's motion to dismiss the action and plaintiff's motion for a directed verdict, and a jury which returned a verdict in
favor of defendant.   From an order denying its motion for judgment in its favor notwithstanding the verdict or for a new trial,
plaintiff appealed.   Affirmed.

William N. M. Crawford, for appellant.

J. H. Driscoll, for respondent.

BUNN, J.

This is an action to recover an assessment levied by plaintiff, a
farmers mutual insurance company, against defendant, on a cyclone
insurance policy theretofore issued to him.   The defense was that
the application was procured by fraudulent representations on the
part of the agent of plaintiff who solicited it.   This issue was submitted to the jury and a verdict for defendant returned.   Plaintiff
appeals from an order denying its motion for judgment notwithstanding the verdict or for a new trial.

As we understand the charge of the trial court the only question
submitted to the jury was whether the contract was procured by
fraud.   The briefs argue another question, the legality or illegality
of the assessment, but we think the case must turn on the sufficiency
of the evidence to sustain a finding of fraud.

The only evidence was the testimony of defendant, which was
substantially as follows: In June, 1912, a stranger came to plaintiff
on his farm in Lac qui Parle county and solicited him for cyclone
insurance.   Plaintiff inquired the cost, and the agent told him it
would cost him $10 the first year and $8 a year thereafter.   Plaintiff then signed the application presented by the agent, and paid
him $10.   Plaintiff could not read or write, and testified that he
relied upon the word of the agent that the writing contained the
"bargain we had been talking about."   This testimony was uncontradicted.   In fact the application contained no language limiting
the amount of assessments, but provided that the applicant agreed

to pay all assessments made on him by the company, with interest, costs of collection and an attorney's fee if suit was brought. The policy contained similar language.

In view of the fact that plaintiff was a foreigner and could not read or write, we think the evidence, though not over-convincing to us, cannot be held insufficient to justify a jury in finding fraud.

Plaintiff contends that it was not bound by the representations made by its agent. This contention is clearly unsound. The representations were made as a part of the very business the agent was employed to do, and were clearly within the scope of his authority. It is not a case of admitting evidence of a prior or contemporaneous oral agreement with the agent, contradicting the written agreement, but a case of fraud. Nor can we sustain the view that the agent's representation of the cost was but his estimate or guess. Nor was defendant necessarily guilty of negligence in failing to ascertain the meaning of the language in the policy after he received it.

Had it appeared that defendant knew that he was applying for insurance in a farmers mutual company, it might well be said that he was bound to know the law applicable to such companies, and that he had no right to rely upon the agent's representations as to the cost. But it fairly appears that defendant knew nothing of the nature of the company or as to the character of the insurance he was to get, or whether he was to pay cash premiums, or assessments levied to meet losses. On the whole we do not feel justified in disturbing the decision of the trial court.

Order affirmed.

THOMPSON-McDONALD LUMBER COMPANY v. EDGAR J. MORAWETZ.[1]

November 6, 1914.

Nos. 18,829—(87).

Mechanic's lien — delivery of material.

1. An actual delivery upon the premises of material sold and furnished a contractor for use in construction of a building thereon is not necessary, as against the owner, to vest in the materialman a right of lien under our mechanic's lien statutes.

Same.

2. In the absence of fraud and collusion between the materialman and the contractor, a good faith delivery of such material to the contractor for use in the building is all that is necessary to protect the rights of the materialman.

Fraud of contractor.

3. The owner may protect himself from fraudulent conduct on the part of the contractor by requiring a bond or other security for the payment of material purchased by him on the credit of the building and premises.

Action in the district court for Dakota county to recover judgment for $297.95 and to foreclose a mechanic's lien for the same upon the premises described in the complaint. The case was tried before Johnson, J., who made findings and ordered judgment in favor of plaintiff. From the judgment entered pursuant to the order for judgment, defendant Morawetz appealed. Affirmed.

Arthur M. Higgins, for appellant.
Josiah E. Brill, for respondent.

BROWN, C. J.
Defendant Morawetz entered into a contract with defendant Offrell for the construction of a building upon premises owned by

[1] Reported in 149 N. W. 300.

Note.—Right to mechanics' lien for materials furnished for structure, but not actually used, see note in 31 L.R.A.(N.S.) 749.

him, Offrell agreeing to furnish all labor and material. On February 27, 1912, Offrell, the contractor, purchased from plaintiff certain material to be used in the construction of the building, of the value of $288.24, and the same was used for that purpose. On March 30, 1912, the contractor purchased other and additional material for the same use and purpose of the value of $9.71. The material so furnished was not paid for, and within 90 days from the date of the second item just mentioned, but not within 90 days from the date of the first item, plaintiff duly perfected a lien against the premises and thereafter brought this action to foreclose the same. Plaintiff had judgment and defendant Morawetz appealed.

The cause comes to this court upon the findings, the evidence not being returned, and the question presented is whether the findings of fact support the conclusions of law. Whether the conclusions of law are so supported depends upon the question, with reference to which the facts are not in dispute, whether the second item of material above mentioned was lienable under the statutes. If it was not, the lien statement was not fixed in time and the lien fails. If it was the judgment must be affirmed. The facts are in brief as follows:

The building under construction was located in Liberty Heights, in Dakota county, and plaintiff's place of business, dealer in lumber and building material, was at Minneapolis. In substance and effect the trial court found, in respect to the item of material in question, that on March 30, 1912, the contractor purchased of plaintiff and plaintiff sold and delivered to him for use in the construction of the building certain material of the value of $9.71; that the contractor ordered the material shipped to him from Minneapolis, and that in pursuance thereof plaintiff delivered the same to a common carrier consigned and to be shipped to the contractor at the place where the building was under construction; that no part of the material was delivered upon the premises or taken there by the contractor or any other person, and no part thereof was ever used in the construction of the building. What became of the material does not appear.

The contention of defendant is that as no part of the material was used in the building, or ever delivered upon the premises where the same was being constructed, the value thereof was not a lienable item, and, further, since the lien was not perfected within 90 days from the date of the first item of material, that the court was in error in ordering judgment for plaintiff.

Our statute, section 7020, G. S. 1913, provides that whoever contributes to the improvement of any real estate by furnishing labor or material for the construction of a building thereon, whether under contract with the owner, contractor or subcontractor, shall have a lien upon the premises for the value of the labor or material so furnished. The statute, being remedial in character, has always received a liberal construction and application. Johnson v. Starrett, supra, p. 138, 149 N. W. 6; 2 Dunnell, Minn. Dig. § 6033. Similar statutes in other states have been construed strictly and the rule announced that there can be no lien for material furnished, unless it be actually incorporated in the building so as to form a part of the structure. Some of the authorities so holding are referred to by Mr. Justice Brown in the Johnson case, supra, and others, including those holding to the contrary, will be found in a note to Pittsburg Plate Glass Co. v. Leary (S. D.) 31 L.R.A.(N.S.) 746. But that rule of strict construction has never been applied in this state. On the contrary we have held that actual incorporation of the material into the building is not essential to the right of lien. Burns v. Sewell, 48 Minn. 425, 51 N. W. 224; Hickey v. Collom, 47 Minn. 565, 50 N. W. 918; Combination Steel & Iron Co. v. St. Paul City Ry. Co. 52 Minn. 203, 53 N. W. 1144. We have consistently followed this rule, and it is supported by the courts of other states having similar statutes. Whether a delivery of material upon the premises where the building is being constructed is essential to the right of lien has not heretofore been presented in a case between the owner of the property and the lien claimant. While such a delivery has been said in some of the opinions to be necessary, the question was not involved in the particular case, and the question is an open one in this state. The case of Wentworth v. Tubbs, 53 Minn. 388, 55 N. W. 543, presented a controversy between a lien claimant and a mortgagee, and involved the question whether the lien there before the court was prior to a mortgage upon the premises, which was executed and recorded before the improvements thereon were commenced. It was held that as against the mortgagee the material must be delivered upon the premises, or the improvement be actually under way, in order that the lien may take priority over a mortgage executed before the commencement of the work. The case is not here in point. We have also held that a delivery of material upon the premises is not necessary to give life to the lien in those cases where a delivery is prevented by the owner. This includes instances where the material is specially prepared in conformity with special orders. John Paul Lumber Co. v. Hormel, 61 Minn. 303, 63 N. W. 718; Berger v. Turnblad, 98 Minn. 163, 107 N. W. 543, 116 Am. St. 353. And notwithstanding expressions found in the opinions that delivery upon the premises is usually necessary, the logical result of our decisions leads to the conclusion that, as against the owner, material sold and in good faith delivered to the contractor for use in the building entitles the materialman to a lien, whether the material be in fact delivered upon the premises or not. If it be delivered to the contractor for use in the construction work, it would seem a strain to hold, and clearly a departure from the logic of prior decisions, that the materialman is bound to follow the contractor to the premises and see to it that the material is taken to and deposited thereon. Our decisions are to the effect that if the material be in fact delivered upon the premises the subsequent act of the contractor, even though fraudulent, in removing the same and converting it to his own personal use does not defeat the lien. If such removal does not defeat the lien, it is a little difficult to understand why the failure of the contractor, to whom possession has been given, to take the material to the premises at all should defeat the lien. If in fact delivered upon the premises the contractor could, under the decisions referred to, within an hour thereafter cart it away without prejudicing the rights of the lien claimant. In view of this situation no benefit can accrue to the owner by an actual delivery upon the premises, and his possession would in no legal respect be protected thereby. If the material in a given case be delivered into the physical possession of the owner, it seems clear that no court would hold that his failure to deliver the same upon the premises would affect the rights of the materialman. We can conceive of no valid reason for applying a different rule where the delivery is to the contractor, the agent and representative of the owner, and for whose acts the owner is responsible to the extent at least that the premises are liable under the statutes for the value of the material so furnished. A rule requiring the materialman to follow the · material to the premises would impose upon him an unnecessary burden and result in no benefit to the owner. In many instances material for the construction of buildings is shipped to the contractor at some distant point. A delivery to the carrier in such case, the material being consigned to the contractor, is a delivery to the contractor, and no useful purpose would be served by requiring the materialman to dispatch a messenger with the material to see that it finally reaches the premises. Of course fraud and collusion between the materialman and the contractor, resulting in a wrongful diversion of material, would destroy the right of lien. But in the absence of fraud we think, and so hold, that a good faith delivery of material to the contractor is sufficient to vest the right of lien. It may at first thought seem that the owner is at a disadvantage and inadequately protected from fraud or collusion, but the matter of his protection is wholly within his own hands. He may require of the contractor a bond as security for the payment for all material purchased for the improvement.

In the case at bar the material was delivered to a carrier, consigned to the contractor at a place where the. building was under construction. The delivery to the carrier was a delivery to the contractor, and plaintiff was not required, in order to protect his lien rights, to accompany the shipment and see that the material was actually delivered upon the premises.

Judgment affirmed.

STATE v. CHARLES A. LESTER.[1]

November 6, 1914.

Nos. 19,000—(13).

Manslaughter — culpable negligence of physician.

1. A medical man, or a person assuming to act as such, will be held guilty of "culpable negligence" within the meaning of G. S. 1913, § 8612, subd. 3, defining manslaughter in the second degree as homicide committed without design to effect death, "by any act, procurement or culpable negligence" not constituting a higher crime, where he has exhibited gross incompetency or inattention, or wanton indifference to his patient's safety.

Same — indictment.

2. An indictment under this statute need not allege knowledge on defendant's part of probability of consequences from the acts or omissions charged; nor is it necessary to charge defendant's duty in the premises, nor set up a specific standard of duty, nor to allege "culpable" or any other degree of negligence *eo nomine*, nor set out defendant's acts in any other than general terms and as ultimate facts.

Judicial notice.

3. The court takes judicial notice that X-ray machines sometimes inflict serious burns.

Indictment sustained.

4. An indictment against a physician, under the statute cited, for manslaughter in the second degree, committed in connection with the operation of an X-ray machine, sustained as against a demurrer, on the ground that the facts charged were not stated with sufficient certainty to, and did not, constitute a public offense.

Defendant was indicted by the grand jury of Douglas county of the crime of manslaughter in the second degree. He was tried before Parsons, J., who overruled defendant's demurrer to the indictment,

---

[1] Reported in 149 N. W. 297.

Note.—Negligent homicide by physician, see note in 61 L.R.A. 287.

Liability of physician for injuries resulting from electrical or X-ray treatment, see notes in 28 L.R.A.(N.S.) 262; 43 L.R.A.(N.S.) 734.

and at the request of defendant certified to this court the question whether the court erred in overruling the demurrer of defendant or in refusing to sustain any of his objections to the indictment.

Lyndon A. Smith, Attorney General, and *John C. Nethaway*, Assistant Attorney General, for the state.

George L. Treat and *Durment, Moore & Oppenheimer*, for defendant.

PHILIP E. BROWN, J.

Defendant demurred to an indictment accusing him of the offense of manslaughter in second degree, on the ground that the acts or omissions charged were not stated with sufficient certainty to, and did not, constitute a public offense. The court below overruled the demurrer and certified the case here.

The indictment was found under G. S. 1913, § 8612, subd. 3, declaring manslaughter to be of this degree when committed without any design to effect death, "by any act, procurement or culpable negligence" not constituting a higher crime. Omitting formal parts, it alleged that defendant:

"Without authority of law, but without a design to effect her death, did feloniously use and employ upon the body of one Ruth Nass, an electrical machine or instrument commonly known as an X-ray machine (a more particular description of said instrument or machine being to said grand jury unknown), for the purpose of taking an X-ray picture of the hip of the said Ruth Nass for the sole use and purpose of said Charles A. Lester, with her consent extracted from her upon his assurance that the exposure of such X-ray would do her no harm, and she relying upon his assurance as a medical man and not otherwise, said Charles A. Lester did then and there attempt to take such picture of subjecting the body of said Ruth Nass to the rays of said machine, and did then and there turn and apply said X-ray upon the body of the said Ruth Nass in and over the region of her right hip, the said machine being a dangerous instrument, except when operated by a skilful manager it was not necessarily dangerous, which danger the said C. A. Lester knew, or in the exercise of the care required under the circumstances he should have known, and said Charles A. Lester did then and there place the tube of the said X-ray unreasonably close to the body of her, the said Ruth Nass, and disregarding the duty he owed her, he did negligently and carelessly fail to give her, during the time of such exposure to such X-ray as aforesaid, such proper and requisite attention as was requisite and proper to prevent burning her, and did operate such X-ray in an unskilful manner and did keep her body so exposed for an unreasonable length of time, thereby inflicting upon the body of her, the said Ruth Nass in the region of the right hip as aforesaid, a mortal burn and injury known as an X-ray burn, from which mortal burn so caused as aforesaid, she, the said Ruth Nass, died."

This court has frequently declared that an indictment must set out the complete criminal offense charged, and every essential element must be alleged directly and certainly; the omission of an allegation without which a criminal offense would not be described being fatal. State v. MacDonald, 105 Minn. 251, 117 N. W. 482. And the essential, ultimate facts alleged must not be consistent with innocency. State v. Erickson, 81 Minn. 134, 83 N. W. 512. Furthermore, the indictment must protect accused from a second prosecution for the same offense. State v. Tracy, 82 Minn. 317, 84 N. W. 1015. It cannot, however, be overturned by technicalities which do not prejudice the substantial rights of defendant. State v. Staples, 126 Minn. 396, 148 N. W. 283.

The only question necessary to be considered in applying the foregoing tests is whether the criminality of defendant's acts as constituting the crime of homicide by "culpable negligence" is sufficiently alleged.

Numerous definitions of this term may be found. 2 Words & Phrases, 1780; 1 Id. (2d Series) 1174. But these would be of little, if any, value in the premises, for the term does not appear in the indictment. Moreover, culpable negligence, that is criminal negligence, is largely a matter of degree, and, as has well been said, incapable of precise definition. Whether it exists to such a degree as to involve criminal liability is a question that must be left, to a great extent, to the common sense of the jury. Hampton v. State, 50 Fla. 55, 64, 39 South. 421; Stehr v. State, 92 Neb. 755, 139 N. W. 676, 45 L.R.A.

(N.S.) 559, Ann. Cas. 1914A, 523, 22 Am. & Eng. Enc. (2d ed.) 810. But not every careless or negligent act whereby death ensues comes within the statute, and something more must appear than the essentials necessary to impose civil liability for damages. 21 Cyc. 766. When considered as the basis of a charge of manslaughter against a medical man, or person assuming to act as such, culpable negligence exists where he exhibits gross lack of competency, or inattention or wanton indifference to the patient's safety; which may arise from his gross ignorance of the science or through gross negligence in either its application or lack of proper skill in the use of instruments. Where, however, he does nothing that an ordinarily skilled and careful practitioner might not do, and death results merely from an error of judgment or accident, no criminal liability attaches. Hampton v. State, supra, decided under a statute like ours; Ferguson's Case, 1 Lewin, 181, Reg. v. Ellis, 2 Car. & K. 470; note 124 Am. St. 330; 22 Am. & Eng. Enc. (2d ed.) 810; 21 Cyc. 769. "Gross" as here used is intended to convey the idea of recklessness with regard to the safety of others, or, as expressed by Mr. Justice Holmes, in Com. v. Pierce, 138 Mass. 165, 52 Am. Rep. 264, "foolhardy presumption."

The failure to allege knowledge on defendant's part that his acts involved probability of serious consequences to the deceased, is not fatal to the indictment, the defect, if any, in this regard, being cured by the presumption of contemplation of probable consequences. Com. v. Pierce, supra. Neither was it necessary to allege defendant's duty to deceased under the circumstances, nor to set up a specific standard by which his acts might be measured, these being matters of law. If, then, the facts alleged sufficiently show such incompetency or inattention or indifference to the safety of deceased as has been indicated as necessary to give rise to criminal liability, the indictment must be upheld, though it charges neither "culpable" nor any other degree of negligence eo nomine, nor defendant's acts in other than general terms and as ultimate facts. To state more as to the latter would be to plead the evidence, which is not required, and "negligence" prefixed by adjectives could not aid the former, unless the facts stated justified such expressions (State v. MacDonald, supra), in which event they would be surplusage.

We must take judicial notice that X-ray machines sometimes inflict serious burns, and the indictment characterizes the instrument used as dangerous unless skilfully handled and presumptively known by defendant to be such, notwithstanding which he placed it too close to his subject, and also failed during an excessive exposure to give her the attention requisite to prevent injury. These allegations import criminal negligence and the questions raised thereby are for the jury. State v. Hardister, 38 Ark. 605, 42 Am. Rep. 5. We sustain the indictment, though it is not a model one.

Order affirmed.

JIM DOBREFF v. ST. PAUL GASLIGHT COMPANY.[1]

November 13, 1914.

Nos. 18,656—(34).

Injury to servant — assumption of risk.

　　Plaintiff was digging a ditch, five feet deep, with sloping sides, the ditch being four feet wide at the top and one and one-half feet wide at the bottom. He piled the dirt from the ditch on the top earth at one side. This top earth was black soil with the admixture of some stones. It did not differ much from the top earth at other points, but by reason of heavy travel was somewhat more crusted. The subsoil was sand and gravel. As the work progressed the sand and gravel rolled into the ditch, leaving the top crust unsupported until it stood out like a shelf. Plaintiff saw this. When the excavation was nearly completed, this top crust fell in on plaintiff. It fell because it was so undermined and because of the weight of earth piled by plaintiff on top of it. Plaintiff was a man 40 years old, experienced in this class of work. *Held*, he assumed the risk of the dangers to which he was exposed and which in fact caused his injury.

[1] Reported in 149 N. W. 465.

Note.—The question of the servant's assumption of risk as to excavations is treated in a note in 19 L.R.A.(N.S.) 350.

Action in the district court for Ramsey county to recover $15,000 for personal injury received while in the employ of defendant. The answer alleged, among other matters, that plaintiff was familiar with the manner and method of digging the trench referred to in the opinion and with the character of the soil in which he was working; that he knew and appreciated the risks and dangers connected with the work in which he was engaged at the time he was injured, and that the risk of injury was assumed by him. The case was tried before Dickson, J., who granted defendant's motion for a directed verdict in its favor. From an order denying his motion for a new trial, plaintiff appealed. Affirmed.

Gustavus Loevinger and *Edward P. Graves,* for appellant.

P. J. McLaughlin, for respondent.

HALLAM, J.

Plaintiff was injured by the caving in of a ditch which he was excavating for defendant on Minnehaha street, in St. Paul. The ditch was about five feet deep with sloping sides, the width at the top being about four feet and at the bottom one and one-half feet. The men worked in sections, that is, each workman would be assigned a section nine feet long which he would himself excavate to the required depth. This work had proceeded for some distance on Minnehaha street. It appears that the character of the soil all along the street was much the same. The top for a depth of about a foot was black dirt and under this was light sand and gravel. The soil at the place of the accident differed from that at other places along the street only in this, that the top soil contained some stones and was packed down harder because of heavy traffic at this point.

One witness for plaintiff, in describing the situation, at this point, said there were some stones as big as your fist, some smaller and some bigger; asked if there were may of them, he answered: "No, it don't was very many." Plaintiff when asked as to the difference between the top crust at the place where this accident occurred and the top soil in other parts of the ditch answered, "There ain't much difference."

Plaintiff dug through the black dirt and stones on the surface, first using a pick, and then shoveling out the earth and stones and the sand and gravel below. As he dug down he noticed the subsoil of sand and gravel sliding or rolling into the ditch. He noticed this about 10 a. m., and this process kept on until the accident at 3 p. m., at which time there was no support to the upper crust on the side on which he was piling the dirt, so that the crust stood out like a shelf. When he was nearly through with his work, this crust which he had undermined fell and caused the injury of which he complains.

It is charged by plaintiff that this work was dangerous and that the defendant was negligent, in failing to shore up or brace the sides of the trench, in failing to slope the sides more by widening at the top, in failing to remove the dirt thrown out by plaintiff from the side of the trench, and in failing to warn plaintiff of the dangers of a cave-in. We do not deem it necessary to discuss these contentions in detail, for whatever may be said as to the precautions necessary to make a pit like this a safe place to work, it seems clear that plaintiff assumed the risk of all the dangers to which he was exposed. The doctrine of assumption of risk has not for years been a favorite with courts anywhere and its application has been much circumscribed, and for the future it has, in this state, and in some other states, and in Federal jurisdictions, been in large part abolished by statute. This injury occurred, however, before the adoption of any applicable statute and, unless we are prepared to abandon the doctrine, it seems applicable to the facts of this case. An employee assumes risks incident to his employment and the method of conducting the work in which he is engaged when the conditions out of which danger arises are known to him or are so obvious that one who owes no duty to inspect is bound to discover them, and when he also understands the risk to which he is exposed, or when, in the exercise of the intelligence with which he is gifted, he ought to understand it. Falkenberg v. Bazille & Partridge, 124 Minn. 19, 23, 144 N. W. 431.

Plaintiff was a man 40 years old and was experienced in this class of work. True, he was a foreigner, a Bulgarian. He had not been in this country long and did not know English well, but this did not detract from his intelligence or his knowledge or appreciation of the risks of his work. He appears to have been an intelligent workman.

He had been engaged in this same class of work in Bulgaria. He understood as well as any one the law of gravitation and the conditions under which earth is liable to fall or cave in. Plaintiff dug this ditch himself. He knew the solid and adhesive character of the top earth. He knew that his own work had undermined this crust and had piled some weight of earth above it. There was no concealed danger. The conditions were all open and apparent. Plaintiff had knowledge, therefore, of the condition out of which the danger arose. He must have known, or, by the exercise of the intelligence which he possessed, he ought to have understood, that a thin shelf of earth might easily collapse of its own weight, and would surely collapse if any considerable weight was added to the top of it, and he must have known that, if a crust of earth were undermined so that it should fall, it would fall in larger and heavier chunks than would soft earth. He had full knowledge of all the conditions, and we cannot escape the conclusion that he understood and appreciated the danger and the risk to which he was exposed.

We are unable to distinguish this case from the numerous cases known as the "gravel pit cases," where a workman engaged in shoveling has been held to assume the risk of the caving in of earth, sand or gravel which he has undermined or assisted in undermining. Pederson v. City of Rushford, 41 Minn. 289, 42 N. W. 1063; Swanson v. Great Northern Ry. Co. 68 Minn. 184, 70 N. W. 978; Reiter v. Winona & St. Peter R. Co. 72 Minn. 225, 75 N. W. 219; Kletschka v. Minneapolis & St. L. R. Co. 80 Minn. 238, 83 N. W. 133. See also Olson v. McMullen, 34 Minn. 94, 24 N. W. 318; O'Neil v. Great Northern Ry. Co. 101 Minn. 467, 112 N. W. 625.

The case differs from the cases cited by plaintiff. In some of these the cave-in occurred by reason of conditions unknown to the plaintiff—or because of blasting of which he had not been advised (Kohout v. Newman, 96 Minn. 61, 104 N. W. 764); or because of cracks in the surface of which he did not know (Hill v. Winston, 73 Minn. 80, 75 N. W. 1030); or because, by reason of darkness, he could not see (Heydman v. Red Wing Brick Co. 112 Minn. 158, 127 N. W. 561; Arnold v. Dauchy, 115 Minn. 28, 131 N. W. 625); or because of other conditions of which he had no knowledge (Lund v. E. S. Wood-

127 M.—19.

worth & Co. 75 Minn. 501, 78 N. W. 81; Bartels v. Chicago & N. W. Ry. Co. 118 Minn. 250, 136 N. W. 760); and in some the employer, possessed of superior knowledge, assured the workman of his safety, (Dimetre v. Red Wing Sewer Pipe Co. supra, p. 132, 148 N. W. 1078).

Plaintiff undertakes to distinguish the case at bar from the "gravel pit" cases, on the ground that the top layer of earth here was crusted more than usual. We have already alluded to this feature of the case. This circumstance was known to plaintiff and the effect of it must have been apparent to him. We do not think it takes the case out of the application of the rules above stated. The case is not like the case of Hill v. Winston, 73 Minn. 80, 75 N. W. 1030, where the crust was of such a character that it would not fall by the operation of ordinary natural causes, but was loosened and fell because of blasting operations with which the plaintiff was not familiar.

Plaintiff clearly assumed the risk of the dangers to which he was exposed and which in fact caused his injury.

Exceptions are taken to some of the rulings of the court in excluding evidence offered by the plaintiff. We have carefully examined these exceptions and the offers of evidence. We shall not discuss these exceptions in detail. None of the offered evidence would, if received, have materially changed the aspect of the case so far as concerns plaintiff's knowledge of the conditions or his appreciation of the risk, and we are of the opinion that if the evidence excluded had been received, the result of the action would necessarily be the same.

Order affirmed.

FELIX G. COLE v. GUST JOHNSON and Another.[1]

November 13, 1914.

Nos. 18,738—(52).

Promissory note — fraud of payee — purchaser for value.
Two issues were submitted to the jury in this action brought upon a promissory note by an alleged *bona fide* holder: One was whether fraud of the payee induced the deal in which the note was given, and the other whether plaintiff was a *bona fide* holder. Upon this appeal by the makers of the note it is *held:*

(1) It cannot be assumed that the jury found against defendants upon the defense of fraud, so as to render error in the submission of the other issue harmless.

(2) The evidence tended to prove circumstances which made it a question for the jury whether plaintiff's testimony, that he had bought the note before maturity and paid $500 therefor, was true, although not contradicted by any direct testimony. An instruction to the contrary was error.

(3) It would seem the jury should have been instructed that the burden was upon plaintiff to show that he became a purchaser for value, before maturity, in the ordinary course of business, and without notice, if they found the defense of fraud true; but since the evidence as to the fraud, which is neither printed nor referred to in the briefs, might have been such that the burden of proof still rested on defendants in this respect we are not required to reverse because the trial court refused to state that it rested on plaintiff.

Action in the district court for Hennepin county to recover $500 upon a promissory note. The defense is stated in the opinion. The case was tried before Steele, J., and a jury which returned a verdict in favor of plaintiff for the sum demanded. From an order denying their motion for a new trial, defendants appealed. Reversed.

John N. Berg and *Adolph E. L. Johnson,* for appellants.
J. H. Green and *James M. Pulliam,* for respondent.

1 Reported in 149 N. W. 466.

HOLT, J.

The suit is upon a promissory note for $500 by one who claims to be a *bona fide* purchaser for value and before maturity. Plaintiff prevailed; and defendants appeal from the order denying a new trial.

The note was given when defendants bought of the payee, W. W. Ehle, a fuel and transfer business including six draft horses. The defendants executed a chattel mortgage on the horses to secure the note, it representing part of the purchase price. The defense alleged that the payee of the note procured the same by fraud and false representation in the sale of the horses mentioned; denied that plaintiff was a *bona fide* holder before maturity; and averred that he had notice of the fraud. Whether there was fraud and false representation in the sale of the horses that cancelled the note, growing out of the transaction, was submitted to the jury, and no complaint is made of the manner thereof. The assignments of error relate wholly to the submission of the issue as to plaintiff being a good faith purchaser, for value, before maturity.

Plaintiff's suggestion of a presumption that the jury found in his favor on the issue of fraud, cannot be entertained, for if error inheres in the submission of the issue of plaintiff's being a *bona fide* holder defendants were necessarily prejudiced, unless it can be clearly demonstrated that the jury found no actionable fraud, or else that there was no evidence for defendants to submit on that issue. Neither can be done in this case, for there was no special verdict, and we have examined that part of the settled case not printed sufficiently to ascertain that the jury might well have found fraud and misrepresentation in the deal and substantial injury therefrom.

In order to determine the correctness and propriety of an instruction assigned as error, it is necessary to state some matters which the testimony either established or tended to prove. The payee of the note, Mr. Ehle, now dead, was a friend of plaintiff. When Ehle was an alderman in the city, plaintiff was street commissioner of the ward. Plaintiff very often visited Ehle's fuel and transfer business before he sold to defendants, and also the one afterwards started by him opposite, across the railroad tracks. Plaintiff frequently accommodated Ehle by signing or endorsing his notes. About a year after the transaction with defendants, Ehle brought an action against them for the possession of the horses for some violation of the conditions in the chattel mortgage. Defendants therein set up a defense of fraud inducing the sale. The trial of that action lasted three days and concluded on January 24, 1912, the verdict being in favor of these defendants. At that trial the note now in suit was received as an exhibit, and so marked. The record is very persuasive that it remained from that time on in the possession of the clerk of the court until the latter part of March following. The chattel mortgage securing this note was not assigned to plaintiff until June 10, 1912. Plaintiff admitted that he knew of the Ehle lawsuit a few days after it was tried. His testimony was very obscure as to dates, but nevertheless he maintained that he received this note on February 5, 1912. He is either mistaken as to this date, or else the other witnesses are that the note was then in the custody of the clerk of court. There is also some testimony to show that Ehle was still interested in the note in May, 1912. Plaintiff testified that he had signed a $900 note for, and with, Ehle which fell due February 3, 1912; that Ehle had not sufficient funds to meet it but obtained the amount lacking, namely, $500, from plaintiff, and in consideration turned over to plaintiff this note. He accounts for the ready money by saying he had it in the house except $150, which he borrowed from a neighbor, but is unable to tell whether this last amount was in check or cash. He knew nothing of the makers of this note, asked Ehle no questions about them or the property covered by the mortgage, and yet accepted this note indorsed "without recourse" by Ehle. Without requesting payment from defendants he gave the note for collection to the attorney who was present and took Ehle's acknowledgment at the assignment of the chattel mortgage in June, 1912. Neither plaintiff nor this attorney could give any definite time when the note was given to the attorney.

We think the cross-examination of plaintiff when considered in connection with the evidence and facts above alluded to made it a question for the jury, and not the court, whether $500 was paid by plaintiff in purchase of this note, or whether, as claimed by defendants, the turning over of the note and assigning the mortgage was only colorable and a scheme to avoid the consequences of the former lawsuit to Ehle. Therefore error is well assigned on this instruction given: "Gentlemen of the jury, I instruct you that there is no testimony in this case to contradict the testimony of Mr. Cole to the effect that he paid $500 for this note to Mr. Ehle, so there was a good consideration for this note." It was for the jury to say upon this record whether plaintiff's testimony was contradicted.

Where there is *mala fides* in a transaction direct proof is scarcely ever available. Proven circumstances might be such that the jury have a perfect right to reject as untruthful a positive statement of a witness though not contradicted by any direct testimony, especially when the witness evinces evasiveness, lack of memory or ignorance on matters which the jury may well conclude to be within his knowledge. Klason v. Rieger, 22 Minn. 59; Brown v. Morrill, 45 Minn. 481, 48 N. W. 328; Hawkins v. Sauby, 48 Minn. 69, 50 N. W. 1015; Los v. Scherer, 90 Minn. 456, 97 N. W. 123; State v. Halverson, 103 Minn. 265, 114 N. W. 957, 14 L.R.A.(N.S.) 947, 123 Am. St. 326. The instruction also tended to advise the jury that plaintiff was protected as a *bona fide* holder. Whether a consideration was paid for the purchase of this note, and the note was then turned over to plaintiff had a vital bearing on the question of good faith and want of notice of a defense, for "want of notice may be inferred from the payment of a valuable consideration where the transaction occurs in the ordinary course of business and is free from suspicious circumstances." Plymouth Cordage Co. v. Seymour, 67 Minn. 311, 69 N. W. 1079. It may be noted also that if plaintiff became the owner after March 14, 1912, there was interest which on the face of the note was overdue and unpaid. And if Ehle at the time did not have possession of the note so that it was not then delivered to plaintiff, there could hardly be a contention that the latter was a good faith purchaser in the ordinary course of business. O'Mulcahy v. Holley, 28 Minn. 31, 8 N. W. 906; First Nat. Bank of St. Paul v. Commrs. of Scott County, 14 Minn. 59 (77), 100 Am. Dec. 194; First Nat. Bank of Waverly v. Forsyth, 67 Minn. 257, 69 N. W. 909, 64 Am. St. 415.

Error is also assigned upon the charge and refusal to charge with respect to the burden of proof as to plaintiff's *bona fides* and want of notice if the jury found fraud in the deal. Judging this issue as made by the pleadings and as submitted to the jury, it would seem that the charge should have been in line with the practice indicated in MacLaren v. Cochran, 44 Minn. 255, 46 N. W. 408; Bank of Montreal v. Richter, 55 Minn. 362, 57 N. W. 61; Park v. Winsor, 115 Minn. 256, 132 N. W. 264; Cochran v. Stein, 118 Minn. 323, 136 N. W. 1037, 41 L.R.A.(N.S.) 391, namely, that, if the defendants established that the transaction wherein the note was procured was induced by fraud and misrepresentation on the part of Ehle, the verdict should go for defendants, unless plaintiff by a fair preponderance of the evidence proved that he purchased the note in good faith, before maturity, for value, and without notice of the fraud. However we would scarcely feel justified upon this record in holding that reversible error is here made to appear. The evidence on the issue of fraud practiced on defendants, inducing the execution of the note, is not printed in the paper book. It may be this would show that defendants' defense against Ehle, had he held the note, was not the right to rescind for the fraud, but partook more of the nature of a breach of contract or of warranty in the sale of the horses so that the burden of proving notice would rest on the defendants within the decision of Merchants & M. S. Bank of Janesville v. Cross, 65 Minn. 154, 67 N. W. 1147; First Nat. Bank of Minneapolis v. McNairy, 122 Minn. 215, 142 N. W. 139, and First Nat. Bank of Wellington v. Person, 101 Minn. 30, 111 N. W. 730. On another trial we apprehend no difficulty will be experienced with the burden of proof nor with instructions relative to circumstantial evidence of *mala fides* in the purchase of negotiable paper, and therefore refrain from further comment on the errors assigned. For the erroneous instruction first discussed a new trial is rendered necessary.

Order reversed.

FIRST NATIONAL BANK OF GILBERT v. C. E. BAILEY.[1]

November 13, 1914.

Nos. 18,758—(63).

Notice to corporation — officer acting for third person.

    The general rule that knowledge possessed by an officer of a corporation is by implication of law imputed to the corporation, has no application where it appears that in a particular transaction the officer acted in an adversary capacity, as the agent of a third person, and did not represent or speak for the corporation, of which agency the other officers of the corporation had full knowledge and information.

Action in the district court for St. Louis county to recover $1,900 upon two promissory notes. The case was tried before Ensign, J., who made findings and ordered judgment in favor of plaintiff. From the judgment entered pursuant to the order for judgment, defendant appealed. Affirmed.

W. G. Bonham, for appellant.
Oliver S. Andresen, for respondent.

BROWN, C. J.

For some time prior to the year 1911, defendant was a resident of this state with property interests in the village of Gilbert, in St. Louis county. One Thompson, from some time in the fall of 1908, was defendant's agent and as such had the control and management of his affairs at Gilbert. Defendant then resided at Eveleth, a short distance from Gilbert. Defendant moved to California in the fall of 1910, and thereafter Thompson had the exclusive management of his Gilbert business interests, and all matters pertaining thereto were committed to his care. Defendant carried an account in plaintiff bank which was in charge of Thompson after defendant moved to

---

[1] Reported in 149 N. W. 469.

Note.—As to imputing to principal notice to agent while acting in other capacity, see note in 3 L.R.A.(N.S.) 444.

California. During the year 1911, Thompson collected rent due to defendant from tenants, depositing the same in defendant's account at the bank; Thompson paid claims arising against defendant, and was authorized to draw upon defendant's bank account for the necessary funds; he was authorized to and did sign defendant's name to many checks on the bank; Thompson was also authorized to borrow money for defendant whenever necessary, and when defendant left for California he delivered to Thompson certain blank promissory notes, signed by defendant, which Thompson was authorized to fill out and negotiate. He sent to Thompson from California two or more blank signed promissory notes with directions to fill them and negotiate them at plaintiff's bank, if necessary to avoid an overdraft of his account, and to deposit the same to his credit. Two of these blank notes were by Thompson filled out and delivered to the bank, one for $1,200, and one for $1,000. He wrongfully converted the proceeds of the $1,200 note to his own use. He had in his possession for collection a promissory note belonging to defendant against one Le Duc which, subsequent to the execution of those two notes, he sold to the bank, crediting defendant's account at the bank with $500, and applying the balance, some $336, upon the above mentioned $1,-200 note. Thompson then took up that note and filled out one of the blank signed notes defendant had sent him from California for the balance due thereon, namely, $900, which the other officers of the plaintiff accepted in renewal of the former note. Neither this note nor the one for $1,000 has ever been paid and this action was brought to recover thereon. Defendant admitted the genuineness and validity of the $1,000 note, but denied that he ever signed or delivered the note for $900, or ever authorized any other person to do so. Defendant also interposed certain counterclaims which do not require special mention. They all depend upon the question whether defendant is liable upon the note referred to, and, as our conclusion is against him on that question, it is unnecessary to make further reference to the counterclaims. It further appears, and there is no controversy about any of the facts in the case, that during all the times stated Thompson was an officer of plaintiff, namely, its president, and with the vice-president and cashier, had charge of its banking affairs. The trial below was without a jury and the court found that both notes were the valid obligations of defendant, that·they were made and delivered to the bank by Thompson under authority from defendant, and judgment was ordered for plaintiff for the amount claimed. Judgment was entered accordingly, and defendant appealed.

The evidence makes it clear that the note for $1,200 heretofore referred to and in renewal of which in part the $900 note in suit was given, was made by Thompson upon a blank furnished him by defendant, but for his own use and purpose and not in the interests or in the transaction of any business for defendant. In short it was a violation of the duties of Thompson as the agent of defendant, and no benefit accrued therefrom to defendant. It is the contention of defendant that since Thompson was at the time an officer of plaintiff, namely, its president, plaintiff is charged with notice of the fraud of Thompson and should not recover. In other words, defendant invokes the general rule, broadly stated in the books, that a corporation is chargeable with notice of facts known to its managing officers. Conceding the rule, as we must, and without stopping to discuss its scope or limitations, it seems clear that it can have no application to the facts here presented. By all well considered authority the rule is now applied only to cases where the officer, whose knowledge is sought to be imputed to the corporation, acts for the corporation in the particular transaction; in other words, where the officer of the corporation conducts both sides of the particular transaction. Morris v. Georgia Loan Co. 109 Ga. 12, 34 S. E. 378, 46 L.R.A. 506; Farrell Foundry v. Dart, 26 Conn. 366; National Security Bank v. Cushman, 121 Mass. 490; First Nat. Bank of Highstone v. Christopher, 40 N. J. Law, 435, 29 Am. Rep. 262. The rule does not apply where the officer does not act for the corporation, and is connected with the transaction only in an adversary capacity, or as the agent for the party dealing with the corporation. Bang v. Brett, 62 Minn. 4, 63 N. W. 1067; E. D. Woodworth & Co. v. Carroll, 104 Minn. 65, 112 N. W. 1054, 115 N. W. 946; First Nat. Bank of West Minneapolis v. Persall, 110 Minn. 333, 125 N. W. 506, 675, 136 Am. St. 479; Tate v. Security Trust Co. 63 N. J. Eq. 559, 52 Atl. 513; National Bank v. Feeney, 9 S. D. 550, 70 N. W. 874, 46

L.R.A. 732; First Nat. Bank of Willimantic v. Bevin, 72 Conn. 666, 45 Atl. 954; Brookhouse v. Union Pub. Co. 73 N. H. 368, 62 Atl. 219, 2 L.R.A.(N.S.) 993, 111 Am. St. 623, 6 Ann. Cas. 679. The evidence in the case at bar clearly shows that Thompson, though president of the bank, did not act for the bank in this transaction, but submitted the matter of accepting the fraudulent note to the other officers of the bank, and they acted upon their own judgment. It also appears that the other officers knew of the fact that Thompson was the agent of defendant; that he had authority to transact all defendant's business at Gilbert, with the right to draw upon defendant's bank account and to fill out and negotiate defendant's blank signed promissory notes. They acted on this information in accepting the note in question, and there is no showing that they were in any way informed that Thompson was defrauding defendant. Clearly these facts, about which there is no controversy, render inapplicable the general rule invoked by defendant.

This disposes of the case. There were no errors in the rulings of the court upon the admission or exclusion of evidence.

Judgment affirmed.

ST. ANTHONY & DAKOTA ELEVATOR COMPANY v. GREAT NORTHERN RAILWAY COMPANY.[1]

November 13, 1914.

Nos. 18,775—(40).

Evidence — state weighmaster's records.

1. The records in the office of the state weighmaster made pursuant to rules established by the Railroad and Warehouse Commission are competent evidence of the facts recorded therein as required by such rules.

Same — cars in bad order.

2. Such rules require state weighers, at the time of weighing loaded cars, to make and enter in the record notations as to any bad order condition of

---

[1] Reported in 149 N. W. 471.

such cars, and such notations so entered become a proper part of such record.

Authenticated copies may be waived.

3. Copies of such records are not admissible in evidence unless duly authenticated, but such authentication may be waived, and was waived in this case.

Estimating value at place of shipment.

4. In the absence of direct evidence as to the value of property at the place of shipment, such value may be determined by taking the value at the place of delivery and deducting therefrom the expense of transportation thereto from the place of shipment.

Action in the district court for Hennepin county to recover $347.-23. The answer, among other matters, alleged that the weights of the grain shipped under the bills of lading mentioned in the opinion when inserted therein were inserted "weights subject to correction" and were inserted by plaintiff or at its dictation and without any knowledge by defendant of the actual weights of the grain so delivered. The case was tried before Bardwell, J., and a jury which returned verdicts upon the three causes of action aggregating $301.06. From an order denying its motion for judgment in its favor notwithstanding the verdict or for a new trial, defendant appealed. Affirmed.

Cobb, Wheelwright & Dille and *H. C. Mackall,* for appellant.
Mercer, Swan & Stinchfield and *C. G. Krause,* for respondent.

TAYLOR, C.

Plaintiff shipped three carloads of grain over defendant's railway from stations in North Dakota to terminal points in Minnesota. When the grain arrived at the place of delivery it was inspected and weighed by the proper state officials, and the quantity then in the cars was found to be less than the quantity loaded therein as shown by the bills of lading. Plaintiff brought this suit to recover for the shortage and obtained a verdict. Defendant thereafter made an alternative motion for judgment notwithstanding the verdict or for a new trial. This motion was denied and defendant appealed.

The appeal is based upon alleged errors in the rulings in respect to the admission of evidence, and in the instructions given to the jury as to the measure of damages.

1. The statutes provide that the State Railroad and Warehouse Commission "shall exercise general supervision over the grain interests of the state, and of the handling, inspection, weighing and storage of grain, * * * and shall make all proper rules and regulations for carrying out and enforcing * * * all laws of the state relating to such subjects." Section 4497, G. S. 1913. The statutes further provide:

"All weighmasters and weighers shall keep such records as may be prescribed by the commission, and shall furnish to any person for whom weighing is done a certificate under his hand, showing the amount of each weight, the number and initial letter or other distinctive mark of each car weighed, place and date of weighing, and contents of car. Such certificate shall be *prima facie* evidence of the facts therein certified." Section 4463, G. S. 1913.

The commission has provided by rule that weighers shall "(a) examine each car very carefully before it is unloaded, and if found to be in a leaky or bad order condition make notations of same in weight record book and in remark column of daily report; also make a special bad order report on blank provided for that purpose."

The weighers who weighed the three cars in question made a notation as to the condition of each car indicating defects therein. The above rule and these notations were received in evidence over defendant's objection, and the chief controversy is whether such evidence was admissible.

Defendant contends that the certificates which section 4463 provides that the weigher shall furnish to the person for whom the weighing is done are competent evidence of the matters which the statute requires to be stated therein, but of nothing else. For the purposes of this case we may concede that such contention is correct, but it does not follow that the evidence received was inadmissible. The statutes require the issuance of such certificates, but they also give the commission general supervision over the entire subject matter of the handling of grain, authorize the commission to make all proper rules and regulations for carrying out and enforcing all laws relating thereto, and require the keeping of such records as the commission shall direct. There is nothing in the law which limits the records to be kept to a record of the certificates required to be issued to the person for whom the weighing was done. On the contrary the provisions referred to clearly indicate that no such limitation was contemplated. Such certificates may properly be recorded in the record, but so may any other pertinent facts which the commission directs the weighers to note therein. Under the statutes, it was within the province of the commission to require the making of the notations in controversy, and to require them to be entered in the official record. The commission made such requirement and the notations were made and recorded in accordance therewith and are a part of the official record.

It is well settled that a record, which the duties imposed upon a public officer required him to make and which was made by such officer pursuant to and in the proper performance of such duties, is competent evidence of the facts properly recorded therein. Healy v. Hoy, 115 Minn. 321, 132 N. W. 208; United States v. McCoy, 193 U. S. 593, 24 Sup. Ct. 528, 48 L. ed. 805; 1 Dunnell, Minn. Dig. § 3347. It follows therefore that the official record containing the notations in question, or a duly authenticated copy thereof, was admissible in evidence.

By virtue of section 4463 certificates issued to the person for whom the weighing is done are competent evidence without other authentication than the signature thereto of the weigher issuing them, but this provision applies only to such certificates and not to other papers which are merely transcripts from the records. It appeared by the testimony of the state weighmaster that the documents offered in evidence, and which contained the notations in controversy, were copies of records in his office. They were not certified copies, and, if objected to upon that ground, would have been inadmissible unless they were certificates within the purview of section 4463, supra. But defendant expressly waived the objection that they were not properly authenticated as copies of the official records, and based its objection solely upon the ground that such notations were inadmissible in evidence because the statute did not expressly authorize the weigher to incorporate them in his certificate.   As already pointed out, they are a proper part of the record, even if not a proper part of such certificates, and such record is competent evidence.   It follows that both the rule established by the commission and the copies of the records made pursuant thereto were properly admitted in evidence.

2. The bills of lading provided that in case of loss the amount of damage should be computed upon the basis of the value of the property at the place and time of shipment.   The court instructed the jury to the effect that the measure of damages, in case there was a shortage for which plaintiff was entitled to recover, was the value of the nondelivered grain at the place of delivery, on the date of shipment, less the freight from the place of shipment.   Defendant challenges the rule given by the court as not in accordance with the contract.   Defendant's contention is not entirely clear, but apparently is to the effect that testimony as to value should have been confined to statements of the value at the place of shipment; and that it was not permissible to determine the value at the place of shipment, by taking the value at the place of delivery and deducting therefrom the expense of transporting the grain from the place of shipment to the place of delivery.   The grain in question was what is known as no-grade.   It was of such inferior quality that it did not come within any established grade having a definite market price.   The evidence indicates that there was no established price for such grain ascertainable from the market reports, but that the value of each lot of no-grade grain was determined by an examination of the grain itself.   There was evidence tending to show the value of the grain at the place of delivery and the expense of transporting it thereto from the place of shipment, but no direct evidence as to its value at the place of shipment.   Under the evidence presented, the only practicable method of determining the value at the place of shipment was that adopted by the court, and the instruction given was correct.

3. The other questions raised are without merit and require no especial mention.

Order affirmed.

.HERMANN KRETZ v. FIREPROOF STORAGE COMPANY.[1]

November 13, 1914.

Nos. 18,787—(47).

Reservation of right of way — modification in later deed.

1. Where a right of way exists over one tract of land as appurtenant to another, the owners of the two tracts may modify the location and extent of the way at their pleasure. A recital in a deed reserving a right of way that the grantor is the owner of the dominant tenement, is proof of the fact of such ownership. A reservation of a right of way in a deed made in 1881 is held to supersede a right of way different in extent created in a deed made in 1866.

Right of way — intention of parties.

2. A right of way appurtenant to one lot cannot be used by the owner thereof as a right of way to another separate tract. But the extent of the tract to be served in connection with the dominant tenement is a question of intention of the parties, and the intent will be determined by the relation of the easement to the land to which it is appurtenant, and other surrounding transactions, including the practical construction of the contract by the parties.

:Same — practical construction.

3. A right of way was reserved by deed to the owner of part of lot 6. The owner of this lot then erected a building covering this part of lot 6 and also part of lots 4 and 5, adjoining. After this, the right of way was confirmed by a later contract. *Held*, an intent was manifested that the right of way shall serve the building as erected at the time the contract was made, the practical construction of the parties being in accord with this construction.

Right of way — use by owner of servient tenement.

4. The owner of the fee of land over which a right of way, not exclusive, is granted, may himself use the land which is subject to the easement, if by so doing he does not unreasonably interfere with the special use for which the easement was created. The way should be maintained at a level reasonably calculated to serve the owner of the fee and the owner of the easement.

[1] Reported in 149 N. W. 955.

Limitation of use.

5. A grant of a right of way to and from an opera house does not limit the use of the way to such time as the property is used as an opera house, but it is available in connection with any proper use of the property.

Action in the district court for Ramsey county to enjoin defendant from using a certain passway 12 feet wide on the easterly side of the northerly 65 feet of lot 6 mentioned in the opinion. The case was tried before Catlin, J., who made findings and ordered judgment in favor of plaintiff. From an order denying its motion for an amendment of the findings and for a new trial, defendant appealed. Reversed and new trial granted.

B. H. Schriber, for appellant.

John F. Fitzpatrick, for respondent.

HALLAM, J.

Action to enjoin defendant from using a right of way.

The facts may be more easily understood by reference to the diagram on page 306.

In 1866 John L. Merriam owned lots 6, 7 and 8, block 23, St. Paul Proper. These lots are each 50 x 150 feet, fronting on Fourth street, and together they form a tract 150 feet square on the southeast corner of Fourth and Wabasha streets. On October 30, 1866, Merriam deeded to one party the north 60 feet, and to another the south 25 feet, of the south 85 feet of the west 38 feet of lot 6. Both deeds conveyed also "a perpetual right of way over and upon a strip of land on the easterly side of said lot 6, 12 feet wide through the whole length of said lot 6, for the purposes of ingress and egress, to and from said described portion of said lot 6, and as appurtenant thereto." By 1881 such conveyances had been made that the north 65 feet of lot 6 was owned by Merriam and William F. Davidson in equal undivided shares. On September 13, 1881, William F. Davidson and wife deeded to Merriam the undivided one-half of the north 65 feet of lot 6, with the following exception: "Excepting and reserving to said parties of the first part as the owners of the southerly 85 feet of said lots 6, 7 and 8

127 M.—20.

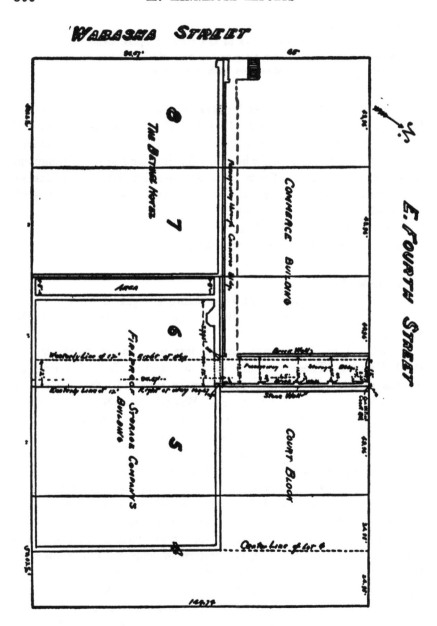

* * * the right of way over a strip of ground twelve feet wide along the easterly side of said lot 6."

In 1882, Davidson commenced the erection of the Grand Opera House, covering the south 85 feet of lot 6 and also of lot 5 and the west one-half of lot 4.

On June 21, 1883, Merriam leased to Davidson for 25 years the east 29½ feet of the north 65 feet of lot 6. This lease contains this clause:

"Subject to the exception and reservation to said William F. Davidson, contained in a certain deed from him and his wife to said party of the first part dated September 13, 1881. * * * whereby a right of way over a strip of ground twelve (12) feet wide along the easterly side of said lot six (6) is reserved to said second party * * * as the owner of the southerly eighty-five (85) feet of lot six (6) seven (7) and eight (8) of said block * * *."

and also this clause:

"It is further agreed that nothing in this contract shall be construed as in any manner changing or vacating the said right of way over a strip twelve (12) feet wide, along the easterly side of said lot six (6) saved and reserved in and by said deed of September 13, 1881, hereinbefore described save and except as such right of way may be temporarily affected during the term hereby granted, and by virtue of this agreement."

The walls of the opera house were then up and reference is made to it in that Davidson was permitted to construct an iron stairway and fire escape leading from the gallery and second floor of the opera house building to a platform on this 29½-foot strip. There was no entrance to the opera house from the 12-foot right of way or from the leased strip save the stairway and fire escape above referred to.

In 1889 the opera house was burned, leaving, however, the walls standing. The building was not rebuilt as an opera house. In 1908 Watson P. Davidson, who had by mesne conveyances acquired the title of William F. Davidson to the opera house property and also to the right of way, leased the same to the defendant for a storage warehouse. In 1908 defendant erected a warehouse four stories high, using the walls of the old opera house as its outer walls, except that the west wall was moved 8 feet further to the east.

In the meantime the Merriam title to the north 65 feet of lot 6 had passed to the Merriam Realty Co., and in 1911 that company deeded it to plaintiff and with it also the north 65 feet of lots 7 and 8. During 1911, plaintiff built on this tract the Commerce Building, 12 stories high. In constructing this building he left a driveway from Fourth street to defendant's warehouse nearly coincident with the right of way in question. This driveway was arched to the height of one story, and above the first story the Commerce Building was built and extended over it. The driveway thus left, varied from the right of way in question in this: Five two foot columns supporting the arch and the building above it were built on the easterly side of the 12-foot strip, and to offset this encroachment plaintiff widened the strip nearly two feet on the westerly side by setting the building that distance in upon his land.

In 1912 plaintiff commenced this action and asked judgment that defendant be excluded forever from the 12-foot passway and enjoined from using the same in any manner or for any purpose. The trial court did not sustain this contention, but held that the passway must be limited in its use to access to and from lot 6, and ordered judgment enjoining the use of it altogether until defendant shall divide its building and erect a solid wall without openings therein on the line between lots 5 and 6.

One of the contentions of plaintiff is that defendant's right of way rests solely on the deeds given by Merriam in 1866, which deeds created an easement of right of way over a 12-foot strip running through the whole length of lot 6. It is claimed that the use of the southerly end of this strip for any other purpose than a way is unwarranted and "deprives him of the right to keep open the rest of the passageway" over plaintiff's land, or at least that it imposes an additional burden on the passageway over plaintiff's land, which should be enjoined. We think it clear that defendant's rights do not rest on the 1866 deeds, but that the later reservations in the deed from Davidson to Merriam made in 1881 superseded the grants in the earlier deeds. The 1881 deed reserved to Davidson, as owner of the south 85 feet of lots 6, 7 and 8, a 12-foot right of way over the north 65 feet of lot 6. Davidson and Merriam owned the northerly 65 feet in common. This deed recited that Davidson owned the south 85 feet. This recital is proof that this was the fact. The parties to a deed are estopped by recitals in it where the facts recited are material to and of the essence of the contract. Bigelow, Estoppel, (6th ed.) p. 408; Herman, Estoppel & Res Judicata, § 618; Daughaday v. Paine, 6 Minn. 304, 310 (443); Holcombe v. Richards, 38 Minn. 38, 45, 35 N. W. 714; Williams v. Swetland, 10 Iowa, 51. It was perfectly competent for these parties, being the owners of all the land involved, to modify or establish this right of way as they saw fit. The effect of this reservation was to establish a right of way from Fourth street to the south 85 feet of lots 6, 7 and 8.

This is the only right of way with which the parties to that transaction were thereafter concerned, and the only one which concerns the parties to this action. We need not consider what the situation would have been if the deed of 1881 had not been given.

2. The important contention in the case is that even this 1881 deed gave to Davidson and his grantees no right to use this right of way as a means of access to a building which covers not only lot 6, but also part of lots 4 and 5. This is not an easement in gross and it exists only as appurtenant to some tract of land. If an appurtenant right of way is granted to A as the owner of lot 6, the easement can be used only in connection with that lot. It cannot be used as a right of way to any other separate tract. It is also contended that such a grant does not give to A the right to inclose additional lands with lot 6 and thus impose upon the easement the burden of serving a larger tract than that contemplated in the deed. The weight of authority seems to sustain this view in the absence of controlling evidence manifesting a different intent. Illustrative cases are: Evans v. Dana, 7 R. I. 306; Albert v. Thomas, 73 Md. 181, 20 Atl. 912; Greene v. Canny, 137 Mass. 64; French v. Marstin, 32 N. H. 316; Harris v. Flower, 91 L. T. 816. Other cases are cited in 14 Cyc. 1209; Washburn, Easements, *60; Gale, Easements, 498. et seq. But we do not find it necessary to determine this as an abstract question. The extent of the tract to be served by the

easement is a matter of intention. Abbott v. Butler, 59 N. H. 317; Sweeney v. Landers, 80 Conn. 575, 69 Atl. 566; Rowell v. Doggett, 143 Mass. 483, 10 N. E. 182. If at the time of the grant of the right of way as appurtenant to lot 6, lot 6 was known to be inclosed by means of permanent walls with lots 4 and 5, we should not doubt that an intention was manifested that the easement should serve lot 6 as it was used in connection with the other lots and in effect serve all three.

Coming then to the facts of this case, we must construe this 1881 deed in connection with the lease in 1883, which confirms this easement, and construe both in connection with attendant circumstances, for when the extent of the easement is not clearly declared the intent of the parties will be determined by the relation of the easement to the land to which it is appurtenant, and other circumstances surrounding the transaction, including the conduct and the practical construction of the contract by the parties. Winston v. Johnson, 42 Minn. 398, 45 N. W. 958; Lidgerding v. Zignego, 77 Minn. 421, 80 N. W. 360; 77 Am. St. 677.

3. At the time the 1883 lease was given, the tract now used by defendant, part of lots 4, 5 and 6, was, as above stated, enclosed within the opera house walls. These walls, and the building they enclosed, were in contemplation a permanent structure. This contemplation has become a reality to the extent that, notwithstanding the fire, the walls still stand and now enclose a building with perhaps greater prospect of permanency than ever before. Yet if the contentions of plaintiff are sound Davidson could not have used this right of way for any practical purpose at all. Had he opened an entrance upon it to the opera house he could not use it to conduct a performer to the stage on lot 4, nor could he permit a patron to enter by means of it and take a seat in the front of the house on lot 5, and if he seated such a patron in the rear of the house on lot 6 he would be obliged to erect a screen between him and the stage. Surely such results were not intended by Merriam and Davidson when this easement was confirmed by the 1883 lease. We think it clear that they intended that the easement so confirmed should permit the enjoyment of a

right of way from Fourth street to the opera house as it was then constructed on parts of lots 4, 5 and 6.

The conduct of later owners, including plaintiff, shows a practical construction of these instruments and leaves no doubt as to their own view of the rights of defendant. At the time the storage warehouse was built the Merriam Realty Co. was the owner in fee of the 12-foot strip. The warehouse was built with its entrance on the strip with the manifest purpose of using the right of way over it as a means of access from Fourth street. Yet the Merriam Realty Co. voiced no word of protest either during the construction of the building or during the years thereafter during which this entrance to the warehouse was used. The deed by which the Merriam Realty Co. conveyed to plaintiff the northerly part of lots 6, 7 and 8, including this strip, excepted this same right of way. It referred to it as reserved or granted by the 1866 deed, but this is not of great importance. It did except it. After plaintiff acquired the property and planned the construction of his 12-story office building, he wrote defendant, "I shall, however, leave a passageway over the easterly 12 feet of the northerly 65 feet of said lot 6, sufficient to answer all the purposes of a right of way to that part of lot 6 which is in the rear of the northerly 65 feet thereof," and he did do so. He entered into negotiations, for the most part fruitless it is true, predicated on the assumption that defendant had a subsisting right of way, and looking toward the adjustment of some small controversies between the parties. He paved this right of way from Fourth street to the entrance to the warehouse with concrete, and he himself habitually passed over it and through defendant's warehouse to the rear of his 12-story building. The recognition of the existence of this right of way as a means of access between Fourth street and the warehouse was decisive and beyond question. Our construction of these instruments is in accordance with the construction placed upon them by the parties concerned, and we hold that defendant has a right of way over this 12-foot strip from Fourth street to its building, and the whole thereof.

4. It is contended the right of way is not maintained at the proper level. The pavement laid by plaintiff is on the level of

Fourth street. Defendant has raised the level at the southerly end. We do not agree with defendant that it has a right to maintain this right of way at the level that existed before the lots were graded. Such a rule in case of city lots would lead to absurd consequences. Nor do we agree with plaintiff that it must necessarily be maintained at the level of Fourth street. Defendant's right to use this strip is not exclusive of plaintiff. Plaintiff no doubt has the right to use this strip, if by so doing he does not unreasonably interfere with the special use for which the easement was created. Thompson v. Germania Life Ins. Co. 97 Minn. 89, 106 N. W. 102. The passway should be maintained at a level reasonably calculated to serve both plaintiff and defendant. See Killion v. Kelley, 120 Mass. 47; Greenmount Cemetery Co.'s Appeals, 4 Atl. 528 (Pa.). There is no finding that the present level is not such a level.

5. In defendant's chain of title is a deed given April 1, 1884, by W. F. Davidson to the St. Paul Opera House Co. This grants a right of way over this strip "to [and] from said opera house." Plaintiff claims this restricts the use of the passway to use in connection with an opera house and that it cannot be used in connection with a storage warehouse. We are of the opinion that the use of the passway was not restricted to such time as the dominant tenement should be used as an opera house, but that it is available in connection with any proper use of the dominant tenement. Bailey v. Agawam National Bank, 190 Mass. 20, 76 N. E. 449, 3 L.R.A.(N.S.) 98, 112 Am. St. 296; White v. Grand Hotel (1913) 1 Ch. 113, 33 Ann. Cas. 472.

Order reversed and new trial granted.

On December 21, 1914, the following opinion was filed:

PER CURIAM.

Appeal from the clerk's taxation of costs. The clerk taxed against respondent the full cost of printing the record, at sixty cents a page. The propriety of this action is the principal question raised on this appeal. This case was tried in the trial court with the case of Davidson v. Kretz, infra, p. 313, and the appeal of Davidson in that case and the appeal of appellant in this were presented together in this court, the same record being used on both appeals. Respondent contends that, in view of this fact, the cost of printing should be apportioned between the two cases and half charged to each case. It appears that all of the record that was printed was necessary to the presentation of the appeal in this case, except twenty-seven pages thereof, the expense of which amounts to $16.20. The appellant now concedes that this may be eliminated. As to the balance of the record, it must be held, following Hess v. Great Northern Ry. Co. 98 Minn. 198, 201, 108 N. W. 7, 803, that under the statutes of this state the court has no discretion in the allowance, disallowance or apportionment of disbursements, and that, inasmuch as this disbursement was necessary to the presentation of the appeal in this case, it must be allowed. The clerk's taxation of costs is affirmed, except as to the item of $16.20 above mentioned.

WATSON P. DAVIDSON v. HERMANN KRETZ and Another.[1]

November 13, 1914.

Nos. 18,787—(46).

Right of way — change of location by parol agreement.

An easement may be extinguished or modified by a parol agreement fully executed, and an oral agreement that the fee owner may erect a permanent building over part of one side of the way and extend the way a like distance on the other side, when executed, extinguishes the old easement to the extent of the obstruction and gives a right to use the new way as a substitute for the old, at least as long as the obstruction continues. Though the new way is narrower than agreed, the owner of the way cannot, after acquiescing in its construction, require that the building be undermined to enlarge the way according to the terms of the oral agreement.

[1] Reported in 149 N. W. 652.

Note.—Upon the question of change of easement by building over right of way, see note in 15 L.R.A. 487.

Action in the district court for Ramsey county to recover $10,000 for interference with a certain easement of plaintiff and for judgment removing all obstructions to the easement in question. The action was tried before Catlin, J., who made findings and ordered judgment in favor of defendants. From an order denying his motion for amendment of the findings and for a new trial, plaintiff appealed. Affirmed.

B. H. Schriber, for appellant.

John F. Fitzpatrick and *Durment, Moore & Oppenheimer,* for respondents.

HALLAM, J.

This action is brought to compel the removal of the supports to the 12-story building mentioned in the opinion in Kretz v. Fireproof Storage Co. supra, p. 304, 149 N. W. 648, which supports were placed on the easterly portion of plaintiff's 12-foot right of way. It appears that plaintiff's 99-year tenant, the Fireproof Storage Co., consented to the placing of these supports in the passway pursuant to a vary informal verbal agreement that defendant would widen the passway the same distance on the other side by setting his building back on his own land. It also appears that plaintiff frequently observed the construction of the building and of these supports and we think acquiesced therein.

It is quite well settled that an easement may be extinguished or modified by a parol agreement granted by the owner of the dominant tenement and executed by the owner of the servient tenement. Boston & P. R. Corp. v. Doherty, 154 Mass. 314, 28 N. E. 277; Morse v. Copeland, 2 Gray, 302; Curtis v. Noonan, 10 Allen, 406. If the owner of an easement of way verbally agrees that the owner of the servient estate may erect thereon an obstruction of a permanent character and substitute another way, this agreement when executed extinguishes the right to the easement to the extent of the obstruction. Boston & P. R. Corp. v. Doherty, 154 Mass. 314, 28 N. E. 277; Pope v. Devereux, 5 Gray, 409; Ebert v. Mishler, 234 Pa. St. 609, 83 Atl. 596; Hamilton v. White, 4 Barb. 60.

Whether the owner of the servient tenement may later close the new and restore the old way is not important here. It is at least certain that the new way cannot be closed unless the old is first restored. Wright v. Willis, 23 Ky. Law Rep. 565; Thompson v. Madsen, 29 Utah, 326, 81 Pac. 160. These same rules apply where the agreement is not to close the old way entirely, but to close part of the way on one side and to enlarge it on the other.

The consent of the parties to the substitution of one way for another may be implied from their acquiescence. Rumill v. Robbins, 77 Me. 193. The storage company agreed to this substitution and plaintiff acquiesced in it and both are bound thereby.

Plaintiff complains that defendant set his building back only one foot seven inches from the west line of the passway and thus narrowed the way five inches, whereas the agreement was that he should set it back two feet, and that defendant had no right to reduce the width of the passway to that extent. It must be borne in mind that the whole matter rested on parol. Both plaintiff and his 99-year tenant watched this building in process of construction and we think acquiesced in it as it was constructed, and acquiesced in the width of the way as the building left it. It is too late now for them to assert that the width of the way is insufficient. They are estopped from so doing. Vogler v. Geiss, 51 Md. 407.

Defendant should not now be compelled to undermine his building even to the extent of the removal of five inches from its support.

Order affirmed.

S. P. CROSBY v. L. P. LARSON.[1]

November 13, 1914.

Nos. 18,822—(83).

Finding sustained by evidence.

Plaintiff sued to recover for services rendered and disbursements made as

---

[1] Reported in 149 N. W. 466.

attorney for a receiver. Upon conflicting evidence, the court found as a fact that plaintiff rendered no services and made no disbursements in the capacity of attorney for the receiver. The evidence is sufficient to sustain the finding.

Action transferred to the district court for Isanti county to ascertain the value of plaintiff's professional services and to recover judgment therefor. The answer specifically denied that plaintiff ever rendered any services to defendant. The case was tried before Giddings, J., who made findings and ordered judgment in favor of defendant. Plaintiff's motion for a new trial was denied. From the judgment entered pursuant to the order for judgment, plaintiff appealed. Affirmed.

S. P. Crosby, pro se.

Godfrey G. Goodwin, for respondent.

HALLAM, J.

Plaintiff, as attorney at law, procured a money judgment in favor of Mrs. S. A. Nebel against Zelma A. Christensen. In proceedings supplementary to execution, defendant Larson was appointed receiver of the property of the judgment debtor. The receiver collected money enough to discharge the judgment and then made application for allowance of his account and for his discharge. The court made an order fixing a time for hearing thereon and directed that a copy of the order be served upon the judgment creditor and also upon this plaintiff. The order was served upon the judgment creditor. Plaintiff was temporarily absent from the state and it was not served upon him. On the hearing the receiver was discharged. Plaintiff, on his return to the state, made application to vacate the order of discharge and also commenced this action. His alleged grievance in both cases is the same and is based on the claim that he was the attorney for the receiver as well as for the judgment creditor and is entitled to compensation for his services and reimbursement for certain expenditures made. The application to vacate the discharge, and the trial of the action to recover fees, came before the court at the same time, and they were considered together. The court found as a fact that plaintiff did not render professional services nor make any disbursements as attorney for the defendant as receiver, and gave judgment for the defendant and denied the motion to vacate the receiver's discharge. The appeal is taken from the judgment alone.

The question whether an attorney for a receiver may maintain an action against the receiver personally for compensation for services rendered in connection with the receivership, is not raised in this case and is not decided. Both parties seemed content to litigate on the trial of this action the question whether plaintiff rendered services for the receiver and, if so, the further question of the value thereof. But one question is presented on this appeal, and that is whether the findings of fact upon that subject are justified by the evidence. Plaintiff testified that the receiver employed him as attorney, and that he rendered services and incurred expenses pursuant to such employment. Defendant, on the other hand, denied that there was any such employment. He admitted conferring with plaintiff, but claimed that he conferred with him as attorney for the judgment creditor. There was no testimony of any other witness. There was some correspondence between these parties, but the nature of it when considered as a whole is not such that it is inconsistent with defendant's claim. The finding of the trial court on this issue of fact is fairly sustained by proof and should not be disturbed.

We are not concerned on this appeal with the question whether plaintiff received proper notice of the receiver's discharge. That question could only arise on appeal from the order denying the motion to vacate the receiver's discharge, and in fact would not be of consequence there in view of the decision that plaintiff had no claim as attorney for the receiver.

Judgment affirmed.

JOHN ANDERSON v. CITY OF LE SUEUR.[1]

November 13, 1914.

Nos. 18,930—(156).

Intoxicating liquor — local option — "majority of the votes cast upon the question."

At the city election in the city of Le Sueur, a city of the fourth class, the question as to whether licenses for the sale of intoxicating liquor should be issued by the city was duly submitted to the electors, under and pursuant to chapter 387 of the Laws of 1913, and a majority of the votes cast upon that question, but not a majority of the whole number cast at the election, were in favor of the issuance of such licenses. As the statute governing the matter provides that such question shall be decided by "a majority of the votes cast *upon the question*," the proposition authorizing the issuance of licenses was adopted.

John Anderson gave notice of contest and appealed to the district court for Le Sueur county from the canvass of votes cast at the annual election of the city of Le Sueur held on April 7, 1914, and the decision of the common council of that city that 225 votes were cast thereat in favor of, and 212 votes were cast thereat against, granting license for the sale of intoxicating liquor in that city. The court appointed referees to inspect the ballots, and the appeal was thereafter heard by Morrison, J., who made findings and dismissed the proceedings. From the judgment entered pursuant to the order of dismissal, contestant appealed. Affirmed.

Francis Cadwell and *Thomas Hessian,* for appellant.

W. C. & W. F. Odell, for respondent.

---

[1] Reported in 149 N. W. 472.

Note.—For the authorities upon what basis majority essential to adoption of constitutional or other special proposition submitted at general or special election is to be computed, see note in 22 L.R.A.(N.S.) 478.

TAYLOR, C.

Whether the city of Le Sueur should issue licenses for the sale of intoxicating liquor was duly submitted to the voters of that city at the city election held on April 7, 1914. The result of the vote, as determined and declared by the city canvassing board, authorized the issuance of such licenses. The appellant, a resident and legal voter of the city, promptly instituted a contest, and, as the result of the trial thereof, the district court found that the total number of ballots cast at the election was 446, of which 222 were in favor of license, 214 were against license, and 10 were blank. The court further found that the proposition authorizing the issuance of such licenses had been adopted by a majority of eight votes, and rendered judgment dismissing the contest. The contestant appealed.

If it required a majority of all the votes cast at the election to authorize the issuance of such licenses, the decision of the trial court was erroneous; if a majority of the votes cast upon that specific question was sufficient to confer such authority, the decision of the trial court was correct. Similar questions have been considered by this court in a number of cases. Prior to the enactment of chapter 387, p. 540, Laws of 1913, the so-called local option statutes applied only to villages and rural towns. Kleppe v. Gard, 109 Minn. 251, 123 N. W. 665. In cities such matters were governed by the provisions contained in their respective charters. The statute which applies to towns and villages prohibits the issuance of such licenses unless "a majority of votes at the last election at which the question of license was voted upon" were in favor of license. Section 1533, R. L. 1905; Section 3142, G. S. 1913. This statute has uniformly been construed to mean that no license could issue, unless more than one-half of all the votes cast at the election were in favor thereof, and that a majority of the votes cast upon that specific question, if less than a majority of the whole number cast at the election, was not sufficient to authorize such issuance. State v. Village Council of Osakis, 112 Minn. 365, 128 N. W. 295; McLaughlin v. Village of Rush City, 122 Minn. 428, 142 N. W. 713. Similar language contained in the charter of the city of Warren was held to have the same meaning. Lodoen v. City Council of City of Warren, 118

Minn. 371, 136 N. W. 1031.   The charter of the city of Ada provided that, "if a majority of the votes cast at such election *on said question* shall be against license, no license for the sale of intoxicating liquors shall be granted by the authorities of the said city of Ada."   In Thune v. Hetland, 114 Minn. 395, 131 N. W. 372, it was held that this provision in the charter of the city of Ada authorized the issuance of licenses, if a majority of the votes cast upon that specific question, although less than a majority of the whole number cast at the election, were in favor thereof.

As already stated, there was no general local option statute applying to cities prior to the passage of the act of 1913.   Each city was governed in respect to such matters by the provisions contained in its own charter.   In 1913, the legislature enacted chapter 387, p. 540, of the laws of that year which is entitled:

"An act authorizing the electors of cities of the fourth class to vote upon the question of licensing the sale of intoxicating liquor in such cities; and prohibiting the sale of liquor in any quantity either wholesale or retail in any such city or the granting of any license for such sale if a majority of the votes on such question at any election hereunder shall be against license, and not otherwise, until such vote shall be reversed at a subsequent election hereunder; and defining terms used herein and prescribing penalties for violations hereof."

This statute provides that, if the license question be submitted to the voters, a separate ballot shall be provided therefor, and, among other things provides:

"The said ballot shall have printed thereon the words 'for license' and 'against license,' and each qualified elector voting upon said question, shall place a cross mark (X) in the place opposite the words 'for license' or in the place opposite the words 'against license,' which ballot shall be deposited in a separate ballot box to be provided for in each voting precinct, and such votes shall be counted for or against said question in accordance with the expressed will of the elector, as provided by the election laws of this state.   The ballots so cast shall be duly canvassed, returned and certified, according to the law governing such city elections and if a majority of the votes cast upon the question shall be in favor of license then license for the sale of intoxicating liquor may be granted, but if such majority shall be against license then no license shall be granted."

This law does not purport to be an amendment of prior laws, but to be an independent act. It applies only to cities of the fourth class, and prior general laws relating to this question did not apply to such cities. The meaning of the language used in the law applying to villages and towns, and the different meaning of the different language used in the charter of the city of Ada, had been determined and announced by this court long before the passage of the act of 1913. With these different rules before them, the legislature, in its title, described the present act, in part, as an act "prohibiting the sale of liquor * * * or the granting of any license for such sale if a majority of the votes *on such question* at any election hereunder shall be against license." They then enacted in the body of the act that "each qualified elector voting *upon said question* shall place a cross mark (X) in the place opposite the words 'for license,' or in the place opposite the words 'against license' * * * and such votes shall be counted *for or against said question* in accordance with the expressed will of the elector. * * * And if a majority of the votes cast *upon the question* shall be in favor of license then license for the sale of intoxicating liquor may be granted, but if such majority shall be against license then no license shall be granted." In view of the language used, and of the circumstances under which it was used, it is entirely clear that the legislature intended to, and did, adopt the rule that cities of the fourth class should be permitted to issue licenses, "if a majority of the votes cast *upon the question,*" although less than a majority of the whole number cast at the election, were in favor of license. The result is to establish a rule for cities of the fourth class different from the general rule which applies to towns and villages; but this is within the discretion of the legislature, and is a matter over which the courts have no control. It may be proper to note, in passing, that chapter 10, p. 20, Laws of 1905, being sections 3129 and 3130, G. S. 1913, may establish a different rule for villages incorporated under the laws therein referred to, than applies to other villages. This question is not considered or determined herein, and is mentioned merely to indicate

127 M.—21.

that the reference herein to villages is not intended to apply to the class of villages governed by the law of 1905.

The city of Le Sueur is a city of the fourth class. The election in controversy was held under and pursuant to the law of 1913. As "a majority of the votes cast *upon the question*" were in favor of license, the decision of the trial court was correct, and the judgment appealed from is affirmed.

BROWN, C. J. (dissenting).

The statutes referred to in the opinion are in *pari materia*, they all relate to the same subject matter, are included in the chapter relating to intoxicating liquors (G. S. 1913, c. 16), and should be construed together for the purpose of gathering the general intent of the legislature. The rule controlling the construction of such statutes is well stated by Mr. Justice Wayne in U. S. v. Freeman, 3 How. (U. S.) 556, 11 L. ed. 724, as follows:

"The correct rule of interpretation is, that if divers statutes relate to the same thing, they ought all to be taken into consideration in construing any one of them, and it is an established rule of law, that all acts in *pari materia* are to be taken together, as if they were one law. Douglas, 30; 2 Term Rep. 387, 586; 4 Maule & Selw. 210. If a thing contained in a subsequent statute be within the reason of a former statute, it shall be taken to be within the meaning of that statute."

The rule for determining the total vote cast upon questions of the kind here involved is well settled by our decisions. State v. Village Council of Osakis, 112 Minn. 365, 128 N. W. 295; McLaughlin v. Village of Rush City, 122 Minn. 428, 142 N. W. 713; Lodoen v. City Council of City of Warren, 118 Minn. 371, 136 N. W. 1031. And the rule should be uniform and applicable alike to all villages and cities operating under the general statutes of the state. It is obvious that the legislature did not deliberately intend by the different statutes referred to in the opinion to provide one rule for cities of the fourth class, another rule for certain villages, and still another for other villages, and the conflict between them, if there be any of a substantial nature, or any ambiguity therein, calls for judicial construction, with a view to making their pertinent provisions a consistent harmonious whole. The subject of so construing separate statutes relating to the same subject is fully discussed in 2 Sutherland, St. Const. § 443, where the authorities are cited, and sustains this view of the law. In my opinion that act of 1913, construed in connection with other statutes upon the same subject, and the construction given thereto by our previous decisions, contains nothing beyond what is necessarily implied in section 3142, G. S. 1913, and the construction given the act of 1913 should follow that heretofore applied to that statute. The case of Thune v. Hetland, 114 Minn. 395, 131 N. W. 372, is not here in point. That case involved the construction of the home rule charter of the city of Ada, which provided a different rule for determining such questions. It is of course clear that, under the constitutional provisions for the adoption by certain cities and villages of home rule charters, charters so adopted may contain such provisions upon this or any other subject, as the people deem for their best interests, provided they do not conflict with the Constitution of the state or its declared policy. But, in determining the intention of such a charter, and what was meant by any particular provision thereof, reference could not be had to acts of the legislature upon the same subject. The charter provisions would be construed without reference to statutory enactments upon similar matters. In this case we are called upon to construe different statutes enacted by the same legislative body, and the rule requiring all thereof to be taken together should be applied. "The letter killeth, the spirit giveth life."

I therefore respectfully dissent.

HOLT, J.

I concur in the foregoing dissent.

P. J. PETERSON v. C. M. E. CARLSON.[1]

November 20, 1914.

Nos. 18,627—(32).

Venue — demand for change.

1. Demand for a change of venue made under G. S. 1913, § 7722, must be made within 20 days after the summons is served. If made after that time, it is too late, even though the time for answering has been extended and has not yet expired.

Same — effect of stipulation.

2. A stipulation extending the time for answering does not extend the time for making application for change of venue.

Demand a nullity if not made in time.

3. In order to effect a change of venue, the defendant must make a record showing him entitled to a change. The essentials are that defendant be a nonresident of the county in which the action is brought and that the demand be made seasonably and in due form. The fact of nonresidence is made to appear by affidavit, and the truth of the affidavit in this particular can be challenged only in the court to which the venue is changed. In determining whether the demand was seasonably made, the court in which the action was commenced will look at its whole record, and, if the record shows on its face that the demand was not made in time, the court will treat the demand as a nullity.

Action in the district court for Waseca county by the executor of the last will and testament of Swan P. Peterson, deceased, to recover $2,100 upon two promissory notes. From an order, Childress, J., granting defendant's motion to strike the case from the calendar and directing the clerk of court to transmit the files to the district court for Hennepin county, plaintiff appealed. Reversed.

E. B. Collester and *Moonan & Moonan,* for appellant.

Olof L. Bruce and *Harry Reuch,* for respondent.

[1] Reported in 149 N. W. 536.

HALLAM, J.

This action was commenced in Waseca county. The summons, with the sheriff's return of service was duly filed with the clerk of the district court of Waseca county. Thirty-seven days after such service, defendant served a written demand for a change of venue to Hennepin county, with an affidavit in proper form alleging that defendant resided in Hennepin county at the time of the commencement of the action. In the meantime the time for answering had been extended by stipulation, and the extended time had not yet expired. Issue was later joined, defendant entitling his answer "Hennepin County" and plaintiff entitling his reply "Waseca County." Plaintiff placed the case on the calendar of the next term of court for Waseca county for trial. When the case was called, the court, on motion of defendant, struck it from the calendar and directed the files to be transmitted to Hennepin county on the ground that the venue had been changed. Plaintiff appeals.

It was error to strike the case from the calendar.

1. The demand for change of venue came too late.

The statute requires that it be made "within twenty days after the summons is served." G. S. 1913, § 7722. This application was not made until 37 days after summons served. A former statute provided that the demand should be made "at any time before the time for answering" expired. G. S. 1878, c. 66, § 51, as amended by chapter 28, p. 147, Laws 1895, and chapter 345, p. 677, Laws 1903. The change to the present language was made in the 1905 Code (R. L. 1905, § 4096). We are asked to "construe" the present statute as meaning the same as the former one. The plain meaning of the language is not the same. The language of the present statute is so clear that there is no room for construction.

2. It is contended that the stipulation extending the time for answering *ipso facto* extended also the time for making demand for change of venue. We cannot so hold. There is simply no connection between the making of an answer and the making of a demand for a change of venue, and a stipulation extending the time for one could not by any permissible construction extend the time for the other.

3. The fact that the time for making demand for change of venue had expired appeared affirmatively on the face of the record of the court. But the trial court held that, the affidavit for change of venue being regular on its face, the court could not go outside of it, even to the extent of examining its own record, to ascertain whether the demand was made in time. In this the court was in error. The court was not obliged to ignore its own record. On the contrary, it was under obligation to consult its record in order to determine whether defendant was entitled to have his motion granted.

Before a defendant can be heard to assert that the venue has been changed, he must present a record that shows him entitled to the change. The essentials are that, at the time of the commencement of the action, the defendant was a resident of a county of the state other than that in which the venue is laid, and that the demand is made seasonably and in due form.

The fact of residence is made to appear by the affidavit for a change of venue, and if the affidavit sets forth such fact and demand is seasonably made, the venue is *ipso facto* changed, and the truth of the affidavit can only be challenged in the court to which the venue is changed. State v. District Court of Meeker County, 77 Minn. 302, 79 N. W. 960; State v. District Court of Pine County, 88 Minn. 95, 92 N. W. 518.

The time of service of the summons is no part of the matter required to be stated in the affidavit for change of venue (Grimes v. Ericson, 92 Minn. 164, 99 N. W. 621), and it was not stated in the affidavit in this case. It usually appears, as it did in this case, from the return of service, upon the summons itself. But the venue is not changed unless the demand is made in time and that fact must be made to appear in some manner before the defendant can demand a transfer of the files. In this case the record shows beyond controversy that the application was not made in time. With the record in this condition the court is not obliged to honor defendant's demand for a change of venue, nor has the venue been changed. Potter v. Holmes, 72 Minn. 153, 75 N. W. 591.

This is in accord with the rulings of the Federal courts in the somewhat analogous case of removal of causes from state to Federal courts on the ground of diverse citizenship, which removal is accomplished by filing a petition and bond in proper form. In such cases the rule is that the state court is not bound to surrender its jurisdiction until a record has been made which on its face shows that the petitioner has a right to the transfer, and the state court has a right to determine, subject to review on appeal, the question of law whether it appears on the face of the record, that is, the petition, the pleadings and the proceedings down to that time, that the petitioner is entitled to a removal of the suit. Stone v. South Carolina, 117 U. S. 430, 6 Sup. Ct. 799, 29 L. ed. 962; Burlington, C. R. & N. Ry. Co. v. Dunn, 122 U. S. 513, 7 Sup. Ct. 1262, 30 L. ed. 1159; Madisonville Traction Co. v. St. Bernard Mining Co. 196 U. S. 239, 25 Sup. Ct. 251, 49 L. ed. 462; Chesapeake & O. Ry. Co. v. Cockrell, 232 U. S. 146, 34 Sup. Ct. 278, 58 L. ed. 544.

If we were to follow the rule adopted by the trial court we would place it in the power of a defendant to stop the progress of a cause at any time, by the mere filing of an affidavit that defendant resided in another county at the time of the commencement of the action, no matter what the stage of the case or the state of the record. Clearly this was not the purpose or proper meaning of the statute.

What may be the proper forum for determining a dispute as to whether a demand for change of venue is in fact made in time, we need not here determine. There is no dispute as to that fact in this case. The record shows affirmatively, and without dispute, that the demand came too late, and the trial court should have treated it as a nullity.

Order reversed and case remanded with directions to proceed in accordance with this opinion.

CARL LARSON v. DULUTH STREET RAILWAY COMPANY.[1]

November 20, 1914.

Nos. 18,744—(59).

Negligence — questions for jury.

In this action to recover damages sustained in a collision with a street car of defendant, it is *held* that the questions of negligence and contributory negligence were for the jury and that the evidence sustains the verdict.

Action in the district court for St. Louis county to recover $6,800 for injury received by plaintiff in a collision with defendant's street car. The answer alleged that the accident was not caused by any negligence on the part of defendant and was caused by plaintiff's negligence. The case was tried before Cant, J., who denied defendant's motion for a dimissal of the action and its motion for a directed verdict, and a jury which returned a verdict for $900. From an order denying its motion for judgment notwithstanding the verdict or for a new trial, defendant appealed. Affirmed.

Thomas S. Wood, for appellant.

C. R. Magney and *John Jenswold, Jr.,* for respondent.

BUNN, J.

Plaintiff recovered a verdict of $900 in the court below, and defendant appealed from an order denying its motion in the alternative for judgment or a new trial.

The assignments of error challenge the sufficiency of the evidence to warrant submitting the issues to the jury and to sustain the verdict rendered.

The action was to recover for injuries to plaintiff and his team sustained in a collision with one of defendant's street cars. The accident happened on Oneota street in Duluth at about 8:30 in the even-

---

[1] Reported in 149 N. W. 538.

ing of March 26, 1913. Plaintiff, a retail coal dealer, in the afternoon loaded his sleigh with coal at a dock at the foot of Fifth Avenue west, and started to return to West Duluth. Reaching Oneota street plaintiff drove west on the northerly or west bound of defendant's tracks on that street. A west-bound car approached him from the rear, and he turned to the left upon the southerly track to let the car go by. The snow was piled up on the right, and plaintiff could not turn that way. After the west-bound car had passed, plaintiff started to turn to the right again when he saw a car coming from the west. Before plaintiff could get out of danger the car struck his sleigh and caused the damages for which he seeks to recover in this action.

The negligence of defendant relied on consists in the alleged excessive speed of the car, the failure of the motorman to give signals, and his not taking measures to avoid striking the sleigh after seeing the danger. The evidence was conflicting, and would perhaps have supported a finding that due care was exercised by the motorman, but we cannot disturb the finding the other way. The motorman did not stop his car or slacken its speed until it struck the sleigh. The question was plainly for the jury, and its decision has the approval of the trial court.

Defendant insists that plaintiff was negligent, first, in driving upon the tracks at all, and second, in starting to turn back instead of crossing over the track when he saw the car approaching. The evidence abundantly establishes the fact that it was not possible to drive on the right hand side of the street because of the icy ridge of snow on that side. This condition did not exist on the other side of the tracks, and it would have been possible, though perhaps inconvenient, for plaintiff to have driven on that side. It was the wrong side of the street, however, and teams traveling there would necessarily be obliged to turn to the right and onto the tracks when meeting vehicles coming from the opposite direction. The street was a main thoroughfare and much traveled. Under all the circumstances, it is not for this court to say as a matter of law that plaintiff was guilty of negligence that bars his right to recover because he traveled on the car tracks instead of along the rather narrow space on the left side. There was more or less danger in using the street at all, but, unless we are prepared to hold that under no conditions may teamsters drive for any distance along street car tracks in the heavily traveled streets of our large cities, we should not say that plaintiff in this case was not entitled to have a jury pass upon his conduct. We hold that the question was properly left to the jury to decide, and that we should not interfere with its conclusion.

As to the claim that plaintiff did not exercise due care after he saw the car approaching, we have no difficulty in holding that the case was for the jury, and that the evidence fairly supports the verdict. An emergency confronted plaintiff. The time for action was shòrt. He instinctively attempted to turn to the right instead of going ahead. It is doubtful whether he could have avoided the accident even had he attempted at first to get over the track and into the space on the left side, instead of trying to turn to the right.

Defendant relies greatly on Carlson v. Duluth Street Ry. Co. 111 Minn. 244, 126 N. W. 825. The case is clearly distinguishable in important particulars. There the street was a broad thoroughfare and in good condition for travel on both sides of the single car track; plaintiff was driving his team rapidly directly toward the approaching car, which could have been easily seen had he been paying any attention. The facts in the instant case are essentially different.

Order affirmed.

FITGER BREWING COMPANY v. AMERICAN BONDING COMPANY OF BALTIMORE and Another.[1]

November 20, 1914.

Nos. 18,748—(243).[2]

Mechanic's lien — action to recover from contractor's surety.
    In this action to recover against the surety on a contractor's bond the

[1] Reported in 149 N. W. 539.   [2] April, 1914, term calendar.

amount of mechanic's liens on the property paid by plaintiff after they had been adjudged valid, it is *held:*

(1) The action is not barred by a limitation in the policy that an action thereon must be brought within six months after the completion of the work under the contract, the breach for which a recovery is sought not arising until after such six months period elapsed.

(2) It is not barred by a limitation of six months after the first breach of the contract. Following Fitger Brewing Co. v. American Bonding Co. of Baltimore, 115 Minn. 78.

(3) The surety was not released by an excess payment made by the owner to the contractor.

(4) It was not released by the failure of the owner to give the surety immediate notice of the failure of the contractor to complete the building by the time specified in the contract.

After the former appeal, reported in 115 Minn. 78, 131 N. W. 1067, the case was tried before Cant, J., who made findings and ordered judgment for $2,122.50 against defendant Hilliard and in favor of defendant bonding company. From an order denying its motion for a new trial, plaintiff appealed. Reversed and new trial granted.

Charles L. Lewis and *J. A. P. Neal,* for appellant.
Washburn, Bailey & Mitchell, for respondent.

BUNN, J.

On a former appeal in this case an order sustaining a general demurrer to the complaint was reversed. 115 Minn. 78, 131 N. W. 1067. Defendant American Bonding Co. then answered, and there was a trial by the court without a jury. The decision was in favor of defendant bonding company, and plaintiff appealed from an order refusing a new trial.

The contention of plaintiff is that the conclusion of law that plaintiff is not entitled to recover is not justified by the findings of fact.

The action as against defendant bonding company is to recover on a contractor's bond given by the company as surety and defendant Hilliard as principal; the recovery sought is for money paid by plaintiff to satisfy lien claims after the same had been adjudged valid charges against its property. The decision of the court below was that the action was barred because not brought within the time limited by the policy. The conditions of the bond pertinent to this question are:

"Any suits at law or proceedings in equity brought or to be brought against said surety to recover any claim hereunder must be instituted within six (6) months after the first breach of said contract; and in no event shall any action or proceeding be brought against the surety hereunder after the expiration of six months after the date of the completion of the work under said contract."

The bond provided that "the 'owner', in estimating his damages, may include the claims of mechanics and materialmen arising out of the performance of the contract, and paid by him only when the same, by the statutes of the state where the contract is to be performed, are valid liens against said property."

Hilliard did not perform the terms of the contract, in that he did not pay for the labor and materials used in the construction of the building. April 23, 1909, plaintiff duly notified defendant bonding company of this fact. Hilliard in fact abandoned the work early in April, 1909, and plaintiff completed the building on or prior to May 1, 1909, expending $56.70 in so doing.

Liens against the property were filed by mechanics and materialmen. An action was begun to enforce these liens. It does not definitely appear from the findings when the liens were filed, or the action commenced, but defendant bonding company was given notice of the pendency thereof in July, 1909, and requested to defend, which it declined to do. Judgment declaring the claims to be valid liens against plaintiff's property was entered February 4, 1910. The bonding company refused to pay, and plaintiff, on February 10, 1910, paid the full amount of the claims adjudged liens against the property.

The present action was commenced April 11, 1910, more than six months after May 1, 1909, the date of the completion of the building, but only two months after the judgment establishing the validity of the lien claims. On the former appeal the complaint did not show when the building was completed, and it was therefore held that the provision of the bond, limiting the right to bring actions thereon to a period ending six months after the date of the completion of the work under the contract, was not involved. The opinion on the former appeal disposed of the provision requiring suits to be brought within six months after the first breach of the contract. It held that the complaint showed no breach that created a liability on the bond until the payment by the owner of valid lien claims. The findings show a breach for which an action on the bond could have been maintained when the contractor abandoned the work, but plaintiff made no claim for such breach. Whether this breach was sufficient to set in motion the first six months limitation, is one of the questions involved here, but it is not this limitation that governed the trial court in its decision.

The decision below was that the action was barred, because not brought within six months after completion of the work under the contract. If this is correct, it disposes of the case, and it will be unnecessary to consider the other limitation, or any other question.

In the former opinion it was held that the complaint showed no breach of the contract that gave plaintiff a right of action on the bond until March 10, 1910, when the lien claims were paid. If the findings show no such breach until this time, we have the absurd situation of the right of action being barred before it accrues. It is true, we think, that this limitation is valid. The parties made their contract, and it is not for the courts to relieve them because it was an unwise or even an absurd contract. It is also true that, standing by itself, the provision that "in no event shall any action or proceedings be brought against the surety hereunder after the expiration of six months after the date of the completion of the work under said contract," is not ambiguous and not open to construction. Nor do we attach any weight to the contention of plaintiff that the work was never completed *"under the contract."* But the provision must be read in connection with the entire bond, and particularly with reference to the chief purpose and object of the bond, which was to insure the faithful performance by the principal of his contract, according to its terms. One of these terms was that "the contractor shall refund to the owner all moneys that the latter may be compelled to pay in discharging any liens on said premises made obligatory in consequence of the contractor's default." The bond itself expressly provided, as before noted, that the owner, in estimating his damages in a claim on the bond against the surety, might include "the claims of mechanics and materialmen * * * paid by him only when the same, by the statutes of the state where the contract is to be performed, are valid liens against the said property." It is clear therefore that one of the main objects of the bond was to insure the owner against lien claims not paid by the contractor, but only when they were valid liens, and were paid by the owner. Under the decision on the former appeal and on reason the owner was not obliged to pay such claims until they were adjudged valid. Indeed he could not safely do so. It is the usual thing that liens are filed after the completion of the work under a building contract, and it usually takes more than six months after the completion of such work to procure the judgment of a court declaring them valid. In the present case it was 10 months afterwards, and there is no suggestion that it could have been done sooner. We have then absolutely inconsistent provisions of the bond; the surety agreed to reimburse the owner when he pays lien claims that are valid claims, and, though it is plain that they probably cannot be adjudged valid before six months or a year after the building is completed, inserts, at the end of the bond it prepares, a proviso that renders its obligation nugatory. It is not only provisions that are ambiguous in themselves that are open to construction. Though a provision of a bond limiting liability be clear when considered by itself, yet, if it is inconsistent with another provision, and particularly with the central idea of suretyship or indemnity, courts will look to the entire instrument and will find ambiguity because of the inconsistent provisions. It is needless to say that such an ambiguity or doubt as to the intention of the parties is to be resolved against the surety. Here the object of the bond would be defeated, if we construed the limitation according to its strict terms when considered alone. A construction which works such a result should not be given, except by plain necessity. We are unable to accede to the idea that these parties intended the absurd result that a right of action on the bond, plainly given by its terms, should be barred before it arose. Defendant seeks to avoid this necessary result by claiming that plaintiff could have brought an action for the breach of the contractor in abandoning the work in April, 1909, and could have had included in his recovery amounts paid by him for the discharge of liens, though paid after the action was brought. Under the decision in Brandrup v. Empire State Surety Co. 111 Minn. 376, 127 N. W. 424, it is true that plaintiff might have taken this course. But it was not obliged to do so. Plaintiff might waive the breach of the contractor in abandoning the work, as in fact it did do. It might well be decidedly difficult to string the case along until the liens had been established as valid in another action, and it would certainly be dangerous for plaintiff to pay them before they were so established. With witnesses who no longer had an interest, it might be impossible and would likely be difficult for plaintiff to prove that the claims paid by it were valid claims against the property, and it might well be that he would fail to recover all that he paid. We are unable to hold that any remedy that plaintiff might have in such an action is sufficient to remove the plain inconsistency between the provision of the bond giving the right of action, and the provision taking it away in the guise of a limitation of time.

It is not necessary to decide within what time after the payment of the lien claims plaintiff might bring its action for reimbursement. The limitation of six months after the breach would begin to run when the claims were paid, if such payment be considered the first breach of the contract. And the action would in any event have to be commenced within a reasonable time. Clearly this action, brought two months after the cause of action accrued, was commenced within such reasonable time. We hold that it was not barred by the limitation of six months after the completion of the work.

This conclusion renders it necessary to consider whether there is any other ground upon which the decision below can be sustained.

The findings that Hilliard did not perform the terms of his contract, in that he did not pay for the labor and materials used in the construction of the building, that he did not complete the building, but abandoned the same in an incomplete condition, show conclusively a breach of the contract in April, 1909, for which plaintiff could have brought an action on the bond. The damages from this breach were small, and plaintiff might well conclude not to go to the trouble and expense of a lawsuit to collect the same. By permitting the six months to elapse plaintiff doubtless lost his right to sue for this breach, but it does not follow that he could not maintain an action based on a breach that occurred afterwards. The abandonment of the work by the contractor, like delay in completing the building, could be waived by the owner, and, if so waived, would not constitute a breach within the meaning of the limitation clause. Lakeside Land Co. v. Empire State Surety Co. 105 Minn. 213, 117 N. W. 431; Fitger Brewing Co. v. American Bonding Co. of Baltimore, 115 Minn. 78, 85, 131 N. W. 1067. Following these decisions, we reach the conclusion that the present action is not barred by the limitation of six months from the first breach.

3. The bond provided that the owner should notify the surety in writing before the last payment or any "reserve" due the principal under the contract shall be paid. The contract provided that 10 per cent of all estimates be retained by the owner until the building is fully completed, and be included and paid in the final payment. It appears that the owner paid the contractor on April 2, 1909, the full amount of an estimate of $3,500, not retaining the 10 per cent reserve, and without notice to the surety. It is claimed that this payment released the surety. We are unable to so hold. If the surety was damaged by the excess payment, it may be that it would be entitled to relief to the extent of the damage it sustained; but this question can be tried and determined on a new trial. We hold that the payment did not in any event release the surety beyond the amount of the excess payment.

4. It is urged that the surety was released by the owner's failure to give immediate notice of the contractor's failure to complete the contract in time, and paying him a large part of the contract price after January 1, 1909, the time specified in the contract for the completion of the building. But the owner was entitled to waive the delay, and making no claim on account of it, was not obliged to give the surety notice. Lakeside Land Co. v. Empire State Surety Co. supra. Notice of the contractor's default was given April 23, 1909. This was clearly within a reasonable time after "any breach of said

contract by said principal or any act on the part of said principal * * * which may involve a loss for which the said surety may be liable."

Order reversed and new trial granted.

THOMAS S. HUTCHINS v. JOHN H. WOLFE.[1]

November 20, 1914.

Nos. 18,765—(38).

Use of scaffold by servant.

1. Where the master selects and furnishes material for scaffolding purposes, to be used for that purpose only, the servants may assume that in selecting the same the master exercised due care, and they are not required before using it to determine whether it is suitable for the purpose.

Same — evidence.

2. Evidence *held* to justify the conclusion that the defendant selected certain material for the purposes stated, that he negligently included therein defective material, the use of which resulted in injury to plaintiff, and that plaintiff was not guilty of contributory negligence.

Action in the district court for Hennepin county to recover $2,550 for injury received while in the employ of defendant. The case was tried before Dickinson, J., who denied defendant's motion for a directed verdict, and a jury which returned a verdict for $1,180. From an order denying his motion for judgment notwithstanding the verdict or for a new trial, defendant appealed. Affirmed.

George E. Young, for appellant.
John M. Berg and *Adolph E. L. Johnson,* for respondent.

BROWN, C. J.
Action for personal injuries in which plaintiff had a verdict and

1 Reported in 149 N. W. 543.

defendant appealed from an order denying his motion for judgment or a new trial.

The facts are as follows: Defendant is a contractor and builder, and at the time of the injury to plaintiff was engaged in the construction of a building on Garfield avenue in the city of Minneapolis. The frame work of the structure had been completed and a scaffold erected to enable the workmen to put up the cornice. This scaffold was constructed by the employees of defendant and from material furnished by defendant for the purpose. It was fully completed and in condition for use prior to the time plaintiff entered into defendant's employ, and plaintiff had no hand either in the selection of material therefor or in its construction. He was not a servant of defendant at that time. It was in the usual form of such structures. After entering defendant's service plaintiff was first put to work inside the building where he remained for three or four days. He was then directed by defendant to go upon this scaffold and assist another workman in laying the cornice of the building. While engaged in this work a plank upon the scaffold and upon which he was required to stand in order to lay the cornice suddenly broke, thereby precipitating plaintiff to the ground, a distance of some 15 feet, resulting in the injuries of which he here complains.

The complaint charged negligence in the failure of defendant to provide plaintiff a safe place in which to do his work; that the material furnished for the scaffold was defective and unsafe; and that the scaffold was improperly constructed. The defense, as disclosed by the answer, in addition to the general denial, was that plaintiff was guilty of contributory negligence, in that by suddenly changing from a standing to a sitting position, he subjected the plank to an unusual and violent strain, thus causing it to break and precipitate him to the ground.

By the verdict the jury found the facts in plaintiff's favor, and against the defense of contributory negligence. Our examination of the record leads to the conclusion that the verdict of the jury finding that the plank was defective and improper for use in the scaffold, and that plaintiff was not guilty of contributory negligence, is sustained by the evidence. The evidence made both issues questions of fact, and we sustain the verdict. It is unnecessary to discuss the evidence. We have examined it with the result stated.

Defendant took exception to the instructions of the trial court, and portions thereof are assigned as error. The court charged, in substance and effect, that since the scaffold was a completed structure before plaintiff entered defendant's employ, the servants who constructed it were not fellow servants of plaintiff, and he did not assume the risk of their negligence in the selection of the material therefor. And further that if defendant made the selection of the material for the scaffold, and failed to exercise due care in such selection, as a result of which the defective plank was made a part of the scaffold, he was liable for such negligence without regard to the fact that his other servants put the scaffold in shape for use. We do not use the exact language of the instructions, but this statement thereof is in substance what the court said to the jury.

The particular objection to the instructions goes to that part wherein the court said to the jury that acts of negligence on the part of defendant's servants preceding the time when plaintiff entered the service, are not chargeable to plaintiff under the fellow-servant doctrine, for he was not at the time of such negligence their fellow servant. We find it unnecessary to determine this question. The authorities are not in harmony thereon, and as a further question disposes of the case we pass it without comment. The question is referred to in 4 Labatt, Master & Servant, 1406, where the authorities upholding both views of the question are cited.

The case on its undisputed facts is controlled by Lee v. H. N. Leighton Co. 113 Minn. 373, 129 N. W. 767, and Falkenberg v. Bazille & Partridge, 124 Minn. 19, 144 N. W. 431. It appears from the evidence, and we discover no real controversy on the subject, that the scaffolding material for this building was all selected by defendant; it was purchased by him and delivered upon the premises to be used for that purpose. It is not a case where the master furnishes a mass of material from which the servants may select suitable pieces for purposes of this kind, but one, like the Leighton case, supra, where the master selects and furnishes material for the particular purpose. In such case the servant is not charged with the duty of

examining the material so furnished to determine whether it is fit
and suitable, but may rely upon the judgment of the master that it
is all proper and safe, and that the master acted with due care in
selecting the same. This is settled law in this state as well as elsewhere. The testimony of defendant makes it clear that he purchased
and delivered upon the premises the material, of which the plank
in question formed part, expressly for scaffolding purposes, and that
it was devoted to that purpose by his servants. The case comes, therefore, within those cited, and defendant is liable irrespective of the
question of the negligence of fellow servants.

All other assignments of error have been considered with the result that no reversible error appears.

Order affirmed.

H. J. VOLLMER and Another v. BIG STONE COUNTY BANK.[1]

November 20, 1914.

Nos. 18,773—(64).

Order on stakeholder — evidence of agreement — priority of claims.

Action to recover on a written order given plaintiffs by a debtor to pay
the amount thereof out of the proceeds of an auction sale of the debtor's
property, which sale was to be held in the future and to be conducted by defendant bank. It is *held:*

(1) The evidence shows an agreement by defendant, made when the order
was presented, to pay the same out of the proceeds of the sale after the
claims which the debtor, prior to the presentation of plaintiff's order, had
ordered defendant to pay.

(2) The evidence was sufficient to support a finding by the jury that plaintiff's order was presented before certain other claims were ordered by the
debtor to be paid.

(3) Defendant, as a stakeholder, was not responsible for the validity of
the claims it was ordered to pay. The evidence was insufficient to show that

1 Reported in 149 N. W. 545.

defendant knew that certain claims were fictitious, and fraudulently conspired with their owners to dissipate the proceeds of the sale so as to prevent the payment of plaintiff's order. It was error to submit this question to the jury.

(4) It was error to instruct the jury that if such claims were fictitious, "*in whole or in part*," to the knowledge of defendant, plaintiffs could recover the full amount of their claim.

(5) The owners of the claims, the priority and validity of which are in controversy, should be made parties to this litigation.

(6) Plaintiffs are the real parties in interest.

Action in the district court for Big Stone county against A. D. O'Brien and the Big Stone County Bank to recover $600 upon the order which appears at the beginning of the opinion. The defense is stated in the opinion. The case was tried before Flaherty, J., who at the close of plaintiff's case denied defendants' motions to dismiss the action, and a jury which returned a verdict for $606.32 in favor of plaintiffs. From an order denying its motion for a new trial, defendant bank appealed. Reversed and new trial granted.

Cliff & Purcell, for appellant.

F. W. Murphy, for respondents.

BUNN, J.

This action is to recover the sum of $600 and interest on the following written order:

"Graceville, Oct. 2, 1912.

"Mr. A. D. O'Brien,

"Cashier Big Stone County Bank, Graceville.

"Please pay to H. J. Vollmer & Co. Six Hundred Dollars out of proceeds of my sale of personal property to be held on Oct. 16th, 1912.

"Wm. Thompson."

The complaint alleged that the order was presented by plaintiffs to defendants on October 2, and accepted by them, but not paid. The case was tried to a jury, and the result was a verdict against defendant bank and in favor of plaintiffs in the full amount of their claim, the case having been dismissed as to defendant O'Brien. Defendant bank appealed from an order denying its motion for a new trial.

The assignments of error call in question the sufficiency of the evidence to sustain the verdict, and certain instructions of the trial court.

The facts, including those which are admitted and those which, though in controversy, the evidence tends to prove, are as follows:

William Thompson, a farmer near Graceville, concluded to quit farming and sell his stock and machinery at auction. He was heavily in debt. He applied to defendant bank to take charge of the auction sale, or, as called in the evidence, to "clerk the sale." This included advertising, employing an auctioneer, receiving the cash realized and passing upon and discounting paper received where cash was not paid. For its services the bank was to receive an agreed commission. It appears that the bank was to pay, out of the proceeds of the sale, certain claims against Thompson. Defendants claimed, and there was testimony tending to show that, on October 1, a list of Thompson's creditors was made, and that Thompson orally directed the bank to pay the claims of these creditors out of the proceeds of the sale. The claims on this list aggregated $1,273.37, including the estimated expenses of the sale, and including a claim of James Fleming for $194, and one of Ignace Windorpski for $354.25. The two claims last mentioned formed the basis of controversy on the trial and will be considered later. Thompson was indebted to plaintiffs in the sum of $327.45, and to McRae & Sons and the First National Bank of Graceville in the sum of $255.84. Neither of these claims was on the list claimed to have been furnished the bank by Thompson October 1. On October 2, Thompson gave plaintiffs the order on which the action is brought. The amount was made up of the claims of plaintiffs, McRae and the First National Bank; this was for convenience, there being no assignment to plaintiffs by McRae or the bank; the difference between the amount of the order and the indebtedness was to be returned to Thompson when the order was paid. The order was presented to the bank by plaintiff H. J. Vollmer on October 3, at about 10 a. m. He testified in substance that he was then told by the cashier and assistant cashier of defendant that there were two claims aggregating some $600 against the expected fund which were ahead of plaintiffs; these two claims, which were mentioned by name, were stated to be all the claims against the fund, and plaintiffs were told that their order would come in next after the payment of these claims and the expenses of the sale, and would be paid. The order was left with the bank and retained by it. Vollmer testified that he called at the bank a week later, when the probable amount to be realized from the sale was figured by him and the assistant cashier at between $1,-600 and $1,700, and when it was again stated by the latter that there was approximately $600 against the fund, ahead of plaintiff's order. Vollmer testified quite positively that nothing was said about any other claims.

The chief witness for defendant was its assistant cashier, who testified to the making up of the list of Thompson's creditors on October 1, and to a verbal order from Thompson to pay these creditors out of the sale proceeds. The witness admitted the presentation of plaintiff's order on October 3, but denied that he agreed to pay it next after the two claims mentioned. His testimony on this point was in effect that he told Vollmer that two mortgages aggregating $600 were prior claims, and that there were other prior claims beside the mortgages. He did not tell Vollmer the amount of these claims, and testified that Vollmer did not inquire the amount, but simply left the order, with the understanding that it would be paid after the claims that were prior.

1. It is apparent, we think, from the evidence as outlined above, that the agreement was that plaintiff's order was to be paid out of the proceeds of the sale after the claims that Thompson had, prior to its presentation, ordered the bank to pay.

2. Therefore the chief question for the trial court and the jury was as to what claims Thompson, before plaintiff's order was presented, had ordered the bank to pay out of the proceeds of the sale. This issue was tendered by the answer, defendants alleging that the property brought $1,400 above expenses at the sale, and that out of this they paid incumbrances on the property and "other claims in accordance with the orders and instructions which said Thompson made prior to the date of the claimed order of plaintiffs," leaving a balance of $177.44, which they had offered to pay to plaintiffs.

The two claims around which the controversy settled were, as stated before, one of Windorpski for $354.25, and one of Fleming for $194. Windorpski was the owner of the farm that Thompson occupied. The claim was for "plowing back" which the tenant had agreed to do, and had not done, and for the landlord's share of certain barley which the tenant had failed to cut. It was represented by a written order dated October 1, 1912, directing the bank to pay the claim out of the proceeds of the sale. The testimony of the assistant cashier, as before noted, was that Thompson, on October 1, verbally directed this and the Fleming claims to be paid. The written order was not given to Windorpski, but seems to have been made on the bank's suggestion and delivered to it by Thompson. Later, and while the order was still unpaid, Windorpski paid Thompson $200 for wheat purchased of him.

The Fleming claim was ostensibly for services of Fleming in cutting and threshing grain for Thompson. The order was dated October 5. Fleming was related to Thompson by marriage. The services had been performed for Thompson a year before the order was given, but no claim had been made for payment. Both Windorpski and Fleming, as well as the other creditors on the list claimed to have been made up October 1, were customers of the defendant bank, and its cashier was active in protecting them.

On the question of priority of presentation as between the claims of Windorpski and Fleming and the order of plaintiffs, an examination of the entire record satisfies us that the issue was for the jury and that it was properly submitted by the trial court. The jury was not bound to believe the testimony of interested witnesses as to the verbal orders claimed to have been given by Thompson on October 1, and we are unable to say that the verdict is not sufficiently supported by the evidence on this point.

3. The trial court submitted another question to the jury, and defendant strenuously insists that it erred in so doing. This was the question whether the claims of Windorpski and Fleming were *bona fide,* or fictitious claims. After fully and correctly instructing the jury on the issue of priority, the court charged that, if the jury should find from the evidence that some of the claims were merely colorable

or fictitious claims, and were known by defendant to be such, then
such claims would not take precedence over the claim of plaintiffs.
The court then called attention to the Fleming and Windorpski
claims, and said in substance that if these claims were fictitious, and
so known to be by the bank, if they were "fabrications, subterfuges,
fictitious arrangements, and were not based on a valid indebtedness in
whole or in part," the claim of plaintiffs would take precedence over
them.

Defendant complains of the submission of this issue to the jury on
several grounds: That fraud was not pleaded in the complaint; that
the evidence showed that the claims were valid; that, though it be
conceded that Thompson did not owe Windorpski and Fleming, yet
this was no concern of the bank, as stakeholder, if it was ordered by
Thompson to pay the claims.

The trial court realized that there were difficulties in the case, and
we have found this true. We have no trouble on the question of
pleading, and we might be able to hold that the evidence cast doubt
enough on the validity and *bona fides* of the Fleming and Windorpski
claims to justify a finding that they were in part at least fictitious.
The chief trouble comes in holding defendant responsible for the validity of these claims. If the evidence showed that the claims were
wholly fictitious, that defendant knew it and conspired with the creditors to dissipate the proceeds of the sale so that there would not be
enough to pay plaintiffs, it might well be said that plaintiffs should
have a remedy for this wrong. But it cannot be doubted that, if defendant did not participate in the fraud, but acted merely as a stakeholder to receive the sale proceeds and pay them out according to the
directions of Thompson, it would not be responsible though Thompson
should order it to pay fictitious claims, or gratuities. The evidence
is not free from suggestions that defendant was not wholly impartial
in its attitude towards the different claimants. It was diligent in
seeing that creditors of Thompson who happened to be customers of
itself presented their claims, while it was not over zealous in protecting creditors like plaintiffs who were not its customers. But we are
unable to find any satisfactory evidence that defendant knew that
Fleming and Windorpski had no claims, and conspired with them to

prevent plaintiffs from receiving payment. Mere knowledge on defendant's part that the claims were in whole or in part invalid would not be sufficient. It was necessary to have evidence of bad faith on defendant's part, actual participation in a scheme to use up the fund by the payment of fictitious claims so as to defeat plaintiffs. We are obliged to hold that the evidence fell short of connecting defendant with the fraud, if any, and that the trial court should not have submitted this issue to the jury.

4. The trial court charged that if the Windorpski and Fleming claims were fictitious *"in whole or in part"* to the knowledge of defendant, plaintiffs could recover the full amount of their order. This was error. Plainly if these claims were simply padded, but were *bona fide* and valid claims in part, and prior to plaintiffs', it cannot be said that they are entirely out of the way.

5. We think that Windorpski and Fleming should be made parties to this action. If the evidence on another trial should not be materially different, the issue would be simply the question of priority of presentation as between plaintiff's order, and the oral or written orders to pay Windorpski and Fleming. And one of these claims might be found to be prior to plaintiffs' and the other subsequent.

6. Defendant's claim that plaintiffs are not the real parties in interest so far as concerns that part of the order which represented the claims of the First National Bank and McRae & Son is not sustained.

Order reversed and new trial granted.

CHARLES M. WAY v. FRED E. BARNEY.[1]

November 20, 1914.

Nos. 18,782—(44).

Liability of stockholder — stock held as collateral security.
Evidence in an action to enforce a stockholder's constitutional liability

[1] Reported in 149 N. W. 462, 646.

Note.—The authorities on the question as to the liability of a pledgee of corporate stock are gathered in notes in 36 L.R.A. 139 and 19 L.R.A.(N.S.) 249.

against one who appeared upon an insolvent local corporation's stock books as a general owner of stock, *held* to sustain a finding that the failure of the corporation's records to show that the stock was issued to and held by defendant as collateral security for an advance made by a third person was not due to the negligence or fraud of the corporation but to his own negligence, wherefore he was estopped, as against creditors, to deny his liability as a stockholder.

Action in the district court for Hennepin county by the receiver of the Winslow Furniture & Carpet Co. to recover $5,000 upon defendant's constitutional liability as a stockholder in that company. The answer among other matters denied that defendant ever subscribed for, acquired, or became either the owner or holder of shares of stock in that company and set up the facts stated in the opinion. The case was tried before Steele, J., who made findings and ordered judgment in favor of plaintiff for the amount demanded. From an order denying his motion to amend the findings or for a new trial, defendant appealed. Affirmed.

Mercer, Swan & Stinchfield, for appellant.

James E. Trask and *John M. Bradford,* for respondent.

PHILIP E. BROWN, J.

This is an action to enforce against defendant constitutional liability as a stockholder of a bankrupt local corporation. Plaintiff prevailed. Defendant appealed from an order refusing amendments of the findings and a new trial.

The complaint was sustained on demurrer in 116 Minn. 285, 133 N. W. 801, 38 L.R.A.(N.S.) 648, Ann. Cas. 1913A, 719, where it was held, among other things, that the discharge of a corporation under the Federal Bankruptcy Act does not discharge or extinguish the constitutional liability of its stockholders for the payment of its debts.

Plaintiff claimed that on April 19, 1905, defendant subscribed for and became the owner of 50 shares of the capital stock of the Winslow Furniture & Carpet Co., the bankrupt corporation, of the par value of $5,000, issued in his name, an entry whereof was then made upon the stock books of the company, and that such ownership continued so to appear until its bankruptcy. Defendant denied subscription for stock in or ever having been a stockholder of the corporation. He admitted the issuance, and delivery, of the shares to him in his name on the date stated, but asserted that he merely held the title in trust for the Winslow Co., as collateral security for a loan and credit aggregating $5,000, made to it by the Salisbury & Satterlee Co., another corporation, pursuant to the terms of a prior agreement between these companies, to which he was not a party; further, that the issuance of this stock and the entry of his name upon the records as a stockholder, without indicating his true relation thereto, was a fraudulent or negligent violation of the corporation's duty, the agreement mentioned, and his rights in the premises. He claimed also to have surrendered the stock in compliance with this agreement while the Winslow Co. was a going concern.

Little dispute exists as to the facts. In April, 1905, the Winslow Co., which had theretofore been a retail furniture dealer in St. Paul, contemplated opening a branch in Minneapolis, and with that end in view conferred, through Mr. Winslow, its president, with Messrs. Salisbury & Satterlee, president and vice president of a company then engaged, under that name, in wholesaling furniture in the latter city, regarding the purchase by it of shares of the former's capital stock. What occurred, the agreement entered into, and how interest was paid on the advances subsequently made, will best be understood by stating the testimony of the last-named officers as witnesses for defendant. Mr. Satterlee, after testifying that Mr. Winslow advised him of the contemplated establishment of the branch, continued:

"And that he wanted to know if he couldn't interest us in taking some financial interest in the business; that he had had some kind of proposition from other people and wanted us to take stock. We told him we wouldn't take stock, couldn't take it and wouldn't. We conversed along that line for some time and then we suggested, I suggested, or Mr. Winslow, in our conversation, it came to this arrangement, that we would let them have approximately $2,500 worth of goods and $2,500 in cash and take stock in the Winslow & Ruff Furniture Co. as security, collateral security, this stock to be issued to Mr. Barney. It was first suggested by Mr. Winslow to issue it to a man in our employ, but we didn't want to have anything to do with it for the reason that with the other trade in the city here it isn't advisable or desirable to have them feel that you are backing competition coming into the city. So we suggested Mr. Barney. He didn't know Mr. Barney, never had heard of him, and said if it was satisfactory to us it would be to him. So we made the deal on that basis."

Mr. Salisbury testified:

"Through Mr. Satterlee I learned Mr. Winslow desired to open a branch in Minneapolis and with Mr. Satterlee had several conferences with Mr. Winslow. It was his desire, as I recollect it, that we should take a certain amount of stock, $5,000 was the ultimate sum that we arrived at as necessary for us to participate in his patronage, to receive his patronage for our line of goods. I was not in favor, nor was Mr. Satterlee at our conferences, of taking stock in the Winslow Furniture & Carpet Co. or in the Winslow & Ruff Furniture Co., as it was at that time. And I presume there was suggestions made along several lines; as I remember it we were trying to reach a point where we could agree upon the conditions under which we could give them $5,000, a loan of $5,000 in credit, partly goods and partly cash. And it was my understanding that when the deal was finally consummated that Mr. Winslow was to issue $5,000 worth of stock to Fred E. Barney which he was to hold to secure us for the payment of the credit which we gave him; that he was to pay us 8 per cent interest, not on the $5,000, but on the cash as soon as it was invested or turned over, and upon the monthly balances of goods. The interest was paid for at least two years if not more. And the time of payment was not definitely settled or promised or understood, except that the success of the business from Mr. Winslow's standpoint would undoubtedly allow him to take up the credit or the loan within two or three years."

After the making of this arrangement defendant, at the request of the Salisbury Co., consented to take the stock in his name, and, likewise, on April 19, 1905, attended a stockholders' meeting of the Winslow Co., at which a resolution was passed to issue the shares to him, which was done, nothing being said about their being collateral. At the same meeting defendant was elected a director of the corporation at Mr. Winslow's request. The original certificate of shares was not offered in evidence, but the stub of the stock book was. It reads as follows:

Certificate
No. 8
For 50 shares
Issued to
Fred E. Barney.
Dated April 19, 1905.
From Whom Transferred.

. . . .

Dated. . . . . 190. . . . .

| No. Original | No. Original | No. of Shares |
| Certificate | Shares | Transferred |

. . . .

Received Certificate No. . . . .

For . . . . Shares

this . . . . day of . . . . 190. . . . .

The within certificate, No. 8, is one of a series, aggregating $25,-000 of preferred stock, and is entitled to the following preference, viz.: To be paid an annual cumulative dividend, on the date of the regular annual meeting of the corporation, of eight per cent, and in case of the winding up of said corporation, said preferred stock shall be paid in full before any common stock shall receive a dividend. The right to redeem the same at any time after five years is reserved.

"Winslow & Ruff Furniture & Carpet Company.
"By Irving M. Winslow, Pres.
"By Alfred Mortenson, Sec."

This was substantially in accord with the resolution authorizing its issuance. Later defendant executed a proxy and the shares were voted thereunder at the annual meeting of the company held in February, 1906. The company's articles of incorporation provided that its government should be vested in a board of three directors, to be elected annually from the stockholders, but defendant was so chosen, with four others. The Salisbury Co. advanced the credit and loan as agreed. In 1908 the Winslow Co. was adjudged bankrupt. Several months prior thereto the Salisbury Co. obtained the stock certificate from defendant, who had retained it in his possession until then, and exchanged it for a note of the Winslow Co.; but no record of this transaction was entered upon the stock books. The Winslow Co. contracted debts after April 19, 1905, which remain unpaid, and for which claims were allowed in the sequestration action subsequently brought against it. The court found the ultimate facts substantially as stated; in effect determined defendant's claim of fraudulent or negligent violation of the duty owing defendant in issuing the stock without indicating its collaterality, unfounded, and concluded that defendant held himself out to creditors as the owner of the shares, and as to them was estopped from denying ownership. Defendant challenges this determination and conclusion as being unsupported by either the evidence or findings.

In this jurisdiction, in harmony with the great weight of authority, one to whom corporate stock has been transferred as collateral security, but who appears upon the books of the corporation as its general owner, is liable as a stockholder for corporate debts. Marshall Field & Co. v. Evans, Johnson, Sloane & Co. 106 Minn. 85, 118 N. W. 55, 19 L.R.A.(N.S.) 249; note 121 Am. St. 197. But the rule is otherwise when the holder's true relation to the stock appears of record (Marshall Field & Co. v. Evans, Johnson, Sloane & Co. supra), or where absence of such disclosure is not due to his failure to exercise reasonable care. Hunt v. Seeger, 91 Minn. 264, 98 N. W. 91. Subsequently to the issue of the stock here in question, the rule stated in the Field case was, to some extent, incorporated in our statutes. See R. L. 1905, § 2863.

At the outset it is to be remembered that we are not dealing with a case where any claim is made that defendant either requested or suggested any notation as to the stock being issued as collateral; and, further, that the root of the rule of estoppel in such cases is protection of creditors, and although stock be issued by a corporation directly to a creditor as collateral security, so that he does not become liable to the corporation for the price of the stock as a subscriber therefor, nevertheless, if he fails to do all that can be expected or required of a reasonably careful and prudent business man in the matter of seeing to it that the character of his holding appear of record, he will not be allowed to deny his liability to creditors not advised to the contrary by the stock books. Hamilton v. Levison, 198 Fed. 444, 446, affirmed 204 Fed. 72, 122 C. C. A. 386; State v. Bank of New England, 70 Minn. 398, 402, 73 N. W. 153, 68 Am. St. 538. Since, therefore, one acting as a dummy for a creditor can stand in no better position than the creditor himself, the Field case must be deemed decisive of the questions here involved, unless it can be said that the evidence required a finding in favor of defendant's claim as to fraud or negligence. Considering the transactions between the two companies from a business standpoint, the inference may fairly be drawn that the Winslow Co.'s purpose was to obtain additional capital, or its equivalent, and that the Salisbury Co. desired patronage from it, but did not wish to be known as a stockholder because other customers might object; wherefore defendant was induced by the latter to act as a "dummy", and to take the stock in his name in order to conceal the real transaction. Furthermore, there is no suggestion of thought, at that time, of liability or of the desirability of any record entry other than made; all evidently believing the branch establishment would. succeed, for, otherwise, neither the Salisbury Co. nor defendant would have entered into the venture. While defendant disclaimed knowledge of the agreement between the two companies, the court was not required to accept this as conclusive. It would have been an unusual transaction for defendant to have accepted shares and a directorship in a corporation in which he had no real interest, without even knowing how many shares had been agreed upon or what he was to do to carry out the purpose of the corporation requesting him to act. Moreover, it is clear from his own statement that he understood the stock belonged to the Salisbury Co., to which he was to deliver it on demand; and, in any event, his lack of knowledge was attributable to his failure to seek it. An entry of the transaction on the books of the Winslow Co., or a statement that the stock was issued as collateral, would have either fully or partially disclosed what was purposed to conceal.

We sustain the findings and hold the court justified in refusing to find either negligence or fraud on the part of the Winslow Co., and that defendant's negligence justified the conclusion of estoppel.

Order affirmed.

On December 11, 1914, the following opinion was filed:

PER CURIAM:

Attention has been called to an omission to make a specific ruling in the opinion on defendant's contention that plaintiff really represents simple creditors with the same standing only as such creditors have under the National Bankruptcy Act (Act July 1, 1898, c. 541, 30 St. 544), and, under the agreement found by the trial court, could not claim the benefit of the estoppel herein declared, except in some such capacity as that of *bona fide* purchasers or lien or judgment creditors; that under that act the creditors here cannot avail themselves of an estoppel which the corporation could not claim. Wherefore, it was urged, plaintiff was precluded from the benefit of an estoppel.

The point has been considered, and is overruled.

CHARLES H. CLARK v. W. A. WELLS and Another.[1]

November 20, 1914.

Nos. 18,823—(78).

Rescission of contract — fraud — return of property.
  1. The party who rescinds a contract on the ground of fraud must, as a

[1] Reported in 149 N. W. 547.

Note.—As to the duty to place other party *in statu quo* upon rescission of contract, see note in 30 L.R.A. 44.

general rule, place the other party *in statu quo* by returning what he received; but "the party guilty of the fraud is not entitled to anything more than substantial justice, and a fair opportunity to receive what he parted with." If, through the fault of the wrongdoer, the party defrauded is unable to return all the property received, in the condition in which he received it, it is sufficient, if he restore the property so far as he is able, and secure to the wrongdoer the equivalent of what cannot be returned.

Same — return of going business.

2. If the wrongdoer refuses to receive the property when tendered back, the defrauded party may properly do what is necessary to conserve its value, and does not thereby waive his rescission. Where he receives a going business, he may, without waiving his rescission, continue it as a going business during the pendency of the suit to recover what he parted with, if he remain ready, at all times, to turn over to the wrongdoer both the business, in substantially the condition in which he received it, and the profits derived therefrom.

Action in the district court for Ramsey county against W. A. Wells and H. W. Mennig to recover $25,000. The facts are stated in the opinion. The case was tried before Brill, J., who made findings and ordered judgment in favor of defendants. From an order denying his motion for a new trial, plaintiff appealed. Reversed and new trial granted.

Christofferson & Burnquist, George T. Olsen and *Durment, Moore & Oppenheimer,* for appellant.

John F. Fitzpatrick, for respondents.

TAYLOR, C.

This is an action to recover back the purchase price paid by plaintiff for the business and property of the Prussian Remedy Co. The complaint, among other things, contains allegations to the effect that plaintiff purchased such business from defendants for the sum of $25,000 paid to them in money and property; that he was induced to make such purchase by fraudulent misrepresentations made by them; that, upon learning of the fraud, he rescinded the purchase, notified defendants thereof, and tendered the business and property back to them in substantially the same condition as when taken over by him; and that defendants refused to return the consideration received therefor. The answer, among other things, denied and put in issue all charges of fraud.

Plaintiff took over the business on July 3, 1912. The action was commenced on September 6, 1912, and was tried on December 2, 1913. Defendants alleged, by supplemental answers, that plaintiff had operated and carried on the business continuously, and for his own profit, after the commencement of the action. At the beginning of the trial, the parties entered admissions upon the record to the following effect:

That plaintiff gave notice of rescission in proper time and brought his action in proper time; that he carried on the business in the usual and customary manner from the time he took it over, on July 3, 1912, until the time of the trial; that, in manufacturing and preparing the remedies for sale, he used the materials and stock on hand, and replaced the same with new stock and materials; that, out of the proceeds of the business, he paid the operating expenses, including a salary to himself, but appropriated no part of the profits other than such salary; that the profits not reinvested in the business were placed in the bank; that, in conducting the business, he had given his notes in the sum of $7,000 and had sold goods upon credit, in the usual course of business, for which accounts receivable were outstanding in the sum of $16,210; and that the business had been conducted in a building leased to him by defendants, at a rental of $150 per month, and for which he had neither paid, nor been asked to pay, any rent.

The misrepresentations charged were set forth in detail in the complaint. After the above admissions had been made, plaintiff sought to prove such misrepresentations, but the testimony offered for that purpose was excluded. Thereupon plaintiff made an offer to prove all the allegations of the complaint. To this offer defendants interposed the following objection:

"The defendants admit that due notice of the rescission of the contract set up in the complaint and answer was given by the plaintiff to the defendants and that the rescission was made within a due

and reasonable time after the transaction, but object to any proof
of any other allegation in the complaint upon the ground that the
plaintiff retained the business of the Prussian Remedy Co. and carried it on as his own from the time of the commencement of this action up to the time of trial, as appears by the facts stipulated in the
record in this action."

This objection was sustained. Thereupon plaintiff further offered
to prove:

"That the plaintiff offered to rescind said contract and that at all
times since the commencement of this action has been ready, willing
and able to deliver to the defendants substantially the property received by the plaintiff from the defendants, and that many times
since the commencement of this action has offered so to do, and that
all such offers have been refused by the defendants, and that plaintiff is now ready, willing and able to return to the defendants said
business and all thereof substantially as received by the plaintiff
from the defendants, and to account to the defendants for any and
all profits and other transactions had in connection with the operation of said business."

In reply to an inquiry by the court, plaintiff stated that this offer
should be taken as qualified by the admissions previously made, and
the proof was excluded as irrelevant and immaterial in view of such
admissions. Both parties then rested without offering any further
evidence. The court held that plaintiff "has disabled himself from
restoring to the defendants the original property and business so
purchased by him. * * * Has waived and abandoned his former
rescission, and is not entitled to any relief," and directed judgment
for defendants. Plaintiff made a motion for a new trial and appealed from an order denying the motion.

The question for decision is whether the carrying on of the business from the commencement of the action until the trial, a period
of about 15 months, in the manner shown by the admissions, bars
plaintiff from recovering as a matter of law.

It is a general rule that a party who rescinds a contract on the
ground of fraud must place the other party *in statu quo* by return-

ing what he has received, but "the party guilty of the fraud is not entitled to anything more than substantial justice, and a fair opportunity to receive what he parted with." I. L. Corse & Co. v. Minnesota Grain Co. 94 Minn. 331, 102 N. W. 728. "There is no reason for the strict application of the rule when substantial justice can be meted out." Marple v. Minneapolis & St. L. R. Co. 115 Minn. 262, 132 N. W. 333. The rule is not based upon any right possessed by the wrongdoer, but upon the natural equity which forbids one party to take back his own property and also retain that of the other. Although the party defrauded may be unable to return all the property received by him, in the condition in which he received it, yet, if such inability resulted from the fault of the wrongdoer, the party defrauded may still rescind the contract and recover back what he parted with, on condition that he return what he received, so far as he is able to do so, and that he secure to the wrongdoer the equivalent of what cannot be returned. McCarty v. New York Life Ins. Co. 74 Minn. 530, 77 N. W. 426; Rase v. Minneapolis, St. P. & S. S. M. Ry. Co. 118 Minn. 437, 137 N. W. 176; Gates v. Raymond, 106 Wis. 657, 82 N. W. 530; Masson v. Bovet, 1 Denio (N. Y.) 69, 43 Am. Dec. 651.

Upon the present record, it must be taken as conceded, for the purposes of this decision, that defendants were guilty of the fraud charged; that plaintiff took over the business and conducted it for about two months before discovering the fraud; that, upon making such discovery, he promptly rescinded the contract, tendered back to defendants what he had received, and demanded the return of what he had parted with; that defendants refused to rescind, or to receive back what they had parted with, or to return what they had received; and that plaintiff forthwith brought suit to recover the consideration which he had paid to them.

When plaintiff tendered back the business, he might, perhaps, have notified defendants that such business and the property pertaining thereto remained at their risk, and have abandoned it; but, as defendants denied his right to turn the business back to them, and refused to take it back, we think he was not required to abandon it, in order to preserve his rights. Barrett v. Speir, 93 Ga. 762, 21 S. E. 168; Potter v. Taggart, 54 Wis. 395, 11 N. W. 678. Under such circumstances it was at least proper for him, if not his duty, to take such steps as were reasonably necessary to conserve the value of the business. That the party rescinding is not required to abandon the property where the other party refuses to receive it, is especially true where the property is of such character that it may depreciate materially in value if abandoned. It is for the benefit of the one ultimately determined to be the owner of the property, that its value be preserved, and the one who refused to receive it is not in a position to complain of any conduct on the part of the other reasonably tending to avert loss.

Defendants sold and plaintiff purchased the business of manufacturing and vending the products of the Prussian Remedy Co. Plaintiff took over a going business, and its value consisted largely in the fact that it was a going business. If it ceased to be such, much of its value would be lost. That it remained under plaintiff's control resulted, not from his own conduct, but from the conduct of defendants; and they cannot complain of any proper action taken by him to preserve it as a going business. He continued to manufacture and sell the remedies in the same manner in which they had previously been manufactured and sold. Defendants contend, however, that, after the rescission, he still conducted the business as his own, and for his own profit. If this be so, it was a waiver of the rescission, but the record does not bear out defendants' contention. Plaintiff offered to prove that, at all times since the rescission, he had been ready to turn the business over to defendants in substantially the same condition in which he received it, and that he is still ready to do so; also that he has appropriated none of the profits, but has kept them on hand ready to be turned over to defendants. It is true that the materials and stock now on hand are not the identical stock and materials received; but this is not important. The business contemplated that stock and materials would be used up and disposed of, and be replaced by new. It could not well be carried on otherwise. It is also true that plaintiff has paid himself a salary.

He was entitled to a reasonable compensation for his services, but could not arbitrarily fix the amount thereof himself. No claim is made, however, that the amount, as fixed by him, was not fair and reasonable. It is also true that, in operating the business, plaintiff has both incurred debts, and acquired outstanding accounts; also that he took over the business without assuming any pre-existing debts, if there were such. He cannot require defendants to assume the debts incurred by him, but must return the business as free and unincumbered as it was when he discovered the fraud. But, if he is able to return the business free and unincumbered, the fact that he is personally liable for the debts, which he has incurred, does not debar him from perfecting the rescission. If, as he claims, he is still able to turn the business back to defendants in substantially the same condition as when he took it over, and is also ready and able to turn over to them the profits which have accrued since he rescinded the contract, he is entitled to recover the consideration with which he parted. Of course, as a condition to such recovery, he must actually turn over the business and profits to, or for, defendants in such manner as the court shall direct.

The amount of the proceeds received from the business, which remain after liquidating the expense necessarily incurred in carrying it on, constitute the profits for which plaintiff must account. The admitted facts would indicate that he has made a substantial profit. To offset the indebtedness of $7,000 he has accounts receivable amounting to the sum of $16,210. If these accounts are good and collectable, and there is nothing to indicate they are not, he should be able to discharge the entire indebtedness and still have a substantial surplus to turn over to defendants as profits.

The order appealed from is reversed and a new trial granted.

JOHN HELPPIE v. NORTHWESTERN DRAINAGE COMPANY.[1]

November 20, 1914.

Nos. 18,830—(76).

Wilful trespass — treble damages.

1. A wilful trespass upon land, as defined by section 8090, G. S. 1913, committed by a servant within the scope of his employment warrants treble damages against the master even though the act was without the master's knowledge or consent.

Same — exclusion of evidence.

2. In an action for treble damages for cutting timber, where the complaint charges wilful and wanton trespass and the answer contains a general denial with what may be construed as an admission of some cutting without lawful authority from plaintiff, it was error to exclude evidence tending to show the cutting by defendant's servant to have been casual or involuntary and to instruct the jury to return treble damages.

Action in the district court for Marshall county to recover $6,000 under R. L. 1905, §§ 4149, 4268, being treble the value of the property destroyed. The case was tried before Grindeland, J., and a jury which returned a verdict for $500. From an order denying its motion for a new trial, defendant appealed. Reversed.

A. N. Eckstrom, Charles Loring and *G. A. Youngquist,* for appellant.

Rieke & Hamrum, for respondent.

HOLT, J.

Plaintiff sued defendant, a corporation, for wilful trespass in cut-

[1] Reported in 149 N. W. 461.

Note.—Upon the master's liability in trespass for wrongful or negligent act of servant, see note in 27 L.R.A. 197.

As to the measure of damages for wrongful cutting or destruction of standing timber, see note in 18 L.R.A.(N.S.) 244; and for the measure of damages for injury to, or destruction of, trees, see note in 19 L.R.A. 653.

ting down a poplar grove on his land. The court instructed the jury to allow treble damages. The appeal is from the order denying defendant a new trial.

The defendant was operating a walking-dredge, in public drainage work, along the boundary of plaintiff's land in Marshall county, this state. The work was in charge of its foreman, Hans Lundstrom. The land in that vicinity was low and soft so that the dredge could not be moved as occasion required, without laying poles or small timber on the ground to give it footing. Upon plaintiff's land was a poplar grove of from five to ten acres in extent. Lundstrom testified that he cut and used poles from this grove, but when he offered to testify that while the cutting was done he supposed the grove was upon the land of a Mr. Sponheim, with whom he had arranged to cut the poles needed, the court sustained plaintiff's objection to the proof. Neither was the defendant permitted to show that it had no knowledge of the trespass and had not authorized it.

Under the rule announced in Potulni v. Saunders, 37 Minn. 517, 35 N. W. 379, defendant claims error in directing a verdict for treble damages. There it is held that such damages cannot be allowed "where defendant is deemed in law to have committed the trespass only by reason of his relation to the actual trespasser." We do not think the language quoted should be taken to have established the doctrine in this state that in no case is the master or principal to be held for treble damages, unless he authorized the servant's or agent's trespass. For, if it does, corporations and large business concerns could scarcely ever be penalized for wilful trespass. A corporation does not by vote of its board of directors, or by its chief executive or managing officer, direct all of its activities. Usually the greater part thereof is entrusted to the judgment and discretion of servants and agents, not officers. The same holds true in the large business enterprises of individuals and partnerships. The law is now thoroughly well settled in this state that the master or principal is responsible for the torts of the servant or agent committed within the scope of the employment even if contrary to orders, Nava v. Northwestern Telephone Exchange Co. 112 Minn. 199, 127 N. W. 935; Barrett v. Minneapolis, St. P. & S. S. M. Ry. Co. 106 Minn. 51, 117 N. W. 1047,

18 L.R.A.(N.S.) 416, 130 Am. St. 585, and cases there cited. That extends also to infliction of punitive damages. Peterson v. Western Union Telegraph Co. 75 Minn. 368, 77 N. W. 985, 43 L.R.A. 581, 74 Am. St. 502; Berg v. St. Paul City Ry. Co. 96 Minn. 513, 105 N. W. 191; Anderson v. International Harvester Co. of America, 104 Minn. 49, 116 N. W. 101, 16 L.R.A.(N.S.) 440. Whatever exceeds compensation for injuries from a tort is in the nature of punitive or exemplary damages, whether fixed by statute or under the ordinary rules of law. When the alleged trespass is shown to have been committed by a servant, it is ordinarily for a jury to determine whether it was done within the scope of the employment. If found so to be, the consequences to the master will be the same as if he personally had done or directed the wrong. As the testimony now stands in this case, the jury might well find that defendant placed the whole management of the drain construction and the operation of the dredge into Lundstrom's hands. The evidence and admissions in the answer would warrant the conclusion that whatever Lundstrom did in the premises was within the scope of his duties, and hence fraught with the same consequences as if he therein had been following the orders of defendant's board of directors.

It therefore becomes a question whether Lundstrom's trespass was such that under section 8090, G. S. 1913, treble damages necessarily follow. This section provides that whoever without lawful authority cuts down any trees or timber on the land of another shall be liable in a civil action to the owner for treble damages, "unless upon the trial it appears that the trespass was casual or involuntary, or that the defendant had probable cause to believe that the land on which the trespass was committed was his own, or that of the person in whose service or by whose direction the act was done, in which case judgment shall be given for only the single damages assessed." This statute is penal in character. Statutes permitting penalties in addition to compensation for torts receive a strict construction. Potulni v. Saunders, supra; Berg v. Baldwin, 31 Minn. 541, 18 N. W. 821. Every trespass is presumptively unlawful, but the law does not give treble damages in every case, where timber is cut on the lands of another without lawful authority. The express provision is that, if, upon the trial, the trespass is shown to be casual or involuntary, the liability shall not exceed actual compensation. Here plaintiff directly charged that the cutting in the grove was an intentional, wanton trespass, known to be unlawful at the time. The answer contained a general denial, except as to certain matters. Plaintiff contends that the answer admits the cutting to have been without lawful authority. We may concede that it does, since it is admitted that some poles were cut by its servants on plaintiff's land, and there is no averment of authority from plaintiff, still it does not follow that defendant must necessarily be mulcted in treble damages. Under the tendered issue defendant was entitled to show that the trespass by its servant was not wilful but casual or involuntary. If Lundstrom had in good faith made arrangement with the owner of a grove to cut poles therefrom, and he thereupon, intending to cut from such grove, through ignorance or mistake came upon the lands of plaintiff and there cut, honestly believing that he was cutting in the grove for which he had permission, the trespass would be casual or involuntary. We think not only should Mr. Lundstrom have been permitted to testify that he supposed he was cutting from Mr. Sponheim's grove, but that he had previously made an arrangement to cut therefrom. It would then be for the jury to say whether his going upon the wrong land was an honest mistake, an involuntary trespass. "The facts upon which the question of treble damages depend must be passed upon by the jury and not by the court." Tait v. Thomas, 22 Minn. 537. The pleadings raised the issue whether the trespass was wilful or involuntary; the evidence tending to show it to be of the latter kind should have been received; and the jury should then, under proper instructions, have been permitted to determine the character of the wrong, to be redressed and punished by treble damages if found by them to have been intentionally and knowingly done against plaintiff's property rights, or to be righted by full compensation only if found to have been involuntary or otherwise within the exception of the statute.

The order denying a new trial is reversed.

DENA UGGEN v. BAZILLE & PARTRIDGE.[1]

November 20, 1914.

Nos. 18,838—(94).

Death of servant — warning of danger — evidence.

1. Evidence in an action against a master, to recover damages for the death of a servant killed while engaged in painting the interior of an elevator shaft by the counterweight of a car moving in an adjacent shaft, considered and *held* sufficient to sustain a finding that defendant failed to give deceased sufficient warning before sending him into the shaft where he was killed.

Motion to discharge the panel — conduct of counsel.

2. Record *held* to disclose no basis for imputation of bad faith on the part of plaintiff's counsel in referring, during his examination of a juror, to a liability insurance company as the real party in interest, and hence denial of defendant's motion to discharge the panel on account thereof was not error.

After the former appeal reported in 123 Minn. 97, 143 N. W. 112, the case was retried before Catlin, J., and a jury which returned a verdict of $5,000. From an order denying its motion for judgment notwithstanding the verdict or for a new trial, defendant appealed. Affirmed.

Wickersham & Churchill, for appellant.
Douglas, Kennedy & Kennedy, for respondent.

PHILIP E. BROWN, J.

This cause was retried to a jury after a reversal reported in 123

[1] Reported in 149 N. W. 459.

Note.—The authorities on the general question of the master's duty to warn or instruct his servants are gathered in a note in 44 L.R.A. 33. And as to the master's duty to instruct servant as to danger to which he is exposed, see note in 41 L.R.A. 143. And for the master's duty to protect or warn servant against dangers not reasonably to be apprehended, see note in 21 L.R.A.(N.S.) 89.

Minn. 97, 143 N. W. 112. Plaintiff had a verdict. Defendant appealed from an order denying its alternative motion.

The nature of the action and the facts showing the general situation are sufficiently stated in the reported case. In addition, however, to what is there set out, it appeared on the second trial that elevator shaft No. 3 was less than six feet square; that deceased was directed to work in shaft No. 2 up to the time he stepped upon the car in shaft No. 3 almost immediately preceding the accident; that no directions or warnings were then given except that the car in shaft No. 2 was about to go up; and that the workman Borchard, who was then standing on the car in shaft No. 3, was the person who responded "all right" before the other car moved.

1. On the former appeal the main contention was whether defendant's foreman, before starting deceased to work on the day preceding the accident, gave the same warning here claimed by defendant as to the dangers incident to the employment in the elevator shafts. Plaintiff made the point in her brief that this warning, if given, was insufficient, but this feature was not particularly pressed, was obscured by other contentions, and only collaterally considered. She now squarely presents the same contention, with others. Whatever instructions or warnings were given affirmatively appear, and there were none other than those about to be recited, all of which were given on the evening of the day preceding the accident. The record discloses that before commencing the work and after a number of the workmen, including deceased, were assembled, some of whom were to work in shaft No. 1, in which no car had been installed, some in shafts Nos. 2 and 3, and others on the outside of the shafts, defendant's foreman gave them some instructions and warnings, when they were close thereto. He testified as follows in this regard:

"The exact wording, of course, I don't remember now. In substance I told him to be very careful in the work in there, explaining how the counterweights were running, that the counterweight of car No. 1 in shaft No. 2 was running in shaft No. 3.

"Q. Now, you say car No. 1?

"A. In shaft No. 2; the first, shaft No. 1, has no car in, so I would like to refer to the car in shaft No. 2 as car No. 1, being that is only two cars in the shaft."

"Q. Now, what was the substance of what you said to Uggen at that time about where the counterweights ran? Tell us that now.

"A. I told him that the counterweight for car No. 2 was running in shaft No. 3, to be careful when the cars were moved.

"Q. Be careful about what?

"A. Well, I don't remember if I said anything more; that is about the substance of what I said at that time." Later the witness admitted that these statements were made to the assembled workmen and not particularly to deceased.

Concerning the same matter, one of the workmen, the witness Borchard, testified:

"Q. Now, before the men started to work in the shaft at the eleventh floor, what did Mr. Shelgren say to the men then?

"A. Well, he explained to us about the running of the elevator and the counterweights in the opposite shaft."

"A. They were that when the elevator in shaft No. 2 was running, why, the weight would move in shaft 3, and that when the elevator in shaft No. 3 was running, why, the weight would be going up and down on the side of the elevator."

"Q. * * * And where, if at all, did he say that the counterweights that were attached to the cable for the middle elevator run in the righthand shaft?

"A. I don't know.

"Q. You don't remember?

"A. I don't remember that."

On plaintiff's part, as on the former trial, there was testimony of a negative nature by some of the workmen who were present when the alleged instructions were given, to the effect that they did not hear the warnings concerning the counterweights.

Under the facts a duty devolved upon defendant to instruct and warn deceased with reference to the running of the counterweights in shaft No. 3, before directing him to enter therein. Furthermore, the instructions given, in order to fill the full measure of this duty, must have been sufficiently clear and plain to be intelligently apprehended. Small v. Brainerd Lumber Co. 95 Minn. 95–98, 103 N. W. 726. Or, as otherwise expressed, they must have been "sufficiently clear, plain and specific to be intelligently observed" (Fitzgerald v. International Flax Twine Co. 104 Minn. 138, 146, 116 N. W. 475, 478); defendant's duty in the premises being not merely to advise deceased of existing conditions, but to see to it that he comprehended the risk and understood the danger. Gillespie v. Great Northern Ry. Co. 124 Minn. 1, 6, 144 N. W. 466. The question, then, is: Can it be held as a matter of law that plaintiff failed to show defendant's neglect, or that deceased must be deemed, under the instructions given or otherwise, to have comprehended the risk incurred in passing on the car in shaft No. 3, and understood the danger of remaining and working there while the other car was in motion? Accepting for the present defendant's version of the instructions as verity, we answer in the negative. The running of two counterweights so near each other and in such a small compartment presented an unusual and dangerous situation to a person on the car in shaft No. 3, requiring greater particularity of warning than can be found in the testimony. Defendant's foreman details no words of explanation either as to the counterweight of the car in shaft No. 3, or as to which weight was used in connection with the car in shaft No. 2, or with reference to the movement of the weights being converse to that of the cars, though Borchard testified shortly in the latter regard. Moreover, the extent of the foreman's directions must be considered in connection with the fact that he did not then contemplate working deceased in shaft No. 3, but in shaft No. 2, where he would incur no danger from the weights. Nor can the usual presumption of care for one's own safety be ignored in considering whether deceased comprehended the danger.

Furthermore, as stated in the former opinion, the negative testimony, which is clearer than on the former trial, cannot be wholly disregarded. If the instructions given had been unquestionably sufficient, and it had been conclusively established that deceased heard them, this evidence would be of doubtful value; but such is not this case. In Seaboard Air Line v. Shanklin, 148 Fed. 342, 345, the court, in considering oral instructions, said:

"But there are certain infirmities which inhere in oral instructions given as a rule of conduct. The language in which they are framed is passing, and not fixed. They are uncertain, and therefore open to constructions partaking of the bias and disposition of the employees. * * * At last, as here, when their existence, meaning, and import are called in question, when these have a vital bearing on the rights of litigants, it is left to the fallible and imperfect memory of witnesses to say that they existed, what they were, and what they meant."

The court there held, in a case quite analogous, on principle, to the present, that the issue was for the jury. We hold likewise.

2. One of the jury panel, during his examination by plaintiff's counsel, stated that he knew a Mr. Neely, but that the latter's connection with the insurance company which insured defendant against liability in the case on trial would not affect him in any way. Plaintiff's counsel then inquired: "The fact that R. M. Neely & Co. are the real party in interest wouldn't affect you?" Whereupon defendant's counsel moved to discharge the panel because of the statement before them that someone other than defendant was the real party in interest, and when, during the argument of the motion, he was called to the stand by defendant, testified that while he was employed in the case by Neely & Co. or the Employers' Liability Assurance Co., as their attorney, he was not paid by them but by defendant, and that the latter was the real party in interest. Plaintiff's counsel thereupon withdrew the question complained of, and admitted that Neely & Co.'s interest was as shown by the testimony of defendant's counsel. The latter, however, insisted upon his motion, which the court denied. We find no basis for an imputation of bad faith on the part of plaintiff's counsel, and therefore no ground for reversal in the ruling. Granrus v. Croxton Mining Co. 102 Minn. 325, 328, 113 N. W. 693.

Order affirmed.

SELMA HEDIN v. NORTHWESTERN KNITTING COMPANY.[1]

November 20, 1914.

Nos. 18,847—(85).

Injury to servant — defective instrumentality.

1. In an action for personal injuries, it is *held* that the evidence supports the verdict to the effect that defendant negligently furnished plaintiff a defective instrumentality with which to perform her work, namely, a sewing machine operated by electric power, and that plaintiff was not guilty of contributory negligence.

Same — assumption of risk.

2. The assurance of defendant, after making repairs upon the machine, that it was in safe working condition, was sufficient to justify the jury in finding that plaintiff did not assume the risk in operating the same.

Quaere — effect of statute.

3. Whether chapter 245, Laws 1913, restricting the right of trial courts to direct verdicts in certain cases, applies to dismissals at the close of plaintiff's case in chief, quaere?

Action in the district court for Hennepin county to recover $15,-200 for personal injury received while in the employ of defendant. The case was tried before Leary, J., who denied defendant's motion to dismiss the action and its motion for a directed verdict, and a jury which returned a verdict for $1,000. From an order denying its motion for judgment notwithstanding the verdict or for a new trial, defendant appealed. Affirmed.

P. J. McLaughlin, for appellant.

John N. Berg and *Adolph P. L. Johnson,* for respondent.

[1] Reported in 149 N. W. 541.

Note.—As to the effect upon the servant's assumption of risk of assurance of safety by master or coservant, see notes in 48 L.R.A. 542; 23 L.R.A.(N.S.) 1014, and 30 L.R.A.(N.S.) 453.

Brown, C. J.

Plaintiff was in the employ of defendant, a manufacturer of knit underwear, in its factory at Minneapolis. She entered the service in January, 1913, and was set to work at sewing machine stitching and finishing garments. The sewing machine was of the ordinary type and was run by electric power, the current of electricity being turned on or off by the operator as occasion required. She was inexperienced in this class of work, but soon became familiar with the operation of the machine and did so successfully for six weeks or two months. She was transferred to another machine in March, of the same kind, and doing the same character of work, and though she successfully operated the first machine, she had difficulty with the second because of the fact the needle frequently broke, thus not only preventing the successful and steady operation of the machine, but endangering her personal safety by flying pieces of the broken needles. The rules of defendant required of the employees whenever a machine did not operate properly, or became out of repair, to report the facts to the foreman in charge, and they were not required or expected to make repairs themselves. Plaintiff so reported this machine, and the foreman or machinist made repairs thereon, but failed to remedy the defect. The needles continued to break, and plaintiff made other reports, and further attention was given the machine by the foreman. He removed the machine from the stand to which it was attached and made repairs, readjusted the parts, smoothed off the surface of the plate through which the needle extends in doing its work, and then said to plaintiff that the machine was all right, and to go on with her work. The machine worked properly for awhile and plaintiff experienced no difficulty with broken needles, but in a short time a needle again broke into pieces, one of which struck plaintiff in the thumb, inflicting the injury of which she here complains. The injury was more or less serious. The broken needle penetrated the flesh of the thumb, and was subsequently removed by an operation, but not until plaintiff had suffered considerably; and she was unable to use her hand or arm for some time thereafter. She brought this action to recover for her injuries, charging in her complaint that defendant negligently failed to provide her with a safe instrumentality with which to do her work; that the sewing machine was defective and out of order to the knowledge of defendant, by reason of which defective condition she was injured. Plaintiff had a verdict and defendant appealed from an order denying its alternative motion for judgment or a new trial.

1. The principal contention of defendant is that the evidence fails wholly to make a case of actionable negligence; that the breaking of the needles was not shown to have been caused by a defect in the machine, or from want of repair, and that the cause thereof was left wholly to speculation and conjecture. In this contention we are unable to concur. It is well settled that negligence may be shown by circumstantial evidence, precisely as any other fact in litigation may be so established. Bruckman v. Chicago, St. P. M. & O. Ry. Co. 110 Minn. 308, 125 N. W. 263. As expressed by Mr. Justice Mitchell in Orth v. St. Paul, M. & M. Ry. Co. 47 Minn. 384, 50 N. W. 363;

"In an action * * * for personal injuries alleged to have been caused by the negligence of defendant, it is not necessary to establish with absolute certainty the connection of cause and effect between the negligent act and the injury. It is sufficient if the evidence furnishes a reasonable basis for satisfying the minds of the jury that the act complained of was the proximate and operating cause."

In this case the evidence is clear, though not pointing out the precise defect which caused, or might have caused, the needles to break, and tends to show that the cause was either a defect in the machine or that in some respect it was out of repair. While it appears that there are various ways by which needles may break when the machine is in operation, as by improper management thereof by the operator, the evidence affirmatively disproves any improper or unskilful operation by plaintiff. She successfully operated the first machine at which she was put to work, had no trouble with breaking needles, and experienced no difficulty whatever until she commenced to work at the one in question. The foreman of defendant was notified of the trouble several times, and he recognized the fact that something was wrong with the machine and he or the machinist repaired and attempted to repair and put it in order but without success. From this the jury was fully warranted in concluding that the machine was defective or out of order, and that the injury to plaintiff by the broken needle was caused thereby. The case therefore is not one where the defect causing the injury is left to conjecture and speculation, and the trial court properly submitted the issue to the jury. Nelson v. St. Paul Plow Works, 57 Minn. 43, 58 N. W. 868; Engler v. La Crosse Dredging Co. 105 Minn. 74, 117 N. W. 242; Mitton v. Cargill Elevator Co. 124 Minn. 65, 144 N. W. 434.

2. We discover no error in the instructions of the court or in the refusal of the requests of defendant. The charge taken as a whole sufficiently included the special requests tendered by defendant, and fairly stated the law controlling the case. In this situation the refusal of the special requests, though they correctly stated the law, was not reversible error. The assurance of the foreman that the machine was all right, given after his last effort to put the same in working order, was sufficient to justify the jury in finding that plaintiff did not assume the risk. Nelson v. St. Paul Plow Works, 57 Minn. 43, 58 N. W. 868; Rogers v. Chicago G. W. Ry. Co. 65 Minn. 308, 67 N. W. 1003; Kerrigan v. Chicago, M. & St. P. Ry. Co. 86 Minn. 407, 90 N. W. 976.

3. The other assignments of error do not require special mention. The question whether the trial court erred in holding that, under chapter 245, p. 336, Laws 1913,[1] restricting the right of the court to direct a verdict, the court is without power to dismiss an action at the close of plaintiff's case in chief, is not properly before the court and is not determined. We had supposed that this statute applied to directed verdicts only, and not to dismissals.

Order affirmed.

1 [G. S. 1913, § 7998.]

WILLIAM OTT v. TRI-STATE TELEPHONE & TELEGRAPH COMPANY.[1]

November 20, 1914.

Nos. 18,867—(108).

New trial — excessive damages.

1. A new trial will not be granted on the ground of excessive damages nor will the verdict be reduced, except upon the ground that the damages were awarded under the influence of passion or prejudice.

Same — discretion of court.

2. The question whether a motion for a new trial on the ground of excessive damages should be granted, or whether the verdict should be reduced, rests in the practical judgment and sound judicial discretion of the trial court. The order of the trial court disposing of such a motion will not be reversed, unless such discretion has been abused.

Action in the district court for Ramsey county to recover $15,668 for personal injury received in a collision with defendant's automobile. The answer alleged that the injuries were caused by plaintiff's negligence. The case was tried before Dickson, J., who denied defendant's motion for a directed verdict, and a jury which returned a verdict for $8,000. From an order denying its motion for judgment notwithstanding the verdict or for a new trial, defendant appealed. Affirmed.

Bracelen & Cronin, for appellant.

Wickersham & Churchill, for respondent.

HALLAM, J.

Plaintiff was injured by collision with an automobile of defendant. He recovered a verdict in the sum of $8,000. The only contention on this appeal is that the damages are excessive. Plaintiff produced testimony of injuries, in general as follows: A fracture of the lower jaw, leaving it in such a condition that it will not nor-

[1] Reported in 149 N. W. 544.

mally open or move from side to side, and leaving it out of adjustment so that the upper and lower jaws do not meet; as a result of these conditions, mastication is imperfect, causing indigestion and dyspepsia; fracture of the nasal bones; this injury has caused disfigurement of the face, and a stoppage of the nasal passages and improper drainage resulting in impaired sense of smell and severe headaches; impaired eyesight; disordered nervous system so that he suffers from sleeplessness, loss of memory and impaired power of cerebration. As to nervous disorder, the testimony is in sharp conflict, but the evidence on behalf of plaintiff tends to prove a condition quite severe. In general, the evidence on behalf of plaintiff tends to prove a substantially impaired capacity for any form of labor. Plaintiff was at the time less than 25 years old, a press feeder by occupation, earning about $14 a week.

We have little trouble in deciding that this verdict should not be disturbed. The rules applicable to such cases are so well-settled that a statement of them should be unnecessary, and yet they seem sometimes to be overlooked. To warrant the court in overruling the verdict of a jury on the ground of excessive damages, the damages must be not merely more than the court would have awarded, but they must so greatly exceed what would be adequate in the judgment of the court, that they cannot reasonably be accounted for, except upon the theory that they were awarded, not in a judicial frame of mind, but under the influence of passion or of prejudice. The damages must be so large that, after making just allowance for difference of opinion among fair minded men, they cannot be accounted for except upon the theory that in the particular case the proper fair mindedness was wanting. Pratt v. Pioneer Press Co. 32 Minn. 217, 18 N. W. 836, 20 N. W. 87; Nelson v. Village of West Duluth, 55 Minn. 497, 57 N. W. 149; Halness v. Anderson, 110 Minn. 204, 124 N. W. 830.

This court and the trial court are not in the same situation, and they are not governed by the same rules. The question whether a motion for a new trial on the ground of excessive damages should be granted, or whether the verdict should be reduced, rests in the practical judgment and sound discretion of the trial court. In reviewing the order of the trial court disposing of such a motion, this court will be guided by the general rules applicable to discretionary orders, and the order will not be reversed unless such discretion has been abused. It is the duty of the trial court to keep the jury within the bounds of reason, and the duty of this court to keep the trial court within the bounds of judicial discretion. Pratt v. Pioneer Press Co. 32 Minn. 217, 18 N. W. 836, 20 N. W. 87; Slette v. Great Northern Ry. Co. 53 Minn. 341, 55 N. W. 137; Mohr v. Williams, 95 Minn. 261, 104 N. W. 12, 1 L.R.A.(N.S.) 439, 111 Am. St. 465, 5 Ann. Cas. 303.

This case well illustrates the wisdom of these rules. This court can see from an examination of the paper record that plaintiff's injuries are severe, but as to the extent of them the trial court is in much the better position to judge. The trial court in its discretion approved the verdict, and we find no abuse of discretion.

Order affirmed.

HENRY SEEWALD v. EDWARD SCHMIDT and Others.[1]

November 27, 1914.

Nos. 18,725—(55).

Contractor's negligence — liability for runaway.

> The defendants Madsen Brothers were operating a concrete mixer, for which a gasolene engine furnished the motive power, immediately adjacent to a public alley in the defendant city of Waseca, but not in the alley. The defendant Schmidt drove his team into the alley upon business and close to the engine. The horses became frightened and ran away and injured a horse of the plaintiff. It is *held*:
>
> (1) That the defendant city was not liable.

[1] Reported in 149 N. W. 655.

Note.—As to the liability for placing near highway object calculated to frighten horse, see note in 12 L.R.A.(N.S.) 1152.

(2) That the evidence did not justify a finding of the jury that the defendant Schmidt was negligent.

(3) That the evidence justified a finding that the defendants Madsen Brothers were negligent.

(4) That whether their negligence was the proximate cause of the injury to the plaintiff's horse was for the jury.

(5) That the defendants cannot avail themselves of a variance between the pleading and proof first suggested on the appeal.

Action in the district court for Waseca county to recover $325 for injury to plaintiff's horse. The facts are stated in the opinion. The case was tried before Childress, J., who when plaintiff rested denied separate motions on the part of defendants to dismiss the action, and a jury which returned a verdict for $250 in favor of plaintiff. From an order denying their separate motions for a new trial, defendants appealed. Reversed as to defendants city and Schmidt and affirmed as to defendants Madsen.

P. McGovern, F. G. Kiesler and *James C. Melville,* for appellants. *Moonan & Moonan,* for respondent.

DIBELL, C.

Separate appeals by the defendants from orders of the court denying their motions for a new trial after a verdict for the plaintiff.

The defendants Madsen Brothers were engaged in the construction of a building in the city of Waseca fronting at the west on Second street and extending easterly to within a few feet of an alley some 20 feet in width. This alley extended through the block from the street at the south to the one at the north. The building in process of erection was toward the north of the block. In doing their work the defendants were using a concrete mixer operated by a gasolene engine. The defendant Schmidt, a farmer residing some seven miles from the city, drove into the southerly end of the alley proceeding northward with a lumber wagon and a somewhat spirited or skittish team. He had some harness which he purposed leaving for repair at a harness shop just south of the concrete mixer. The concrete mixer and gasolene engine were close to the alley but not in it. The defendant stopped his team when he reached the harness shop, jumped out, holding to the lines. Just then the team became frightened, turned around to the right and to the south, got away from him, and ran into and injured a horse of the plaintiff.

The verdict was against all three defendants.

1. The city is not liable. The concrete mixer was not in the alley. There was building material, used by Madsen Brothers, in the alley; but the obstruction resulting from it had no causal connection with the runaway.

There is nothing in the case of City of Winona v. Botzet, 169 Fed. 321, 94 C. C. A. 563, 23 L.R.A.(N.S.) 204, cited by the respondents, nor in the cases cited therein, suggesting a liability on the part of the city. In that case a team was frightened by a blast of the whistle of the city waterworks.

The cases hold that under certain circumstances a city is negligent in failing to guard a street by barriers against pitfalls or dangers on adjoining private property. Grant v. City of Brainerd, 86 Minn. 126,.90 N. W. 307, and cases cited. This is merely a matter of keeping the streets safe. In some cases it is held that a city may be liable for injuries sustained by travelers on the street from the fall of adjacent buildings or walls which have become dangerous to the public, and which the city has charter authority to abate, though they are privately owned and are on private property. The rule has been stated as follows:

"Municipal corporations to whom the state has delegated ample power to abate common nuisances are bound to exercise that power for the removal of such of them as they know, either actually or constructively, to exist. This duty, it seems, is positive." Williams, Municipal Liab. Tort, § 186.

If there is liability it should be confined to injuries sustained by a traveler on the streets.

"A failure by the corporation to exercise its charter power to abate nuisances not rendering its streets unsafe does not give a person who is injured by such failure a private action against the corporation." 4 Dillon, Mun. Corp. § 1628.

This limitation is illustrated by Davis v. City of Montgomery, 51 Ala. 139, 23 Am. Rep. 545; Cain v. City of Syracuse, 95 N. Y. 83.

So it has been held that a city is liable for injuries sustained by one in a street caused by the falling of burned walls of a building standing upon adjacent premises of private persons where they constituted a nuisance. Parker v. City of Macon, 39 Ga. 725, 99 Am. Dec. 486; City of Savannah v. Waldner, 49 Ga. 316; Kiley v. Kansas City, 87 Mo. 103, 56 Am. Rep. 443; Grogan v. Broadway Foundry Co. 87 Mo. 321. The principle sustaining such liability has been denied. Howe v. City of New Orleans, 12 La. Ann. 481; Hixon v. City of Lowell, 13 Gray, 59. In Lincoln v. City of Boston, 148 Mass. 578, 20 N. E. 329, 3 L.R.A. 257, 12 Am. St. 601, the court said that "noises outside the limits of the highway amounting to a public nuisance are not a statutory defect in the way."

It is not necessary to determine the correct rule or the limits of its application. There was not a nuisance which could be abated by the city. At most there was negligence in the operation of the engine and mixer. There is no principle of law upon which liability on the part of the city can be rested.

2. The evidence was not such as to justify a finding that defendant Schmidt was negligent. He drove into the alley from the street south of the block and some distance from the engine. He knew that the theater building was being constructed. There is evidence that when he got into the alley he saw the mixer and knew that the engine was running. The evidence is that the exhaust of the engine could be heard for some distance. The character of the noise depended upon the amount of material being fed into the mixer. It was more or less intermittent. Schmidt was driving a lumber wagon, the ground was frozen, and the wagon made some noise. His team was young and spirited and needed careful control. He was in pursuit of his business and making use of the public alley to reach the harness shop. The character of his team was not such that he was precluded from using it in his ordinary business when in town. He was not lacking in care in driving. He held to the lines and was dragged until they broke. Viewing the question of liability from a practical, common-sense standpoint, a jury should not be allowed to find that one using a team as the defendant was using his, driving with the care he was exercising, though his team was spirited and somewhat unused to the

noises of a busy town, was negligent. Such a burden of liability is too onerous.

3. It is claimed that the defendants Madsen Brothers were negligent in not sufficiently muffling the exhaust of the engine. The muffler was attached to the engine. The claim is that the defendants should have attached a pipe of some length to the exhaust, attached the muffler to the end of it, and thereby such noise as there was would have been at a greater distance from the alley. There is some evidence that because of the noise of the engine trouble was had with the teams which were hauling material for the building.

A majority of the court are of the opinion that the question of the negligence of defendants Madsen Brothers was for the jury.

The alley was narrow and was much in use by the public. The farmers used it to unload their produce at the rear of the stores and to load their supplies. The merchants used it to receive their freight and to load out their merchandise. The mixer, while not in the alley, was immediately adjacent to it. The view that the defendants may be held liable finds support in Wolf v. Des Moines Elevator Co. 126 Iowa, 659, 98 N. W. 301, 102 N. W. 517. There the exhaust pipe from a gasolene engine used in connection with a grain elevator extended through the roof of the engine room and was about 40 feet from the traveled way. It seems that the muffler was defective. The court refers to the fact that an extension of the exhaust pipe might have been made, or that the engine might have been made to exhaust into a vat of water, and the noise thereby lessened. In the course of its opinion the court said:

"The basic principle upon which the doctrine of all the cases is bottomed is found in the maxim old as the books, in substance, that no man shall make use of his own property in such manner as to unreasonably interfere with the enjoyment on the part of others of the rights conferred upon them by law. Of necessity it follows that in each individual case the question must resolve itself to this: Was the use being made of the adjacent property such in character as to be an unnecessary interference with or unnecessarily dangerous to persons making lawful use of the street or highway? And whether or not improper use amounting to negligence has been made to appear in any given case is generally a question to be determined by the jury. Taking the facts as shown by the record in the instant case, we think it cannot be doubted but that the elevator was located at a place where it might properly be. So, too, as we think, the use of a gasolene engine in connection with the operation of such elevator was proper and lawful, and cannot therefore be said to have been per se negligent. The use of gasolene in the creation of motive power has become general throughout the country, not only in the operation of mills and factories, but as well for the purposes of locomotion, and there can be no grounds upon which to predicate at this time a holding that such use is in and of itself wrongful. As in the use of steam and electricity, it becomes wrongful only when the use is attended with negligence."

Applying the reasoning of that case we hold that the jury could find negligence in Madsen Brothers.

4. Whether the negligence of the defendants Madsen Brothers was the proximate cause of the injury to the plaintiff's horse was at least for the jury. Griggs v. Fleckenstein, 14 Minn. 62 (81), and cases cited thereto in 1 Notes on Minn. Reports, 556.

5. The complaint alleged that the engine and mixer were in the alley and that the defendant Schmidt left his team in the alley unhitched. The questions of negligence already discussed were litigated without objection. The claim of a variance is now for the first time made. It is too late. Johnson v. Avery, 41 Minn. 485, 43 N. W. 340; Lemon v. DeWolf, 89 Minn. 465, 95 N. W. 316; Raitila v. Consumers Ore Co. 107 Minn. 91, 119 N. W. 490.

Other assignments of error do not require specific mention. They have been considered.

Reversed as to defendants city of Waseca and Schmidt and affirmed as to defendants Madsen Brothers.

NELLIE BOOS v. MINNEAPOLIS, ST. PAUL & SAULT STE. MARIE RAILWAY COMPANY.[1]

November 27, 1914.

Nos. 18,793—(48).

Death of servant — negligence of foreman.

1. Evidence in an action to recover damages for the death of one of defendant's yard employees killed while attempting to couple cars standing on a spur track, considered and *held* such as would support a finding that the foreman of a switching crew working on the lead track from which the spur branched was bound to anticipate deceased's presence on the spur in the performance of his duties, so that it was negligence for him to cut loose other cars and allow them to run down grade, without warnings, lights or attendants, to and upon the spur, where they collided with the cars between which deceased was working.

Questions for jury.

2. Whether deceased assumed the risk or was himself negligent, *held* for the jury.

Negligent custom unavailing.

3. Defendant could not toll its duty to use reasonable care in keeping safe the place where deceased was required to work by invoking a negligent custom or usage with respect to the handling of its cars and the conduct of operations in the yards.

Offer of evidence — when inadmissible.

4. If any of the matters embraced in a joint offer of evidence are inadmissible, it is not error to reject the whole.

Action by wife — inquiry into relation with husband.

5. In an action by a wife, as administratrix of her husband's estate, to recover damages for his death, the state of the domestic affairs between plaintiff and deceased at or preceding the time of his death, short of desertion by her or forfeiture of her right to support, cannot be inquired into for the purpose of defeating a recovery or reducing the damages.

Excessive damages.

6. $7,500 damages for the death of a foreman of a switching crew, who was earning from $90 to $100 per month, *held*, under the circumstances of the case, excessive.

1 Reported in 149 N. W. 660.

Action in the district court for Ramsey county by the administratrix of the estate of Martin J. Boos, deceased, to recover $7,500 for the death of her intestate while in the employ of defendant. The case was tried before Kelly, J., and a jury, 10 members of which signed a verdict for the amount demanded. From an order denying its motion for judgment notwithstanding the verdict or for a new trial, defendant appealed. New trial granted unless plaintiff consents to a reduction of the verdict to $5,000.

J. L. Erdall and *M. D. Munn,* for appellant.

C. D. & R. D. O'Brien and *Wondra & Helm,* for respondent.

PHILIP E. BROWN, J.

Action by the administratrix of Martin J. Boos to recover damages caused by his death alleged to have resulted from defendant's negligence. Plaintiff had a verdict. Defendant appealed from an order denying its alternative motion.

Plaintiff's deceased was killed on January 9, 1913, in defendant's yards at Shoreham, Minneapolis. These yards were known as the east and west end. The former consisted of two lead tracks extending from the main line, with 12 other tracks radiating between and connecting them, each long enough to hold a train of about 48 cars. Trains coming into the yard were set on one of these radiating, or spur, tracks for inspection, and cars found to be in bad order were so marked. At night a switching crew worked in each yard, sorting the cars and setting them on the various spur tracks in order to make up outgoing trains. Bad order cars were placed on one of the spurs selected each night by the assistant yard master or the foreman of the switching crews, from which they were transferred to the repair tracks. At the time of the accident, and for some time prior thereto, plaintiff's deceased was employed in defendant's yards as foreman of the repair track switching crew, with sole authority to direct its movements and work. He had charge of a switch engine and his crew consisted of an engineer, a fireman and two helpers. Among other duties, he was required to take the bad order cars each night from the track on which they were collected to the repair tracks. On the night of January 9, 1913, spur track No. 4, located south of the center of the east end yard, was designated to receive the bad order cars, and two had been placed thereon from the east lead track, the first having the draw-bar in its east end pulled out. Thereafter, at about 4:35 o'clock in the morning, deceased, with his crew, backed his engine, to which several cars were attached, on track 4 from the west lead track, leaving one of his helpers at the switch, and, with the other helper, attempted to hook the car with the defective coupler to the other car. While so engaged, and from 15 to 30 minutes after the placing of the first two cars on the spur, two more bad order cars were cut loose, by the same switching foreman who had placed the others, from a train at the upper, or northerly, end of the east lead track, and allowed to run down the grade thereof, with neither lights nor attendants, to track No. 4, where the switch, an unlighted and unguarded one, had been set for them, whence they continued down the slight grade of the latter some 10 or 15 car lengths, until they collided with the cars between which deceased and his helper were working, killing them. The place of the accident was not visible from the point where the second two cars were cut loose, and the crew releasing them, not knowing of deceased's presence on track 4, gave him no notice of the operation. His engineer neither saw nor heard the cars approaching, nor felt the impact. No work was done at night in the repair shops to which the bad order cars were to be taken, and the shift of deceased and his crew ended at 6, while that of the other switching crews ended at 7, a. m.

1. Plaintiff claims defendant was negligent in failing to use due care to make the place where deceased was required to work reasonably safe. Defendant denies negligence on its part and contends that deceased assumed the risk and was himself negligent; predicating its position upon the ground that the work was being done, on the night in question, by all of its employees, save deceased and his crew, in the usual manner and in accordance with the custom theretofore obtaining. It argues that the evidence conclusively established a custom or usage of notifying deceased of the track selected for the bad order cars, all of which were accordingly set thereon and notice then given him of such fact, when, and not before, he would

take them out, and that, if he had occasion to go upon the bad order track before receiving the last mentioned notice, it was his duty to protect himself by advising the other switching crews of his presence or by taking possession of the switches; wherefore, deceased having failed to do either and gone upon this track without having received such notice, plaintiff cannot recover.

The record contains no direct testimony tending to show any notification of deceased that any bad order cars had been placed on track 4, or that the operation of collecting them thereon had been completed so that he should go in and get them. On the contrary it affirmatively appears by the testimony of the foreman of the switching crew which released the last two cars, who, in accordance with the alleged custom or usage, would have given the notice, that none such was given. But notwithstanding this, defendant's contention must fail; for the custom or usage upon which it is founded was neither so conclusively established as to require the jury to find it nor of a character sustainable by law. Insofar as its existence depends upon the testimony of the foreman whose crew released the cars which caused this accident, no great reliance can be placed thereon, for it would have been but natural under the circumstances that he should make the best explanation possible of his conduct. Furthermore, while his testimony tends generally to support defendant's hypothesis, he admitted, while claiming the fact to be otherwise, that there was no general custom or rule requiring deceased to protect himself; and his insistence that deceased should not have gone after the cars until notified is contradicted by the testimony of defendant's assistant night yard master that it was left to deceased entirely as to when he would do so, and that such was customarily done at any time during the night, though usually after midnight. Moreover, since deceased's shift ended at 6 o'clock a. m., he would naturally, at 4:35, have been looking to the finishing of his work. The evidence, therefore, would clearly support a finding that, when the last two cars were turned loose, the foreman of the crew releasing them was bound to anticipate deceased's presence on track 4, engaged in attempting to remove the defective car, from which the conclusion of negligence on defendant's part would, under the further facts disclosed, necessarily follow. Likewise, under the circumstances, it was fairly for the jury to say whether deceased was required to anticipate that this foreman, who was thoroughly familiar with the general situation, would send uncontrolled cars down upon him without warning, or whether he assumed the risk.

Nor could defendant toll its duty to use reasonable care in keeping safe the place where deceased was required to work, by invoking a custom or usage of handling its cars in such an inherently dangerous manner as that disclosed by this record. As said in Hamilton v. Chicago, B. & Q. Ry. Co. 145 Iowa, 431, 436, 124 N. W. 363, 365: "It is practically the universal rule that custom or usage will not justify a negligent act." To the same effect see Braaflat v. Minneapolis & Northern Ele. Co. 90 Minn. 367, 369, 96 N. W. 920; Wiita v. Interstate Iron Co. 103 Minn. 303, 309, 115 N. W. 169, 16 L.R.A.(N.S.) 128; The P. P. Miller, 180 Fed. 288; Thompson, Negligence, §§ 30, 3777; White's Supp. Id. (Vol. VIII.) same sections. And, as declared by Mr. Thompson in his Commentaries on Negligence, § 4528, note: "It would be difficult to state a proposition more careless of justice and absolutely brutal, than the proposition that a railroad company can shunt its cars along its tracks at night with no light upon them to apprise its yardmen of their approach, and with no man upon them to give warning to those who may be on the track in front of them." See sections 4512–4543, Vol. VIII. (White's Supp.) of the same work. See also, Bordeaux v. Atlantic, 150 N. C. 528, 64 S. E. 439. Defendant could not have contracted for immunity from liability for negligence, and so much the more can it not be permitted to stand behind a negligent custom. Nor would an employee readily be charged with assuming the risks involved in such a custom, and the evidence in this case falls short of establishing any such assumption as a matter of law.

2. Deceased was between 32 and 33 years old, strong and healthy, and earning from $90 to $100 per month. He was married, but had no children. Plaintiff, his wife, admitted she had not lived in the same house with him for about three years prior to his death, claiming that this state of affairs was brought about solely by his desire that they should live with his parents. She testified, how-

ever, that during that period they were together a good deal, the last time being about a week prior to the accident, and that their relations as husband and wife continued up to the time of his death, though he contributed only about $10 per month towards her support. She knew of his death, but did not attend the funeral. Later during the trial, defendant, as a part of its case, offered to prove a different reason for the separation, that his mother received his wages, and that none thereof was given to plaintiff after she left him, together with other matters, all embraced in a joint offer, which was rejected. If, therefore, any of the matters were inadmissible, it was not error to reject the whole. 3 Dunnell, Minn. Dig. § 9717, note 8. Some were improper. If defendant had attempted to show desertion by plaintiff of forfeiture of her right to support, a different question would be presented, namely, whether such would defeat her right to recover or might be considered in mitigation of damages. See Stimpson v. Wood, 59 L. T. (N. S.) 218; Fort Worth v. Floyd (Tex. Civ. App.) 21 S. W. 544. But the offer as made was not broad enough to raise those questions, failing, among other things, to include discontinuance of the marital relations, and short of this it was not competent for defendant to inquire into the state of the domestic affairs of deceased and his wife. Dunbar v. Charleston & W. C. R. Co. 186 Fed. 175. See, also, Central of Georgia Ry. Co. v. Bond, 111 Ga. 13, 36 S. E. 299; Boswell v. Barnhart, 96 Ga. 521, 23 S. E. 414.

3. Were the damages excessive? These must be confined to the pecuniary loss sustained by plaintiff. Hutchins v. St. Paul, M. & M. Ry. Co. 44 Minn. 5, 46 N. W. 79. And their amount is arrived at by considering the circumstances of each case. The jury awarded $7,500, the highest statutory allowance. Defendant, in this connection, and others, contends that counsel for plaintiff was guilty of misconduct in summing up to the jury. His remarks go beyond legitimate argument and are disapproved. But a majority of the court hold that they do not warrant a reversal. They have, however, been considered in connection with the verdict. We are unable to say that plaintiff was entitled to the highest sum allowable under any circumstances in an action for death.

It is therefore ordered that if plaintiff, within 10 days after the remittitur goes down, files consent to a reduction of the verdict to the sum of $5,000, the order appealed from will stand affirmed; otherwise a new trial is granted.

HALLAM, J. (dissenting).

Deceased was 32 years old, earning $90 to $100 a month. Plaintiff his widow is 30. If, as the opinion indicates, it is "not competent for defendant to inquire into the state of the domestic affairs of deceased and his wife" short of showing "discontinuance of marital relations" it seems to me there is no ground for a reduction of this verdict.

If such matters are proper to be considered at all, then defendant's proffered evidence should have been received and its rejection was error and a new trial should be granted to defendant without condition.

Neither does it seem to me that objectionable remarks of counsel furnish any ground for reduction of the verdict of a jury.

I can see no justification for a conditional affirmance of the order of the trial court.

STATE ex rel. E. L. LARSON v. EVEN HALVERSON and Others.[1]

November 27, 1914.

Nos. 18,802—(65).

Care of infant — father's right.
> Evidence considered and *held* to show that the best interests of a minor child of the age of about five years, and her general welfare, will be best

1 Reported in 149 N. W. 664.

Note.—As to the denial of custody of child to parent for its well-being, see note in 41 L.R.A.(N.S.) 564.

served and protected by remaining with her grandparents where she has
been since her birth and the subsequent death of her mother, and that the
natural right of the father to her custody and control must yield thereto.

Upon the relation of E. L. Larson, the district court for Houston
county issued its writ of *habeas corpus* directed to Even Halverson,
Anna Halverson and Sophia Halverson. The matter was heard by
Kingsley, J., who ordered judgment awarding the custody of re-
lator's minor child to respondents. From that order relator appealed.
Affirmed.

Catherwood & Nicholsen, for relator.

Gray & Thompson and *Duxbury & Duxbury,* for respondent.

BROWN, C. J.

Relator, E. L. Larson, and Julia Halverson, were duly married
to each other some time in the year 1907, and thereafter continued to
reside together as husband and wife until the death of the wife in
December, 1909. A daughter was born to them in April, 1909,
who, since the death of the mother, has been in the custody and care
of respondents, the mother and father and sister of the deceased.
The child is now about five years of age. She was so committed to
the custody of her grandparents and her aunt under arrangements
made with them by relator immediately following the death of the
mother, and when the child was only a few months old. The home
of the grandparents during all this time was and still is on a farm
in Houston county, this state, while relator resided, from a time
prior to the death of his wife and since, at St. Paul, and in the employ of the street railway company. Relator remarried in November, 1912. Subsequent to this marriage this proceeding was instituted to gain possession and control of the child, respondents having
refused to surrender her on the demand of the father. The court
below, after hearing and duly considering the evidence presented,
ordered and directed the entry of judgment awarding the custody of
the child to respondents until the further order of the court. Judgment was so entered and relator appealed.

It is thoroughly settled law that the parent's right to the care, custody and control of his minor children is paramount to all other considerations, save the best interests of the child, and his ability and fitness being established the custody and control follow as a matter of course. But in all controversies involving the custody of minor children the welfare and best interests of the child are the chief consideration and prevail over the natural right of the parent. This is too well settled to require the citation of authorities. We apply the law as thus stated to the case at bar. The evidence before us discloses the ability and fitness of the father, from a pecuniary point of view, to support his daughter, but whether her interests and welfare, in view of her physical condition, will justify taking her from her present home and surroundings, is so clouded in doubt and uncertainty, with the force of the evidence against the change, that we conclude that she should for the present, and until the further order of the court below, remain with her grandparents and her aunt, where she has been since her birth, and from whom she has received the most tender and affectionate care.

It appears, as already stated, that relator remarried in November, 1912, and resides with his present wife in rented apartments in St. Paul. In addition to the care of the home and the discharge of her household duties, the present wife also conducts a small grocery store in the vicinity of the place of their residence, and this necessarily occupies a considerable portion of her time during the day. Relator is engaged as car conductor for the street railway company and he is away from home during the working hours. The child, according to the testimony of the relators and also physicians called to treat her, has not enjoyed perfect health since her birth. Her mother was afflicted with tuberculosis and died of that ailment a few months after the birth of the child. The child, a year or two ago, was taken with a serious eye trouble which the physicians attributed to the tubercular condition of the mother. This trouble is likely to recur and for this reason, coupled with her physical condition, attributable to the same cause, the physicians testified that it would be detrimental to her health and welfare to remove the child from her present sur-

roundings and take her to either St. Paul or Minneapolis.   It is
their opinion that the child requires an outdoor life, and among
congenial surroundings, and that the home life on respondents' farm
is best suited to the improvement, now under way, of her general
health and condition.   The child will receive tender care and attention at the hands of its grandparents and aunt, the respondents.
And though a stepmother might extend the same care and attention
to her stepchild, and no doubt relator's present wife would endeavor
to do so, we are not justified in ignoring the evidence of the physicians above referred to, or in concluding that their judgment of
what is best for the child is not sound.   This situation differentiates
the case from any of those where the natural right of the father has
been given effect, for it centers around and aims at the welfare of
the child, which is paramount to the natural paternal right.

Judgment affirmed.

GERMAN AMERICAN STATE BANK OF RITZVILLE v. P. J. LYONS.[1]

November 27, 1914.

Nos. 18,828—(91).

Promissory note — title of indorsee — case followed.
　　1. Rosemond v. Graham, 54 Minn. 323, to the effect that an indorsee of
　　negotiable paper, taken before maturity as collateral security for an ante-
　　cedent debt, in good faith and without notice of defenses, holds the same
　　free from such defenses, followed and applied.

No error.
　　2. The record presents no reversible error.

Action in the district court for Hennepin county to recover $2,500
upon defendant's promissory note.   The defense is stated in the
opinion.   The case was tried before Booth, J., and a jury which

[1] Reported in 149 N. W. 658.

returned a verdict in favor of plaintiff. From an order denying his motion for a new trial, defendant appealed. Affirmed.

Booth & McDonald, for appellant.

Koon, Whelan & Hempstead, for respondent.

BROWN, C. J.

On June 9, 1910, defendant made and delivered his promissory note to one McLean for the sum of $2,500, due and payable on December 24, 1911. McLean was indebted to plaintiff bank in a sum exceeding the amount of this note, and before the maturity thereof and in the usual course of business transferred the note to plaintiff as collateral security to that indebtedness. Plaintiff thereafter brought this action to recover upon the note. Defendant interposed in defense that the note was obtained from him by McLean by fraud and fraudulent representation; that it was delivered upon certain conditions which were never complied with; that plaintiff took the note with notice and knowledge of the terms and conditions upon which it was delivered to McLean, and was not a *bona fide* holder of the same. Upon the issues so presented the cause went to trial, resulting in a verdict for plaintiff. Defendant appealed from an order denying his motion for a new trial, based in part upon the ground of newly discovered evidence.

The assignments of error challenge the sufficiency of the evidence to support the verdict, the refusal of certain requested instructions, and two or more rulings on the admission of evidence.

The defense of fraud and fraudulent representations interposed by defendant was available to him only in the event plaintiff was not a *bona fide* holder of the note. If plaintiff was such a holder, the note being negotiable, then, under the authorities, here and elsewhere, the defense fails. Roach v.. Halvorson, supra, p. 113, 148 N. W. 1080, and authorities there cited. So the primary inquiry is whether the evidence supports the verdict affirming such *bona fides* in plaintiff's title. Our examination of the record leads to an affirmative answer to the question. We find ample evidence to support the conclusion that no officer or agent of plaintiff having the transaction in charge had any notice or knowledge of the alleged fraud or fraudulent representations, and that the bank acquired the note in the usual course of business before maturity. In this view of the evidence, which has been given credence by the jury and trial court, it only remains to consider whether plaintiff is a holder for value, within the meaning of the law.

It appears, and there is no controversy upon the subject, that, at the time the note was transferred to plaintiff, it then held the obligations of McLean to an amount exceeding the amount of this note. The note was transferred to plaintiff as collateral security to that indebtedness. The trial court instructed the jury that the pre-existing indebtedness was sufficient to constitute a valuable consideration. Exception was taken to the charge and it is assigned as error. The instructions of the court were in harmony with the rule adopted many years ago by this court, and since adhered to, and the exception must be overruled. It was expressly held in Rosemond v. Graham, 54 Minn. 323, 56 N. W. 38, 40 Am. St. 336, that an indorsee of negotiable paper, taken before maturity as collateral security for an antecedent debt, in good faith and without notice of defenses, such as fraud, which might have been available as between the original parties, holds the same free from such defenses. Counsel for defendant contend that the decision there rendered was erroneous and should be overruled. In this we do not concur. The decision is in harmony with the general trend of our decisions in analogous cases. Horton v. Williams, 21 Minn. 187; 1 Notes on Minn. Reports, 882, and has consistently been followed and applied. 3 Notes on Minn. Reports, 1013, where all the decisions are collected and cited. And moreover the rule of the Graham case is in accord with the provisions of the Negotiable Instruments Act of 1913 (chapter 272, § 25) which, though not in force at the time of this transaction, is confirmatory of the rule there laid down.

The other assignments of error do not require special mention. We discover no error of a character to justify a reversal, either in the instructions of the court, or in its rulings excluding evidence, nor in denying a new trial on the ground of newly discovered evidence.

Order affirmed.

HERBERT HAWKINS v. MELLIS, PIRIE & COMPANY.[1]

November 27, 1914.

Nos. 18,868—(90).

Evidence of value — qualification of witness.

1. Where the assets of a corporation were shown to include various items of property, the court ruled properly that a witness should not give an opinion as to the aggregate value until he had shown qualification to estimate the value of the several items.

Value of stock — charge to jury.

2. The instructions of the court to guide the jury in finding the value of corporate stock do not contain reversible error in view of the evidence showing that the stock had no market value, that there had been no actual sales to outsiders, and that, during the short time the corporation had been in existence, its capital stock was speedily being depleted so that the par value of the stock could not be taken as *prima facie* evidence of its actual value.

Verdict sustained by evidence.

3. The verdict finds fair support in the evidence.

Action in the district court for Hennepin county to recover the value of 220 shares of defendant's stock which it was alleged defendant had converted. The case was tried before Waite, J., who denied defendant's motion for an instructed verdict and a jury which returned a verdict for $71.25. Defendant's motion for a new trial was denied. From the judgment entered pursuant to the verdict, plaintiff appealed. Affirmed.

H. W. Volk, for appellant.

Edwin S. Slater, for respondent.

HOLT, J.

The action is against the corporation for the conversion of 220 shares of its capital stock, issued to plaintiff and fully paid for. The corporation denied the conversion and counterclaimed for

[1] Reported in 149 N. W. 663.

$1,000, the price of 100 additional shares issued to plaintiff but not paid for. The defendant recovered a verdict for $71.15. Plaintiff appeals from the order denying a new trial.

The verdict must be based upon the conclusion that defendant had converted 220 shares of the 320 belonging to plaintiff and also that he had not paid for the 100 shares not converted. The first proposition is of course in accord with plaintiff's contention and of the latter he does not complain. The errors assigned relate wholly to the ascertainment of the damages for the shares converted; and include a ruling touching the admissibility of evidence bearing upon value, an instruction to guide the jury in the determination thereof, and their estimate of the value or damages.

Only one ruling on the reception of evidence is questioned. Plaintiff, who had been the secretary of the corporation from its inception until about a month prior to the alleged conversion, when on the witness stand, was asked this question in regard to the assets: "Now, kindly state what was the value in dollars and cents as near as you can state, on November 22, 1910?" An objection that no foundation was laid was interposed and sustained. The court then reminded counsel that the witness would not be permitted to give a blanket value before he had first shown some qualification to testify as to the value of the various items composing the assets. Thereupon appellant's counsel said "I will excuse him from answering more at present, and try to get the matter in better shape." No further attempt was made to elicit estimates of the value of the assets from the witness. It is clear that no reversible error is found in the ruling of the court.

The substance of the part of the charge upon which error is predicated stated: That in case the conversion was proven the measure of the damages would be the actual value of the stock converted; that ordinarily that would be the measure, but it appeared that the stock had no market value since it was not listed, quoted or offered for sale; that evidence had been introduced tending to show the condition of the business of the company; that the par value of the stock was to be considered by the jury, but was not to be taken, as contended by plaintiff, to be the measure of recovery in the absence of absolute proof by defendant that it was not worth that amount. The court then continued: "I am of the opinion that the par value of the stock is one of the things to be considered by you, and in doing so you should take into account the financial condition of the company, the nature of the business and all other things which will enable you to form an opinion as the actual value of the stock. I am aware of the fact that when I say value of the stock I am using an ambiguous term, because we have to have some kind of yard stick to measure the value, as the ordinary standard does not apply in this case. I know of no better rule for you to adopt, if you get that far in the case, than to ascertain and determine from the evidence what a person who wanted to buy stock in this corporation would reasonably expect to pay for this block of 220 shares." There were no instructions requested, and no corrections or modifications asked when the case was submitted to the jury. As the evidence stood we believe the substance of the charge pertinent and proper. It is true that the par value of the shares of corporate stock may be taken as the actual value in the absence of other evidence bearing on the question. Thompson, Corporations, § 3496; Harris Appeal, 12 Atl. 743 (Pa.) ; Brinkerhoff-Farris Trust & Sav. Co. v. Home Lumber Co. 118 Mo. 447, 24 S. W. 129; Moffitt v. Hereford, 132 Mo. 513, 34 S. W. 252. In the case at bar it was shown that after the corporation had been in operation a little over a year its original capital of $10,000 had dwindled to $6,846.69 in book assets. This is adequate reason for saying that the par value was not presumptively the actual value of the stock. In Uncle Sam Oil Co. v. Forrester, 79 Kan. 611, 100 Pac. 512, it was held that, where in an action for conversion the complaint alleged the value to be less than par, the introduction of the share certificate of stock showing its par value, was not sufficient evidence to permit a recovery for the damages alleged. The rule given by the court that the jury was "to ascertain and determine from the evidence what a person who wanted to buy stock in this corporation would reasonably expect to pay for this block of 220 shares," may not have furnished a great deal of assistance. But in view of the evidence we are not prepared to say it was misleading. When stock in a corporation has not figured in the markets, and there have been no sales or dealings therein, its actual value must be determined at the fair price which a person who desires to buy would be willing to pay, taking into consideration the original capital, how far there has been profit or loss in the business carried on, the assets and liabilities, the future prospects, and everything that goes to affect the value of the shares of stock.

It is also claimed that the verdict is perverse, or demonstrably wrong. The record is very meager as to the nature of the business undertaken by this corporation. It would seem however that three or four men formed the corporation presumably to examine, audit or open books of account. They agreed upon the salary each was to draw. Some real estate was held, but whether this was in part payment for stock or a side issue in the business does not appear; also furniture and fittings were acquired; and some loans made or credits given. There is no evidence as to the actual value of these items, save the value as carried on the corporation books on March 31, 1911, at which time there was cash on hand or in bank of $5,327.57. The books also show that during less than a year while plaintiff was connected with defendant, there was an impairment of the capital of more than $2,000 and, as stated above, five months later an impairment of more than $3,000. No dividend was ever declared, but the salaries of the officers were speedily depleting the capital. We have looked in vain for any earnings from the business carried on. Under these circumstances we are not prepared to hold that the verdict of the jury, fixing the value of the 220 shares of stock converted at $71 less than the price plaintiff agreed to pay for the 100 shares, is not fairly supported by the evidence.

Order affirmed.

MAX R. CLUSS v. MINNIE HACKETT.[1]

November 27, 1914.

Nos. 18,871—(109).

Adverse possession — evidence.

  Evidence examined and *held* not to establish title to real property by adverse possession.

Action of ejectment in the district court for Houston county. The answer set up title by adverse possession of one of the village lots described in the complaint and disclaimed title or possession to the other lot. The case was tried before Kingsley, J., who denied plaintiff's and defendant's motions for directed verdicts, and a jury which returned a verdict in favor of defendant. Plaintiff's motion for judgment notwithstanding the verdict was granted. From the judgment entered pursuant to the order for judgment, defendant appealed. Affirmed.

John F. Doherty, for appellant.

Duxbury & Duxbury, for respondent.

BROWN, C. J.

Action in ejectment in which defendant set up title to the property by adverse possession. Defendant had a verdict in the court below, but upon motion the court directed the entry of judgment for plaintiff notwithstanding the verdict. Judgment was so entered and defendant appealed.

The only question presented is whether the evidence reasonably tends to support the defendant's claim of title by adverse possession. Our examination of the record leads to the conclusion that it does not. Defendant has been in the actual possession and occupancy of the premises for 13 years. To make up the necessary 15 years she attempted to show that her predecessor in the occupancy of the prop-

[1] Reported in 149 N. W. 647.

erty had remained in the actual, open and hostile possession thereof, under claim of title, for several years immediately preceding the date on which defendant took possession. Defendant or her husband paid $50 to the prior possessor for his rights. Defendant has the right to tack on this prior possession to complete the necessary fifteen years, but the evidence wholly fails to show that the prior possessor, if anything more than a naked trespasser, was holding the property under any color or claim of title. He entered into possession without permission of the owner, and under no claim of right as against such owner. During the time of his possession he entered into negotiations with the holder of the record title for the purchase of the property, at least for a quitclaim deed of the same, and agreed to pay therefor the sum of $50. He paid $10 down, but made no further payments, though the quitclaim deed was tendered to him. This contract, though verbal, negatives any inference of an adverse claim. Olson v. Burk, 94 Minn. 456, 103 N. W. 335; Johnson v. Peterson, 90 Minn. 503, 97 N. W. 384. He also contemplated at one time during his possession acquiring a tax title to the property, but the delinquent taxes at that time amounted to about $200, and he dropped the matter. Neither he nor defendant ever paid any taxes upon the property, and the prior possessor testified on the trial that he never made any claim to the ownership of the property. While an affirmative claim of ownership is not necessary in such cases, where the acts and conduct of the person in possession clearly and unequivocally indicate such claim in fact, the evidence in this case wholly fails to show acts or conduct of that nature. From the evidence the court below was fully justified in concluding that the prior possessor entered upon the property as a trespasser, under no claim of title or right as against the true owner, and that he remained in that status until he vacated the same. The case comes within several of our later decisions. Mitchell v. Green, 125 Minn. 24, 145 N. W. 404; Mattson v. Warner, 115 Minn. 520, 132 N. W. 1127, and the cases therein cited.

Judgment affirmed.

JACK HARRIS v. HOBART IRON COMPANY.[1]

November 27, 1914.

Nos. 18,887—(99).

Workmen's Compensation Act — election not to accept — when effective.
Construing the Workmen's Compensation Act (Laws 1913, c. 467), approved April 24, 1913, effective from October 1, 1913, it is *held* that an employee accepts the provisions of the act until he makes an election not to accept; that under the proviso contained in section 12 of said chapter his election, made within 30 days after October 1, is effective at once, notwithstanding the clauses of sections 11 and 12 relative to a 30 days' notice; and that an employee injured on October 15, 1913, perfecting his election not to be bound by the act on October 29, 1913, is, until that date, bound by the act and cannot maintain a common law action for his injury.

Action in the district court for St. Louis county to recover $25,350 for personal injury received while in the employ of defendant. From an order, Hughes, J., sustaining defendant's demurrer to the complaint, plaintiff appealed. Affirmed.

D. D. Morgan and *James J. Giblin,* for appellant.

Washburn, Bailey & Mitchell, for respondent.

DIBELL, C.

This action was brought by the plaintiff to recover damages for personal injuries sustained on October 15, 1913, while in the employ of the defendant. The plaintiff appeals from an order sustaining the defendant's demurrer to his complaint.

The sole question is whether the plaintiff at the time of his injury was subject to the provisions of the so-called Workmen's Compensation Act (Laws 1913, p. 675, c. 467).[2] If he was the demurrer was rightly sustained. If he was not it was wrongly sustained.

It is an essential feature of the act that every employer and employee coming within its terms is bound by it unless he makes an

---

[1] Reported in 149 N. W. 662. [2] [G. S. 1913, §§ 8195–8230.]

election not to accept it. No provision is anywhere in the act for an acceptance. There is always an acceptance, unless there be an election not to accept. See Mathison v. Minneapolis Street Ry. Co. 126 Minn. 286, 148 N. W. 71, where the the constitutionality of the act was under consideration.

The act was approved April 24, 1913, to be in effect on October 1, 1913. Section 11 of the act provides, among other things, that every employer and employee is presumed to have accepted the act unless 30 days prior to the accident he elects not to accept its provisions and signifies his election by giving a notice in a manner specifically prescribed. Section 12 provides that either party may terminate his acceptance, or his election not to accept, by 30 days' written notice to the other given in a manner specified. It contains this proviso:

"Provided, however, that during the thirty (30) days immediately succeeding the taking effect of this act, notice of election not to accept the provisions of Part 2 may be given by either party to the other as above provided, and shall be immediately effective as a notice of election, upon filing duplicate thereof with the labor commissioner."

This proviso furnishes the key to the situation presented. Its evident purpose is to permit either party to give notice of his election not to accept within 30 days after the taking effect of the act, and to make the same immediately effective, so as to obviate what might otherwise be the effect of the statutory requirement of a 30 days' notice.

After the plaintiff served and filed his election not to accept, that is, on October 29, 1913, he was not subject to the provisions of the compensation act. Prior to that time he was. He was injured while subject to the act.

The construction of the statute presents no difficulty and justifies no further discussion.

Order affirmed.

LAURA B. CHASE v. TINGDALE BROTHERS.[1]

November 27, 1914.

Nos. 18,976—(200).

Automobile — proof of negligence — charge to jury.

In this action to recover damages to plaintiff's automobile sustained in a collision with the automobile of defendant it is *held:*

(1) G. S. 1913, § 2634, providing that all motor vehicles must be kept to the right of the center of the street, has no application under the facts in this case and the burden of proof to show that defendant was negligent was upon plaintiff.

(2) An inadvertently inaccurate instruction was not reversible error, the inaccuracy not being seasonably called to the attention of the trial court.

(3) There was no prejudicial error in an instruction on the subject of damages or in a ruling on the admission of evidence relating to damages.

(4) The evidence made a case for the jury and supports the verdict.

Action in the district court for Hennepin county to recover $300 for injury to plaintiff's electric automobile, caused by the negligence of defendant and its servants. The case was tried before Montgomery, J., and a jury which returned a verdict in favor of defendant. From an order denying her motion for a new trial, plaintiff appealed. Affirmed.

Jay W. Crane, for appellant.

Keith, Evans, Thompson & Fairchild, for respondent.

BUNN, J.

Plaintiff was driving her electric automobile south on Park avenue, Minneapolis, at about 6:30 p. m. on October 28, 1913. She was on the right hand side of the street about three feet from the curb and was driving in a lawful and careful manner, when her car was struck by an automobile belonging to defendant and driven by its chauffeur. This action was to recover the damages sustained to plaintiff's car by the collision. The case was submitted

---

[1] Reported in 149 N. W. 654.

127 M.—26.

to the jury and a verdict for defendant was the result. Plaintiff appeals from an order refusing a new trial.

Plaintiff claims prejudicial errors in the charge, and error in denying her motion for an instructed verdict in her favor. These claims are largely based upon the premises that plaintiff was driving on the right side of the street, and that defendant's car was on the wrong side of the street when the collision occurred. This is true only in a technical sense. The facts which the jury was justified in finding are these: Defendant's car was being driven north along the right hand side of Park avenue about six feet from the curb, at a speed of from 10 to 15 miles per hour, when an electric car backed out of an alley or driveway in front; there were no lights on this car and no warning had been given of its approach; defendant's chauffeur saw the electric car suddenly loom up ahead, applied his brakes and attempted to make a quick turn to the left to get around the rear of the electric; the pavement was wet and slippery because of the weather, the rear wheels of defendant's car skidded to the right, striking the right rear-wheel of the electric; at substantially the same moment the front of defendant's car collided with plaintiff's automobile, causing the damage complained of.

Plaintiff's claims here are centered upon the proposition that the burden of proof was upon the defendant. This is contended on the ground that there was a violation of G. S. 1913, § 2634, providing that "all vehicles * * * must keep to the right of the center of the street," and of section 2635, limiting the rate of speed of motor vehicles to 15 miles an hour on public highways that pass through the residence portion of a city. As to the matter of speed, the evidence did not show it was in excess of 15 miles an hour. As to defendant's car not keeping to the right of the center of the street, plainly the statute has no application where a motor vehicle, through no fault of its driver, skids on a slippery pavement and is thus thrown across the center line. No violation of the statute was conclusively shown, and therefore the burden of proof to show the absence of negligence was not with defendant. The case of

Molin v. Wark, 113 Minn. 190, 129 N. W. 383, 41 L.R.A.(N.S.) 346, relied on by plaintiff, is not in point.

Plaintiff criticizes an instruction of the trial court to the effect that, if the jury found that defendant violated the statute, and that plaintiff's damages resulted proximately from such violation, a *"prima facie"* case of negligence was made. The use of the words *"prima facie"* was obviously an inadvertence which would have been corrected had it been seasonably called to the attention of the court. The inaccuracy cannot avail plaintiff now. Steinbauer v. Stone, 85 Minn. 274, 88 N. W. 754.

There is a claim of error in an instruction on the measure of damages, and in permitting a witness to testify as to the cost of repairs to the damaged car. As the jury never reached the question of damages, it is plain that there is nothing to decide here.

Plaintiff asked an instruction that she was entitled to a verdict on the evidence of defendant's driver. Insofar as the claim that the refusal of this instruction was error, is based upon the speed of the car, or upon its being to the left of the center of the street when the collision occurred, it is sufficient to say, as we have already practically said in discussing the statute, that the evidence does not conclusively show negligence on the part of the driver. Taking all the circumstances surrounding the accident, including the emergency that confronted the driver, and his conduct in this emergency, we are satisfied that the case was one for the jury, and that the verdict absolving the driver from blame is fairly supported by the evidence.

Order affirmed.

MARY HAYES v. MINNIE MOORE.[1]

November 27, 1914.

Nos. 19,048—(81).

Landlord and tenant — action for use and occupation.

1. An action in the nature of assumpsit for the use and occupation of real property lies only where the relation of landlord and tenant subsists between the parties, founded on an agreement express or implied.

Same — evidence.

2. Evidence examined and *held* to show neither an express nor implied agreement creating the relation of landlord and tenant between plaintiff and defendant.

Action in the municipal court of Mankato to recover the reasonable value of the use of plaintiff's building from October, 1913, to November, 1914. The case was tried before Comstock, J., who denied the motion of defendant Moore to dismiss the action and a jury which returned a verdict for $87.50. From an order denying defendant Moore's motion for judgment notwithstanding the verdict or for a new trial, she appealed. Reversed and judgment for defendant ordered.

Ivan Bowen, for appellant.
John E. Regan, for respondent.

BUNN, J.

This appeal is by the defendant Minnie Moore from an order denying her motion in the alternative for judgment notwithstanding the verdict or for a new trial, after a trial to a jury and a verdict for plaintiff. The action was against Fong Moon and Minnie Moore to recover the reasonable value of the use and occupancy by them of a building owned by plaintiff. The original complaint alleged

[1] Reported in 149 N. W. 659.

Note.—The question as to when an action for use and occupation of premises will lie is treated in a note in 26 L.R.A. 802.

that on September 7, 1912, Fong Moon leased the premises, to be used as a laundry, at the agreed rental of $25 per month, that on October 1, 1913, defendant Moore purchased the laundry machinery and equipment from Fong Moon, took possession thereof, and that said machinery and equipment "has been ever since said date, and still is, in the building owned by this plaintiff." This complaint was subsequently amended so as to allege that Minnie Moore took possession of the premises October 1, 1913, and remained in possession thereof and "kept and used said building," until February 15, 1914. Fong Moon did not answer. Defendant Moore admitted in her answer her purchase of the machinery and equipment from Fong Moon, but alleged that prior to November 1, 1913, she demanded of plaintiff the possession of such machinery and equipment and offered to remove the same from the building, but that plaintiff at all times refused to permit her to do so.

The case was tried to a jury. The court denied a motion to dismiss made on the ground that the complaint did not state a cause of action, a like motion made at the close of plaintiff's case, and motions to dismiss and to direct a verdict made at the close of all the evidence. These rulings are assigned as error.

We will pass the question of the sufficiency of the complaint as amended, and consider whether the evidence shows any liability on the part of defendant Moore. Plaintiff's agent was the only witness on her behalf; he testified to the leasing of the premises to Fong Moon in September, 1912, for a Chinese laundry; that the laundry "moved out" October 1, leaving the machinery in the building; that about December 1, witness met defendant's husband who told him he owned the outfit in the laundry and wanted to look at it; witness told Moore that somebody would have to pay the rent, and that he would hold the machinery until the rent was paid; Moore wanted to remove the machinery, but witness refused to allow him to do so until the rent was paid; witness told Moore that he would have to pay rent, but Moore did not agree to do so. February 15 the premises were leased to a third person who had before that time purchased the machinery. The other testimony showed clearly that plaintiff had insisted on holding the machinery in the building.

until somebody paid the rent, and that defendant Moore had never used the premises except in the sense that her machinery and equipment had remained there against her wishes and because plaintiff refused to allow it to be removed.

Under these facts it is quite clear to us that defendant Moore is not liable for rent or for the use and occupation of the premises. It is elementary that an action in the nature of assumpsit for use and occupation will not lie unless the relation of landlord and tenant subsists between the parties, founded on agreement, express or implied. Hurley v. Lamoreaux, 29 Minn. 138, 12 N. W. 447; Crosby v. Horne & Danz Co. 45 Minn. 249, 47 N. W. 717; Hackney v. Fetsch, 123 Minn. 447, 143 N. W. 1128. No such relation existed in this case; admittedly there was no express agreement constituting the relation of landlord and tenant as between plaintiff and defendant Moore, and no implied agreement to that effect can possibly be spelled out of the evidence.

Order reversed and judgment for defendant ordered.

FRANK V. KRIHA v. CHARLES G. KARTAK and Others.[1]

November 27, 1914.

Nos. 19,077—(92).

Service of summons — finding — evidence.

1. A finding of the trial court that there was no fraud in obtaining service of the summons in a divorce action *held* sustained by the evidence.

Divorce — action to set aside decree — agreement of separation.

2. Conceding without deciding that an agreement of separation between the parties, entered into after the desertion charged in the complaint, would be material evidence on that issue, the failure to disclose on the trial the existence of such agreement, though intentional, is not fraud or perjury for which the judgment can be set aside under the statute.

[1] Reported in 149 N. W. 666.

Action in the district court for Ramsey county against the administrator of the estate of Elizabeth M. Kartak, deceased, and the heirs at law of the decedent, to set aside a decree of divorce, to declare plaintiff to be the lawful surviving spouse of decedent, and that he be allowed to share in her estate. The case was tried before Dickson, J., who made findings and ordered judgment in favor of defendants. From an order denying his motion for a new trial, plaintiff appealed. Affirmed.

Willis & Cahill, for appellant.

Allen & Straight, for respondents.

BUNN, J.

This is an action to set aside, as obtained by fraud, a judgment of divorce. The decision was in favor of defendant, and plaintiff appeals from an order denying a new trial.

The contention of plaintiff is that the finding of the trial court that there was no fraud in obtaining the judgment is not sustained by the evidence.

The evidentiary facts upon which this finding was made are as follows:

Plaintiff and Elizabeth M. Kartak were married in St. Paul December 30, 1909; in September, 1910, they went to Grand Forks, North Dakota, and began keeping house and living together in that city as husband and wife. Early in November of the same year plaintiff left his wife and went to a hotel in the city to live. Some three weeks later he returned to her, and they lived together until Christmas day, 1910, when plaintiff again left. The court finds that this was wilful desertion by plaintiff. January 27, 1911, plaintiff caused to be prepared by a lawyer in Grand Forks a written agreement of separation, which was on the next day signed by plaintiff and his wife. This agreement provided, in addition to the main features of separation, absolving each other from all claims by reason of the marriage relation, releasing the husband from all obligation to support his wife, and arranging property matters, that plaintiff would pay the railway fare of his wife from Grand Forks to St. Paul, and the expenses of removing her personal effects to

that city.   Plaintiff paid his wife $100 to cover these expenses, and
she shortly thereafter moved to St. Paul, where she lived separate
and apart from her husband until her death, never demanding and
never receiving from him any support or maintenance.   Kriha remained in Grand Forks, being employed there in a candy factory.
In October, 1912, Mrs. Kriha employed attorneys of St. Paul to
bring an action for divorce against her husband on the ground of
desertion; they prepared and signed a summons and complaint, and
between October 1 and December 12 made efforts to locate Kriha
and obtain personal service upon him.   He was supposed to be still
in Grand Forks, and the papers were sent to the sheriff there for
service; they were returned with the information that Kriha had
left Grand Forks and was in Aberdeen.   The summons and complaint were then sent to Aberdeen for service, but were returned
by the sheriff there with the information that Kriha had gone to
Fargo.   Inquiry of the sheriff at Fargo elicited the information that
Kriha was in Wahpeton.   The sheriff at Wahpeton reported that
he was unable to find Kriha.   In fact Kriha's movements had been
exactly as reported, except that he had left each place shortly before
the papers were received there.   Kriha left Wahpeton for Winnipeg
on November 2, but his wife or her attorneys did not ascertain this
fact until later; they then tried to locate Kriha in Winnipeg, but
he had disappeared.   These efforts to personally serve the summons and complaint proving fruitless, the attorneys prepared to
serve the summons by publication.   It was necessary to prepare a
new summons (complaint filed), and at the same time the old
complaint was added to so as to ask leave for plaintiff in the action
to resume her maiden name.   The complaint was filed December
12, 1912, and an application made to a judge of the district court for
an order of publication.   This application was based upon an affidavit of plaintiff setting forth in detail the efforts of herself and
her attorneys to locate Kriha and serve him personally.   The order
was made and the summons published.   Defendant made no appearance, and the case was heard in May, 1913.   Mrs. Kriha and her
witnesses testified to the desertion, but she did not disclose to the
court the separation agreement.   The divorce was granted, and

the judgment entered on May 17, 1913. Mrs. Kriha, or Elizabeth Kartak, using her maiden name, died May 26, 1913. Immediately afterwards Kriha appears and retains counsel to "look after [his] interests." This action followed.

It is claimed that there was fraud in not making further efforts to serve Kriha personally, and in concealing from the court the existence of the separation agreement. The first claim relates to the matter of invoking the jurisdiction of the court, the other to the merits of the cause of action.

1. The importance of personal service in divorce actions is recognized by the statute, by this court, and uniformly, we think, by the trial courts. We do not doubt that where substituted service instead of personal is made through fraud of the plaintiff, with intent to keep the institution of the action a secret from defendant, a judgment procured by such fraud will be set aside in a suit brought for that purpose, even after the death of the plaintiff, unless there is some element of estoppel. But we see no fraud in this case. The learned counsel for plaintiff calls the divorce suit in question a "blot upon the judicial records of Ramsey county" "founded in fiction and perversity, maintained in fraud, and consummated by deceit." This is strong language, but we think it is wholly unwarranted by the facts. It is based upon the facts that Kriha returned from Winnipeg to Grand Forks November 17, 1912, and remained a resident of that city until March, 1913, and that Mrs. Kriha and her attorneys, after their unavailing efforts to find Kriha, did not, when the new summons was prepared, renew their efforts. We are unable to agree to the claim that what was done to locate Kriha before the summons was changed is "utterly immaterial." That those efforts show the utmost good faith and diligence in endeavoring to obtain personal service is very clear. Are plaintiff and her attorneys to be charged with fraud, with a studied attempt to conceal from the defendant the fact that the suit was brought, just because they did not cover again the same ground they had shortly before gone over, or start new inquiries? We think not. It is plain that they did not know that Kriha had returned to Grand Forks, or where he was. Their prior efforts justified them in the belief that further effort would be

futile. They might, it is true, have written again to Grand Forks, or inquired of relatives and friends of defendant in St. Paul. But their information was that Kriha had left Grand Forks permanently, and had disappeared. They had no reason to suppose that further inquiry would disclose any new information. The trial court has found that there was no fraud in obtaining the order for publication or in acquiring jurisdiction over Kriha. We hold that this finding is amply supported by the evidence.

2. As to the claim of fraud in not disclosing to the court in the trial of the divorce action the existence of the separation agreement, in the first place it is questionable as a matter of law, whether this agreement was a defense to the charge of desertion. The desertion had occurred a month or more before. Whether the agreement should be considered as merely an arrangement of the property rights of the parties, not affecting the question of desertion, is perhaps a doubtful question. It might depend upon the facts surrounding its execution. Weld v. Weld, 27 Minn. 330, 7 N. W. 267; 14 Cyc. 636; Ogilvie v. Ogilvie, 37 Ore. 171, 61 Pac. 627; Walker v. Walker, 14 Cal. App. 487, 112 Pac. 479; Nichols v. Nichols, 11 S. W. 286, 10 Ky. Law Rep. 930. In this state of the law, we can hardly impute fraud to the plaintiff or her attorneys in determining that the agreement was not material. In addition it appears that Mrs. Kriha was unable on account of illness to be in court when the case was tried, her testimony being given by deposition taken at the hospital. Her attorneys had seen the agreement some time before in another connection, but did not have possession of it or have it in mind at the time of the trial.

But though it is conceded that the failure to disclose to the court the agreement of separation was intentional, this is not fraud or perjury which is ground for setting aside the decree. The complaint advised the defendant that his wife charged and would attempt to prove desertion. It is immaterial that he did not answer, or that in fact he did not know of the suit. The concealment of the separation agreement, if it was material evidence, and intentional, was at least no worse than would be the giving of false testimony as to the fact of desertion. This would not be ground for setting aside the decree. When the issues are clearly defined in the pleadings and no fraud is practised which misleads a party as to the character of the proofs intended to be offered, or tends to induce the party to refrain from defending, fraud or perjury in establishing the issue pleaded is not ground for setting aside the judgment under R. S. 1905, § 4277 (G. S. 1913, § 7910). There must be fraud in invoking the jurisdiction of the court, or in preventing the party from defending the action, or inducing him not to do so. McElrath v. McElrath, 120 Minn. 380, 139 N. W. 708, 44 L.R.A.(N.S.) 505, and cases there cited. National Council of Knights and Ladies of Security v. Ruder, 126 Minn. 154, 147 N. W. 959.

We find it unnecessary to discuss or decide whether plaintiff would be estopped to question the decree. We hold that it is valid.

Order affirmed.

BERNARD SILBERSTEIN v. WILLIAM I. PRINCE.[1]

November 27, 1914.

Nos. 19,104—(291).

Election — validity of ballot.

Failure to vote for the requisite number of commissioners as required by the Duluth charter establishing a commission form of government, does not vitiate a ballot to such extent that it cannot be counted in canvassing the votes for mayor.

From a decision of the common council of the city of Duluth, acting as a canvassing board after the general municipal election in that city for the election of a mayor and commissioners thereof

[1] Reported in 149 N. W. 653.

held on April 1, 1913, determining that William I. Prince had received 3,132 votes for mayor at that election and was duly elected mayor of that city, Bernard Silberstein, candidate for the office of mayor at that election, appealed to the district court for St. Louis county. The appeal was heard before Cant, J., who made findings and ordered judgment in favor of the contestee Prince. From the judgment entered pursuant to the order for judgment, contestant appealed. Affirmed.

John B. Richards, for appellant.

O. J. Larson and *Neil E. Beaton,* for respondent.

PHILIP E. BROWN, J.

The parties were rival candidates for the office of mayor of Duluth, at the first election, held April 1, 1913, under the new charter establishing a commission form of government. Contestee was declared elected, whereupon contestant commenced this contest, which, after trial to the court, resulted in findings and judgment confirming contestee's title. Contestant appealed.

The court found that contestee received 3,148 votes, and contestant 3,139; these totals being reached by including 109 votes cast on ballots which failed to designate the requisite number of commissioners, of which 66 were counted for contestee and 43 for contestant. It follows that if these 109 votes be excluded contestant would have a majority of 14, and this he urges should be done; founding his claim on the contention that under the charter the ballots containing them are either totally void or at least not proper to be considered in canvassing the votes for mayor. The relevant charter provisions relied on, with special stress upon the words we have italicized, are as follows:

"Section 41. The clerk shall cause ballots for each general and special election to be prepared, printed and authenticated. The ballots shall contain a complete list of the offices to be filled and the names of the candidates nominated therefor. When the number of candidates is more than three times the number of offices to be filled, the form of ballot shall be substantially as follows:

GENERAL (OR SPECIAL) MUNICIPAL ELECTION.
CITY OF DULUTH (INSERTING DATE THEREOF).
INSTRUCTIONS.

To vote for any person, mark a cross (X) in a square to the right of the name.

Vote your first choice in the first column.

Vote your second choice in second column.

Vote only one first choice and only one second choice for any one office.

Vote in the third column for all the other candidates whom you wish to support.

Do not vote for more than one choice for one person, as only one choice will count for any candidate.

Any distinguishing mark makes the ballot void.

If you wrongly mark, tear or deface this ballot, return it and obtain another from the election officers.

For Mayor Vote for one first choice	First Choice.	Second Choice.	Additional Choices.
....	....	....	....
....	....	....	....
For Commissioners *Vote for first choices or* *ballot will be void.*			
....	....	....	....
....	....	....	....
For other officers			
....	....	....	....
....	....	....	....

(Charter amendments, ordinances or other referendum matters to be voted upon to appear here.)

* * * * * * * * * * *

No votes shall be counted on the election of commissioners unless the votes mark as many first choices as there are commissioners to be elected, and instructions to that effect shall be printed in an appropriate place on the ballot.

Section 42.   All official ballots used at any election shall be identical in form.   Space shall be provided on the ballot for charter amendments or other matters to be voted upon at municipal elections. * * *

Section 43.   The clerk, at least, ten (10) days before the election shall cause to be printed not less than two thousand (2,000) sample ballots, upon paper of different color but otherwise identical, except numbering, with the ballot to be used at the election, and shall distribute the same to registered voters at his office.   Sample ballots shall be posted at the polls on election day.

Section 44.   Canvass of Returns and Determination of Results of Elections: * * *

(b) If a ballot contain more than one vote for the same candidate, only the one of such votes highest in rank shall be counted. *All ballots shall be void which do not contain first choice votes for as many candidates for commissioners as there are commissioners to be elected.*   If a ballot contain either first or second choice, votes in excess of the number of offices to be filled, no vote in the column showing such excess shall be counted.

(c) The foregoing portion of this section shall be printed conspicuously on the tally sheets furnished by the clerk to the election officers."

Contestant argues that the prime purpose of the charter was to compel, in the interest of good government, the electorate to vote for the requisite number of commissioners as the fittest possible governing body, wherefore, by way of penalty for a voter's noncompliance with its directions in this regard, the counting of his ballot cast for mayor is prohibited; the language of the charter being claimed to be so unequivocal as to admit of no other interpretation, or, in any event, properly susceptible of no other construction without defeating the cardinal object indicated.

This court, in Farrell v. Hicken, 125 Minn. 407, 147 N. W. 815, recently sustained and gave effect to the provisions quoted so far as concerns the counting of votes for commissioners; and, assuming without deciding that no constitutional objections stand in the way of so holding, we will confine ourselves to consideration of the question whether the ruling there made can or, as in effect demanded by contestant, should be extended to votes for mayor, notwithstanding the entailed disfranchisement of many electors as to the head of the ticket. Certainly no court would declare such a drastic result unless imperatively constrained so to do. Our Constitution vests in electors the right to vote for all officers elective by the people, and no one should be deprived thereof upon doubtful construction of election laws. Bloedel v. Cromwell, 104 Minn. 487, 116 N. W. 947. Indeed, it is a rule of universal application that all statutes tending to limit the citizen in the exercise of his right of suffrage must be construed liberally in his favor. 15 Cyc. 281. Hence a literal and isolated reading of the vitiating words, upon which alone, if at all, contestant's position is tenable, cannot be adopted unless there is no other recourse; and that they were not intended so to be taken seems clear upon several considerations: First, the reason for their appearance on the ballot is found in the last paragraph of section 41, quoted and italicized above, which significantly refers only to the counting of ballots "on the election of commissioners," and which likewise furnishes a most persuasive suggestion as to the proper interpretation of the language of section 44, subdivision (b); second, if the radical and far-reaching departure from established usage demanded by contestant were intended, why did not the framers of the charter incorporate such intention as one of the leading features in the instruction to be printed at the head of the ballot provided for by section 41, instead of leaving the voter to be first so apprised by the notation in the form of ballot under the head "For Commissioners?" Finally, reading all sections *in pari materia* together, what would be the effect of contestant's contention upon votes for amendments, ordi-

nances, referendum matters and judicial candidates, all of which
may be presented to the voters by the same ballots used in election
of commissioners, and the last of which were actually included on
the ballots under consideration? Manifestly they would have to
be rejected, with the resultant wholesale disfranchisement of voters,
merely because they failed, even innocently, to comply with the
directions as to voting for commissioners. We are satisfied that
no such result was intended. Nor have we overlooked the claim
that the mayor is practically "a fifth commissioner;" but giving
due weight thereto we are unable to reach the conclusion that the
ballots in controversy should not have been counted.

Judgment affirmed.

ROBERT SEEGER v. MARGARET YOUNG and Others.[1]

December 4, 1914.

Nos. 18,777—(30).

Pendency of prior action — findings.

　　1. Evidence in an action to determine adverse claims to real property,
wherein defendant pleaded in abatement the pendency of a prior proceeding
by her to register her title, in which plaintiff in the action was made a
defendant and answered claiming title, considered and *held* to sustain findings
that the prior proceeding was instituted and still pending.

Same.

　　2. The action and the proceeding were within the rule of abatement for
another suit pending.

Same.

　　3. The trial court did not err in applying the rule and abating the action.

Action in the district court for Ramsey county to determine adverse claims. The case was tried before Kelly, J., who made findings and ordered that the action be dismissed because of the pendency

---

1 Reported in 149 N. W. 735.

of a former action. From the judgment of dismissal, entered pursuant to the order, plaintiff appealed. Affirmed.

William G. White, for appellant.

William W. Fry, for respondent.

PHILIP E. BROWN, J.

Action to determine adverse claims to four lots in St. Paul. Defendant Young answered, setting up the pendency of a former action for the same cause, and alleging ownership in herself. The trial court sustained the defense of former action pending, and dismissed the case. Plaintiff moved for findings on the merits. The motion was denied, and judgment of dismissal entered. Plaintiff appealed.

Plaintiff contends: (1) That there was no evidence to sustain the finding that the former action, which was a proceeding by Young to register her title under the Torrens Act, was ever instituted; (2) that the evidence did not show that the proceeding was still pending; (3) that the pendency of a registration proceeding does not in any event operate to abate a subsequent action by a party thereto to determine adverse claims.

The facts necessary to an understanding of the points involved are as follows: The present action was commenced July 12, 1913. On the trial plaintiff introduced evidence making a *prima facie* case of title in himself. Defendant offered no evidence tending to show any title, but did offer in evidence "No. 1122 of the registration files of this (district) court, being the application of Margaret Young to register the title to the lots in question." There was an objection on the ground that the offered evidence did not show another action pending between the same parties. Upon an examination of the files offered it appeared that the application was filed October 25, 1910, that the proceeding was referred to the examiner of titles, who reported that the title of the applicant was proper for registration and recommended that Robert Seeger, plaintiff herein, and certain others be made parties. A petition for summons and an order directing the issuance of the same, dated November 29, 1910, appeared in the files, all in due form. There also appeared an answer of Robert Seeger filed May 12, 1913, in

127 M.—27.

which he alleged that he was the owner in fee of the lots and prayed judgment to that effect. No summons was found among the papers in the file offered. Objection was made on this ground, but the record was received as a whole. The case was taken under advisement by the court; and a day or two thereafter defendant's counsel handed the trial judge the summons in the registration proceeding, which was regular in form and appeared to have been issued November 29, 1910, received by the sheriff for service April 15, 1913, and filed with the clerk April 23, 1913. The trial court found as facts that the summons was so issued and received by the sheriff for service, and that it was served on one of the parties named as defendant, and as to the others, including Seeger, that the sheriff certified and returned that he was unable to find said defendants in his county. The court found further that the registration proceeding was pending and undetermined.

1. Plaintiff's first claim, that the evidence does not show that the registration proceeding was ever instituted, cannot be sustained. The reception by the court of the land title summons after the case had been submitted was irregular and not to be commended, but this irregularity does not, under the circumstances, call for a reversal, though the issuance and service of the summons constituted the only evidence of the commencement of the proceeding. Robert Seeger, plaintiff in this action, answered in the Torrens proceeding. He appeared generally and the jurisdiction of the court over him was complete. He joined issue with the applicant on the question of title, and asked the court to determine the issue in his favor. The proceeding was clearly pending at that time.

2. We are unable to hold that the finding that the proceeding was still pending and undetermined is not sustained by the evidence. No judgment appeared in the files, nor any order of dismissal or other evidence that the proceeding had been determined or dismissed. It was clearly pending when Seeger's answer was filed in May, 1913, and in the absence of evidence to the contrary it should be considered as still pending a few months later. See G. S. 1913, § 7707. An action is commenced in this state as to each defendant when a summons is served upon him, or when he appears without service, and

is deemed pending until its final determination. Smith v. Hurd, 50 Minn. 503, 52 N. W. 922, 36 Am. St. 661; H. L. Spencer Co. v. Koell, 91 Minn. 226, 97 N. W. 974. Plaintiff relies on Phelps v. Winona & St. Peter R. Co. 37 Minn. 485, 35 N. W. 273, 5 Am. St. 867, to sustain his contention that the finding that the proceeding was still pending has no evidence to support it. In that case the former action had been dismissed by the plaintiff, and while Mr. Justice Mitchell does say that proof that the action had been commenced was insufficient to prove it was still pending, the statement was in no way necessary to the decision and is not in harmony with the statute and other decisions referred to. It is true that the effective part of a plea of former action pending is that the action is still pending, and this must be proved; but we know of no rule which makes direct evidence of the fact necessary. Nor do we see why the presumption arising as to the continuation of a state of things shown once to have existed is not to have some weight under circumstances of this kind.

3. This brings us to the question whether a party defendant to a Torrens proceeding, who has set up title in himself, may, during the pendency of that proceeding, maintain an action to determine the adverse claim of the applicant and to have his own title adjudicated, without the action being subject to abatement because of the pendency of the registration proceeding.

In Merriam v. Baker, 9 Minn. 28, 31 (40), this court expounded the principle underlying the rule of abatement for another suit pending as follows:

"The great end to be subserved by the rule which recognizes the plea of another action pending between the same parties, for the same cause of action, as a good defense, is to prevent a party from being harrassed by a multiplicity of suits for the same cause of action, and that he may not be compelled to maintain the issues on his part in any action so long as they are in possession of another tribunal competent to determine such issues, where they may be disposed of. We believe the true test in such cases (where there is no question as to the identity of the issues involved) is the existence of such an action in any court or tribunal having jurisdiction of the subject-matter of the controversy; and that the plea is maintained if such court or other tribunal have authority to entertain such a cause of action."

In full accord with the above the rule itself was declared in Disbrow Mnfg. Co. v. Creamery Package Mnfg. Co. 115 Minn. 434, 132 N. W. 913:

"But the ultimate inquiry," said the present Chief Justice, at page 437, after alluding to lack of harmony in the authorities, "seems to be whether a judgment in the first, if one be rendered, would be conclusive upon the parties, in respect to the matters involved in the second action. If so, a plea in abatement should be sustained."

And again, at page 438:

"Whether it comes within the language of the rule in such cases as technically expressed in the books, the fact that a recovery in the former suit will finally determine the principal issue in both actions, the present action should be abated. * * * It is not essential that the same specific relief be demanded in each action. It is sufficient that the subject-matter of the actions are the same."

With this authoritative declaration of the rule and the comprehensive statement of its basic principle, we need only to analyze the proceeding and the action here involved in order to determine the point in controversy. The purpose of the Torrens Act is to provide a speedy and summary remedy to settle the title to land (Reed v. Siddall, 94 Minn. 216, 102 N. W. 453; Peters v. City of Duluth, 119 Minn. 96, 106, 137 N. W. 390, 41 L.R.A.[N.S.] 1044); the adverse claims statute has the same object (Dunnell, Minn. Pl. § 898), and, though the former is more comprehensive in some respects, the general rules of procedure apply in both (Owsley v. Johnson, 95 Minn. 168, 103 N. W. 903), and, as between applicant and any defendant who subsequently brings action against him to determine the adverse claim of the former against the latter, the issues are identical. Hence a judgment registering applicant's title, if such should be rendered, would unquestionably "be conclusive upon the parties, in respect to the matters involved in the second action;" and this, regardless of the reversal of the position of the parties in the latter (Disbrow Mnfg. Co. v. Creamery Package Mnfg. Co.

supra); for the court in the registration proceeding not only has
authority' to adjudicate the issues (Hendricks v. Hess, 112 Minn.
252, 255, 127 N. W. 995; Peters v. City of Duluth, supra), but is
required to do so, as in civil actions, before awarding applicant
relief. Owsley v. Johnson, supra. The only doubt, therefore, which
can be suggested as to the applicability of the rule of abatement
as between the proceeding and the action, must inhere in the nature
of the judgment or decree which the court must render where applicant fails to establish title, the court having no power in such case
to decree title in defendant or to order such title registered, but only
to dismiss the application. G. S. 1913, § 6888. In this connection,
however, it must be remembered that the applicability of the rule
under consideration turns upon the effect of a judgment in the first
action, *"if one be rendered,"* without regard to the contingencies
consequent upon a possible dismissal. And from this it follows
that, except upon the hypothesis of a defendant's prevailing upon
an issue of title set up by him, a registration proceeding is not, by
section 6888, or otherwise, differentiated with respect to dismissal
from any ordinary action, in which both the court and plaintiff have
the power to dismiss. G. S. 1913, § 7825. But plaintiff insists
that the rule of abatement does not apply, because though he should
prevail in the registration proceeding he would be dismissed therefrom without relief, whereas in his present action he may have a
decree establishing his title as against defendant therein. Section
6888 reads:

"If the court shall find after hearing that the applicant has not
a title proper for registration, an order shall be entered dismissing
the application which may be made without prejudice. The applicant may upon motion dismiss the application at any time before
the final decree is entered upon such terms as shall be fixed by the
court."

Undoubtedly, under this section, the court may, in a proper case,
dismiss or allow dismissal without prejudice, as in any other action,
and must, furthermore, dismiss where applicant fails to establish
title, whether because a defendant has established title in himself
or otherwise; but what court would, after trial on the merits of a

defendant's claim of title, fail to make findings according to the facts proved? Indeed, failure to make such findings to a defendant's prejudice would be reversible error. Owsley v. Johnson, supra, 170. And these, if in defendant's favor, would estop applicant in any subsequent proceeding between the parties involving the same subject matter (2 Dunnell, Minn. Dig. § 5162), the judgment of dismissal which would be entered thereon being sufficient to satisfy the requirements of the rule, stated in Child v. Morgan, 51 Minn. 116, 121, 52 N. W. 1127, that findings, in order to operate by way of estoppel, must be carried into judgment. In short, where the defendant establishes title the court must so find, and thereupon dismiss, not without prejudice as between applicant and such defendant but absolutely. Hence the defendant in a registration proceeding may have all the relief usually available in an action to determine adverse claims wherein he is plaintiff (see Sache v. Wallace, 101 Minn. 169, 170, 178, 112 N. W. 386, 11 L.R.A.[N.S.] 803, 118 Am. St. 612, 11 Ann. Cas. 349), and all demanded by the complaint in the present action, which is in the usual form. The proceeding and the action here involved, therefore, are squarely within the principle and rule first above stated. Furthermore, the action was subject to abatement under any and all the tests which might be applied; for the same evidence would sustain or defeat the title asserted in both it and the former proceeding, as full and as adequate relief is obtainable in the one as in the other, so far as the present plaintiff is concerned, and the determination of the merits in the former would conclude the parties in the second.

This conclusion, however, does not determine the appeal, for we must still inquire whether the court erred in applying the rule under the particular circumstances of the case. As we have seen, the reason of the rule is prevention of vexatious litigation. 1 R. C. L. p. 10, § 1. Hence the rule itself "is not one of unbending rigor or of universal application, nor is it a principle of absolute law," but is "rather a rule of justice and equity, generally applicable, and always so where the two suits are virtually alike and in the same jurisdiction." 1 Cyc. 22. Moreover, the pendency of the former action being merely matter of abatement and not in bar (Stephens v. Monongahela Nat. Bank, 111 U. S. 197, 4 Sup. Ct. 336, 28 L. ed. 399; Hurst v. Everett [C. C.] 21 Fed. 218), the rule in relation thereto is one of procedure and policy, and in modern practice the court will inquire into the circumstances in order to determine, as a question of fact, whether the second action should be abated as vexatious. Note 84 Am. Dec. 453. But we have already seen that plaintiff's action was not necessary, at least in the absence of special circumstances not here disclosed; and where, as here it appears, the trial court has given the matter of vexatiousness careful attention, its determination should not be disturbed except for cogent reasons. A pertinent inquiry, and one difficult to answer consistently with any theory favorable to plaintiff, is: Why did he bring this second action? The inconvenience, evils and emasculation of the registration act which would result from permitting the proceeding and the action to run along together before the same or separate courts are apparent. If it had appeared that the second action was essential to conserve any right or remedy claimed by plaintiff, as ejectment, or for foreclosure of a mortgage or lien, the reason of the rule thus ceasing, the court would have had power to refuse to apply it or else limit its application according to the necessity, at the same time protecting applicant in the registration proceeding by any proper order of stay or continuance in the action. But no such considerations were presented or invoked. If any such had appeared, as, for further example, the running of the statute of limitations against plaintiff's title, and the trial court had abused its discretion in the premises, its action would have been reviewable by this court. Furthermore, in the example stated, plaintiff would have ample remedy under G. S. 1913, § 7825, to expedite the trial of the issues in the registration proceeding, and, if this were not effective to save his right from the bar of the statute, he would still be protected, insofar as he was prevented by the registration proceeding from asserting it in such manner as to save it, by the rule that where one is prevented from exercising his remedy by some paramount authority the statute of limitations is tolled *pro tanto*.

See St. Paul, M. & M. Ry. Co. v. Olson, 87 Minn. 117, 91 N. W. 294, 94 Am. St. 693; Sage v. Rudnick, 91 Minn. 325, 98 N. W. 89, 100 N. W. 106.

We hold that the court did not err in abating the action.

Judgment affirmed.

BROWN, C. J.

BUNN, J.

We concur in the views expressed in the opinion save the conclusion that the action to determine adverse claims should be abated.

Our view of the question is that full and adequate relief cannot be granted a defendant in the Torrens proceeding, and he should not therefore be barred from the right to institute an independent action to determine his title to the property. No judgment affirming title in a defendant can be rendered in that proceeding, and for this reason the remedy is not full and complete. While it is true as stated in the opinion that findings should be made in the Torrens proceeding which, if to the effect that a defendant owns the property, would estop the applicant in another action, or subsequent Torrens proceeding, the defendant in whose favor such finding is made is not entitled to judgment thereon, and, to give effect to the findings, and the resulting estoppel, he must bring a subsequent action in which such judgment may be rendered. He is entitled to a final judgment but cannot get it in the Torrens proceeding. That proceeding should not therefore be held a bar to the second action in which the relief may be granted. Koch v. Peters, 97 Wis. 492, 73 N. W. 25; Carr v. Lyle, 126 Mich. 655, 86 N. W. 145; Reis v. Applebaum, 170 Mich. 506, 136 N. W. 393; Pratt v. Howard, 109 Iowa, 504, 80 N. W. 546. The proper practice in such case would seem a stay of the second action until the final determination of the Torrens proceeding, and not an absolute abatement.

CHARLES W. NICHOLS v. F. B. ATWOOD.[1]

December 4, 1914.

Nos. 18,815—(70).

Special verdict — evidence.

1. The evidence sustains the special finding of the jury that the subscription contract upon which the action is brought was made with a corporation other than plaintiff's assignor.

New trial — no cause of action.

2. The reception in evidence of an exhibit bearing solely upon another issue properly in the case, even if technical error, did not warrant a new trial since the special finding above mentioned determined that plaintiff could have no cause of action no matter how such other issue was decided. Furthermore, the trial court properly received the exhibit and correctly instructed the jury how and when to consider the same, and hence, in ordering a new trial because of the reception thereof, erred.

New trial.

3. The record presents no erroneous rulings or instructions which entitled plaintiff to a new trial.

Action in the district court for Hennepin county to recover a balance of $2,500 alleged to be due under a certain contract. The facts are stated in the opinion. The case was tried before Dickinson, J., and a jury which returned a verdict in favor of defendant, and special findings as stated in the opinion. From an order granting plaintiff's motion for a new trial, defendant appealed. Reversed.

Hall, Tautges & Loeffler and *Robert S. Kolliner,* for appellant.
Mercer, Swan & Stinchfield, for respondent.

HOLT, J.

Plaintiff, claiming to be owner by assignment of a subscription contract executed by defendant for 45 shares of the treasury stock of the Colorado-Yule Marble Co., sued to recover the amount unpaid.

[1] Reported in 149 N. W. 672.

The answer alleged that plaintiff was not the owner of the contract; that his purported assignor was not the party with whom defendant contracted, but was the mere agent of the corporation mentioned; and that defendant's signature was obtained by means of false representations in regard to its business and property. This appeal by defendant is from an order granting plaintiff a new trial after verdict and special findings in defendant's favor.

Early in 1910 defendant's attention was called to the stock and business of the Colorado-Yule Marble Co., hereafter called the marble company, a ten million dollar Colorado corporation, owning extensive marble quarries and equipments in that state. From the start the corporation had in the Knickerbocker syndicate a fiscal and transfer agent to dispose of its stock and securities. In 1907 the Knickerbocker corporation was merged in the then organized Fidelity Bond & Mortgage Co., hereinafter referred to as the bond company, a New York corporation, in 1912 purporting to have a capital and surplus of $1,321,509.54. Plaintiff procured the subscription from defendant. He claims that he was then the western sales agent of the bond company, but had no connection with the marble company except as stockholder until in December, 1911, when he entered its employ. The subscription contract here involved was signed January 13, 1911. About six months previously defendant had bought through plaintiff, five shares of the marble company stock. By means of plaintiff's personal solicitations and literature mailed or handed to defendant, he was importuned to purchase more, which finally culminated in the contract mentioned the day after the president and vice-president of the marble company, at a meeting or luncheon arranged for by plaintiff, had made certain representations to defendant concerning the property and prospects of the corporation. It is not necessary to particularly refer to the alleged false representations which induced defendant to subscribe. It is sufficient to state that the evidence at the trial centered on these propositions: Was plaintiff the real party in interest? Was the marble company in fact a party to the subscription contract with defendant? Was the subscription for 45 shares of stock obtained from defendant by means of fraud and deceit? The jury by special findings answered the first in the negative, and the other two in the affirmative, in addition to rendering a general verdict in favor of defendant. The court granted a new trial on the sole ground that prejudicial error was committed in receiving parts of an exhibit numbered 7 in evidence.

The contention of appellant is that Exhibit 7 was admissible and, even were it otherwise, no prejudicial error resulted from its reception since the jury found that defendant's contract was not with plaintiff's assignor, and that plaintiff is not the real party in interest. The respondent retorts that there is no evidence to sustain either the general verdict or special findings and that the record discloses prejudicial errors, other than the one appearing to the trial court, therefore the order must be affirmed. This result is inevitable, if the verdict lacks support or there be rulings raised by the motion for a new trial disclosing prejudicial error. Fitger v. Guthrie, 89 Minn. 330, 94 N. W. 888; Poirier Mnfg. Co. v. Griffin, 104 Minn. 239, 116 N. W. 576.

Plaintiff on the trial disclaimed a cause of action if defendant's contract was with the marble company, for plaintiff does not claim through it. It follows that, if the special finding that defendant contracted with the marble company is supported by the evidence, the general verdict must stand, unless the rulings complained of and assigned as error on the motion for new trial affect or prejudicially bear on the determination of the special finding mentioned. The issue of fraudulent representations becomes immaterial. We now call attention to some of the matters from which the jury could draw the conclusion that defendant contracted with the marble company. The printed form or blank of the subscription contract signed by defendant, in itself, justifies his contention that he dealt with the marble company. Circulars or literature had either been handed to him by plaintiff or mailed, disclosing that one Meek was the president of the marble company and Charles Austin Bates its vice-president and director. Bates was also the president of the bond company. In one of these circulars, over the name of Mr. Bates, we read: "We are selling something we already own and have paid for. We do not have to make the marble. All we have to do is to cut it out and put it on the cars." This must refer to the marble company, for the bond company owned no quarries. The same circular gives the residence and character of the directors of the marble company and we read concerning director Bates: "Charles Austin Bates is president of the Fidelity Bond and Mortgage Company of New York, and to him has fallen the task of disposing of the company's securities, from time to time, as the cash was needed for development work. The Fidelity Bond and Mortgage Co. is the registrar and transfer agent of the Marble Co." In addition to the president of one corporation being the vice-president and director of the other, they had a treasurer in common, and shared the same office in New York City. The record suggests the thought that the chief reason for calling the bond company into existence was the use of a desirable fiscal, sales and transfer agent by the officials of the marble company. Plaintiff, Mr. Meek and Mr. Bates came to Minneapolis on January 12, 1911, invited defendant and other prospective subscribers for lunch at the West Hotel, ostensibly to induce the guests to subscribe for stock in the marble company. Mr. Meek then in the presence of Mr. Bates and plaintiff made an extended statement in respect to the properties, condition and prospects of the marble company to defendant and the other invited persons. Plaintiff at no time informed defendant that he or the bond company acted in any other capacity than sales agent for the marble company. It may well be surmised that if prospective subscribers had been told facts such as now claimed by plaintiff, namely, that this so-called fiscal agent, registrar and transfer agent was owner of the stock, having purchased it from the marble company, it would have deterred them from subscribing. In view of the facts alluded to, no fault should be found with the jury for attaching little importance to this direction, in small print, on the subscription contract below the blank for the signature of the subscribers: "Send subscriptions and make checks payable to Fidelity Bond & Mortgage Co. 2 West 33rd street (at Fifth avenue) New York." The jury were amply justified in finding that defendant contracted with the marble company. The special finding that plaintiff is not the real party in interest is but corollary and inevitable conclusion from the one mentioned before.

And in passing we may say that it is not surprising that plaintiff's testimony concerning the assignment to him by the bond company of the cause of action failed to carry conviction. It was to the effect that, when he transferred his services from it to the marble company, he was unable to get either his pay or a statement of the amount due, and finally after waiting almost a year he had to accept an assignment of defendant's contract from an employer having a capital and surplus exceeding a million dollars.

Plaintiff also claims that it conclusively appears that defendant, after knowledge of the deceit, made payments on the subscription and received shares for the amounts paid, thereby precluding a rescission, and further there being no proof of damages judgment should go for plaintiff. Even were the premise true, the conclusion does not follow, for plaintiff is again met with the special findings. However, we may remark that it was for the jury to accept or reject defendant's testimony that, when the last payment was made, he had not ascertained all the facts as to the fraud practiced upon him and that plaintiff's explanation, when called to his attention, was such that defendant's aroused suspicions were abated.

We are forced to the conclusion that the issue of fraud and deceit is now of no importance, and that no error in the admission of evidence relating thereto was prejudicial, unless it is made to appear that it affected the controlling finding that defendant contracted with the marble company. "Where upon a special verdict upon one issue the party is entitled to the judgment rendered, error in the charge or admission of evidence as to another issue will be disregarded," Whitacre v. Culver, 9 Minn. 279 (295); Cole v. Maxfield, 13 Minn. 220 (235). The court might have properly told the jury that, if they found that the subscription contract was with the marble company, they need give no further consideration, or any answer, to the other two questions submitted. If immaterial issues are injected into a trial, we may concede that the litigant who is not to blame therefor or who has objected thereto is prejudiced. But this is not such a case in respect to the defense that the contract was procured by false representations. Defendant was not bound to anticipate a favorable finding on the controlling issue indicated. He had a right to tender and litigate the issue of fraud. The connection between plaintiff and the two corporations and their relation to each other was such that it opened wide the door of inquiry. If defendant was able to prove the deception pleaded, he was entitled to so do, and need not place his whole reliance on the other defenses set up. Hence we may not say that plaintiff was prejudiced by the litigation of an irrelevant and immaterial issue, or that the cry of fraud and false representations needlessly obscured or prejudiced the pivotal question. Rauma v. Bailey, 80 Minn. 336, 83 N. W. 191. We are therefore of opinion that no prejudice resulted to plaintiff from the reception of the parts of Exhibit 7 read to the jury, assuming the same inadmissible. It does not touch or bear upon the controlling special finding.

But that aside we are of the opinion that no error was committed in the reception of Exhibit 7, in view of the instructions given the jury. They were told that, if the subscription contract was between defendant and the bond company, these statements made by the marble company, or issued by it or by its officers, would not be competent evidence against plaintiff. "If the marble company was not the principal in these transactions, then the paragraphs and figures from Exhibit 7, which have been read to you, should be disregarded, as well as any other statements appearing in the evidence which you cannot find were authorized by plaintiff or the bond company. And, gentlemen of the jury, no evidence as to the condition of the company subsequent to January 13, 1911, is of any materiality or relevancy to the issues here, except as they may show or tend to show what the true state of facts was at that date, or prior thereto, and then only insofar as they may show or tend to show the falsity of any of the alleged representations which I have pointed out." The learned trial court rightly and clearly limited and guided the jury not only in the consideration of Exhibit 7, but also of other exhibits and testimony bearing on the alleged representations.

Several matters in the record are urged as sufficient errors justifying a new trial. We have examined all, but only two, apart from those already considered, require notice. One who became president of the marble company long after the defendant signed the subscription was a witness for plaintiff. He had previously been a director. Plaintiff attempted to prove by him that the marble company had sold to the bond company its treasury stock of 6,270 shares out of which came the 45 shares subscribed for by defendant. It was elicited that the alleged sale was not evidenced by any writing, unless a resolution passed by the board of directors of the marble company was contained in its records which were not within the state. Several pages of the settled case are filled with counsel's unsuccessful attempts to have the witness state the legal conclusion that the resolution effected a sale of the stock, and to show an oral acquiescence by an officer of the bond company, but he nowhere asks the witness to give either the language or the substance of the resolution. No attempt was made to offer secondary evidence thereof. It is taxing the credulity of a court and jury beyond limit to attempt to prove a transaction involving more than half a million dollars between two corporations by the mere say so, or conclusions, of a director or officer, without producing either the original minutes or a copy containing the resolution embodying the deal, or even offering testimony as to the substance of the resolution. There was no error in the ruling. The authorities cited by respondent to sustain his position are not in point. There was here no attempt to prove what actually took place.

A refusal to give this instruction is one of the errors urged as valid reason for sustaining the new trial awarded: "It makes no difference in this case whether or not the defendant knew that the plaintiff Nichols was acting in making this contract of sale for the Fidelity and Bond Company and Mortgage Company or for the Colorado-Yule Marble Company, if you find in fact that he was acting only for the Fidelity Bond and Mortgage Company. If the Fidelity Bond and Mortgage Company was in fact the principal in the sale of these securities and no statement or representation to the contrary was made to the defendant by the plaintiff or any other representative or agent of the Fidelity Bond and Mortgage Company, then the said Fidelity Bond and Mortgage Company was the owner of whatever cause of action, if any there was, in this case, and was entitled to assign that cause of action to this plaintiff."

The instruction was not proper. The first sentence thereof is palpably misleading as applied to the issues in this case. If defendant knew that plaintiff represented only the bond company, he, in entering the contract, could place no reliance upon unauthorized representations made by the marble company, but if justified in the belief that he was dealing with the latter he could rely on its statements.

We consider plaintiff had a fair trial. The decisive issue as to which corporation defendant became obligated to was decided against plaintiff. No error inheres in that determination. We are inclined to the opinion that no technical error was made by the trial court in the reception of Exhibit 7, especially in view of the clear instructions when and how to apply the portions received, and are firmly convinced that in no event was plaintiff prejudiced by the ruling thereon at the trial, nor by any other ruling. Consequently the new trial should not have been granted.

Order reversed.

SAMUEL BENENSON v. SWIFT & COMPANY.[1]

December 4, 1914.

Nos. 18,858—(110).

Negligence of master — questions for jury.

1. Evidence in an action by a servant to recover damages for injuries received by him in a fall from an elevated platform, *held* to make a case for the jury on the issue of defendant's negligence with regard to the place where plaintiff was required to work, and also as to assumption of risk and contributory negligence.

Charge to jury.

2. Instructions *held* erroneous.

Action in the district court for Ramsey county to recover $3,000 for personal injuries received while in the employ of defendant.

1 Reported in 149 N. W. 668.

The answer denied negligence or want of care on defendant's part, and alleged that the accident and injury were in part at least caused or induced by the negligence of plaintiff, that the conditions under which plaintiff was working at the time of the accident were patent and observable, and that he appreciated the risk. The case was tried before Stolberg, J., and a jury which returned a verdict in favor of plaintiff for $400. From an order denying defendant's motion for judgment notwithstanding the verdict or for a new trial, it appealed. Reversed.

Barrows, Stewart & Ordway, for appellant.

A. J. Hertz, for respondent.

PHILIP E. BROWN, J.

Action to recover damages claimed to have been caused by defendant's failure to furnish plaintiff, its servant, a safe place in which to work. Defendant denied negligence on its part and alleged contributory negligence and assumption of risk. Plaintiff had a verdict. Defendant appealed from an order denying its alternative motion.

Plaintiff's duties required him to pull a truck along an elevated platform, to and from defendant's icing plant, in connection with the icing of refrigerator cars by means of chutes. The truck had two wheels 18 inches in diameter, set three feet apart, the extreme width. The platform was parallel to the railroad track and some 16 feet above it, being 20 feet wide and more than 50 feet long. A shed 12 feet wide, open in front, supported by posts, was situated along a portion of the opposite side thereof from the track, and was devoted to the storage of boxes used in the business but not in connection with the icing department. The only guard on the other side of the platform was a 4x4 inch timber nailed to the floor on the extreme outer edge. Plaintiff had been employed in the same work at the same place for some six days prior to the accident. Others were likewise employed; the rule being that a truckman without a load should stop and the one with a load pass. Plaintiff was 23 years old, a foreigner with slight knowledge of our language, having been in this country only a few months prior to the accident. The proofs would support. a finding that just before he was injured he was drawing his empty truck in the usual manner along the platform, and on reaching a point opposite the shed saw another workman loading a truck with boxes.   There being only a little more than sufficient room to pass, plaintiff stopped, whereupon the assistant foreman of the icing gang told him to come on, and just after he had passed, but before his truck was by, the other workman raised his truck so that it collided with plaintiff's, throwing plaintiff and his truck to the tracks below to his injury.

1. Defendant insists that no breach of duty on its part was established, and that the place was safe.   The inquiry should start here, for if this position be well taken plaintiff has no case.   In addition to the facts stated, defendant offered evidence of the impracticability of putting a higher railing or guard along the outside of the platform; but there was no proof that the 4x4 could not have been elevated to some extent without interfering with the work, and it is significant in this connection that defendant claimed there was no collision, but that, when plaintiff attempted to pass, the wheel of his truck went up on the rail and over the side.   The assistant foreman referred to testified: "He (plaintiff) was a new man there and so we always take care of them and look after them a little more than the old fellows there because the old fellows are used to it, they try to look after themselves."   This, coming from an experienced man, is at least indicative of attendant dangers not obvious to plaintiff. This witness insisted plaintiff had ample room to pass, but made the inconsistent admission that "to be on the safe side" he told him to stop.   The platform at the place of the accident was not over seven feet eight inches in the clear, and it is apparent that there could not have been much room to spare when it was occupied by the other truck.   We do not sustain defendant's contention as to the safety of the place as a matter of law.

If its negligence in this regard proximately contributed to the injury, and if there was no assumption of risk or contributory negligence, defendant is liable, notwithstanding that, as must be held, the two truckmen were fellow servants, and even though it be conceded that the box truckman was negligent; for if defendant was also negligent in the regard mentioned we would have the combined negligence of the master and a servant concurring to cause the injury of a fellow servant, in which case the master is not absolved. Franklin v. Winona & St. P. R. Co. 37 Minn. 409, 34 N. W. 898, 5 Am. St. 856; 2 Notes on Minn. Reports, 1114. The evidence is insufficient to constitute the assistant foreman a vice principal. It is important, however, on assumption of risk, which issue cannot on this record be determined as a matter of law in defendant's favor. Nustrom v. Shenango Furnace Co. 105 Minn. 140, 142, 117 N. W. 480. It is also material on plaintiff's alleged contributory negligence, which cannot be predicated upon compliance with a superior's orders unless the danger is obvious.

2. The court should have qualified its instruction defining a reasonably safe place by limiting the standard of comparison to "the same or similar circumstances."

The general instructions were not in harmony with the views above expressed.

The case is not one, however, for judgment notwithstanding the verdict, but for a new trial.

Order reversed.

C. D. RODGERS v. UNITED STATES AND DOMINION LIFE INSURANCE COMPANY.[1]

December 4, 1914.

Nos. 18,863—(113).

Vacating default judgment.

 1. The matter of opening a default judgment rests in the discretion of the trial court, and its action in opening default will not be reversed except for palpable abuse of discretion.

Same.

 2. The court may in its discretion open a default judgment obtained

---

[1] Reported in 149 N. W. 671.

against a corporation because of bad faith or intentional neglect of the officer who is charged with the duty of making defense.

Same — stipulation of attorney for judgment.

3. An attorney has power to bind his client by a stipulation for judgment, but where an attorney, from ignorance of facts or from bad faith, stipulates for judgment against a client who has a just defense, the court may, in its discretion, open the judgment and permit the defense to be interposed, if no substantial prejudice will result to the opposing party from the incident delay.

Same — affidavit by officers of corporation.

4. An affidavit by an attorney, based upon knowledge acquired from investigation of the affairs of the corporation, *held* to contain sufficient showing of facts to sustain an order opening a default judgment. The affidavit of all officers and directors as to ignorance of the entry of the judgment is not necessary.

From an order of the district court for St. Louis county, Fesler, J., granting defendant's motion to set aside a judgment against it for the sum of $5,201.90, for the reason that the judgment was entered because of its excusable neglect, and permitting it to defend the action, plaintiff appealed. Affirmed.

William P. Harrison, for appellant.

James A. Wharton, for respondent.

HALLAM, J.

Appeal from an order opening a judgment and granting leave to answer. Defendant is an insurance corporation. The moving affidavit alleges that certain of its officers and directors, including its president, dissipated and squandered all of the assets of the company in the purchase of certain gold bonds of the Williamsville, Greenville & St. Louis Railway Co., and also gave notes of the company in part payment. The notes sued on in this action are some of these. This suit was commenced in January, 1913. It is alleged that at that time the affairs of the company were in the control of its president; that he handed the summons to an attorney whom he had secured to look after the interests of himself and his associates; that this attorney interposed an answer, but later withdrew it and stipulated for judgment, and on July 8, 1913, judgment was entered for

$5,201.90, the amount demanded in the complaint. In July, August and September, 1913, three blocks of said gold bonds, of the face value of $27,000, were sold at three separate execution sales for the aggregate amount, over expenses, of $2,906.70. The affidavit further states, that the stockholders and directors knew nothing of this suit; that the company in fact had a good defense to the notes and the president had personal knowledge of facts sufficient to make a defense, but that he did not act in good faith toward defendant and withheld such information and allowed judgment to go against defendant; that the acts of the president and the attorney were indifferent, careless and negligent and amounted to excusable neglect on the part of defendant. There is no direct allegation of bad faith on the part of the attorney, but from all of the allegations of the affidavit it is fairly inferable either that he was ignorant of the facts constituting the defense, or that through indifference, which could amount to no less than bad faith, he ignored them.

It is further alleged that, on September 1, 1913, the stockholders had a meeting and appointed a committee to make an investigation, that at a meeting on September 15 a new board of directors was elected, and that on the conclusion of the investigation, and about the last of November, this application was made. The trial court made an order that the judgment be vacated and the answer allowed to stand on condition of payment to the attorney for the plaintiff the sum of $250. It appears that plaintiff himself purchased the bonds sold at the execution sale and, so far as it appears, still has them. In view of the payment required of defendant as a condition to opening the judgment, it is not apparent that plaintiff will suffer any substantial prejudice from the delay in determination of the case on its merits.

The matter of opening a default judgment rests in the discretion of the trial court. That discretion is a judicial one and is not to be exercised capriciously or arbitrarily, yet the discretion of the court should be liberally indulged to relieve a party from default, to the end that the judgment of the court should be rendered in a controverted case only after a trial on the merits. The action of the trial court in relieving a party of a default will not be reversed except for palpable abuse of discretion.   Where there has never been a trial on the merits and the defendant shows that he has a good defense, and no substantial prejudice appears to the plaintiff from the delay, it is the duty of the trial court to relieve the defendant of his default if he furnishes any reasonable excuse therefor, and the action of the court in so doing will not be disturbed.   Jorgensen v. Boehmer, 9 Minn. 166 (181); Martin v. Curley, 70 Minn. 489, 73 N. W. 405; White v. Gurney, 92 Minn. 271, 99 N. W. 889; Barrie v. Northern Assurance Co. 99 Minn. 272, 109 N. W. 248; Hendricks v. Conner, 104 Minn. 399, 116 N. W. 751; Dr. Shoop Family Medicine Co. v. Oppliger, 124 Minn. 535, 144 N. W. 743.

It is well settled, a corporation may have opened a judgment entered by default because of the intentional neglect or bad faith of the officer on whom the summons is served or who is charged with the duty of making defense.   Bray v. Church of St. Brandon, 39 Minn. 390, 40 N. W. 518; J. H. Queal & Co. v. Bulen, 89 Minn. 477, 95 N. W. 310.   Corporation officers are trustees and, while their acts in general bind the corporation, still in the event of bad faith their acts may be repudiated by the stockholders who are the beneficiaries of the trust.

Beyond doubt an attorney has authority to bind his client by a stipulation for judgment.   G. S. 1913, § 4950; Bray v. Doheny, 39 Minn. 355, 40 N. W. 262; Wells v. Penfield, 70 Minn. 66, 72 N. W. 816.   At the same time it is clear that a party may, in a proper case, be relieved from a stipulation made by his attorney. This has been recognized in this state from early times.   Bingham v. Board of Supervisors of Winona County, 6 Minn. 82 (136).   In several cases it has been said that the court may relieve a party from the stipulation of his attorney if improvidently made, or made under a clear mistake or procured by fraud or collusion; Hildebrandt v. Robbecke, 20 Minn. 83 (100); Bray v. Doheny, 39 Minn. 355, 40 N. W. 262; Eidam v. Finnegan, 48 Minn. 53, 50 N. W. 933; or if in equity and good conscience it ought not to stand; Wells v. Penfield, 70 Minn. 66, 72 N. W. 816.   The same principles are generally recognized in other jurisdictions.   Thompson, Trials, 195; 36 Cyc. 1295.   The circumstances under which the court may relieve against a stipulation of an attorney are not clearly defined. In Bingham v. Board of Supervisors of Winona County, 6 Minn. 82 (136), it was said the settlement of issues by stipulation should have as much effect as their determination by the verdict of a jury, and it should require the same or as strong reasons to set the stipulation aside as would be required to set aside a verdict. It is not necessary to define the precise limits of the power of the court in this particular. It is sufficient for purposes of this case to say that the court may, in its discretion, open a judgment entered upon stipulation of an attorney and allow a trial on the merits, where the attorney has, from ignorance of facts or from bad faith, stipulated for judgment against a client who has a just defense, and where no substantial prejudice will result to the opposing party from the incident delay.

Applying the foregoing rules, it must be held that the order of the trial court in opening this judgment must be sustained.

The affidavit on which the application is based was made by the present attorney for defendant. It was made upon knowledge acquired as a member of the investigating committee above mentioned. It is urged that he could not in this or any other manner, except from hearsay, know that the directors of the corporation, other than those acting with its president, were ignorant of the entry of the judgment until September, 1913. It is true he could have no other than hearsay knowledge of the state of mind of these directors, but from his investigation he could determine whether notice of such facts was ever conveyed to them through the usual channels. There is no intimation that any of these directors did in fact have any such knowledge. Two parties claimed by plaintiff to be directors were brought into the case, but they each denied being even stockholders. We do not wish to relax the rule that a party asking to have a default judgment opened bears the burden of excusing his default, but it is not necessary for a corporation defendant to produce the affidavit of all its officers and directors as to ignorance of the entry of judgment in order to make out a *prima facie* case, at least where no likelihood of knowledge on their part appears.

The delay until November in making the application, was not, under the circumstances above disclosed, an inexcusable delay.

Order affirmed.

CARL ANDERSON v. LANDERS-MORRISON-CHRISTENSON COMPANY.[1]

December 4, 1914.

Nos. 18,873—(116).

Obstruction of public alley — injunction by abutting owner.

1. An owner of property abutting upon a public alley may maintain an action to restrain and enjoin an unlawful attempt permanently to obstruct the alley and prevent the free use thereof by such abutting owner.

Same.

2. In such case the abutting owner has an interest in the use of the alley different in kind and degree from that of the public at large which equity will protect as against a wrongdoer. Kaje v. Chicago, St. P. M. & O. Ry. Co. 57 Minn. 422, followed and applied.

Action in the district court for Hennepin county to restrain defendant from obstructing a certain street and alleyway or from further excavating or constructing or maintaining a tunnel or maintaining or operating any cars or other devices in said excavation or tunnel in any way to interfere with the free use of the alley or street as a public highway, and that they be restored to their normal condition. From an order, Steele, J., overruling defendant's demurrer to the complaint, it appealed. Affirmed.

James C. Melville, for appellant.

Julius E. Miner and *Stevens & Stevens,* for respondent.

BROWN, C. J.

Appeal from an order overruling a general demurrer to plaintiff's

1 Reported in 149 N. W. 669.

complaint. The facts as disclosed by the complaint, and to some extent explained on the oral argument, are substantially as follows: Twenty-ninth street in the city of Minneapolis extends along blocks 19 and 20 in Windom's addition parallel with the right of way of the Chicago, Milwaukee & St. Paul Railway Co. The railroad tracks have recently been ordered lowered and depressed by the city authorities. The lowering of the tracks has left a high bank along the street, rendering approach to the railroad yards difficult and inconvenient for those in the immediate vicinity having business with the company in the way of freight shipments. Defendant owns and occupies all of block 20 fronting on Twenty-ninth street, and also a part of block 19. Defendant has continuous relations with the railroad company in the matter of shipment and transportation of its commodities, and in the transaction of the same is considerably inconvenienced by the embankment caused by the lowering of the railroad tracks fronting its premises. To overcome this and to aid and facilitate the loading and transfer of such commodities defendant applied to the city council for permission to construct a tunnel under Twenty-ninth street from the railroad right of way to its premises. In response the city council duly enacted an ordinance granting such right. The ordinance provided that defendant might construct and maintain a tunnel under and across the street, the same to be constructed at a point corresponding with the center of block 20. This would bring the tunnel directly opposite an alley extending through the center of block 20 from Twenty-ninth street to Lake street, the latter being a street one block removed from Twenty-ninth street and running parallel therewith. The alley is 12 feet wide and has always been open and in use by the abutting property owners, and the public generally. The ordinance provides that the tunnel should be constructed according to plans approved by the city engineer, and when completed that the street should be by defendant restored to its natural condition. Provision was made also to the effect that defendant should save the city harmless from any and all damages occasioned by the construction of the tunnel, and the city reserved the right to use the tunnel whenever it had occasion to do so. The level of the street at the intersection of the alley is considerably higher than the level of the alley, and the tunnel, if constructed, will leave a high embankment at the point of intersection and wholly obstruct ingress to the alley from that street. The tunnel as proposed also contemplates excavations in and the exclusive use of the alley for a distance of about 100 feet from the street line, for which no authority is granted by the ordinance. Plaintiff is the owner of lots 7 and 8 of block 20, immediately adjoining defendant's premises, upon which he has constructed a flat building, which is occupied by tenants. The lots abut upon the alley, and the construction of the tunnel will wholly prevent access to his property by way of Twenty-ninth street, the obstruction being the high bank occasioned by the tunnel at the intersection of the alley with that street. He brought this action to restrain the construction of the tunnel, and the resulting interference with his right of access to his property, alleging that the acts of defendant in this respect are wrongful, without authority of law and in violation of plaintiff's vested right to the free and uninterrupted use of the alley. The trial court overruled the demurrer and certified that the questions presented are doubtful and defendant appealed.

The only question presented is whether the complaint, in any view of the facts alleged, shows a right in plaintiff to any specific relief. 2 Dunnell, Minn. Dig. § 7549. If it does the demurrer was properly overruled. That the complaint shows such right is clear. It appears that the construction of the tunnel will wholly prevent access to plaintiff's property from Twenty-ninth street, and effectually prevent the use of the alley in connection with that street. That plaintiff has a vested right to the free and unobstructed use of the alley, to and from Twenty-ninth street, cannot well be questioned, and it requires no argument to demonstrate the existence of the same. The construction of the tunnel, leaving as it will a barrier preventing passage onto the street from the alley will interrupt, without authority, that right and plaintiff is entitled to appropriate relief. The injury to plaintiff is continuing, and may be restrained by injunction. Colliton v. Oxborough, 86 Minn. 361, 90 N. W. 793; Baldwin v. Fisher, 110 Minn. 186, 124 N. W. 1094; Chadbourne v. Zilsdorf, 34 Minn. 43, 24 N. W. 308; Horton v. Williams, 99 Mich. 423, 58 N. W. 369; 2 Dunnell, Minn. Digest, § 4476. The question is fully discussed in the cases cited, and others therein referred to, and need not be repeated. That plaintiff has a special interest in the free and open way from his property to Twenty-ninth street, and one distinct from that of the general public, is settled and disposed of by the case of Kaje v. Chicago, St. P. M. & O. Ry. Co. 57 Minn. 422, 59 N. W. 493, 47 Am. St. 627. The precise question, here presented, was involved in that case and ruled favorably to the property owner. Vanderburgh v. City of Minneapolis, 98 Minn. 329, 108 N. W. 480, 6 L.R.A.(N.S.) 741, is not in point. That case involved the lawful vacation of the street there in question, and it was held that plaintiff's remedy was an action at law for damages. The alley in the case at bar has not been vacated, nor has the defendant been authorized by the city authorities or otherwise to obstruct the alley leading to plaintiff's property. This differentiates the cases.

In view of this conclusion it becomes unnecessary to consider the validity of the ordinance granting tunnel privileges to defendant. The rights so granted are not here involved, for no authority was there conferred upon defendant beyond the lines of Twenty-ninth street. It does not attempt to authorize an obstruction or an encroachment upon the alley.

Order affirmed.

ST. PAUL MOTOR VEHICLE COMPANY v. A. D. S. JOHNSTON.[1]

December 4, 1914.

Nos. 18,889—(121).

Facts conceded by attorney — dismissal of action.
    When counsel in his opening statement to the jury makes a deliberate concession as to the facts, and chooses to abide by it after his attention

[1] Reported in 149 N. W. 667.

is called to its effect, the court may act upon the facts conceded and grant defendant's motion for dismissal if, with such facts conceded, there can be no recovery under the complaint.

Action in the district court for Ramsey county to recover $750 balance alleged to be due for services and supplies. The case came on for trial before Dickson, J., who granted defendant's motion to dismiss the action. From an order denying plaintiff's motion for an order vacating the dismissal of the action and for a new trial, plaintiff appealed. Affirmed.

Duxbury, Conzett & Pettijohn, for appellant.
Barrows, Stewart & Ordway, for respondent.

Dibell, C.

The complaint is in the common law form of *indebitatus assumpsit* for goods sold and delivered and services rendered for which a balance of $750 is claimed. In his opening statement counsel for the plaintiff stated the nature of the claim for $750, and from his statement it must be conceded that he could not recover under the allegations of the complaint, the claim for the $750 being substantially a claim for damages for the breach of an executory contract of sale. Counsel for the defendant then, before the introduction of any testimony, moved for a dismissal of the action upon the ground that, taking the facts conceded by counsel to be true, no recovery could be had under the complaint. A colloquy was then had between counsel and the court, the narration of which requires several pages of the paper book, counsel for the plaintiff insisting that he had a right of recovery upon the complaint as it was and the facts as he conceded them to be.

In Barrett v. Minneapolis, St. Paul & S. S. M. Ry. Co. 106 Minn. 51, 117 N. W. 1047, 18 L.R.A.(N.S.) 416, 130 Am. St. 585, Start, C. J., stated the rule relative to the effect of an opening statement of counsel as follows:

"A trial court has the right to act upon facts deliberately conceded by counsel in his opening statement and to direct a verdict against the plaintiff upon such concession, if such facts, if proven, would not entitle the plaintiff to a verdict. Such power, however, must be exercised sparingly, and never without full consideration and opportunity for counsel to explain and qualify his statement so far as the truth will permit."

An examination of the record shows that the facts were deliberately conceded by counsel and that he chose to abide by them. Under these circumstances the trial court expeditiously and with propriety disposed of the case by granting defendant's motion.

Order affirmed.

STATE v. PETER L. NEWMAN and Another.[1]

December 11, 1914.

Nos. 18,796—(3).

Criminal law — evidence upon former trial.

Defendants were convicted of the crime of kidnapping, and appealed. It is *held:*

(1) The verdict is sustained by the evidence.

(2) The evidence of one of the defendants given on a former trial was properly received in evidence as against such defendant. It was given voluntarily, and its admission in evidence on the second trial was not a violation of said defendant's privilege against self incrimination.

(3) The evidence of one of the defendants given on the former trial was not admissible as against the other defendants on trial. It being a joint trial, the evidence was properly in the case, and the jury should have been instructed that it was not evidence as against the other defendants. There being no request or suggestion to the trial court to give such an instruction, it was not error to fail to do so.

Peter L. Newman and William J. Sullivan were indicted by the grand jury, tried in the district court for Crow Wing county before McClenahan, J., and a jury, and convicted of the crime of kid-

[1] Reported in 149 N. W. 945.

napping. From an order denying their motion for a new trial, defendants appealed. Affirmed.

Alderman & Clark and *M. E. Ryan,* for appellants.

Lyndon A. Smith, Attorney General, *Alonzo J. Edgerton,* Assistant Attorney General, and *G. S. Swanson,* County Attorney, for the state.

BUNN, J.

Defendants Newman and Sullivan, with two others, were tried jointly on an indictment charging them with the crime of kidnapping. The jury acquitted the other defendants, but found Newman and Sullivan guilty. They moved for a new trial, and appealed from an order denying the same.

It is claimed, though not very strenuously, that the evidence is not sufficient to justify a verdict of guilty.

G. S. 1913, § 8628, so far as material here, reads as follows: "Every person who shall wilfully: 1st. Seize, confine or inveigle another, with intent to cause him, without authority of law, to be secretly confined or imprisoned within the state, or sent out of it, to be sold as a slave, or in any way held to service, or kept or detained against his will, * * * shall be guilty of kidnapping, and punished," etc.

The indictment charged that the defendants on April 17, 1913, at the village of Crosby in Crow Wing county, did wilfully, unlawfully and feloniously seize, confine and inveigle one Theodore Sjogren, with intent to cause him, without authority of law, to be secretly confined within the state, and set out the acts constituting the seizure, confinement and inveigling of Sjogren.

The evidence justified the jury in believing beyond a reasonable doubt that the following facts were true:

Sjogren was a miner and had come from his home in Michigan to work in one of the mines near Crosby. The miners started a strike and Sjogren was a member of a committee appointed to confer with the superintendent and the "captain" of the shaft. Several conferences had been held prior to the evening of April 17, 1913. On that evening Sjogren visited a pool hall in Crosby and attended a moving picture show. After coming out from this show with two companions, and as he was passing an automobile standing near the sidewalk, revolvers were pointed at his face, and he was ordered to step into the automobile. He complied, and the automobile drove off. Defendants Newman and Sullivan were two of the men, the others being the two defendants who were acquitted and one Payne, who was indicted but not tried. All of the men had revolvers, and dark handkerchiefs over their faces. They gagged Sjogren and went through his pockets, though they took nothing from him. The machine was driven to Brainerd, with more or less of threats and shooting on the way. In Brainerd the five men conducted Sjogren to a room in a hotel, where they had refreshments. Sjogren was told that if he would not go back to the mines, but go home to Michigan, the men would let him go, but would shoot him full of holes if he ever came back or wrote to his friends in Crosby. Sjogren promised, and his captors left him in charge of Payne, one of their number, the others going back to Crosby. Payne, with the help of a revolver, kept Sjogren in charge, saw that he bought a ticket for Duluth, and took the train with him. Payne got off at Deerwood, Sjogren continuing to Duluth.

It is manifest that this story, if believed, was sufficient to convict defendants of wilfully seizing, confining or inveigling Sjogren, with the intent to cause him, without authority of law, to be secretly confined or imprisoned within the state. There is little room to question the substantial features of Sjogren's tale, as told above, and we are obliged to hold that the conviction was justified by the evidence. We are not concerned with the motives of the men who thus attempted to get out of the way one of the committee of strikers. It is not pretended that they acted with any legal authority.

. The only question in the case that merits special mention is one of evidence. This was the second trial. On the first defendant Newman testified on his own behalf. On this trial, the state offered his testimony given on the first trial. The attorney for all of the four defendants on trial entered a general objection that the testimony was incompetent, irrelevant and immaterial. The objection was overruled, and defendants excepted.

It is claimed that the admission of this evidence was error as to defendant Newman, on the ground that it was a violation of his constitutional privilege to refuse to incriminate himself. We cannot adopt this view. The evidence was given voluntarily on the former trial. We see no distinction between his declarations there under oath, and voluntary statements made out of court. He is not deprived of his constitutional privilege, where the declarations offered against him were made voluntarily. It is otherwise where the statements offered were made under legal compulsion. The distinction is clearly perceived by comparing State v. Strait, 94 Minn. 384, 102 N. W. 913, and State v. Drew, 110 Minn. 247, 124 N. W. 1091, 136 Am. St. 491, the former a case of declarations made by a bankrupt in voluntary bankruptcy proceedings, which were held admissible, the latter a case where the declarations were made in involuntary proceedings and held inadmissible. The authorities elsewhere support the view that the evidence of Newman on the former trial was admissible as against him on this trial. 40 Cyc. 2541, and cases cited. Commonwealth v. Reynolds, 122 Mass. 454; People v. Kelley, 47 Cal. 125; People v. Arnold, 43 Mich. 303, 5 N. W. 385, 38 Am. Rep. 182; State v. Gilman, 51 Me. 206; State v. Witham, 72 Me. 531; Dickerson v. State, 48 Wis. 288, 4 N. W. 321.

It is equally plain that Newman's testimony on the former trial was not admissible as against defendant Sullivan. This is conceded. But it was properly received as against Newman. It was a joint trial, defendants not availing themselves of their right to be tried separately. The evidence was therefore rightly in the case, but could not be used as against the defendants other than Newman. The court, on such a suggestion being made, would undoubtedly have so instructed the jury. But the attention of the court was in no way called to this situation by any request or suggestion fro·ı counsel. There was no error under the circumstances. It should be added that it is difficult in any event to see how the admission of this evidence prejudiced defendant Sullivan. He went on the stand himself and gave substantially the same story of the automobile ride and supper in Brainerd that Newman gave in his testimony on the former trial.

Order affirmed.

E. V. LOMBARD v. P. H. RAHILLY.[1]

December 11, 1914.

Nos. 18,809—(79).

Contract — plaintiff not entitled to directed verdict.

1. In an action to recover upon a contract implied in fact for material and labor furnished, it is *held* that the evidence did not justify a direction of verdict in favor of the plaintiff. A "contract implied in fact" requires a meeting of the minds, an agreement just as much as an "express contract." The difference between the two is largely in the character of the evidence by which they are established.

Same — pleading.

2. In an action to recover upon such a contract, the making of it being denied, it is not necessary for the defendant to plead facts tending to show that the material and labor were furnished without expectation of pay and that the minds of the parties never met in an agreement.

Action in the district court for Wabasha county to recover $170.04 upon an implied contract. The facts are stated in the opinion. The case was tried before Snow, J., and a jury which returned a verdict in favor of plaintiff for the amount demanded. From an order denying defendant's motion to vacate the verdict and for a new trial, he appealed. Reversed.

Lawler & Mulally and *John W. Murdock,* for appellant.

Wesley Kinney and *F. M. Wilson,* for respondent.

DIBELL, C.

This is an action to recover for material and labor furnished the defendant in the repair of a heating plant and plumbing work in his house.

For the purposes of this appeal it is to be considered that on January 24, 1911, the plaintiff entered into a contract for the installation of a heating plant in the defendant's house and completed it in April, 1911. On January 3, 1912, the tank heater exploded and did certain damage for the repair of which substantially all of the

[1] Reported 149 N. W. 950.

work and material for which suit is now brought were furnished. The defendant makes two claims. One is that the plaintiff furnished the material and labor without any contract and without expectation of pay in repairing damage done by reason of the defective work under the original contract of January, 1911. The other is that his house was injured by the explosion and that the plaintiff is liable for the damage done, and for this he counterclaims. There was a verdict for the plaintiff for the full amount claimed and the defendant appeals from the order denying his motion for a new trial.

1. After the explosion the plaintiff went to the house of the defendant and made an examination. There was some communication by telephone between the house of the defendant and plaintiff's place of business. Just what this communication was does not very definitely appear. Because of it the plaintiff went to the defendant's house. He claims that he met the defendant there, and that they entered into an express contract for doing the work of repair but without an agreement as to price. The defendant claims that he did not see the plaintiff at all. That the plaintiff did repair work is not disputed. The court substantially instructed the jury that the plaintiff was entitled to recover the amount of his claim and that the verdict would depend upon the determination of the counterclaim for damages, which, according to defendant's claim, exceeded in amount the plaintiff's claim. In so instructing the jury the court proceeded upon the theory that there was an agreement to pay for the repair work necessarily implied. It disregarded the defendant's claim that the circumstances were such that the jury might infer that the work was done without expectation of pay and because of a defective performance of the original contract. A contract implied in fact requires a meeting of the minds, an agreement, just as much as an express contract. The difference between the two is largely in the character of the evidence by which they are established. It is sometimes said that a contract implied in fact is established by circumstantial evidence. The statement is often made that when the work is done by one on the property of another, with the knowledge of such other, a presumption of an agreement to pay is implied. This is well enough if it is understood that this presumption is one of fact, evidentiary

in nature, not necessarily controlling the determination of the issue being tried, and to be weighed with other circumstances of evidentiary force upon such issue. It is true that a situation may be such that the presumption is controlling and justifies the direction of a verdict. The question whether there is such a contract is usually to be determined by the jury as an inference of fact. See Keener, Quasi Contracts, pp. 3–14, where the subject is discussed.

We have examined the evidence with care and we are of the view that the jury, if it chose to accept the version of the defendant, might conclude that the work done by the plaintiff in the repair of the heating plant and plumbing was done without expectation of pay; or, in other words, that the inference did not follow from the evidence as a matter of law that there was a contract. Therefore it was error to take the defendant's contention from the jury.

2. It is suggested by the plaintiff that the defendant did not plead that the work was done in performance of the old contract and without expectation of pay. Conceding, without holding, that there was no pleading to the effect stated, the result claimed by the plaintiff does not follow. In an action upon a contract, either express or implied in fact, it is for the plaintiff to prove the meeting of the minds. In doing this he may be aided by presumptions. To rebut it the defendant may show circumstances, without pleading them, tending to justify an inference that there was not a meeting of minds.

The general verdict for the plaintiff for the exact amount of his claim necessarily determined the defendant's counterclaim contrary to his contention. There should not be a new trial of the counterclaim. The new trial will be upon the cause of action alleged in the complaint.

Order reversed.

STATE ex rel. LYNDON A. SMITH v. VILLAGE OF GILBERT and Others.[1]

December 11, 1914.

Nos. 18,819—(16).

Construction of statute.

1. Properly construed chapter 113 of Laws 1909, providing for annexation of territory to villages and cities, applies both to existing and to future municipal corporations of that kind. The clear intent expressed in the first part of the first section to include future as well as existing villages, aided by the presumption that the legislature intended to pass a constitutional act, leads to the conclusion that the word "present" in the latter part of said section refers to the village limits as "present" or existing at the time of the institution of the annexation proceedings and not to the time of the passage of the statute.

Village — annexation of territory.

2. It is no valid objection to village annexations that territory properly conditioned to be annexed was not included.

Fraudulent votes did not change result.

3. The fraudulent and unlawful colonization of the annexed territory by residents of the village prior to the election and their taking part therein, assuming that it can be raised in this proceeding, did not change the result, for if all such illegal votes are rejected and that number deducted from the votes cast in favor of annexation, the proposition still received a majority.

Annexation of territory.

4. Territory annexed to a village, like territory originally incorporated, must be so conditioned as properly to be subjected to village government.

Same.

5. It does not appear from the record herein that the territory annexed was not within the condition mentioned.

Upon the petition of Lyndon A. Smith, as attorney general of the state of Minnesota, this court granted its writ directing the village

[1] Reported in 149 N. W. 951.

of Gilbert and the trustees of that village to show *quo warranto* they held and exercised their authority and offices in certain territory described in the writ, and to show cause why the annexation proceedings mentioned in the opinion should not be declared illegal and void, and why the individual respondents should not be ousted. The respondents answered. Writ discharged.

Lyndon A. Smith, Attorney General, *Baldwin, Baldwin & Holmes* and *Washburn, Bailey & Mitchell,* for relator.

Warner E. Whipple, W. H. Radermacher and *O. J. Larsen,* for respondents.

HOLT, J.

This is a *quo warranto* proceeding brought in this court to test the legality of the annexation of certain territory to the village of Gilbert in St. Louis county. The village as originally incorporated included 2,240 acres. In *quo warranto* proceedings, reported in 107 Minn. 364, 120 N. W. 528, a writ of ouster was granted because the territory lacked urban qualification. Thereupon, in virtue of chapter 148, p. 160, of the Laws of 1909 and the general law relating to village organization, the village again incorporated, retaining 80 acres of the original territory and adding on the south of the west 40 thereof a wedge-shaped piece of 53 acres. The annexation now attacked was made under and in conformity to chapter 113, p. 103, Laws of 1909, which was enacted and went into effect prior to the incorporation of the present village of Gilbert.

The principal reasons for asserting the illegality of the annexation are: (1) The unconstitutionality of the law under which it was attempted; (2) its inapplicability, even if constitutional, to the village of Gilbert; (3) if the foregoing propositions are not sustained, irregularity and fraud in the proceedings vitiated the attempted annexation; and (4) the territory annexed is not so conditioned that it is proper to come under village government.

Section 1 of chapter 113, p. 103, Laws of 1909 (section 1800, G. S. 1913), reads: "Any territory containing a population of not less than 75 persons, and not included in any incorporated city or village, but adjoining any city or village now or hereafter existing under the laws of the state of Minnesota, and no part of which territory is more than one and one-half miles from the present limits of the city or village which it adjoins, may be annexed to such city or village and become a part thereof." Then follow sections prescribing the procedure. It is contended that the section quoted, properly construed, applies only to cities and villages in existence when the law was enacted. If true, the act is void. Nichols v. Walter, 37 Minn. 264, 33 N. W. 800; State v. Cooley, 56 Minn. 540, 58 N. W. 150; State v. Ritt, 76 Minn. 531, 79 N. W. 535; Alexander v. City of Duluth, 77 Minn. 445, 80 N. W. 623. The first part of this section is clearly indicative of an intent to embrace all cities and villages whether then in existence or thereafter organized. The only doubt arises from the use of the words "present limits" in the last part of the section. The use of the word "present" unquestionably injects an ambiguity, if a literal and strict interpretation is attempted. But courts often, and without serious misgivings, convict legislators of inaccuracy in the use of words, in order to absolve them from the more serious charge of attempting to pass a law in conflict with the Constitution. It must be presumed that the legislature intends to enact valid laws. If there be reasonable room to construe a statute so that it will not offend the Constitution, it must be done. We find no difficulty in holding that the word "present" refers to the limit of the village at the time of the institution of annexation proceedings, and not to village limits at the time of the enactment of the law. This construction also refutes the claim that the law is not applicable to the village of Gilbert. Annexation in virtue thereof can be made to existing and future villages and cities alike.

As to irregularity, the contention is that there was territory immediately north and east of the village having streets laid out conforming to those in the village and a large population essentially urban in character which was not included in the annexation, but purposely excluded, because it was known that the voters thereof would have defeated the project, as was done two years previously when such territory, together with part of that in the present annexation, was attempted to be added to the village. A sufficient answer is that the legislature has not made it a condition that all the suitable territory adjoining a village or city shall be included in an annexation attempt. Indeed, if the several statutes now existing be examined, it would seem that the policy is to permit piecemeal annexations as well as detachments. G. S. 1913, §§ 1226, 1228, 1230, 1233, 1241, 1798. However, it is clear that the act under consideration does not contemplate that the annexation of any particular territory shall depend upon the nonexistence of other urban or semi-urban territory adjacent to the village. It is made to rest upon the sole determination of the electors of the territory proposed to be annexed and its fitness for village government, save that the governing body of the village possesses the discretionary right to order the election to be held in such territory. The original incorporation of a village is not open to attack, because there was left out other adjoining territory which properly could have been included. State v. Village of Dover, 113 Minn. 452, 130 N. W. 74, 539. No reason or law calls for a different rule in respect to subsequent extensions of a village. So that we cannot hold that the governing body of the village exercised an arbitrary discretion in ordering an election for this annexation, because it did not include other adjoining urban or semi-urban territory. It must be remembered that the formation of municipalities and the annexing or detaching territory therefrom is with the legislature and not the courts. We cannot question the wisdom of the statutes regulating the same, nor the expediency of the conditions prescribed for the right to organize or to change.

The relator earnestly insists that there was such fraud practiced by village officers and residents of the village that the election must be declared invalid. The evidence is convincing that colonization of prospective voters in the territory to be annexed was attempted by residents of the village. Connected with the under-handed and unlawful plan we find an employee and an officer of the village. The opponents of annexation were not asleep; their methods of frustrating the scheme were as cunning; and are excusable only on the theory that the end justifies the means. It is not necessary to go into details. For, conceding that the result of the election can be questioned by this proceeding, a point we do not decide, it cannot be held that the ballots fraudulently cast by persons not entitled to vote render void the ballots duly cast by the qualified voters at a lawfully called and conducted election, upon a proposition which they had the right to determine. At the most, the ballots fraudulently cast may be rejected. Here 60 ballots were cast in favor of annexation, 33 against, and one was spoiled. We do not understand that it is claimed that more than 16 ballots were cast by those who had no right to vote— who were colonizers. If we assume that every one of these illegal ballots was cast for annexation and hence deduct them from the 60 affirmative votes, we still have a decisive majority in favor of annexation. Even if all challenged votes—25—were assumed to be fraudulent and considered cast in favor of annexation, there would still be a majority for the proposition. The opponents of annexation were closely watching the election, assisted by lawyers of rare ability, and we may rest assured that no questionable vote went unchallenged.

By chapter 113, p. 103, Laws of 1909, no condition at all is prescribed for the territory proposed to be annexed, except that it must contain a population of not less than 75 persons, that it must not then be within the limits of any city or village, but must adjoin the limits of an existing village or city to which it is proposed to attach it, and that no part thereof can be more than one and one-half miles from such limits. The territory here annexed contained a population of 590 persons, was not within the limits of any existing village or city, it adjoined the then limits of the village of Gilbert, no part thereof was more than one and one-half miles from the then village limits. It contained 1,880 acres. So that there was a literal compliance with the statute. But we may assume, and so hold, that the same qualifications extend to territory sought to be annexed as to territory included in the original incorporation, namely, it must be "so conditioned as properly to be subjected to village government." And whether it reasonably comes within this definition is, we take it, the only question open for consideration by the court. The record discloses that Gilbert is a flourishing mining village of nearly 2,000 inhabitants, with some 500 more in contiguous territory other than the 1,880 acres mentioned. The annexed territory, with the wedge-shaped 53 acres of the village projecting into the northerly side, is in compact form, almost square. In the northeasterly part there are groups of settlements unquestionably semi-urban in character, and the same applies to a 40-acre tract or two in the southwesterly part. On some of the intervening ground are mines in operation containing the necessary buildings and equipment. The mines employ several hundred men working in shifts night and day who reside either at the village or, in the settlements referred to, in the annexed territory. The people in the southwest corner have convenient communication with the city of Eveleth to the southwest and not much more distant than Gilbert, but the testimony shows that by far the greater amount of their trade and intercourse is with Gilbert. Although part of the territory not occupied by habitations, mines or mining equipment, is devoted to garden patches, the greater part thereof is either wild cut-over land, or ground utilized for dumps in the mining operations. It is not contended that any substantial portion thereof is adapted for agricultural purposes. A mine near the southwest limits has supplied the village so far with water, but it is claimed that the village stands in need of the annexed territory through which to reach a large lake on the south boundary for future water supply. This is of no great weight since under section 1819, G. S. 1913, villages may obtain access to water, and furnish those outside the village limits therewith. Under the whole annexed territory valuable ore deposits are supposed to exist, so that while the assessed valuation of the property in the village proper is less than a quarter of a million dollars, that in the annexed territory is over five millions. In the great possibilities of revenue from the taxation of these valuable mining lands, no doubt, is found one of the chief motives for and against annexation. But the legislature has not made the value of either the territory to be incorporated into a village, or that to be annexed, a condition for or against. There would be no village here but for the existence and operation of the mines. The men inhabiting the so-called locations, surrounding the mines, resort to the village proper for their needs. The churches, lodges, stores and places of amusement are in the village proper. So is the high school. There is a certain dependence of a mining or manufacturing community upon the adjacent village or city different from that of the agricultural community. This the legislature has recognized in provisions permitting purely agricultural lands to be detached. Hunter v. City of Tracy, 104 Minn. 378, 116 N. W. 922.

Relator relies on the decision holding the original corporation vulnerable, because it included a large extent of territory not so conditioned as to be proper for village government. The argument is that the annexed territory is largely the same in kind. But it must be remembered that the facts now disclosed are very different from the ones then pleaded. Then it appeared that on the platted portion in the incorporated village resided only 98 persons, now in the village reside 1,800 people, and in it those in the surrounding locations within the one and one-half mile limit transact most of their business. It is the nucleus to which the people in the annexed territory are drawn. In the mines within the annexed part several hundred men work, many of whom reside in the village, and pass back and forth. From the valuable mineral deposits, assumed to be in the ground, it is reasonable to believe that the ore will be mined, and thus give employment to a great number of men for years to come. From our decisions it is apparent that land may be included which is not needed for present village purposes. Future necessities and growth may be anticipated. What territory shall and what territory shall not be included in a village incorporation or annexation is a question of fact to be determined by the people immediately interested within the limits placed by the legislature. "The soundness of their judgment in passing on the question must be tested as questions of fact * * * are tested on appeal." State v. Village of Dover, 113 Minn. 452, 130 N. W. 74, 539. In State v. Village of Alice, 112 Minn. 330, 127 N. W. 1118, the conditions of the lands incorporated into a village were very similar to the territory here in question. It comprised two sections, on one of which were no dwellings. It was wild land, except for a mine in operation on one of the forties and this was located half a mile from any of the platted part. The population was only 233 persons. The opinion, after referring to the rule that creation of municipal corporations is solely for the legislature—the same holds true in respect to annexations—and that in an attack upon the legality of such corporations courts can do noth-

ing more than determine whether the conditions prescribed by the
legislature existed when organized, states: "No inflexible rule can
be laid down by which the question can be answered; for each case
must depend, to some extent at least, on its own particular facts.
Neither the extent of the adjacent territory nor its relative value to
the platted territory is one of the conditions found in the statute.
* * * The fact that the lands included in this village are suitable for mining purposes might be a reason why it would be proper
so to include them; for lands of that class may, and usually do, de-
rive a benefit in many ways from being included within the limits
of a municipality, such as the benefit of police protection, water,
lights, and sewage." Assuming that territory annexed must like
that in the original incorporation be "so conditioned as properly to
be subjected to village government," nevertheless we are not justified
in overruling the finding of the electors that the territory in this case
was so conditioned. The precedent established in the Alice village
case, where the disclosed conditions were not as favorable for village
government as in the instant case, sustains our conclusion. It is not
for this court to determine whether the legislature is wise in the extensive additions permitted, or the people wisely covet the chance
to place additional burdens of village improvements on mine owners
who have so far, apparently without objection, sustained the heavy
end of, perhaps, the heaviest burden of every village or city, namely,
that of education. The village is part of an independent school district 18 miles long and from three to six miles wide, the center of
which is in the village, where are located a costly high school and
grade schools conducted under the very latest methods, with nurses,
medical attendance, evening school, vocational schools, entertain-
ments, free conveyance of pupils, etc.

To the effect that the creation of municipal corporations, change
in their boundaries by annexation or severance of territory, and the
conditions upon which such creation or change may be made, are
legislative and not judicial questions may also be cited: State v.
Simons, 32 Minn. 540, 21 N. W. 750; City of Winona v. School
District No. 82, Winona County, 40 Minn. 13, 41 N. W. 539, 3
L.R.A. 46, 12 Am. St. 687; People v. City of Riverside, 70 Cal.

461, 11 Pac. 759; State v. City of Waxahachie, 81 Tex. 626, 17 S.
W. 348; Kelly v. Pittsburg, 104 U. S. 78, 26 L. ed. 659, and section
265, McQuillin, Municipal Corporations.

In our opinion the writ should be discharged. So ordered.

CHRISTIAN CARLSON v. JOHN WENZEL.[1]

December 11, 1914.

Nos. 18,837—(100).

Judgment on the pleadings.

> Construing a farm lease giving to the vendee of the owner the right of
> possession upon sale, it is *held* that the court erred in granting the de-
> fendant lessee's motion for judgment on the pleadings.

Action to recover possession of certain land. Defendant's motion
in the district court for McLeod county for judgment on the pleadings was granted, Morrison, J. From the judgment entered pursuant to the order for judgment, plaintiff appealed. Reversed.

C. G. Odquist and *Anderson & Kube,* for appellant.

G. W. Brown, for respondent.

DIBELL, C.

This was an action in unlawful detainer brought in the municipal
court of Hutchinson and removed to the district court on appeal for
a trial *de novo.* The court granted defendant's motion for judgment
on the pleadings. From the judgment plaintiff appeals.

The defendant is the owner, by assignment, of a lease of a farm
dated September 9, 1912, made by one Richards, the then owner.
The lease ran to October 9, 1915, at a specified cash rental, payable
semiannually, commencing April 1, 1913.

---

[1] Reported in 149 N. W. 937.

The lease, which is of a form in common use, contains these provisions:

"That if the said first party sells said premises during the life of this lease and before the crop is in the ground, and desires to give possession to the purchaser, that the second party will forthwith surrender possession of said leased premises upon payment to him of $1.50 per acre for each acre of said premises newly plowed by said second party at the time said possession is demanded; if sold after the crop is in, then said second party shall have the right to remove such crop when ready to be harvested. That if said first party sells said premises during the term of this lease, the purchaser may at any time enter upon the leased premises for the purpose of plowing, breaking more land, summer-fallowing, cultivating or otherwise improving any part of said premises not in actual cultivation by said second party, and without such entry working any forfeiture of the rents herein agreed to be paid."

On January 22, 1914, the plaintiff bought the farm from Richards. There was then in the ground some eight acres of winter rye sown by the defendant. The defendant had done some plowing for the 1914 crop season. On February 4, 1914, the plaintiff tendered payment for the plowing and demanded possession.

In Minnesota the usual cropping season is the spring season. Farm leases are made with reference to the spring crop. It cannot be held that the planting of the rye in the fall saved the defendant's right of possession for the purpose of planting the spring crop of the following season or his right of occupancy of the premises. The defendant does not lose his crop of rye. By the terms of the lease he has a right of removal and that carries with it whatever right of possession is necessary to make the removal effective.

Under the lease, which is indefinite and perhaps inconsistent in its terms, it may be, as the defendant's counsel contends, that the crop is in the ground within the meaning of the lease when in the ordinary course of husbandry the ground is prepared and the cropping commenced; or it may be that upon sale the vendee has no right of possession, except for the purpose of cultivating or improving the portion of the premises not in cultivation, if the cropping season is at hand and the ground is under cultivation. These questions are not before us.

Under the pleadings it was error to hold that the plaintiff was not entitled to possession.

Judgment reversed.

CHARLES JOHNSON v. HARRY G. YOUNG.[1]

December 11, 1914.

Nos. 18,866—(105).

Impeachment of witness.

1. Failure to lay a technically perfect foundation as regards time and place is not ground for rejecting testimony of prior contradictory statements made by a witness out of court, where it is clear that neither he nor the impeaching witness is misled thereby.

Street car discharging passenger — motor vehicle — lookout by driver.

2. G. S. 1913, § 2632, requiring operators of motor vehicles to slow down in approaching or passing a street car which has been stopped to allow passengers to alight or embark, and to stop if necessary for the safety of the public, was intended to create a zone of safety around and about the entrance of such car by placing the burden of the lookout upon the driver of the motor vehicle; and hence one alighting from a standing street car is not obliged to keep a lookout for automobiles, under penalty of being charged with contributory negligence if he fails to do so.

Charge to jury.

3. Instruction *held* erroneous as depriving plaintiff of the benefit of this statute, and also as introducing an irrelevant issue as to the duty to look out for vehicles in general.

Taxing disbursements.

4. Disbursement for printing paper book and appellant's brief taxed at 60 cents per page. In no case will a larger sum be allowed unless such expense has actually been incurred. [Reporter.]

1 Reported in 149 N. W. 940.

Note.—As to the duty of the operator of an automobile near street cars, see notes in 38 L.R.A.(N.S.) 493; 42 L.R.A.(N.S.) 1184, and 51 L.R.A.(N.S.) 1003.

Action in the district court for Stearns county to recover $10,113 for personal injury received by plaintiff's minor son while alighting from a street car, by collision with defendant's automobile. The answer denied negligence on defendant's part and alleged that plaintiff's son not only contributed to, but proximately caused, the collision. The case was tried before Roeser, J., and a jury which returned a verdict in favor of defendant. From an order denying plaintiff's motion for a new trial, he appealed. Reversed.

Harry S. Locke, for appellant.

J. D. Sullivan, for respondent.

PHILIP E. BROWN, J.

Action to recover damages for personal injuries suffered by plaintiff's minor son Elmer, alleged to have been caused by defendant's negligent operation of an automobile. Defendant had a verdict. Plaintiff appealed from an order denying a new trial.

The accident happened near the crossing of an east and west street in St. Cloud, at about 8:10 p. m., July 2, 1913. Elmer, aged 19, and an acquaintance contemplated taking a westerly-bound street car running on this street, and as it appeared both walked out to the crossing, but before it arrived there the latter turned and went back without Elmer's knowledge. Defendant was then approaching from the east on the right side of the street, driving his automobile. The street car stopped a short distance beyond the crossing and several passengers alighted. Plaintiff claims his son immediately put one foot on the step of the standing car, but when, on looking backward, he observed his companion on the sidewalk, he turned and started to walk there and was immediately struck and run over by defendant's automobile, which he had not previously seen. Defendant admitted he was looking at the car and saw people getting off and on, and also the striking and injury of the boy near the crossing. He claimed, however, that his approach thereto was at a speed of not to exceed five miles an hour, with his machine under perfect control and decreasing speed. Further, that after all passengers desirous of so doing had apparently alighted and the car had started and moved a short distance westerly, and when his machine was 10 or

12 feet from the crossing, Elmer swung off the car backwards some 8 or 10 feet beyond the crossing, when he was struck and knocked down almost instantly; whereupon defendant stopped immediately before running over him, but not until the front wheel reached his right foot. Testimony was given to the effect that the boy was picked up six or seven feet from the crossing and about four feet from the street car. He admitted he could have seen the approaching automobile had he looked when turning around. The evidence, which would have warranted a finding of considerably higher speed than defendant claimed, was sharply conflicting, and made a case for the jury on the question of defendant's negligence but not of wilfulness. Whether plaintiff's or defendant's version of the accident was the true one was likewise for the jury.

1. One Huhn testified for defendant to the effect that he was a passenger on the street car and was standing on the vestibule when the accident happened, and that the car had not only then started, but had proceeded from 8 to 12 feet. On cross-examination he admitted having a conversation with one Knutsen on the following morning, in the latter's tailor shop, but denied that he then stated in substance that the street car was standing perfectly still when the accident occurred or that the front wheel of the automobile ran over Elmer's leg. Later plaintiff called Knutsen and interrogated him concerning these alleged statements, and after proving the holding of the conversation between the latter and Huhn on the day following the injury, but not the place where or the hour when it occurred, asked him in almost the identical language previously used if he had so stated. The court, however, sustained an objection thereto as "incompetent, irrelevant, immaterial, inadmissible, no foundation laid." This was error. The object of the rule requiring the attention of the witness to be first called to statements made out of court contradictory to his testimony before he can be contradicted, is that in fairness to him he should be afforded an opportunity to recollect and explain his former statement, if one was made. The record contains no intimation of any conversation between these persons concerning this matter at any other time or place, and evidently neither witness was misled as to the occasion. This testimony related to material

and important subjects, and its exclusion was a too technical application of the rule of impeachment. 3 Dunnell, Minn. Dig. § 10,351 (b); Jones, Ev. (1914) § 846; Wigmore, Ev. § 1029.

2. The court charged at defendant's request:

"The law requires that a person attempting to alight from or embark upon a street car use ordinary care. He must use his faculty of seeing and hearing and he must under the circumstances of this case be chargeable with notice that upon the evening when the accident occurred vehicles of different kinds, including automobiles, were liable to be passing upon the street where this accident occurred, and it was his duty under all the circumstances to keep a lookout for such vehicles for his own safety." This is assigned as error.

G. S. 1913, § 2632, provides:

"In approaching or passing a car of a street railway, which has been stopped to allow passengers to alight or embark, the operator of every motor vehicle shall slow down, and if it is necessary for the safety of the public, he shall bring said vehicle to a full stop not less than ten feet from said street car."

Before considering the instruction or the effect of the statute, it will be well to review shortly our holdings made prior to the passage of the latter.

Stillman v. Shea, 99 Minn. 422, 109 N. W. 824, involved an injury to plaintiff caused by a collision with a horse and wagon while she was crossing a street. The court said at pages 425, 426:

"In a case like the one before us, the driver of a team has almost as complete control of his team as a pedestrian has of his movements. The relative rights of pedestrians and vehicles in a public highway are equal and reciprocal—one has no more rights than the other, and each is obliged to act with due regard to the movements of others entitled to be upon the street. Neither is called upon to anticipate negligence on the part of the other. It is no more the duty of a pedestrian to continually look out for approaching vehicles than it is the duty of drivers to look out for pedestrians. No pedestrian has a right to pass over a public thoroughfare without regard to approaching vehicles, nor has any vehicle a right to appropriate the

127 M.—30.

public street for the purpose of transacting business without regard to its use by pedestrians."

In Arseneau v. Sweet, 106 Minn. 257, 119 N. W. 46, plaintiff was struck by defendant's automobile while she was in the act of boarding a street car. The court said at page 259:

"Respondent was in lawful possession of the street. She had a right to walk out from the curb to the car tracks, in anticipation of the approaching car, and, if she took a position in the street within three or four feet of the car tracks with the intention of boarding the approaching car, she was not required absolutely to keep a lookout for vehicles at that point. The law governing the conduct of foot passengers and vehicles in the public streets is well settled. Stallman v. Shea, 99 Minn. 422, 109 N. W. 824; Thies v. Thomas (Sup.) 77 N. Y. Supp. 276; Huddy, Laws of Automobiles, p. 58. Respondent had no exclusive right to the street for the purpose of boarding a street car. She was not entitled to take a position even three or four feet from the car tracks and remain oblivious to her surroundings. But she was not guilty of contributory negligence simply because she did not look and did not see or hear the approaching machine. Her attention was naturally concentrated on the street car, and she was entitled to assume that others would exercise due care with reference to her position."

This case was followed in Liebrecht v. Crandall, 110 Minn. 454, 456, 126 N. W. 69; and to the same effect see Johnson v. Scott, 119 Minn. 470, 474, 138 N. W. 694.

It is doubtful if the instruction could be sustained under these authorities; but in addition thereto we have the statute subsequently passed. The purpose of the latter was, by creating a zone of safety, to protect the many who use street cars as against the comparatively few who, in driving automobiles, might render ingress to and egress from the former dangerous. It modified the doctrine of reciprocal rights in the street in all cases falling within its terms, and obviates the necessity, if any theretofore existed, on the part of those boarding or leaving standing cars, of looking out for approaching automobiles. In such case they have the right to presume that persons using so dangerous an agency will perform their duty and obey the statute, and, in the absence of reasonable ground to think otherwise, they are not guilty of negligence in assuming freedom from a danger which can come only from such violation. Whatever the rule may heretofore have been, the burden of the lookout is now upon the automobile driver, and the duty of the street-car passenger is diminished accordingly. Medlin v. Spazier, 23 Cal. App. 242, 137 Pac. 1078.

The instruction, therefore, cannot be sustained. In effect the jury were advised that, even under the view of the testimony most favorable to plaintiff, his son was obliged to "keep a lookout" for automobiles, which, as we have seen, is not the law, and also for other vehicles liable to be passing, though such were in nowise involved in the case, thus introducing an irrelevant issue likely to confuse and mislead the jury.

We find no other error.

Order reversed.

On January 5, 1915, the following opinion was filed:

PER CURIAM.

Appellant taxed, against respondent's objection, for printing the paper book and brief in this cause, 75 cents a page. For many years the practice has been to allow only 60 cents when the printing was done in the three large cities, and 75 cents in other cases. In no case will a larger sum be allowed, and these only when such expenses have actually been incurred.

The clerk is directed to reduce the amount allowed to 60 cents a page.

WILLIAM KLING v. THOMPSON-McDONALD LUMBER COMPANY.[1]

December 11, 1914.

Nos. 18,869—(114).

Verdict sustained by evidence.

1. It is admitted that plaintiff, a street car conductor, was injured by defendant's auto truck. He claimed that the truck ran into him while he was standing in the street adjusting the trolley upon his car. Defendant claimed, and the great preponderance of the evidence indicated that, while attempting to adjust the trolley, he fell from the platform of the car in front of the truck. The evidence is sufficient to sustain the verdict, if the accident happened in either manner, and the failure to sustain plaintiff's claim in this respect does not require a reversal.

Motor vehicle and street car — construction of statute.

2. The conductor of a street car is within the class of persons for whose benefit the statute requires motor vehicles to slow down, and, if "necessary for the safety of the public," to stop not less than 10 feet from a street car which is receiving and discharging passengers.

Same.

3. While a street car is receiving and discharging passengers, pedestrians to and from the car have the right of way, and it is the duty of an auto driver to stop, if necessary for their safety, and, if he does not stop, to exercise such care in the management of his machine as, under the circumstances, shall appear to be reasonably necessary to guard against injury to any one.

Harmless error.

4. There was no reversible error in the rulings of the court, or in the charge to the jury.

Action in the district court for Hennepin county to recover $10,-170 for personal injury sustained through collision with defendant's

[1] Reported in 149 N. W. 947.

Note.—The question of the duty of the driver of an automobile when near street cars is discussed in notes in 38 L.R.A.(N.S.) 493; 42 L.R.A.(N.S.) 1184, and 51 L.R.A.(N.S.) 1003.

motor truck. The facts are stated in the opinion. The case was tried before Hale, J., and a jury which returned a verdict in favor of plaintiff for $2,166. From an order denying defendant's motion for a new trial, it appealed. Affirmed.

P. J. McLaughlin, for appellant.

Stan J. Donnelly & Stan Dillon Donnelly, for respondent.

TAYLOR, C.

This is an action to recover damages for personal injuries. Plaintiff had a verdict, and defendant appealed from an order denying a motion for a new trial.

The errors assigned are: That the evidence does not sustain the verdict; that the charge to the jury was prejudicial; that two instructions requested by defendant were not given; that an objection to the admission of testimony was overruled; and that a request to submit a special question for the jury to answer was denied.

Plaintiff was the conductor of an interurban street car running between St. Paul and Minneapolis. While his car was crossing the tracks of the Chicago, Milwaukee & St. Paul Railway Co., in Minneapolis, the trolley came off the wire. The momentum of the car carried it across the tracks, and to the usual place for discharging and receiving passengers beyond such tracks, where it was brought to a stop by the motorman. Three passengers entered the car but none alighted therefrom. After the car came to a stop, plaintiff's attention was called to the fact that the trolley was off the wire. He was inside the car but hastened to the rear vestibule and, while standing upon the platform, tried to put the trolley back in place. He testified that he worked in this manner for three or four minutes without succeeding; and then stepped into the street, at the side of and facing the rear vestibule of the car, and, while in this position, had worked for two or three minutes trying to replace the trolley, when he was struck and knocked down by defendant's auto truck. He also testified that he had not seen the truck and did not know that it was approaching.

The truck was going in the same direction as the street car. It stopped at the railroad tracks, then crossed the tracks, and proceeding slowly attempted to pass the street car which still remained stationary. The driver of the truck testified that, when he was at the railroad crossing, he saw the conductor standing upon the platform of the car trying to put the trolley in place; that when the front of the truck was about opposite the rear of the car, the conductor gave the trolley rope a jerk and, apparently losing his balance, fell from the platform in front of the truck. Of the passengers upon the street car, six were called as witnesses—two by plaintiff and four by defendant. Each of the four called by defendant testified positively that plaintiff, while attempting to fix the trolley, slipped, or lost his balance, and fell from the platform directly in front of the truck, substantially as stated by the driver. Of the two called by plaintiff, one testified that he was upon the platform; saw the conductor upon the platform trying to put the trolley in place; looked into the car for a seat, then looked back and saw the wheel of the truck shoving the conductor along the pavement. The other testified that he was upon the platform; that he stepped out of the way of the conductor who was working at the trolley; turned to go into the car; felt a jar; thought the truck struck the car; turned back and the conductor was then under the truck. Neither of them saw the conductor leave the platform, but, during the moment when they were looking elsewhere, his position was changed from that of standing upon the platform to that of lying upon the pavement against the wheel of the truck.

Plaintiff's statement that he stepped from the platform to the street and attempted to put the trolley in place while standing in the street is not corroborated by any other witness, not even by the motorman. A light rain was falling, and had been nearly all day, and both the street and the steps of the car were wet, muddy and slippery. When the car came to a stop, the gates were opened and remained open until after the accident. The truck was going very slowly. Of four witnesses who estimated the speed, none placed it above three miles per hour. Plaintiff apparently fell crosswise of the street and directly in front of the left front wheel of the truck, which struck him about midway between his hips and his shoulders. The wheel did not run over him, but pushed him along the pavement for some distance and fractured several of his ribs. The slow speed of the truck, the way in which he fell, and the testimony of all the other witnesses, including those called by himself, render the claim that plaintiff was standing in the street, and was there run down, so improbable that, if the jury, by their verdict, necessarily found that the accident happened in that manner, a new trial should be granted under the rule applied in the following cases: Voge v. Penney, 74 Minn. 525, 77 N. W. 422; Messenger v. St. Paul City Ry. Co. 77 Minn. 34, 79 N. W. 583; Baxter v. Covenant Mut. Life Assn. 77 Minn. 80, 79 N. W. 596; Gammons v. Gulbranson, 78 Minn. 21, 80 N. W. 779; Schmeltzer v. St. Paul City Ry. Co. 80 Minn. 50, 82 N. W. 1092; Peterson v. Chicago Great Western Ry. Co. 106 Minn. 245, 118 N. W. 1016; Patzke v. Minneapolis & St. Louis R. Co. 109 Minn. 97, 123 N. W. 57; Hill v. Jones, 109 Minn. 370, 123 N. W. 927, 18 Ann. Cas. 359.

In the charge the court defined in general terms, but quite fully and correctly, the care required of an auto driver to prevent injury to others and then stated:

"The negligence which the defendant is charged with here, or the driver, is the failure to use reasonable and ordinary care; such as a reasonably prudent man would be expected to use under the same circumstances." He then read the following paragraph from the statute:

"In approaching or passing a car of a street railway, which has been stopped to allow passengers to alight or embark, the operator of every motor vehicle shall slow down, and if it is necessary for the safety of the public, he shall bring said vehicle to a full stop not less than ten feet from said street car."

He then continued:

"That is the rule by which the defendant's conduct is to be measured in this case. The law does not require him absolutely to stop when the gates are open, ten feet from the gates; but he is required to take that into consideration, and if it is necessary for the safety of the public, he is required to stop ten feet before he gets to the gates.

"It is claimed on the part of the plaintiff that the fact that the gates were open was a sign, an indication, to this driver or to anybody that came along, that people might be getting on or off the car.

"It is claimed on the part of the defendant that the plaintiff fell off the steps onto the ground. Now it makes no difference that he may have fallen out, so far as the liability of the defendant is concerned; that is, I mean if the driver, under the circumstances, was not using reasonable and ordinary care, such as he ought to have used under the circumstances, and because of the failure to use such reasonable and ordinary care this man was run over. A man is entitled to recover, if he falls down in a street, or if he lies down in a street; he is entitled to just as much protection as a man that stands up on the street. The only object of that evidence, that I can see, was this: That the conductor, as they claim, was not standing upon the street, therefore there was no evidence visible to the driver that the conductor was there, and that because of this he was not required to use the same care that he would have been required to use if the conductor had been, as he claims he was, standing upon the street fixing this trolley. But if the driver was not using reasonable and ordinary care under the circumstances, and the plaintiff did, as the defendant claims, fall out onto the street and was run into, then the defendant in this case is liable. There is no claim here that the plaintiff was himself guilty of negligence, or that he assumed the risk. The only question is, as I have stated, was the driver of this machine, under all the circumstances, guilty of negligence such as I have stated, and was the injury to this plaintiff the proximate result of such negligence."

After the jury had been out about three hours they returned and requested further instructions "as to the duty of the driver of an auto truck when approaching a street car with the gates open." The court responded by again reading the portion of the statute above quoted but added no comment thereto.

Defendant contends, at the outset, that the only purpose of the statute above quoted is to protect passengers while entering or leaving a street car, and that it was not intended for the benefit of the men operating the car, and does not apply in case of injury to them. We cannot give the statute such a narrow construction. It requires the auto to slow down, and, if "necessary for the safety of the public," to come to a full stop. It expresses an intention to protect, not merely those entering or leaving the car, but the public generally, and we think the operatives upon the car are within its purview. Fairchild v. Fleming, 125 Minn. 431, 147 N. W. 434.

The statute casts upon an auto driver approaching a street car, stopped to allow passengers to alight or embark, the burden of keeping watch and taking such action as may be necessary to guard against injury to persons coming into the street. He is required to slow down, and, if necessary for the safety of the public, to stop. In effect, under such circumstances, pedestrians are given the right of way to and from the car, and the auto driver must govern himself accordingly. If he does not stop, he must exercise a high degree of care to avoid injury to those who may be, or may come, upon the street. He is not an insurer against accidents, however, and, if the roadway is clear and appears likely to remain clear, so that, apparently, he can proceed without endangering anyone, and he goes forward with due caution, and with his machine under such control as to enable him to avert any danger that could reasonably be anticipated, he is not liable for the happening of an accident which, in the exercise of reasonable caution and prudence he could not have foreseen or guarded against.

It is undisputed that plaintiff was struck and injured by the truck. If he was standing upon the street, as he claimed, and, while in plain view and engaged in replacing the trolley, was run down by the truck, defendant's negligence is clear. If he fell from the car, as the great weight of evidence indicates, whether defendant is chargeable with negligence depends upon whether the circumstances were such as to justify the driver of the truck in undertaking to pass the car, and whether in passing the car he exercised that degree of care and caution, in the operation of his machine, which, under the circumstances, appeared to be reasonably necessary for the safety of those in a position where they might suddenly come in front of the truck as it passed the car entrance. Several passengers entered the car after it stopped, but this was while the truck was back at the railroad tracks. When the truck approached the car, no one was either entering or leaving it, and no one was upon the street. The driver saw the conductor attempting to put the trolley in place, and might

reasonably have assumed, as seems to have been the fact, that the
car was no longer waiting for passengers to alight or embark, but
was merely waiting for the conductor to reconnect it with its source
of motive power.   It cannot be held that the statute makes an attempt to pass, under such circumstances, negligence *per se*.   But, in
attempting to pass, the driver is required to exercise such care as,
under the circumstances, shall appear to be reasonably necessary to
guard against injuring any one then in a position to move suddenly
either toward or from the car.   Plaintiff fell under the truck and, as
expressed by the witnesses, was shoved along the pavement by the
wheel for a considerable distance.   The driver estimates it as six or
eight feet.   Several of the witnesses state the distance as more than
half the length of the street car, which was over 40 feet long.   Considering the distance which the truck ran after striking plaintiff, in
connection with its slow speed and all the other facts and circumstances, it was a fair question for the jury whether the driver was
exercising proper care in the management of his machine at the time
of the accident, and the evidence is sufficient to sustain their verdict.

We have quoted the portion of the charge to which exceptions
were taken, and have considered such portion in connection with that
which preceded it, and are of the opinion that the charge, taken as
a whole, submitted the case to the jury substantially in accordance
with the views above expressed, and that, considered as a whole, it
contains no reversible error, although, in answering the request of the
jury for further instructions, the court might well have explained
the duty of the driver more fully.

Defendant requested the court to instruct the jury that plaintiff
could not recover, if he fell from the car upon the street in front of
the truck.   Conceding that the accident happened in that manner,
the evidence still made a question for the jury, as already stated, and
the refusal to give this instruction was correct.   Defendant also requested the court to instruct that "if * * * a person of ordinary care and prudence would have attempted to pass the street car
at the time and in the manner the driver of the truck in question
attempted to pass," the plaintiff could not recover.   This instruction

did not mention the statute, nor the duty imposed thereby upon the driver of an automobile. In view of this omission, and of the fact that the court, early in its charge, told the jury that it was the duty of the driver to use such care, "as a prudent, reasonably careful man would be expected to use under the same circumstances," and later defined the negligence charged as "the failure to use reasonable and ordinary care, such as a reasonably prudent man would be expected to use under the same circumstances," the refusal to give the instruction in the form requested did not constitute error.

It was within the discretion of the trial court to grant or refuse defendant's request to submit a special interrogatory for the jury to answer. 3 Dunnell, Minn. Digest, § 9802. It was also within the discretion of the trial court to permit plaintiff to answer the question as to whether he was married and had a family. No abuse of discretion appears.

As the evidence is sufficient to sustain the verdict, notwithstanding the rejection of plaintiff's version of the manner in which the accident happened, the order appealed from is affirmed.

ERNEST MAHR v. JAMES FORRESTAL and Another.[1]

December 11, 1914.

Nos. 18,872—(115).

Evidence — verdict.

1. The evidence in this personal injury action justified submitting to the jury the question of defendant's liability, and justified the verdict.

Charge to jury.

2. There was no reversible error in certain instructions.

Damages.

3. The damages are excessive.

[1] Reported in 149 N. W. 938.

Action in the district court for Hennepin county to recover $30,-000 for personal injuries received while in the employ of defendants. The answer denied negligence on defendants' part, and alleged that the physical conditions under which plaintiff was working at the time of injury were easily observable and well known to him, and that he assumed the risks. The facts are stated in the opinion. The case was tried before Olin B. Lewis, J., and a jury which returned a verdict for $11,337.50. From an order denying defendants' motion for judgment notwithstanding the verdict or for a new trial, they appealed. Affirmed on condition.

Barrows, Stewart & Ordway, for appellants.

Larrabee & Davies, for respondent.

BUNN, J.

The verdict in this personal injury action was for the plaintiff in the sum of $11,337. Defendants appeal from an order denying their motion for judgment or for a new trial.

The facts surrounding the accident are substantially as follows: In the spring and summer of 1913, defendants were operating a self-propelling or "walking" dredge near Marathon, Iowa. For some weeks prior to May 3, the crew had been engaged in repairing the dredge. Youngquist was defendant's foreman in charge of the repair work on this and other dredges of defendant. Russell was the foreman in charge of this particular dredge. The repair work was finished on the morning of May 3, and the crew commenced "walking" the dredge to the place where digging was to be done. In this crew were the foreman, an engineer, a blacksmith and assistant, a "runner" and a "craner." One Marvin was the "runner," and plaintiff was the "craner." The "runner" had control of the levers which threw the machinery in and out of gear, and charge of the operation of these levers in walking the dredge and in digging. The "craner" operated the swinging of the crane, or machinery which did the digging. It was his duty to trip or empty the scoop when digging operations were going on. This was done by means of a trip rope, the end of which was coiled upon a hook which hung above the machinery. To reach this rope it was convenient to stand upon a pulley on the backing shaft which was stationary when the dredge was not walking or digging. After the dredge had "walked" some 50 feet on the day in question, it became necessary to stop and do some digging in order to cross a ditch. Russell, the foreman, was not on the dredge at the time. Marvin was in his place near the levers on the front of the dredge, and plaintiff was standing near Marvin. Plaintiff testified that Marvin told him to go and fix the trip rope. He got upon the pulley in order to comply with the order, Marvin at first standing upon the floor assisting, but afterwards going over to the levers. While plaintiff was standing upon the pulleys, fixing the trip rope, the machinery started, the pulley began to turn, and plaintiff fell between the pulley he was standing on and the master pulley on the main shaft, and received the injuries complained of.

When the dredge stopped prior to the accident, the engine and main shaft were left running. To start the machine to walking or digging, it was necessary to throw in the levers.

This would start the entire machinery, including the shaft on which was the pulley on which plaintiff stood. This pulley, when at rest, was about half an inch from the revolving pulley on the main shaft. They were friction pulleys, and throwing the levers operated to make them come in contact.

Plaintiff's case rests upon the claim that Marvin ordered him to fix the trip rope and, while he was engaged in doing this, started the machinery in motion. In other words, the theory is that Marvin was a vice principal, and that his negligence was the negligence of the master. Defendants contend that they had not delegated to Marvin their absolute duties to furnish their servants a safe place to work, and to use reasonable care to keep the place safe; they further claim that in starting the machinery Marvin was engaged in one of the details of his work as a servant of defendants, and was not acting as their *alter ego,* or vice principal. The evidence was abundantly sufficient to warrant the jury in finding that Marvin was boss on the dredge when Russell was not there, and that plaintiff and the other employees were under his orders. We must take as established the fact that Marvin ordered plaintiff to fix the trip rope, and knew that he was in a position of extreme danger should the machinery that moved the pulley he was standing on be started without warning. The jury was justified in finding that Marvin did so start this machinery. These facts bring the case within a familiar line of decisions of this court: Hess v. Adamant Mnfg. Co. 66 Minn. 79, 68 N. W. 774; Barrett v. Reardon, 95 Minn. 425, 104 N. W. 309; Cody v. Longyear, 103 Minn. 116, 114 N. W. 735; Dizonno v. Great Northern Ry. Co. 103 Minn. 120, 114 N. W. 736; Lohman v. Swift & Co. 105 Minn. 150, 117 N. W. 418; Raitila v. Consumers Ore Co. 107 Minn. 91, 119 N. W. 490; Aho v. Adriatic Mining Co. 117 Minn. 504, 136 N. W. 310; Kempfert v. Gas Traction Co. 120 Minn. 90, 139 N. W. 145. It is sought to distinguish the cases cited from the present case by reason of the particular facts here. It is urged that Marvin, in moving the levers that started the machinery, was performing a detail of his work as a fellow-servant of plaintiff. The same contention was made and overruled in many of the cases cited. In the Cody case, the foreman was also a fellow-workman in the ordinary work of defendant, but it was held that his act in starting the machinery was the act of the master and not a mere detail of the work. In the Lohman case the same contention was made and elaborately argued but overruled. As stated by the present Chief Justice in the case last referred to: "It is not the rank or title the employee in charge as foreman sustains to the master which determines whether his particular act was that of the master or a fellow servant, but rather the nature of the act, and whether it involved one of the personal duties the master owed to other servants." We think that the act of Marvin involved one of the personal duties that defendant owed its servants, the duty to exercise reasonable care to provide them a safe place to do their work, and not to subject them to unnecessary risks or dangers. And we think the evidence warrants the conclusion that defendant had delegated the performance of these duties to Marvin, when the foreman was not on the dredge. Counsel argue that the facts here bring the case within the rule applied in Jemming v. Great Northern Ry. Co. 96 Minn. 302, 104 N. W. 1079, 1 L.R.A.(N.S.) 696; Doerr v. Daily News Pub. Co. 97 Minn. 248, 106 N. W. 1044; Berneche v.

Hilliard, 101 Minn. 366, 112 N. W. 392, and similar cases. We are unable to agree to this. The above cases have so often been distinguished from cases like the present that it seems unnecessary to again point out the differences. It is enough to say that they lack the peculiar features of the present case that make the negligent act that of the defendants themselves rather than the act of a fellow-servant of plaintiff.

It is true that Marvin did not order plaintiff to stand upon the pulley, and that it was probably not necessary to do so in order to fix the trip rope. But it was convenient and customary to stand upon the pulley to reach the rope, instead of procuring a box or barrel upon which to stand, and Marvin knew that plaintiff was in the habit of so using the pulley, and that he was actually standing thereon at the time. The position was not particularly dangerous while the pulley was stationary, but became extremely dangerous if the pulley moved. This was the situation in most of the cases in which the master has been held liable for the negligent act of his vice principal. We conclude that the evidence justified submitting to the jury the question of defendants' liability for the negligence of Marvin, and justified the verdict finding them liable.

The trial court submitted the question whether Marvin was a vice principal to the jury. The instructions are criticized as laying down a wrong test for the determination of this question, as making the rank of Marvin the criterion, rather than the delegation to him by the master of the performance of an absolute duty of the latter. It is argued that the instructions assigned as error practically permitted a recovery, if Marvin was a superior servant with the right to give orders to plaintiff, and if he negligently started the machinery, thus failing to distinguish between the negligence of a servant in his capacity as such, and his negligence in the performance of absolute duties of the master intrusted to him. But, in each of the instructions criticized, the liability of defendants is made dependent upon the question whether Marvin was acting for the defendants, and there was no request to have this more particularly defined, and no exception taken at the time. We find no reversible error here, and there is no claim of error elsewhere.

The verdict is large, but the injuries were very serious. Plaintiff was in the hospital five months. The muscles of his left leg were torn, and numerous skin grafting operations were only partially successful. The external "hamstring" muscle was destroyed. The surface of the injured leg has healed over, except at one place, but it is an unhealthy dry surface, and will always need applications of oil to keep it from cracking. The injured leg will never be as large or as strong as the other leg, and there is and probably always will be a partial paralysis in the injured muscles. Plaintiff is able to walk a little without crutches or cane, but with difficulty, owing to the muscles of the injured leg not being under control. It was left more or less a matter of speculation whether the future would bring material improvement. Without minimizing the nature or probable duration of the condition, and giving due regard to plaintiff's suffering, and his loss of earning capacity, we think the verdict is still excessive. There was no evidence that plaintiff would not be able to earn a good living in spite of his injury, which, serious as it undoubtedly is, does not equal in gravity of consequences the loss of a leg. We feel that $8,500 is ample compensation, and that anything beyond that savors of punishment. If plaintiff, within 10 days after the remittitur goes down, files his consent to a reduction of the verdict to $8,500, the order appealed from will stand affirmed. Otherwise a new trial is granted.

CHARLES HOWELL v. CUYUNA NORTHERN RAILWAY COMPANY.[1]

December 11, 1914.

Nos. 18,914—(123).

Mineral lease construed.

    1. A lease of real property construed and *held* to confer upon the lessee

---

[1] Reported in 149 N. W. 942.

Note.—Upon the right of the owner or lessee of mineral in place as to the use of the surface, see note in 48 L.R.A.(N.S.) 883.

the right to explore for, remove and transport to market, all iron ore found therein, and such additional rights of possession and control of the premises as are necessary to the proper conduct of the mining operations.

Same — possessory action by owner.

2. Except insofar as necessary to such mining operations the lessor, the fee owner of the land, retains the right of possession of the surface of the land and may maintain an action against any third person entering into the possession thereof without right or authority.

Same — construction of railroad.

3. The lessee, though the lease grants him the right to construct upon the premises all facilities necessary to market the ore taken from the land, including railroads, has no right to authorize the construction of a railroad upon the premises, except for the purpose of aiding in the mining operations and the transportation of ore to market.

Action in the district court for Crow Wing county to recover possession of land or $11,300 damages caused by the construction of a railroad upon it. The facts are stated in the opinion. The case was tried before McClenahan, J., who ordered judgment on the pleadings in favor of defendant. From the judgment entered pursuant to the order for judgment, plaintiff appealed. Reversed and new trial granted.

Clapp & Randall, for appellant.

C. W. Bunn and *D. F. Lyons,* for respondent.

BROWN, C. J.

The complaint in this action alleges, in substance and effect, that during all the times therein stated plaintiff was and still is the owner and entitled to the possession of the land mentioned therein, and that on September 1, 1908, defendant wrongfully and unlawfully entered upon the land and constructed thereon a line of railroad and ever since has operated it as a common carrier for general commercial purposes; that no proceedings were ever had or·taken to acquire the right to so occupy the land and no damages were ever assessed or paid therefor; that the land so taken is of the value of $2,000, and that the reasonable value of the use thereof since it was so taken by defendant is the sum of $1,000. The demand for relief is that

127 M.—31.

plaintiff have judgment for the possession of the land or, in lieu
thereof, damages in the sum of $11,300. Defendant answered ad-
mitting plaintiff's ownership of the land, and the construction thereon of its line of railroad, and the operation of the same as alleged
in the complaint; admitting also that no damages have ever been ascertained or paid to plaintiff for the right thus taken, and alleging
in defense and justification that the road was so constructed upon
the land "upon the request and with the express consent and authority
of plaintiff's lessee, the Northwestern Improvement Company," and
that defendant's occupancy of the land is with the full authority of
that company. Defendant further alleged that plaintiff, prior to the
act complained of, leased the land to the Howell Mining Co., which
company subsequently sublet to the improvement company. A copy
of the lease was attached to and made a part of the answer. The
reply admitted the lease and the rights granted thereby, and that defendant constructed its line of road upon the land at the request
and with the authority and consent of the lessee, the improvement
company. All other allegations of the answer were denied.

When the cause came on for trial the court granted defendant's
motion for judgment on the pleadings. Judgment was so entered
and plaintiff appealed.

It is the contention of defendant that the lease in question granted
to the improvement company for the term of 50 years the exclusive
right of possession of the land, that plaintiff, the fee owner, has no
present right of possession and cannot therefore maintain an action
either in ejectment or for damages against this defendant, who holds
under the improvement company. Whether this contention is sound
depends upon the construction to be given the lease, and the determination of the question whether it is anything more than an ordinary mining lease, granting to the company the right of possession
and control of the land insofar as necessary to remove iron ore therefrom. If the latter, it would seem clear that the improvement company would have no right to grant surface rights to third persons, the
rights so granted having no reference to or in furtherance of the
mining operations. In other words, the company would not be authorized if that be the construction of the lease to impose upon the

land an additional servitude, having no relation to the mining or transportation of the iron ore.

The lease treats fully of the rights of the parties, and provides that, in consideration of the covenants therein contained, the land is leased and let to the improvement company for the term of 50 years from the first day of September, 1908; it authorizes the lessee to explore for, mine and remove the merchantable iron ore which is or may be found deposited in or upon the land; "and to construct all buildings, make all excavations, openings, ditches, drains, railroads, wagon roads, and other improvements thereon suitable for the mining and removal of iron ore; and may cut and use timber from the leased premises for the purpose of carrying on any operation, or constructing, repairing or carrying on any building or work authorized by this lease." It further provides that at certain stated times the lessee shall pay to the lessor for all ore taken from the land at the rate of twenty cents per ton of 2,240 pounds; and pay for 5,000 tons of ore each year whether mined or not. It also requires the lessee to furnish the lessor with monthly statements showing the quantity and amount of ore taken from the land; and that the lessee shall pay all taxes assessed against the land, or improvements thereon, or iron ore produced therefrom. It provides that the lessee shall open, use and work the mines in such manner only as is usual and customary in skilful and proper mining operations of similar character; that the lessor may enter upon the premises for the purpose of inspecting the mining operations and measuring the quantity of ore taken or removed, "not unnecessarily or unreasonably hindering or interrupting the operations of the lessee." It gives the lessor a lien upon all ore taken from the mine, and all improvements upon the premises as security for the payment of the royalties for ore taken out. The lessor is given the option to terminate the lease at any time upon 90 days' notice, and when so terminated, or at the expiration of the term of the lease, the lessee agrees to surrender possession of the premises to the lessor; in the meantime the lessor covenants to defend the title and the right of possession in the lessee.

The foregoing embodies substantially all the elements of the contract which are relevant to the question of its construction as respects the present controversy. We are unable, after a somewhat careful consideration of the matter, to construe the lease otherwise than an ordinary mining lease, by which the rights conferred upon the lessee relate to and are confined exclusively to mining operations, and granting to it such right of exclusive possession as may be necessary to the conduct of the same. The question would seem to be controlled by Diamond Iron Mining Co. v. Buckeye Iron Mining Co. 70 Minn. 500, 73 N. W. 507, where a similar contract or lease was construed and held to vest in the lessor a right to payment of royalties only in the event that iron ore was found upon the land; that the lease was not one for the general use and possession of the land but one for mining purposes only, and, there being no ore to mine, there was no liability on the part of the lessee to pay royalties on a given number of tons of ore whether mined or not. The same stipulation is found in the lease here involved. While the lease involved in that case stated that the premises were leased for mining purposes, and no such express language is found in the lease here before the court, we are unable to hold that this fact differentiates the cases. It is manifest, taking this lease as a whole, that the sole purpose was to vest in the lessee mining privileges only. Under the rule of that case the improvement company in the case at bar could not be compelled to pay royalties unless ore was present in the land, suitable for marketing, from which it necessarily follows that the parties did not intend to confer upon the lessee all surface rights, or the exclusive right of possession. It seems clear that the lessee could not, though the lease contains a clause permitting a sublease, sublet the premises for agricultural or for any other purpose not connected with and having some relation to the mining operations. If this be true, and there would seem no sufficient answer to it, it follows that the right of possession and control of the premises remained in the lessor insofar as not inconsistent with or obstructive of the rights of the lessee in working the mine. Erickson v. Iron Co. 50 Mich. 604, 16 N. W. 161; 3 Lindley, Mines, § 813; Fowler v. Delaplain, 79 Oh. St. 279, 87 N. E. 260, 21 L.R.A.(N.S.) 100.

It is true that the lease authorizes the lessee to construct buildings, railroads and wagon roads, and such other facilities as may be necessary to a successful operation of the mine, but it does not appear from the answer that such was the purpose of the railroad in question. So far as disclosed by the pleadings the railroad was constructed for the purpose of general traffic, and has no relation to the shipment of ore from the land. The construction of the road upon the premises was, therefore, an unlawful encroachment upon the paramount estate of plaintiff, the lessor, an appropriation of his property for a purpose not contemplated or authorized by the lease, for which he is entitled to redress. We do not consider whether, or to what extent, the terms of the lease would be violated by the construction of the road, if it shall appear that the purpose thereof was the transportation of the ore to market in connection with the general traffic of the company. If the construction of the road was for that double purpose, even though an additional servitude upon the land by reason of the general commercial traffic conducted by it, and therefore perhaps a technical violation of plaintiff's rights, it would seem that the damages claimed should be very substantially reduced.

Judgment reversed and new trial granted.

STATE v. JOHN TROCKE.[1]

December 11, 1914.

Nos. 18,959—(10).

Criminal law — conviction sustained by evidence.

1. Defendant was convicted of the crime of carnally knowing a female child under the age of 18 years. Such conviction may rest upon the uncorroborated testimony of the prosecutrix, unless such testimony be discredited by facts and circumstances casting doubt upon the truth thereof. Evidence examined and *held* sufficient to sustain such conviction.

Same — cross-examination of prosecutrix.

2. In such a prosecution, defendant is entitled to much latitude in his

[1] Reported in 149 N. W. 944.

cross-examination of the prosecutrix, but it is not error to exclude a question as to her testimony before the grand jury, asked merely for the purpose of testing her memory.

Contradictory testimony — request to charge.

3. Where the prosecutrix and the defendant flatly contradict each other, the jury should be cautioned to weigh carefully all the facts and circumstances tending to show where the truth lies, but a request, so framed as to be liable to mislead them, is properly refused; and giving the substance of so much of the caution embodied therein as is proper, is sufficient.

Appeal by defendant from an order of the district court for McLeod county, Morrison, J., denying a motion for a new trial, after a trial and conviction of the crime stated in the opinion. Affirmed.

Lawler & Mulally, for appellant.

Lyndon A. Smith, Attorney General, and *Alonzo J. Edgerton,* Assistant Attorney General, for respondent.

TAYLOR, C.

Defendant was convicted of the crime of carnally knowing a female child under the age of 18 years. The case has been tried twice. At the first trial, the jury returned a verdict of guilty, but a motion for a new trial was made and granted. At the second trial, the jury again returned a verdict of guilty. A motion for a new trial was made and denied and defendant appealed.

The assignments of error challenge: (1) The sufficiency of the evidence to sustain the verdict; (2) the ruling of the court in sustaining an objection to a question asked the complaining witness, on cross-examination, concerning her testimony before the grand jury; (3) the refusal of the court to give two of the instructions requested by defendant.

1. The testimony is not elevating and we shall not rehearse it. The prosecutrix testified to the commission of the act charged in the indictment, at the time therein charged, and to the commission of numerous similar acts prior thereto. Her testimony was contradicted by defendant, but, if believed by the jury, was sufficient to sustain the verdict. State v. Newman, 93 Minn. 393, 101 N. W. 499; State v.

Johnson, 114 Minn. 493, 131 N. W. 629. She was also corroborated to some extent by the conduct of the defendant.

2. The prosecutrix had testified, on cross-examination, that acts of intercourse had taken place, at intervals, from March until December 28, 1912; that such an act took place on December 28, but that she could not give the specific date on which any other such act took place. She was then asked: "Do you remember what you testified before the grand jury as to dates of [such] intercourse?" The question was objected to as immaterial and excluded, and the ruling is urged as error. The purpose of the question, as stated by defendant in his brief, was to test the memory of the witness; and the only complaint made is that the ruling unduly restricted his cross-examination. No claim is made that the witness testified differently before the grand jury, nor that the question was asked for the purpose of laying a foundation for impeachment. The defendant, in such a prosecution, is entitled to much latitude in his cross-examination, and the question asked might properly enough have been permitted. The fact that it related to testimony given before the grand jury did not render it inadmissible. 4 Wigmore, Evidence, § 2362. Under the circumstances, however, the admission or exclusion of the testimony rested in the judicial discretion of the trial court. The ruling did not prejudice any of defendant's substantial rights; and was not reversible error, even if based upon a wrong reason.

3. Besides a request for a directed verdict, defendant presented 11 instructions which he requested the court to give to the jury. Eight of these were given, another was given in substance in the general charge, and two were refused. One of those refused directed the jury to take into consideration, "any credible evidence tending to show an attempt on the part of the prosecutrix or her relatives or representatives to extort money from the defendant." This was correctly refused for the reason that there was no evidence of any such attempt. The other, of the two refused, requested the court to instruct as follows concerning the testimony of the prosecutrix:

"The jury are warned that it would be dangerous to convict on her testimony, unless they also find that it is sustained by facts and circumstances corroborating it, and such corroboration should go to the commission of the offense and not to the defendant's opportunity to commit it or similar collateral or indirect facts and circumstances."

Some states, by statute, have adopted the rule that no conviction shall be had in such cases, unless the testimony of the prosecutrix be corroborated by other evidence tending to show the commission of the offense, and perhaps some courts apply the same rule without statutory authority therefor; but Minnesota, in common with the great majority of the states, holds that a conviction for such an offense may rest upon the uncorroborated testimony of the prosecutrix, unless her testimony be discredited by facts and circumstances casting doubt upon its reliability. It is recognized, however, that the character of the offense is such that there is rarely any direct testimony other than that of the parties themselves; that the charge is not only difficult to prove, if true, but is extremely difficult to defend against, even if utterly untrue; and that, where the testimony of the parties is flatly contradictory, the jury should be cautioned to scrutinize, with care, all the facts and circumstances disclosed at the trial, which tend either to corroborate, or to discredit, the testimony or claims of the one or the other. But, as consent is not a defense to such a prosecution, the rule, applied in prosecutions for rape, that suspicion is cast upon the claim of the prosecutrix by failure to make an outcry, or to make prompt complaint, or by the absence of facts and circumstances which indicate that a struggle has taken place, has no application in such cases.

The instruction requested, as framed, is objectionable, in that the jury were liable to understand from it that corroboration going to the actual commission of the offense was essential to justify a conviction. The charge repeatedly called the attention of the jury to the necessity of carefully considering all the facts and circumstances, disclosed at the trial, which tended to indicate where the truth lay. It is too long to quote, and the cautionary expressions are interspersed throughout its entire length; but the following summary of the cautions given is sufficient to show that they were ample:

The jury were told, in substance, that, to warrant a conviction, all the evidence, when carefully considered and weighed, must produce in their minds a settled and abiding conviction, to a moral certainty, of the truth of the charge, and satisfy them beyond a reasonable doubt that every material fact necessary to show defendant's guilt has been established; that, if they found that the testimony of the prosecutrix was not corroborated, the crime charged required special scrutiny and a careful weighing of the evidence, and of all remote and near circumstances and probabilities, especially if they should find that such testimony is at all improbable or suspicious; that the accusation is easily made and hard to prove, and, perhaps, harder still to disprove, be one ever so innocent; that, as such acts are not committed in the presence of witnesses, it is important that all the attending circumstances be given such weight in corroborating the truth of the charge, or in casting doubt upon the truth of the charge, as they are fairly and reasonably entitled to, when taken in connection with all the evidence in the case; that the jury should give careful consideration to prosecutrix' subsequent conduct as to complaining of the offense or accusing the defendant, her probable motive in shielding another, and all like testimony as to the probability of the commission by defendant of the act charged; that, in weighing the testimony of the prosecutrix, they must weigh carefully, as affecting her credibility, all testimony tending to show a motive on her part to concoct a false charge against defendant; and that she had admitted acts of immorality with others, which admissions were admitted for the purpose of bearing upon her credibility as a witness, and that, "the testimony of a woman of immoral or unchaste character should be regarded with caution and discrimination, and should be carefully weighed."

The court, in cautioning the jury, gave as much of the substance of the caution embodied in the instruction requested as defendant was entitled to have given, and properly refused to give the instruction as framed.

Order affirmed.

JOHN G. JOHNSON v. WILD RICE BOOM COMPANY.[1]

December 18, 1914.

Nos. 18,670—(35).

Harmless error.

1. The refusal to require plaintiff to elect between different causes of action which in fact were tried as one, even if error, was without prejudice to defendant.

New trial — error in charge — two causes tried as one.

2. The cause of action for diverting more water than agreed from the navigable stream by which plaintiff operated his flour mill, and the one for detaining waters unreasonably, by flooding dams at the source of the same stream, being tried as one cause, the verdict rendered may include damages for both causes, hence error in an instruction relating to one of the causes of action necessarily requires a new trial.

Case followed.

3. The same error which inhered in the charge in the case of Heiberg v. Wild Rice Boom Co. supra, page 8, exists here, with reference to the rights of defendant to temporarily detain water in the flooding dams.

Use of water for driving logs.

4. The defendant had the right to accumulate and detain water by flooding dams for such time and in such quantities as was reasonably necessary to enable it to drive with reasonable efficiency and dispatch the logs which were to be floated by it upon that part of the stream over which it operated, and this notwithstanding that such detention of the water so lessened the supply in the stream that plaintiff meanwhile was unable to run his mill.

Charge to jury.

5. The injury to the mill dam is not so clearly shown to have resulted wholly from diversion of the water, that the error in the charge, in respect to the right to accumulate and detain the quantity of water needed by defendant, was without prejudice.

[1] Reported in 150 N. W. 218.

Note.—As to the right of a riparian owner to impound water for the purpose of floating logs, see note in 35 L.R.A.(N.S.) 832.

The question of the correlative rights of log owners and riparian owners is discussed in notes in 41 L.R.A. 377 and 32 L.R.A.(N.S.) 376.

Action in the district court for Norman county upon four causes of action to recover $10,000, damages caused by the wrongful diversion of water from plaintiff's mill. The answer alleged defendant's incorporation under sections 2933 and 2934, R. L. 1905; that its principal business consisted in driving and handling logs and timber from the upper tributaries of Wild Rice river; that prior thereto no other corporation organized under that law had taken possession of the river or its tributaries for the purpose of handling or driving logs therein, and that defendant had ever since maintained its dams and works in carrying on the driving, handling and transportation of logs and timber through the river; that the maintenance and operation of the dams and the flooding dams were necessary to enable it to drive, handle and transport logs on said waters and that the dams had been maintained and operated for that purpose and no other. The case was tried before Grindeland, J., and a jury which returned a verdict for $2,000 on the first, second and third causes of action and a verdict for $800 on the fourth cause of action. From an order denying defendant's motion for a new trial, it appealed. Reversed.

Lind, Ueland & Jerome, for appellant.
Peter Sharpe and *Christian G. Dosland,* for respondent.

HOLT, J.

Damages were claimed because defendant's interruption of the natural flow of water in Wild Rice river and diversion of part of such water prevented plaintiff from operating his flour mill, and also for injury to the mill dam. The jury awarded plaintiff $2,000 for the loss sustained from inability to run the mill because of defendant's interference with the water, and $800 for injury to the dam. Defendant appeals from the order denying a new trial.

The Wild Rice river has its source in the westerly part of Clearwater county and runs in a westerly direction through Mahnomen and Norman counties to the Red River of the North. It is the outlet for several large lakes near its source, and along its course streams and tributaries empty into it. The channel is tortuous, exceeding 200 miles in length. It is a navigable stream, at least for the transportation of logs and timber products. The village of Ada is a short distance north of the river, and on Long lake, near the village, is a saw mill owned and operated by the Wild Rice Lumber Co. The lumber company since prior to 1904 brought the logs and timber cut near the head waters of Wild Rice river to its mill pond in Long lake by floating them down the river to a point near Ada, where are its booms. There by means of an 8-foot sluiceway, cut through the north bank of the river, and an artificial channel into Long lake the logs are brought from the river to its saw mill. The lumber company had improved the river, and, in 1908, when defendant was incorporated under section 6263, G. S. 1913, as a public service corporation, it took possession of the river for the purpose of handling and driving logs therein, and acquired the improvements and facilities which the lumber company had constructed. Since the last named date defendant has annually transported several million feet of logs on the river down to the lumber company's saw mill. It appears that to drive the logs it usually is necessary to impound the waters in the lakes near the source of the river so as to obtain a head of water sufficient to carry the logs down to the booms. In dry seasons it may be necessary to dam up the water for successive intervals before the drive reaches the booms. Considerable quantities of water are used in flushing or floating the logs from the boom through the sluiceway and channel mentioned into Long lake. The water thus going into Long lake is not returned to the Wild Rice river, but passes into another stream which empties into Red river direct. Many years before the lumber company began to drive logs and operate its mill, plaintiff owned and operated a flour mill on Wild Rice river at a place more than 50 miles by the river below defendant's sluiceway and artificial channel. He obtained power by maintaining an 8-foot dam across the river. Shortly before 1904 he instituted a suit to enjoin the lumber company from diverting any of the waters from the river into Long lake, but before the trial the action was dismissed pursuant to a stipulation which contained an agreement that in the future no more water should be diverted but what sufficient remained to enable plaintiff to operate his flour mill. Johnson v. Wild Rice Boom Co. 118 Minn. 24, 136 N. W. 262, was for violation of this agreement, and a recovery was sustained. So also was the case of Johnson v. Wild Rice Boom Co. 123 Minn. 523, 143 N. W. 111, for a subsequent period and up to August 1, 1911. In neither of these actions were damages claimed for interrupting the flow of the water by the detention or flooding dams at the outlet of the lakes near the source of the river. However, in Heiberg v. Wild Rice Boom Co. supra, page 8, 148 N. W. 517, and in Juhl v. Wild Rice Boom Co. infra, page 537, 148 N. W. 520, the maintenance and operation of these detention dams constituted the basis for the damages claimed, and the rule of law there announced applies to this case, insofar as damages are based upon the temporary withholding of the water by the dams mentioned. The diversion of part of the waters of the river into Long lake did not cause any damage to the plaintiff mill owners in the last-named cases, because their mills were situated above the sluiceway. In the present case plaintiff set forth four causes of action. The first for wrongfully diverting too much water into Long lake; the second for detaining the waters at intervals by the dams near the source of the river, being the same dams involved in the Heiberg and Juhl cases; the third was for both diversion and detention, virtually joining the first and second causes of action; and the fourth was for damages from the combined wrongs causing the ice to sink and injure the mill dam.

The appeal presents for review the ruling of the court upon defendant's motion to require plaintiff to elect between the first two and the third causes of action; also the charge in respect to the rights of the parties in the stream.

The court refused to require plaintiff to make an election. Although there appears to be no good reason for stating the facts upon which damages are asked for inability to operate the flour mill, because of defendant's interference with the natural flow of the river under three causes of action, we would not grant a new trial for refusing to require an election. It is not perceived how defendant was prejudiced by the ruling. We may say that the better practice would be to eliminate either the first two or the third. No effort was made to prove damages in each cause of action separately, and in the nature of things this could not be done, especially to separate that claimed in the third from either of the other two causes.

The decision in the Heiberg case, supra, is controlling here, so far at least as to require a new trial in respect to the first three causes of action, if the challenged instructions to the jury are substantially alike. For if any damages other than from diversion were allowed they are included in the $2,000 awarded. One sentence, found in the charge in the Heiberg case, namely: "The defendant has no rights which are paramount to those of the plaintiff," is omitted here. This sentence was but a summary of the tenor of the whole charge, to the effect that the rights of plaintiff and defendant to use the waters in the stream were equal. The charge in the instant case is open to the same criticism, namely, the relative rights of the parties to the use of the waters, of vital importance to a correct determination of the case, were not defined. Nowhere is the jury told that in taking possession of the river and tributaries and improving the same to facilitate the handling and floating of logs, and in the handling and floating of logs for the public the defendant was, as aptly stated by the Chief Justice in the Heiberg case, in the exercise of "a power and right not possessed by riparian owners or other persons. The power and authority so granted, being for a public purpose and in aid of navigation, is superior and paramount to the rights of riparian owners." This doctrine is fully and sufficiently discussed, and the authorities supporting it cited in the decision mentioned, and need not be here repeated.

We are also of opinion that defendant was entitled to have more specific instructions given the jury for guidance in determining when its use of the waters of the stream became wrongful as against plaintiff. The defendant's right to use the waters for transportation purposes being superior to that of the riparian owners for power purposes, the proper use must be measured by what is reasonably required to transport with ordinary diligence and by customary methods the property intrusted to it for transportation. On this subject the court refused to give this instruction requested by the defendant: "Defendant had the right to accumulate and retain water by the flooding dams referred to in the complaint for such length of time and in such quantities as was reasonably necessary to enable it to drive with reasonable efficiency and dispatch the logs which were to be floated from Lower Rice lake to Ada, and this notwithstanding that such accumulation and retention of the water may have impaired the supply of water for plaintiff's mill to such an extent that it could not be operated by water while the water was so accumulated and retained." We deem this instruction to be accurate and appropriate, with perhaps the substitution of "defendant's boom in Wild Rice river near Ada" in place of "Ada." The substance should have been given.

Plaintiff places unwarranted reliance on Crookston Waterworks, Power & Light Co. v. Sprague, 91 Minn. 461, 98 N. W. 347, 99 N. W. 420, 64 L.R.A. 977, 103 Am. St. 525, wherein it is stated that it was intended by the then existing sections 2385 and 2386 of the General Statutes of 1894 "to recognize the rights of the riparian owner in the construction of the dam, and the public in the use of the stream, and that neither one is granted a paramount right." It is evident that reference is had to the right possessed by both the riparian owner and the one floating logs to make use of the stream, each for a legitimate purpose of his own, but neither to make a negligent use thereof to the injury of the other. A corporation which is authorized to improve streams so as to facilitate the driving of logs, and to handle and drive logs for the public, is also given the right to construct flooding dams to detain the water necessary to float the logs it is required to handle. This right was not involved in the case last mentioned, but simply an alleged injury to a power dam through the negligence of one who was using the stream to thereon float his own logs. The decision of Red River Roller Mills v. Wright, 30 Minn. 249, 15 N. W. 167, which the trial court closely followed in framing its charge to the jury, related entirely to the alleged wrongful use which an upper riparian owner made of the stream to the injury of a lower. Page v. Mille Lacs Lumber Co. 53 Minn. 492, 55 N. W. 608, 1119, was between two parties who both used the stream to float their logs. In none of these cases did the question arise whether a corporation like defendant may temporarily detain and accumulate water in flooding dams when reasonably necessary to carry on its work, although it prevents a lower riparian owner, for the time being, from using the stream for power purposes. Such corporation, having the superior right to the use of the water for the public purpose for which it was created, cannot be held liable for impairing the use of power dams, unless it be proven that there has been more of a detention or accumulation than was reasonably necessary for the driving, in a proper manner, of the logs which it was required to drive. It is only for the needless or negligent interference that damages may be claimed. A use of the waters may not be held needless or negligent, so long as it is required in order to properly do the work defendant is authorized and intrusted by law to do. To illustrate: Suppose defendant had been driving logs to a point below plaintiff's mill through a sluiceway in the dam, and the water supply in the river were such that logs could not be sluiced and the mill operated at the same time. In such a situation defendant would have the superior right to open, and keep open, the sluiceway for the passage of the logs, and plaintiff could not complain. But if defendant in sluicing its logs negligently injured plaintiff's dam, or kept the sluice gates open when there were no logs to float through, or in an unworkmanlike manner negligently protracted the passing of the drive through the sluiceway, an actionable injury would arise.

We suggested above that the instruction requested by defendant was technically faulty in that the terminus of defendant's right to use the waters was stated to be Ada instead of the booms at the sluiceway near Ada. The present action was tried, and so were the prior ones between these parties, upon the theory, as we understand it, that both parties consider their rights as to diversion of water into Long lake governed by the stipulation made when, in 1904, the injunction suit against defendant's predecessor in interest was dismissed.

In respect to the injury to the mill dam the court instructed the jury: "If you should find that during the winter of 1911 and 1912 the defendant diverted water from the river through its sluiceway in violation of the contract, and also find that defendant wrongfully and unreasonably retained the water by dams, then you will proceed to determine whether this caused the damage to plaintiff's dam.

* * * Was the damage to the dam caused by the unlawful diversion of the water, or was it caused by the unreasonable retention of the water, or was it caused by both? If it was caused by either or both, the defendant would be liable." Defendant's exception to the instructions appears well taken, unless it may be said that it conclusively appears that the injury was caused solely by the wrongful diversion of water to Long lake, so that no prejudice resulted from a failure to define the relative rights of the parties in respect to the detention of waters in Wild Rice river. Plaintiff claimed that during the last days of December, 1911, when ice had formed on his mill pond to considerable thickness, defendant detained and diverted the water so that not enough came down to support the ice and it, sinking in the middle of the pond, pressed against the dam, causing a crack in the concrete wall thereof and breaking or displacing some of the piling. He strenuously insists that there is nothing to contradict the testimony of Mr. Sharpe that he, as agent for plaintiff, made an arrangement with defendant's manager that defendant could turn water from the river into Long lake during the last few days of December, 1911, provided it was not done in such quantity as to impair the stability of the ice on the mill pond. There is also testimony that the sluiceway was open, or had a hole in it at that time. It is true that there is no direct testimony contradicting this alleged arrangement. However, there is evidence from which the jury would be warranted in drawing the conclusion that the ice fell not alone from the water diverted, but because at that time a head of water was being accumulated at the flooding dams mentioned. There was also testimony from which the jury could find that a reasonable use by defendant permitted, or required, an accumulation of water in the flooding dams during the winter months, in order to obtain a sufficient supply for floating the logs in the spring. Admissions made by plaintiff in the summer of 1912 were also of a nature to make the cause and extent of the damage to the dam a close question of fact. The evidence is far from satisfactory that any considerable quantity of water was diverted into Long lake during the last days of December, 1911, and the first part of January, 1912. We may also take cognizance of the fact that, in the more than 50-mile course of the river between the sluiceway and plaintiff's dam, no doubt, tributary creeks and rivulets furnish a considerable flow of water to replenish the waters supporting the ice in his mill pond. If it failed to do this the inference is that the dam must have been exceedingly leaky and out of repair before the alleged wrongful acts of defendant took place. Under this situation we are not able to say that the error in the charge on this phase of the controversy was without prejudice.

Order reversed.

DEOLENA CRANDALL v. CHICAGO GREAT WESTERN RAILROAD COMPANY.[1]

December 18, 1914.

Nos. 18,820—(66).

Injury to switchman — interstate commerce.

1. The plaintiff's intestate, a switchman, was employed by the defendant in its yards at Oelwein, Iowa, making up a train destined for Minnesota, some of the cars to be set out at stations in Iowa and some carrying local freight to be unloaded on the way, some of the cars in the train being made up having been transported by the defendant from points in Illinois to its Oelwein yards, destined some to Iowa points and some to points in Minnesota, and some of them originating in Iowa, destined some to Iowa points and some to points in Minnesota. The deceased was run over by an intrastate car and the negligence found was in respect of the brake-step of an intrastate car. It is *held* that the defendant was at the time engaged as a common carrier in interstate commerce and that the deceased was employed by it in such commerce, and that the Federal Employers' Liability Act (35 St. 65, c. 149), applied.

Negligence — proximate cause.

2. The evidence justified a finding that the defendant was negligent in respect of the brake-step; and the jury could find, as a legitimate inference,

1 Reported in 150 N. W. 165.

Note.—Upon the question of the constitutionality, application and effect of the Federal employers' liability act, see note in 47 L.R.A.(N.S.) 38.

without indulging in conjecture that the defendant's negligence in this respect was the proximate cause of the death of the deceased.

Action in the district court for Mower county by the administratrix
of the estate of Clifford Crandall, deceased, to recover $35,000 for
the death of her intestate while in defendant's employ. The answer
denied any negligence on the part of defendant, and alleged that
the death of the intestate was caused by his own negligence; that
he knew and appreciated the hazards of the employment and assumed
the risk. The case was tried before Kingsley, J., and a jury which
returned a verdict for $10,625. From an order denying defend-
ant's motion for judgment notwithstanding the verdict or for a new
trial, it appealed. Affirmed.

Briggs, Thygeson & Everall, Monte Appel and *Catherwood &
Nicholsen,* for appellant.

Sasse & French and *Dunn & Carlson,* for respondent.

DIBELL, C.

The plaintiff's intestate, Clifford Crandall, was killed on October 14, 1912, while in the employ of the defendant as a switchman
in its yards at Oelwein, Iowa. In an action based upon the Federal
Employer's Liability Act (35 St. 65, c. 149), to recover damages
for his death, the plaintiff recovered a verdict. The defendant
appeals from an order denying its alternative motion for judgment
or for a new trial.

1. It is the contention of the defendant that the record does not
present a case within the Federal act. The trial court instructed
the jury that the Federal act applied. To be within the act the
defendant must have been engaged at the time as a common carrier
in interstate commerce and Crandall must have been employed
by it in such commerce. Second Employers' Liability Cases, 223
U. S. 1, 32 Sup. Ct. 169, 56 L. ed. 327; Pedersen v. Delaware
L. & W. R. Co. 229 U. S. 146, 33 Sup. Ct. 648, 57 L. ed. 1125, Ann.
Cas. 1914C, 153, and cases cited.

The important facts, determinative of the question, are substantially these: The defendant was making up a train in its yards

at Oelwein, Iowa. The train was destined to a point in Minnesota, though some of the cars were to be set out at stations in Iowa, and some local freight was to be unloaded on the way. Some of the cars, destined for points in Iowa, originated in Iowa, and some came from points in Illinois where the defendant received them for transportation. Some of the cars, destined for Minnesota, originated in Iowa, and some came from Illinois, where the defendant received them for transportation. These cars, some intrastate and some interstate, were being made into the Minnesota train. Crandall was foreman of the switching crew engaged in this work and was run over and killed by an intrastate car, which was one of a string of cars containing both intrastate and interstate cars then being moved in making up the train. The car which ran over him was at the time intended for the Minnesota train; and the negligence found was in respect of the brake-step on this car. Under these facts the case is within the Federal Employer's Liability Act. St. Louis, S. F. & T. R. Co. v. Seale, 229 U. S. 156, 33 Sup. Ct. 651, 57 L. ed. 1129, Ann. Cas. 1914C, 156; Pedersen v. Delaware, L. & W. R. Co. 229 U. S. 146, 33 Sup. Ct. 648, 57 L. ed. 1125, Ann. Cas. 1914C, 153; North Carolina R. Co. v. Zachary, 232 U. S. 248, 34 Sup. Ct. 305, 58 L. ed. 591, Ann. Cas. 1914C, 159, and cases cited. The court rightly instructed the jury that the Federal act applied.

2. It is the contention of the defendant that a causal connection between the defective brake-step and the death of Crandall is not shown.

In making up the train the switching engine and crew went from the lead track south onto a side track, which extended in a northerly and southerly direction, to take out some cars from a string of cars standing thereon. The crew worked on the west side of the train, or the left side looking north toward the engine. Crandall uncoupled the rear car of those to be taken out. This car belonged to the defendant. The evidence supports a finding that the brake-step on the forward end of the car, to the right or east of the center line, was loose and in a defective condition, and that it was so as the result of the negligence of the defendant.

There is no direct evidence as to how Crandall came to his death. Becker, the switchman working with him, climbed up the rear end of the third hind car after Crandall uncoupled and the cars were ready for the movement north. He went forward and released the brake at the forward end of the third car, returning to the rear end of the second car. He says he either released the brake of the hind car or found it released. He rode the second car north to the lead, standing on the running-board near the center. The theory of the plaintiff is that after Becker went on top Crandall climbed up the second car, started to release the brake on the rear car, using the brake-step, and because of its defective condition fell and was run over. Sometimes in the course of the work he released the brake of the rear car. There is evidence that a lantern, evidently that of Becker, went up onto the rear end of the cars as they started. There is evidence that another lantern followed, though it does not appear that it was seen on top of the cars. There was a heavy white frost. There were marks of steps from the top of the ladder of the second hind car to the running-board, turning thence toward the hind car. The frost about the brake-step was disturbed. The frost on the brake-step was scraped off. Opposite the brake-step on the rear end of the second hind car was a spot of oil such as is used in railroad lanterns. Crandall's body was found a few car lengths north of where the cars were uncoupled. His lantern was near. His head was severed from his body and lay on the right or east side of the outer rail and his body was between the rails. The right or east forward trucks of the hind car were bloody.

It is familiar law that a causal connection between the act of negligence found and the injury for which damages are given must be established. It is not enough that the evidence be consistent with the theory that the negligent act caused the injury; it must be such as to show, by legitimate inferences of fact, that it did cause it. The evidence need not be direct; it may be circumstantial. Mitton v. Cargill Elevator Co. 124 Minn. 65, 144 N. W. 434, and cases cited.

We are of the opinion that from the evidence the jury might find by legitimate inference, without a resort to conjecture or speculation, that Crandall's death came from the defective brake-step.

A number of assignments challenge rulings on evidence and instructions to the jury. We have examined them in detail and thoroughly. We find no error.

Order affirmed.

JOHN RIPA and Others v. JOHN D. HOGAN and Others.[1]

December 18, 1914.

Nos. 18,834—(97).

Money had and received — findings.

In this action for money had and received the evidence sustains the findings.

Action in the district court for Hennepin county to recover $667.29 for money had and received. The answer was a general denial. The case was tried before Booth, J., who made findings and ordered judgment in favor of plaintiffs for $513.84. From an order denying defendants' motion for judgment notwithstanding the verdict or for a new trial, they appealed. Affirmed.

Mansfield & Jones, for appellants.

Keith, Evans, Thompson & Fairchild, for respondents.

HOLT, J.

In this action, for money had and received, findings were made in favor of plaintiffs and defendants appeal from the order denying a new trial.

The sole question which may be considered under the assignments of error is the sufficiency of the evidence to sustain the findings of fact. The following facts were either undisputed or else there was

[1] Reported in 150 N. W. 167.

evidence justifying the court in considering them established: The defendants were partners dealing in real estate both on their own account and as agents, having an office at Aberdeen, South Dakota. In May, 1908, plaintiffs came from their homes in Nebraska, looking for land investments near Aberdeen. They met defendants and negotiations resulted in a sale of half a section of land in McPherson county, South Dakota, to plaintiffs. One of the plaintiffs received a deed of 160 acres thereof, and the others took each 80 acres. Parts of the half section were under cultivation, and there was a tenant on the land who had a lease for the cropping seasons of 1908 and 1909 under which a share of the crops was reserved in lieu of rent. Plaintiffs agreed to be partners in respect to the rent or income from the half section, and defendants agreed to act as their agents in disposing of plaintiffs' share of the crops for 1908 and to transmit the proceeds to them. They did so. In the spring of 1909 the tenant moved away, and defendants found one Scully with whom they executed a cropping contract for that season, signing it as agents for plaintiffs. Under this contract the title to the whole crop remained in the landowners until divided. Scully was to furnish the seed, plant, cultivate, harvest and thresh the crop, and deliver the landowners' share at the elevator. Upon division one-third was to be retained by plaintiffs, and Scully was to receive two-thirds. After seeding and before harvest Scully, who also cultivated other land bought from defendants on contract, left the country because of some trouble. He had given a banker of Leola security on his share of the crop on the lands farmed by him and a partner. This partner's interest does not seem to bear on the determination of this case. When Scully left, defendants arranged with the banker mentioned to procure some one to harvest and market the crop and attend to the distribution of the proceeds to the proper parties. Plaintiffs testified that defendants had agreed in the fall of 1909 to thresh and market the crop, collect the money for plaintiffs' share thereof and send it to them. On October 21, 1909, when the banker had received the returns from the lands which Scully and his partner had seeded, he transmitted to defendants a draft for $667.29. This he stated to be the landowners' share of the crop raised on plaintiffs' half section during the cropping season of 1909. There was also evidence tending to show that the yield on plaintiffs' land was such that the one-third thereof would exceed the sum mentioned, being well within the amount which the court found that defendants had received.

Complaint is made of the finding that defendants were plaintiffs' agent, on the ground that there was no such issue. The fact of agency was not the ultimate fact necessary to plead in this case, for it makes no difference in what capacity the money was had and received so long as it belonged to plaintiffs. Brand v. Williams, 29 Minn. 238, 13 N. W. 42. But, whether agency was pleaded or not, the court had the right to ascertain the relation in which defendants stood to plaintiffs when it was shown that the proceeds of the crop from plaintiffs' land were traced into defendants' hands. In view of the situation in which the evidence placed defendants, we think it devolved upon them to show how much, if any, of the $667.29 which actually came into their hands did not come from plaintiffs' one-third share of the crop. By the very contract which defendants as agents made, plaintiffs held the legal title to the whole of the crop on the half section until a division thereof. By defendants' procurement the whole crop was sold without division— they, knowing the situation, caused an intermingling of the proceeds. The one with whom defendants arranged to dispose of the crop, and to apportion the proceeds among those entitled thereto, states that the amount which came into defendants' hands was plaintiffs' share. The court did not find that all thereof was plaintiffs', and we fail to discover, upon this record, any justification for defendants' claim that they are the ones aggrieved by the finding.

The judgment is affirmed.

STATE v. MARY LE FLOHIC.[1]

December 18, 1914.

Nos. 18,845—(4).

Motion to dismiss indictment.

1. The court did not err in denying defendant's motion to dismiss an indictment not tried within the time fixed by R. L. 1905, § 4786 (G. S. 1913, § 8510), and in holding that the state showed reasonable cause why it should not be dismissed.

Evidence.

2. The evidence justified the conviction.

Defendant was indicted by the grand jury, tried in the district court for St. Louis county before Cant, J., and a jury, and convicted of keeping a house of ill-fame. From an order denying her motion for a new trial, defendant appealed. Affirmed.

John H. Norton, for appellant.

Lyndon A. Smith, Attorney General, *Warren E. Greene,* County Attorney, and *Mason M. Forbes,* First Assistant County Attorney, for respondent.

DIBELL, C.

The defendant was indicted at the September, 1913, term of the district court of St. Louis county for keeping a house of ill-fame. When the indictment was called for trial at the January, 1914, term, she moved for a dismissal upon the ground that the indictment against her was not tried at the next term of the court at which it was triable. The motion was denied. The defendant was convicted. She appeals from the order denying her motion for a new trial.

1. The defendant based her motion for dismissal upon R. L. 1905, § 4786 (G. S. 1913, § 8510), which, so far as here material, is as follows:

"If indicted, and trial is not postponed upon his own application,

[1] Reported in 150 N. W. 171.

unless tried at the next term of the court in which it is triable, the indictment shall be dismissed, unless good cause to the contrary be shown."

Terms of the district court in St. Louis county convene in the months of September, November, January, March and May. The trial was continued from the September term to the November term at the request of the defendant. There was a trial at the November term which resulted in a disagreement.

The state contends that there was a trial in November within the meaning of the statute. There is authority for this contention. State v. Enke, 85 Iowa, 35, 51 N. W. 1146; Ochs v. People, 124 Ill. 399, 16 N. E. 662; Gillespie v. People, 176 Ill. 238, 52 N. E. 250. It was not urged below. We do not determine it, but pass directly to a consideration of the ground upon which the trial court placed its decision.

The phrase, "good cause to the contrary," contained in the statute, refers to cause shown when the motion to dismiss the indictment is made. When the defendant's motion was made it appeared from a colloquy between counsel, which it was agreed should stand for the purposes of the motion as if embodied in affidavit, in addition to facts before recited, that upon the disagreement of the jury it seemed impracticable to get another jury; that difficulty had been experienced in getting the jury which disagreed; that the facts claimed in connection with the prosecution were of notoriety in the community; that the county attorney did not move the case for trial; that the defendant did not ask another trial at that term; that nothing was done by either; and that the case was continued to the January term by a general order of continuance made at the close of the November term.

It was for the court to determine from the facts before it whether good cause was shown why the indictment should not be dismissed. There had been no considerable delay. There was no complaint that the defendant had not been accorded a speedy trial. She had not been urgent for an earlier trial. The prosecuting authorities had not been lax or dilatory. The state and the defendant were ready for trial. No prejudice was suggested because of the delay.

The motion to dismiss the indictment was not based on the provision of the Bill of Rights, art. 1, § 6, of the Constitution, guaranteeing a "speedy public trial." It was based upon the statute quoted. Whether a trial is a speedy trial within the Constitution is a judicial question. The legislature cannot say and does not say that a trial is speedy if had within the time and under the conditions mentioned in the section of the statute quoted. It does say, and it properly may say in regulating criminal procedure, that an indictment not tried as therein provided shall be dismissed.

Upon the facts disclosed when the motion was made the court was justified in finding that there was good cause why the indictment should not be dismissed.

2. It is claimed that the evidence is insufficient to justify a conviction. Naturally enough the witnesses were not the choicest. Their credibility and the weight of their testimony were for the jury. It is unnecessary to review the evidence. It is enough to say that the court has read it and is satisfied of its legal sufficiency.

Objections are made to rulings upon evidence. We have examined them and find nothing requiring mention.

The case was fairly and carefully tried and submitted to the jury and the conviction should stand.

Order affirmed.

W. W. PULS v. CHICAGO, BURLINGTON & QUINCY RAILROAD COMPANY.[1]

December 18, 1914.

Nos. 18,846—(101).

Negligence of master.

    1. The evidence justified a finding that the defendant was negligent in

---

[1] Reported in 150 N. W. 175.

Note.—As to the servant's assumption of risk of the master's breach of statutory duty, see notes in 6 L.R.A.(N.S.) 981; 19 L.R.A.(N.S.) 646; 22 L.R.A.

having dull or nicked knives on a hand jointer on which the plaintiff was working and that such negligence caused the plaintiff's injury.

Same — failure to guard knives of jointer.

2. The evidence justified a finding that the defendant was liable for a failure to guard the knives on such jointer as required by the order of the Industrial Commission of Wisconsin.

Expert witness.

3. A witness held competent to testify as an expert.

Assumption of risk.

4. The plaintiff did not, as a matter of law, assume the risk.

Damages not excessive.

5. An award of $2,000 for the loss of the little finger at the knuckle joint, and the next finger at the second joint, of the left hand, to a carpenter 35 years of age, who is left-handed, is not excessive.

Action in the district court for Ramsey county to recover $3,500 for personal injury received while in the employ of defendant. The answer alleged that the injuries were in part at least caused by negligence on the part of plaintiff and that plaintiff knew and assumed the risks incident to his employment. The case was tried before Kelly, J., and a jury which returned a verdict in favor of plaintiff for $2,000. From an order denying defendant's motion for judgment notwithstanding the verdict or for a new trial, it appealed. Affirmed.

Barrows, Stewart & Ordway, for appellant.
Barton & Kay, for respondent.

DIBELL, C.

Appeal by the defendant from an order denying its alternative motion for judgment notwithstanding the verdict or a new trial after a verdict for the plaintiff in an action to recover for personal injuries sustained while in the employ of the defendant.

The plaintiff was injured while working for the defendant on a hand jointer at Grand Crossing, in Wisconsin. Two acts of negli-

(N.S.) 634; 33 L.R.A.(N.S.) 646; 42 L.R.A.(N.S.) 1220, and 49 L.R.A.(N.S.) 471.

On the question of the servant's assumption of obvious risks of hazardous employment, see note in 1 L.R.A.(N.S.) 272.

gence are alleged: (1) That the knives of the jointer were dull
and nicked; (2) that the defendant failed to guard the knives.

1. There is evidence that the knives were dull and nicked and
that their condition in this respect tended to throw or kick back the
boards. If they were kicked back, there was a likelihood that the
operator's hands would come in contact with the knives. The evidence was such as to make a question for the jury upon the negligence charged.

2. Under authority of the statutes of Wisconsin the Industrial
Commission made the following order assumed to be of statutory
effect:

"All hand jointers must be equipped with safety cylinder heads
and a guard must be placed over the knives to protect the hands of
the operator."

It defined "guarded" as follows:

"The term 'guarded' when used in these orders shall mean so
covered, fenced or inclosed that a person in the course of his employment is not liable to come in contact with the point of danger
and be injured."

The defendant complied so far as to furnish safety cylinder heads.
It did not place a guard over the knives. There is evidence that it
was practicable to do so. There is evidence that a guard of some
kind had at one time been over the knives. There was evidence
that it was impracticable. There was testimony on the part of the
defendant that guards could not be placed over the knives without
destroying the character of the machine as a jointer. The court
submitted the case to the jury substantially upon the theory that
the defendant was liable only in the event that it was practicable to
place a guard over the knives; and that it negligently failed so to
place guards. Upon the theory upon which the case was submitted
the questions of practicability and negligence were for the jury.

3. The witness Dagnon gave expert testimony as to the character
of the machine and the practicability of guarding the knives. It
is urged that he was not sufficiently qualified to testify as an expert. He had worked several years about machinery of this kind.

We think he was qualified to testify; or at least that the question of his competency was for the court.

4. The plaintiff had considerable experience in work of this and a similar kind. It is claimed that he assumed the risk of his work, whether his injury came from dull or nicked knives or a failure to guard. We think there is no question of the assumption of risks which survives an adverse finding of the jury.

5. The plaintiff was a carpenter 35 years of age. The injury resulted in the loss of the little finger of his left hand at the knuckle joint and the next finger at the second joint. He is left-handed. The verdict was for $2,000. It is claimed that this amount is excessive but we do not think it is.

Order affirmed.

———

STATE v. ROBERT WARD.[1]

December 18, 1914.

Nos. 18,854—(5).

Malicious injury to property — indictment — evidence.

Defendant was convicted under an indictment charging malicious injury to property and appealed. It is *held:*

(1) The indictment was not bad because it failed to charge that defendant acted "maliciously."

(2) It was not error to receive as evidence the opinions of qualified witnesses as to whether logs found in defendant's possession came from stumps on the land of the complaining witnesses.

(3) Jurors on a former trial may testify on a subsequent trial as to physical facts coming to their knowledge during a view made by them on the former trial. It is not material that the former verdict was set aside because of the misconduct of the jury in conducting unauthorized experiments during the view.

(4) It was not error to permit jurors on the former trial to give their

1 Reported in 150 N. W. 209.

opinions or conclusions derived from and based upon the knowledge acquired on the view.

(5) There was no error in rulings in the admission or rejection of evidence, or in failing to give a requested instruction.

(6) The evidence sustains the verdict.

Defendant was indicted by the grand jury, tried in the district
court for Wright county before Giddings, J., and a jury, and convicted of the crime of wilfully cutting down standing timber on the
land of others. From the judgment of conviction, defendant appealed. Affirmed.

W. H. Cutting and *James E. Madigan,* for appellant.

Lyndon A. Smith, Attorney General, *John C. Nethaway,* Assistant Attorney General, and *Stephen A. Johnson,* County Attorney,
for respondent.

BUNN, J.

Defendant was convicted under an indictment charging malicious
injury to property, and appealed from the judgment.

The sufficiency of the indictment is challenged, as are certain rulings in the admission of evidence, and the sufficiency of the evidence
to warrant the conviction.

1. The indictment was in the language of the statute, G. S. 1913,
§ 8934, subd. 1. It charged that defendant on or about March
10, 1912, at the town of Maple Lake in Wright county, wilfully
and unlawfully cut down two maple trees then standing and growing upon the lands of others, the owners being named and the lands
particularly described. The alleged defect in the indictment is that
it did not allege that the cutting was done "maliciously." There
is no doubt that to constitute an offense under the statute, there
must be an element of malice. Price v. Denison, 95 Minn. 106, 103
N. W. 728. But it is not necessary to use the word malicious in
the indictment. The words "wilfully and unlawfully" embody the
idea of maliciousness, and they are the words used in the statute.
We think the indictment was sufficient.

The rulings on evidence that are complained of may be grouped
into two classes: (1) Receiving expert opinion evidence on the

question whether two logs found with defendant's name on them came from the stumps on the land of the complaining witnesses; (2) permitting jurors on a former trial to testify as to their observations and experiments on a view they were permitted to take during the trial, and their opinions derived from such observations and experiments.

The facts are as follows: The land involved was timber land owned by certain sisters, and known as the Butler woods. A brother "looked after" it. Two maple trees were found to be cut down and the logs hauled away. Two green maple logs were afterwards found in a nearby mill yard, both marked "R. Ward" on the end. The logs were measured, and then the stumps in the woods and the distances between them and the tree tops on the ground. It was testified that defendant, when asked where he got the logs, replied that he cut them on "our own place," referring to the farm of his father. It was shown that there were no recently cut maple stumps on the Ward land, and no stumps or trees as large as the logs in controversy. The tops of the stumps in the Butler woods and the ends of the two logs were cut off and used as exhibits in the case. It was in evidence that defendant had never asked for permission to cut any logs in the Butler woods. He did not take the stand on this trial, though he did on the former one. It appears that his defense and testimony then was that the logs were cut on his father's land.

2. We think it was a proper case for expert opinion evidence. The opinions of woodsmen who had examined the logs and stumps and measured the distance between the latter and the tree tops, and who had examined the stumps on the Ward land, would naturally be of assistance to the jury in determining whether the logs were from the trees in the Butler woods or from the Ward land. This is the consideration which should in the main govern the admission or exclusion of opinion evidence. We see no abuse of discretion in receiving this testimony.

3. On the former trial the jurors were permitted to go to the woods and view the stumps and tree tops. They conducted experiments, and their verdict of guilty was set aside because of this impropriety. On this trial many of them were called as witnesses

by the state, and were permitted over objections not only to testify as to what they observed on the view, and their experiments, but to state their opinions derived from such observations and experiments. It is quite clear upon principle and well established by decided cases that jurors upon a former trial may testify on a subsequent trial as to physical facts coming to their knowledge during a view made by them on the former trial. Hughes v. Chicago, St. P. M. & O. R. Co. 126 Wis. 525, 106 N. W. 526; Cramer v. Burlington, 42 Iowa, 315; Woolfolk v. State, 85 Ga. 69, 99, 11 S. E. 814; Hull v. Seaboard Air Line, 76 S. C. 278, 57 S. E. 28, 10 L.R.A.(N.S.) 1213; 40 Cyc. 2236. It is not material that the former verdict was set aside because of the misconduct of the jury in conducting unauthorized experiments. This was not receiving the evidence or affidavits of jurors to impeach their verdict. That verdict had already been set aside.

4. It is a question of more doubt whether the opinions of the jurors, derived from the knowledge acquired on the view, were properly received. The opinions might be influenced by the testimony on the former trial, and not wholly based on the view. But this bears rather on the weight of the evidence than on the question of its admissibility. Holding as we have that opinion evidence was properly received, and that the former jurors were competent witnesses, it would seem to follow that their opinions, based on the facts ascertained on the view were properly received. In Woolfolk v. State, 85 Ga. 69, 11 S. E. 814, cited above, defendant was convicted of the murder of his father, and a new trial was granted. On the first trial certain drawers with blood stains thereon were in evidence and taken to the jury room when the jury retired. On the second trial two of the former jurors were allowed to testify as to their conclusions that there was the bloody print of a hand on the drawers. It was contended that it was impossible for the witnesses to say what effect the other testimony on the trial had, in causing their minds to form the conclusions that they saw the print of a hand. It was held that the evidence was admissible, the objection going more against its weight rather than against its admissibility. In the case at bar the jurors declared that their opinions were based

127 M.—33.

upon the facts learned on the view. We cannot say that they were influenced by evidence received on the trial. While for the reasons suggested, we do not approve of the practice, we are unable to hold that it was error to permit the jurors, as well as the other witnesses, to state their conclusions based upon the knowledge acquired on the view. We have no right to say, as counsel for defendant does, that the former jurors were allowed to give generally their conclusions as to defendant's guilt, and the reasons why they convicted him. We must assume as true their sworn statements that they based their opinions wholly on the facts that came to their knowledge while viewing the stumps and logs, and conducting their experiments.

5. We see no error in sustaining objections to cross-examination of these jurors directed to showing their misconduct on the former trial. This appeared clearly enough, if it was material on the question of their credibility, and restricting the cross-examination in this regard was well within the court's discretion. We find no error in any other ruling on evidence, or in failing to give an instruction on the weight to be given circumstantial evidence.

6. Defendant claims that the verdict is not sustained by the evidence. We think that the evidence, though circumstantial, points pretty clearly to the conclusion that defendant cut the logs from the property of the complaining witnesses. The chief claim, and one not wholly without merit, is that the evidence fails to show that defendant cut down the trees "maliciously." The owners of the land did not testify, and there is no separate evidence that defendant was actuated by malice, or an intent to injure the owners. But the malice which is an essential ingredient of the offense need not be proved directly or as a separate fact. When the act is wrongfully and wilfully done, and the necessary result is to injure the property of another, malice may be inferred. Defendant had no permission to cut down trees in the Butler woods. He was not laboring under any belief that he had a right to do so, or under any mistaken impression that the land belonged to himself or his father. He insisted at all times that the logs came from the farm of his father, some distance away. On the whole we are unable to say

that the necessary malice was not shown, or that the verdict is not sustained by the evidence. Defendant has been tried twice. The trial that resulted in the judgment from which this appeal was taken was a fair one, and the trial court has approved the verdict. We think it should stand.

Judgment affirmed.

BERTHA GRONLUND v. CUDAHY PACKING COMPANY and Others.[1]

December 18, 1914.

Nos. 18,862—(112).

Negligence — question for jury.

1. Plaintiff sued for damages for the death of her intestate caused by a collision between a two-horse wagon belonging to defendant packing company and driven by defendant Mosberg, and a one-horse wagon driven by the deceased. The evidence as to negligence and contributory negligence was conflicting, and made a question for the jury and is sufficient to sustain their verdict.

Appellants cannot raise point on appeal.

2. As the evidence and the instructions bearing upon the question as to whether defendant Lounsberry was also liable to plaintiff in damages had no bearing upon the claim made against appellants, appellants are not in position, upon this appeal, to question the rulings in respect thereto.

Refusal to charge jury.

3. The law of the road applicable to the case having been stated fully and clearly in the general charge, the court did not err in refusing to give the special instructions in respect thereto requested by appellants.

Action in the district court for St. Louis county by the administratrix of the estate of Henry O. Gronlund, deceased, to recover $7,500 for the death of her intestate. The case was tried before Dancer, J., and a jury which returned a verdict in favor of plain-

[1] Reported in 150 N. W. 176.

tiff for $4,187.50. From an order denying their motion for judgment notwithstanding the verdict or for a new trial, defendants Mosberg and the packing company appealed. Affirmed.

Washburn, Bailey & Mitchell, for appellants.
Abbott, MacPherran, Lewis & Gilbert, for defendant Lounsberry.
Charles L. Lewis, Neil E. Beaton and *O. J. Larson,* for respondents.

TAYLOR, C.

Plaintiff is the widow of Henry O. Gronlund, deceased, and the executrix of his estate. Alleging that his death was caused by the negligence of defendants, she brought this suit to recover damages therefor. The trial resulted in a verdict against defendants Mosberg and the Cudahy Packing Co., but in favor of defendant Lounsberry. Thereafter defendants Mosberg and the Cudahy Packing Co. made a motion for judgment notwithstanding the verdict, and, in case that should be denied, for a new trial. Both motions were denied and they appealed.

The accident happened upon Michigan avenue in the city of Duluth. This street extends east and west and crosses Lake street, at nearly a right angle, underneath a bridge or viaduct which extends the entire width of Lake street. The roadway of Michigan avenue under this bridge is about 32 feet wide between curbs. Defendant Lounsberry was constructing an addition to a large building near by, and had placed a quantity of broken brick, plaster and other refuse from this building under the bridge and along the curb on the south side of Michigan avenue. At the farthest point, this refuse extended into the roadway a distance of 12 or 14 feet from the south curb. The remainder of the roadway, 18 or 20 feet in width, was clear and unobstructed. At the time the accident occurred, Gronlund, driving a one-horse wagon, was proceeding west along Michigan avenue, and Mosberg, driving a two-horse wagon for the Cudahy Packing Co. was proceeding east. They attempted to pass each other under the bridge and opposite the pile of rubbish above mentioned, but their wagons collided and Gronlund was thrown from his wagon to the pavement with sufficient force to fracture his skull and cause his death.

In the complaint, Lounsberry is charged with negligence in placing the rubbish in the street; and the packing company and its driver, Mosberg, are charged with negligence in failing to keep to the right of the center of the traveled portion of the street opposite the rubbish; in failing to exercise due care in passing Gronlund's wagon; in driving at a high and negligent rate of speed, and in negligently causing the packing company's wagon to collide with the wagon of Gronlund.

1. The evidence indicates that the teams could have passed each other without difficulty, and that the collision resulted from lack of due care on the part of one, or both, of the drivers. It does not indicate that either was driving at an improper rate of speed. It is conflicting, however, as to the manner in which the collision occurred. There is testimony tending to show that the packing company's wagon ran against Gronlund's wagon while the latter was close to the north curb; there is also testimony tending to show that Gronlund's wagon ran against the packing company's wagon while the latter was well south of the center of the unobstructed portion of the roadway. Whether Mosberg was at fault, and, if so, whether he alone was at fault, or whether Gronlund was also at fault, were fair questions for the jury, and were properly submitted to them. They have determined these questions in favor of plaintiff, and the evidence is such that this court is not justified in setting aside their conclusions.

2. Appellants complain of certain rulings made in respect to the admission of evidence offered by defendant Lounsberry. Plaintiff does not complain of such rulings, and, as the evidence in question had no bearing upon plaintiff's claim against appellants, nor upon appellants' defense thereto, appellants are not in position to question such rulings.

3. Appellants also challenge the action of the court in refusing to give certain instructions, and in giving certain other instructions concerning the negligence charged against Lounsberry. What is said above also applies here. Plaintiff does not complain, and, as

these instructions had no bearing upon the charge of negligence made against appellants, appellants were not prejudiced by the action of the court in either giving them or refusing to give them.

4. Appellants also assign as error the failure of the court to give to the jury certain requested instructions concerning the law of the road. That the refusal to give specific requests is not error, if the points embodied therein are sufficiently covered by the general charge, is well settled. The charge, as given, was full, clear and accurate. The law of the road was clearly and correctly explained, and the court did not err in refusing to instruct further in respect thereto.

Order affirmed.

GREGORY E. SNYDER v. GREAT NORTHERN RAILWAY COMPANY.[1]

September 25, 1914.

Nos. 18,714—(230).

Damages.

Action for personal injury. A verdict for $1,750, approved by the trial court, *held* not excessive. Plaintiff was 37 years old, was under treatment in the hospital 10 days, for five months after the injury had been unable to work and probably would be unable so to do for several months more. [Reporter.]

Action in the district court for Anoka county to recover $27,000 for personal injury received while in the employ of defendant. The answer alleged that if plaintiff sustained any injury, it was through his own negligence and failure to exercise the care of an ordinarily prudent person for his own safety. The case was tried before Giddings, J., and a jury which returned a verdict for $1,750 in favor of plaintiff. From an order denying its motion for a new trial, defendant appealed. Affirmed.

Cobb, Wheelwright & Dille and *C. M. Bracelen,* for appellant.

Thomas D. Schall, T. D. Sheehan and *B. C. Thayer,* for respondent.

[1] Reported in 148 N. W. 617.

PER CURIAM.

A verdict for $1,750, approved by the trial court, cannot be held excessive on appeal where the evidence was such that the jury might well find that plaintiff, a brakeman 37 years old in defendant's employ, because of a defective grab-rod on a freight car was thrown from a moving train with such violence that he was rendered unconscious and, as a result, was under treatment in a hospital some 10 days and confined to his room longer; that he received such shock that a partial or incomplete hernia developed which can be cured only by an operation; that his back became lame and painful and so remained at the trial about five months after the injury; that his nervous system was affected and he is now subject to dizzy spells; that he, by reason of the injuries, had not been able to work since the accident and in all probability would be unable to so do for several months more; and that prior to the injury he was in good health and earning more than one hundred dollars a month.

Order affirmed.

STATE ex rel. VIRGINIA & RAINY LAKE COMPANY v. STANLEY BASHKO.[1]

October 9, 1914.

Nos. 18,827—(295).

Certiorari — stipulation not equivalent to writ.

Where the time had expired within which findings of the district court can be reviewed (no judgment having been entered), a stipulation of the parties to submit the matter to this court as though a writ of certiorari had been applied for or issued gives this court no jurisdiction. [Reporter.]

Action in the district court for St. Louis county by Stanley Bashko against the Virginia & Rainy Lake Co. to recover for personal injury received while in its employ. The case was tried before Fesler, J., who made findings and ordered judgment for $1,000, payable at the rate of $10 per week for a period of 100 weeks, in favor of plaintiff. Thereupon the stipulation mentioned in the opinion was entered into between the attorneys of the parties to the action, that the clerk of the district court should certify and return to the supreme court all of the pleadings, record of testimony and all proceedings, with the same effect and in all respects the

---

[1] Reported in 148 N. W. 1082.

same as though a petition for a writ of *certiorari* had been made in due time and form to the supreme court by the defendant, and the court acting on the petition had caused a writ to be issued, and that all the proceedings should be reviewed by the supreme court bearing upon the questions involved, in all respects as might be done if the proceedings were before that court on a writ of *certiorari* duly issued. Dismissed.

Abbott, MacPherran, Lewis & Gilbert, for relator.

Charles E. Adams, for respondent.

PER CURIAM.

The attorneys have stipulated that this case shall be deemed to be before this court as upon a writ of *certiorari*, but no such writ was ever applied for or issued. They seek to review the findings of the district court in this manner, although no judgment has been entered in that court. Even if such findings could be reviewed by writ of *certiorari*, and if the parties could substitute a stipulation in place of the writ, neither of which can be conceded, the time within which such findings could be so reviewed had expired before the making of the present stipulation.

This court has never acquired jurisdiction of the case and the proceedings in this court are dismissed.

WILSON & THOREEN v. N. F. W. HENNINGSEN.[1]

October 16, 1914.

Nos. 18,877—(124).

Appeal dismissed.

Appeal from a judgment was dismissed, where there was no settled case or bill of exceptions, no assignments of error, and appellant sought to have reviewed claimed defects in the evidence and errors in the charge to the jury. [Reporter.]

From a judgment for $47 entered in favor of plaintiff in the district court for Washington county, defendant appealed. Dismissed.

N. F. W. Henningsen, pro se.

Wilson & Thoreen, for respondents.

[1] Reported in 148 N. W. 1081.

PER CURIAM.

The defendant appeals from a judgment. The so-called paper book does not contain the judgment, but the original judgment roll is in the return to this court. An inspection thereof reveals no error. In the litigation defendant has been his own attorney. Because of his apparent inexperience in legal procedure, we have examined the documents in the return and the files herein with a view to discover his grievances (there being no assignments of error), and we find these relate to claimed defects in the evidence and errors in the charge of the court. There is no settled case or bill of exceptions. We are therefore not in a position to consider any matter which the appellant intended to raise by his appeal, and it should be dismissed. So ordered.

GEORGE H. GOODSPEED v. JULIUS A. SCHMAHL.[1]

October 17, 1914.

No. 19,117.

Constitutional amendment — ballot.

Secretary of state directed to have the official ballot for the seventh proposed amendment printed with the words "Seven Senator Amendment" as provided by the statute. [Reporter.]

Upon the application of George H. Goodspeed, this court directed Julius A. Schmahl, as secretary of the state of Minnesota, to desist from further printing, circulating and distributing and furnishing to the proper officials of the state the ballot prepared by him for the submission of the proposed amendments to the Constitution of the state at the general election in November, 1914, and to proceed to prepare and make as the official ballot upon which should be submitted the constitutional amendments, a ballot whereon should be printed in reference to the submission of the amendment to section 2, article 4, of the Constitution, the words printed in capitals at the end of the opinion herein, and nothing else, so far as related to that proposed amendment, or show cause why he had not done so. The respondent made return that his acts in having printed the proposed constitutional amendment, with the omission of the words "Seven Senator Amendment" were done unintentionally and through inadvertence. Application granted.

Haycraft & Palmer and *Moonan & Moonan*, for petitioner.

[1] Reported in 149 N. W. 1069.

Lyndon A. Smith, Attorney General, and *Clifford L. Hilton*, Assistant Attorney General, for respondent.

PER CURIAM.

The application of George H. Goodspeed for an order requiring this respondent, secretary of state, to correct the official state ballot containing the proposed Constitutional Amendments to be voted upon at the November, 1914, general election, having been duly heard and considered and it appearing that error has been made in the preparation of said ballot, it is ordered:

That you, the said Julius A. Schmahl, the respondent herein, as secretary of state of the state of Minnesota, do immediately upon receipt of a copy hereof:

Desist from further printing, circulating and distributing and furnishing to the proper officials of said state the ballot prepared by you for the submission of the proposed amendments to the Constitution of said state at the general election to be held in November, 1914.

That you proceed to prepare and make as the official ballot upon which will be submitted the constitutional amendments proposed, a ballot whereon shall be printed the following in reference to the submission of the amendment to section 2, of article 4, of the Constitution, to-wit:

"SEVEN SENATOR AMENDMENT—AMENDMENT OF SECTION 2 OF ARTICLE 4 OF THE CONSTITUTION, RELATING TO THE NUMBER OF MEMBERS OF THE SENATE AND HOUSE OF REPRESENTATIVES AND THE BASIS OF APPORTIONMENT THEREOF.

    "YES...................NO...................

HENRY HANSEN and Others v. NORTHWESTERN TELEPHONE EXCHANGE COMPANY and Others.[1]

October 23, 1914.

Nos. 18,762—(62).

Appeal dismissed — moot question.

Action to enjoin a city council from enacting an ordinance granting defendant corporation the right to construct a telephone exchange. After the restraining order was set aside, the ordinance was passed, accepted by defendant and

[1] Reported in 149 N. W. 131.

the work of construction begun. Thereafter plaintiffs appealed from an order sustaining defendants' demurrers to the complaint. Appeal dismissed, because there was no real controversy involved. [Reporter.]

Action by 28 plaintiffs against defendant telephone exchange company and the aldermen and recorder of the city of Luverne to restrain the passage and publication of a city ordinance. The defendants demurred individually and collectively to the complaint. The matter was heard before Nelson, J., who denied plaintiffs' application for a temporary injunction, set aside the temporary restraining order made by the court commissioner, and sustained the demurrers. From that order plaintiffs appealed. Dismissed.

A. J. Daley, M. H. Chunn and *W. N. Davidson*, for appellants.
Edmund A. Prendergast, for respondent telephone company.

PER CURIAM.

This action was brought by plaintiffs, as taxpayers, against the members of the city council of the city of Luverne, the city recorder, and the Northwestern Telephone Exchange Co., a corporation, to restrain and enjoin the passage by the council, the recording or publication by the recorder, and the acceptance by the Telephone Co. of an ordinance pending before the council, by which a franchise was intended to be granted to the Telephone Co. to construct and operate a telephone exchange within the city. The city officers and the Telephone Co. interposed separate general demurrers to the complaint. At the time of commencing the action, plaintiffs procured from the court commissioner an order temporarily restraining the council from passing the ordinance, and an application was made to the court for a temporary injunction restraining further proceedings by defendants pending the action. At the hearing on the application for an injunction, the demurrers to the complaint were submitted, and the court thereafter made an order discharging the order made by the court commissioner, denying the motion for a temporary injunction and a further order sustaining the demurrers to the complaint. It appears that the ordinance in question had been passed by the council and that the mayor of the city had vetoed the same. The action was commenced immediately after this action by the mayor, and the purpose thereof was to restrain and enjoin the council from passing the same over the veto. After the court had denied the temporary injunction and sustained the demurrers to the complaint, the council passed the ordinance over the veto and the Telephone Co. duly filed its acceptance thereof, and entered upon the work of constructing and putting in operating shape the telephone exchange authorized by the ordinance. Thereafter plaintiffs appealed from the orders sustaining the demurrers to the complaint. It will thus be seen that what the plaintiffs by the action sought to prevent, namely, the passage of the ordinance and the acceptance thereof by the Telephone Co., has been consum-

mated, and the action necessarily must fail. It now involves no real controversy
in respect to the purpose of the action, and the appeal presents a moot case.
If it be conceded that the action can be maintained at all, being one to restrain
the passage of an ordinance, the validity of the same and of the contract resulting from the acceptance thereof by the Telephone Co., are not involved in
the action, for the passage and acceptance of the ordinance occurred subsequent
to the commencement thereof, and can only be made issues therein, if the remedy is here available, by supplemental complaint, no application to file which
appears to have been made. Section 7763, G. S. 1913; 2 Dunnell, Minn. Dig.
§§ 7634, et seq.

We therefore dismiss the appeal as one involving no real controversy.

Appeal dismissed.

Justice Phillp E. Brown took no part.

JOHN F. MELBERG v. WILD RICE LUMBER COMPANY.[1]

November 6, 1914.

Nos. 18,671—(36).

Negligence — finding not sustained by evidence.

The evidence was insufficient to sustain a finding that the driver of a team
was negligent in permitting them to get beyond his control or in failing to direct their course so as to avoid collision with plaintiff. [Reporter.]

Action in the district court for Norman county to recover $5,000 for per-
sonal injury received by plaintiff's minor son through defendant's negligence.
The case was tried before Grindeland, J., who denied defendant's motion to dismiss the action, and a jury which returned a verdict for $600 in favor of plain-
tiff. From an order denying its motion for judgment notwithstanding the verdict or for a new trial, defendant appealed. Reversed with directions to enter
judgment for defendant.

Lind, Ueland & Jerome, for appellant.

Christian G. Dosland, for respondent.

PER CURIAM.

Action to recover damages alleged to have been sustained by plaintiff's minor

[1] Reported in 149 N. W. 1069.

son through defendant's negligence. Plaintiff had a verdict and defendant appealed from the denial of its alternative motion.

The injuries complained of were claimed to have been caused by the same runaway accident involved in plaintiff's case against this defendant, reported in 125 Minn. 469, 147 N. W. 427. The present case was tried at a term subsequent to the trial of that case, but before the decision of this court therein. The negligence charged was that the team were runaways, which defendant, with knowledge of that vice, permitted to be driven on the public highway in charge of an incompetent driver. On the trial, however, the occurrence was inquired into with particularity, and each party offered evidence regarding the driver's management of the horses from the time they started to run until the accident. The instructions were to the effect that the evidence failed to establish the stated negligence, but, as we construe them, they also submitted as the sole question of negligence whether the driver could have avoided the accident by the exercise of due care while the horses were running away. On the trial defendant excepted to the giving of this portion of the instructions, on the ground that no such negligence was alleged, and argues that therefore this issue should not have been submitted. In refutation, plaintiff contends that the matter was fully litigated and the defect is one remediable by amendment.

However, if the evidence was insufficient to sustain a finding in this regard, these questions are clearly immaterial. True it is, testimony was given by witnesses not called on the former trial, but it was of slight, if any, consequence, except as bearing on the issues disposed of by the court adversely to plaintiff; and while the driver was more fully examined and, to some extent, contradicted his former testimony in matters of detail, the evidence was substantially the same on both trials.

We are unable to sustain the verdict either on the theory, suggested by plaintiff, that the jury may have believed the driver guided the horses against plaintiff's wagon in order to stop them, or on any other, or to differentiate the case as to liability from the former.

There being no probability of making a stronger case, the order is reversed, with directions to enter judgment for defendant notwithstanding the verdict.

JOHN QUIRK v. CONSUMERS POWER COMPANY.[1]

November 6, 1914.

Nos. 18,761—(37).

New trial.

New trial granted because of conduct of the trial court which it is thought
prejudiced defendant. [Reporter.]

Action in the district court for Ramsey county to recover $50,000 for personal
injury received while in the employ of defendant. The case was tried before
Kelly, J., who denied defendant's motions for dismissal of the action and for a
directed verdict in its favor, and a jury which returned a verdict of $10,000.
From an order denying its motion for judgment notwithstanding the verdict or
for a new trial, defendant appealed. Reversed and new trial granted.

Briggs, Thygeson & Everall and *Denegre & McDermott,* for appellant.
Markham & Calmenson, for respondent.

PER CURIAM.

Plaintiff recovered a verdict of $10,000. Defendant appeals from an order
denying its motion in the alternative for judgment notwithstanding the verdict
or for a new trial.

Plaintiff received serious personal injuries from an electric current, while he
was engaged in working in the vicinity of heavily charged wires in the "pent
house" of defendant on top of its building on Third street in St. Paul. Defendant claims that it was not negligent, that plaintiff was, and that he assumed the risk. These issues were the vital ones on the trial below, and were
closely contested. We think they were for the jury on the evidence presented.
We do not make a further statement of the facts or the evidence, or further
discuss these issues, beyond the statement that on the record a verdict either
way would be sustained if there had been a fair trial.

But there was conduct on the part of the trial court which, considered with
the size of the verdict, forces us to the conclusion that in justice to defendant the case should be tried again. It will do no good to rehearse here the unfortunate episode on the trial which we think prejudiced defendant's case. Defendant's counsel, apparently through no fault of his own, but through a misunderstanding on the part of the court, was put in a bad light in the eyes of the
jury by a trial judge who is well known for his fairness. What the trial court

afterwards, during the trial and in its charge, said to the jury on the subject was not calculated to remove the sting. The verdict is so large that we think it very probable that the jury was influenced in fixing the damages, if not in determining the question of liability, by the attitude of the trial court.

It was error also to receive evidence of negotiations for a settlement. Other rulings complained of are not likely to be made on another trial and we do not discuss them. We do not approve of the action of the trial court in reading the pleadings to the jury.

Order reversed and new trial granted.

TOWN OF ERDAHL v. TOWN OF SANFORD.[1]

November 6, 1914.

Nos. 18,821—(84).

Pauper — error to dismiss action.

Action to recover moneys expended for the support of a pauper. Whether the pauper had a settlement in defendant town was a question for the jury, and the court erred in dismissing the action. [Reporter.]

From a judgment in justice court in favor of defendant, plaintiff appealed to the district court for Grant county. The appeal was heard before Flaherty, J., who when plaintiff rested granted defendant's motion to dismiss the action. From an order denying its motion for a new trial, plaintiff appealed. Reversed.

E. J. Scofield, for appellant.

R. J. Stromme, for respondent.

PER CURIAM.

In this action, brought to recover moneys expended for the support of a pauper, the issue was whether the pauper had obtained a residence or settlement, under section 3071, G. S. 1913, in the defendant town so as to make that town liable. An examination of the testimony introduced by plaintiff leads to the conclusion that the question of the pauper's residence or settlement in the defendant town was for the jury, and the court erred when dismissing the case. This being the result it is deemed best not to set out or discuss the testimony. It would not benefit the profession nor aid the parties in another trial.

Order reversed.

[1] Reported in 149 N. W. 1070.

ROBERT J. ELLIOTT v. H. L. BARKER.[1]

November 6, 1914.

Nos. 18,883—(129).

Corporation.

 Where a corporation takes a lease of premises and before the lease goes into effect the corporation is dissolved by judicial proceedings, it is bound by the lease and is liable for a breach of it, even if it does not take possession under the lease. In this case the lease and a prior lease constituted but one transaction. [Reporter.]

 In proceedings in the district court for Hennepin county for the dissolution of the Waterbury Implement Co., Robert J. Elliott filed a claim for $1,125 for rent. The allowance of the claim was objected to by H. L. Barker, receiver and trustee of that company. The matter was heard before Jelley, J., who made findings amending the claim, and ordered judgment in favor of claimant for the sum of $2,458.25. From the order allowing the claim, the trustee and receiver appealed. Affirmed.

Herbert T. Park, for appellant.

William W. Bartlett, for respondent.

PER CURIAM.

 Appeal by the receiver from an order of the district court allowing the claims of the claimant.

 On March 1, 1912, the claimant Elliott made two leases to the Waterbury Implement Co., one expiring on December 1, 1912, and the other, which included some property additional to that included in the first, commencing on that date at an increased rental. The company abandoned the premises in November, 1912. Rent was paid to the first of that month. On December 6, 1912, the company was dissolved by judicial proceedings and a trustee appointed. Upon its dissolution Elliott was entitled to damages in some amount. The propriety of the measure adopted by the court is not drawn in question.

 The trustee claims that nothing can be allowed because of the breach of the lease which was to commence December 1, 1912, for the reason that possession was not taken under it. Clearly this is wrong. The company was bound by the second lease and liable for a breach of it. Besides the two leases constituted but one transaction.

---

[1] Reported in 149 N. W. 1070.

It is a further contention of the trustee that there was a constructive eviction and that the claimant took possession of the property and occupied and used it during the period for which he seeks rent. We have carefully examined the record bearing on these questions. They were for the trial court. They do not require review nor discussion.

Order affirmed.

JOSEPH P. WHITWELL v. ERIC WOLF.[1]

November 13, 1914.

Nos. 18,814—(67).

Negligence — finding of court sustained.

The court did not err in finding that plaintiff's *prima facie* case of negligence was not rebutted by defendant's evidence. [Reporter.]

Action in the municipal court of St. Paul to recover $400. The case was tried before Hanft, J., who made findings and ordered judgment for $250 in favor of plaintiff. From an order denying his motion for a new trial, defendant appealed. Affirmed.

John J. Kirby, for appellant.

Denegre & McDermott, for respondent.

PER CURIAM.

This is an action to recover damages for the death of a horse, alleged to have been caused by defendant's negligent management of an automobile. The cause was tried by the court without a jury, and findings made for plaintiff. Defendant appealed from an order denying a new trial.

The accident occurred on a street, running north and south, in St. Paul. Plaintiff tied his horse to a hitching post at the curb on the east side of the street, leaving the animal facing north. A few feet further north, on the opposite side of the street, stood a covered automobile. Some 15 minutes later plaintiff discovered that the animal had been so badly injured by defendant's automobile that it had to be killed. After proving these facts and the value of the animal, plaintiff rested.

Under the doctrine of *res ipsa loquitur* the burden of explaining that the accident did not occur from want of care then devolved upon defendant. He

1 Reported in 149 N. W. 299.

127 M.—34.

testified, in his own behalf, that, while he was driving south on the west side of the street, but near the center, at a speed of ten or twelve miles an hour, and when he was from seven to eight feet from the horse, and passing the standing automobile, one Peterson, whom he did not see until he was five or six feet away, came towards him from behind the latter on a bicycle, and to avoid colliding with him he turned his machine almost at right angles to the left and applied the brakes; but the pavement was wet and in bad condition, and the machine, slipping, struck the horse, causing the injury.

The street was of average width, but the lay of the ground did not appear. Defendant's car was new, but no proof was made of its condition, nor of defendant's competency as a driver, except that he had driven an automobile for about a year, nor within what distance the car could be stopped when going at the rate of speed claimed under any circumstances. Defendant produced no other witness, nor was Peterson's absence explained. After the accident the automobile was found facing towards and directly square with the horse.

In this state of the record we cannot hold that the trial court erred in finding that plaintiff's *prima facie* case of negligence was not rebutted.

Order affirmed.

ROBERT SINCLAIR v. JOHN F. FITZPATRICK.[1]

November 13, 1914.

Nos. 18,898—(135).

Work and labor — findings.

The necessary conclusion from the findings is that the wife was held out by her husband as his agent in ordering a small change in their homestead to recover the cost of which the action was brought. [Reporter.]

Action in the municipal court of St. Paul to recover $46.01. The action was tried before Hanft, J., who made findings and ordered judgment in favor of plaintiff for the amount demanded. From the judgment entered pursuant to the order for judgment, defendant John F. Fitzpatrick appealed. Affirmed.

R. G. O'Malley and *John F. Fitzpatrick*, for appellant.

John S. Crooks, for respondent.

1 Reported in 149 N. W. 1070.

PER CURIAM.

This action was brought against the huband and wife to recover the reasonable value for changing, at their request, a woodshed into a garage. Judgment was rendered against both. The husband alone appeals therefrom, upon the sole ground that there is no finding that he requested the work to be done. The findings are not to be commended. But since there was no application either for a new trial or for an amendment of the findings to more definitely state whether or not appellant requested plaintiff to render the services, we should construe the findings so as to sustain the judgment, if possible. The findings relative to appellant's responsibility are: That he with his wife and family lived upon the premises where respondent did the work; that he had previously made smaller repairs thereon upon the wife's order which appellant paid for; that the alteration in question was made upon the wife's request; that appellant was about the premises part of the time every day while the work was being done; and that the premises thus improved constituted the homestead of the defendants. The fair and necessary conclusion from these findings is that the wife was held out by appellant as his agent in ordering this trifling change in the homestead of which he was at least a part owner. Adams v. Eidam, 42 Minn. 53, 43 N. W. 690; Clark v. Thorpe Bros. 117 Minn. 202, 135 N. W. 387.

Judgment affirmed.

CHARLES H. JOHNSTON v. ILLINOIS CENTRAL RAILROAD COMPANY.[1]

November 27, 1914.

Nos. 18,839—(89).

Question for jury.

Whether plaintiff was employed by defendant or by another company was, under the evidence, a question for the jury. [Reporter.]

Action in the district court for Ramsey county to recover $25,000 for personal injury received while in the employ of defendant. The case was tried before Brill, J., who when plaintiff rested granted defendant's motion to dismiss the action. From an order denying his motion for a new trial, plaintiff appealed. Reversed.

Samuel A. Anderson and *A. F. Storey*, for appellant.

Butler & Mitchell, for respondent.

PER CURIAM.

Plaintiff, a member of a switching crew employed in the railroad yards at Memphis, Tennessee, brought this suit to recover damages for personal injuries sustained through the negligence of another switching crew employed in the same yards. He alleged, in his complaint, that defendant and the Yazoo & Mississippi Valley Railroad Co. operated the yards in question jointly, and that he and all other switchmen, at work therein, were employed by these two companies jointly. He brought suit against the defendant, the Illinois Central Railroad Company, only. Defendant, in its answer, denied ever employing him, and alleged that he was employed solely and exclusively by the Yazoo & Mississippi River Railroad Co. At the close of plaintiff's evidence, defendant made a motion to dismiss the suit, which was granted upon the ground that plaintiff had failed to prove that he was in the employ of defendant. Plaintiff moved for a new trial, and appealed from an order denying his motion.

The only question presented is whether the evidence was sufficient to make a question for the jury as to whether plaintiff was in the employ of defendant at the time of the accident. It would require considerable space and serve no useful purpose to recapitulate the evidence. It is sufficient to say that there was substantial evidence tending to show that plaintiff was in the employ of defendant. There was also substantial evidence tending to show that he was in the employ of the other company. Whether he was employed by the defendant, either alone or in connection with the other company, or by the other company only, was a fair question for the jury, under all the evidence, and should have been submitted to them.

Order reversed.

GEORGE H. WINTERS v. MINNEAPOLIS & ST. LOUIS RAILROAD COMPANY.[1]

December 4, 1914.

Nos. 18,655—(184).[2]

Remittitur without paying costs.

Motion to send remittitur to court below without payment of costs denied. No showing of inability of guardian *ad litem* to pay. [Reporter.]

After the decision in the appeal reported in 126 Minn. 260, 148 N. W. 106, plaintiff moved that the remittitur be sent to the court below without payment of the judgment for costs. Motion denied.

Barton & Kay, for plaintiff.

W. H. Bremner and *F. M. Miner*, for defendant.

[1]   orted in 148 N. W. 10

PER CURIAM.

Plaintiff's motion that the remittitur be sent to the court below without payment of the judgment for costs is denied. By G. S. 1913, § 7983 (R. L. 1905, § 4347), the infant plaintiff and his guardian *ad litem* are liable for costs. There is no showing of the inability of the guardian to pay.

STATE ex rel. E. F. KELLY v. ARTHUR B. CHILDRESS.[1]

December 4, 1914.

No. 19,164.

Settlement of case.

A trial court has jurisdiction to settle and allow a case after an appeal has been taken from an order denying a new trial. Loveland v. Cooley, 59 Minn. 259, 61 N. W. 138. The rule was not changed by G. S. 1913, § 7996. [Reporter.]

Upon the relation of E. F. Kelly this court granted its order directing Honorable Arthur B. Childress, as judge of the district court for Rice county, to show cause why a peremptory writ of *mandamus* should not issue commanding him to settle a proposed case in the action entitled State ex rel. Klemer v. Kelly. Writ granted.

Lucius A. Smith and *Anson L. Keyes,* for relator.
E. H. Gipson and *Robert Mee,* for respondent.

PER CURIAM.

In the proceeding entitled State ex rel. Klemer v. Kelly, in the court below, judgment was ordered in favor of relator. Defendant therein moved for a new trial, which motion the court denied. Defendant promptly appealed, and a certified copy of the bond and notice of appeal was transmitted to this court. The appeal was so taken on October 3, 1914. Thereafter and on October 5, 1914, defendant served a proposed case upon relator, to which no amendment was proposed. The proposed case was upon proper notice presented to the trial judge for allowance on October 22, 1914. The court refused to hear the matter or to settle the case on the sole ground that the appeal to this court from the order denying a new trial divested the district court of further jurisdiction, and hence that the court was without authority to act in the matter. This proceeding was thereafter brought to compel the trial court to settle the proposed case, and sign and certify the same as containing a correct record of the pro-

[1] Reported in 149 N. W. 550.

ceedings had on the trial. On the hearing in this court respondent moved to dismiss the proceeding on the ground that the court below had no jurisdiction to act because of the fact that the appeal had deprived it of further authority in the case.

It was held in Loveland v. Cooley, 59 Minn. 259, 61 N. W. 138, that the trial court has jurisdiction to settle and allow a case after an appeal has been taken from an order denying a new trial. The decision there rendered disposes of the question in the case at bar. The rule there announced was not changed, as contended by counsel, by chapter 55, p. 47, Laws 1913 (G. S. 1913, § 7996).

It is therefore ordered that respondent proceed, upon proper notice, to hear the parties upon an application to settle the case, and make such order in the premises as shall conform to the facts and be consistent with the statutes in such cases provided.

WILLIAM JENTZ v. TOWN OF TYRONE.[1]

December 11, 1914.

Nos. 18,843—(102).

Highway.
    Petition to lay out a highway. Verdict in district court in favor of petitioners. *Held:* The court did not abuse its discretion in denying a new trial. [Reporter.]

From an order of the board of supervisors of the town of Tyrone denying his petition to lay out and establish a certain highway, William Jentz appealed to the district court for Le Sueur county, where the appeal was heard before Morrison, J., and a jury which returned a verdict in favor of appellant. From an order denying its motion for a new trial, defendant appealed. Affirmed.

Thomas Hessian, for appellant.
Francis Cadwell, for respondent.

PER CURIAM.
Plaintiff and others petitioned the supervisors of the town of Tyrone in Le Sueur county to lay out and establish a public highway. The board denied the petition, and plaintiff appealed to the district court, where the case was tried

---

[1] Reported in 149 N. W. 1069.

to a jury. There was a verdict reversing the action of the board, and defendant appealed to this court from an order denying a new trial.

Defendant claims that the verdict is not justified by the evidence, and that there were prejudicial errors in rulings on the admission of evidence and in the charge. We have examined the record, and reach the conclusion that the verdict should stand. It will be of no value as a precedent to detail the evidence, or to state or discuss the alleged errors on the trial. The questions were purely questions of fact, and the evidence is such that we cannot say the court abused its discretion in refusing a new trial. We find nothing in any of the rulings or instructions of the trial court that calls for a reversal.

Order affirmed.

WYMAN, PARTRIDGE & COMPANY v. MIKE HENNE.[1]

December 11, 1914.

Nos. 18,899—(119).

Evidence — loose leaf ledger.

Action for balance of price of merchandise. The evidence tended to prove that as orders were filled and before delivery they were entered upon charge sheets, and the amount of the sales was entered from the sheets upon the ledger by the bookkeepers before delivery. The sheets were not destroyed after the ledger entries were made. *Held:* The loose leaf ledger, containing entries for moneys received and merchandise sold, was properly received in evidence. [Reporter.]

Action in the municipal court of Minneapolis to recover $365.95 for goods sold and delivered. The case was tried before Bardwell, J., who made findings and as conclusion of law ordered judgment in favor of plaintiff for the amount demanded. Plaintiff's motion for a new trial was denied. From the judgment entered pursuant to the order for judgment, defendant appealed. Affirmed.

Paul J. Thompson and *M. A. Hessian*, for appellant.

Dodge & Webber and *Arthur T. Conley*, for respondent.

[1] Reported in 149 N. W. 647.

Note.—The authorities on the question of the admissibility of a party's books as evidence in his own favor are gathered in an extensive note in 52 L.R.A. 546.

PER CURIAM.

. Plaintiff alleges that, between given dates, it sold and delivered to defendant, at his request, "certain goods, wares and merchandise, of the actual and reasonable value of $2,222.32, which sum defendant agreed to pay therefor." That no part of said sum has ever been paid, save and except the sum of $1,956.71. The answer admits that defendant purchased merchandise of plaintiff and has paid it "a large amount of money on account thereof." It alleges that defendant "has paid the plaintiff in full either in cash or by return of merchandise for all goods, wares and merchandise sold to him either as alleged in the complaint or otherwise," and denies every allegation in the complaint except as admitted. Defendant appeals from the judgment rendered against him for $265.61 and costs.

The only ground urged for reversal of the judgment is that the court erred in receiving in evidence defendant's loose leaf ledger. The head bookkeeper testified in respect to this ledger that it was one of plaintiff's account books, containing the record of goods sold and moneys paid, entered at the time of the transactions by the persons authorized to make them under the direct supervision of the witness, and that the book was just and true to the best of his knowledge and belief. It also appeared that the usual way in which plaintiff did business was to enter the goods as the orders were filled in its place of business, and before delivery, upon charge sheets. Before the goods were delivered these sheets went to the bookkeepers, who therefrom entered the amount of the sales on the ledger. The sheets were kept, and were not mere memoranda which were destroyed after the ledger entry. When this loose leaf ledger was offered in evidence, defendant objected on the ground that no foundation was laid. There was also special objection to certain pencil memorandum of interest computation therein, not here material since the court disallowed the interest claims. The court in ruling on the objection stated: "The objection so far as the original entries is concerned is good; that is, you should bring your original record here. I will receive the books subject to objection, ignoring the pencil memorandum." The printed record contains but a fragment of the settled case. The loose leaf ledger page received is printed. It shows entries for money received as well as for merchandise sold. There is no evidence that the moneys received were entered in any other place than in this ledger. It was properly admissible, for the payments were also in issue. The settled case is not here. What if anything was done to convince the court that the value of the merchandise sold and delivered was the amount stated in the findings is not made to appear. We therefore deem it unnecessary to determine in this case whether the entries upon the ledger leaf of the merchandise sold were admissible as tending to prove a sale or delivery thereof under chapter 251, p. 297, Laws of 1909.

Judgment affirmed.

CHRIS N. JUHL and Another v. WILD RICE BOOM COMPANY.[1]

July 31, 1914.

Nos. 18,486–(69).[2]

New trial — general verdict upon two causes of action.

A new trial granted because the verdict was a general verdict, and the amount awarded for damages upon the second cause of action could not be separated. [Reporter.]

Action in the district court for Norman county to recover $4,000. The case was tried before Grindeland, J., who denied defendant's motions for a directed verdict on each cause of action and on both causes of action, and a jury which returned a verdict for $1,700 in favor of plaintiff. From an order denying its motion for judgment notwithstanding the verdict or for a new trial, defendant appealed. Reversed and new trial granted.

Lind, Ueland & Jerome, for appellant.

Christian G. Dosland, for respondent.

PER CURIAM.

The facts in respect to the principal question involved in this case are the same as those presented in Heiberg v. Wild Rice Boom Co. supra, page 8, 148 N. W. 517, and the decision therein rendered controls the result here. In this case there are two causes of action, namely: (1) For the alleged wrongful damming of the tributaries of the river; and (2) withholding the water therein until a large quantity had accumulated and then casting the same down in destructive quantities and washing out a part of plaintiff's mill dam. There was a general verdict for plaintiff, and though plaintiff showed a clear right to recover on the second cause of action, at least the evidence presented a case for the jury, the amount awarded for the injury there complained of cannot be ascertained because the verdict covered both causes of action. It cannot be separated, and for the error pointed out in the other case, which is also presented here, there must be a reversal.

Order reversed and new trial granted.

---

1 Reported in 148 N. W. 520.   2 April, 1914, term calendar.

INDEX

ABATEMENT AND REVIVAL—Continued.
>   upon him or when he appears without service, and is deemed to be
>   pending until its final determination.
>   —Seeger v. Young, 418.

ABBREVIATION.

See EVIDENCE, 7.

ACCRETION. See NAVIGABLE WATER, 9.

ACTION. See ABATEMENT AND REVIVAL, 5; EJECTMENT; FORCIBLE ENTRY AND
>   UNLAWFUL DETAINER, 1; MINE AND MINERAL, 2; NEGLIGENCE, 1.

SURVIVAL OF CAUSE OF ACTION.

See DEATH.

SPLITTING CAUSE OF ACTION.

See JUDGMENT, 4.

ENJOINING ACTION IN FOREIGN STATE.

See INJUNCTION.

WHEN ACTION IS PENDING.

See ABATEMENT AND REVIVAL, 1, 2, 4, 6.

DISMISSAL OF ACTION.

See ABATEMENT AND REVIVAL, 4; CONTEMPT; PAUPER; SPECIFIC PERFORMANCE;
>   TRIAL, 3, 10.

ADMISSION. See EVIDENCE, 10–13.

ADVERSE CLAIM. See ABATEMENT AND REVIVAL, 1; REGISTRATION OF TITLE,
>   1, 2.

ADVERSE POSSESSION.
>   1. An oral contract to buy a quitclaim deed from the record holder of title
>   to land negatives any inference of adverse possession of the land by the
>   proposed purchaser.
>   —Cluss v. Hackett, 398.
>   2. Evidence examined, and *held* not to establish title to real property by
>   adverse possession.
>   —Cluss v. Hackett, 397.

AFFIDAVIT. See JUDGMENT, 2; MORTGAGE, 5.

ALIMONY.

FOR LIFE.

See DIVORCE, 2.

AMENDMENT. See PLEADING, 1.

APPEAL AND ERROR. See CRIMINAL LAW, 8; PLEADING, 1.

OBJECTION TO QUESTION IN TRIAL COURT.

1. An objection that a question is incompetent, irrelevant and immaterial does not raise the point that it is improper as calling for an opinion of the witness on the whole issue in the case.
   —Thoreson v. Susens, 84, 86.

FAILURE TO OBJECT TO CHARGE TO JURY.

2. An inadvertently inaccurate instruction was not reversible error, the inaccuracy not being seasonably called to the attention of the trial court.
   —Chase v. Tingdale Brothers, 401.

NOTICE OF APPEAL.

3. The notice of plaintiffs' appeal from the order granting their motion for a new trial does not in terms embrace an appeal from the court's orders on the demurrers interposed, even if such orders were appealable.
   —Bjorgo v. First National Bank of Emmons, 105.

RECORD—SETTLED CASE.

4. The original verdict filed with the clerk is part of the record proper, and is no proper part of a settled case. If the verdict as incorporated in the settled case conflicts with the original verdict as so filed, the latter will be regarded in this court as the true verdict.
   —Sonnesyn v. Hawbaker, 16.

5. A trial court has jurisdiction to settle and allow a case after an appeal has been taken from an order denying a new trial. Loveland v. Cooley, 59 Minn. 259, 61 N. W. 138. The rule was not changed by G. S. 1913, § 7996.
   —State ex rel. v. Childress, 533.

ASSIGNMENT OF ERROR.

See APPEAL AND ERROR, 10.

6. The defendants cannot avail themselves of a variance between the pleading and proof first suggested on the appeal.
   —Seewald v. Schmidt, 376.

DISCRETION OF TRIAL COURT.

7. The matter of opening a default judgment rests in the discretion of the trial court, and its action in opening default will not be reversed except for palpable abuse of discretion.
   —Rodgers v. United States and Dominion Life Insurance Co. 435.

APPEAL AND ERROR—Continued.

8. A new trial will not be granted on the ground of excessive damages, nor will the verdict be reduced, except upon the ground that the damages were awarded under the influence of passion or prejudice.

—Ott v. Tri-State Telephone & Telegraph Co. 373.

REVIEW.

See COSTS, 3.

9. Where a charge is not excepted to on the trial or at all, it is not before this court for review upon an appeal.

—Rademacher v. Pioneer Tractor Manufacturing Co. 177.

10. Appeal from a judgment was dismissed, where there was no settled case or bill of exceptions, no assignments of error, and appellant sought to have reviewed claimed defects in the evidence and errors in the charge to the jury.

—Wilson & Thoreen v. Henningsen, 520.

11. It would seem the jury should have been instructed that the burden was upon plaintiff to show that he became a purchaser for value, before maturity, in the ordinary course of business, and without notice, if they found the defense of fraud true; but since the evidence as to the fraud, which is neither printed nor referred to in the briefs, might have been such that the burden of proof still rested on defendants in this respect, we are not required to reverse because the trial court refused to state that it rested on plaintiff.

—Cole v. Johnson, 291.

12. As the evidence and the instructions bearing upon the question as to whether defendant Lounsberry was also liable to plaintiff in damages had no bearing upon the claim made against appellants, appellants are not in position, upon this appeal, to question the rulings in respect thereto.

—Grondlund v. Cudahy Packing Co. 515.

13. Under rule 9 of this court, where the sufficiency of the evidence to sustain the verdict is challenged, the portions of the record printed must be in substantial conformity with the settled case, and not be in the nature of a bill of exceptions.

—Watre v. Great Northern Railway Co. 119.

14. Action in ejectment. Defense, that defendant is in possession under an oral contract of sale, with such part performance as to take the case out of the statute of frauds. The court found no oral contract was made. To entitle the defendant to the relief asked for, such contract must be clearly proved and its terms so specific and distinct as to leave no reasonable doubt of their meaning. The finding should not be set aside

APPEAL AND ERROR—Continued.

unless it is manifestly and palpably against the weight of the evidence. The evidence is conflicting and it well sustains the finding of the trial court, and the finding must be sustained.

—Berndt v. Berndt, 238.

REVIEW ON CROSS APPEAL.

15. A party whose motion for new trial has been granted is not aggrieved by the order, so that the rulings adverse to him on the trial may be reviewed on his cross appeal.

—Bjorgo v. First National Bank of Emmons, 105.

HARMLESS ERROR.

See MUNICIPAL CORPORATION, 17.

16. It was not prejudicial error to reject an offer of evidence to prove fraud upon the vendor of land by plaintiff acting as his agent and purchasing in his own interest, and to deny a motion to amend to allege fraud, it not appearing that further material evidence could be produced.

—Sonnesyn v. Hawbaker, 15.

17. The defendant claimed title through a chattel mortgage executed by plaintiff's husband, but failed to show any authority from plaintiff, either direct or by way of estoppel, to mortgage the mares. Such being the case, no prejudicial error can be asserted by defendant on the immaterial issue whether the mortgage purported by its terms to include this team. If plaintiff proved ownership, she was entitled to a verdict, regardless of what was included in her husband's unauthorized mortgage.

—Klein v. Frerichs, 177.

18. Two issues were submitted to the jury in this action brought upon a promissory note by an alleged *bona fide* holder: One was whether fraud of the payee induced the deal in which the note was given, and the other whether plaintiff was a *bona fide* holder. Upon this appeal by the makers of the note it is *held:*

It cannot be assumed that the jury found against defendants upon the defense of fraud, so as to render error in the submission of the other issue harmless.

—Cole v. Johnson, 291.

19. The injury to the mill dam is not so clearly shown to have resulted wholly from diversion of the water that the error in the charge, in respect to the right to accumulate and detain the quantity of water needed by defendant, was without prejudice.

—Johnson v. Wild Rice Boom Co. 490.

20. The reception in evidence of an exhibit bearing solely upon another issue

APPEAL AND ERROR—Continued.

properly in the case, even if technical error, did not warrant a new trial, since the special finding above mentioned determined that plaintiff could have no cause of action no matter how such other issue was decided. Furthermore, the trial court properly received the exhibit and correctly instructed the jury how and when to consider the same, and hence, in ordering a new trial because of the reception thereof, erred.

—Nichols v. Atwood, 425.

ELECTION BETWEEN CAUSES OF ACTION.

21. The refusal to require plaintiff to elect between different causes of action which in fact were tried as one, even if error, was without prejudice to defendant.

—Johnson v. Wild Rice Boom Co. 490.

DECISION UPON FORMER APPEAL.

22. A proposition decided upon a former appeal becomes the law of the case, and should not be re-examined in a subsequent appeal in the same action.

—Orr v. Sutton, 37, 41.

MOOT QUESTION.

23. Action to enjoin a city council from enacting an ordinance granting defendant corporation the right to construct a telephone exchange. After the restraining order was set aside, the ordinance was passed, accepted by defendant and the work of construction begun. Thereafter plaintiffs appealed from an order sustaining defendants' demurrers to the complaint. Appeal dismissed, because no real controversy was involved.

—Hansen v. Northwestern Telephone Exchange Co. 522.

ASSIGNMENT. See JUDGMENT, 8.

ASSUMPTION OF RISK. See MASTER AND SERVANT, 14–22.

ATTORNEY AND CLIENT. See JUDGMENT, 2.

AUTHORITY TO STIPULATE FOR JUDGMENT.

See JUDGMENT, 3.

ALLOWANCE OF FEE BY COURT.

See MECHANIC'S LIEN, 9.

ACTION FOR COMPENSATION.

Plaintiff sued to recover for services rendered and disbursements made as

ATTORNEY AND CLIENT—Continued.

attorney for a receiver. Upon conflicting evidence, the court found as a fact that plaintiff rendered no services and made no disbursements in the capacity of attorney for the receiver. The evidence is sufficient to sustain the finding.

—Crosby v. Larson, 315.

AUCTION.

ACTION ON ORDER UPON PROCEEDS OF AUCTION SALE.

See BILLS AND NOTES, 4.

AUCTIONEER.

There are important distinctions between the business of an auctioneer and that of a peddler. The auctioneer does not sell his own goods; he acts, in making a sale at auction, primarily as the agent of the seller; when the property is struck off, he becomes also the agent of the purchaser, at least to the extent of binding him by his memorandum of sale. He is liable to the seller for a loss due to his negligence, or to his deviating from instructions, as well as for money paid him by purchasers. He is liable to a purchaser under certain circumstances.

—Wright v. May, 152.

AUCTIONEER'S LICENSE.

See CONSTITUTION, 2.

AUTOMOBILE. See HIGHWAY, 2, 3; NEGLIGENCE, 4, 12; RAILWAY, 4.

LAW OF THE ROAD—SECTION 2634, G. S. 1913.

See MUNICIPAL CORPORATION, 18.

STREET CAR—SECTION 2632, G. S. 1913.

See MUNICIPAL CORPORATION, 12-17.

BANK AND BANKING. See BILLS AND NOTES, 3.

The fact that a bank draft issued by a small village bank was made payable to the order of the defendant bank is held sufficient to put the defendant bank on inquiry as to the ownership of the proceeds before paying the same to the person presenting the draft.

—Bjorgo v. First National Bank of Emmons, 105.

BANKRUPTCY.

PREFERENCE.

See FRAUDULENT CONVEYANCE, 1.

127 M.—35.

BILL OF EXCEPTIONS. See APPEAL AND ERROR, 10, 12.

BILL OF LADING. See EVIDENCE, 7.

BILLS AND NOTES. See EVIDENCE, 13; PLEDGE.

VALUABLE CONSIDERATION.

1. A pre-existing debt is a valuable consideration.
　　—German-American State Bank of Ritzville v. Lyons, 392.

BONA FIDE PURCHASER.

See APPEAL AND ERROR, 18.

2. Action upon a promissory note by an alleged *bona fide* holder. *Held:* the evidence tended to prove circumstances which made it a question for the jury whether plaintiff's testimony that he had bought the note before maturity and paid $500 therefor was true, although not contradicted by any direct testimony. An instruction to the contrary was error.
　　—Cole v. Johnson, 291.

ACTION UPON NOTE SIGNED IN BLANK.

3. Action upon promissory notes, one signed in blank by defendant and filled in by his agent, who was president of plaintiff bank and in charge of its business with the vice president and cashier, and both notes negotiated with the bank. The proceeds were converted by the agent. *Held:* Plaintiff was liable on the notes.
　　—First National Bank of Gilbert v. Bailey, 296.

ACTION ON WRITTEN ORDER.

4. Action to recover on a written order given plaintiffs by a debtor to pay the amount thereof out of the proceeds of an auction sale of the debtor's property, which sale was to be held in the future and to be conducted by defendant bank. It is *held:*

(1) The evidence shows an agreement by defendant, made when the order was presented, to pay the same out of the proceeds of the sale after the claims which the debtor, prior to the presentation of plaintiff's order, had ordered defendant to pay.

(2) The evidence was sufficient to support a finding by the jury that plaintiff's order was presented before certain other claims were ordered by the debtor to be paid.

(3) Defendant, as a stakeholder, was not responsible for the validity of the claims it was ordered to pay. The evidence was insufficient to show that defendant knew that certain claims were fictitious, and fraudulently conspired with their owners to dissipate the proceeds of the sale so

BILLS AND NOTES—Continued.

as to prevent the payment of plaintiff's order. It was error to submit this question to the jury.

—Vollmer v. Big Stone County Bank, 340.

5. It was error to instruct the jury that if such claims were fictitious "*in whole or in part*," to the knowledge of defendant, plaintiffs could recover the full amount of their claim.

—Vollmer v. Big Stone County Bank, 340.

SAME—PARTIES TO ACTION.

6. Plaintiffs are the real parties in interest.

—Vollmer v. Big Stone County Bank, 341.

7. The owners of the claims, the priority and validity of which are in controversy, should be made parties to this litigation.

—Vollmer v. Big Stone County Bank, 341.

DEFENSE TO ACTION AGAINST MAKER.

8. Where defendant executed a promissory note for a valid pre-existing debt, and, for at least five years after full knowledge of the transaction, recognized the note as valid and repeatedly promised to pay it, he cannot thereafter interpose as a defense thereto that he was intoxicated when he signed it, and testimony to prove such intoxication may properly be stricken from the record.

—Matz v. Martinson, 262.

DEFENSE AVAILABLE BY INDORSEE FOR COLLATERAL SECURITY.

9. Rosemond v. Graham, 54 Minn. 323, 56 N. W. 38, to the effect that an indorsee of negotiable paper, taken before maturity as collateral security for an antecedent debt, in good faith and without notice of defenses, holds the same free from such defenses, followed and applied.

—German American State Bank of Ritzville v. Lyons, 390.

BOND.

CONTRACTOR'S BOND.

See LIMITATION OF ACTION; MECHANIC'S LIEN, 7; PRINCIPAL AND SURETY, 1-4.

BROKER. See JOINT ADVENTURE, 3.

BY-LAW. See INSURANCE, 10, 11.

CARRIER.

DISCRIMINATION IN RATES.

1. Contracts made prior to statutory rate regulation *held* no justification for downward departure from freight tariffs thereafter established, whereby plaintiffs, shippers who were charged with the legal rates for the same services, were discriminated against.

—Seaman v. Minneapolis & Rainy River Railway Co. 180.

2. Decision in Sullivan v. Minneapolis & R. R. Ry. Co. 121 Minn. 488, 142 N. W. 3, adhered to.

—Seaman v. Minneapolis & Rainy River Railway Co. 180.

ACTION TO RECOVER OVERCHARGE.

3. The favored shipper's alleged payment to defendant of the difference between the discriminatory rate and the regular tariff, after the discriminations complained of had occurred, *held* no defense against the disfavored shipper's right to recover.

—Seaman v. Minneapolis & Rainy River Railway Co. 181.

SAME—COMPETITION IN BUSINESS.

4. Business competition is essential to a recovery of rate differentials by a shipper who is discriminated against, where no proof is made of damage other than the difference in the rates charged.

—Seaman v. Minneapolis & Rainy River Railway Co. 181.

5. Where both shippers were dealing in the same products in the same general market, shipping from practically the same place, they must be said to have been competitors within any reasonable meaning of the term.

—Seaman v. Minneapolis & Rainy River Railway Co. 186.

SAME—EVIDENCE.

6. Evidence *held* to show business competition, between plaintiff Seaman and a favored shipper, within the rule requiring such competition, where rate differentials are sought to be recovered, but the contrary was established in Sullivan v. Minneapolis & R. R. Ry. Co. 121 Minn. 488, 142 N. W. 3.

—Seaman v. Minneapolis & Rainy River Railway Co. 181.

CASES (MINNESOTA) DISTINGUISHED.

Amann v. Minneapolis & St. L. R. Co. 126 Minn. 279, 146 N. W. 101.
   —Sikorski v. Great Northern Railway Co. 112.
Arnold v. Dauchy, 115 Minn. 28, 131 N. W. 625.
   —Dobreff v. St. Paul Gaslight Co. 289.
Barron v. Liedloff, 95 Minn. 474, 104 N. W. 289.
   —Daley v. Towne, 234.
Bartels v. Chicago & N. W. Ry. Co. 118 Minn. 250, 136 N. W. 760.
   —Dobreff v. St. Paul Gaslight Co. 290.
Berneche v. Hilliard, 101 Minn. 366, 112 N. W. 392.
   —Mahr v. Forrestal, 478, 479.
Carlson v. Duluth Street Ry. Co. 111 Minn. 244, 126 N. W. 835.
   —Larson v. Duluth Street Railway Co. 330.
Corrigan v. Elsinger, 81 Minn. 42, 83 N. W. 492.
   —Jewison v. Dieudonne, 171.
Crookston Waterworks, P. & L. Co. v. Sprague, 91 Minn. 461, 98 N. W. 347.
   —Johnson v. Wild Rice Boom Co. 495, 496.
Dimetre v. Red Wing Sewer Pipe Co. 127 Minn. 132, 148 N. W. 1078.
   —Dobreff v. St. Paul Gaslight Co. 290.
Doerr v. Daily News Pub. Co. 97 Minn. 248, 106 N. W. 1044.
   —Mahr v. Forrestal, 478, 479.
Erickson v. Paulson, 111 Minn. 337, 126 N. W. 1097.
   —Johnson v. Slapp, 36.
Farley v. Byers, 106 Minn. 260, 118 N. W. 1023.
   —Daley v. Towne, 234.
Forest Lake State Bank v. Ekstrand, 112 Minn. 412, 128 N. W. 455.
   —Orr v. Sutton, 49.
Good v. Von Hemert, 114 Minn. 393, 131 N. W. 466.
   —Daley v. Towne, 234.
Heydman v. Red Wing Brick Co. 112 Minn. 158, 127 N. W. 561.
   —Dobreff v. St. Paul Gaslight Co. 289.
Hill v. Winston, 73 Minn. 80, 75 N. W. 1030.
   —Dobreff v. St. Paul Gaslight Co. 289, 290.
In re Doll, 47 Minn. 518, 50 N. W. 607.
   —State ex rel. v. Wolfer, 105.
Isham v. Broderick, 89 Minn. 397, 95 N. W. 224.
   —Daley v. Towne, 234.
Jemming v. Great Northern Ry. Co. 96 Minn. 302, 104 N. W. 1079.
   —Mahr v. Forrestal, 478, 479.
Kaaterud v. Gilbertson, 96 Minn. 66, 104 N. W. 763.
   —McKnight v. Minneapolis Street Railway Co. 210.

CASES (MINNESOTA) DISTINGUISHED—Continued.
Rossman v. Tilleny, 80 Minn. 160, 83 N. W. 42.
  —McKnight v. Minneapolis Street Railway Co. 209, 210.
Spencer v. Levering, 8 Minn. 410 (461).
  —Sucker v. Cranmer, 126.
Staples v. East St. Paul State Bank, 122 Minn. 419, 142 N. W. 721.
  —Orr v. Sutton, 49.
State v. Nolan, 108 Minn. 170, 122 N. W. 255.
  —Wright v. May, 152.
State Bank of Boyd v. Hayden, 121 Minn. 45, 140 N. W. 132.
  —Orr v. Sutton, 49.
State ex rel. v. Village of Gilbert, 107 Minn. 364, 120 N. W. 528.
  —State ex rel. v. Village of Gilbert, 458.
Stitt v. Rat Portage Lumber Co. 101 Minn. 93, 111 N. W. 948.
  —McKnight v. Minneapolis Street Railway Co. 210.
Swanson v. Great Northern Ry. Co. 68 Minn. 184, 70 N. W. 978.
  —Dimetre v. Red Wing Sewer Pipe Co. 135.
Swanson v. Great Northern Ry. Co. 73 Minn. 103, 75 N. W. 1033.
  —McKnight v. Minneapolis Street Railway Co. 209, 210.
Vanderburgh v. City of Minneapolis, 98 Minn. 329, 108 N. W. 408.
  —Anderson v. Landers-Morrison-Christianson Co. 443.
Village of Wayzata v. Great Northern Ry. Co. 67 Minn. 385, 69 N. W. 1073.
  —McKnight v. Minneapolis Street Railway Co. 209, 210.
Wentworth v. Tubbs, 53 Minn. 388, 55 N. W. 543.
  —Thompson-McDonald Lumber Co. v. Morawetz, 279, 280.
West v. Hennessey, 58 Minn. 133, 59 N. W. 984.
  —McKnight v. Minneapolis Street Railway Co. 209, 210.
Williams v. Dickson, 122 Minn. 49, 141 N. W. 849.
  —Daley v. Towne, 234.

CASES (MINNESOTA) FOLLOWED.
Ames v. Brandvold, 119 Minn. 521, 138 N. W. 786.
  —Daley v. Towne, 233.
Ames v. Richardson, 29 Minn. 330, 13 N. W. 137.
  —Imperial Elevator Co. v. Bennett, 261.
Bechtel v. Bechtel, 101 Minn. 511, 112 N. W. 882.
  —Fitzpatrick v. Fitzpatrick, 98.
Davis v. Woodward, 19 Minn. 137 (174).
  —Mastin v. May, 93, 95.
Diamond Iron Mining Co. v. Buckeye Iron Mining Co. 70 Minn. 500, 73
  N. W. 507.
  —Howell v. Cuyuna Northern Railway Co. 484.

CASES (MINNESOTA) FOLLOWED—Continued.

Mitchell v. Green, 125 Minn. 24, 145 N. W. 404.
—Cluss v. Hackett, 398.

Orr v. Sutton, 119 Minn. 193, 137 N. W. 973.
—Orr v. Sutton, 41.

Peterson v. City of Rushford, 41 Minn. 289, 42 N. W. 1063.
—Dobreff v. St. Paul Gaslight Co. 289.

Reiter v. Winona & St. P. R. Co. 72 Minn. 225, 75 N. W. 219.
—Dobreff v. St. Paul Gaslight Co. 289.

Rosemond v. Graham, 54 Minn. 523, 56 N. W. 38.
—German American State Bank of Ritzville v. Lyons, 390, 392.

Rother v. Monahan, 60 Minn. 186, 62 N. W. 263.
—Orr v. Sutton, 44.

State v. Fitzgerald, 117 Minn. 192, 134 N. W. 728.
—Orr v. Sutton, 41.

State v. Kerr, 51 Minn. 417, 53 N. W. 719.
—Orr v. Sutton, 41.

State v. Village of Alice, 112 Minn. 330, 127 N. W. 1118.
—State ex rel. v. Village of Gilbert, 459.

Sullivan v. Minneapolis & R. R. Ry. Co. 121 Minn. 488, 142 N. W. 3.
—Seaman v. Minneapolis & Rainy River Railway Co. 180.

Swanson v. Great Northern Ry. Co. 68 Minn. 184, 70 N. W. 978.
—Dobreff v. St. Paul Gaslight Co. 289.

Terryll v. City of Faribault, 84 Minn. 341, 87 N. W. 917.
—Orr v. Sutton, 41.

Thompson v. Myrick, 24 Minn. 4.
—McKnight v. Minneapolis Street Railway Co. 208, 210.

Wherry v. Duluth M. & N. Ry. Co. 64 Minn. 415, 67 N. W. 223.
—Sikorski v. Great Northern Railway Co. 112.

Williams v. Williams, 101 Minn. 400, 112 N. W. 523.
—Fitzpatrick v. Fitzpatrick, 98.

CASE (MINNESOTA) LIMITED.

Potulni v. Saunders, 37 Minn. 517, 35 N. W. 379.
—Helppie v. Northwestern Drainage Co. 361.

CERTIORARI. See MUNICIPAL CORPORATION, 8.

JURISDICTION NOT GIVEN BY STIPULATION OF PARTIES.

Where the time had expired within which findings of the district court can
be reviewed (no judgment having been entered), a stipulation of the

COMMERCE—Continued.

siderable extent not precisely ascertainable, interstate commerce, to which the Federal rule of damages applied.

—Seaman v. Minneapolis & Rainy River Railway Co. 181.

COMMUTATION OF SENTENCE. See PARDON, 1, 2.

COMPETITION. See CARRIER, 4–6.

CONSIDERATION. See BILLS AND NOTES, 1.

CONSTITUTION. See ELECTION, 4; NAVIGABLE WATER, 5.

VESTED RIGHT.

See STREET RAILWAY, 3.

CONSTITUTIONALITY OF STATUTE.

1. Courts often, and without serious misgivings, convict legislators of inaccuracy in the use of words, in order to absolve them from the more serious charge of attempting to pass a law in conflict with the Constitution.

—State ex rel. v. Village of Gilbert, 454.

LICENSING AUCTIONEER.

2. The statutes of this state (G. S. 1913, §§ 6083 to 6088), providing that the county board or auditor may license any voter in its county as an auctioneer, and providing a penalty for selling property at auction without such license, violate neither section 2, art. 4, of the Constitution of the United States, section 1 of the Fourteenth amendment to the Constitution of the United States, or section 2, art. 1, of the state Constitution. Nor are they invalid as delegating legislative power to the county board or county auditor.

—Wright v. May, 150.

ORDINANCE REQUIRING CONSTRUCTION OF STREET CAR LINE.

3. An ordinance requiring defendant, a street railway corporation, to construct a new and additional car line, enacted under the authority reserved by the terms of the franchise granted to defendant, *held* not to violate any of the constitutional rights of defendant.

—State ex rel. v. St. Paul City Railway Co. 191.

CONTEMPT.

Proceeding in contempt for alleged violation of a judgment enjoining defendants from maintaining a dam or obstructing the flow of a river. *Held:* The findings of fact are amply sustained by the proof, and show

CONTEMPT—Continued.

that respondent has not been guilty of violation of the injunctional part of the judgment. Upon such findings the contempt proceeding was properly dismissed, and appellants are not prejudiced by the order refusing to set aside the findings and dismissal.

—Simons v. Munch, 267.

CONTRACT. See FRAUDS (STATUTE OF); JOINT ADVENTURE, 1, 2.

AMBIGUOUS CONTRACT.

See EVIDENCE, 6.

DIFFERENCE BETWEEN EXPRESS AND IMPLIED CONTRACT.

1. In an action to recover upon a contract implied in fact for material and labor furnished, it is *held* that the evidence did not justify a direction of verdict in favor of the plaintiff. A "contract implied in fact" requires a meeting of the minds, an agreement, just as much as an "express contract;" the difference between the two being largely in the character of the evidence by which they are established.

—Lombard v. Rahilly, 449.

IMPLIED CONTRACT.

2. The statement is often made that when work is done by one on the property of another, with the knowledge of such other, a presumption of an agreement to pay is implied. This is well enough if it is understood that this presumption is one of fact, evidentiary in nature, not necessarily controlling the determination of the issue being tried, and to be weighed with other circumstances of evidentiary force upon such issue.

—Lombard v. Rahilly, 450.

ACTION ON IMPLIED CONTRACT—PLEADING DEFENSE.

3. In an action to recover upon an implied contract, the making of it being denied, it is not necessary for the defendant to plead facts tending to show that the material and labor were furnished without expectation of pay and that the minds of the parties never met in an agreement.

—Lombard v. Rahilly, 449.

MODIFICATION.

See EASEMENT, 6.

CONSTRUCTION OF BUILDING CONTRACT.

See MECHANIC'S LIEN, 8; PRINCIPAL AND SURETY, 2.

QUESTION FOR JURY.

4. The contract for the construction of a church building provided that cer-

CONTRACT—Continued.

tain of the windows of the building should be set with art or cathedral glass. A subcontractor agreed to furnish all "mill work" for the structure. It is *held* that on the evidence presented to the court below the question whether the contract to furnish the "mill work" included the cathedral glass should have been disposed of by the trial court as a question of fact or mixed law and fact and a finding made thereon.

—Foltmer v. First Methodist Episcopal Church of St. Cloud, 129.

5. The construction of the contract, the same being ambiguous and the parol evidence in explanation thereof not being conclusive of the intention of the parties, was properly submitted to the jury.

—Blocher v. Mayer Brothers Co. 242.

RESCISSION—RESTORATION OF BENEFIT.

6. The party who rescinds a contract on the ground of fraud must, as a general rule, place the other party *in statu quo* by returning what he received; but "the party guilty of the fraud is not entitled to anything more than substantial justice, and a fair opportunity to receive what he parted with." If, through the fault of the wrongdoer, the party defrauded is unable to return all the property received in the condition in which he received it, it is sufficient, if he restore the property so far as he is able, and secure to the wrongdoer the equivalent of what cannot be returned.

—Clark v. Wells, 353.

SAME—RETURN OF GOING BUSINESS.

7. If the wrongdoer refuses to receive the property when tendered back, the defrauded party may properly do what is necessary to conserve its value, and does not thereby waive his rescission. Where he receives a going business, he may, without waiving his rescission, continue it as a going business during the pendency of the suit to recover what he parted with, if he remain ready, at all times, to turn over to the wrongdoer both the business, in substantially the condition in which he received it, and the profits derived therefrom.

—Clark v. Wells, 354.

8. The defrauded party cannot require that the wrongdoer assume the debts he has contracted in conducting the business, but he must return the business as free and unencumbered as it was when he discovered the fraud.

—Clark v. Wells, 359.

DEFENSE OF INTOXICATION.

9. A contract entered into by a person in such a state of intoxication that he

CONTRACT—Continued.

is unable to comprehend its terms is voidable, but not void. If, after having knowledge of and comprehending its terms, he affirms it, it becomes valid and binding. His failure to disaffirm it within a reasonable time after having such knowledge is deemed an election to affirm it.

—Matz v. Martinson, 262.

COPY. See EVIDENCE, 3; EXECUTION, 2.

CORPORATION. See EMINENT DOMAIN, 2; JUDGMENT, 1, 2; NAVIGABLE WATER, 17.

ACTION ON SUBSCRIPTION TO STOCK.

1. The evidence sustains the special finding of the jury that the subscription contract upon which the action is brought was made with a corporation other than plaintiff's assignor.

—Nichols v. Atwood, 425.

ACTION FOR CONVERSION OF STOCK—VALUE OF STOCK.

2. The instructions of the court to guide the jury in finding the value of corporate stock do not contain reversible error, in view of the evidence showing that the stock had no market value, that there had been no actual sales to outsiders, and that, during the short time the corporation had been in existence, its capital stock was speedily being depleted, so that the par value of the stock could not be taken as *prima facie* evidence of its actual value.

—Hawkins v. Mellis, Pirie & Co. 393.

CONSTITUTIONAL LIABILITY OF STOCKHOLDER.

3. Evidence in an action to enforce a stockholder's constitutional liability against one who appeared upon an insolvent local corporation's stockbooks as a general owner of stock *held* to sustain a finding that the failure of the corporation's records to show that the stock was issued to and held by defendant as collateral security for an advance made by a third person was not due to the negligence or fraud of the corporation, but to his own negligence, wherefore he was estopped, as against creditors, to deny his liability as a stockholder.

—Way v. Barney, 346.

KNOWLEDGE OF OFFICER.

4. The general rule that knowledge possessed by an officer of a corporation is by implication of law imputed to the corporation has no application, where it appears that in a particular transaction the officer acted in an adversary capacity, as the agent of a third person, and did not repre-

CORPORATION—Continued.

sent or speak for the corporation, of which agency the other officers of the corporation had full knowledge and information.

—First National Bank of Gilbert v. Bailey, 296.

Tort of Servant.

5. A corporation does not by vote of its board of directors, or by its chief executive or managing officer, direct all of its activities. Usually the greater part thereof is intrusted to the judgment and discretion of servants and agents, not officers. The same holds true in the large business enterprises of individuals and partnerships.

—Helppie v. Northwestern Drainage Co. 361.

Combination in Restraint of Trade.

See Criminal Law, 8.

Dissolution of Corporation—Liability to Landlord.

6. Where a corporation takes a lease of premises and before the lease goes into effect the corporation is dissolved by judicial proceedings, it is bound by the lease and is liable for a breach of it, even if it does not take possession under the lease. In this case the lease and a prior lease constituted but one transaction.

—Elliott v. Barker, 528.

COSTS.

Taxation of Disbursements.

1. Under the statutes of the state, the court has no discretion in the allowance, disallowance or apportionment of disbursements.

—Kretz v. Fireproof Storage Co. 313.

Liability of Intervener.

2. Where an intervener, claiming a lien on property for the negligent loss of which the action is brought, reiterates the allegations of the complaint in the action and becomes practically a coplaintiff, he is liable, under G. S. 1913, § 7766, jointly with plaintiff for costs, upon the setting aside of separate verdicts in their favor, including the expense of a transcript and two copies of the testimony.

—McKinley v. National Citizens Bank of Mankato, 212.

3. The trial court's determination, made on conflicting affidavits, as to the number of folios charged for in taxing disbursements, cannot be disturbed.

—McKinley v. National Citizens Bank of Mankato, 212.

COUNTY AND COUNTY OFFICERS.

CRIMINAL LAW.

EVIDENCE—JUDICIAL NOTICE.

1. The court takes judicial notice that X-ray machines sometimes inflict serious burns.
   —State v. Lester, 282, 286.

EVIDENCE OF MALICE.

2. The malice which is an essential ingredient of malicious injury to property need not be proved directly or as a separate fact. When the act is wrongfully and wilfully done, and the necessary result is to injure the property of another, malice may be inferred.
   —State v. Ward, 514.

OPINION EVIDENCE.

3. It was not error to permit jurors on the former trial to give their opinions or conclusions derived from and based upon the knowledge acquired on the view.
   —State v. Ward, 510.

4. It was not error to receive as evidence the opinions of qualified witnesses as to whether logs found in defendant's possession came from stumps on the land of the complaining witnesses.
   —State v. Ward, 510.

TESTIMONY AT FORMER TRIAL.

5. The evidence of one of the defendants given on a former trial was properly received in evidence as against such defendant. It was given voluntarily, and its admission in evidence on the second trial was not a violation of said defendant's privilege against self-incrimination.
   —State v. Newman, 445.

REQUEST FOR INSTRUCTIONS.

6. The evidence of one of the defendants given on the former trial was not

127 M.—36.

CRIMINAL LAW—Continued.

admissible as against the other defendants on trial. It being a joint trial, the evidence was properly in the case, and the jury should have been instructed that it was not evidence as against the other defendants. There being no request or suggestion to the trial court to give such an instruction, it was not error to fail to do so.

—State v. Newman, 445.

TIME OF TRIAL—DISMISSAL OF INDICTMENT.

7. The court did not err in denying defendant's motion to dismiss an indictment not tried within the time fixed by R. L. 1905, § 4786 (G. S. 1913, § 8510), and in holding that the state showed reasonable cause why it should not be dismissed.

—State v. Le Flobic, 505.

DISMISSAL OF APPEAL.

8. The defendant, a foreign corporation, indicted for a violation of the statute prohibiting an unlawful combination in restraint of trade, sought an opportunity to change its plea of not guilty to guilty and receive sentence. The sentence immediately imposed was a fine, which was at once paid. Six months thereafter, lacking a few days, this appeal was taken. Upon the state's motion to dismiss the appeal it is made to appear that appellant paid the fine voluntarily, with the intention to abide by and comply with the sentence of the court, and hence the appeal should be dismissed.

—State v. People's Ice Co. 252.

HOMICIDE—CULPABLE NEGLIGENCE OF PHYSICIAN.

9. A medical man, or a person assuming to act as such, will be held guilty of "culpable negligence" within the meaning of G. S. 1913, § 8612, subd. 3, defining manslaughter in the second degree as homicide committed without design to effect death, "by any act, procurement or culpable negligence" not constituting a higher crime, where he has exhibited gross incompetency or inattention, or wanton indifference to his patient's safety.

—State v. Lester, 282.

10. An indictment under this statute need not allege knowledge on defendant's part of probability of consequences from the acts or omissions charged; nor is it necessary to charge defendant's duty in the premises, nor set up a specific standard of duty, nor to allege "culpable" or any other degree of negligence *eo nomine*, nor set out defendant's acts in any other than general terms and as ultimate facts.

—State v. Lester, 282.

CRIMINAL LAW—Continued.

KEEPING HOUSE OF ILL-FAME.

11. The evidence justified the conviction of defendant.
—State v. Le Flohic, 505.

KIDNAPPING.

12. Defendants were convicted of the crime of kidnapping, and appealed. It is *held* that the verdict is sustained by the evidence.
—State v. Newman, 445.

MALICIOUS MISCHIEF.

See CRIMINAL LAW, 2.

13. Defendant was convicted under an indictment charging malicious injury to property, and appealed. It is *held:* The indictment was not bad because it failed to charge that defendant acted "maliciously," and the evidence sustains the verdict.
—State v. Ward, 510, 511.

RAPE—TESTIMONY OF PROSECUTRIX.

14. Defendant was convicted of the crime of carnally knowing a female child under the age of 18 years. Such conviction may rest upon the uncorroborated testimony of the prosecutrix, unless such testimony be discredited by facts and circumstances casting doubt upon the truth thereof. Evidence examined and *held* sufficient to sustain such conviction.
—State v. Trocke, 485.

15. Where the prosecutrix and the defendant flatly contradict each other, the jury should be cautioned to weigh carefully all the facts and circumstances tending to show where the truth lies, but a request, so framed as to be liable to mislead them, is properly refused; and giving the substance of so much of the caution embodied therein as is proper is sufficient.
—State v. Trocke, 486.

COMMUTATION OF SENTENCE.

See PARDON, 1, 2.

CROSS-EXAMINATION. See WITNESS, 4, 8.

CUSTOM. See MASTER AND SERVANT, 11, 12; NEGLIGENCE, 2; TRIAL, 7.

DAM. See NAVIGABLE WATER, 12, 13, 15.

DAMAGES. See CARRIER, 7, 9; MUNICIPAL CORPORATION, 21; NAVIGABLE WATER, 11, 12.

DAMAGES—Continued.

MEASURE OF DAMAGES.

See FRAUD.

TREBLE DAMAGES.

See LOG AND LOGGING, 2; MASTER AND SERVANT, 29; TRESPASS.

DAMAGES FOR FRAUD.

See VENDOR AND PURCHASER, 2.

IN ACTION FOR DIVERSION OF SURFACE WATER.

See WATER AND WATERCOURSE, 2.

1. In the nature of things damages in this case cannot be ascertained with mathematical certainty, nor is it necessary that they should be to entitle plaintiff to a recovery. A liberal discretion is vested in the jury to determine, from all the facts shown, what part is caused by defendant's acts. Mere difficulty in getting at the amount of damages is no reason for denying them altogether.
   —Watre v. Great Northern Railway Co. 122.

IN ACTION FOR DEATH BY WRONGFUL ACT.

2. $7,500 damages for the death of a foreman of a switching crew, who was earning from $90 to $100 per month, *held*, under the circumstances of the case, excessive. Verdict reduced to $5,000, or new trial granted.
   —Boos v. Minneapolis, St. Paul & Sault Ste. Marie Railway Co. 381.

IN ACTION FOR PERSONAL INJURY.

DAMAGES NOT EXCESSIVE.

3. Action for personal injury. Verdict for $39,000. Plaintiff suffered the loss of both arms and the virtual loss of a leg. *Held:* The damages awarded are not excessive.
   —McMahon v. Illinois Central Railroad Co. 2, 8.

4. In an action by a railway switchman 29 years old, with an earning capacity of $105 a month, a verdict for $2,050 for injuries consisting of the loss of two teeth, a serious ankle sprain, aggravation of appendical trouble, and alleged injury to the back, sustained as against the contention that it was excessive.
   —O'Brien v. Great Northern Railway Co. 87.

5. Action for death of plaintiff's intestate, an experienced switchman. Verdict for $4,660. *Held:* The verdict was not excessive since the jury might have found that the death was not instantaneous.
   —Capital Trust Co. v. Great Northern Railway Co. 144.

DAMAGES—Continued.

    6. Action for personal injury. Plaintiff was a pressfeeder under 25 years of age, earning $14 a week. Evidence that his lower jaw was fractured, leaving it out of adjustment with the upper, causing indigestion and dyspepsia; disfigurement of the face with impaired sense of smell and eyesight, and a severe nervous disorder. *Held:* A verdict of $8,000 was not excessive.

    —Ott v. Tri-State Telephone & Telegraph Co. 373, 374.

    7. An award of $2,000 for the loss of the little finger at the knuckle joint, and the next finger at the second joint, of the left hand, to a carpenter 35 years of age, who is left-handed, is not excessive.

    —Puls v. Chicago, Burlington & Quincy Railroad Co. 508.

    8. Action for personal injury. A verdict for $1,750, approved by the trial court, *held* not excessive. Plaintiff was 37 years old, was earning more than $100 a month, was under treatment in the hospital 10 days, for five months after the injury he had been unable to work and probably would be unable so to do for several months more.

    —Snyder v. Great Northern Railway Co. 518.

SAME—DAMAGES EXCESSIVE.

See APPEAL AND ERROR, 8; NEW TRIAL, 4.

    9. Action for personal injury. Verdict for $11,300. Plaintiff was in the hospital five months. His left leg will never be as large or strong as the other, and a partial paralysis in the muscles which were torn will probably continue. He walked with difficulty. Whether the future would bring material improvement was left uncertain. *Held:* The verdict was excessive, and was reduced to $8,500.

    —Mahr v. Forrestal, 475.

    10. There was no reversible error in the rulings of the court or in the charge to the jury.

    —Kling v. Thompson-McDonald Lumber Co. 468.

DANGEROUS MACHINERY. See MASTER AND SERVANT, 7, 8.

DEATH.

    When a person lives an appreciable length of time after receiving an injury through a defendant's negligence, even though in a state of unconsciousness, his cause of action survives under section 9 of the Federal Employer's Liability Act. Testimony that plaintiff's intestate after the injury moaned and breathed for ten minutes justified the court in submitting the question of the survival of his cause of action to the jury.

    —Capital Trust Co. v. Great Northern Railway Co. 144.

DEATH BY WRONGFUL ACT. See DAMAGES, 2; MASTER AND SERVANT, 1, 4, 5. 13, 19, 24; MUNICIPAL CORPORATION, 19.

DEATH BY WRONGFUL ACT—Continued.
> In an action by a wife, as administratrix of her husband's estate, to re-
> cover damages for his death, the state of the domestic affairs between
> plaintiff and deceased at or preceding the time of his death, short of
> desertion by her or forfeiture of her right to support, cannot be in-
> quired into for the purpose of defeating a recovery or reducing the
> . damages.
>> —Boos v. Minneapolis, St. Paul & Sault Ste. Marie Railway Co. 381.

DEED.
RESERVATION OF RIGHT OF WAY.
See EASEMENT, 3, 5.

DELIVERY. See INSURANCE, 4; MECHANIC'S LIEN, 4–6.

DEMAND. See EVIDENCE, 8.

DISBURSEMENT. See COSTS, 1.

DISCRETION OF COURT. See APPEAL AND ERROR, 7; COSTS, 1; EVIDENCE, 12;
> HIGHWAY, 1; JOINT ADVENTURE, 4; JUDGMENT, 1, 3; MECHANIC'S LIEN,
> 9; NEW TRIAL, 4; TRIAL, 5.

DISCRIMINATION. See CARRIER, 1–7.

DISMISSAL OF ACTION. See ABATEMENT AND REVIVAL, 4; CONTEMPT; PAUP-
> ER; SPECIFIC PERFORMANCE; TRIAL, 3, 10.

DISORDERLY HOUSE. See CRIMINAL LAW, 11.

DIVORCE. See INJUNCTION.
> 1. In an action for divorce on the ground of cruel and inhuman treatment,
> it is *held* that the evidence supports the findings of the trial court,
> and, further, that the divorce was not granted on the consent of the
> parties.
>> —Fitzpatrick v. Fitzpatrick, 96.

DECREE FOR ALIMONY MODIFIED.

> 2. An award of alimony *held* not out of proportion to what is reasonable
> and fair, in view of the facts presented, but that the judgment should
> be modified to secure the relief intended to be granted, namely, life
> support of the wife.
>> —Fitzpatrick v. Fitzpatrick, 96.

ACTION TO SET ASIDE JUDGMENT.

> 3. Where substituted service instead of personal is made in a divorce ac-

DIVORCE—Continued.

tion through fraud of plaintiff, with intent to keep the institution of the action a secret from defendant, a judgment procured by such fraud will be set aside in a suit brought for that purpose, unless there is some element of estoppel.

—Kriha v. Kartak, 409.

4. A finding of the trial court that there was no fraud in obtaining service of the summons in a divorce action *held* sustained by the evidence.

—Kriha v. Kartak, 406.

5. Conceding without deciding that an agreement of separation between the parties, entered into after the desertion charged in the complaint, would be material evidence on that issue, the failure to disclose on the trial the existence of such agreement, though intentional, is not fraud or perjury for which the judgment can be set aside under the statute.

—Kriha v. Kartak, 406.

DRAIN. See MASTER AND SERVANT, 16.

DYNAMITE. See MECHANIC'S LIEN, 1.

EASEMENT.

RIGHT OF WAY.

1. The owner of the fee of land, over which a right of way, not exclusive, is granted, may himself use the land which is subject to the easement, if by so doing he does not unreasonably interfere with the special use for which the easement was created. The way should be maintained at a level reasonably calculated to serve the owner of the fee and the owner of the easement.

—Kretz v. Fireproof Storage Co. 304.

2. A right of way appurtenant to one lot cannot be used by the owner thereof as a right of way to another separate tract. But the extent of the tract to be served in connection with the dominant tenement is a question of intention of the parties, and the intent will be determined by the relation of the easement to the land to which it is appurtenant and other surrounding transactions, including the practical construction of the contract by the parties.

—Kretz v. Fireproof Storage Co. 304.

3. A right of way was reserved by deed to the owner of part of lot 6. The owner of this lot then erected a building covering this part of lot 6 and also part of lots 4 and 5, adjoining. After this, the right of way

EASEMENT—Continued.

was confirmed by a later contract. *Held*, an intent was manifested
that the right of way shall serve the building as erected at the time
the contract was made; the practical construction of the parties being
in accord with this construction.

—Kretz v. Fireproof Storage Co. 304.

4. A grant of a right of way to and from an opera house does not limit
the use of the way to such time as the property is used as an opera
house, but it is available in connection with any proper use of the property.

—Kretz v. Fireproof Storage Co. 305.

SAME—MODIFICATION OF RIGHT.

5. Where a right of way exists over one tract of land as appurtenant to
another, the owners of the two tracts may modify the location and extent of the way at their pleasure. A recital in a deed reserving a right
of way that the grantor is the owner of the dominant tenement is
proof of the fact of such ownership. A reservation of a right of way
in a deed made in 1881 is *held* to supersede a right of way different in
extent created in a deed made in 1866.

—Kretz v. Fireproof Storage Co. 304.

SAME—ESTOPPEL.

6. An easement may be extinguished or modified by a parol agreement fully
executed, and an oral agreement that the fee owner may erect a permanent building over part of one side of the way and extend the way
a like distance on the other side, when executed, extinguishes the old
easement to the extent of the obstruction, and gives a right to use the
new way as a substitute for the old, at least as long as the obstruction
continues. Though the new way is narrower than agreed, the owner of
the way cannot, after acquiescing in its construction, require that the
building be undermined to enlarge the way according to the terms of
the oral agreement.

—Davidson v. Kretz, 313.

EJECTMENT. See APPEAL AND ERROR, 14; FORCIBLE ENTRY AND UNLAWFUL
DETAINER, 2.

Before the commencement of this action plaintiff sold the land to other
parties under contract which provided for payment of the price, delivery of a deed, and delivery of possession at a time fixed. That time
arrived soon after commencement of this action. Payment has not yet
been made and no deed given. The purchasers are accordingly not yet

EJECTMENT—Continued.

entitled to possession. Ejectment is a possessory action. Plaintiff is entitled to the possession of the land and is entitled to maintain ejectment.

—Berndt v. Berndt, 238.

ELECTION. See INTOXICATING LIQUOR.

NOTICE OF ELECTION.

See SCHOOL AND SCHOOL DISTRICT.

BALLOTS FOR TOWN OFFICERS.

1. In a contest for the office of town clerk, and a contest for the office of town supervisor, tried together, it is *held,* upon an examination of the evidence and a construction of certain ballots, that in each contest the contestant and contestee received an equal number of votes.
—Johnson v. Slapp, 33.

2. At a town election where there was no official ticket, each voter was given two tickets, one of each faction. A ticket on which a voter had crossed off the name of the candidate and written the name "Alfret Johnson" was counted by the court for F. A. Johnson, commonly known as Alfred Johnson, the evidence indicating there was no other Alfred Johnson in town.
—Johnson v. Slapp, 35.

BALLOT UNDER CHARTER OF DULUTH.

3. Failure to vote for the requisite number of commissioners, as required by the Duluth charter, establishing a commission form of government, does not vitiate a ballot to such extent that it cannot be counted in canvassing the votes for mayor.
—Silberstein v. Prince, 411.

OFFICIAL STATE BALLOT.

4. Secretary of state directed to have the official ballot for the seventh proposed constitutional amendment printed with the words "Seven Senator Amendment" as provided by the statute.
—Goodspeed v. Schmahl, 521.

COLONIZATION OF VOTERS.

See MUNICIPAL CORPORATION, 3.

ELECTION OF REMEDY. See SPECIFIC PERFORMANCE.

EMINENT DOMAIN.

EXERCISE OF POWER.

1. The power of eminent domain rests exclusively in the legislature and can be exercised only as authorized by the legislature.
   —Minnesota Canal & Power Co. v. Fall Lake Boom Co. 23.

SAME—BY PUBLIC SERVICE CORPORATION.

2. Under the statutes relating to public service corporations, it is the duty of the court to determine, in each particular case, whether the taking of the designated property is necessary for the purposes of the proposed enterprise, and whether such property may lawfully be taken for such purposes.
   —Minnesota Canal & Power Co. v. Fall Lake Boom Co. 23.

SAME—FOR PUBLIC USE.

3. Private property can be condemned only when it can be made to subserve some public use. If the purpose for which it is sought to take private property cannot be accomplished, such taking will not subserve public purposes, is not necessary within the meaning of the statute, and is unauthorized.
   —Minnesota Canal & Power Co. v. Fall Lake Boom Co. 24.

BURDEN OF PROOF ON PETITIONER.

4. The burden of showing that such purpose can be accomplished is upon the petitioner.
   —Minnesota Canal & Power Co. v. Fall Lake Boom Co. 24.

EVIDENCE.

5. The evidence justifies the conclusion of the trial court that the purpose of the proposed enterprise cannot be accomplished without impairing the navigability of the navigable waters of the Birch Lake drainage basin.
   —Minnesota Canal & Power Co. v. Fall Lake Boom Co. 24.

EQUITY. See MORTGAGE, 5; MUNICIPAL CORPORATION, 11.

We do not believe provisions of the redemption statute can be abrogated, or in particular cases relieved against by the courts in the absence of some agreement or act of waiver of the party whose rights are to be affected.
   —Orr v. Sutton, 48.

ESTOPPEL. See APPEAL AND ERROR, 17; BILLS AND NOTES, 8; CORPORATION, 3; DIVORCE, 3; EASEMENT, 6; NEGLIGENCE, 5.

EVIDENCE. See CARRIER, 10; TRIAL, 1.

CORROBORATION.

See CRIMINAL LAW, 14; EVIDENCE, 16; JOINT ADVENTURE, 4.

ADMISSIBLE EVIDENCE.

See CRIMINAL LAW, 6; JUDGMENT, 7; RAILWAY, 8.

SUFFICIENCY.

See MASTER AND SERVANT, 1.

STRIKING OUT.

See BILLS AND NOTES, 8; TRIAL, 2.

OF CUSTOM.

See MASTER AND SERVANT, 11, 12; NEGLIGENCE, 2.

OF RAINFALL AT DISTANCE.

See WATER AND WATERCOURSE, 3.

OF MALICE.

See CRIMINAL LAW, 2.

JUDICIAL NOTICE.

See CRIMINAL LAW, 1.

PRESUMPTION.

See ABATEMENT AND REVIVAL, 6; CONTRACT, 2; EXECUTION, 1; MASTER AND SERVANT, 2; SCHOOL AND SCHOOL DISTRICT.

BURDEN OF PROOF.

See APPEAL AND ERROR, 11; EMINENT DOMAIN, 4; INSURANCE, 5, 14; MUNICIPAL CORPORATION, 18; NEGLIGENCE, 9.

DOCUMENTARY.

See APPEAL AND ERROR, 20.

RECORDS OF STATE WEIGHMASTER.

1. The records in the office of the state weighmaster made pursuant to rules established by the Railroad and Warehouse Commission are competent evidence of the facts recorded therein as required by such rules.
    —St. Anthony & Dakota Elevator Co. v. Great Northern Railway Co. 299.

2. Such rules require state weighers, at the time of weighing loaded cars,

EVIDENCE—Continued.

> to make and enter in the record notations as to any bad order condition
> of such cars, and such notations so entered become a proper part of
> such record.
>> —St. Anthony & Dakota Elevator Co. v. Great Northern Railway Co.
>> 299.

SAME—COPY OF RECORD INADMISSIBLE.

3. Copies of such records are not admissible in evidence unless duly authenticated, but such authentication may be waived, and was waived in this
case.
> —St. Anthony & Dakota Elevator Co. v. Great Northern Railway Co.
> 300.

WRITTEN REPORT OF ACCIDENT.

4. A jury is justified in taking into consideration the circumstances usually
surrounding reports and statements of accidents made by an employee
to an employer or his claim agent. There may be reasons that appear
good to the servant at the time, why the giving of full details should
be unnecessary. Some, because of an aversion to appear as a witness
if a suit results, may make as noncommittal report as possible, others
may omit an important detail, thinking its legal bearing trivial. Again,
a servant's desire to retain his place may be sufficiently persuasive to
him to induce only a partial disclosure of his knowledge, if he thinks
himself or a foreman or fellow servant at all to blame. And, unless compelled by the authority of the law, many persons would hesitate to make
written statements which charged any fellow being with having been,
even remotely, the cause of the death of another.
> —Capital Trust Co. v. Great Northern Railway Co. 147.

LOOSE LEAF LEDGER.

5. Action for balance of price of merchandise. The evidence tended to prove
that as orders were filled and before delivery they were entered upon
charge sheets, and the amount of the sales was entered from the sheets
upon the ledger by the bookkeepers before delivery. The sheets were
not destroyed after the ledger entries were made. There was no evidence that moneys received were entered elsewhere than in this ledger.
Held: The loose leaf ledger, containing entries for moneys received and
merchandise sold, was properly received in evidence.
> —Wyman, Partridge & Co. v. Henne, 535.

PAROL EVIDENCE TO EXPLAIN AMBIGUOUS CONTRACT.

6. The contract set out in the opinion *held* ambiguous and uncertain in its

EVIDENCE—Continued.

terms as respects the subject matter of the litigation, and that parol evidence was admissible in explanation of the same.

—Blocher v. Mayer Brothers Co. 241.

PAROL EVIDENCE TO EXPLAIN TRADE ABBREVIATION.

7. Upon an issue as to the amount of coal delivered to a carrier for transportation testimony of competent witnesses is admissible to prove that figures in the weight column of the bill of lading are trade abbreviations.

—Lampert Lumber Co. v. Minneapolis & St. Louis Railroad Co. 195.

ADMISSION BY ACQUIESCENCE.

8. Evidence of a demand for money to which no reply is made may be received, when the demand is made under such circumstances that a reply would ordinarily be made.

—Sonnesyn v. Hawbaker, 15.

CONDUCT OF PARTY TO ACTION.

9. While the conduct of a person, subsequent to an alleged transaction, may be used against him to disprove the position he takes in a litigation involving the same transaction, it may not be offered to corroborate or prove the correctness of such position.

—Ikenberry v. New York Life Insurance Co. 215.

ADMISSION BY FORMER OWNER TO DEFEAT TITLE.

10. The general rule that admissions of a former owner of property in disparagement of his title, made after he had parted with the title and possession, cannot be received in evidence against his successor in interest, applies to commercial paper.

—Roach v. Halvorson, 113.

PROOF OF ADMISSION AGAINST INTEREST.

11. When it appeared that a purported sender of a telegram was in a state of coma from a paralytic stroke, so that it was impossible for her to have caused or directed a message to be sent, the telegram is properly excluded, when offered as an admission against interest.

—Ikenberry v. New York Life Insurance Co. 215.

12. In the reception in evidence of acts or conduct in collateral matters tending to prove admissions against interest upon an issue in litigation, the trial court must exercise discretion and consider whether, in view of surrounding circumstances, the matter offered is likely to aid the jury. No abuse of such discretion is found in the ruling excluding the will of

EVIDENCE—Continued.

plaintiff's testate, in which no mention is made of this insurance payable
to her estate.

—Ikenberry v. New York Life Insurance Co. 216.

HEARSAY.

13. Under the rule, admissions made by the payee of a negotiable promissory
note after he has transferred the same to a third person, tending to
show that the note was by him obtained in fraud, are hearsay and inadmissible against the indorsee, in an action against the maker.

—Roach v. Halvorson, 113.

OPINION EVIDENCE.

See APPEAL AND ERROR, 1; CRIMINAL LAW, 3, 4.

14. A witness *held* competent to testify as an expert.

—Puls v. Chicago, Burlington & Quincy Railroad Co. 508.

OPINION EVIDENCE OF VALUE.

15. Where the assets of a corporation were shown to include various items
of property, the court ruled properly that a witness should not give an
opinion as to the aggregate value, until he had shown qualification to
estimate the value of the several items.

—Hawkins v. Mellis, Pirie & Co. 393.

TESTIMONY AT FORMER TRIAL.

See CRIMINAL LAW, 5, 6; WITNESS, 1.

16. Testimony on a former trial is not conclusive against the party giving it,
where his testimony on the later trial is corroborated, even though his
explanation of the discrepancy may not impress this court with favor.

—Pogue v. Great Northern Railway Co. 79.

EXCEPTION. See APPEAL AND ERROR, 9.

EXECUTION.

ALIAS WRIT.

1. An original writ of execution must be returned before an *alias* writ can
issue. Where the evidence shows the original writ returned and the
alias writ issued on the same day, it will be presumed, in the absence
of evidence to the contrary, that these acts were done in such order as
to render both valid.

—Carlson v. Smith, 203, 206.

2. No order of court is necessary for the issuance of an *alias* writ of execution. The fact that the copy of the execution served on the judgment

EXECUTION—Continued.

> debtor does not bear the signature or seal of the clerk of the court, does not invalidate a sale of real estate made under the execution.
> —Carlson v. Smith, 203.

LEVY AND RETURN.

3. No formal levy is necessary to be made on real estate in order to sell the same on execution. Failure of the sheriff to make return after the execution sale does not invalidate the sale.
> —Carlson v. Smith, 204.

EXPULSION OF MEMBER. See INSURANCE, 9, 14; PLEADING, 2.

FEDERAL EMPLOYER'S LIABILITY ACT.

DEFAULT.

See DEATH.

Action for personal injury to brakeman. *Held:* Defendant was not entitled under the act to a deduction because of the contributory negligence of plaintiff.
> —McMahon v. Illinois Central Railroad Co. 8.

FINE. See CRIMINAL LAW, 8.

FIRE. See MASTER AND SERVANT, 1, 2.

FORCIBLE ENTRY AND UNLAWFUL DETAINER.
1. Proceedings under the forcible entry and detainer statute to recover the possession of land alleged to be unlawfully and forcibly detained cannot be maintained against a person who peaceably and under claim of right entered into possession of the property and does not forcibly detain the same. Davis v. Woodward, 19 Minn. 137 (174), followed and applied.
> —Mastin v. May, 93.
2. The unlawful detention, unaccompanied with force, where the original possession was taken peaceably and under claim of right, is not sufficient to authorize proceedings under section 7657, G. S. 1913. Ejectment is the remedy in such cases.
> —Mastin v. May, 93.

FORFEITURE. See WAIVER.

FRAUD. See CONTRACT, 6, 8; CORPORATION, 3; DIVORCE, 3–5; INSURANCE, 1; JOINT ADVENTURE, 3; MECHANIC'S LIEN, 6, 7; SPECIFIC PERFORMANCE; VENDOR AND PURCHASER, 2.

FRAUD—Continued.

MEASURE OF DAMAGES.

The amount of damages recoverable for fraudulent misrepresentation as to
the quality of the property sold is the difference between the purchase
price and the value of the property in its true condition.

—International Realty & Securities Corporation v. Vanderpoel, 89.

FRAUDS (STATUTE OF). See APPEAL AND ERROR, 14.

A contract to buy land for joint benefit of plaintiff and defendant and to divide the profits when plaintiff obtains a purchaser for it is in the nature
of a partnership or joint adventure, and is not the sale to plaintiff of
an interest in land, and is not within the statute of frauds.

—Sonnesyn v. Hawbaker, 15.

FRAUDULENT CONVEYANCE.

ABSENCE OF INTENT TO DEFRAUD CREDITORS.

1. In the absence of an actual intent to defraud creditors, a transfer by a
debtor to a creditor of property to pay or secure a valid debt, though it
may be a preference, is not deemed fraudulent in law, unless some insolvent or bankrupt law makes it so, and then only in aid of an insolvent or bankruptcy proceeding. The assignment in this case was not
fraudulent in law.

—Imperial Elevator Co. v. Bennett, 256.

EVIDENCE OF INTENT TO DEFRAUD.

2. A debtor assigned to a creditor as security for his debt the proceeds of
an insurance policy on property that had been destroyed by fire. It is
held that a finding of the trial court that there was no intent to defraud
creditors is sustained by the evidence.

—Imperial Elevator Co. v. Bennett, 256.

GASOLENE. See MECHANIC'S LIEN, 1.

GLASS. See CONTRACT, 4.

GRAVEL PIT CASES. See MASTER AND SERVANT, 14.

HABEAS CORPUS.

ISSUE OF WRIT BY SUPREME COURT.

1. It is the practice of this court to refuse to issue writs of *habeas corpus*

HABEAS CORPUS—Continued.

in ordinary cases and unless the circumstances are exceptional. In view of the importance of the case and the importance of an early final determination of it, this original proceeding is entertained.

—State ex rel. v. Wolfer, 102.

CUSTODY OF CHILD.

2. Evidence considered, and *held* to show that the best interests of a minor child of the age of about five years, and her general welfare, will be best served and protected by remaining with her grandparents, where she has been since her birth and the subsequent death of her mother, and that the natural right of the father to her custody and control must yield thereto.

—State ex rel. v. Halverson, 387.

HEARSAY. See EVIDENCE, 13.

HIGHWAY.

1. Petition to lay out a highway. Verdict in district court in favor of petitioners. *Held:* The court did not abuse its discretion in denying a new trial.

—Jentz v. Town of Tyrone, 534.

FRIGHTENING HORSES WITH AUTOMOBILE.

2. It is the duty of the person operating an automobile upon a public highway, when meeting a team of horses being driven thereon, to exercise reasonable care to avoid frightening the team, and, if necessary, to slow down or stop his car, as the situation presented may require.

—Nelson v. Halland, 188.

3. The operator of the automobile is not relieved from this duty by the failure of the driver of the team to signal him to stop his car. Whether the failure to so signal will constitute contributory negligence will depend upon the facts presented in the particular case.

—Nelson v. Halland, 188.

HOMESTEAD.

The necessary conclusion from the findings is that the wife was held out by her husband as his agent in ordering a small change in their homestead to recover the cost of which the action was brought.

—Sinclair v. Fitzpatrick, 530.

HOMICIDE. See CRIMINAL LAW, 9, 10.

127 M.—37.

HUSBAND AND WIFE. See APPEAL AND ERROR, 17; DEATH BY WRONGFUL ACT; HOMESTEAD; INSURANCE, 11.

ALLOWANCE OF PERSONAL PROPERTY TO WIDOW.

See WILL.

INDICTMENT AND INFORMATION. See CRIMINAL LAW, 7, 10, 13.

MOTION TO DISMISS.

See CRIMINAL LAW, 7.

An indictment against a physician, under G. S. 1913, § 8612, subd. 3, for manslaughter in the second degree, committed in connection with the operation of an X-ray machine, sustained as against a demurrer on the ground that the facts charged were not stated with sufficient certainty to, and did not, constitute a public offense.
—State v. Lester, 282.

INJUNCTION. See APPEAL AND ERROR, 23; CONTEMPT; MUNICIPAL CORPORATION, 10, 11.

Judgment was entered in a court in Minnesota in favor of the plaintiff, the wife of the defendant, in an equitable action for separate support. The defendant, having become a resident and citizen of Illinois, brought an action for divorce against the plaintiff in a court of that state. It is held that the trial court did not err in denying the plaintiff's application for a temporary injunction restraining defendant from proceeding with his action for divorce in Illinois.
—Merriam v. Merriam, 21.

INSURANCE.

ACTION TO RECOVER ASSESSMENT.

1. In this action to recover an assessment against a member of a farmers mutual insurance company, it is held that the evidence sustains the verdict of the jury to the effect that defendant was induced to make application for the insurance by fraudulent representations on the part of the agent of plaintiff who solicited the application. Held, further, that plaintiff was bound by such representations, and that defendant was not guilty of negligence.
—Minnesota Farmers Mutual Insurance Co. v. Djonne, 274.

FIRE INSURANCE.

See FRAUDULENT CONVEYANCE, 2.

2. A fire insurance policy is a mere personal contract of indemnity against

INSURANCE—Continued.

a loss by the person insured. It does not attach to the property or go with the same as an incident.

—Imperial Elevator Co. v. Bennett, 261.

No SUBROGATION IN FAVOR OF MECHANIC'S LIEN CLAIMANT.

3. Where the owner of real estate insures his interest therein against loss by fire, in the absence of contract obligation, the holder of a mechanic's lien on the property has, after a loss by fire, no claim upon the proceeds of the insurance money.

—Imperial Elevator Co. v. Bennett, 256.

LIFE INSURANCE.

4. The evidence examined and *held* to make the payment of the first premium on a life insurance policy and its delivery to and receipt by the insured questions of fact for the jury.

—Ikenberry v. New York Life Insurance Co. 215.

PROOF OF INSURABLE INTEREST.

5. Where a person procures insurance upon the life of another, it is the general rule that he must prove an insurable interest in such life in order to recover upon such policy; but, where a person insures his own life and appoints another to receive the proceeds of such insurance, the appointee establishes a *prima facie* right to recover by proving the contract of insurance and the happening of the event upon which it is to become payable. If facts exist which preclude such recovery, they are matters of defense.

—Christenson v. Madson, 225.

6. Under the evidence in this case, the court did not err in refusing to find that immoral relations existed between the insured and his beneficiary.

—Christenson v. Madson, 225.

MUTUAL BENEFIT INSURANCE.

See PLEADING, 2.

7. A death benefit certificate issued by a mutual aid association, wherein it was provided that all obligations thereunder should cease if the member "at the time of his death belonged to a secret, non-Catholic aid association or for any reason could not be considered as a rightful and reputable member of his respective society or this association," *held*, when construed, as required, most favorably to assured, not forfeited by his membership in a secret aid association open to Roman Catholics,

INSURANCE—Continued.

> sanctioned by their actual membership, and not shown to have been disapproved by that church, though in no way affiliated therewith.
> —Geronime v. German Roman Catholic Aid Association, 247.

8. The above provision is not invalid as being against public policy.
> —Geronime v. German Roman Catholic Aid Association, 248.

NECESSITY OF TENDER TO AVOID FORFEITURE.

9. After notice to deceased that she was expelled from membership and no further assessments would be received from her, no further tender of assessments was necessary to keep her certificate in force. Her obligation to the defendant was not thereby discharged. The conduct of defendant simply waived payment of assessments at the times stipulated in the contract. Under such circumstances, if the member stands on the contract and seeks to enforce it he must discharge his obligation of payment as a condition to such enforcement, and should the society change its attitude and again recognize the contract, the member must continue to discharge the obligations of the contract if he would continue it in force.
> —Marcus v. National Council of Knights and Ladies of Security, 197.

WHO MAY BE BENEFICIARIES UNDER CERTIFICATE.

10. The classes of persons eligible as beneficiaries under policies issued by a fraternal association are to be determined by the rules adopted for the express purpose of governing such matters, and not by general statements made for the purpose of indicating the general object of such association, and restrictions limiting the classes who may be so designated must be expressed in positive terms and cannot be inferred from general statements.
> —Christenson v. Madson, 225.

11. The by-laws of the association having provided that policies may be made payable to the affianced wife of the insured, a policy so payable is valid, although the object of the association, as stated in its constitution, is to provide insurance for the surviving relatives of its members.
> —Christenson v. Madson, 225.

NOTICE OF PROOF OF DEATH.

12. The conduct of defendant in repudiating the contract of deceased relieved her from making application to join another council on dissolution of the council to which she belonged, and waived the requirement that

INSURANCE—Continued.

> plaintiffs make proofs of death and of their claim on blanks to be furnished by defendant.

> —Marcus v. National Council of Knights and Ladies of Security, 197.

ACTION ON CERTIFICATE—PLEADING.

13. The pleadings in this case raise the question of waiver of nonpayment of assessments, of waiver of a law of the order requiring members of a dissolved council to take certain steps to preserve their membership, and waiver of proofs of death.

> —Marcus v. National Council of Knights and Ladies of Security, 196.

SAME—BURDEN OF PROOF.

14. Defendant notified deceased that she was expelled from membership and her certificate cancelled, and that no further assessments would be received from her. The burden is on the defendant to prove that its repudiation of its contract was rightful. Its assertion of due expulsion in its notice of repudiation of membership furnishes no evidence of expulsion, even though the plaintiff offers the notice of repudiation in evidence.

> —Marcus v. National Council of Knights and Ladies of Security, 197.

INTENT. See EASEMENT, 2, 3; FRAUDULENT CONVEYANCE, 2; MUNICIPAL CORPORATION, 1.

INTERVENTION. See COSTS, 2.

INTOXICATION. See BILLS AND NOTES, 8; CONTRACT, 9.

INTOXICATING LIQUOR.

LOCAL OPTION.

MAJORITY OF VOTES CAST UPON THE QUESTION.

At the city election in the city of Le Sueur, a city of the fourth class, the question as to whether licenses for the sale of intoxicating liquor should be issued by the city was duly submitted to the electors, under and pursuant to chapter 387 of the Laws of 1913, and a majority of the votes cast upon that question, but not a majority of the whole number cast at the election, were in favor of the issuance of such licenses. As the statute governing the matter provides that such question shall be decided by "a majority of the votes cast *upon the question*," the proposition authorizing the issuance of licenses was adopted.

> —Anderson v. City of Le Sueur, 318.

JOINT ADVENTURE. See FRAUDS (STATUTE OF).

1. It is well settled in this state that an agreement between two parties to purchase real property for the purpose of selling again for a joint profit is a contract in the nature of a partnership and is valid though not in writing.

—Sonnesyn v. Hawbaker, 18.

2. Plaintiff procured the sale of a tract of land from a third party to defendant, the contract being taken in the name of defendant. The evidence sustains the finding of the jury that it was agreed between plaintiff and defendant that the land was bought for their joint benefit, and that, on plaintiff's procuring a sale, the parties should divide the net profits.

—Sonnesyn v. Hawbaker, 15.

3. Evidence was received upon the question whether plaintiff committed a fraud upon the vendor by acting as agent and purchasing in his own interest, without the consent of the vendor, and the question was submitted to the jury, and they were instructed that, if such conditions existed, their verdict must be for defendant. The verdict for plaintiff is a finding that there was no such fraud, and defendant cannot obtain relief on that ground.

—Sonnesyn v. Hawbaker, 15.

EVIDENCE—DISCRETION OF TRIAL COURT.

4. The reception of certain evidence as to collateral facts was within the discretion of the trial court, and was properly received as corroborative of plaintiff's testimony.

—Sonnesyn v. Hawbaker, 15.

JUDGMENT. See DIVORCE, 2.

ACTION TO SET ASIDE JUDGMENT.

See DIVORCE, 3, 4.

VACATING JUDGMENT.

See APPEAL AND ERROR, 7.

1. The court may in its discretion open a default judgment obtained against a corporation because of bad faith or intentional neglect of the officer who is charged with the duty of making defense.

—Rodgers v. United States and Dominion Life Insurance Co. 435.

2. An affidavit by an attorney, based upon knowledge acquired from investigation of the affairs of the corporation, held to contain sufficient showing of facts to sustain an order opening a default judgment. The affidavit of all officers and directors as to ignorance of the entry of the judgment is not necessary.

—Rodgers v. United States and Dominion Life Insurance Co. 436.

JUDGMENT—Continued.

SAME—STIPULATION FOR JUDGMENT.

3. An attorney has power to bind his client by a stipulation for judgment, but where an attorney, from ignorance of facts or from bad faith, stipulates for judgment against a client who has a just defense, the court may, in its discretion, open the judgment and permit the defense to be interposed, if no substantial prejudice will result to the opposing party from the incident delay.

—Rodgers v. United States and Dominion Life Insurance Co. 436.

SPLITTING SINGLE CAUSE OF ACTION.

4. A single and entire cause of action cannot be split up into several suits, and the judgment in a suit brought upon such cause of action is a bar to a second suit thereon, although the complaint in the second suit may set forth grounds for relief which were not set forth in the complaint in the first suit.

—McKnight v. Minneapolis Street Railway Co. 207.

DECREE CONSTRUED.

5. In arriving at the meaning of a judgment or decree, it is improper to rely wholly on the literal reading of clauses severed from the sentence in which they are placed. The judgment as a whole should be considered in interpreting any particular clause or sentence therein, and if so considered there be any doubt, or it be open to two constructions, the pleadings and findings or verdict may be resorted to, and that construction given which harmonizes with the record. *Held*, that the trial court properly construed the judgment and decree herein.

—Simons v. Munch, 266.

WHEN SECOND SUIT IS BARRED BY PRIOR JUDGMENT.

6. A judgment, rendered in a suit brought by a passenger to recover for injuries sustained while alighting from a street car, is a bar to a subsequent suit brought by the same passenger against the same defendant to recover for the same injuries, although the particular acts of negligence charged may be different in the two suits, as the cause of action in both suits is the violation of the ultimate duty to afford safe egress from the car.

—McKnight v. Minneapolis Street Railway Co. 207.

7. The test is not whether the two complaints are so drawn that the same evidence would be admissible under both. but whether the same evidence which will sustain the cause of action upon which a recovery is sought

JUDGMENT—Continued.

in the second suit, would also have sustained the cause of action upon which a recovery was sought in the first suit.

—McKnight v. Minneapolis Street Railway Co. 211.

ASSIGNMENT.

8. The statute providing for filing of assignments of judgments with the clerk of court, and for a docket entry thereof, affects the validity of assignments only as to subsequent purchasers and attaching creditors. As between the parties, an assignment of a judgment is valid without compliance with these formalities.

—Carlson v. Smith, 203.

PAYMENT.

See CRIMINAL LAW, 8; MORTGAGE, 1–4; QUIETING TITLE; TRIAL, 13.

JUDGMENT NOTWITHSTANDING VERDICT.

On the evidence in this case the questions were for the jury, and it was error to grant judgment notwithstanding the verdict.

—Moe v. Kekos, 117.

JUDICIAL SALE.

REDEMPTION BY JUDGMENT CREDITOR.

Assuming a valid tender proven it is *held:*

(a) That the defendant Torinus, the holder of the title acquired through the mortgage foreclosure sale, by accepting the redemption money paid by plaintiffs, judgment creditors, with full knowledge of the facts showing that they had no right to redeem, thereby suffered plaintiffs to succeed to his title and cannot now question the validity of their redemption.

(b) That the evidence does not show any rights or equities which required the court to relieve the defendant William Sutton, junior to plaintiffs in the line of redemptioners, who attempted to redeem under a mortgage, recorded without the prepayment of the registry tax. Nor has Sutton alone, or in conjunction with any other defendant, any equities through which to attack plaintiffs' title.

(c) That the defendant Sauntry, the owner, after the expiration of the year of redemption had no interest in the land so as to question plaintiffs' redemption, and his right to have the land applied to the payment of such of his debts as were liens thereon depended entirely upon the lienholders making redemption in strict conformity with the statute.

—Orr v. Sutton, 38.

JURISDICTION. See APPEAL AND ERROR, 5; CERTIORARI.

KIDNAPPING. See CRIMINAL LAW, 12.

LACHES. See SPECIFIC PERFORMANCE.

LAKE. See NAVIGABLE WATER, 2, 6–10.

LANDLORD AND TENANT. See USE AND OCCUPATION, 1, 2.

CONSTRUCTION OF LEASE.

See MINE AND MINERAL, 1-3.

FARM LEASE.

1. Construing a farm lease giving to the vendee of the owner the right of possession upon sale, it is held that the court erred in granting the defendant lessee's motion for judgment on the pleadings.
   —Carlson v. Wenzel, 460.

2. In Minnesota the usual cropping season is the spring season. Farm leases are made with reference to the spring crop. It cannot be held that the planting of rye in the fall saved the defendant's right of possession for the purpose of planting the spring crop of the following season or his right of occupancy of the premises.
   —Carlson v. Wenzel, 461.

ACTION UPON LEASE.

See CORPORATION, 6.

LIABILITY FOR DEFECTIVE PREMISES.

3. When a landlord does not covenant to keep the demised premises in repair, and such defects as exist therein are obvious, and there is no concealment, and the defects do not constitute a nuisance, the lessee takes the risk of their safe occupancy, and the landlord is not liable to him for an injury sustained in their use, or to one occupying under him.
   —Daley v. Towne, 231.

4. Applying this doctrine, it is *held* that the court properly directed a verdict for two of the defendants, occupying the position of landlords.
   —Daley v. Towne, 231.

LEGISLATURE. See CONSTITUTION, 2; EMINENT DOMAIN, 1.

LICENSE. See NEGLIGENCE, 4.

AUCTIONEER'S LICENSE.

See CONSTITUTION, 2.

LIEN. See MECHANIC'S LIEN; MORTGAGE, 5.

LIMITATION OF ACTION. See PRINCIPAL AND SURETY, 4.

We are unable to accede to the idea that the parties to a contractor's bond
given plaintiff intended the absurd result that a right of action on the
bond, plainly given by its terms, should be barred before it arose.
—Fitger Brewing Co. v. American Bonding Company of Baltimore,
334.

LOG AND LOGGING. See CRIMINAL LAW, 4; NAVIGABLE WATER, 11–16.

CORPORATION FOR DRIVING LOGS.

1. Section 6263, G. S. 1913, granting corporations for driving logs certain
rights in navigable rivers, is constitutional, provided the exemption from
liability is limited to merely consequential injuries. In respect to all
other injuries, the liability of the corporation must be limited to due
care.
—Heiberg v. Wild Rice Lumber Co. 13.

2. Section 8090, G. S. 1913, providing a person who, without lawful authority, with certain exceptions specified, cuts down any trees or timber on
the land of another shall be liable for treble damages, is penal in character and is to be strictly construed.
—Helppie v. Northwestern Drainage Co. 362.

LOOSE LEAF LEDGER. See EVIDENCE, 5.

MACHINERY. See MECHANIC'S LIEN, 1, 2.

MALICIOUS MISCHIEF. See CRIMINAL LAW, 2, 13.

MASTER AND SERVANT. See WORKMEN'S COMPENSATION ACT.

LIABILITY FOR INJURY—DEATH OF SERVANT.

1. Plaintiff's intestate was killed by fire in defendant's factory. The portion
burned consisted of a frame building with a shingled roof. It was the
custom of defendant's employees to burn rags and greasy waste in the
heating furnace. Just before the fire the furnace was full and ready
to be fired. A few hours after the fire it was found to be empty. In the
meantime smoke was seen indicating a fire in the furnace. The burning
of the rubbish usually emitted sparks. The fire started on the shingled
roof. The inside of the building was lined with tar paper, and in it
were various forms of combustible material. The evidence is sufficient
to sustain a finding that the rubbish in the furnace was burned by de-

MASTER AND SERVANT—Continued.

ing dull or nicked knives on a hand jointer on which the plaintiff was working and that such negligence caused the plaintiff's injury.

—Puls v. Chicago, Burlington & Quincy Railroad Co. 507.

FAILURE TO GUARD MACHINERY.

8. The evidence justified a finding that the defendant was liable for a failure to guard the knives on such jointer as required by the order of the Industrial Commission of Wisconsin.

—Puls v. Chicago, Burlington & Quincy Railroad Co. 508.

LIABILITY OF RAILROAD COMPANY FOR INJURY OR DEATH OF SERVANT.

See COMMERCE, 1; DAMAGES, 2–5, 7, 8.

9. Plaintiff was run over by a freight train of defendant. He testified that he was ordered by the conductor to go under the train to fix something that was dragging, and that while he was under the car for that purpose the conductor started the train, without notice to him. This story is denied by the conductor. Some of the circumstances corroborate plaintiff. The evidence is sufficient to sustain the jury's finding that plaintiff's injury was caused by the negligence of the conductor.

—McMahon v. Illinois Central Railroad Co. 1.

10. There was no error in charging the jury that, unless plaintiff was injured while under the car fixing a broken brake rod, there is no evidence as to how the accident happened, nor in refusing to charge that, if he was not under the car for that purpose, the verdict must be for the defendant. There was no theory advanced on the trial that the accident happened in any other manner, and the conduct of all parties has conceded that at the time plaintiff was injured he was under the car for the purpose claimed by him.

—McMahon v. Illinois Central Railroad Co. 2.

11. An offer of evidence that on other roads it is customary for a trainman, before going under a train, to personally notify the engineer, was properly rejected, since defendant's witnesses testified that on this division of defendant's road personal notice to the engineer was not required, if the conductor was notified.

—McMahon v. Illinois Central Railroad Co. 2.

12. Defendant could not toll its duty to use reasonable care in keeping safe the place where deceased was required to work by invoking a negligent custom or usage with respect to the handling of its cars and the conduct of operations in the yards.

—Boos v. Minneapolis, St. Paul & Sault Ste. Marie Railway Co. 381.

13. Evidence, in an action to recover damages for the death of one of defendant's yard employees killed while attempting to couple cars standing on

MASTER AND SERVANT—Continued.

a spur track, considered, and *held* such as would support a finding that the foreman of a switching crew working on the lead track from which the spur branched was bound to anticipate deceased's presence on the spur in the performance of his duties, so that it was negligence for him to cut loose other cars and allow them to run down grade, without warnings, lights, or attendants, to and upon the spur, where they collided with the cars between which deceased was working.

—Boos v. Minneapolis, St. Paul & Sault Ste. Marie Railway Co. 381.

FELLOW SERVANT.

See MASTER AND SERVANT, 4, 9.

ASSUMPTION OF RISK.

See MASTER AND SERVANT, 22.

14. The rule of the "gravel pit" cases does not apply where the embankment consists of material of such adhesiveness, or so placed or supported, that it may reasonably be expected to withstand the effect and operation of the law of gravitation.

—Dimetre v. Red Wing Sewer Pipe Co. 132.

15. Whether it would be unreasonable for the servant to rely upon the assurances given him is a question for the jury, unless the court can say that reasonable minds could reach only one conclusion. The present case is within the rule-requiring the question to be submitted to the jury.

—Dimetre v. Red Wing Sewer Pipe Co. 133.

16. Plaintiff was digging a ditch, 5 feet deep, with sloping sides, the ditch being 4 feet wide at the top and 1½ feet wide at the bottom. He piled the dirt from the ditch on the top earth at one side. This top earth was black soil with the admixture of some stones. It did not differ much from the top earth at other points but by reason of heavy travel was somewhat more crusted. The subsoil was sand and gravel. As the work progressed the sand and gravel rolled into the ditch, leaving the top crust unsupported until it stood out like a shelf. Plaintiff saw this. When the excavation was nearly completed, this top crust fell in on plaintiff. It fell because it was so undermined and because of the weight of earth piled by plaintiff on top of it. Plaintiff was a man 40 years old, experienced in this class of work. *Held*, he assumed the risk of the dangers to which he was exposed and which in fact caused his injury.

—Dobreff v. St. Paul Gaslight Co. 286.

17. Where the master selects and furnishes material for scaffolding purposes, to be used for that purpose only, the servants may assume that in selecting the same the master exercised due care, and they are not re-

MASTER AND SERVANT—Continued.

quired, before using it, to determine whether it is suitable for the purpose.

—Hutchins v. Wolfe, 337.

18. The assurance of defendant, after making repairs upon a sewing machine operated by electric power, that it was in safe working condition, was sufficient to justify the jury in finding that plaintiff did not assume the risk in operating the same.

—Hedin v. Northwestern Knitting Co. 369.

19. Whether deceased assumed the risk or was himself negligent *held* for the jury.

—Boos v. Minneapolis, St. Paul & Sault Ste. Marie Railway Co. 381.

20. Evidence, in an action by a servant to recover damages for injuries received by him in a fall from an elevated platform, *held* to make a case for the jury on the issue of defendant's negligence with regard to the place where plaintiff was required to work, and also as to assumption of risk and contributory negligence.

—Benenson v. Swift & Co. 432.

21. The plaintiff did not, as a matter of law, assume the risk.

—Puls v. Chicago, Burlington & Quincy Railroad Co. 508.

CONTRIBUTORY NEGLIGENCE.

See MASTER AND SERVANT, 20.

22. Where the master directs the servant to perform specific work, and assures him that he can do so in safety, if the servant, in reliance upon such assurance, proceeds to perform the work, he is usually not chargeable either with contributory negligence or with a voluntary assumption of the risk, unless the danger be so obvious and imminent and so apparent to the ordinary mind that it would be unreasonable for him to rely upon the assurances given him.

—Dimetre v. Red Wing Sewer Pipe Co. 133.

23. In an action for personal injuries, it is *held*, that the evidence supports the verdict to the effect that defendant negligently furnished plaintiff a defective instrumentality with which to perform her work, namely, a sewing machine operated by electric power, and that plaintiff was not guilty of contributory negligence.

—Hedin v. Northwestern Knitting Co. 369.

PROXIMATE CAUSE OF DEATH.

24. The evidence justified a finding that the defendant was negligent in respect of the brakestep; and the jury could find, as a legitimate inference, without indulging in conjecture, that the defendant's negligence in this respect was the proximate cause of the death of the deceased.

—Crandall v. Chicago Great Western Railroad Co. 498.

MASTER AND SERVANT—Continued.

QUESTION FOR JURY.

25. The evidence in this personal injury action justified submitting to the jury the question of defendant's liability, and justified the verdict.
—Mahr v. Forrestal, 475.

CHARGE TO JURY.

26. In an action for injuries to a servant, the court should have qualified its instruction defining a reasonably safe place by limiting the standard of comparison to "the same or similar circumstances."
—Benenson v. Swift & Co. 435.

27. There was no reversible error in certain instructions.
—Mahr v. Forrestal, 475.

LIABILITY FOR INJURY TO THIRD PERSON—TORT OF SERVANT.

See CORPORATION, 5.

28. The law is now thoroughly settled in this state that the master or principal is responsible for the torts of the servant or agent committed within the scope of the employment, even if contrary to orders.
—Helppie v. Northwestern Drainage Co. 361.

WILFUL TRESPASS BY SERVANT.

29. A wilful trespass upon land, as defined by section 8090, G. S. 1913, committed by a servant within the scope of his employment, warrants treble damages against the master, even though the act was without the master's knowledge or consent.
—Helppie v. Northwestern Drainage Co. 360.

MECHANIC'S LIEN. See INSURANCE, 3.

WHAT MATERIALS GIVE RIGHT TO LIEN.

1. Coal and gasolene for generation of power, dynamite for blasting, lubricant, lighting materials and supplies, and materials for erection of a tool-house, furnished excavating contractors, held lienable under G. S. 1913, § 7020, as being contributions to the improvement of defendant's realty. Supplies for and repairs and parts of the excavating machinery held not lienable, being merely contributions to the personal property of the contractors.
—Johnson v. Starrett, 138.

2. Where the excavation and removal of earth in a building contract are performed by machinery, by the use of power obtained from materials

MECHANIC'S LIEN—Continued.

    furnished by the lien claimants, instead of by common labor, such materials are within the terms of the mechanic's lien statute.

    —Johnson v. Starrett, 143.

3. Materials furnished in good faith for the improvement of realty may be lienable, though not actually used in the work.

    —Johnson v. Starrett, 138.

DELIVERY OF MATERIAL.

4. An actual delivery upon the premises of material sold and furnished a contractor for use in the construction of a building thereon is not necessary, as against the owner, to vest in the materialman a right of lien under our mechanic's lien statutes.

    —Thompson-McDonald Lumber Co. v. Morawetz, 277.

5. Material was ordered by a contractor for a certain building and was delivered to a common carrier, consigned to the contractor at the place where the building was under construction. No part of the material was delivered upon the premises or used in the building. *Held*, such a delivery is a delivery to the contractor, and the materialman was entitled to a lien.

    —Thompson-McDonald Lumber Co. v. Morawetz, 277, 281.

6. In the absence of fraud and collusion between the materialman and the contractor, a good-faith delivery of such material to the contractor for use in the building is all that is necessary to protect the rights of the materialman.

    —Thompson-McDonald Lumber Co. v. Morawetz, 277.

PROTECTION OF OWNER AGAINST FRAUD.

7. The owner may protect himself from fraudulent conduct on the part of the contractor by requiring a bond or other security for the payment of material purchased by him on the credit of the building and premises.

    —Thompson-McDonald Lumber Co. v. Morawetz, 277.

CONSTRUCTION OF BUILDING CONTRACT.

8. The term "mill work," as used in building contracts, has a well defined and well understood meaning. As applied to window sash, it includes ordinary glass properly set into the sash and ready to be placed in position in the building.

    —Foltmer v. First Methodist Episcopal Church of St. Cloud, 131.

ENFORCEMENT OF LIEN—ALLOWANCE TO ATTORNEY.

9. The allowance of an attorney's fee of $25 in an action to foreclose a mechanic's lien was within the discretion of the court.

    —Foltmer v. First Methodist Episcopal Church of St. Cloud, 130, 132.

MINE AND MINERAL. See NAVIGABLE WATER, 8.

CONSTRUCTION OF LEASE.

1. A lease of real property construed, and *held* to confer upon the lessee the right to explore for, remove, and transport to market all iron ore found therein, and such additional rights of possession and control of the premises as are necessary to the proper conduct of the mining operations.
—Howell v. Cuyuna Northern Railway Co. 480.

LESSOR'S RIGHT TO SURFACE.

2. Except insofar as necessary to such mining operations, the lessor, the fee owner of the land, retains the right of possession of the surface of the land, and may maintain an action against any third person entering into the possession thereof without right or authority.
—Howell v. Cuyuna Northern Railway Co. 481.

CONSTRUCTION OF RAILWAY.

3. The lessee, though the lease grants him the right to construct upon the premises all facilities necessary to market the ore taken from the land, including railroads, has no right to authorize the construction of a railroad upon the premises, except for the purpose of aiding in the mining operations and the transportation of ore to market.
—Howell v. Cuyuna Northern Railway Co. 481.

MONEY RECEIVED.
In this action for money had and received, the evidence sustains the findings.
—Ripa v. Hogan, 502.

MOOT QUESTION. See APPEAL AND ERROR, 23.

MORTGAGE.

REGISTRY TAX.

See JUDICIAL SALE.

REDEMPTION BY JUDGMENT CREDITOR.

1. No one in the line of redemptioners, nor an intermeddler, may, by tender of payment of a judgment, impair or destroy a judgment creditor's right to use the judgment to effect redemption.
—Orr v. Sutton, 37.

2. To destroy a judgment creditor's right to use the judgment as a means for obtaining certain land through redemption, it is not indispensable that the judgment debtor, in addition to tender of payment, bring suit to 127 M.—38.

GE—Continued.

compel satisfaction of the judgment and deposit the money tendered in court.

—Orr v. Sutton, 37.

EFFECT OF TENDER.

3. A tender by the judgment debtor of the full amount due on a judgment, under which the judgment creditor has filed an intention to redeem land, before the arrival of the time when the judgment could be used for such purpose, and under circumstances clearly disclosing that both parties appreciated the purpose of such tender, destroys the right of the judgment creditor to thereafter use the judgment as a basis for redeeming such land.

—Orr v. Sutton, 37.

4. But if a redemption is made by a judgment creditor whose right to make it, though good on the face of the record, has, in fact, been destroyed by the tender of the payment of the judgment, the title of the purchaser at the sale nevertheless passes to him if the holder thereof accepts the redemption money with full knowledge of the tender.

—Orr v. Sutton, 38.

COMPENSATION FOR TAXES PAID BY MORTGAGEE'S ASSIGNEE.

5. A mortgage, containing stipulations that the mortgagee might pay taxes and charge the amount to the mortgagors, or at his option buy and hold in his own right tax title on the mortgaged premises, was foreclosed and at the sale plaintiff, the assignee of the mortgagee, bid in the premises for the amount of the debt and expenses of sale; while the year of redemption was running plaintiff redeemed from tax sales and paid taxes to prevent the penalty from being added, but through inadvertence failed to file and furnish the affidavit required by section 8172, G. S. 1913, so that defendants, the mortgagors, within the year, redeeming, as owners, did so without reimbursing plaintiff. In this action to recover of defendants the sums thus paid by plaintiff subsequent to the sale and to enforce a lien therefor against the land it is *held:*

That, even though the court cannot restore the statutory remedy lost through plaintiff's failure to comply with the requirements of the statute, and though it be conceded, without so deciding, that under the terms of the mortgage and the facts of the case no personal claim exists against defendants, still plaintiff's payment of the tax liens was, under the mortgage and statute, authorized and lawful, so that in equity he should be subrogated to the rights of the holders of such liens.

—Sucker v. Cranmer, 124.

OTOR VEHICLE. See AUTOMOBILE.

MUNICIPAL CORPORATION.

ANNEXING TERRITORY.

1. Properly construed, chapter 113, Laws 1909, providing for annexation of territory to villages and cities, applies both to existing and to future municipal corporations of that kind. The clear intent expressed in the first part of the first section to include future as well as existing villages, aided by the presumption that the legislature intended to pass a constitutional act, leads to the conclusion that the word "present," in the latter part of said section, refers to the village limits as "present" or existing at the time of the institution of the annexation proceedings, and not to the time of the passage of the statute.

—State ex rel. v. Village of Gilbert, 452.

2. It is no valid objection to village annexations that territory properly conditioned to be annexed was not included.

—State ex rel. v. Village of Gilbert, 452.

3. The fraudulent and unlawful colonization of the annexed territory by residents of the village prior to the election, and their taking part therein, assuming that it can be raised in this proceeding, did not change the result; for if all such illegal votes are rejected, and that number deducted from the votes cast in favor of annexation, the proposition still received a majority.

—State ex rel. v. Village of Gilbert, 452.

4. Territory annexed to a village, like territory originally incorporated, must be so conditioned as properly to be subjected to village government.

—State ex rel. v. Village of Gilbert, 452.

5. It does not appear from the record herein that the territory annexed was not within the condition mentioned.

—State ex rel. v. Village of Gilbert, 452.

ORDINANCE.

See APPEAL AND ERROR, 23; CONSTITUTION, 3; STREET RAILWAY, 1-3.

REMOVAL OF OFFICER—CHARTER OF ST. PAUL.

6. The St. Paul City charter, by amendment effective June 1, 1914, gives to heads of departments the right to remove subordinates by the methods prescribed in the chapter on civil service. This provision restricts the right of removal inherent in the power to appoint, and there is no right of removal except upon compliance with the requirements of the civil service chapter.

—State ex rel. v. McColl, 155.

7. The amended charter contains a chapter regulating what is known as the classified civil service, provides that appointments to positions in the

MUNICIPAL CORPORATION—Continued.

    classified service shall be based on merit, and provides that the comptroller shall frame rules subject to the approval of the council, which rules shall provide "for discharge * * * only where the person * * * discharged * * * has been presented with the reasons for such discharge * * * specifically stated in writing, and has been allowed a reasonable time to reply thereto in writing." This provision is self-executing, and it became operative when the amended charter went into effect.

    —State ex rel. v. McColl, 156.

  8. This provision does not contemplate that the officer sought to be removed shall be accorded a formal trial, but it does contemplate that removals shall only be for some cause touching the fitness and qualifications of the officer to discharge the duties of the office. The cause is to be determined by the removing officer, and his determination is quasi-judicial, and may be reviewed on *certiorari*. The fact that the removing officer does not assume to proceed under the provisions which the charter required him to follow does not alter the case. The writ lies even if the action was arbitrary and without jurisdiction and void.

    —State ex rel. v. McColl, 156.

  9. The amended charter provides that: "All persons holding positions in the classified service of the city as established by this charter, at the time it takes effect, shall retain their positions until discharged, reduced, promoted or transferred in accordance therewith." Under this provision the right of the relator to hold his office is confirmed, and it cannot be urged against his right to contest an irregular removal that he was over age when appointed.

    —State ex rel. v. McColl, 156.

OBSTRUCTION IN ALLEY.

See NEGLIGENCE, 4.

  10. An owner of property abutting upon a public alley may maintain an action to restrain and enjoin an unlawful attempt permanently to obstruct the alley and prevent the free use thereof by such abutting owner.

    —Anderson v. Landers-Morrison-Christenson Co. 440.

  11. In such case the abutting owner has an interest in the use of the alley different in kind and degree from that of the public at large, which equity will protect as against a wrongdoer. Kaje v. Chicago, St. P. M. & O. Ry. Co. 57 Minn. 422, 59 N. W. 493, followed and applied.

    —Anderson v. Landers-Morrison-Christenson Co. 440.

STATUTE REQUIRING VEHICLES APPROACHING STREET CAR TO SLOW DOWN.

  12. G. S. 1913, § 2632, requiring operators of motor vehicles to slow down in

MUNICIPAL CORPORATION—Continued.

approaching or passing a street car which has been stopped to allow passengers to alight or embark, and to stop, if necessary, for the safety of the public, was intended to create a zone of safety around and about the entrance of such car, by placing the burden of the lookout upon the driver of the motor vehicle; and hence one alighting from a standing street car is not obliged to keep a lookout for automobiles, under penalty of being charged with contributory negligence if he fails to do so.

—Johnson v. Young, 462.

PEDESTRIANS HAVE RIGHT OF WAY.

13. While a street car is receiving and discharging passengers, pedestrians to and from the car have the right of way, and it is the duty of an auto driver to stop, if necessary for their safety, and, if he does not stop, to exercise such care in the management of his machine as, under the circumstances, shall appear to be reasonably necessary to guard against injury to any one.

—Kling v. Thompson-McDonald Lumber Co. 468.

14. The conductor of a street car is within the class of persons for whose benefit the statute requires motor vehicles to slow down, and, "if necessary for the safety of the public," to stop not less than 10 feet from a street car which is receiving and discharging passengers.

—Kling v. Thompson-McDonald Lumber Co. 468.

15. Where an auto truck approached a standing street car, with gates wide open, which no one was either entering or leaving, when no person was upon the street, it cannot be held that, under G. S. 1913, § 2632, it was negligence *per se* for the truck driver to attempt to pass the car.

—Kling v. Thompson-McDonald Lumber Co. 473, 474.

16. Instruction *held* erroneous, as depriving plaintiff of the benefit of this statute, and also as introducing an irrelevant issue as to the duty to look out for vehicles in general.

—Johnson v. Young, 462.

17. It is admitted that plaintiff, a street car conductor, was injured by defendant's auto truck. He claimed that the truck ran into him while he was standing in the street adjusting the trolley upon his car. Defendant claimed, and the great preponderance of the evidence indicated, that, while attempting to adjust the trolley, he fell from the platform of the car in front of the truck. The evidence is sufficient to sustain the verdict, if the accident happened in either manner, and the failure to sustain plaintiff's claim in this respect does not require a reversal.

—Kling v. Thompson-McDonald Lumber Co. 468.

MUNICIPAL CORPORATION—Continued.

COLLISION BETWEEN MOTOR VEHICLES.

18. In this action to recover damages to plaintiff's automobile sustained in a collision with the automobile of defendant it is *held:* G. S. 1913, § 2634, providing that all motor vehicles must be kept to the right of the center of the street, has no application under the facts in this case, and the burden of proof to show that defendant was negligent was upon plaintiff.
    —Chase v. Tingdale Brothers, 401.

COLLISION BETWEEN WAGONS.

19. Plaintiff sued for damages for the death of her intestate caused by a collision between a two-horse wagon belonging to defendant packing company and driven by defendant Mosberg, and a one-horse wagon driven by the deceased. The evidence as to negligence and contributory negligence was conflicting, and made a question for the jury and is sufficient to sustain their verdict.
    —Grondlund v. Cudahy Packing Co. 515.

STREET.

20. The defendants Madsen Brothers were operating a concrete mixer, for which a gasolene engine furnished the motive power, immediately adjacent to a public alley in the defendant city of Waseca, but not in the alley. The defendant Schmidt drove his team into the alley upon business and close to the engine. The horses became frightened and ran away and injured a horse of the plaintiff. It is *held* that the defendant city was not liable.
    —Seewald v. Schmidt, 375.

LAW OF THE ROAD.

21. There was no prejudicial error in an instruction on the subject of damages or in a ruling on the admission of evidence relating to damages.
    —Chase v. Tingdale Brothers, 401.

NAVIGABLE WATER. See EMINENT DOMAIN, 5.

WHAT CONSTITUTES NAVIGABLE WATER.

1. Natural bodies of water are classed as navigable or non-navigable. The term navigable, as used in this connection, has been extended beyond its technical signification. It is unnecessary that the water should be capable of commerce of pecuniary value. The division of waters into navigable and non-navigable is but another way of dividing them into

NAVIGABLE WATER—Continued.

public and private waters. If a body of water is adapted for use for public purposes it is a public or navigable water.

—State v. Korrer, 60.

MEANDERED LAKE.

2. A meandered lake, approximately 150 acres in extent, naturally suitable for boating, bathing, hunting, fishing, and other beneficial public uses, on the shore of which is situated a village of 2,000 inhabitants, is a public or navigable body of water.

—State v. Korrer, 60.

3. The question is not wholly one of interference with present public use. The fact that in the opinion of the court the portions of the lake in controversy are, during low-water mark, not capable of any substantial beneficial use does not prevent the state from objecting to its diversion to a private use foreign to the public uses of the water and the soil under it.

—State v. Korrer, 61.

OWNERSHIP OF SOIL UNDER NAVIGABLE WATER.

4. Under the English common law the crown owned the soil under the tide water and also the soil under the water of navigable rivers up to the point reached by the flow of the tide. The soil under fresh water rivers above tide water and the soil under fresh water lakes belonged to the owners of the shore land.

—State v. Korrer, 60.

5. The soil under navigable waters was not granted by the Constitution to the United States, but was reserved to the states respectively, and the new states had the same rights.

—State v. Korrer, 70.

6. In the United States each state determines for itself the question of the ownership of the soil underlying its public waters. The United States government never owned the soil under public waters, and its patent to the shore land does not pass title to the land under the water. This belonged to the states, and if the riparian owner has acquired it at all it is by the favor or concession of the state. In Minnesota the title of the proprietor of abutting lands extends to low-water mark. The title to the soil under the waters below low-water mark is held by the state, not in the sense of ordinary absolute proprietorship, but in its sovereign governmental capacity, for common public use, and in trust for the people of the state, for the public purposes for

NAVIGABLE WATER—Continued.

which they are adapted. This rule applies to all public waters, lakes as well as streams.

—State v. Korrer, 61.

7. When a lake is so small in size as to constitute merely a pond and to be entirely upon the land of one individual, no question of public ownership is raised. The shore owner of land on such lake takes title to the middle of the lake.

—State v. Korrer, 71.

OWNERSHIP OF SOIL BETWEEN HIGH AND LOW WATER.

8. The fee to the soil between high and low water is in the abutting owner subject to the right of the public to use or reclaim it for public purposes. The shore owner has the right during periods of recession of water to take ore from this space, provided the state does not require it for public purposes and provided he shall not measurably interfere with the utilization of it for such prospective uses.

—State v. Korrer, 61.

RIPARIAN RIGHTS.

9. The shore owner has well-defined riparian rights in the adjacent water and the soil under it below low-water mark. These rights include the right of access, the right to accretions and relictions, the right to wharf out and the right, absolute as respects every one but the state, to improve, reclaim and occupy the surface of the submerged land out to the point of navigability for any private purpose.

—State v. Korrer, 61.

10. These rights are not unrestricted, but are subject to the control of the state. The state has power to conserve the integrity of its public lakes and rivers. The riparian owner has no right against the protest of the state to destroy the bed of a public lake for the private purpose of taking ore therefrom.

—State v. Korrer, 61.

RIGHT OF CORPORATION FOR DRIVING LOGS.

See APPEAL AND ERROR, 19; LOG AND LOGGING, 1, 4.

11. The rights of mill and other riparian owners upon navigable rivers are subordinate to the right of the state to improve the river for navigation, and to the rights conferred upon logging corporations organized under section 6263, G. S. 1913, with the limitation that the rights so conferred must be exercised in a reasonable manner and so as not unnecessarily to injure or damage riparian rights.

—Heiberg v. Wild Rice Boom Co. 8.

NEGLIGENCE.

See CARRIER, 11; CORPORATION, 3; INSURANCE, 1; JUDGMENT, 6; MASTER AND
    SERVANT, 1, 4, 6, 7, 9, 12, 13, 19, 20, 23, 24; MUNICIPAL CORPORATION,
    15, 19; NAVIGABLE WATER, 16; RAILWAY, 4, 7; WATER AND WATER-
    COURSE, 1.

WHAT CONSTITUTES CAUSE OF ACTION.

1. In suits based upon negligence, the cause of action is the violation of
   the ultimate duty to exercise due care that another may not suffer
   injury.
       —McKnight v. Minneapolis Street Railway Co. 207.

WHAT CONSTITUTES DUE CARE.

2. Proof of custom is some evidence as to whether an act is negligent. What
   is usually done may be evidence as to what ought to be done. General custom is not, as a matter of law, in itself due care, but it is
   proper to show that the act claimed to be negligent was not done in
   the usual mode of doing such things, for the amount or degree of care
   required by men in general in similar circumstances is the test of
   ordinary care.
       —McMahon v. Illinois Central Railroad Co. 6.

CULPABLE NEGLIGENCE.

See CRIMINAL LAW, 9, 10.

3. Culpable negligence, that is, criminal negligence, is largely a matter of
   degree, and, as has well been said, incapable of precise definition.
   Whether it exists to such a degree as to involve criminal liability
   is a question that must be left, to a great extent, to the common sense
   of the jury.
       —State v. Lester, 284.

WILFUL NEGLIGENCE.

See RAILWAY, 6.

INJURY TO LICENSEE.

4. Where plaintiff, a farmer, was injured by an automobile while he was
   passing through the rear portion of a village automobile repair and
   farm implement shop in order to transact business in the front, the
   fact that he reached the place where he was injured by passing through
   a rubbish-strewn alley and the rear entrance of the building did not,
   upon the facts of the case, constitute him a bare licensee, so as to
   preclude him from invoking the rights of one upon premises by invitation.
       —Jewison v. Dieudonne, 163.

NEGLIGENCE—Continued.

5. Where there is a holding out of a partnership relation concerning the control of a place where business is transacted and an invitation extended, under such circumstances of publicity as to warrant the inference that a person subsequently injured therein through the negligence of an employee of those in charge must have had the right to believe that those extending the invitation were in control of the premises, a recovery may be had without regard to the actual existence of the partnership relation; liability in such case, however, depending, not wholly upon the doctrine of estoppel, nor that of *respondeat superior*, but upon the assumption of a definite status with reference to the property and a specific relation to the person injured, to which the law attaches direct and positive duties.

—Jewison v. Dieudonne, 163.

PROXIMATE CAUSE.

See MASTER AND SERVANT, 24; NEGLIGENCE, 11.

CONTRIBUTORY NEGLIGENCE.

See FEDERAL EMPLOYER'S LIABILITY ACT; HIGHWAY, 3; MASTER AND SERVANT, 6, 19, 20, 22, 23; MUNICIPAL CORPORATION, 12, 19; NEGLIGENCE, 13; RAILWAY, 5, 6; STREET RAILWAY, 4.

EVIDENCE.

6. The evidence did not justify a finding of the jury that defendant Schmidt was negligent in driving his horses into an alley near a concrete mixer operated by a noisy gasolene engine, by reason of which they became frightened, ran away and injured plaintiff's horse.

—Seewald v. Schmidt, 375, 376.

7. The evidence was insufficient to sustain a finding that the driver of a team was negligent in permitting them to get beyond his control or in failing to direct their course so as to avoid collision with plaintiff.

—Melberg v. Wild Rice Lumber Co. 524.

8. The evidence justified a finding that the defendants Madsen Brothers were negligent.

—Seewald v. Schmidt, 376.

BURDEN OF PROOF.

9. Under the doctrine of *res ipsa loquitur* the burden of explaining that the accident did not occur from want of care devolved on defendant. The court did not err in finding that plaintiff's *prima facie* case of negligence was not rebutted by defendant's evidence.

—Whitwell v. Wolf, 529.

NEGLIGENCE—Continued.

REFUSAL TO INSTRUCT JURY.

See TRIAL, 8.

CHARGE TO JURY.

10. An instruction that the violation of a penal statute, as to starting trains without signal, constituted a breach of duty owed by defendant to plaintiff, could not prejudice defendant, where the employee on whom the statute imposes the duty of giving the signal is the engineer, and the finding of the jury negatives negligence on the part of the engineer.

—McMahon v. Illinois Central Railroad Co. 1.

QUESTIONS FOR JURY.

11. Whether the negligence of Madsen Brothers was the proximate cause of the injury to plaintiff's horse was for the jury.

—Seewald v. Schmidt, 376.

12. Whether an employee of the repair shop, who was handling the automobile at the time of the accident, was guilty of negligence, *held* for the jury.

—Jewison v. Dieudonne, 163.

SAME—CONTRIBUTORY NEGLIGENCE.

13. The question of negligence on plaintiff's part was also for the jury.

—Jewison v. Dieudonne, 163.

NEW TRIAL. See APPEAL AND ERROR, 3, 5, 8, 15, 20; TRIAL, 5, 6.

SETTLEMENT OF CASE, AFTER NOTICE OF APPEAL.

See APPEAL AND ERROR, 5.

PREJUDICIAL CONDUCT OF COURT.

1. New trial granted because of conduct of the trial court which it is thought prejudiced defendant in view of the large verdict returned for plaintiff.

—Quirk v. Consumers Power Co. 526.

TWO CAUSES OF ACTION—ERROR IN CHARGE ON ONE.

2. The cause of action for diverting more water than agreed from the navigable stream, by which plaintiff operated his flour mill, and the one for detaining waters unreasonably, by flooding dams at the source of the same stream, being tried as one cause, the verdict rendered may

NEW TRIAL—Continued.

include damages for both causes; hence error in an instruction relating to one of the causes of action necessarily requires a new trial.

—Johnson v. Wild Rice Boom Co. 490.

SAME—GENERAL VERDICT INCLUDED BOTH CAUSES.

3. A new trial granted because the verdict was a general verdict, and the amount awarded for damages upon the second cause of action could not be separated.

—Juhl v. Wild Rice Boom Co. 537.

EXCESSIVE DAMAGES.

4. The question whether a motion for a new trial on the ground of excessive damages should be granted, or whether the verdict should be reduced, rests in the practical judgment and sound judicial discretion of the trial court. The order of the trial court disposing of such a motion will not be reversed, unless such discretion has been abused.

—Ott v. Tri-State Telephone & Telegraph Co. 373.

NOTICE. See APPEAL AND ERROR, 3; BANK AND BANKING; CORPORATION, 4; INSURANCE, 9; JUDGMENT, 8; MASTER AND SERVANT, 11; SCHOOL AND SCHOOL DISTRICT; VENDOR AND PURCHASER, 1, 3.

NUISANCE. See LANDLORD AND TENANT, 3.

OFFICER.

KNOWLEDGE.

See CORPORATION, 4.

REMOVAL.

See MUNICIPAL CORPORATION, 6-9.

ORDINANCE.

REQUIRING CONSTRUCTION OF STREET RAILWAY.

See CONSTITUTION, 3; STREET RAILWAY, 1-3.

PARDON.

COMMUTATION OF SENTENCE.

1. It is well settled that a commutation of sentence is a substitution of a less for a greater punishment. After commutation the commuted sen-

PARDON—Continued.

tence is the only one in existence. After commutation, the sentence has the same legal effect, and the status of the prisoner is the same, as though the sentence had originally been for the commuted term.
—State ex rel. v. Wolfer, 103.

2. A prisoner sentenced to the state prison for life, whose sentence is commuted to one for a term of years, is entitled to a diminution of that sentence by reason of good conduct commencing on the day of his arrival in prison, and not from the time of commutation of his sentence.
—State ex rel. v. Wolfer, 102.

PARENT AND CHILD. See HABEAS CORPUS, 2.

PARTIES TO ACTION. See BILLS AND NOTES, 6, 7.

PARTNERSHIP. See FRAUDS (STATUTE OF); JOINT ADVENTURE, 1, 2; NEGLIGENCE, 5.

The fact that two of defendants were sued as copartners did not make a recovery necessarily depend upon the establishment of such relation.
—Jewison v. Dieudonne, 163.

PAUPER.

Action to recover moneys expended for the support of a pauper. Whether the pauper had a settlement in defendant town was a question for the jury, and the court erred in dismissing the action.
—Town of Erdahl v. Town of Sanford, 527.

PAYMENT. See BILLS AND NOTES, 4; CARRIER, 3; INSURANCE, 4, 13; PRINCIPAL AND SURETY, 1; TENDER; VENDOR AND PURCHASER, 2.

PEDDLER. See AUCTIONEER.

PHYSICIAN AND SURGEON. See CRIMINAL LAW, 9.

X-RAYS.

See INDICTMENT AND INFORMATION.

PLEADING. See JUDGMENT, 5.

COMPLAINT.

See APPEAL AND ERROR, 23; JUDGMENT, 4, 7.

ANSWER.

See CONTRACT, 3.

PRINCIPAL AND AGENT. See BILLS AND NOTES, 3; CORPORATION, 3; HOME-STEAD; INSURANCE, 1; JOINT ADVENTURE, 3; WITNESS, 3.

PRINCIPAL AND SURETY.

RELEASE OF SURETY.

1. The surety was not released by an excess payment made by the owner to the contractor.

—Fitger Brewing Co. v. American Bonding Co. of Baltimore, 330.

2. It was not released by the failure of the owner to give the surety immediate notice of the failure of the contractor to complete the building by the time specified in the contract.

—Fitger Brewing Co. v. American Bonding Co. of Baltimore, 331.

CONSTRUCTION OF BOND.

3. It is not only provisions that are ambiguous in themselves that are open to construction. Though a provision of a bond limiting liability be clear when considered by itself, yet, if it is inconsistent with another provision, and particularly with the central idea of suretyship or indemnity, courts will look to the entire instrument and will find ambiguity because of the inconsistent provisions. It is needless to say that such an ambiguity or doubt as to the intention of the parties is to be resolved against the surety.

—Fitger Brewing Co. v. American Bonding Company of Baltimore, 334.

ACTION ON BUILDING CONTRACTOR'S BOND—LIMITATION OF ACTION.

4. In this action to recover against the surety on a contractor's bond the amount of mechanic's liens on the property paid by plaintiff after they had been adjudged valid, it is *held:*

(1) The action is not barred by a limitation in the policy that an action thereon must be brought within six months after the completion of the work under the contract; the breach for which a recovery is sought not arising until after such six months' period elapsed.

(2) It is not barred by a limitation of six months after the first breach of the contract. Following Fitger v. American Bonding Co. of Baltimore, 115 Minn. 78, 131 N. W. 1067.

—Fitger Brewing Co. v. American Bonding Co. of Baltimore, 330.

PROCESS. See SUMMONS.

PUBLIC LAND.

PATENT.

See NAVIGABLE WATER, 6.

PUBLIC POLICY. See INSURANCE, 8.

PUBLIC USE. See EMINENT DOMAIN, 3; NAVIGABLE WATER, 1-3, 6, 8.

QUIETING TITLE.

CONSTRUCTION OF FINDINGS.

The pleading and evidence required a finding on the issue of tender of payment by the judgment debtor of the judgment under which plaintiffs effected redemption. If the findings in this case are to be construed to the effect that by direct authority of the judgment debtor a tender in lawful money of the full amount of plaintiffs' judgment was not made to them personally prior to the time when they could use the same for redemption purposes, they are not justified by the evidence.
—Orr v. Sutton, 37.

RAILROAD AND WAREHOUSE COMMISSION.

RECORDS OF STATE WEIGHMASTER.

See EVIDENCE, 1-3.

RAILWAY. See CARRIER, 11.

CONSTRUCTION OF ROAD ON LEASED LAND.

See MINE AND MINERAL, 3.

RULES OF COMPANY.

See RAILWAY, 8.

CONSTRUCTION OF COMPANY RULES.

1. A train made up ready for travel, in charge of a road crew, overdue to start, and which has attempted to leave the station, but is unable to make a heavy grade without application of additional power, which, however, is right at hand, is a train "on the road" as distinguished from a train "standing in a yard."
—McMahon v. Illinois Central Railroad Co. 2.

LIABILITY FOR INJURY OR DEATH OF SERVANT.

See COMMERCE, 1; EVIDENCE, 4; MASTER AND SERVANT, 9-13; NEGLIGENCE, 10.

ACCIDENT AT HIGHWAY CROSSING—DUTY OF TRAVELER.

2. A railroad track is in itself a danger signal. The duty of a traveler approaching a railroad track to look and listen for trains is the rule. 127 M.—39.

RAILWAY—Continued.

It is only under exceptional circumstances that he is relieved of this duty. Failure of the railroad company to give expected signals may excuse him in relaxing somewhat in his vigilance, but it does not dispense with vigilance altogether. An instruction which gives the jury to understand that the traveler may wholly omit the duty of looking and listening, simply because he hears none of the customary or required signals of the approach of the train, is erroneous.

—Pogue v. Great Northern Railway Co. 79.

3. Any circumstance which impedes the exercise of the sense of hearing renders more imperative the duty of the traveler to use his sense of sight.

—Pogue v. Great Northern Railway Co. 79.

4. A person approaching a railroad track in a lighted automobile in the dark of evening will not be held negligent as a matter of law in not seeing a train approaching without a headlight, where his view is obscured until he is within less than 30 feet of the track, and there is testimony that he looked as soon as he could, but did not see the train until it was upon him.

—Pogue v. Great Northern Railway Co. 79.

CONTRIBUTORY NEGLIGENCE.

5. In this action to recover for injuries received by plaintiff while attempting to cross between cars of a train standing on a crossing, it is held that it conclusively appears from the evidence that plaintiff was guilty of contributory negligence.

—Sikorski v. Great Northern Railway Co. 110.

QUESTIONS FOR JURY.

6. In an action by the plaintiff to recover damages for the death of his intestate who was run over and killed by a car of the defendant which was blocking a crossing and was put in motion by cars switched against it, as he was crossing behind it, it is held: (1) That the question whether the plaintiff's intestate was guilty of contributory negligence was one of fact and was properly submitted to the jury. (2) That the court was in error in submitting to the jury the question whether the defendant, by the act of its conductor, was guilty of wilful or wanton negligence.

—Gillespie v. Great Northern Railway Co. 234.

EVIDENCE.

7. There is evidence in this case that defendant was negligent in operating

RAILWAY—Continued.

a train without a headlight on the engine, and without giving proper signals of its approach.
—Pogue v. Great Northern Railway Co. 79.

8. The private rules of a railroad company, adopted for the guidance of its trainmen, not known to the deceased, are inadmissible in an action to recover damages caused while he was crossing the tracks behind a string of cars blocking the crossing.
—Gillespie v. Great Northern Railway Co. 234, 235.

RAPE. See CRIMINAL LAW, 14, 15; WITNESS, 4.

RECORD. See APPEAL AND ERROR, 4; EVIDENCE, 1–3.

REDEMPTION. See EQUITY; JUDICIAL SALE; MORTGAGE, 1–5; QUIETING TITLE.

REGISTRATION OF TITLE. See ABATEMENT AND REVIVAL, 1, 4.

1. The defendant in a registration proceeding may have all the relief usually available in an action to determine adverse claims wherein he is plaintiff.
—Seeger v. Young, 422.

2. As between an applicant to register title to land and any defendant who subsequently brings action against him to determine the adverse claim of the former against the latter, the issues are identical.
—Seeger v. Young, 420.

RELICTION. See NAVIGABLE WATER, 9.

RES IPSA LOQUITUR. See NEGLIGENCE, 9.

RESPONDEAT SUPERIOR. See NEGLIGENCE, 5.

RESTRAINT OF TRADE. See CRIMINAL LAW, 8.

RIGHT OF WAY. See EASEMENT, 1; MUNICIPAL CORPORATION, 13.

RIPARIAN RIGHT. See NAVIGABLE WATER, 6–12.

Riparian rights are incident to the ownership, not of the bed of the water, but of the shore land.
—State v. Korrer, 71.

SALE. See BILLS AND NOTES, 4.

SCHOOL AND SCHOOL DISTRICT.

The last day for posting notices of election in proceedings for the consolidation of school districts, under G. S. 1913, §§ 2686–2694, was Monday, February 10, The notices were tacked up on Sunday, February 9, but remained up to Monday, the tenth. The notices were valid. Where such

SCHOOL AND SCHOOL DISTRICT—Continued.

a notice is left posted on Sunday, the court may presume that it remained posted on Monday, there being no evidence to the contrary.

—Thoreson v. Susens, 84.

SPECIFIC PERFORMANCE. See APPEAL AND ERROR, 14.

ELECTION OF REMEDY.

Bringing an action to rescind an executory contract for fraudulent misrepresentations as to the quality of the land, and thereafter voluntarily dismissing such action because the right to rescind had been lost by laches, is not such an election of remedies as will debar plaintiff from subsequently bringing an action to enforce specific performance of such contract.

—International Realty & Securities Corporation v. Vanderpoel, 89.

STATE. See NAVIGABLE WATER, 3–11.

STATUTES CITED BY THE COURT.

CONSTITUTION OF UNITED STATES.

UNITED STATES STATUTES AT LARGE.

GEORGIA.

ILLINOIS.

CONSTITUTION OF MINNESOTA.

GENERAL STATUTES 1878.

STATUTES CITED BY THE COURT—Continued.

STATUTES CITED BY THE COURT—Continued.

STATUTES CITED BY THE COURT—Continued.

SESSION LAWS—GENERAL.

STIPULATION. See CERTIORARI; JUDGMENT, 3; VENUE, 3.

STREET RAILWAY. See CONSTITUTION, 3; JUDGMENT, 6; MUNICIPAL COR-
PORATION, 12–17.

ORDINANCE REQUIRING CONSTRUCTION OF LINE.

1. Whether public interests require the building of a new and additional
line of road is largely a question of fact, and addressed primarily to
the judgment and discretion of the city council, whose determination
thereof will be interfered with by the courts only when arbitrary and
clearly unreasonable.
   —State ex rel. v. St. Paul City Railway Co. 193.

2. The finding of the trial court that the proposed new line was justified
by public necessity and convenience *held* sustained by the evidence.
   —State ex rel. v. St. Paul City Railway Co. 191.

3. Under the reserved authority of the city to order the construction of
new lines of street railway, the city may direct whether the new line
shall be a single or double track line; and defendant possesses under

STREET RAILWAY—Continued.
>
> its franchise no vested right or option to determine the character of the line in this respect.
>
> —State ex rel. v. St. Paul City Railway Co. 191.

ACTION FOR INJURY.

4. In this action to recover damages sustained in a collision with a street car of defendant, it is *held* that the questions of negligence and contributory negligence were for the jury, and that the evidence sustains the verdict.
>
> —Larson v. Duluth Street Railway Co. 328.

SUBROGATION. See INSURANCE, 3; MORTGAGE, 5.

SUMMONS. See VENUE, 1.

SERVICE OF SUMMONS.

See DIVORCE, 3, 4.

TAXATION.

ACTION TO RECOVER TAXES PAID.

See MORTGAGE, 5.

TELEGRAPH AND TELEPHONE. See APPEAL AND ERROR, 23; EVIDENCE, 11.

TENDER. See INSURANCE, 9; JUDICIAL SALE; MORTGAGE, 1–4; QUIETING TITLE; TRIAL, 13; VENDOR AND PURCHASER, 3.
Tender never discharges an obligation. It simply excuses the person owing it from the consequences of failure to make payment at the time the contract requires.
>
> —Marcus v. National Council of Knights and Ladies of Security, 200.

THEATRE. See EASEMENT, 4.

TIDE. See NAVIGABLE WATER, 4.

TIME. See EXECUTION, 1.

TITLE. See EVIDENCE, 10; NAVIGABLE WATER, 4–8; PLEDGE; RIPARIAN RIGHT; TROVER AND CONVERSION, 1.

TOWN. See ELECTION, 1, 2.

TRESPASS.

WILFUL TRESPASS BY SERVANT.

See MASTER AND SERVANT, 29.

In an action for treble damages for cutting timber, where the complaint charges wilful and wanton trespass and the answer contains a general denial, with what may be construed as an admission of some cutting without lawful authority from plaintiff, it was error to exclude evidence tending to show the cutting by defendant's servant to have been casual or involuntary and to instruct the jury to return treble damages.

—Helppie v. Northwestern Drainage Co. 360.

TRIAL.

ELECTION BETWEEN CAUSES OF ACTION.

See APPEAL AND ERROR, 21.

OBJECTION TO QUESTION.

See APPEAL AND ERROR, 1.

JOINT OFFER—EVIDENCE INADMISSIBLE.

1. If any of the matters embraced in a joint offer of evidence are inadmissible, it is not error to reject the whole.

—Boos v. Minneapolis, St. Paul & Sault Ste. Marie Railway Co. 381.

MOTION TO STRIKE OUT EVIDENCE.

2. Section 7998, G. S. 1913, does not deprive the court of the power to strike out immaterial evidence, nor require it to submit to the jury questions having no bearing upon the outcome of the suit. Where the court states the case as it is, explains the rules of law which apply, and permits the jury to return such verdict as they may deem proper under the circumstances, the court has fully performed the duty imposed upon it by this statute.

—Matz v. Martinson, 262.

OPENING STATEMENT OF COUNSEL.

3. When counsel in his opening statement to the jury makes a deliberate concession as to the facts, and chooses to abide by it after his attention is called to its effect, the court may act upon the facts conceded and grant defendant's motion for dismissal if, with such facts conceded, there can be no recovery under the complaint.

—St. Paul Motor Vehicle Co. v. Johnston, 443.

REFERENCE BY COUNSEL TO INDEMNITY INSURANCE.

4. Record *held* to disclose no basis for imputation of bad faith on the part

TRIAL—Continued.

of plaintiff's counsel in referring, during his examination of a juror, to a liability insurance company as the real party in interest; and hence denial of defendant's motion to discharge the panel on account thereof was not error.

—Uggen v. Bazille & Partridge, 364.

ACTION OF COURT ON COUNSEL'S ARGUMENT.

5. Determination of the question whether improper remarks of counsel were prejudicial rests largely in the discretion of the trial court. Counsel made improper remarks in his address to the jury. The court directed him to desist, and he did so, and the court directed the jury not to consider such matters as were the subject of the remarks. The case presented does not warrant this court in granting a new trial on this ground.

—Sonnesyn v. Hawbaker, 15.

CHARGE TO JURY.

See APPEAL AND ERROR, 2, 9, 11, 20; CORPORATION, 2; CRIMINAL LAW, 6; MASTER AND SERVANT, 26.

6. The record presents no erroneous rulings or instructions which entitled plaintiff to a new trial.

—Nichols v. Atwood, 425.

7. Where the court, in an action to recover for personal injuries, instructed the jury that plaintiff could not recover unless a custom existed to give warning of the danger, and there is no evidence tending to prove the existence of such custom, a verdict for plaintiff cannot be sustained.

—Marshall v. Chicago, Rock Island & Pacific Railway Co. 244.

REFUSAL TO INSTRUCT JURY.

See CRIMINAL LAW, 15.

8. Refusal of instruction upon the necessity of differentiating the loss occasioned by defendant's negligence from that due to other causes *held* not reversible error.

—Watre v. Great Northern Railway Co. 119.

9. The law of the road applicable to the case having been stated fully and clearly in the general charge, the court did not err in refusing to give the special instructions in respect thereto requested by appellants.

—Grondlund v. Cudahy Packing Co. 515.

RIGHT TO DIRECT VERDICT.

10. Whether chapter 245, Laws 1913 (G. S. 1913, § 7998), restricting the

TRIAL—Continued.

 right of trial courts to direct verdicts in certain cases, applies to dismissals at the close of plaintiff's case in chief, quære?
 —Hedin v. Northwestern Knitting Co. 369.

11. Whether the court, since the enactment of section 7998, G. S. 1913, no longer possesses the power to direct a verdict in any case, if objection be made thereto, is neither involved nor decided herein.
 —Matz v. Martinson, 266.

12. That section has no reference to the reception or rejection of evidence, and in no way changes or restricts the power of the court to determines questions arising in respect thereto.
 —Matz v. Martinson, 265, 266.

VERDICT.

See APPEAL AND ERROR, 4; NEW TRIAL, 2–4.

FINDINGS OF COURT.

See APPEAL AND ERROR, 14; JUDGMENT, 5; QUIETING TITLE.

13. In an action to quiet title tender of the amount of a judgment under which plaintiffs subsequently redeemed was a defense to the validity of the redemption. The trial court failed to make a definite finding on this issue, as it should have done. This court *held* the evidence did not warrant a finding that a tender had not been proven and assumed that a tender was in fact made.
 —Orr v. Sutton, 42, 43.

14. The evidence is sufficient to sustain a finding that a judgment against plaintiff and his cosurety was assigned to defendant.
 —Carlson v. Smith, 203.

TROVER AND CONVERSION. See BILLS AND NOTES, 3.

 In an action for conversion of a team, if plaintiff proves title, the defendant has not made out a defense by showing merely that the team, taken under a writ of replevin from plaintiff's husband, was afterwards returned because rebonded by him.
 —Klein v. Frerichs, 177.

USE AND OCCUPATION.

WHEN ACTION LIES.

1. An action in the nature of assumpsit for the use and occupation of real property lies only where the relation of landlord and tenant subsists between the parties, founded on an agreement express or implied.
 —Hayes v. Moore, 404.

USE AND OCCUPATION—Continued.

2. Evidence examined, and *held* to show neither an express nor implied agreement creating the relation of landlord and tenant between plaintiff and defendant.

    —Hayes v. Moore, 404.

VALUE.

EVIDENCE.

See CARRIER, 10; CORPORATION, 2; EVIDENCE, 15.

VARIANCE. See APPEAL AND ERROR, 6.

VENDOR AND PURCHASER. See APPEAL AND ERROR, 14, 16; EJECTMENT.

AFTER STATUTORY NOTICE TO TERMINATE CONTRACT OF SALE.

1. Where the vendor has given the statutory notice to terminate the contract for nonpayment of overdue instalments, and the time limited by statute for making such payment has expired, the vendee cannot reinstate the contract by thereafter electing to apply his claim for damages in discharge of such instalments.

    —International Realty & Securities Corporation v. Vanderpoel, 89.

2. As damages for the fraud cannot be applied upon the purchase price unless the vendee so elects, they do not operate as payment thereon until he has made such election.

    —International Realty & Securities Corporation v. Vanderpoel, 89.

SAME—TENDER OF PRICE.

3. The notice provided by G. S. 1913, § 8081, for the termination of an executory contract of sale is in effect a statutory foreclosure of the contract, and a tender of payment after the expiration of the 30 days is of no avail.

    —International Realty & Securities Corporation v. Vanderpool, 92.

VENUE.

CHANGE OF VENUE.

1. Demand for a change of venue made under G. S. 1913, § 7722, must be made within 20 days after the summons is served. If made after that time, it is too late, even though the time for answering has been extended and has not yet expired.

    —Peterson v. Carlson, 324.

2. In order to effect a change of venue, the defendant must make a record showing him entitled to a change. The essentials are that defendant be

VENUE—Continued.

a nonresident of the county in which the action is brought and that the demand be made seasonably and in due form. The fact of nonresidence is made to appear by affidavit, and the truth of the affidavit in this particular can be challenged only in the court to which the venue is changed. In determining whether the demand was seasonably made, the court in which the action was commenced will look at its whole record, and if the record shows on its face that the demand was not made in time, the court will treat the demand as a nullity.

—Peterson v. Carlson, 324.

3. A stipulation extending the time for answering does not extend the time for making application for change of venue.

—Peterson v. Carlson, 324.

VILLAGE. See MUNICIPAL CORPORATION, 1–5.

ANNEXATION OF TERRITORY.

WAIVER. See CONTRACT, 7; EQUITY; EVIDENCE, 3; INSURANCE, 9, 12, 13.

WAREHOUSEMAN. See CARRIER, 11.

WATER AND WATERCOURSE. See CONTEMPT; NAVIGABLE WATER; NEW TRIAL, 2.

NEGLIGENT FLOODING OF LAND.

1. Jury's finding that the flooding of plaintiff's land was due to defendant's negligence sustained.

—Watre v. Great Northern Railway Co. 118.

EVIDENCE.

2. Evidence *held* to afford a sufficient basis for a reasonable approximation of the portion of the damage attributable to defendant's acts.

—Watre v. Great Northern Railway Co. 119.

EVIDENCE OF RAINFALL.

3. Trial court *held* not to have abused its discretion in excluding evidence of the amount of rainfall at distant points.

—Watre v. Great Northern Railway Co. 118.

WILL. See EVIDENCE, 12.

ALLOWANCE TO WIDOW.

Under subdivision 1, R. L. 1905, § 3653 (G. S. 1913, § 7243), the widow is entitled to the allowance of personal property to the amount of $500 provided thereby, though she assents to her husband's will at the time of

WILL—continued.

> its execution and accepts its provisions in lieu of the provisions made
> for her by law; the subdivision cited providing that she shall receive
> such allowance as well when she takes the provisions made by her hus-
> band's will as when he dies intestate.
>> —Horbach v. Horbach, 223.

WITNESS. See CRIMINAL LAW, 5.

JUROR AT FORMER TRIAL.

1. Jurors on a former trial may testify on a subsequent trial as to physical
   facts coming to their knowledge during a view made by them on the
   former trial. It is not material that the former verdict was set aside
   because of the misconduct of the jury in conducting unauthorized experiments during the view.
   > —State v. Ward, 510.

CONVERSATION WITH DECEASED PERSON—CONSTRUCTION OF STATUTE.

2. The statutory provision (G. S. 1913, § 8378) which forbids a person interested in the result of an action from giving evidence therein concerning
   any conversation with a deceased person relative to any matter at issue,
   should be strictly construed.
   > —Ikenberry v. New York Life Insurance Co. 219.

COMPETENCY—CONVERSATION WITH DECEDENT.

3. The agent of defendant who negotiated the insurance, to whom the insured
   made and delivered a note for the amount of the first premium, and to
   whom the defendant sent the policy after its issue, is *held* not interested
   in the event of the action, so as to prevent his testifying to conversations
   with the insured, now deceased.
   > —Ikenberry v. New York Life Insurance Co. 216.

CROSS-EXAMINATION.

4. In a prosecution for carnal knowledge of a female child under 18 years of
   age defendant is entitled to much latitude in his cross-examination of
   the prosecutrix, but it is not error to exclude a question as to her testimony before the grand jury, asked merely for the purpose of testing her
   memory.
   > —State v. Trocke, 485.
5. There was no error in rulings in the admission or rejection of evidence, or
   in failing to give a requested instruction.
   > —State v. Ward, 511.

WITNESS—Continued.

CREDIBILITY.

6. Where there is *mala fides* in a transaction direct proof is scarcely ever available. Proven circumstances might be such that the jury have a perfect right to reject as untruthful a positive statement of a witness though not contradicted by any direct testimony, especially when the witness evinces evasiveness, lack of memory or ignorance on matters which the jury may well conclude to be within his knowledge.
   —Cole v. Johnson, 294.

IMPEACHMENT—EVIDENCE OF CONTRADICTORY STATEMENTS.

7. Failure to lay a technically perfect foundation as regards time and place is not ground for rejecting testimony of prior contradictory statements made by a witness out of court, where it is clear that neither he nor the impeaching witness is misled thereby.
   —Johnson v. Young, 462.

8. The testimony of a witness which concededly made defendant's negligence a question for the jury, in this a personal injury action, was not so discredited by prior written statements and reports, or by his cross-examination, that a verdict based thereon, and approved by the trial court, should not stand. The jury have a right to consider the circumstances under which such statements are made.
   —Capital Trust Co. v. Great Northern Railway Co. 144.

WORDS AND PHRASES.

INACCURATE USE OF WORDS.

See CONSTITUTION, 1.

WHAT CONSTITUTES NAVIGABLE WATER.

See NAVIGABLE WATER, 1, 2.

CONSTRUCTION OF DECREE.

See JUDGMENT, 5.

CONSTRUCTION OF WORD "PRESENT."

See MUNICIPAL CORPORATION, 1.

"MILL WORK."

See CONTRACT, 4.

TRAIN "ON THE ROAD."

See RAILWAY, 1.

WORDS AND PHRASES—Continued.

1. "Good cause to the contrary" in G. S. 1913, § 8510, refers to cause shown when the motion to dismiss the indictment is made.

    —State v. Le Flohic, 506.

2. The prefix "non" denotes mere negation or absence of the thing or quality to which it is applied.

    —Geronime v. German Roman Catholic Aid Association, 250.

3. The words "wilfully and unlawfully" embody the idea of maliciousness.

    —State v. Ward, 511.

WORKMEN'S COMPENSATION ACT.

Construing the Workmen's Compensation Act (Laws 1913, c. 467, G. S. 1913, §§ 8195–8230), approved April 24, 1913, effective from October 1, 1913, it is *held* that an employee accepts the provisions of the act until he makes an election not to accept; that under the proviso contained in section 12 of said chapter his election, made within 30 days after October 1, is effective at once, notwithstanding the clauses of sections 11 and 12 relative to a 30 days' notice; and that an employee injured on October 15, 1913, perfecting his election not to be bound by the act on October 29, 1913, is, until that date, bound by the act, and cannot maintain a common law action for his injury.

    —Harris v. Hobart Iron Co. 399.

WRIT. See CERTIORARI; EXECUTION; HABEAS CORPUS; REPLEVIN.

X-RAY. See CRIMINAL LAW, 1; INDICTMENT AND INFORMATION.

[END OF VOLUME]

E₄ J H J
5/19/13 -

5216 - 7

Lightning Source UK Ltd.
Milton Keynes UK
UKHW011237050119
334854UK00009B/1546/P